THE
INTEGRAL URBAN HOUSE

SELF-RELIANT LIVING IN THE CITY

by the Farallones Institute   *Introduction by Sim Van der Ryn*

Sierra Club Books   San Francisco

The Integral Urban House

The Sierra Club, founded in 1892 by John Muir, has devoted itself to the study and protection of the earth's scenic and ecological resources—mountains, wetlands, woodlands, wild shores and rivers, deserts, and plains. The publishing program of the Sierra Club offers books to the public as a nonprofit educational service in the hope that they may enlarge the public's understanding of the Club's basic concerns. The point of view expressed in each book, however, does not necessarily represent that of the Club. The Sierra Club has some 50 chapters coast to coast, in Canada, Hawaii, and Alaska. For information about how you may participate in its programs to preserve wilderness and the quality of life, please address inquiries to Sierra Club, 530 Bush, San Francisco, California 94108.

The publisher gratefully acknowledges the interest of The Open Space Institute in the publication of this book.

Library of Congress Cataloging in Publication Data

Farallones Institute.
The integral urban house.

Bibliography
Includes index.
1. Dwellings.   2. Environmental engineering (Buildings)   3. City and town life.   I. Title.
TH4812.F37   1978   643   78-8592
ISBN 0-87156-213-8

Book design by Jon Goodchild.

Cover design by Gordon Ashby and Bill Wells.
Part illustrations by Bill Wells.
Illustrations for Chapter 12 by David Critchfield and Scott Matthews, unless credited in the Acknowledgments.
Other line illustrations provided by Jon Goodchild, by the Farallones Institute and by Lisa Haderlie.
Photographs by Pat Goudvis.

10 9 8 7 6 5 4 3 2 1

Printed in the United States of America.

Grateful acknowledgment is made to the following individuals, organizations, and publishers:

Academic Press, N.Y., for permission to reprint material from *Pest Control*, by Wendell W. Kilgore and Richard L. Doutt, copyright © 1977 by Academic Press; and for permission to reprint material from *Theory and Practice of Biological Control*, edited by C.B. Haffacker and P.S. Messenger, copyright © 1977 by Academic Press.

Addison-Wesley Publishing Co., Reading, Mass., for permission to reprint material from *Fundamentals of Air Pollution*, by Samuel J. Williamson, copyright © 1973 by Addison-Wesley Publishing Co.

Agricultural Research Service, ERDA, Washington, D.C., for permission to reprint material from *Proceedings, Solar Greenhouse Conference, 1977*.

The American Association for the Advancement of the Sciences, Washington, D.C., for permission to reprint material by D. Pimental, et al., from *Science*, Vol. 182, November, 1973; and material by H.J. Evans and L.E. Barker from *Science*, Vol. 197, July, 1977.

Annual Review of Energy, for permission to reprint material from "Raising the Productivity of Energy Use," by Lee Schipper, from LBL data, Art Rosenfeld.

Burgess Publishing Company, Minneapolis Minn., for permission to reprint material from *Experiments in Soil Bacteriology*, 1951 Edition, by O.N. Allen, copyright © 1957 by Burgess Publishing Company; some material after Gsin 1948.

California Energy Commission for permission to reprint material from *Solar for Your Present Home*, copyright © 1978 by California Energy Commission.

Peter Calthorpe, for permission to reprint diagrams of houses designed by Calthorpe, copyright © 1978 by Peter Calthorpe.

Cheshire Books, N.H., for permission to reprint material from *The Solar Home Book*, by Bruce Anderson with Michael Riordan, copyright © 1976 by Cheshire Books.

The Clivus Multrum Co., Cambridge, Mass., for permission to reprint material on the Clivus Multrum.

The Columbia University Press, N.Y., for permission to reprint material from *Urban Planning Aspects of Water Pollution Control* by Sigurd Grava, copyright © 1969 by Columbia University Press.

The Consumers Cooperative-Twin Pines, Berkeley, Calif., for permission to reprint material from *The Co-op News*, copyright Consumers Co-op-Twin Pines.

C.R.C. Press, Cleveland, Ohio, for permission to reprint material from *Man, Food and Nutrition*, by Miloslaw Bechigl, Jr., copyright by C.R.C. Press.

Doubleday & Company, N.Y., for permission to reprint material from *Architecture and Energy* by Richard G. Stein, copyright © 1977 by Richard G. Stein. Reproduced by permission of Doubleday & Co., Inc.

The East Bay Municipal Utility District for permission to reprint material from its booklet *Meet Your Meter*.

Ernest Benn Limited, London, for permission to reprint material from *The Food and Health of Western Man*, by J.L. Mount, copyright © 1975 by Ernest Benn Limited.

M.L. Flint and Dr. Robert Van den Bosch for permission to reprint material from *A Source Book for Integrated Pest Management*, 1977.

W.H. Freeman and Company, San Francisco, for permission to reprint material from *Ecoscience: Population, Resources and the Environment*, by Paul R. Ehrlich, Anne H. Ehrlich, and John P. Holdren, copyright © 1977 by W.H. Freeman and Company; and for permission to reprint material from *Plant Science*, Second Edition, by Jules Janick, R.W. Schery, F.W. Woods, and V.W. Ruttang, copyright © 1974 by W.H. Freeman and Company.

Longman Group Limited, Essex, England, for permission to reprint material from *Soil Conditions and Plant Growth*, by E.J. Russell, copyright by the Longman Group Limited, based on material given in N.H.J. Miller, *J. Agric. Sci.* 1906, 377, and E.J. Russell and E.H. Richards, ibid., 1920, 1922.

McGraw-Hill, Inc., N.Y., for permission to reprint material from *Man's Physical World*, by Joseph E. Van Riper, copyright © 1962 by McGraw-Hill, Inc.

Macmillan Publishing Co., Inc., N.Y., for permission to reprint material from *The Nature and Properties of Soils*, Fifth Edition, by Lyon, Buchman, and Brady, copyright © by Macmillan Publishing Co.

Acknowledgements, continued

Morgan and Morgan, Inc., Dobbs Ferry, N.Y., for permission to reprint material from *Harnessing the Sun*, by John Keyes, copyright © by Morgan and Morgan, Inc.

C.V. Mosby Co., St. Louis, for permission to reprint material from *Chemical Villains: A Biology of Pollution*, by James W. Berry, David W. Osgood, and Philip A. St. John, copyright © 1974 by C.V. Mosby Co., and for permission to reprint material from *Introductory Nutrition*, Second Edition, by H.A. Guthrie, copyright © 1971 by C.V. Mosby Co.

The North Country Star, Willits, Calif., for permission to reprint material from its issue of October, 1977.

The Population Reference Bureau, Washington, D.C., for permission to reprint material by A.R. Omran from *Population Bulletin* 32(2) 1977. Copyright © 1977.

Rodale Press Inc., Emmaus, Pa., for permission to reprint material from *Goodbye to the Flush Toilet*, by Carol Hupping Stoner, copyright © 1977 by Rodale Press Inc., Emmaus, Pa. 18049.

W.B. Saunders Co. Philadelphia, for permission to reprint material from *Nutrition and Pysical Fitness*, Ninth Edition, by Bogert, Briggs, and Calloway, copyright © 1973 by The W.B. Saunders Co.; for permission to reprint material from *Contemporary Biology*, by Mary E. Clark, copyright © 1973 by the W.B. Saunders Co.;

and for permission to reprint material from *Fundamentals of Ecology*, by Eugene P. Odum, Third Edition copyright © 1971 by the W.B. Saunders Co.

Sierra Club Books, San Francisco, for permission to reprint material from *Other Homes and Garbage*, by Jim Leckie, Gil Masters, Harry Whitehouse, and Lily Young, copyright © 1975 by Sierra Club Books.

The University of Michigan Press, Ann Arbor, for permission to reprint material from *Soil Animals*, by Friedrick Schaller, copyright © by University of Michigan Press.

The University of Pennsylvania Press, Philadelphia, for permission to reprint material from *Biological Control of Water Pollution*, edited by Joachim Tourbier and Robert W. Pierson, Jr. Reprinted by permission from an article by Robert W. Harris. Copyright © by the University of Pennsylvania.

USDA, for permission to reprint material from *Yearbook of Agriculture, 1957.*

The Vermont Crossroads Press, for permission to reprint material from *Woodburners Encyclopedia*, by J.W. Shelton, copyright © 1976 by Vermont Crossroads Press, based on data from H.C. Hotten and J.B. Howard, *New Energy Technology—Some Facts and Assessments*, MIT Press, 1971.

John Wiley and Sons Publishing Co., for permission to reprint material from *Handbook for Vegetable Owners*, by James Edward Knott, copyright © 1957 by John Wiley and Sons.

CONTENTS

INTRODUCTION

In late 1972 a group of architects, engineers, and biologists in the San Francisco Bay Area began meeting with the aim of joining our professional skills to create dwellings that would translate into physical form the central principles of the emerging environmental movement. Each of us—often feeling isolated by the narrow perspective of our specialties—was looking for ways to extend and integrate ideas and practice, to teach others, and continue his or her own learning. We saw the potential of integrating principles of biology, food and energy production, and the design of living space and community to create places where one might function without total dependence on an "artificial," centralized technology; at the same time, we saw the need for a center where people could combine theoretical and philosophical learning with practical experience in our areas of expertise: agriculture, architecture, building, engineering, biology and natural systems. Our immediate goal became the combination of all of our skills toward the design and construction of a place that would test experimental, ecologically stable and resource-conserving living systems.

Many people at that time seemed to be giving up on cities, attempting to reconnect to the earth by moving to rural areas. I was one of these. In our group Bill and Helga Olkowski argued persuasively for another approach. "Cities are where people are," they said. "Everyone can't move to the country or there won't be a country any more, and besides, if people move to the country with their urban consciousness, the country will be transformed into the city just as happened with the suburbs. The challenge is to make cities ecologically stable and healthy places to live."

The Olkowskis had already acted on their beliefs. Over a period of years they had redesigned their home space and their lives so that they were raising a good portion of their own food, wasting nothing, and enthusiastically experimenting with dozens of little and big ways for average city people to reduce their dependence on centralized systems and become more connected to the basics of life support. When I first heard of Bill and Helga over twelve years ago, I nodded, thinking to myself, "Yes, Berkeley is full of eccentrics."

In 1973, the big news was the energy crisis as the Mid-East oil producers withheld their production from the U.S. and European markets. More of us discovered in coping with this "crisis" just how dependent our technology and economy had become on nonrenewable resources. Few persons heard about another significant event of 1973, though many were touched by it. For the first time since the Great Depression of the thirties, rising incomes did not keep pace with the increasing cost of goods and services. Real income in this country began to fall in 1973 and has been falling ever since (that is, the dollars it costs to buy homes, food, clothing, education, health care are outdistancing dollar increases in income). This little-noticed statistical event marked an important turning point whose full significance most of us have yet to grasp. It comes down to this: more and more energy—material and human—is used to maintain present wasteful habits and pay for their effects. More government to administer and regulate the complex effects of centralized technologies. More dollars to treat the social and environmental diseases that result from the way we live, and more and more energy required to secure the usable energy needed to run our homes, businesses, transportation, agriculture—all the pieces that make up our society. We *are* on a treadmill running a rat race in which we move harder and harder, faster and faster simply to stay in place.

By 1973 some of the practices the Olkowskis had begun years before no longer seemed strange. In fact, I was doing many of them myself: growing vegetables, composting, raising chickens, learning how to heat water and houses with the sun and wood, helping people design and build places they could build and maintain themselves, designing and building sanitary systems that didn't pollute or waste water or nutrients.

Our group—established as the Farallones Institute—bought the Olkowskis' dream, and added to it and developed the Integral Urban House in Berkeley as a Farallones Institute research and educational center to develop urban-scale appropriate technology. We have been pursuing that vision for several years; it has been a difficult and rewarding journey. In the first months of designing and building the Integral Urban House there were almost daily conflicts growing out of the selective vision bred by our own particular specialties. Tom Javits and Jim Campe almost came to blows over how the concrete floor would be poured. Jim wanted to bring a concrete truck down the driveway for the pour and Tom vowed to lay his body in front of the wheels before he would allow the precious soil to be compressed by the giant truck. So we wheel-barrowed in many yards by hand. The builders learned that what they called "dirt" was living, organic matter, and Tom learned that concrete is heavy and dries fast. Should we cut a tree to allow more sun to fall on the solar collector? Was space to store wood scraps for the stove more important than space for the chickens? The learning still continues, and we now know a whole lot more about how to live lightly and well in the city. And through your use of this book, we will all come to know more, possibly enough to make a way for ourselves, our children, and grand-children, to a sustainable future urban life.

This book, then, is the result of four years' experience in living with and refining the systems of the Integral Urban House. Many people contributed to making the house and this book a reality. Jim Campe, Jeff Poetsch and Sheldon Leon were responsible for much of the construction of the house. Since the beginning, Tom Javits has been the resident manager and the sparkplug that has made the house a vital part of the community. A grant from the Heller Charitable Trust made it possible for the Institute to develop a syllabus on integrated systems which was the seed that led to this book. And Harlow Daugherty provided the original grant that made the project possible. In addition to the principal authors, key chapters have been contributed by Sterling Bunnell (part of Chapter 11), Scott Matthews (Chapter 12) and myself (Chapter 2). Stuart Leiderman typed much of the manuscript. We are indebted to Jon Beckmann, Director of Sierra Club Books who first suggested that our work deserved a wider audience. Our editor, Wendy Goldwyn, has patiently and tenaciously seen the book project through over the three years it took to get it together.

This book shows you how to achieve a high quality urban way of life using a fraction of the resources we are accustomed to, at lower cost, with less waste, pollution and ugliness. At the center of the concept is a view that envisions a new connection between urban habitat and natural systems. Any of us can learn to live better and with more satisfaction by employing ecological principles in designing how we live. At the present point in history, when monoculture-promoting human organizations have become unviably gigantic while their resource base is rapidly contracting, the application of ecological principles is imperative to the well-being of individuals, households, and communities.

The house and this book are the collective product of many different people. We don't always agree about everything, and we are all still learning and improving ways of living lightly on earth. As I see it we have no other choice but to learn—however haltingly—to walk the path towards our sustenance and the survival of this beautiful and fragile blue-green planet we call Earth, our only home.

Sim Van der Ryn
President and Founder, Farallones Institute

Part One:
The Concept

1. BEGINNINGS

This book is about an idea. We call this idea the integral urban house. The idea is not original with us, but its physical actualization has become an urgent concern of ours over the last several years. An example of an Integral Urban House exists in Berkeley, California (throughout this book the capitalized title Integral Urban House refers to the house in Berkeley, while the lower-cased words refer to the concept of an integral urban house), as a demonstration project of the Farallones Institute, a nonprofit educational and research organization with administrative offices in Berkeley, California. Other examples are the Ouroborus House in Minneapolis, the East Eleventh Street project in New York City, and the Office of the Institute for Self-Reliance in Washington, D.C. Many similar projects are being developed throughout the United States as well as in other countries.

Many people participated in the realization of the Integral Urban House in Berkeley. Some were founders of the institute along with us, providing the original support that made the project possible. Others were dedicated designers, builders, educators, urban farmers, students, and helpers who provided the many skills needed to create and experiment with the systems developed.

This Integral Urban House project in Berkeley is open to the public for casual visits and to students for critical examination. Hopefully, it serves as an inspiration and catalyst for new ideas on how to implement the primary goal: the creation of a self-reliant urban household, an urban residence that helps to support its residents while they support it. This house integrates the life-support systems of its residents in such a manner as to conserve energy and resources and provide a healthy environment in which humans may survive and thrive.

However, this book is not solely about the Integral Urban House we helped to create, because that is only one example of the idea. Indeed, we learned so much in the process of developing this one that we will surely do some things quite differently in the integral urban houses we help to realize in the future. Therefore, we shall be considering the idea in its broadest sense, drawing examples from other such efforts with which we are familiar, and giving details regarding those specific aspects with which we have had first-hand experience. We have no intention of implying that ours are the only available or suitable approaches to reaching the same goal.

The Integral Urban House as an Idea: The idea of the integral urban house arose from our felt need to elaborate a model life-support system that large numbers of people could use preparing for their future while simultaneously improving their daily life. Forecasting the future is usually a value-laden process in which, simply speaking, one documents past activities, events, and changes, and then, on the assumption that the same basic processes will continue to operate, projects the perceived patterns into the future. Clearly, certain worldwide patterns will not change radically in the immediate future. These include widespread social inequalities and continued population growth and their attendants—famine, poverty, disease, and human conflict.

Against this somber prophecy we propose that people need to feel that they have some control over their own lives in order to come together in constructive groups to reform their communities. And they need to believe in their own ability to create and maintain their basic life-support systems in order to feel at least somewhat in control. To use a metaphor for our automobile-addicted culture, we need to feel that we are in the driver's seat rather than merely passengers in our own lives.

Nowhere is the sense of victimization greater than among those of us who live in urban areas or who, though living in a rural setting, have adopted urban (nonagricultural) lifestyles. If you fall into one of these cate-

Figure 1-1. **The Integral Urban House, Site Plan**

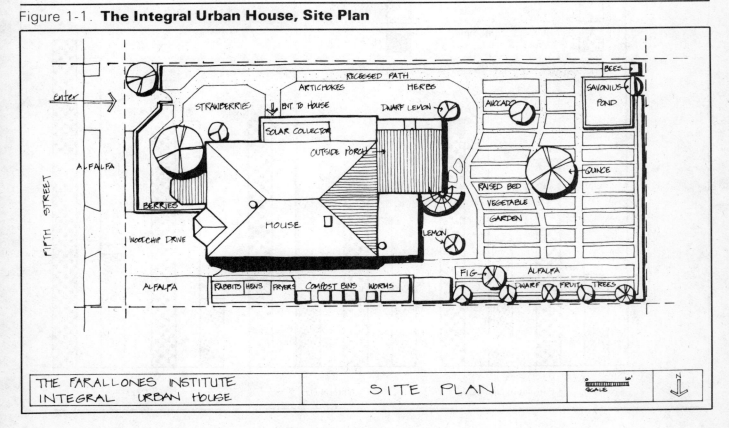

gories, what will you do when a transit strike closes your local grocery store, when there is no more gasoline at the local service station, no natural gas in the pipes to the furnace or heater, and so on? What are you doing as food, gasoline, electricity, and natural gas prices rise and water becomes scarce? How will you react as an increasingly large number of your acquaintances die from various types of cancers that experts now agree are in large measure caused by toxic materials in the environment? Ironically enough, the majority of these chemical compounds result from activities that are said to make our lifestyles possible. Table 1-1 shows how the mortality patterns have changed in the United States. Where we once died from infectious diseases we now are subject to degenerative diseases triggered by the stress of modern urban lifestyle, diet, and exposure to toxic materials. Table 1-2 is presented to give some perspective on the mortality figures in Table 1-1.

We do not think the solution to environmental crises is self-sufficiency, because such a condition is not possible even if it were desirable. If self-sufficient human communities exist at all, they are extremely rare. One might argue that no such community ever existed by interpreting "self-sufficient" to mean independent of other humans. Can an isolated Brazilian jungle tribe be considered self-sufficient when it is showered with radioactive fallout from nuclear tests conducted by major world political powers thousands of miles away? Tribespeople might protect themselves from poisonous snakes but not from, for example, increased ultraviolet radiation at

Source: Ehrlich, Ehrlich, and Holdren, *Ecoscience: Population, Resources, Environment.*

Figure 1-2. **Perspectives on World Fuel Reserves**

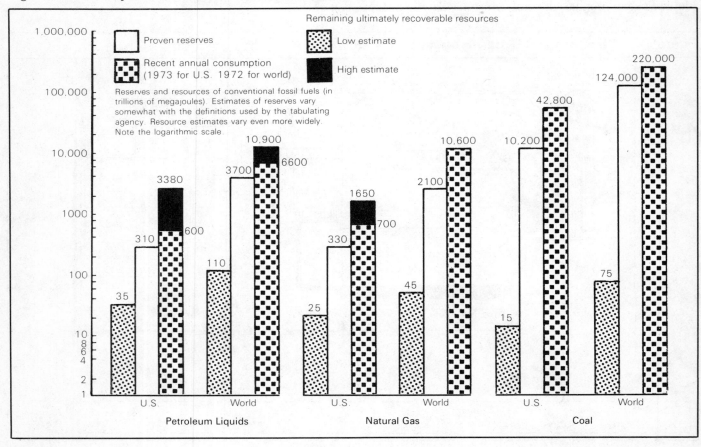

the earth's surface due to depletion of the ozone layers in the upper atmosphere, or large-scale weather modifications inadvertently caused by human activities on other continents.

In spite of the awesome interdependence of all humans, a large number of us, including the most apartment-constrained inner-city resident, can cultivate a measure of self-reliance, or what was once referred to as "Yankee ingenuity." We can learn to use what resources we already have right where we are to keep ourselves warm in winter; raise some of our own food on rooftops, porches, patios, backyards, and community gardens; obtain some of the nonhuman energy we need from nonpolluting sources; recycle and compost our wastes through homesite and neighborhood centers; and repair and maintain our own habitat (in spite of its capricious-seeming intention to pursue the laws of thermodynamics and lapse into disorder).

Five basic needs define our basic life-support systems (see margin). When they are not met it becomes difficult to maintain the simplest human interactions, much less engage in social reform or create works of technology or art that manifest culture. When you are unhealthy it literally costs more to support your life.

As our homes are now structured, satisfying most of these basic life-support needs requires that we be dependent on resources originating far away. We consume vast amounts of nonrenewable or, worse yet, dangerous forms of energy in the process of bringing these resources to ourselves and then carting away our wastes. Though we eat California lettuce and Mexican tomatoes in New York, we become vulnerable to the vagaries of complex distribution systems that are subject not only to human error but also to all the political and social pressures of the times.

Our schools did not teach us such simple things as how to manage flies

A first step toward self-reliance is to list our most basic needs

1. Food that provides us with sufficient calories or energy, and a balanced nutrition for our bodies to carry on normal metabolic processes as well as to resist invasion by pathogens or assaults by toxicants
2. Uncontaminated water to drink and clean air to breathe
3. A method of managing our own wastes so they do not create conditions that impair our health
4. Protection from the extremes of weather
5. Freedom from pests and pestilence

Table 1-1. Ten Leading Causes of Death, United States: 1900, 1970

Cause	Rank 1900	Rank 1970	Percent of Total Deaths 1900	1970
Accidents (non-vehicular)	6	5	4.5	3.1
Accidents, motor vehicle		6		2.8
Arteriosclerosis		9		1.7
Brights disease (chronic nephritis)	5		4.7	
Cancer	9	2	3.7	17.2
Cirrhosis of the liver		10		1.6
Congestion and brain hemorrhage	7		4.2	
Diabetes		8		2.0
Diarrhea and enteritis	3		8.1	
Diphtheria	10		2.3	
Diseases of early infancy	8	7	4.2	2.3
Heart disease	4	1	8.0	38.2
Influenza/pneumonia/bronchitis	1	4	14.4	3.6
Stroke		3		10.8
Tuberculosis	2		11.3	
			65.4%	**83.3%**

Table 1-2. United States Deaths from Various Causes

Cancer deaths (1969)	323,000
World War II battle deaths	292,000
Auto accident deaths (1969)	59,600
Vietnam war deaths (six years)	41,000
Korean war deaths (three years)	34,000
Polio deaths (1952, worst year)	3,300

Source: Epstein, "Potential Carcinogenic Hazards Due to Contaminated Drinking Water."

Source: Adapted from Omran, "Epidemiological transition in the United States."

and cockroaches without poisoning ourselves, process our own manure safely without using up gallons of pure water and the energy needed to pump it to us, use the sun and wind to create heat, light, and the energy to run machinery. Few of us learned the other simple home-scale technologies that are appropriate to the resources and climate of the regions we live in. Most of us grew up believing that improving the quality of our lives over that of our pioneer ancestors requires completely giving up a sense of self-reliance in the home to become totally dependent on energy sources far away and controlled by powerful international corporations almost entirely beyond the influence of the communities they serve.

Yet it is possible to construct, or renovate, a house so that it does an excellent job of protecting its residents from the weather with very little addition of energy from somewhere else. (Recent studies by the Federal Department of Energy suggest that houses built as passive solar systems could furnish 99.9 percent of the heat needed in a Los Angeles residence, 60 percent in New York, 57 percent in Boston, 52 percent in Seattle, and 42 percent in Madison, Wisconsin.) Similarly, process one's own household organic wastes in a space three by eight feet, and use the product to raise tomatoes or other vegetables in a five-gallon can. Water for drinking can be obtained from contaminated water through the use of a solar still. To some

Table 1-3. **Energy Used in Construction***

Materials	Units	Btu/Unit
Framing lumber (rough)	Board feet (bd ft)	7611
Glass, double strength sheet	Square feet	15,430
Ready-mix concrete	Cubic yards	2,594,338
Paint (oil and alkyd)	Gallons	488,528
Asphalt roofing shingles	Square feet	25,334
Steel, hot rolled structural	Pounds	18,730
Aluminum, rolled structural	Pounds	92,146
Insulation (4.5 inches thick)	Square feet	6860
Common brick	One brick	14,291

*The energy reported here is that used to mine, extract, transport, refine, fabricate and incorporate the materials in buildings of any sort, and includes administrative activities.

Source: Stein, *Architecture and Energy*.

Table 1-4. **Carcinogens Discovered in a Nationwide Drinking Water Survey***

Compound	Number of Cities Detected	Concentration in Ppm†
Chloroform§	80	less than 0.1 to 311
Bromodichloromethane§	78	0.3 to 116
Dibromochloromethane§	72	less than 0.4 to 100
Bromoform§	26	less than 0.8 to 92
Carbon tetrachloride	10	less than 2.0 to 3
1,2 Dichloroethane	26	less than 0.2 to 6

*Of eighty cities tested by the Environmental Protection Agency
† Ppm is the abbreviation for parts per million, or one gram in one million grams of water.
§ These have been found to arise primarily from the chlorination of drinking water, rather than from industrial sources.

Source: Harris, "Carcinogenic Organic Chemicals in Drinking Water."

degree—small though it may be in some cases but substantial in others—we can gain a measure of control over our own lives by creating integrated life-support systems in our homes that conserve energy and resources. These houses can then be used as bases for creating more self-reliant neighborhoods and communities. When we engage in such activities to increase our self-reliance the quality of life improves rather than continues to degenerate.

It is a paradox that the way to becoming more self-reliant is through increased understanding of our dependence upon the physical and biological processes of our planet and the social inventions that use them. By getting to know these processes, we can stop interfering with and destroying them and can make them work for us. Aiding in such understanding is one of the goals of this book.

Why House?   The house is the interface between the body and the environment, a physiological buffer. The house, though not necessarily the family home, is the key social environment (the birth, growing, living, dying, meeting, and learning place). The house structure itself, and the systems operating within it, are presently key consumers of energy, resources, and information. The house is a symbol of both ourselves and the world, our earth. It is a good place to begin to examine how we live now and how we might change for the better. Your "house" can be an apartment, a room, or any place where you get your necessities of life.

Why Urban House?   It doesn't matter whether the population of the local community is eight million (New York City), one million (Baltimore, Maryland), one hundred thousand (Dearborn, Michigan), or one thousand (Arapahoe, Nebraska). People across the United States follow the same urban lifestyles we see illustrated on television: they buy their food at the store, prepare and cook it with a wide array of energy-consuming appliances, and throw their wastes, unsorted, into a can to be carted off to the dump. They manage the interface between themselves and other species they dislike by using chemical poisons. They work away from their home, if they are lucky enough to find a job (47 percent of United States farmers have off-the-farm income), and get to work by automobile. They live and work in structures that waste prodigious amounts of energy. And they go through their daily lives largely out of touch with the regional and seasonal rhythms of which they are a part except, perhaps, as these relate to the pocketbook, and in disasters like floods, tornadoes, and hurricanes.

The city is a funnel for resources. From the rest of the country resources pass through the city on the way to the dump—for example, trees → paper → dump. This funnelling effect is illustrated in Figure 1-3. At the same time, urbanites largely determine public policy. The price of agricultural land and the management of wildlands and forests, either by unconscious consumer behavior or deliberate decision through the political process, are largely under the influence of people who live in urban areas and/or follow urban lifestyles.

Why "Integral"?   Integral means together, whole or complete, and at the same time, essential. We chose the term integral urban house because we

Figure 1-3. **The Urban Funnel: Food Passed through Cities to Dumps**

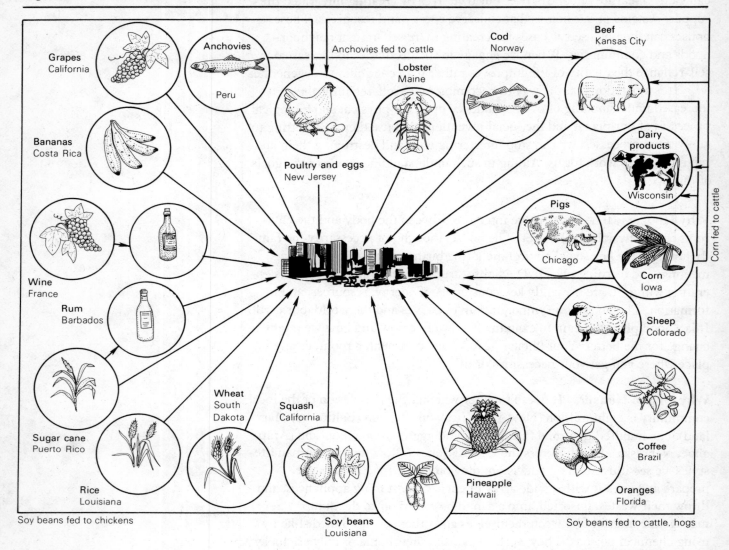

Grapes California
Anchovies Peru
Anchovies fed to cattle
Cod Norway
Beef Kansas City
Lobster Maine
Bananas Costa Rica
Poultry and eggs New Jersey
Dairy products Wisconsin
Wine France
Pigs Chicago
Corn fed to cattle
Rum Barbados
Corn Iowa
Sheep Colorado
Sugar cane Puerto Rico
Wheat South Dakota
Squash California
Coffee Brazil
Rice Louisiana
Soy beans Louisiana
Pineapple Hawaii
Oranges Florida

Soy beans fed to chickens

Soy beans fed to cattle, hogs

were striving for an integration of ideas about structure both as habitat and life-support system. There is a need for a new synthesis of biological and architectural ideas (biotecture or ecotecture, if you will). To integrate these areas, models for new ways of life and corresponding structures are needed that will show the way to a solar economy and demonstrate energy and resource-conserving methods and lifestyles. These models must show an integration with the biophysical region in which they are situated. One model for the country or the world is not enough.

New or Used: We decided to focus our efforts on the rehabilitation of an existing home rather than building from the ground up. We considered the tremendous investment of materials, natural resources, and energy that society has already committed to the maintenance of existing structures. To allow housing to deteriorate in favor of new construction would be essentially to waste precious resources. Also, we know that if our efforts were to become a national model, then demonstrating retrofit technologies would be most appropriate, since only a small percentage of the population has the capital to finance construction of a new home. The building costs associated with renovating houses are generally only a fraction of those for new construction. For example, Oakland Better Housing, a private firm that specializes in rehabilitating older homes in the San Francisco Bay Area, usually budgets $15 to $20 a square foot in construction costs for the complete overhaul of a house. Compare that figure with the typical construction costs of a new northern Californian house, $35 to $45 per square foot.

Housing rehabilitation is recycling in its most profound sense. In many rundown neighborhoods where inexpensive older homes are found the renovation of one could inspire other householders to refurbish their property. For example, when the Farallones Institute purchased what was to become the Integral Urban House, the neighborhood was in serious jeopardy of being lost to land speculators. Industry and Berkeley city officials were considering condemning the dilapidated homes on our block and converting the neighborhood into an industrial park. Our remodeling of the Integral House not only dignified this one particular residence, but uplifted the spirit of the neighborhood. Soon other energetic families purchased homes nearby and started rehab efforts of their own. In three years, eight homes in the neighborhood were restored and once again occupied by families. Vegetable gardens sprang up in backyards and the neighborhood became a community of integrity and purpose. Its residential character was restored and the effort of business to convert the block into an industrial park was headed off.

Changing One's Lifestyle

The realities of a growing human population and finite earth resources make clear that present United States urban lifestyles will have to change. Whether they will do so largely because of catastrophe or by design remains to be seen.

It is not easy to modify one's habits, as all of us know who have struggled to make such personal changes as losing weight, stopping smoking, or cutting out caffeinated beverages. Some years ago, before the Integral Urban House project, two of us (the Olkowskis) decided to make some massive changes in our daily behavior in order to achieve a personal lifestyle that was both more self-reliant and less environmentally destructive. It seemed essential that we experience first-hand the kinds of psychological and physical problems that might be associated with making the changes we felt would eventually be required in the society around us.

In our case, the motivation for change was based on a series of convictions derived from academic training as biologists and from certain current information sources. The challenge for us was how to change a whole series of our own behavior patterns in order to bring them into harmony with our general self-image and our beliefs regarding the consequence of our actions. Through initial introspection and discussion we came to the conclusion that certain factors were crucial in influencing the comfort we felt or the ease and speed with which we were able to take on new behavior patterns. It seemed that for each individual and each kind of behavior these factors would vary, and that their negative or positive contributions to ease of change could be measured and compared. These factors are as follows:

Motivation for change is based on understanding that:

- much significant environmental disturbance is directly due to the activities of humans;
- such disturbance is resulting in a deterioration of our own lives through a direct decrease in comfort and pleasure (some simple examples are the unwanted defrosting of foods in the freezer due to power blackouts, the clouding of a favorite view by smog, and increased noise from a new freeway);
- this environmental deterioration may be directly affecting our health and length of life—for example, by increasing our chances of developing cancer because of the chloroform in the municipal water supply (see Table 1-4), or exposure to pesticides in our surroundings and on our food (see Table 7-2, pages 148–49);
- this degradation is affecting the life of other species on the planet and increasing the physical constraints under which life operates (examples are heavy-metal pollution of the San Francisco Bay resulting from waste-management practices in the area, or the potential increase in ultraviolet radiation through use of fluorocarbons in aerosol cans);
- these recorded disturbances among other species, because of the interrelatedness of all living things, must ultimately affect all human lives and thus our own welfare;
- life coevolves with the environment, and environmental changes must ultimately affect the life that is dependent upon it.

Figure 1-4. **Habitat & Life Support System of an Integral Urban House**

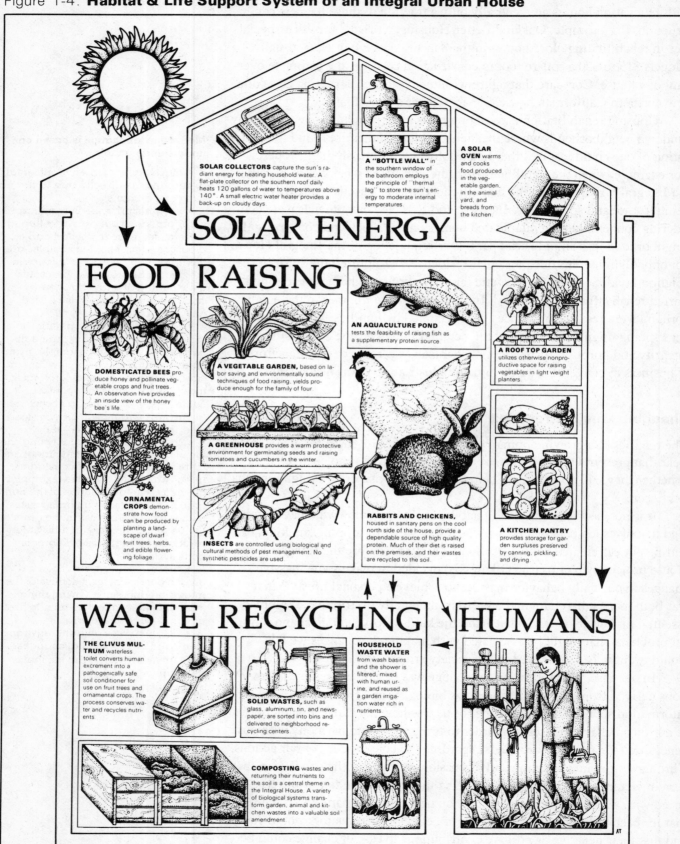

SOLAR ENERGY

SOLAR COLLECTORS capture the sun's radiant energy for heating household water. A flat-plate collector on the southern roof daily heats 120 gallons of water to temperatures above 140°. A small electric water heater provides a back-up on cloudy days.

A "BOTTLE WALL" in the southern window of the bathroom employs the principle of "thermal lag" to store the sun's energy to moderate internal temperatures.

A SOLAR OVEN warms and cooks food produced in the vegetable garden, in the animal yard, and breads from the kitchen.

FOOD RAISING

DOMESTICATED BEES produce honey and pollinate vegetable crops and fruit trees. An observation hive provides an inside view of the honey bee's life.

A VEGETABLE GARDEN, based on labor saving and environmentally sound techniques of food raising, yields produce enough for the family of four.

AN AQUACULTURE POND tests the feasibility of raising fish as a supplementary protein source.

A ROOF TOP GARDEN utilizes otherwise nonproductive space for raising vegetables in light weight planters.

ORNAMENTAL CROPS demonstrate how food can be produced by planting a landscape of dwarf fruit trees, herbs, and edible flowering foliage.

A GREENHOUSE provides a warm protective environment for germinating seeds and raising tomatoes and cucumbers in the winter.

INSECTS are controlled using biological and cultural methods of pest management. No synthetic pesticides are used.

RABBITS AND CHICKENS, housed in sanitary pens on the cool north side of the house, provide a dependable source of high quality protein. Much of their diet is raised on the premises, and their wastes are recycled to the soil.

A KITCHEN PANTRY provides storage for garden surpluses preserved by canning, pickling, and drying.

WASTE RECYCLING

HUMANS

THE CLIVUS MULTRUM waterless toilet converts human excrement into a pathogenically safe soil conditioner for use on fruit trees and ornamental crops. The process conserves water and recycles nutrients.

SOLID WASTES, such as glass, aluminum, tin, and newspaper, are sorted into bins and delivered to neighborhood recycling centers.

HOUSEHOLD WASTE WATER from wash basins and the shower is filtered, mixed with human urine, and reused as a garden irrigation water rich in nutrients.

COMPOSTING wastes and returning their nutrients to the soil is a central theme in the Integral House. A variety of biological systems transform garden, animal and kitchen wastes into a valuable soil amendment.

1. Cultural and/or Personal Taboos: For example, some designs for composting or waterless toilets require physical manipulation or direct visual confrontation of human manure and other wastes.

2. The Apparent Immediacy of Catastrophe: For example, the California drought and consequent water rationing in the San Francisco Bay Area were perceived as threatening when cherished home landscape vegetation began to turn yellow and die. This situation paved the way for a speedy adoption of greywater (used water from sinks and showers) technologies.

3. Amount of Sustained Awareness Generated: Using the above example, constant daily media reference to the drought helped to create a climate of reminders.

4. Family and Community Support: The actual or anticipated reaction of family members, neighbors, and landlords to digging up the front lawn in order to plant corn, for example, could affect the home food-raising experiment considerably if the front lawn is the only sunny area available for the effort. This also relates to larger systems within the community that may exist to support that behavior. It is easier to begin recycling your newspapers in a community like Berkeley, California, where a regular monthly, city-wide pickup exists and where other people's neatly tied bundles are visible to remind you, than in a location where you must actively seek out the one or two places that provide that service to only a few households and only through special efforts on their part.

5. Amount of Stress Experienced from Not Changing a Behavior: A circumstance that encouraged us to recycle was that we could rarely fit all of the household garbage into the garbage can. In our large household, almost every week we had to deal with the hassles of trying to force all the garbage in the can, leaving some of it outside or around the house (particularly paper and cardboard), or paying extra to have it hauled away.

6. Amount of Information Available on Options for Change: We could switch to a car with better mileage performance only when reliable information from consumer testing services was easily obtainable to help us choose wisely.

7. Immediate Rewards Available: These we provided for each other through verbal praise and expressions of admiration. We were living up to our image of each other as responsible citizens and flexible individuals.

8. Self-Image: Obviously whether our self-image corresponded with "waste not, want not," or "fly now, pay later" influenced the amount of pleasure we could receive from activities with delayed rewards. For example, with respect to storing organic kitchen wastes, later to turn them into garden compost that would then be useful in the growing of plants, the ultimate reward of harvested food comes many months, or sometimes seasons, after the initial effort.

9. Concrete Models Available: With all the sets of matching kitchen or household containers on display in a typical large hardware/variety store, we have yet to see an attractive set marked "aluminum," "bi-metal," "glass," "paper," "organic wastes," and "nonrecyclables." Nor did we know of a single household we could visit that was so equipped at the time we began our recycling efforts. In fact, the reverse was true. Family and friends happily dumped all these wastes together in a single can, just as we had done. Nor was provision made for the convenient sorting of wastes in the design of any of the households that we were aware of. No practical hands-on models existed at all.

Table 1-5 shows how we rated the significance of each of these factors in relation to one desired behavior change, the sorting of garbage. You may enjoy a similar exercise in attempting to predict the success of a venture to change your own personal lifestyle.

By analyzing what we went through to set up a home recycling center—where the organic waste, glass, paper, metal, and other materials could be sorted for processing—and actually beginning to sort out our household wastes, several insights emerged. The process looked something like this:

Problem Perception: First of all we formulated the problem by bringing our ecological knowledge to bear upon the pollution problems evident around us and at that time just beginning to break into the national and local media. We saw that separation of wastes at the source in the home was the critical step, not the creation of a machine, for example, that sorts what was once sorted. That was 1969, the year of Earth Day as well as much Save the (San Francisco) Bay activity. The latter directed the public's attention to the fact that San Francisco Bay was rapidly being filled in by dumps, or "sanitary land fills," among other things. Within various predicted lengths of time, the Bay Area cities would run out of places to dump their garbage.

This table is a rating made by the Olkowskis of the positive and negative influences they experienced in 1969 when they were teaching themselves to sort their own garbage and recycle their household wastes.

Table 1-5. Some Major Predisposing Conditions Needed for Behavior Change

Predisposing Conditions	Degree of Influence*								
	Negative					Positive			
	4	3	2	1	0	1	2	3	4
Cultural and/or personal taboo					★				
Immediacy of catastrophe					★				
Sustained awareness of problem							★		
Family support				★					
Community support							★		
Stress if change didn't occur						★			
Positive incentives (verbal reinforcement)									★
Information on options						★			
Self-image									★
Availability of concrete model				★					

*A value of zero (0) represents neutral influence. The authors felt that personal and cultural feelings pro and con about handling their own wastes averaged out, leaving them neutral on this aspect. Community support was expressed by the willingness of the Consumers' Cooperatives of Berkeley to establish a weekend recycling center on one of their parking lots, and the City Health Department signifying their approval of the development of home composting systems by issuing a pamphlet on the subject written by the Ecology Center. Obviously, the total points on the positive side showed that the attempt at behavior change was very likely to be successful. It was, and has persisted, and has been thoroughly integrated into the rest of our living habits.

Goal Articulation: Nature recycles, humans do not. Humans should!
(Our species is paying a heavy price for not recognizing that humans are a part of nature.) Once the goal of recycling our "waste" had been articulated, we spent a great deal of time talking about it. We were preparing ourselves for the question, What are *we* doing about environmental pollution? "If we are not part of the solution, we are part of the problem."

Visualization: What did the solution to the problem of recycling our homesite wastes look like? A period of extensive discussion ensued with attempts to visualize exactly how all the changes in our lifestyle could take place and what some of the consequences would be. We had to investigate a route for each type of household waste and imagine our personal interactions with the materials.

We knew it was simple to sort the waste at the home but now we needed a way to get the materials from the home back into industrial pathways. There were already models in the society for use of certain industrial secondary materials. One of the authors had participated in aluminum and paper drives during World War II. Another had participated in newspaper pick-up drives as a Boy Scout. It was really a matter of weighing the pros and cons of two obvious models: materials could be collected from the home to a collection center by a city service or brought by residents to a collection center directly.

We decided on the latter, since it seemed easiest to accomplish at the start. It also would be a good way of testing and demonstrating motivation in the community. The Berkeley Ecology Center provided a meeting place where others we were able to interest in the project could come together. These included Cliff Humphries who had started the group Ecology Action, whose members recycled newspapers in their own neighborhood. Eventually, through the help of Don Rothenburg, Education Director of the Consumers' Cooperatives of Berkeley (a consumer-owned chain of supermarkets and other stores with a consumer-community orientation), a recycling center was established on the parking lot of the CO-OP. It thrived. Within two years there were seventy-five recycling centers in the Bay Area, and others began to appear across the country. Obviously a social need existed and the motivation was there; all that was lacking was a model for behavior change.

These recycling centers, however, did not deal with the organic wastes, only glass, metal, and some paper. The problem with organic kitchen wastes at the home level was more difficult to solve. No acceptable urban model existed for coping with these materials. Carrying the stuff out in a pail and dumping it on the compost heap may work in a rural area where residents live far apart, but smells and problems with rats and flies precluded this solution in the city. The period of visualization and verbalization around this problem was lengthy. Gradually, we worked out what seemed to be a viable solution. We would keep separate, clearly designated, attractive bins under the sink in the kitchen for each category of inorganic material. Organic wastes would be drained in a colander by the side of the sink, transferred periodically to one of several small covered plastic garbage cans just outside the kitchen door on the back porch, and covered with a couple inches of sawdust so the smell didn't attract flies. This material would then be stored

Figure 1-5. **Integral Urban House Floor Plans**

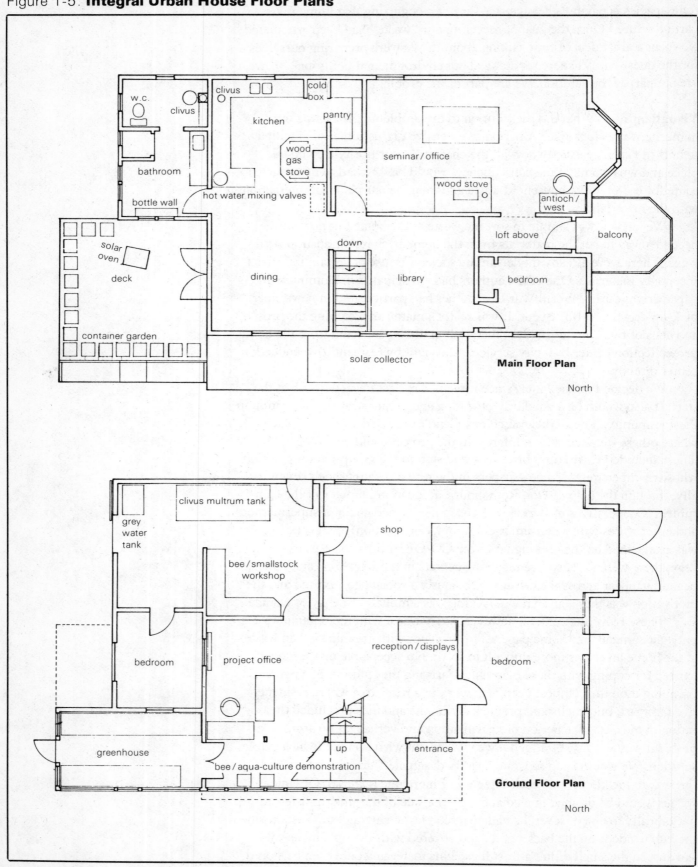

Main Floor Plan

North

Ground Floor Plan

North

until enough small cans of kitchen garbage, as well as weeds, leaves, and other garden debris, had been accumulated to enable the building of a one-cubic-yard batch of hot compost in a bin constructed for the purpose. (For a detailed discussion of this method, see pages 125–37.)

Internalization or Incubation: We found it significant that after we had clearly visualized the plan and accepted the proposition that implementing it was desirable a period ensued in which only continued talk but no action took place. Apparently, it was necessary to repeatedly confirm to each other the importance of the goal, the correctness of the model, and the details of the behavior change to which we were committing ourselves. As in Alcoholics Anonymous or Weight Watchers, we needed to reinforce our resolution through extensive verbalizing. This period of inactivity before taking the plunge we call internalization, or incubation. It seemed that something below the level of consciousness had to happen before we could actually shift our behavior in the desired direction.

Behavior-change Implementation: Finally, one day, we went out and bought the containers and began sorting our own garbage. It was easy. We couldn't figure out why it had taken us so long to actually do it. Once we were doing it and could describe or show the model, it was easy to effect a similar behavior change in others similarly motivated.

The Importance of Having a Model: One of our conclusions from this and similar experiences was the importance of having a model. This insight inspired us to develop the Integral Urban House in Berkeley as a model that people could come and visit. Another insight was the importance of providing adequate reinforcement for each other, through verbal approval, when we were the only ones we knew who were trying something different and everyone else thought we were a little crazy. Perhaps most important was the respect we gained for the difficulties of changing one lifestyle deliberately in the ways the Integral Urban House represents. Equally significant was the confirmation that the changes were worth making.

We believe that we have discovered a process for accomplishing environmental change that people in large numbers can easily adopt and learn. We have demonstrated that changes in behavior ultimately lead to environmental changes and that, conversely, in order to change any environmental condition one needs to first identify and evaluate the necessary behavioral changes. The Integral Urban House incorporates a set of solutions to the problems of living in the city that we have tested and believe to be valuable.

2. INTEGRAL DESIGN

In the preface, we discussed the basic motivation that led to the development of the Integral Urban House. The idea shared by the original group was the desire to create an urban living place—or habitat—whose humanly developed design organization would be analogous to the features of a healthy natural system, and in so doing begin to approximate the economy, efficiency, and simple elegance inherent in any natural system.

The word we use to describe the tendency to approximate the features of a natural system is *integral,* meaning "connected or unified whole." The dictionary meaning is "essential to completeness." In this chapter we will explore some of the principles of integral systems and how they are applied to the design of an integral urban house. At the outset, it is important to keep in mind that *no* human-designed system can ever achieve the organization of natural systems that have evolved over millions of years. We also should keep in mind that integral design has as much to do with *process* as it does with realized *form.* A house whose shape is analogous to that of a natural form—for example a house shaped like a nautilus shell or a dome emulating the natural structure of a microscopic creature—is not inherently "organic" or "natural." We do, however, tend to associate houses built of native unprocessed materials—earth, stone, or unsawn wood—as more "natural" than those built of industrial materials such as glass, steel, concrete.

Integral Design

Integral design applies lessons from the biology of natural systems to the design of environments for people. This emerging integration of architecture and ecology—some have dubbed it bioarchitecture or ecotecture—is in its infancy although we can identify principles and patterns that earlier cultures have known and applied. This discussion is necessarily more speculative and philosophical than the "how-to" chapters in the book, yet it is at the center of what this book is all about.

An obvious question is, "Why emulate natural design; what is there about the behavior of natural systems that we should pay attention to in designing our cities, towns, and houses?" The answer is framed by the most basic observed fact on earth: that the source of all life energy is the sun. But the earth is only habitable through the action of autotrophs—green plants (from the lowly algae to the towering redwoods) that capture a small percentage (about 1 percent) of solar energy and transform and fix it into useful forms of energy for other forms of life. Without complex natural systems to fix and transform energy, all solar energy would be lost as waste heat and life would not be sustained. We call this process entropy, the tendency of all energy to degrade into unusable waste heat, radiated back into space. Negentropy—the sum total of all life processes that capture and transform energy into usable forms—is the basis for life and civilization.

Evolution is the process by which natural systems become increasingly diverse, complex, and differentiated in order to counteract entropy. Evolution through negentropy may be seen as nature's slow but certain strategy to achieve stability in the face of the inevitable entropic degradation and eventual death of the planet.

Human beings cannot hope to improve on the efficiency of natural negentropic processes. However, a goal can be to design habitat and culture in such a way that natural systems and the information contained in them are not degraded and destroyed. Humans as a species are uniquely adapted to process and store information in abstract and symbolic forms. This characteristic gives us our unique ability to manipulate our surroundings as no other species can. Some people would claim that modern societies are somehow more callous about their effect on natural systems than cultures of earlier times. While there are important exceptions, the rule seems to be that throughout history, cultures have gained short-term advantage by exploiting for maximum productivity, ignoring long-term stability. As ecosystems deteriorated, people had to take the consequences or move on. Edward Hyams, in his classic *Soil and Civilization,* documents the ecological destruction of vast areas of the planet by earlier cultures in Europe, Africa, Asia, and this continent:

Most were destroyed by the use of early succession monoculture techniques that produced large yields for a relatively short period of time. It is like the story of the goose that laid the golden eggs. Her keepers were not satisfied with getting the eggs one at a time so they killed her to get them all out at once, only to find that once the goose was dead there were no more golden eggs.

What has changed is the scale of the potential destruction of natural systems. It has grown enormously through a dizzying array of new technologies, spiraling populations, and the increasing insulation of modern urban populations from the first-round effects of ecological deterioration. This insulation and the accompanying false sense of security is rooted in a massive but short-lived dowry of fossil fuels—the stored product of tropical-forest ecosystems many eons old.

It is instructive to plot graphically the use of fossil fuels that presently provide a minority of the earth's population with the basis for a high material standard of life against a time axis encompassing most of known human history. The image is that of a needle, perhaps symbolic of our collective addiction to the fossil fuel fix providing the euphoric feeling that we can es-

Figure 2–1. **The Fossil Fuel Needle**

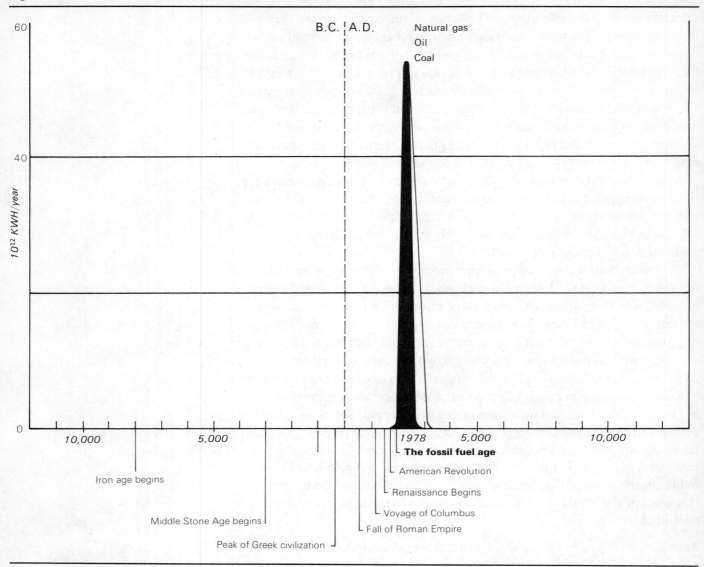

cape the destiny that other careless cultures suffered. Or some might see in this image the fickle finger of the fossil fuels themselves.

The point here is that we can do something about the destructive course our culture is now on by learning how to make the transition to an integrally designed way of life.

The Integral System

To those familiar with the jargon of electronics, circuitry, and related fields, some of this language may sound familiar, for indeed many of the patterns that explain the flow of energy and materials in natural systems have been adapted in all kinds of human-designed systems. However, ecological reality is more complex, less mechanistic, and more indeterminate than any mental map is capable of representing. In this limited space it is not our intent, nor would it be possible, to give a definitive picture of what distinguishes a living system from an inanimate one, or how to construct a habitat that fully integrates the inanimate and the living form. At this time, only the vague outlines of this knowledge are there, and much of what we can learn is by comparison.

We can contrast the properties of the integral system with what we call the *linear* system—the "early-succession ecology" or monoculture that seems to characterize most human societies:

Integral	*Linear*
* Energy flows through loops	* Energy flows along straight line
* Parts fit overlapping functions	* Parts are specialized modular components
* Low entropy/high information	* High entropy/low information
* Open system/closed loops	* Closed system/no loops
* Memory stored in many different cells	* Memory stored in specialized component
* High rate of material recovery	* High rate of material loss
* Multiple alternate channels	* Single channels
* No waste	* High waste
* Self-regulating	* Imbalance passed along
* Multipurpose	* Single purpose
* Steady flow of energy	* Surging flow of energy
* Diversity, complexity, stability	* Uniformity, simplicity, instability
* High number of species	* Low number of species
* Biomorphic aesthetic	* Linear aesthetic

Main Features of Integral Systems

1. Process materials and energy through closed loops and webs of multiple channels;
2. Release energy within the system in small increments;
3. Maintain a steady state (homeostasis) through negative feedback loops and permeable boundaries;
4. Store information in a decentralized genetic memory.

Figure 2-2. **Energy Flow in a Closed System Habitat**

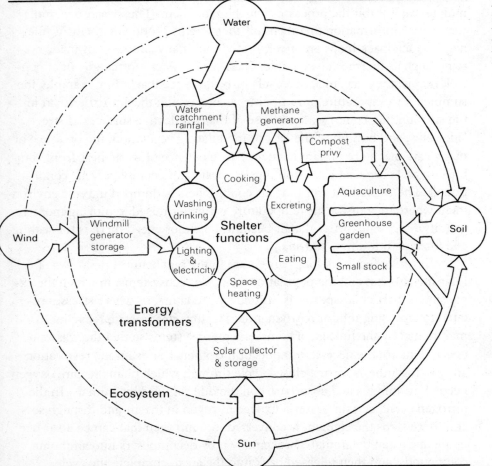

A schematic diagram of nutrient and energy cycles in an integral habitat. Note that technology (the middle ring) mediates between ecosystem resources (the outer ring) and human needs and functions (the inner ring).

These properties exist on a continuum. The important thing is to get a feeling for when the design of a particular system approaches the integral and when it approaches the linear.

The closed integral loop is fundamental to the nature of living systems. Many benefits are realized from the intentional application of this concept to the design of the built environment.

Living organisms exist as complex eddy pools in a continuously flowing stream of energy and material elements. That energy from the sun which is caught by life processes is sooner or later radiated away into space where it is forever lost to us. Nutrient elements released from the earth's rocks eventually accumulate in sediment in the bottom of the seas; it takes many millions of years for them to be recycled back to the land. The trickle of energy and nutrients available to life is not infinite and must be conserved if living things are to prosper.

Webbing implies multiple channels and loops. Webbing allows the meaningful transfer of energy, materials, and information, and constitutes the connections that comprise living systems, whether they are called cells, organisms, or ecosystems. If energy and nutrients flow along webs or pathways, they can be retained longer within living boundaries, and thus an internal steady state environment for life systems is established. Multiple parallel pathways allow compensating flow to take place when a channel is impaired. Loops allow both cycling and self-regulation. For example, each subsystem processes its input to release output products which, as they accumulate, can inhibit the processes which made them. Thus waste accumulation can be information that turns off the systems producing them. While negative feedback loops are incorporated into many simple man-made systems, such as thermostats, complex man-made systems often go out of control, that is, they get stuck in a cycle of positive feedback. For example, the summer air temperature in most cities is higher and the air dirtier than in the surrounding countryside because of many reflective surfaces of streets, sidewalks, and buildings; the lack of modulating vegetation; the presence of many cars that store radiant heat; and the existence of waste heat from combustion and electrical use. Buildings are sealed and completely air conditioned. The waste heat from the air conditioners is dumped into the environment where the outside air temperature is further raised, requiring more air conditioning. The dirtier the air becomes, the more need there is for sealing and filtering buildings, and so on.

Negative feedback loops are found in the biochemical pathways of cellular metabolism and the population swings of ecosystems, in which the expansion of particular species is limited by predators, or where stresses related to crowding inhibit reproduction. Healthy steady-state recycling is maintained by the linkage of complementary systems so that the wastes of one system are the necessary inputs of the other. For example, respiration and photosynthesis form a closed cycle through which plants respire oxygen needed by animals and absorb carbon dioxide respired by animals. In the nitrogen cycle, certain bacteria fix free nitrogen in the air and through several more steps the element is converted into nitrogen that can be absorbed by plants, eaten by animals, broken down by decomposers into ammonia compounds, and then released back into the air to complete the cycle.

Another principle contributing to homeostasis is that in natural systems energy is most efficiently used by organisms when released in small increments. The long enzyme chains that metabolize sugar in our cells or the long food chains that utilize energy in such complex and elegant ecosystems as the oceans or tropical forests are good examples. Mature natural systems consist of many different nested stages, each of which can store energy for a long time and transport it along a multiplicity of routes. This structure has the effect of minimizing the waste when a sudden surge of potential energy is released in a simple system, and very little of it can be stored. We all know what happens when a watershed is denuded of vegetation and no longer can absorb a sudden heavy rain. The result is flooding downstream, waste of soil and water, and further regression of the system. In an ecosystem, many little steps tend to be gentle and subtle while a few big steps tend to be harsh and destructive.

A part of our concern here is the boundaries between systems. In integral systems, boundaries are permeable and systems mesh together with such intricacy that transactions across the boundaries of systems flow without waste or upheaval. By contrast, our modern urban systems are monocultural crazy quilts stitched loosely together with waste.

Information is the pattern that organizes form. The energy-materials pattern crystallized *is* form, and the pattern when transmitted is information. In simplest terms, "inform"—"in-form"—means "to give form to." Within any living system, evolutionary information is contained within the DNA of every cell and in the learned experience of the food chain. The DNA is the code that determines the formal organization and structure of the organism. In human societies, information is stored in the cultural pattern, which includes the built environment, the institutional structure, and patterns of communication.

In the continued cycling of energy and materials through time, information is stored as genetic evolution and culture. Information is precious and needs to be conserved. While species have continuously appeared and disappeared throughout earth's history, every major information advance has been retained. *The real harvest of the ecological fabric evolving through time is information,* including human culture. A return to a higher degree of regional autonomy and responsibility will not be a return to the Dark Ages, as some have claimed, as long as information is conserved and enhanced. Protecting information is a necessary accommodation to the ecological rules by which living beings can maintain themselves in a healthy relationship with their world.

Too much energy flow is detrimental to ecological systems. An overload or surge of energy flowing through a system can be destructive to the informational content that is embodied in its structure and form. This is true for natural as well as man-made systems. Run too much current through an appliance and it burns out. Overload an aquatic system with nutrients suspended in sewage and its natural health and structure is destroyed. A dam bursting upstream releases a sudden surge of energy and wipes out entire valleys and communities downstream.

Early succession monocultures (such as our present society) process energy and materials so rapidly that the outflow overwhelms systems on the

An Ecosystem Includes Five Functions:

1. Fixation of sunlight into biomass;
2. Cycling of nutrients (for example, nitrogen cycling between the living and nonliving components);
3. Self-regulation of population size;
4. Succession of components (for example, one species following and displacing a previous species);
5. Self-reproduction and maintenance.

receiving end. The result is loss of information and loss of structure. Unfortunately, economists—the shamans of the modern industrial system—know nothing about the behavior of natural systems. In economics, flow measured in money is everything; the destruction of information embedded in the structure of living communities is not measured. The increased entropy that results from the loss of information is never calculated. Keynesian economics seeks to maximize energy and money flow. Stable and diverse natural and cultural systems are seen as obstacles to progress or resources to be transformed into cash flow. Some see this approach as burning down the house of life to toast marshmallows.

The distribution of information in living systems varies with their scale and function. We consider three basic life scales: the ecosystem, the organism, and the cell.

The structure of information in the ecosystem follows the general principles mentioned as typical of integral systems, that is, the presence of closed loops and multiple channels, energy distribution in many stages and small increments, the presence of negative feedback loops and of permeable boundaries between distinct subsystems, and an information system decentralized in each cell. An ecosystem can last indefinitely and compensate for major disturbances and dislocations. A lost part or species can usually be compensated for by other parts with similar functions. Information is re-

Figure 2–3. **Schematic of a Generalized Ecosystem**

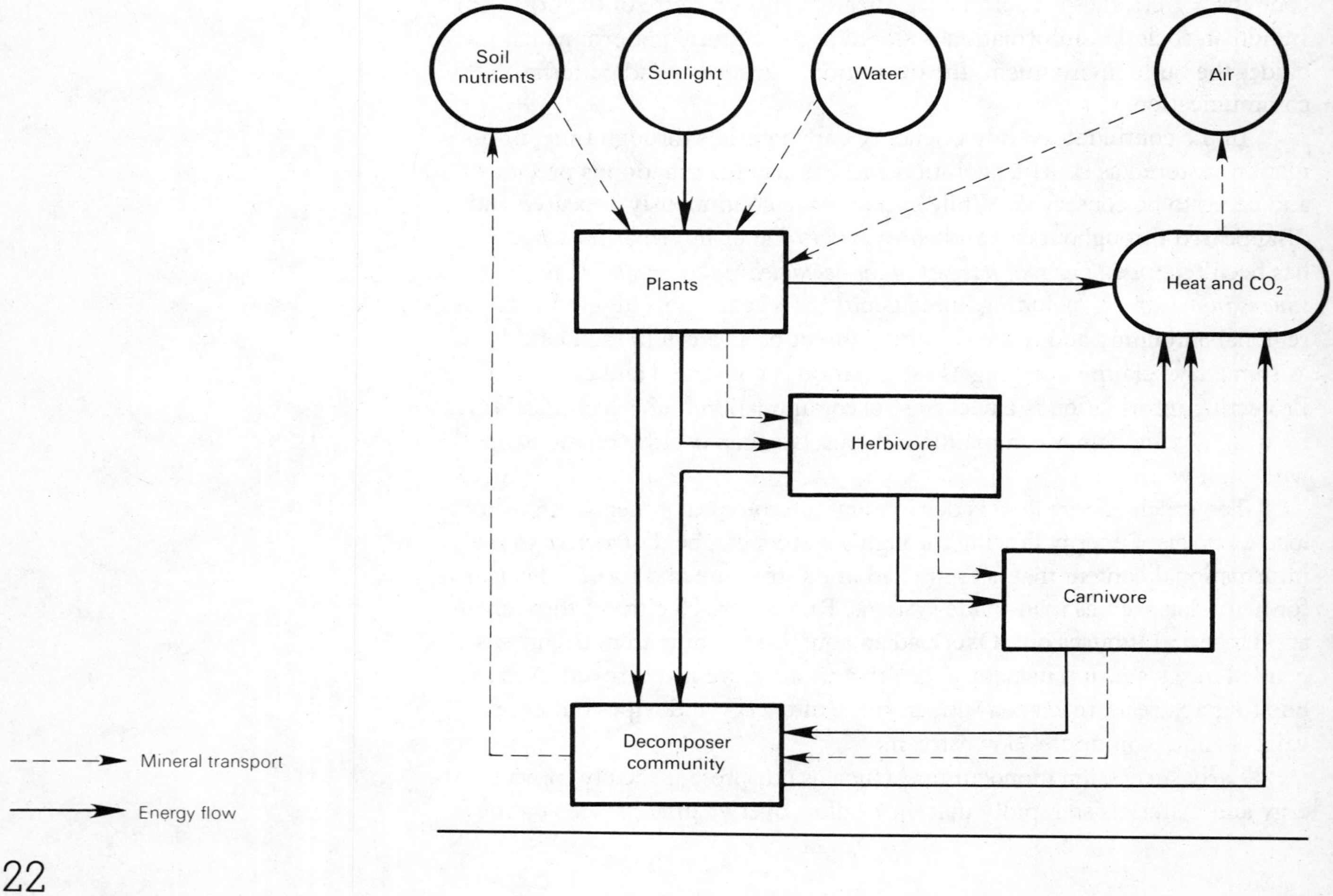

- – – → Mineral transport

———→ Energy flow

tained within the genetic, and sometimes learned, patterns of various species. No purely human-designed system extant is analogous to an ecosystem; however, gardens and other agricultural systems are comparable to many natural ecosystems. The more pathways, steps, and loops that can be included in a man-made system the more stable and healthy the system will be.

Organisms, especially animals with central nervous systems, are much more centralized with regard to their information, and have comparatively little redundancy of functioning parts. The loss of an important organ commonly results in death. The highly directed design of organized parts allows such organisms to focus energy very effectively while they are alive. The organ is the precursor and analog of the machine and indeed the body, and its parts and process can be the analog for the design of an integral house. Houses are like bodies in that their components are designed like organs to perform specific functions. Some degree of backup and shunting allows compensation for changes and breakdowns. Information is centralized in the humans who operate the household system.

The cell is the intermediate between ecosystem and organism in design. Its information is relatively centralized in its nucleus but it has many parallel and redundant metabolism channels. It thus combines potential immortality with the direction of energy toward specific tasks. Communities are like cell tissue in their spatial arrangement and metabolic looping. To the extent that they conserve energy and materials effectively, they place less strain on the surrounding and supporting system.

Multiple Pathways

On average it takes as much energy to heat and cool the U.S. building stock for three years as it took to build it in the first place. Home furnaces are the largest source of air pollution after automobiles, dumping an estimated 8.4 million tons of air pollutants into the atmosphere each year. . . .

The materials currently used in modern American architecture are among the most energy intensive materials there are. . . .

In many parts of the U.S., domestic utility bills currently exceed mortgage payments. . . .

All water used in buildings, no matter for what purpose, exists as sewage. Our water and sewage systems are coupled in series. We quite literally defecate in our water systems in the name of personal hygiene. An average house uses between 150–200 gallons of water per inhabitant per day. . . .

The average home produces 4.5 pounds of garbage per person per day or anywhere from 2.5 to 5 tons per year. Fibers, plastics, paper, wood, glass, metal and food scraps are usually thrown in the same trash can. A lot of highly organized material input channels are combined in one "noisy" exit channel and dumped; disorder or entropy is maximized. Subsequent sorting costs make recycling uneconomic in many cases. . . .

Homes pollute flows of materials as thoroughly as they infect water systems. Mixing organic and inorganic wastes makes frequent trash collection a necessity if disease vectors imparted by waste food putrefaction are to be avoided. . . .

The BTU value of garbage thrown out by a family of four over a year in Boston is equal to between a quarter and a third of the winter heating requirements of a conventional house. . . .

—Wellesley-Miller, 1977

A contrast between Wellesley-Miller's description of the typical U.S. home and urban pattern and the organization and flow of the integral house is useful. It is important to remember that no exotic or breakthrough technology is required to make the integral house concept work. The components or parts of the system are all available. Integration is the key. By themselves, a solar collector, waterless toilet, and windowsill garden do not constitute a system. Figure 2-4 provides an inclusive view of the integral house's basic components organized around three areas: food production, resource recovery, and energy generation.

Multiple Pathways in an Integral House: In an integral house, each major functional system employs multiple pathways for material and energy flow. The heating system, for example, includes direct solar gain through windows, a solar air space heating system, and a wood stove space heater for cloudy cold days. Organic wastes can be shunted in a variety of ways. Human fecal matter decomposes in the Clivus Multrum, and when fully decomposed is used as a soil amendment on ornamentals. Urine is diluted and used as a nitrogen-rich fertilizer. Kitchen scraps are fed to the chickens, which convert them into edible protein and eggs, and the chicken manure is recycled in the garden. Garbage can also be composted or fed to worm cultures, which make a nutrient-rich casting for garden use; the worms themselves are fed to the chickens or the fish in the pond. Duckweed in the pond absorbs toxic fish waste and in turn can be dried and fed to the chickens.

These are only several examples of the principle of multiple pathways, which is closely linked to the diversity and stability associated with natural healthy systems. Multiple pathways constitute an interactive process within any food or nutrient chain. For example, a diversity of types of plants in a garden insures a diversity of insect life; this condition in turn insures that no particular insect population is likely to get out of control and become a pest. Diverse plant and insect life attracts birds and other natural predators on the food chain that help to maintain balance.

These simple examples of the closed integral loop with multiple pathways enhancing stability and diversity can be contrasted with their linear equivalents. To heat a house electrically, for example, requires that many more times the energy equivalent of high quality fuels be consumed than will finally result in useful heat in the home. Moreover, a large investment is required to process, transform, and distribute the energy from source to use location. Most of the energy is wasted. In the case of the waste or garbage cycle, in the linear mode "wastes" are simply hauled to land-fills and buried. Most urban areas, not surprisingly, are running out of available land-fill space and many cities are now hauling garbage to remote locations, sometimes hundreds of miles away. Human wastes are diluted in the ratio of 100 to 1 with potable water and piped to large sewage factories where the solids are removed through mechanical and bacterial action. The polluted,

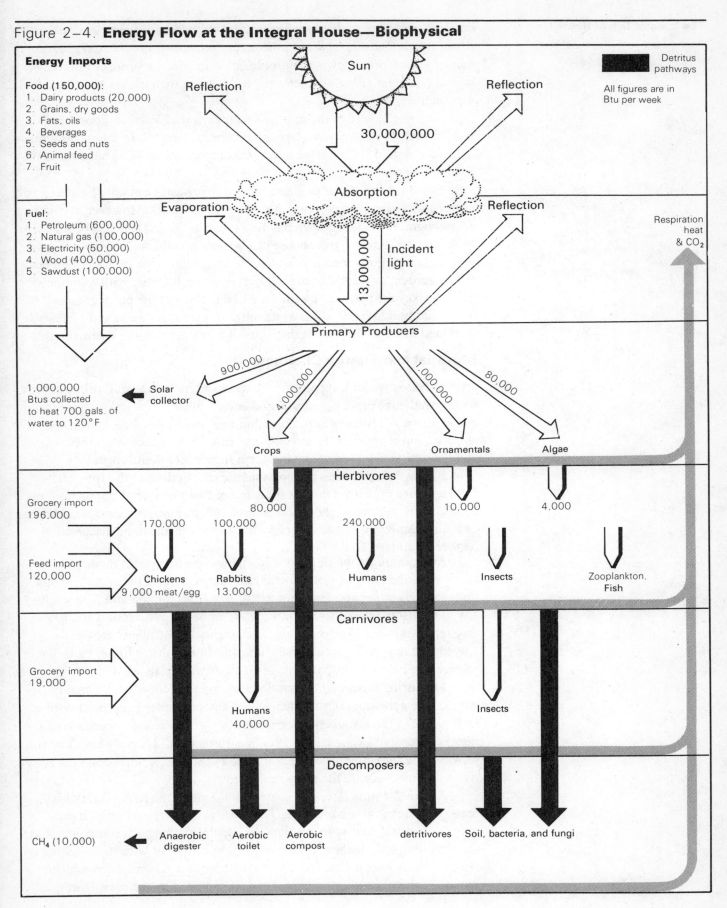

Figure 2–4. **Energy Flow at the Integral House—Biophysical**

nutrient-rich effluent that remains is then dumped into rivers or oceans where it overloads the ability of the natural system to provide oxygen, producing a condition known as eutrophication in which a surge of microbiological and algal growth depletes the oxygen and then decays to further foul the water.

Another feature of the multiple pathway is that each component of the system tends to perform overlapping functions. One test of the integral quality of any system is the extent to which components are integrated into multiple functions.

Consider our earlier example. An electric heater can only be an electric heater and a garbage truck can only be a garbage truck. However, a window admits light, provides a view, may be a place to sit, and can also be a solar collector. An attached greenhouse can be a solar collector and storage system, a place to grow seedlings and winter vegetables, the location for a hot tub. A garden, or planting boxes, however small, together with a composting bucket, takes the place of the smelly garbage can and the noisy garbage truck, and besides processing waste nutrients, provides a source of beauty, food, and flowers, and can be the focus of many pleasurable leisure hours.

Material and Energy Channels

In this section we look at some of the ways systems of integral urban houses work together to process material and energy flows.

Figure 2-2 illustrates in diagrammatic form a possible set of relationships among ecosystem resources (outer ring), basic functions (inner ring), and the designed systems that transform inputs into useful form.

Figure 2-5 illustrates the ecosystemic transactions at the Integral Urban House organized into its three major functions: food production, resource recovery, and energy and resource generation. This view is useful because it organizes into one diagram all the components to be discussed in further detail later in the book.

As an examination of Figure 2-3 shows, the ecosystem model traditionally is described in terms of mineral and energy flows. Energy, in terms of this model, is understood to enter the system from the sun and then gradually to be lost to outer space as heat, while minerals cycle round and round through the system. The minerals, or elements, of the planet are our "givens." They are finite and make up what Buckminster Fuller calls our "Spaceship Earth." They also make up all the materials we use.

Measuring input and output flows within the ecosystemic diagram begins to give a measure of the efficiency of any particular household system. In Figure 2-4 the actual energy transactions within selected portions of the integral household system have been measured in BTUs per week. The sun provides the initial input, while plant photosynthesis, animals, and the activity of decomposers are the main subsystems.

Figure 2-4 illustrates the energy flow through the living (biotic) systems of the integral urban house. This view is important because it provides a quantitative way to evaluate the capability that each component has for providing food for the residents. The large amount of sunlight falling on the yard undergoes a series of transformations as it powers the system and mobilizes the parts. As the sun's energy is captured by the plants through

Figure 2-5. **Integral House Ecosystem**

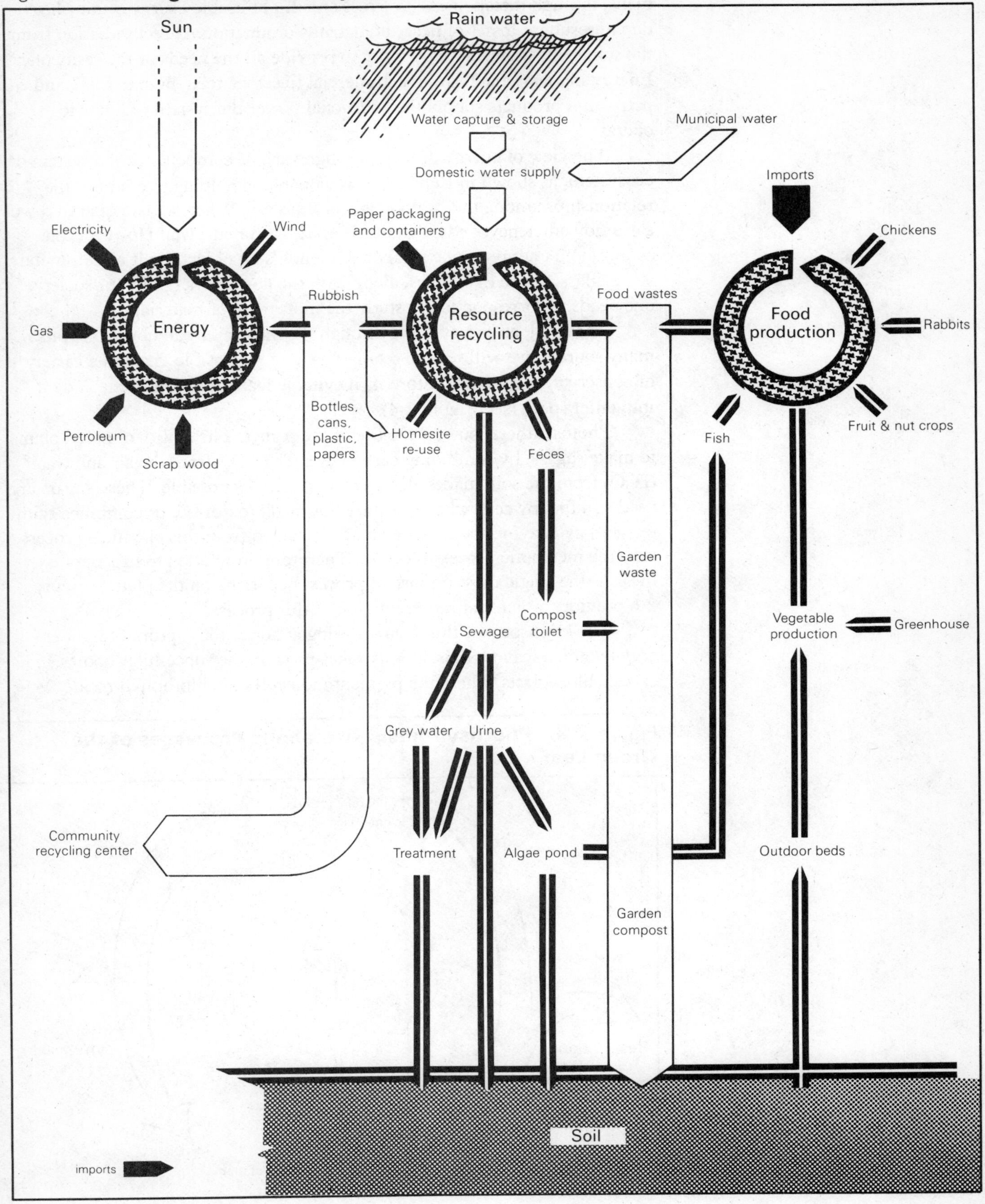

Sun

Rain water

Water capture & storage

Municipal water

Domestic water supply

Imports

Electricity

Wind

Paper packaging and containers

Chickens

Gas

Energy

Rubbish

Resource recycling

Food wastes

Food production

Rabbits

Petroleum

Scrap wood

Bottles, cans, plastic, papers

Homesite re-use

Feces

Fish

Fruit & nut crops

Community recycling center

Sewage

Compost toilet

Garden waste

Vegetable production

Greenhouse

Grey water

Urine

Treatment

Algae pond

Outdoor beds

Garden compost

Soil

imports

27

photosynthesis and as plant energy is captured by animals, including humans, through metabolism, the gross amount of usable energy diminishes due to resultant losses of heat and detritus production. Direct radiation from the sun is not sufficient in quantity to provide all the needs of the residents. Energy inputs in the form of commercial livestock feed, human food, and petroleum products supply the additional power the system requires to operate.

The view of energy flowing through various components of a system or ecosystem, as shown in Figure 2-4, is valuable in helping to quantify the relationships among the components of a system. When we can quantify, we can study efficiency, and efficiency is essential for survival. However, one cannot hold energy in one's hands. One holds an object, be it a fuel, metal, stove, glass, or the like. Thus, along with the flow of energy in our society, one needs to correspondingly study the movement of materials.

Above all, as energy flows through the integral urban house from its many sources, we will seek to retain it as long as possible through a variety of conservation methods before its inevitable leak out of the home and off into outer space (see Figure 2-4).

Photosynthesis powers the life of the planet. The ability of green plants to make sugars, by combining carbon dioxide (CO_2) from the air and water (H_2O) from the soil, makes all other life processes possible. These sugars are used as a fuel by cells where they are "burned" (oxidized, or combined with oxygen) by enzyme action. The energy obtained from this chemical process runs the metabolic processes of life. Therefore, in relation to life, photosynthesis is the single most important process occurring on the planet. Figure 2-6 provides a pictorial representation of this process.

The key aspect of this sugar-making action is the capture of light energy by green leaves. This activity takes place in the subcellular bodies called chloroplasts, where the pigment molecules of chlorophyll reside.

Figure 2-6. **Photosynthesis: Metabolic Processes of the Green Leaf**

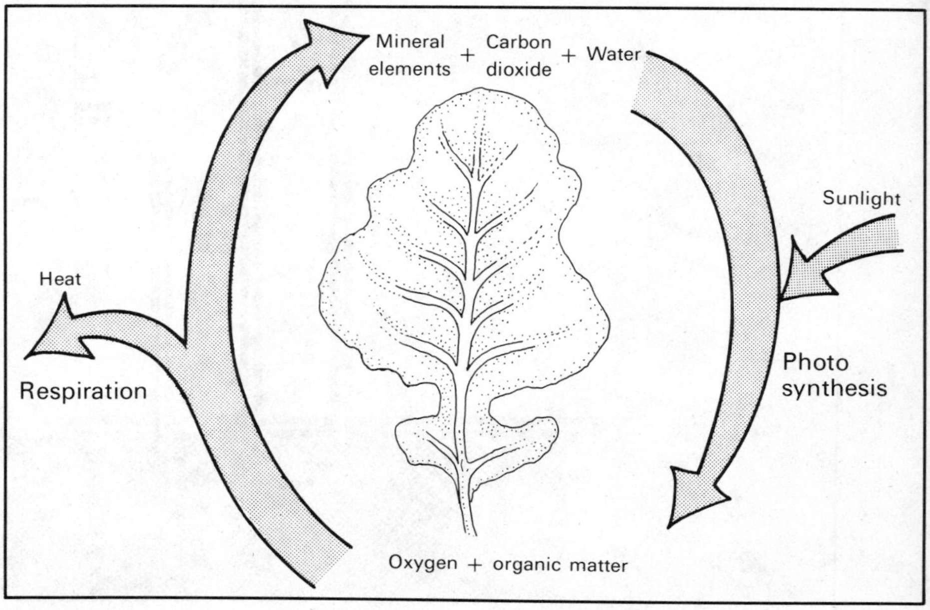

Mineral elements + Carbon dioxide + Water

Sunlight

Heat

Respiration

Photosynthesis

Oxygen + organic matter

Chlorophyll absorbs light waves predominantly in the blue and red areas of the electromagnetic spectrum, reflecting green (and yellow, which is masked until the chlorophyll dies). Thus the leaves appear green.

These pigment molecules are photosensitive, and when the light reaches them, they store the incoming energy in the form of excited electrons. These excited electrons then create new chemical bonds, resulting in molecules that are more complex and whose chemical bonds contain more stored energy. Thus light energy is converted to, and stored as, chemical energy in sugars and starches.

Minerals: Every home, human process, and organism on the earth utilizes minerals. They are the "stuff" of life. A very useful way to visualize the flow of these materials through the human ecosystem is to imagine a series of wheels, each one of which is a cycle for a particular mineral or material.

Figure 2–7. **Nitrogen Cycling in the Integral House**

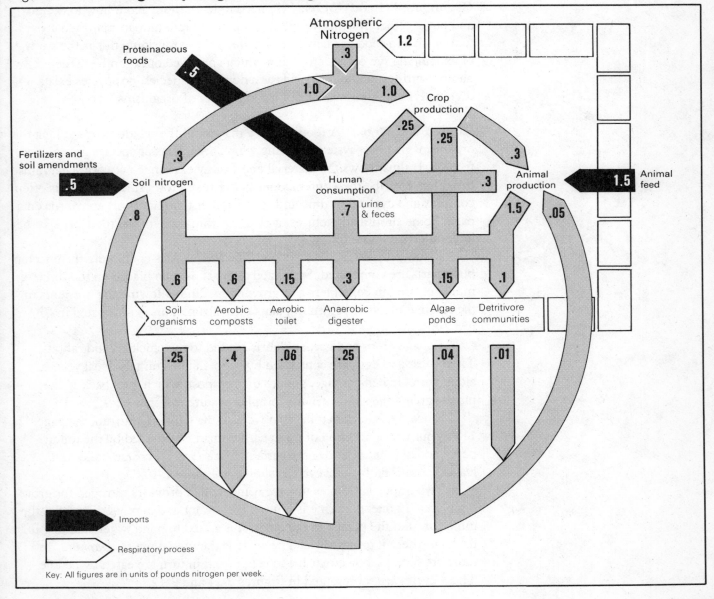

Key: All figures are in units of pounds nitrogen per week.

Although these minerals are represented as atoms, they are actually taken in by an organism in particular forms and combinations. A good example is hydrogen (H). Hydrogen is not absorbed by humans directly in its molecular form (H_2), but is probably most commonly absorbed in water (H_2O). Yet atomic hydrogen is also a major component of many other materials—sugars, starches, fats, proteins, methane, petroleum, and so on.

Ecologists have worked out some of the key cycles for use in managing resources. The idea is to discover how natural ecosystems process minerals so that these patterns can be used as models for human ecosystem management and design. The nitrogen cycle of the integral urban house is presented in Figure 2-7. It differs from a classical picture of the nitrogen cycle in that it represents a mechanistic view of nitrogen in a managed life-support system rather than simply as a biophysical process. The nitrogen cycle is used because it is a "key" or macronutrient needed in large quantities. Using this sort of design tool helps make a tighter, more integrated system.

Organismal (Food) Webs: We need to learn more about how to design and put together systems of living components into human-managed ecosystems such as a food garden. The knowledge base for doing this is the study of existing native ecosystems from which contrived ones can be modeled. In natural settings, without humans as a dominant species, no species exists individually. Each is a member of a community of organisms.

Home Food Webs: A food web is a map of all the relationships among the organisms in an ecosystem showing which organisms or species group they feed on. It thus shows the material and energy exchange network. Diagrams can often describe these interactions better than prose, since the web is often complex and cyclical in time and space, rather than linear, as are words on a page. Some simplified pictures of cycles within some of the food webs at the integral urban house follow.

Plants provide food for people. The food wastes containing the uneaten plant parts are composted. Stabilized compost is then placed on the soil as a mulch or used in containers as a growing medium allowing the nutrients in the original plants to return to plants once again. This is illustrated in Figure 2-8.

Foliage crops and garden debris are fed to the chickens and rabbits. Their meat and eggs are consumed by people. The animals' fecal wastes, along with kitchen garbage, go into the compost, which goes back to the plants, giving the slightly more complex picture in Figure 2-9.

Since the waterless toilet that we use (the Clivus Multrum, see page 113) requires the addition of more carbon than is provided by the toilet paper added to it, we add some garden debris (weeds, coarse stalks and leaves) occasionally. The cycle is shown in Figure 2-10.

Two important cycles involve urine, which provides nitrogen for growing plants. In one, the urine is diluted with water and applied directly to the mulch around the plants; in the other, it is added to pond water standing in the sun, where it grows algae. The algae is then fed upon by *Daphnia,* and these are fed upon by crayfish and fish, which in turn are eaten by people. These cycles are represented in Figures 2-11 and 2-12.

Figure 2–8. **Human Food-Compost Cycle**

Mulch, as a growing medium for plants

Plants

Compost

People

Kitchen garbage

Figure 2–9. **Small Stock Food Cycle**

Plants

Compost

People

Kitchen garbage

Chickens, rabbits

Figure 2–10. **Human Waste Cycle**

People

Kitchen garbage

Bacteria, fungi and other micro-organisms in the Clivus Multrum (waterless toilet)

Plants

Figure 2–11. **Urine/Marine Cycle**

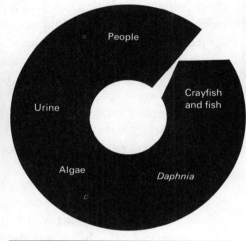

People

Urine

Crayfish and fish

Algae

Daphnia

Figure 2–12. **Urine Cycle**

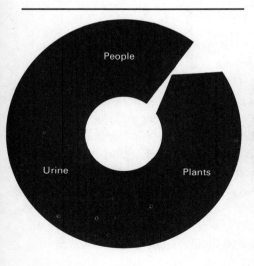

People

Urine

Plants

Figure 2–13. **Insect Food Cycle**

Chickens

Feces

Traps

Flies

In another simple food cycle, the flies attracted to and/or feeding in the chicken manure are trapped and fed to the chickens, Figure 2-13.

An interesting food web was developed by siting the beehive over the fish pond. In a big, healthy hive, about a thousand new bees are born each day and a thousand die. These latter leave the hive to do so, or are carried away and dropped by the worker bees. The many dead bees from our hive are eaten by the fish, as shown in Fig. 2-14.

Many other food cycles and webs surround us, both inside and outdoors. Some, such as those of the decomposer organisms that break down complex plant and animal materials into their simplest components, are essential to life. Those of others, such as the house spiders that control insect pests within our home, work, unappreciated, to our advantage. Still others, for instance those involving the cockroaches, flour moths, and carpet beetles, are annoying or damaging to our possessions.

Water: The hydrologic, or water, cycle is continuous, and is driven by the sun (see Figure 2-15). The sun evaporates water from the surfaces of plants, soil, bodies of water, and structures. Through photosynthesis, it supplies the energy that plants use for their metabolic processes, an integral part of which is the transpiration of water vapor into the air. The sun heats the air itself, causing it to rise, and the moving air speeds evaporation. This water-laden air rises, cools, condenses and falls to earth again.

In the integral urban house, water is used for drinking, cooking, washing, and raising animals and plants. The challenge is to take the water from the point where it enters the home and use it frugally. As it becomes increasingly contaminated with wastes from cooking and bathing, it can either be recycled through a still to restore it to drinking-water purity, or sent through compost and soil to raise plants and eventually replenish the groundwater supply. In those solar space heating systems in which water is used to capture heat from the sun and transfer it to the air throughout the house, there may be large amounts of water stored within the house that become a permanent part of the house structure. Figure 2-16 shows the water pathways through the integral urban house and how various functions of the home can be integrated with a carefully planned water system.

Economy, Energy, and Aesthetics

In terms of human purpose, integral design produces value in three spheres: (1) economy, (2) energy use, and (3) aesthetics. Economics measures the short-term costs of energy and material transactions in money terms. Costs are set by the availability of materials or services, the demand for them, and other constraints on the marketplace such as government actions that affect or distort the economic transaction. The individual decision-maker is concerned with costs that his or her actions can affect directly, and the priorities of our early succession, production-oriented economy is such that integral design in itself very often does not result in short-term economic advantage for its practitioner. In the short run, a farmer who grows diversified crops and returns wastes to the soil may not do as well as one whose profits depend on strip-mining the soil of its nutrients and quality. The urban dweller who

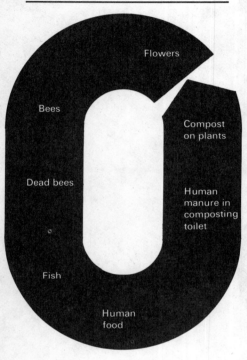

Figure 2-14. **Insect/Marine Food Cycle**

Flowers

Bees

Compost on plants

Dead bees

Human manure in composting toilet

Fish

Human food

Figure 2–15. **Hydrologic Cycle**

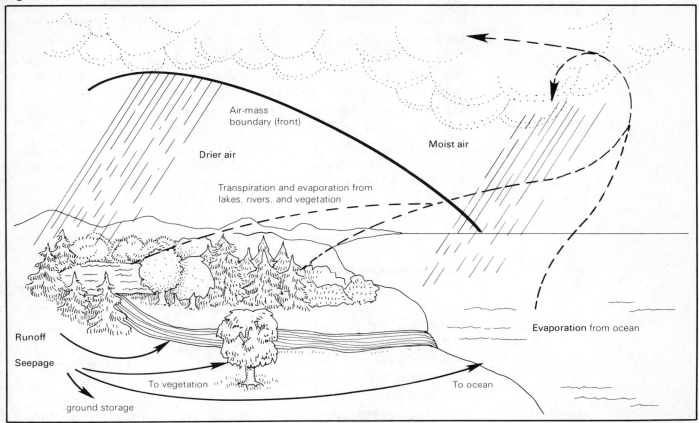

Air-mass boundary (front)

Drier air

Moist air

Transpiration and evaporation from lakes, rivers, and vegetation

Evaporation from ocean

Runoff

Seepage

To vegetation

To ocean

ground storage

Figure 2–16. **Water Pathways through Integral Urban House**

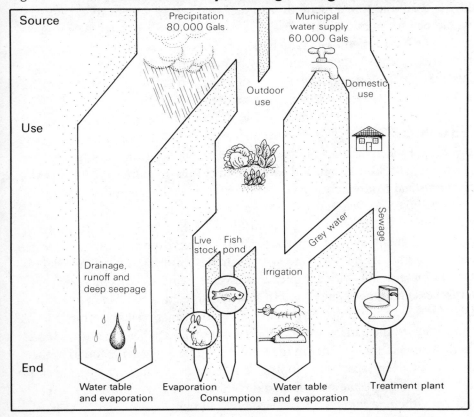

Source

Precipitation 80,000 Gals.

Municipal water supply 60,000 Gals

Outdoor use

Domestic use

Use

Grey water

Sewage

Live stock

Fish pond

Irrigation

Drainage, runoff and deep seepage

End

Water table and evaporation

Evaporation Consumption

Water table and evaporation

Treatment plant

makes the effort to install a waterless recycling toilet still has to pay the tax burden of a wasteful centralized sewer system. The homeowner who installs solar heating equipment still has to underwrite the cost of expensive conventional centralized generating equipment, and must compete against the low price—relative to their fuel value—of fossil fuels. In each case, the boundaries of the economic system do not conform to the boundaries of the integral system. The costs of destroying the fertility of the soil are not charged against the soil miner, and no economic incentives are offered to the individual who does not wish to participate in institutionalized pollution, such as is practiced in the public sewer. However, as the pioneer-style industrial culture runs up against the limits imposed by resource scarcity, breakdowns in its overextended networks, and the simple entropy of bloated size, economics will begin to reflect the advantages of working with the natural grain rather than against it.

As a rule, in any integrally designed system, total energy flow through the system will be much lower than in the linear system. The linear, early-succession system pulses energy through at a maximum rate, with a high rate of waste, in order to achieve maximum product flow. As mentioned previously, the economic costs are often not borne by the immediate user but get buried in the increasing entropy of the larger system. For example, home heating using nuclear electrically generated heat as compared with the direct storage of solar energy is extremely inefficient when comparing potential fuel value to end use. Similarly, modern agriculture may use ten to twenty calories of energy to produce one calorie of food. In traditional agricultural practices, the ratio is reversed. Wasteful modern practices are rationalized on the basis that the total productivity of energy-intensive agriculture are far higher than traditional methods, and that we would starve or food prices would be astronomical if the fossil fuel subsidy were removed. At a time when our food system is so largely dependent on energy-wasteful monoculture, these claims, sadly enough, may be all too true. More than anything else this conclusion points up the need to begin rebuilding the network of a regional, energy-efficient agriculture before it is too late.

Finally, we touch on the aesthetic sphere, which too often is neglected and without which neither economy nor the efficient use of energy have any meaning. Indeed, aesthetics *is* the meaning we find in form. Aesthetics, then, is conceptual information, and varies from culture to culture. A friend from the industrial Midwest remarked that while he and his neighbors were surrounded by ecological devastation, they were tool literate because they were surrounded by a forest of tools and machines. The meaning we derive from our environment is limited by the form of that environment and how we are able to interact with it. We start with a simple assumption: regular participation and interaction with complex and diverse living systems increases our awareness and renews the spirit. In short, the meaning that we derive from life is enriched and constantly recharged by the functional and ritualistic connection to the natural world. The preindustrial aesthetic is always based on this connection, whether in the miniature Japanese garden found in the densest towns in Japan, the simple Arab courtyard fountain, the shade elms and sheep sward of the New England commons, or the picturesque "architecture without architects" of an earlier world that adapted habitat to local materials, site, climate, and ecosystem.

For the most part, Americans have lost that intimate connection and awareness of their place in the natural world. The "natural" has been reduced to empty symbols such as the tract house lawn (which started out as a sheep meadow), and ecosystems have become landscapes to be peered at out of car windows: another low-information image like the TV screen.

The task, then, of integral design at the household level is to begin to recreate the opportunities for people to derive meaning and satisfaction from their experience of natural cycles as these occur in the household. This assumes that the occupant becomes an active and intelligent participant in managing, maintaining, and adapting the dwelling. The "hot rod" is one example of an aesthetic that grows out of the young American male's attempt to find meaning in everyday industrial culture. Maybe the day is not too far off when millions of Americans will be "hot rodding" their now denatured houses into finely tuned, multichanneled, closed-looped, organic instruments for processing nature's flow.

A Walking Tour of the Integral Urban House

Front of the Integral Urban House

The Integral Urban House is the Urban Center of the Farallones Institute, a nonprofit organization devoted to the study and teaching of environmentally sound lifestyles and life-support systems. The house demonstrates the integration of food-raising, waste recycling, and natural energy systems within the context of an urban home.

Photographs by Pat Goudviz

Modifications have been made in the front of the house to demonstrate sound management of urban resources. Wood chips are used in the sidewalk area to absorb rainfall and reduce runoff, alfalfa for our rabbits is planted in raised beds along the street as an alternative to traditional lawns, and mulberry trees are planted next to the fence to provide a source of leaves that may ultimately be fed to silkworms to produce cocoons for stuffing garments.

Side Yard

The south side of the Integral Urban House displays two types of solar collectors: the glass-covered, copper flat-plate unit positioned on the sloping roof heats the household water supply, and the green plants which convert sunlight into food through photosynthesis. Banana squash is trained up a supporting post of the house to demonstrate efficient use of vertical space. Ground covers of strawberries, comfrey, rhubarb and culinary herbs provide food as well as ornamental beauty.

Backyard Vegetable Garden

The vegetables most likely to be raised in the urban backyard—lettuce, tomatoes, squash, carrots, beets, peas, and beans—are the ones that require the most energy (both in the various forms of fossil-fuel and human energy) when grown on the farm. Approximately three to four hours of work a week is all that is required to produce enough vegetables for a family of four in a backyard garden such as the one developed by the Integral Urban House. Vegetables are grown close together in raised beds (there is no point in growing things in rows since we do not need to leave room for a tractor's movement; the beds are raised to permit good drainage—a consideration for this particular area of the country). The methods used in the garden are specifically designed to deal with the constraints of time, light, and space experienced by the average urban gardener.

37

Back Porch

Planter boxes on the porch supplement the production of food provided by the vegetable garden in the rear of the lot. The containers, filled with a mixture of compost and soil and watered by a drip-irrigation system, provide herbs and salad greens for the adjacent kitchen. The porch also accommodates a self-contained chicken house, making morning collection of eggs convenient, and a solar oven that cooks garden produce and home-raised meat.

The inset photograph shows the back of the house before the conversion.

Aquaculture Unit

In an aquaculture system in the southwest corner of the lot several species of fish in the 2000–gallon pond convert garden debris and insects into fish protein for human consumption. A wind machine above, constructed from oil drums and recycled wood, operates a pump that cycles the water from the pond through a drum purification filter. The drum is filled with oyster shells coated with bacteria that remove nitrogen and growth-inhibiting enzymes from the water. The water picks up oxygen as it descends from the filter bed into the pond.

Beehives on an elevated platform to the rear of the pond produce some one hundred pounds of honey each year. The location of the hive keeps the bees away from human traffic and allows the dead bees to fall into the pond below, where they are consumed by the fish (see Chapter 11).

Experiments are being conducted to determine the optimal mix of fish species, the preferred types of food, pumping efficiencies of the wind machine, and the water purification capabilities of various filtration media.

Compost Bins and Animal Shelter

Animal pens and compost bins are located on the north side of the house to make use of an area too dark for raising vegetables. The rabbit and chicken cages (see Chapter 10) are arranged to allow rabbit manure from the bottom tier of cages to fall into the chicken yard where it is picked over by the birds, which eat any fly larvae. Eight hens produce an average of thirty eggs per week. The offspring from four doe rabbits and one buck yield approximately 5 pounds of dressed meat each week.

Plant wastes from the garden, manure from the livestock area, and food garbage from the kitchen are composted in a set of three wooden bins. The bins retain the heat of the biological decomposition process, reduce fly breeding and access by rodents, protect the compost from rain, and facilitate turning the pile.

A flytrap constructed of screen and wood attracts and traps neighborhood flies by means of an odiferous bait. The dead flies are fed to the chickens.

Greywater System and Clivus Multrum

The Clivus Multrum composting toilet, positioned in the basement underneath the bathroom and kitchen, collects human wastes and kitchen garbage. The inclined orientation of the tank and air ducts within facilitate biological decomposition of the wastes. Waste gases exit through a roof vent. After thirty months of decomposition, the finished product is removed from the lower chamber and used as a soil amendment in the garden.

Wastewater drainpipes (greywater) have been rerouted from the sewer to a 55-gallon storage drum for reuse in the garden. A system of valves in the waste line regulates seasonal use. Collected greywater is allowed to cool in the tank and then drains through a hose to the garden when it is distributed to the various garden beds.

Greenhouse

A greenhouse built onto the south-west corner of the house is useful for raising vegetable seedlings, producing tomatoes in winter, and as a source of warmth for the adjacent rooms (see Chapter 9).

An observation beehive and aquarium located in the reception room of the house allow a close inspection of these biological communities.

Kitchen

In the kitchen of the Integral Urban House a combination gas/wood range cooks the food, a cool closet attached to the north side of the house utilizes natural convection of air to maintain fresh fruits and vegetables, and a pantry provides storage space for canned garden surpluses and dry goods. Above the stove, a donut-shaped stovepipe provides additional space heating from the wood burner.

Bottle Wall

Outside View: One-gallon apple juice containers filled with blackened water face the sun to collect daytime solar energy for nighttime use. Insulated shutters are opened during the day and their white surface reflects sunlight onto the "bottle wall," which screens the south-facing bathroom window (see Chapter 4).

Indoors View: In the late afternoon, the shutters are closed on the outside of the house so that the heat collected in the bottles is reradiated into the bathroom for evening warmth.

3. DESIGN PROCESSES

Design for Designing

I. *The Idea: Determining the purpose*
A. Stating the desired effect for the system to be created as it relates to large-scale environmental and human living conditions
1. Stating the overall purpose (without time frame)
2. Stating the function (what ought the system to do?)
3. Stating the goals within a time frame
B. Determining constraints: conceptual, biophysical, ecological, ethical, economic, political, social, and personnel (personal)
C. Insuring commitment from active members of effector group(s)

II. *The Design: Determining the components*
A. Deciding who will be involved, and when, where, how and with what the design will be implemented
B. Inventorying the existing state of the system
C. Developing component models
D. Integrating component models: the grand design
E. Making a materials list
F. Making an economic estimate
G. Making a time schedule
H. Creating a control hierarchy and decision-making plan
I. Reviewing and approving the final design

III. *The Plan: Determining the method*
A. Developing models and representation
B. Making a time table and contingency plan
C. Making work schedules
D. Delegating responsibilities
E. Analyzing budget and finance

Nearly everything around us is designed in accordance with a plan—from the utensils with which we cook and eat, the appliances and furniture in our house, the clothes we wear, the material we read, and the music we sing or play, to the radio, television, cinema, plays, and art exhibits we see and hear. All the structures and vehicles we use are designed—the residential homes and apartment houses, factories, airports, theatres, the cars, busses, airplanes, bicycles—as are the materials used to make all these things. The wood, paper, stone, mortar, glass, metals, textiles, paints, plastics, inks and dyes, and the fuels are manufactured from raw materials for various purposes that dictate their design, and the manufacturing processes themselves are planned for efficiency. The personnel who perform manufacturing processes are hired, trained, and put to work according to a design.

The size, appearance, cost, content, texture, taste, and smell of the foods we eat are all determined according to plan. The same is true of the processes for creating this food from seed to plate—how it is grown, harvested, shipped, stored, processed, sold, prepared, and eaten. The interior air space surrounding us is designed—its temperature, light, moisture, dust, toxicants, smells, and noise. The domestic organisms that share our habitats with us are there according to plan. The pets we keep—cats, dogs, birds, fish, and others—are selectively bred to fulfill certain needs. House plants, most garden plants, and all residential and municipal landscaping are consciously selected. Our lifestyle habits, from brushing our teeth to eating and defecating are all learned for a reason; none are innate. These habits in part constitute our cultural and individual designs for living.

Plainly, we live in a human-designed environment, although just as clearly our conscious participation in it is less through deliberation than by default. If we don't use intelligence to shape our surroundings and life-support systems others will do it for us, and their notions may not be to our advantage.

The integral urban house is intended as a habitat purposefully designed from the very broad perspective of where humans fit into the ecosystem.

How can one arrive at such a design, tailored to the needs of a specific group of people living together in a particular spot on the earth?

A Design for Designing

By "design for designing" we mean a plan for deliberately altering the state of a system. No matter where you live or what you do you are changing the environment around you. The object of making a design for designing, or a design process, is to make such alterations more consciously. If you choose a design process that accounts for the ecosystem realities discussed in the last chapter, hopefully the end result will be an increase in your survival capabilities. A design process can also provide you an opportunity to take a step back from your daily tasks, look at your overall life-support system, and plot future changes. By comparing the existing system with where you want to be, you may find the motivation for change.

The following information is necessary for creating even the simplest habitat design:
1. Your objectives or purpose for doing what you are doing; 2. An inventory of your needs and resources; 3. A list of the physical components and behavioral processes you intend to incorporate in the overall plan; 4. A blueprint of the physical structure incorporating those components; 5. A budget for the project that includes expenditures anticipated as well as materials that will be required.

If the project is to be performed by a group of people—as was the development of the Integral Urban House in Berkeley—the process becomes much more complex, and the design must then include detailed plans of what will be done in what order by whom. The margin shows a comprehensive design for designing.

Box 3-1 presents a technique useful in planning such a group project. The use of a PERT diagram helps fix the components of a project in time so more accurate scheduling can occur. The process in Box 3-1 specifies twenty-two jobs and allocates various time periods for accomplishing them. The total completion time is thirty-eight days, with the longest tasks being plastering, bricklaying, and landscaping. Such a schedule helps in organizing labor, particularly if you are subcontracting. If you are doing all the building yourself, it can help you organize your own time commitments, materials purchase, and job sequencing. Coordinating simultaneous jobs, as with the outside and inside work, becomes easier through using such a visual tool. In short, PERT diagrams can help organize complex tasks.

Determining Objectives

Once at a Farallones Institute staff meeting to discuss the future direction of the institute Max Kroschel made the comment that for himself, he was out to develop a bioethic, not just build a little hardware to help him over the rough spots of an energy or resource crisis. This same objective motivated us when we first conceived of the integral urban house idea. Whatever such a home might be, it is not merely a collection of solar or energy-saving devices, or even a backyard garden to help save on high food prices. Those components are admirable, but, as we have pointed out before, collected to-

F. Securing supplies and resources
G. Developing performance specifications

IV. *The Work: Putting it together*
A. Preparing the site
B. Training personnel: use of teaching programs
C. Agreeing on final plan
D. Assembling materials
E. Monitoring systems: choosing type and methods, assessing cost
F. Recording time and materials used, ecological impact, conditions of design, and construction

V. *The Finish: Closure, or What to do after it is built*
A. Collecting data
B. Evaluating result in terms of performance specifications
C. Comparing expectations and actualities
D. Eliciting feedback: recommendations for design and construction changes
E. Assessing and correcting errors
F. Maintaining the long-term system
G. Other considerations: deciding on personnel (operators, administrators, managers); determining social organization; identifying continuing operating constraints; building in self-correction mechanisms; end design process or begin a new design (social acknowledgment of finish)

VI. *Evaluating the work: How thoroughly does the thing or process created fulfill the initial goals?*

Box 3-1. **A Graphic Organizing Technique: PERT**

In order to develop a more precise plan, certain graphic conventions have been invented by planners. The following table and diagram show the steps in construction of a house, using such a graphic tool, commonly called a PERT (or *Planning Evaluation Review Technique*).

Job Name	Description	Time (Days)
A	Excavate, pour footers	4
B	Pour concrete foundations	2
C	Erect frame and roof	4
D	Lay brickwork	6
E	Install drains	1
F	Pour basement floor	2
G	Install rough plumbing	3
H	Install rough wiring	2
I	Install air conditioning	4
J	Fasten plaster and plasterboard	10
K	Lay finished flooring	3
L	Install kitchen equipment	1
M	Install finished plumbing	2
N	Finish carpentry	3
O	Finish roofing and flashing	2
P	Fasten gutters and downspouts	1
Q	Lay storm drains	1
R	Sand and varnish floors	2
S	Paint	3
T	Finish electrical work	1
U	Finish grading	2
V	Pour walks, and landscape	5

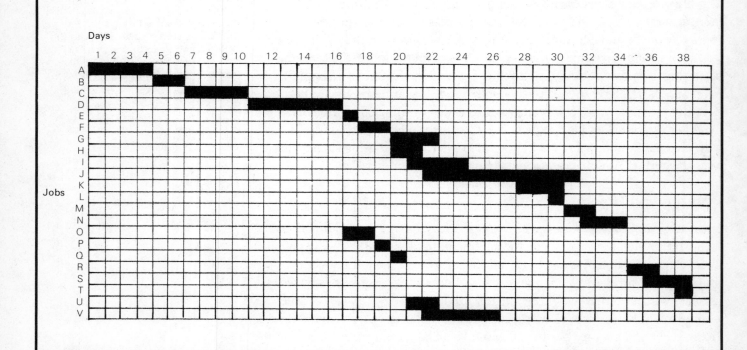

gether they are not an integral urban house. Nor would they justify the writing of this book, since adequate how-to literature is being produced on every side for those who want to learn the basics. In fact, some of the appropriate technology fields are expanding so rapidly that any book must necessarily be quickly outdated. The latest news on energy- and resources-conserving hardware can best be obtained through staying current with the many available periodicals. But in surveying the literature, it becomes apparent that little aid is given on how this hardware can be rated in terms of its value for increasing survival capability.

A bioethic is a system of moral concepts that deal with the relationship of humans to all other living organisms and with the conditions that sustain life and thus ultimately make continued human survival possible. In a chapter titled "Energetic Basis for Religion" in *Environment, Power and Society,* Howard T. Odum suggests that the Ten Commandments of such an ethical system should be based on the wise use and conservation of energy. We offer the ten "thrival" commandments (see margin note) as a basis for an ecosystem ethic that maximizes the capacities of the creative and responsible individual.

Obviously, the true planetary energy costs of our own home lifestyles must be examined, and Odum is in a sense the father of the popularization for that kind of evaluation. But besides being conceptually aware, people need a way to express that bioethic through their everyday activities. The integral urban house meets this need by providing a way of actualizing a bioethic through the structure and function of the home.

What we described earlier as the emergent quality of the system we were hoping to create in the Integral Urban House can thus be restated as the overall objectives in our design plan for the project:

1. To encourage a way of living that minimizes negative impact upon the larger environment.

2. To provide a habitat that promotes as much self-reliance as possible, given the constraints of climate, urban lifestyles, and varying individual circumstances such as income, family structure, health, and personal aesthetics.

Taking Inventory

Analyzing Present Lifestyles and Habitats: A fundamental part of designing is assessment. One must know some basic figures relating to personal and household consumption of resources in order to formulate and then implement a comprehensive plan for reducing one's impact on the environment. The important areas of analysis are energy use, waste generation, and food consumption. By detailing existing patterns of resource use, you will be able to determine which conservation measures are most economically and technologically feasible. In this section we present a procedure for assessing the quantities of resources you presently use and review a decision-making process that will help you make the right choices in developing your own home-resource management plan.

If you examine urban lifestyles from the perspective of the objectives stated above and ask, "What do I do in my own life that creates the greatest negative impact on the planet?" the answer that might come most readily to

The Ten Thrival Commandments

1. Thou shalt honor the mystery and subtlety of the universe which brought forth the ecosystem which is thy source; and recognize that its design exceeds the crude capacity of thy mind.

2. Thou shalt not compartmentalize the ecosystem or assume that by knowing a part thou understands the whole.

3. Thou shalt resist the narrowing of thy appreciation of the whole system by the preoccupations of thy work.

4. Honor all experiences. Don't perpetuate their mistakes. Respect the integrity of information.

5. Thou shalt not reduce the information of the biosphere through extermination of species, destruction of unique configurations, or significant individual organisms.

6. Thou shalt not take from the ecosystem more than is consistent with its continual well-being. The energy and materials that flow through you are a temporary privilege providing opportunities for reasonable self-expression.

7. Thou shalt not divert more energy, material or space to the human species than is consistent with the continued health of the biosphere. Thou shalt not waste energy, materials or information.

8. Thou shalt not spread false information. Thou shalt not pervert information to enhance profit or status.

9. Do not exchange your best understanding of how things work for cheap social concensus.

10. Look to thyself and thy surroundings. Do not try to be anyone else. Respect for self and nature have a common root.

mind is, "I drive a private automobile." Consider the features of the automobile and its effects: its planned obsolescence, its use of fossil fuels, its creation of life-destroying waste products, the seemingly endless variation in models requiring tremendous use of resources in duplication of parts, the rate at which farmlands and wild areas are turned into freeways, parking lots, and filling stations, and the costly, enigmatic hassle to the average owner in terms of maintenance and repairs. In this light the private automobile certainly deserves prominent mention.

However, it is difficult to see how modification of the home itself can affect a person's dependence on an automobile, unless it be to include bicycle racks in a place secure from theft but convenient to exits, and a writing corner equipped with lists of local, state, and national representatives to whom letters can be addressed supporting improved mass transportation systems, diversified fuels, smaller cars, and so on. Another approach, however, is to design a source of income that will allow you to have your office, studio, or production unit in the home or within walking or biking distance. Surely such an alternative is worth considering as you critically evaluate your current lifestyle.

Still looking at the larger picture, it would seem obvious that small, isolated living units lack what larger groups sharing a household offer in real energy and resource saving. Each person or couple owning their own com-

Box 3-2. **Worksheet for Monitoring Home Energy Consumption***

Gas					**Electricity**				
Month	Therms Consumed	×	Btu per Therm	= Btu Consumed	Month	Kilowatt-hours Consumed	×	Btu per Kilowatt-hour	= Btu Consumed
example:	80	×	100,000	= 8,000,000	example:	360	×	3414	= 1,230,000
January		×	100,000	=	January		×	3414	=
February		×	100,000	=	February		×	3414	=
March		×	100,000	=	March		×	3414	=
April		×	100,000	=	April		×	3414	=
May		×	100,000	=	May		×	3414	=
June		×	100,000	=	June		×	3414	=
July		×	100,000	=	July		×	3414	=
August		×	100,000	=	August		×	3414	=
September		×	100,000	=	September		×	3414	=
October		×	100,000	=	October		×	3414	=
November		×	100,000	=	November		×	3414	=
December		×	100,000	=	December		×	3414	=
Total Btu of Gas Used				_____	**Total Btu of Electricity Used**				_____

*For Btu values of fuel other than gas and electricity, consult your dealer or utility company.

plete set of household appliances, for example, is unnecessary waste; many such items can be shared. (Doubtless, this idea will strike many readers as heresy in this private possession-oriented society.) While some neighborhood zoning ordinances discourage groups of nonrelated adults from living together (for moral or other reasons), increasing rents and costs of all consumer goods may make these arrangements more attractive and common in the future. Such modern versions of the extended family or old-time boardinghouse can also enhance the household's self-reliance by increasing the range of skills brought to the unit through the increase in members.

Home modifications to accommodate larger groups living together would include installing the same kinds of sound- and heatproof partitions that might be used to increase energy conservation in any household, arranging storage bins for consumable materials such as grains and canned goods, so these goods can be bought in bulk, and putting up communication devices such as bulletin and blackboards to facilitate the more complex social organization required by larger groups. This section is intended to apply to such large groups as well as to the smaller households more common in our cities.

Useful Questions to Ask Yourself and Your Co-Inhabitants: One way to get a clearer picture of the components that need to be designed into or modified in your integral urban house is to make a systematic assessment of your current living space. Several kinds of analyses can be made, but we suggest at least the following: 1. An energy audit; 2. A waste-resource inventory; 3. A life-support needs survey; 4. A determination of how best to make use of the sun's energy, which also involves developing an urban food-raising plan; 5. Determining how to manage the interface between the integral urban house and the larger human and nonhuman community.

We will examine these assessments one by one in the following sections.

An Energy-Use Inventory: Home energy audits have become more common, thanks to the consciousness-raising experiences of the 1974 oil crisis and the cold winters and drought of the mid- and late-1970s. With the exception of wood that you cut and haul yourself and electricity or methane from homesite generators, and the like, all other fuels brought into the home provide a record in the form of bills and receipts. The first step in making an audit is to gather together these fuel bills for the past year (gas, electricity, tons of coal, cords of wood, and so on) and sort them by the intervals to which they correspond. Next, construct a chart such as the example in Box 3-2. For each month or other interval for which you have receipts list the amount of energy used as therms of gas, kilowatt-hours of electricity, or other appropriate energy unit. (A therm is equal to 100,000 Btu of energy, or approximately one hundred cubic feet of natural gas. A kilowatt-hour is the amount of energy burned by 10 one-hundred-watt bulbs over one hour. For other useful conversion factors, see the Appendices of this book.) Make the conversion into British Thermal Units (Btu) so that you can appreciate the magnitude of use. (One Btu is roughly equivalent to the amount of heat energy represented by the burning of a wooden match.) It is likely that your power bills will be greater during the winter than in the summer. Construct

One therm of gas is equal in heat value to about 30 kilowatt-hours. For December, 1977 the national average cost of energy was 4 cents per kilowatt-hour of electricity and 20 cents per therm of natural gas. Translated into units of energy equivalents, it cost 20 cents to purchase 100,000 Btu worth of gas and $1.35 to purchase 100,000 Btu of electricity.

a graph plotting energy use against a month to illustrate seasonal trends in energy consumption and to compare use before and after you adopt a conservation program. The difference between the average summer and winter months will give you an indication of how much energy you are using for heating in those cases where it is not otherwise obvious. Summer expenditures will reflect nonheating uses: air conditioning, cooking, hot water, pilot lights on appliances, and so on.

You can get another kind of handle on your energy expenditures by calculating how long you use various electric appliances and checking their consumption against Table 3-1. In many cases, using small cooking appliances that heat just what you need will save energy compared with stoking

Table 3-1. Energy Consumption of Common Household Appliances

Appliance	Power Rating (in Watts)	Normal Monthly Use (in Hours)	Kilowatt-Hour Consumption per Month*	Dollars Consumed per Month
Water heater (quick recovery)	4500	82.9	373	14.92
Water heater (standard)	3000	113.3	340	13.60
Lights	1200†	160	192	7.68
Refrigerator/freezer (frostless)	425	317	135	5.40
Air conditioner	1300	80	105	4.20
Range	11,720	60	102	4.08
Clothes dryer	4800	17	80	3.20
Food freezer	300	250	76	3.04
Refrigerator	235	161	38	1.52
Television (color)	300	125	37.5	1.50
Dishwasher	1190	24	28	1.12
Television (b/w)	255	114	29	.96
Frying pan	1170	14	16	.64
Heater (radiant)	1300	10	13	.52
Iron (hand)	1050	10	11	.44
Coffee maker	850	9	8	.32
Broiler	1375	6	8	.32
Radio	80	90	7.5	.30
Washing machine (automatic)	375	14.6	5.5	.22
Toaster	1100	2.7	3	.12
Vacuum cleaner	540	5.6	3	.12
Food wastes disposer	420	5	2	.08
Clock	2	750	1.5	.06
Food blender	290	3	1	.04
Sewing machine	75	13.3	1	.04
Hair dryer	300	2	0.5	.02
Shaver	15	13.3	0.2	.008

Source: Adapted from Leckie, Masters, Whitehouse, and Young. *Other Homes and Garbage*.

Note: Electricity costs computed at 4¢ per kilowatt-hour.
*To compute monthly kilowatt-hour consumption for an appliance, multiply its power rating (in kilowatts) by the amount of hours used monthly.
† Cumulative rating of several light-bulbs.

up an entire oven to cook a small amount of food. The mining of the materials to make the appliance, and then the manufacturing and transporting of it consumed energy which is not calculated in home use estimates, but is important for overall social net energy assessments.

Gasoline use can best be measured by filling the tank of your car, driving for a few days and noting the number of miles driven, and then dividing that number by the number of gallons it takes to re-fill the tank.

A look at your home consumption of energy makes the inherent limitation of city life very clear. In no other area of life-support is the incongruity between what we consume and what we produce more pronounced than in the area of energy. Consider that the average American's *daily* consumption of energy for residential purposes is equivalent in magnitude to the physical labor one person could exert on a job over a thirty-five-day period. In the kitchen alone, a family using a gas range to cook their food can consume some one hundred cubic feet of natural gas each day. That translates to 25,000 kilocalories of fossil-fuel energy to cook an average of only 10,000 kilocalories of food energy.

The combination of sunlight falling on your home, wind blowing past your yard, and organic matter generated by your waste, probably provides only a fraction of your total energy requirements, even for the most conservation-minded family. Obviously, energy self-sufficiency is not obtainable in an urban area. However, some ideas on how energy can be conserved are given in Chapter 4.

A Waste-Resource Inventory: An energy audit will tell you how much energy you are using. A slightly different tactic should be taken to determine how resources already passing through the household can be conserved or recycled. The best place to start with this assessment is at your household wastebasket and garbage can. Are you throwing away organic materials that could provide food for growing plants? Are you mending, patching, converting, or otherwise reusing all the objects and materials you can? Some strong value judgments are involved here, since most of us are enmeshed in a product-oriented race to keep up with the Joneses by continually buying new stuff. For example, mended socks are so rare now it is hard to find the yarns with which to repair them, yet surely socks continue to wear out at the toe and heel, leaving the bulk of the cloth in good condition, just as they did years ago. Nowadays it is considered easier to put more hours into one's job in order to earn the cash to buy new goods than to take the time to weave over a hole in the old.

What about paper, glass, and metal? What in your present garbage is going into the local dump and what could be recycled? And, particularly important, for which nonrecyclable materials that you are presently bringing into the house—plastics, for example—could you find substitute materials? To encourage you in this respect, consider that the compounds put into plastic jars and bottles to keep them flexible slowly migrate out of them, leaving the containers brittle and prone to cracking. At the same time, these migrating plasticizers go into your milk, shampoo, and other household products, and into the air you breathe. The amount of these substances migrating out is small, particularly if the temperature is low, but it is constant, virtually ubiquitous, and probably a health hazard. In addition, many plastics give off toxic fumes when they are burned and are very resistant to decay when they are buried (as in landfills). Can you reduce the amount of plastics you bring into your household?

Box 3-3 has been prepared to assist you in conducting a waste-product inventory in your home. It has been arranged to allow you to compare your figures with the national averages and to assist you in estimating quantities of certain waste materials, such as sewage, that are difficult to measure directly in the home. In Part Two of the book we will discuss how many of these resources, now wasted, can be conserved and/or recycled for use again. Once you implement a conservation program in your home, you can return to this worksheet again and determine the extent of your resource savings. The quantities of waste production that correspond to the first five items on the worksheet can be determined by separating the various frac-

Box 3-3. Worksheet for Monitoring Family Waste Production

Week ending:

Waste Product		Pounds Produced at Present	Pounds Produced* after Conservation Program Is Begun	National Average
Newspaper	household			
	per capita†			8.4 lb.
Tin, aluminum, glass containers	household			
	per capita			6.0 lb.
Plastic	household			
	per capita			4.5 lb.
Food wastes	household			
	per capita			10.5 lb.
General trash	household			
	per capita			14.0 lb.
Waste water	household			
	per capita			245 gal.
Human urine	household			
	per capita			7 qt.
Human feces	household			3.5 lb. (wet weight)
	per capita			
Total sewage, including water flushing toilets	household			
	per capita			420 gal.

*Refers to the amount of wastes (trash, sewage, water, and so on) leaving your house.

† To arrive at per capita (per person) figure, divide the total household production by the number of individuals in the house.

tions of your domestic rubbish and weighing each individually at the end of a week's (or a month's) accumulation.

Your family's production of urine and feces probably won't be measurably different from the national average, and most likely will remain constant unless your family reduces its consumption of food. Of course, the amount of waste actually left at home will vary according to the work and recreational schedule that determines how much time is spent away or in the house.

Water is an often-wasted resource essential to life. You can get a sense of your overall use from your monthly bill. Box 3-4 shows some sample water meters and explains how to read them. Reading the meter will give you a daily figure and from that you can calculate some big expenditures, for example, periodic watering of the lawn. Another way to determine outdoor use is to monitor the length of time you run the garden hose and compute

Box 3-4. **How to Read the Water Meter**

All customers of the East Bay Municipal Utility District have their water supply measured by a meter. This results in each customer paying his share of operating the system based on the amount of water used since the last billing.

All EBMUD meters measure water in cubic feet (one cubic foot equals about seven and a half gallons). EBMUD charges for the amount of water consumed based on the number of units of 100 cubic feet (748 gallons) that you use, as shown by the meter.

There are two basic types of water meters, the straight-reading meter which resembles the mileage indicator in an automobile speedometer, and the round-reading meter which has several separate dials.

Straight-Reading Meter

EBMUD eventually will use this type of meter exclusively, largely because it is easy to read. In Figure A, the reading is taken from the figures shown under the words "cubic feet." Including the zero painted on the face, the meter reads 81710, which is the total number of cubic feet of water recorded since the meter was installed. Because our charge is based on units of 100 cubic feet, the meter reader disregards the last two figures, so he would record a reading of 817 units. If you used 1200 cubic feet of water by the next time he read the meter, the next reading would be 81710 plus 1200 or 82910—829 units. Your bill would thus be based on the difference in the two readings, or 12 units (8976 gallons).

The large hand is used only for testing purposes.

Figure A

Round-Reading Meter

The meter most widely in use today by EBMUD has several small dials in a circle, and is a little more difficult to read. The dials are marked off in ten divisions, and are read much like a clock, except that the hand on every other dial turns counterclockwise. To tell which way any one hand goes, look to see which way the numbers are printed around the face of the dial.

To check the reading on the meter in Figure B begin with the "100,000" dial and read each dial around the meter to the "10" dial. If the hand is between numbers, use the lower number. The dials register 8, 0, 6, 3, and 2, respectively (80,632 cubic feet). Again, since a unit is composed of 100 cubic feet, the last two figures are not counted, so the number of units registered is 806. (The "one foot" dial is to show that the meter is functioning.)

By following these directions, you should be able to read your meter accurately. There are many variations in meters within the EBMUD system, so be sure you check which way each dial is turning when you make a reading.

Figure B

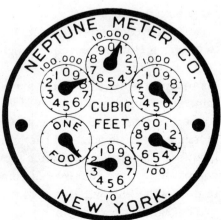

how much water is used per minute. Commonly, the flow for an outdoor spigot is five to eight gallons per minute, but you can check this by timing how long it takes to fill up a five-gallon bucket.

Since it can be assumed that all the water used in the home ultimately becomes sewage, total volume of sewage production can be calculated by subtracting from the total quantity of water used (as read from your water meter) the amount used outdoors for watering the garden, car washing, and so on. Wastewater production, referred to in later chapters as greywater, is the nontoilet flush water used in the home. Its volume can be estimated by subtracting the quantity of water used for flushing the toilet (assuming five gallons per flush—a conservative estimate)—from the total sewage production of the home.

One way to conserve water is to recycle it. However this cannot be done indiscriminately, since the quality of greywater varies greatly. We discovered this when we decided to develop a water recycling system at the Integral Urban House in Berkeley. An analysis of the wastewater production data of the house revealed that 90 percent came from the bathroom tub and sink and only 10 percent from the sink in the kitchen. By examining samples of the drainage water from the different sources, we determined that a good three-quarters of the solid matter flushed from the sinks into the sewer originated at the kitchen sink and only a fraction had its origins in the shower or bathroom sink. It is the solid matter (food wastes, hair, grease, and grit) conveyed in wastewater that makes re-use for garden irrigation difficult.

Since the house had a hook-up to the municipal sewage lines, we thought it made better sense to discharge the kitchen sink water, heavily laden with particulates, grease, and detergents, into the sewer, and alter the household wasteline plumbing so that we could reuse only the bathroom greywater in the yard. This simplified plumbing modifications and also circumvented the problems of salt and detergent toxicity and accumulation of solids in the garden, which would have resulted had we tried to reuse the kitchen sink wastewater.

You can assume that every gallon of nonflush water consumed in your home will produce one gallon of wastewater, but you will need to check the quality of the water emanating from the different drains in your house. If you keep a record of how much water your household is using *before* you begin a conservation effort and your outdoor water use remains much the same both before and after, you can assume that any difference is due to reduced water consumption indoors. See Chapter 5 for a discussion of how to develop a greywater recycling program and other water conservation ideas.

Examining Your Life-Support Needs: Another perspective can be obtained by examining the needs of your household in terms of the other life-support systems for the residents. One such analysis is offered in Table 3-2. Here are the basic needs and activities of the human residents of our house, from bed to mortuary. Examine these needs from the viewpoint of their compatibility with your overall objectives, as well as for resource-use patterns. You will realize from reading the right-hand column that the activities you engage in determine many of the resources you use. Those activities and the needs they generate flow, in turn, from your life-support needs. Each activity requires tools, artifacts, furniture, clothing, utensils, machines, setting, and so on. The personal need for supportive contact or our need for recreation means one may engage in sports, for example, and then require sporting equipment. Since each particular item or device requires energy and minerals as well as human time to fabricate, each represents an extremely large investment that may or may not be clear from its purchase price or from the time the need arose.

Such a survey offers you an opportunity to sensitize yourself to the value and organization of the articles you keep in your home. It also may help you to rethink the need, use, composition, wear, lifetimes, and eventual ends for all these materials.

Assessing the Potential for Using Solar Energy: Answering the question, "How can my home make use of solar energy?" requires knowing first of all how much sun is actually available to your house and grounds. Second, you need to consider the cost and complexities of the various systems or hardware you wish to integrate into your homestead. For the first assessment you need to become conscious of how the sun moves during each day and through the seasons of the year in relation to your house, the open space around it, and the various sun-obstructing structures within and adjacent to your home.

The Amount of Sun Available to You for Raising Food: In addition to simply observing where the shadows fall in your yard, you may wish to make a more sophisticated analysis based on the amount of sun's energy available to

---

Table 3-2. **Life-Support Needs and Some Associated Activities**

Basic Resource Needs	Personal and Social Needs	Basic Activities and Tools
Air	Good health	Sleeping (mattress, bed, sheets, pillows, and blankets)
Water	Supportive human contact	Waking (clock, rooster)
Food	Sensual and conceptual pleasure	Defecating and urinating (waste-management system)
Shelter from weather	Belief systems	Dressing (clothing)
Energy from nonhuman sources to accomplish work	Meaningful work	Washing (water, sink, soap, and tooth cleaner)
Cash income to obtain what cannot be produced or bartered for	Education (formal and informal) and access to a supportive environment	Eating (food, cooking and eating implements, stove and fuel)
	Recreation (space, time and resources for its pursuit)	Transporting (vehicle, corridor, and fuel)
		Working (setting, tools, knowledge, resources)
		Playing (setting, information, equipment, other people)
		Learning (educators, equipment, settings)
		Maintaining one's habitat (tools, supplies)
		Reproducing (a partner of the opposite sex and medical care)
		Dying (medical care and mortuary)

your geographic location on the planet. Part of this process is determining how much sun is available to you for food production. One thousand kilocalories of light energy can produce ten kilocalories of food energy, assuming a photosynthetic conversion rate of 1 percent—that is, the rate by which the green plant can convert the radiant energy of the sun into chemical energy of plant cells. Simply computing the amount of light energy falling on a square yard (.83 square meters) of your garden during the growing season and then multiplying it by the size of the garden would provide a rough sense of how many calories of food energy the residents eating these plants might hope to obtain each day. (See below for a discussion on insolation.) However, there are some complications to this, since under the usual urban and suburban constraints, trees, buildings, and other structures will shade different parts of your growing area during various times of the day and season. Thus, an estimate must be made of the percent of the area receiving only partial sunlight. The degree of shading can be roughly correlated to a corresponding drop in insolation. Land in the full shadow of a building all day long will only receive 15 to 20 percent of the daily insolation of a similar piece of land in full light. Land shaded by evergreen trees may receive only 35 to 50 percent as much insolation.

Next, one must make an estimate of the percent of the garden ground area that is actually covered by plant leaves on which the sunlight falls, referred to as the photosynthetic canopy. This will also vary from week to week, seedlings occupying only a small part of the space around them as compared to mature plants. Of course, companion planting, where fast-growing plants are grown temporarily among slower maturers, and then harvested before the slow-growers have taken all the space, helps to maximize use of space where sunlight is available. (See pages 155–57 for a discussion of how to use space intensively.) Starting seedlings indoors and setting them out where others have just been harvested after they are already a fairly good size, is another tactic for capturing as many calories as possible. (See pages 172–77 on starting seedlings indoors.) On the average, throughout the year only 33 percent of the land area of a garden will be covered by leaves.

Another factor in this equation must be the efficiency with which the plants are able to fix the sunlight into sugars. This amount varies somewhat according to the specific species, the bioregion, and the conditions. Temperature, concentration of carbon dioxide (CO_2), and availability of water can all effect the photosynthetic conversion rate. In the laboratory, under various experimental conditions, chlorophyll molecules have demonstrated efficiencies as high as 75 percent. Laboratory experiments with growing plants under similar enhanced conditions have shown efficiencies from 15 to 22 percent. Algae, grown in small cylinders in water with dissolved nutrients agitated so that all the organisms were exposed to a diffused light, have reached efficiencies of 20 to 50 percent. However, the rate drops to 2 to 6 percent when the algae are grown in large tanks. Nevertheless, these laboratory results indicate that a tasty algae, grown in clear tanks aerated by wind-driven pumps, has the potential to produce substantial calories for human or other animal diets, since by comparison only 1 percent of the total radiation received from the sun is fixed by many common vegetable crops under typical field conditions.

Objective: To determine the amount of food energy (expressed as kilocalories per day) potentially available from your home garden. Your geographic location, length of growing season, and local bioclimatic conditions are basic determinants.

Procedure: With the aid of information in the appendices, enter the figures that are relevant to your situation. By multiplying the six determined values you will determine the food-raising potential of your specific ground-space in terms of kilocalories per day.

Computation: Multiply, in sequence, the figures entered in A, B, C, D, and E.

A. Daily solar insolation, in Btu per square foot per day.

B. Amount of land available for garden production, in square feet. Estimate the proportion of land receiving only partial sunlight and reduce the total by that amount.

C. Percentage of usable land covered by plant leaves—the *photosynthetic canopy*—for the particular month for which you are performing these calculations. If, for example, you anticipate that one-third of your garden space will be covered by plant leaves, enter 0.33.

A [　　　　　] × B [　　　　　] × C [　　　　　]

D. Plant biomass conversion rate. This accounts for photosynthetic conversion by the plant (i.e., sun energy to food energy), as well as losses due to respiration, disease and insect damage. This figure is generally considered to be 1 percent (0.01) for vegetables.

E. Percentage of net production actually consumed by humans. Subtract the stems, roots, and other inedible plant parts. An accepted estimate for vegetables is 35 percent (0.35).

× D [　　　　　] × E [　　　　　] = **Btu**

For comparison, here are the values and computation performed for the Integral Urban House for the month of June:

A [**1600 Btu**] × B [**2500 sq. ft.,**] × C [**0.33**]

per foot per day

2000 square feet of land receiving full sunlight, plus 1000 square feet of additional land receiving partial sunlight estimated at 50 percent

general figure for common vegetables

× D [**0.01**] × E [**0.35**] = **4900 Btu**

general figure for common vegetables

general figure for common vegetables

So, for the month of June, at the Integral Urban House there are a potential 4900 Btu (1,234.8 kilocalories) of food energy available per day from the garden.

Evaluation: Determine the percentage of your family's total daily food-energy requirement that could potentially come from the space you have available (that is, your potential food-energy value computed above, divided by your family's daily food-energy needs). Generally, a young (18–35 years) active person re-

quires a minimum of 10,000 Btu of food energy per day.

At the Integral Urban House, the four residents' collective food requirement is 40,000 Btu. The 4900 Btu potential daily production in the garden is approximately 12.5 percent of the total food-energy requirement.

But of course not all of the energy fixed by the plant is then built into plant tissue. At least 35 percent of the energy captured is lost through plant respiration. Furthermore, you do not eat the entire plant (even with lettuce or similar leafy plants, you do not eat the roots), so you must estimate the amount of the plant consumed and enter that into your computation. Use Box 3-5 to compute the amount of food calories a piece of land might provide.

An Urban Food-Raising Plan: Once you have estimated the food-energy potential of your growing space, how do you choose the plants that will use the sun-calories available to you? You may find it interesting to see the reasoning we used at the Integral Urban House when faced with this same question. We knew from an energetics standpoint that complete self-sufficiency was impossible on our small lot. There simply were not enough calories of sun-energy falling on our property to produce all the food the four young people living there would consume. So we had to make some choices.

We started with an analysis based upon economics and energetics. It is fascinating to see how intimately the two are connected. To a large extent, the price of food reflects the amount of energy, both biological and mechanical, contributing to the production of that food. (Of course government subsidies to the energy industries can make foods appear cheaper than they really would be otherwise.) Our objective was to use the space we had available to raise the largest amount of food possible, and to do it profitably.

We began by comparing the options of using a small city plot of one hundred square feet for the production of a vegetable, say broccoli, or the raising of a grain, for example, wheat. Even though our food-raising techniques produced high yields, we knew from previous experience with grain production that fifteen square feet of land was required to produce one pound of wheat worth fifteen cents. (Prices are from the CO-OP Market, Berkeley, California, December 1977. We expect the relation to be fairly consistent.) That translates to one penny of crop per square foot of space used. To raise a pound of broccoli, however, which has a market value of thirty-nine cents, only one square foot of space is required for two and a half months. Compared to wheat production, the dollar-value yield per square foot area of broccoli is thirty-nine times as great. In addition, many climates will allow two or three crops of some vegetables, such as broccoli or cabbage, per year, but few regions will permit multiple crops of grain in one year.

Home-raising of broccoli and other garden vegetables makes sense from a standpoint of net energetics as well. The term net energetics refers to the ratio between the amount of energy consumed by a system (including the costs of developing the system) and the amount of energy produced by the system. The energy produced by the system is the energy value of the actual crop, measured in kilocalories. Because agricultural practices vary so much from crop to crop, each food has its own net energy ratio. Table 3-3 gives the net energy figures for a variety of agricultural commodities. Broccoli has a net energy value of 0.2, meaning that only 0.2 energy units of food value is derived from each unit of energy fuel invested in the production of the crop.

In the case of wheat flour, for every unit of fuel energy invested in its production, 5.4 units of food energy is available to the consumer through the crop. Accordingly, wheat flour has an overall net energy efficiency ratio twenty-seven times as great as broccoli. These figures are fairly representative for other grains and vegetables. It is evident that the commercial production of fresh vegetables is supported by the extensive use of fossil fuels, which up until now have been an inexpensive source of energy. (For more on this subject, see Chapter 7.)

Commercial grain production is relatively efficient in the use of fuels. That makes sense, because the field management and marketing practice as-

Table 3-3. **Energy Efficiencies of Different California Crops**

Commodity	Crop Calorie Content (A) 1,000 kcal/ton	Fuel and Electrical Energy Input (B) 1,000 kcal/ton	A/B* (Efficiency)
Field Crops			
Barley	3166.1	479.0	6.6
Beans (dry)	3084.4	2683.1	1.2
Corn	3338.4	1027.3	3.3
Rice	3293.1	1289.3	2.6
Sorghum, grain	3011.8	1188.8	2.6
Sugar	3492.6	6654.2	.5
Wheat flour	3020.9	563.3	5.4
		Average	3.2
Raw Vegetables and Fruits			
Beans, green	1115.8	2048.0	.5
Broccoli	290.3	1178.6	.2
Carrots	381.0	359.8	1.1
Cauliflower	244.9	986.4	.2
Celery	154.2	351.5	.4
Lettuce	163.3	484.3	.3
Melons	235.9	636.6	.4
Onions	344.7	390.3	.9
Potatoes	689.5	325.4	2.1
Strawberries	335.6	727.6	.5
Tomatoes	199.6	262.2	.8
Apples	508.0	401.1	1.3
Apricots	462.6	840.4	.6
Grapefruit	371.9	1165.5	.3
Grapes	607.8	576.9	1.1
Oranges	462.6	1089.5	.4
Peaches	344.7	471.6	.7
Pears	553.3	964.2	.6
Plums	598.7	1650.9	.4
		Average	.7
Canned Vegetables and Fruits			
Beans, green	870.9	3021.5	.3
Tomatoes	190.5	1138.9	.2
Apples	371.9	1397.8	.3
Grapefruit	272.2	1797.7	.2
Grapes	462.7	1115.3	.4
Pears	417.3	1734.1	.7
		Average	.3
Frozen Vegetables and Fruits			
Beans, green	925.3	2856.1	.3
Broccoli	254.0	1911.2	.1
Cauliflower	199.6	1619.8	.1
		Average	.2
Dried Fruits and Nuts			
Almonds	5424.9	7086.7	.7
Prunes	3120.7	4447.1	.7
Walnuts	5697.1	10745.6	.5
		Average	.6

Source: Cervinka, Chancellor, Coffelt, Curley, and Dobie, *Energy Requirements for Agriculture in California.*

Note: A/B = ratio of caloric content/fuel and electrical energy (the larger the number the greater the efficiency).

sociated with grain production are much less intensive than those associated with the production of fresh vegetables. So, from the standpoint of energy resource conservation, homesite production of fresh vegetables made very good use of the backyard of the Integral Urban House and grain production did not.

To make the choice for vegetables over grain is not precise enough. One needs to know what types of vegetables and how much of each to grow. This is as much a matter of energetic efficiency as it is a matter of food preference. Table 3-4 cites the amount of land required for production of various fractions of a family's diet. Salad vegetables such as lettuce, green onions, and small carrots can be supplied for a family of four from the cultivation of some 150 square feet of space (a 10 foot by 15 foot garden plot) during the months the weather permits. Although salads do not represent a high caloric contribution to one's diet, they do provide minerals and vitamins and add to the pleasure of each meal. Also, salad crops are easy to raise and can be cultivated throughout a large part of the year in many regions of the country.

Dinner vegetables are those which are commonly cooked and served as a major portion of the meal. Examples are cauliflower, squash, and fresh beans. During the growing season, a family of four that consumes a moderate amount of fresh vegetables at dinner can probably produce this part of their diet, plus leafy salad crops, on approximately 600 square feet of land: a plot 20 feet by 30 feet. That is an impressive yield considering what a large percentage of their total food bill can be saved by raising vegetables on such a small amount of land.

If you have a large piece of land for gardening, say 50 feet by 50 feet, you might be able to produce your family's entire yearly vegetable supply. This would include storage and preserve crops such as winter squash, tomatoes, cabbage, and onions.

The average family consumes some 151 pounds of fresh fruits each year. This amount represents 5 percent of their yearly monetary food ex-

Table 3-4. **Land Required to Produce Portions of a Family Diet***

Fraction of Diet Grown	Square Feet Required	Percent of Total Food Costs Saved†	Percent of Total Calories Required‡
A) Leafy greens	150	6	2
B) Dinner vegetables, plus (A)	600	18	6
C) Entire vegetable supply	2500	32	16
D) Entire fruit supply, plus (C)	3500	40	20
E) Grains and cereals plus all fruits and vegetables	25,000	55	47
F) Forage crops for livestock, plus (E)	100,000	80	75

Note: An acre is 43,560 square feet.

*Assuming a family of two adults and two children having a total food-energy requirement of 8000 kilocalories per year and consuming a proportionately higher percentage of fresh vegetables than the average family.
† Growing rates for Berkeley, California.
‡ Typical values for an American family.

Source: Asbrook, *Butchering, Processing and Preservation of Meat.*

penditure (see Table 3-5). Between 750 and 1250 square feet is the minimum amount of soil that would be required to produce a family's entire fruit supply. At the Integral Urban House, we decided to raise strawberries instead of lawn as a ground cover and to espalier dwarf varieties of deciduous apples and plums along a back fence. Essentially, we raise species of fruit trees and shrubs not only as food producers, but also for the beauty of their flowers and shapes.

The amount of land needed to raise a family's supply of grain is conservatively estimated at 21,500 square feet, nearly half an acre. Obviously, grain production would require a tremendous jump in land requirement (600 percent) relative to the amount of increased economic self-reliance (40 percent) over the previous level of sustenance discussed (see Table 3-5). For the backyard urban gardener, grain raising clearly is not appropriate. However, there are some circumstances under which urban grain raising could make better sense. For instance, where there is an entire vacant lot available,

Table 3-5. **Average U.S. Food Consumption per Person**

	Energy Value (Kcal/lb)		Average Cost/lb (Dollars)		Lb Consumed per Capita per Year	Percent of Diet	Total Energy per year (Kcal/yr)	Percent of Energy	Cost per Year (Dollars)	Percent of Total Cost
Leafy vegetables	100 } 150		.32 } .43		308	23	46,200	3	132.44	12.5
All other vegetables	200		.53							
Fruit	200		.35		151	11	30,200	2	52.85	5
Grains and cereals	1600		.26		129	9	206,400	18	33.54	3
Meat and eggs	1000		1.95		287	21	287,000	25	555.65	52.5
Dairy	1200		.68		285	21	342,000	32	193.80	18.5
Fats	4000		.63		54	4	216,000	19	34.02	3
Sugars and nonalcoholic beverages	} 175		.39		130 } 148 18	11	25,900	2	57.72	5.5
Total					1362 lb/yr	100%	1,153,700 kcal/yr	100%	$1060.02/yr	100%

a late-fall sowing of winter wheat could possibly yield a reasonable crop of grain come spring. (For more details on this, see Logsdon, *Small-Scale Grain Raising,* listed in the bibliography.)

Obviously, use of city soil for producing grain for livestock feed does not make sense. However, the raising of livestock can be worthwhile if garden and grocery-store wastes are fed to the animals as a supplement to their ration of feed-store-purchased concentrate. With livestock you are no longer depending solely on the amount of sunlight falling on your property. The raising of some species of animals, principally rabbits and chickens, begins to make even better sense if you have space to raise some forage crops such as alfalfa, comfrey, or jerusalem artichokes.

Assessing for the Integration of Components: Many of the food-raising components, evaluated independently as separate units, will not appear to be terribly profitable. But considered as part of a larger, more diverse food-raising program for your home, their economic appeal may improve. The interrelationship between the livestock and garden at the Integral Urban House demonstrates the point. Weeds and inedible portions of food crops from the garden are fed to the rabbits and chickens. In turn the animals' manure is composted and the finished product used as fertilizer for the plants. The two components, in their interaction, tend to promote the usefulness of each other. We have already discussed some examples of this in Chapter 2, pages 30–32, on home food webs.

Assessing for Other Solar Components: An energetic economic assessment should be made regarding the value of including other solar components, such as hot water or space heating, into your overall integral urban house plan. While we have no doubt as to the value of these methods in regard to new construction, renovation of an already existing structure requires different and often more costly strategies. We are assuming you will use all available outdoor ground space for plant and food production because this space is usually very small already. Therefore, south-facing roof and wall surfaces on the house or other structures remain as additional potential areas for collection of solar energy and are a better option than building new additions that will take valuable yard growing space.

Window and wall heaters are a definite possibility if unimpeded exposure is available, or if enough reflective surface can be constructed to utilize sunlight during the fall and spring when the sun is higher in the sky and the side of the house may be partially shaded by the eaves. However, the best choice for a solar collector is a south-facing roof. It does not have to be due

Table 3-6. **Costs & Savings Estimates Using Active Solar Energy**

Application	Swimming Pool Heater	Domestic Water Heater	Whole House Air Heater	Electrical Supply
Present annual fuel and operating costs	$300	$125	$500	$70
Units consumed annually*	1500 therms of gas	630 therms of gas	2500 therms of gas	1200 KWH electricity
Btu consumed annually (in millions)	150	63	250	4
Square feet of collector surface**	200†	80††	400‡	500‡‡
Cost per ft² of collector§	$1200	$1200	$8000	$10,000
Estimated energy savings in first year§§	$225	$93.75	$375	$52.50
Pay-back period if energy costs remain constant (in years)	5.3	12.6	21.3	9
Pay-back period if energy costs rise 10 percent per year (in years)	4.5	8.3	12.5	32

*Calculated at 20¢ per therm (100,000 Btu), and 4¢ per kilowatt-hour (3414 Btu).
**Assuming that solar system provides 75 percent of total service needed and conventional system provides 25 percent.
† Collector area sized at 50 percent of surface area of 400–square foot pool.
†† Based on average-sized heater required by four-person family in northern California.

‡ Assuming average annual isolation values of 1,000 Btu per square foot per day.
‡‡ Calculated at 2 watts of power production per square foot of photovoltaic cells.
§ Includes costs for all system components.
§§ Calculated at annual savings of 75 percent of annual costs with a conventional system.

south, and can deviate up to 20 degrees in either direction. It is best to know your microclimate conditions precisely, however, since afternoon or mornings may be sunnier in your particular location. This should be factored into your assessment concerning the feasibility of using solar energy.

Table 3-6 shows the costs of various solar technology applications relative to that of conventional methods. The figures in the table are hypothetical and do not necessarily reflect the national average for the actual cost of solar units or the economics for any one particular home. However the figures are accurate from a relative standpoint and they should help you understand how to determine the pay-back periods for a capital investment in solar equipment as well as the rate of return on investment for various types of energy applications. The table is oriented toward nonintegrated applications of active solar collection, simply because those types of systems are most widely used at present. The economics of solar technologies that integrate passive systems (those in which there are no moving parts) and active systems (which rely on air or water movement) for providing a variety of uses will be considerably different than the systems suggested by Table 3-6.

To assess the situation accurately for your residence, you need to construct such a table, filling in real numbers that are pertinent to your home. You can determine your present expenditure of money and energy using conventional fuels by studying your fuel bills and making estimates of use of each utility in the home. You may have done this already, if you've made an energy-use inventory. Conversion of units of fuel, such as kilowatt-hours of electricity and cubic feet of gas to Btu can be made by consulting Box 3-2. Get estimates from local distributors of solar energy equipment to determine the size of solar panels you'll need and the cost of installation and to determine what percentage of the total energy for a specific application will be solar. Rarely is a solar system sized to provide 100 percent of the energy requirement for a particular use. An auxiliary unit using conventional sources of fuel is usually employed to provide a back-up to the solar system during periods of cloudy weather. Solar distributors will often provide a series of estimates for different percentages of service delivered by the solar system. You will see that the marginal return for your investment will peak at about 60 to 85 percent of service depending upon where you live and your level of use.

The annual savings in energy can be estimated by multiplying your current energy costs by the percentage of service expected from the solar system.

The percentage of your investment returned to you each year is found by dividing the annual savings in energy by the total cost of your solar system. (Thus, after a certain number of years, your solar system will have entirely paid for itself.)

Finally, the pay-back period—the time needed to recoup your investment—should be evaluated. It is approximately the anticipated cost of the solar system, divided by the yearly savings in energy costs, adjusted for the ever-increasing costs of fuel and delivery. (We have assumed a 10 percent yearly rise in energy costs.) When you calculate pay-back period, remember that your current energy systems do not offer such a possibility. The way conventional systems are structured now, you will continue to pay for their operation as long as you live. Appreciating this difference is, in a way, the major change in thinking required to understand the promise of many of the systems this book is advocating.

In our own assessments of the best ways to use the sun's energy in the integral urban house, we have concluded that the most rewarding are the most obvious and the simplest:

1. Open the window curtains on the sunny side of the house during the day and close them at night to hold the heat in; follow the reverse procedure when you wish to keep the heat out. In other words, conserve the sun's energy from which you are already benefiting directly.

2. Use the sunlight to raise plants and to raise animals that can feed on those plants.

3. Use the sun's energy directly to heat water.

4. Build a small attached or free-standing greenhouse, or a sunporch for prolonging the growing season.

Everyone should be able to modify his or her household to conserve the energy already being received from the sunlight directly. Many people will be able to grow a portion of their own food. Some will want to go further and buy or build various types of solar hardware. We have therefore structured the "how to" sections—Parts Two and Three—to correspond with this order of interest.

The Interface Areas: Humans & Wildlife, House & Street, and House & Neighborhood: Assessing your present lifestyle and home design in terms of managing interface areas between house and neighborhood requires that you become sensitive to problems of toxic materials, status displays, competitiveness, and the lack of current working models for neighborhood cooperative organizations.

With respect to nonhuman, nondomestic life that shares your home and garden habitat, you need to consider the four basic questions shown in the margin.

In looking out at the neighborhood, one might ask, "What cooperative ventures might be undertaken to improve life in all the houses in line with our objectives?" Joint food raising? Seed, vegetable, and home-raised meat swapping? Bulk food or materials buying? Collection and transporting of recycled materials? Management of organic wastes? Consider what efforts have been made to influence city or county governments with respect to the following matters: traffic diversion, noise abatement, wastewater treatment, municipal composting, leaf banks, methane recovery from sewage treatment and dump sites, recycling centers with regular pick-ups for wastepaper and other waste materials, community gardens, bikeways and bike racks, benches to encourage pedestrians, better mass transit, zoning to preserve open land for parks and surrounding agricultural land for raising food, farmers' markets in town, municipal pest-control programs that reduce the use of poisons, and many other similar ventures that harmonize and enhance the efforts of the integral urban house and that can only be undertaken by larger groups cooperating together. A few of the components that we personally have been involved in are discussed in Chapter 15.

The design for the physical structure of an integral urban house and

1. Have the habitat and food resources of beneficial organisms been maximized to encourage natural suppression of pest species? Examples of beneficial organisms are insect-eating birds, lizards, frogs, snakes, spiders, and bees.

2. Has the house been constructed or modified to exclude and/or reduce the habitat and food for such pest organisms as rats, mice, termites, cockroaches, ants, and flies?

3. What alternatives to using poisons in managing this interface are available?

4. What are the hazards associated with the poisons to which the residents are now exposing themselves?

garden, criteria derived from the assessments described above will help you make a list of components or behaviors you would like to develop or modify. The design we arrived at for ourselves in preparing the way for the Integral Urban House in Berkeley is listed in the margin.

What to Do First?

Now that you have developed your own list of objectives, where should you start? The parable quoted below may be of some use to you. It illustrates a systems idea called hierarchial growth. The story describes two ways of going about organizing a project: (1) working from beginning to end, and (2) assembling subcomponents and then integrating these into the total system.

We advise people to develop an overall plan for the total integrated system but when beginning the actual work to start small. Choose to develop first those areas of life-support that have immediate economic rewards, that are easiest to establish and manage, and for which you either already possess or can easily obtain the expertise. Gradually build towards greater self-reliance as the initial projects prove successful. If you start by conserving the energy and resources you already have, your efforts will make an immediate difference and give you a base from which to approach the more difficult tasks of producing your own food or the more glamorous ones of creating and installing hardware of solar technology.

The Two Watchmakers

There were once two fine watchmakers, Hora and Tempus. Each was a skilled craftsman and the watches of both were very much in demand. New customers were constantly calling on them to place orders. Yet strangely enough while Hora prospered, Tempus became poorer and poorer; he could not compete with Hora and finally he went out of business. What could account for the difference between the two?

Each of the watches the men were constructing consisted of a hundred parts. When Tempus assembled his, he started with part one and attempted to complete the entire hundred. But every time he set down his work to answer the phone, the watch would promptly decompose into its individual pieces again and he would have to start all over. The more interruptions he had to deal with, the slower the assembly process went and the more his output decreased.

Hora, by contrast, had developed a system of assembling the individual parts into small subcomponents of ten parts each. Whenever he had ten all completed, he would then bring them together into a whole. If he was interrupted by a phone call, the worst that would happen would be that one of his subassemblies had to be rebuilt. Thus his output was steady, his customers satisfied, and his business successful.

Deciding on components

1. Create structural additions, room furnishings, and appliances that moderate climate and conserve energy resources, so that the least amount of supplemental energy will be needed for us to live comfortably within the house and reuse the greatest possible amount of materials.

2. Carry water from source point (rain, well, municipal delivery system) through the system, reusing it as often as possible before it leaves the property.

3. Take advantage of all direct sunlight falling on the property, to:
a. raise food plants
b. heat water
c. heat indoor space for humans and for raising plants

4. Design outdoor areas to:
a. maximize use of space in producing food with the least labor input, once the systems are developed
b. use shaded areas for compost bins, animal cages, and storage of compostable materials until processed
c. provide space for drying clothes and for other direct uses of sun's energy

5. Design kitchen and storage areas to:
a. make it easy to clean and prepare garden vegetables and home-raised meat, and to extract honey
b. provide storage for foods in bulk at proper temperature
c. provide storage for recycling: (1) organic materials to the compost (2) inorganic and noncomposted organic (paper) materials to the recycling center

Part Two:
Conserving Energy and Resources

4. CONSERVATION OF ENERGY

Some of the key joints that may need weatherizing:

1. Between the bottom exterior wall plate and floor sheathing

2. Between the top of the foundation wall and the edge joist (the board that goes around the edge of the floor frame on the outside in a wood-frame house) or sill plate (the board covering the space under the window sill)

3. Junctures in exterior covering materials such as siding and masonry, especially where water can be trapped, as in exposed butt joints ("T"-shaped joints) and some board-and-batten joints (where the siding of the house is joined to the vertical boards, called "batts" on the exterior of the house)

4. Where chimneys or pipes pass through the roof

5. In old homes where the roof joins the walls

Weatherizing means making a structure more weatherproof. Solarization is using solar energy in designing or operating the home. Although using solar energy, particularly if it involves obtaining new equipment, has a glamour and adventure not associated with the usual sort of activities required in weatherizing a structure, weatherizing is without doubt more effective in conserving energy in terms of time and money expended. If your home is like most, it probably loses more energy due to faulty construction and wear than can be gained from installing a solar system. Although this is a generalization it is logically true, since the same losses of heat will occur after solarization as before. Therefore, if you want to reduce your energy consumption and consequent impact on the planet, weatherize first and solarize second, or if you can, do them simultaneously.

Weatherization Before Solarization

In building new or retrofitting old homes to conserve energy, it is useful to determine how the structure loses heat. Table 4-1 illustrates how a "characteristic house" in the Baltimore/Washington, D.C. area loses heat in the winter and lets heat in during the summer. "Heating load" here refers to the percentage of the home's total heating requirements that are attributed to loss of heat through the specified parts of the home. For instance, heat loss through the windows accounts for 13.6 percent of the heating requirement of the average home that has an insulated ceiling or attic. Similarly, cooling load refers to the percentage of the total air conditioning requirement that each part of the building contributes. One of the major sources of the cooling requirement is from the "interval load," that is, the amount of heat input into the home resulting from appliances and the metabolic activities of people.

If your house is located in an area of the country where it is colder or warmer for a longer period than the average, more emphasis should be placed on the heating load or cooling load respectively. Although the "characteristic" house described in the table has an insulated ceiling or attic, which many homes in the country do not (but should), the data presented should help you determine priorities for changing the space heating or cooling systems of the house. We are assuming that attic insulation would be one of the first improvements.

Another useful point made by Table 4-1 concerns the great influence of infiltration—the free flow of air in and out of a home through the cracks around doors and windows—on the energy balance of the average home. Because infiltration is the most important load factor in both the heating and

Table 4-1. **Heating and Cooling Loads in a Typical House, N.E. Region***

Components	Percent of Heating Load	Percent of Cooling Load
Doors	1.4	0.4
Floors	2.2	2.4
Ceilings (insulated)	3.7	2.3
Windows	13.6	4.1
Walls (uninsulated)	23.9	14.2
Infiltration	55.2	41.5
Internal Load†	———	35.1
Total	100	100

*Baltimore, Washington. Walls are uninsulated, but ceiling is insulated.   † Appliances, lights, and physiological heat from occupants.

Source: Report Number HUD-HAI-2, *Residential Energy Consumption, Single-Family Housing.*

cooling systems of a house, preventing it will affect both systems simultaneously. It follows that if all the factors can be simultaneously affected, to some degree the total energy use by the structure will decrease. Of course, energy savings will ultimately be measured in direct proportion to how much energy (labor and materials) you put into the changes.

Minimizing Infiltration: Infiltration is the single most important aspect of weatherizing and should be considered first. Frequently, it is the easiest aspect to correct. Cold air entering a home through cracks can account for 30 to 50 percent of the load on a heating system, even in a well-insulated house. This figure can be cut in half by making windows and doors tighter. Weatherstripping can reduce air infiltration by as much as 60 percent.

Securing a weatherstripped window to the frame of a window through some sort of latch can further reduce infiltration by 15 percent, since by itself latching can be even more effective than most weatherstripping. Installation of storm windows (not aluminum, since it conducts away heat), can reduce cold-air leakage by 30 percent. If you go beyond weatherizing and decide to increase the glass area on south-facing walls for purposes of solar-heat collection (see Chapter 12), pay particular attention to controlling air leaks by proper framing and trim around opening. If the framing and trimming is poor, any gains in heat collection capability could be offset by heat lost to infiltration.

The infiltration of air into and out of a structure occurs primarily through the trim and frames of windows and doors, up through chimney flues (see diagram), through exhaust-fan air vents, and around key joints in the house.

In these and other places, especially where exposure to outside water and wind occurs, use of a good sealer or caulking compound can help reduce air infiltration and effect significant reductions in the cooling and heating requirements of your home.

Technically, weatherstripping is anything that closes off space around doors and windows. The names of weatherstripping materials vary. When used to fill air spaces around windows and along the top and sides of doors, the material is called weatherstrip. The material placed on the bottom edge of a door is referred to as door bottom, or door sweep. On the plate the door swings off of, it is called a threshold. Table 4-2 indicates the advantages and disadvantages of general types of weatherstripping. This information may help you to choose among the brands available in your local stores.

The Chimney Effect

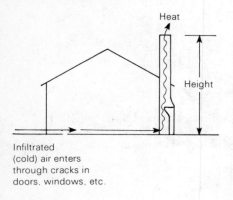

Heat

Height

Infiltrated (cold) air enters through cracks in doors, windows, etc.

Table 4-2. **Types of Weatherstripping for Doors & Windows***

Type	Composition	Use
Felt	Wool or other cloth	Where material will not get wet
Reinforced felt	Wool felt and aluminum	Where material will not get wet
Reinforced basket	Vinyl-covered aluminum	Versatile; can be stapled easily and removed easily in case of error; waterproof
Tubular reinforced basket	Vinyl-covered aluminum with hollow or foam-filled tubes	Good where pressure seals are desired
Rigid strips	Aluminum and vinyl best	Because of expense, use only in visible places

*Foam strips, neoprene, rubber, vinyl, or polyurethane with adhesive backs are poor materials not recommended.

Box 4-1. **Computing Degree-Days for Weatherizing**

No structure or heating or cooling system can be designed until an assessment of the local climatic conditions at the proposed site is conducted. The temperature difference between the outside and inside of a structure, the wind condition, and the shading on and around the building are the chief climatic factors that affect the indoor temperatures. To design a structure that will operate as a physiological buffer, ameliorating the extremes of outdoor temperatures, one needs to determine the range of these conditions and to adjust the design in anticipation of them. A good way to begin this process is to obtain weather data from the nearest weather station and make extrapolations to the particular site.

Minimum design temperature and degree-day tabulations are two means of assessing climatic extremes. Minimum outside design temperatures—the lowest likely outdoor winter temperature—are tabulated for cities and towns throughout the United States (see *ASHRAE Handbook of Fundamentals* or Leckie, *et al.*, *Other Homes and Garbage*). The concept behind these temperatures is that structures should be designed to withstand the most severe conditions, or the periods of lowest or highest temperature.

Degree-days is another design aid that indicates long-term energy requirements. The greater the number of degree-days, the greater the need for heating a structure. One degree-day accumulates for every degree *below* 65°F (18.3°C) over a twenty-four-hour period. Daily average outside temperatures are used to make this calculation. The daily average temperature is determined by adding the maximum and minimum temperatures, and then dividing by 2. Thus, a day with a maximum of 60°F (15.6°C) and a minimum of 30°F (−1.1°C) has an average of 45°F (7.2°C). This is 20 degrees below 65°F (18.3°C). Hence 20 degree-days accumulate for this day. Degree-day calculations start on January 1, and for different areas of the United States, particularly the more northern climates, can go up to 10,000 degree-days, or more. Like the minimum design temperature, degree-day calculations have been tabulated and are available from local and national weather data sources.

Computing Degree-Days and Energy Costs: Once infiltration has been reduced through the application of weatherstripping and caulking, a plan for working toward the optimal combination of energy-conserving home improvements, or weatherizing, is needed. A process for developing such a plan has been outlined by the National Bureau of Standards and applied throughout the United States by the Community Services Administration. This process is based on a theoretical 1200-square foot house. In order to use the data on this model house in designing your own plan, you must first have information about energy costs in your area and about your climate, expressed in degree-days (the amount of days the outside temperature drops below 65°F multiplied by the amount of degrees below 65° for each of those days). See Box 4-1 for details on how to compute degree-days.

Source: Community Services Administration, *A Community Planning Guide to Weatherization.*

Table 4-3. Heating Index for Different Types of Fuel

Fuel																
Gas (Therm)	11¢	14¢	18¢	21¢	25¢	27¢	29¢	31¢	35¢	41¢	51¢	61¢	72¢	82¢	$1.03	$1.23
Oil/Kero (Gallon)				30¢	34¢	37¢	40¢	43¢	50¢	51¢	71¢	86¢	$1.00	$1.15	$1.44	$1.72
Electric (KWH)				1¢	1.2¢	1.3¢	1.4¢	1.5¢	1.7¢	2¢	2.5¢	3¢	3.5¢	4¢	5¢	6¢
Coal (Ton)	$21	$28	$35	$42	$49	$53	$57	$62	$70	$82	$102	$123	$144	$164	$205	$246
Degree Days:																
1000	2	2	3	3	4	4	4	4	5	6	7	9	10	12	15	18
2000	3	4	5	6	7	8	8	9	10	12	15	18	21	23	29	35
3000	5	6	8	9	11	11	12	13	15	18	22	26	31	35	44	53
4000	6	8	10	12	14	15	16	18	20	23	29	35	41	47	59	70
5000	8	10	13	15	18	19	21	22	25	29	37	44	51	59	73	88
6000	9	12	15	18	21	23	25	26	30	35	44	53	62	70	88	105
7000	11	14	18	21	25	27	29	31	35	41	51	61	72	82	103	123
8000	12	16	20	24	28	30	33	35	40	47	59	70	82	94	117	141
9000	14	18	23	27	32	34	37	40	45	53	66	79	92	105	132	158
10000	15	20	25	30	35	38	41	44	50	59	73	88	103	117	147	176

Table 4-4. Optimal Combinations of Energy Conservation Techniques

Heating Index	Attic Insulation	Wall Insulation*	Floor Insulation†	Duct Insulation	Storm Doors	Long Life $25	$8	$4	Short Life $25	$8	$4
1–3	R-0	0	0	R-8			None				
4–6	R-11		0	R-8						None	
7–10	R-11		R-11	R-8	None	None	20	15			
11–12	R-19	Full	R-11	R-8		20	15	10	None	20	15
13–15	R-19	Wall	R-11	R-8		15	12	8	None	20	15
16–19	R-30	Insula-	R-19	R-16		12	9	6	20	15	10
20–27	R-30	tion	R-19	R-16	Optional	9	7	5	15	12	8
28–35	R-33	R-11	R-19	R-16	Optional	6	5	all	12	9	6
36–45	R-38	to		R-24		4	all	all	9	7	5
46–60	R-44	R-14		R-24					6	5	all
61–85	R-49		R-22	R-32	all	all windows			4	all	all
86–105	R-57			R-32	doors					all windows	
106–130	R-60			R-32							
131–	R-66			R-40							

*Insulation blown into walls
† Floors over unheated areas
‡ Minimum economical size in square feet of window to be covered:

$25.00 window is triple track (long life = 15 years; short life 7.5 years)
$8.00 window is double plastic (long life = 5 years; short life 3 years)

$4.00 window is single plastic (long life = 5 years; short life 3 years)

You may have already compiled costs while making the energy assessment suggested in Chapter 3. It can be obtained from the utility or fuel dealers in your area. Usually, only a phone call is needed. Be sure that quoted energy costs include all the taxes, surcharges, delivery charges, and fuel adjustments that you will actually have to pay. Gas is sold by the therm (10^5 Btu), oil and kerosene by the gallon, electricity by the kilowatt-hour (KWH), and coal by the ton. Use Tables 4-3 and 4-4 to determine the basic aspects of a weatherizing plan based on a minimum cost for improvements where major changes such as installation of a new furnace or solar heating system are not possible.

First, using your computations of degree-days and energy costs, select your heating index from Table 4-3. Then, with this number, use Table 4-4 to select the appropriate combination of factors needed for an energy-conserving heating system. For example, gas at 29¢ per therm in a 5000-degree-day area, gives a heating index of 21. The table specifies that with this index you would need R-30 attic insulation, R-19 floor insulation, R-16 duct insulation, etc. "R" stands for thermal resistance.

A digression is necessary here to define and show the relationship among k, R, and U values. A k value is a measurement of heat transfer through a specific type of material. Heat transfer, referred to as thermal conductivity, is measured by how many Btu will travel through one inch of a material every hour per square foot of surface area, for every degree difference between the temperature on the two sides of the material ($Btu/in/hr/ft^2/°F$). The smaller the k number, the greater the potential in-

Table 4-5. Thermal Conductivity (k) of Materials at Room Temperature

Material	Conductivity (k) ($Btu/in/hr/ft^2/°F$)	Material	Conductivity (k) ($Btu/in/hr/ft^2/°F$)
Air (still)	0.169–0.215	Limestone	10.8
Asbestos		Mineral wool	
board with cement	2.7	board	0.33
wool	0.62	fill-type	0.27
Brick		Paper	0.9
common	5.0	Paraffin	1.68
face	9.2	Plaster	
fire	6.96	cement	8.0
Cellulose, dry	1.66	gypsum	3.3
Cinders	1.1	Redwood bark	0.26
Clay		Rock wool	0.27
dry	3.5–4.0	Sand, dry	2.28
10 percent moisture	5.5	Sand (Fairbanks)	
20 percent moisture	10.0	4 percent moisture	8.5
Concrete		10 percent moisture	15.0
cinder	4.9	Sandy Loam	
stone	12.0	4 percent moisture	6.5
Corkboard	0.28	10 percent moisture	13.0
Cornstalk, insulating board	0.33	Sandstone	12.6
Cotton	0.39	Stone (crushed quartz,	
Foamglas	0.40	4 percent wet)	11.5
Glass wool	0.27	Water, fresh	4.1
Glass		Wood	
flint	5.1	fir	0.8
pyrex	7.56	maple	1.2
Gypsum, solid	3.0	red oak	1.1
Hair felt	0.26	white pine	0.78
Ice	15.6	Wood fiber board	0.34
Lime, mortar	2.42	Wool	0.264

Source: Selected from Table 4-8, Leckie *et al.*, *Other Homes and Garbage.*

sulating value of a material (because it will let less heat flow through it; see Table 4-5).

The R value, or "resistance," is the total thickness (t) of a particular item, such as a piece of insulation, divided by its k value; that is, $R = t/k$. So, for example, when you buy insulation, the label should tell the k value of the material from which it is made, and the R value of a piece of that particular thickness. The higher the R, the less heat will be lost through the walls, floors, or ceiling of a home. Table 4-6 below shows the R value and thickness of insulation. For R values of materials not listed, check with manufacturers or read labels carefully. Remember that two materials may have the same thickness, but the one with the higher R value will reduce heat loss more.

The opposite way of describing the same phenomenon, resistance to heat transfer, is to describe the rate at which a material lets heat through. This is the U value, and is equal to $1/R$. U values are discussed in Chapter 12 in relation to windows as solar collectors.

Why would anyone want to know about k and R values? Besides being able to evaluate a particular product, you can use these values to calculate how much of the heat inside your house is being lost to the outside through a particular wall. Say that a wall is composed of building material having a composite R value of 15, which includes the sum of R values for the outside sheathing, insulation material, inside wallboard, and air spaces. Using this value, you can calculate the rate of heat loss for a 50–square-foot section of wall over a 10–hour period if the internal and outside temperatures are assumed to be constant at 65°F (18.3°C) and 35°F (1.7°C) respectively. Figure that $1/15$ Btu of heat will be lost each hour for each square foot of wall surface for every degree difference. Thus,

$$\frac{1/15 \text{ Btu} \times 50 \text{ ft}^2 \times 10 \text{ hr} \times 30°F}{\text{ft}^2 \times F° \times \text{hr}} = 1000 \text{ Btu}$$

(Note that all the units cancel out except Btu.)

For a thorough discussion with examples, consult: Leckie, *et al., Other Homes and Garbage*, Anderson, *The Solar Home Book*.

Table 4-6. **How Thick Should Insulation Be?**

| R | Batts or Blankets, Inches of | | Loose Fill, inches of | | |
	Glass Fiber	Rock Wool	Glass Fiber	Rock Wool	Cellulose Fiber
11	3.5–4	3	5	4	3
13	4	4.5	6	4.5	3.5
19	6–6.5	5.25	8–9	6–7	5
22	6.5	6	10	7–8	6
26	8	8.5	12	9	7–7.5
30	9.5–10.5	9	13–14	10–11	8
33	11	10	15	11–14	9
38	12–13	10.5	17–18	13–14	10–11

Note: It is best to check the specification on the insulation itself before purchase, since actual materials can vary and manufacturers may also provide slightly different products in different areas.

Source: U.S. Department of Housing and Urban Development, *In the Bank or Up the Chimney?* Also in Federal Energy Administration, *Home Energy Savers Workbook*.

Insulation: Selecting the proper type and amount of insulation is an important decision. Types range from mineral wool, air spaces, glass and wood fiber, pulverized paper, treated sawdust or cellulose, to the newer types of plastic, which may be preformed into boards and sheets, sprayed on, or foamed in place. See Table 4-6 for R values of several types of insulation materials. The basic factors to consider besides cost and effectiveness include resistance to rodents and insects, resistance to decay and shrinkage, flammability rating, presence of objectionable vapors and odors, amount of particles present that irritate the skin, eyes, and lungs, performance in the presence of moisture, energy consumption used in manufacture and transport, and overall environmental impact. See Table 4-7 for a comparison of some of these factors for different materials.

Choosing and Using Insulations: Studies conducted at the National Bureau of Standards on the thermal performance of cellulose fiber, fibrous glass wool, and urea-formaldehyde provided some surprises. The results are of importance to designers, architects, builders, and homeowners. These studies were conducted with a 2×4 standard constructed wall (studs 16 inches on center), insulated with all three materials. The wall was subjected to temperatures of 5°F (-15°C) on one side, and normal indoor temperatures, about 75°F (23.9°C), on the other for a two-month period. The same tests were also conducted on a test house similarly insulated over a winter period of seventy-six days. The results of these studies show cellulose and fiber glass to be roughly equal in thermal conductance (k) and thermal resistance (R), with urea-formaldehyde foam having a much lower conductance (higher resistance to heat transfer).

The measured thermal conductance, k, of cellulose and glass fiber was

Table 4-7. The Advantages and Disadvantages of Different Types of Insulation

Type of Insulation	Advantages	Disadvantages
Cellulose fiber	Loose form settles better and has a higher R value than loose mineral wool.	Unless specified on the bag, it is not vermin- or fireproof; also, needs a separate vapor barrier.
Mineral wool (fiber glass)	Inexpensive; standard material in house construction; available in many forms (blankets, blankets with vapor barrier, loose); fire-resistant.	Loose form settles and leaves uninsulated gaps; low R value/thickness ratio.
Vermiculite and perlite	Pours and distributes well, especially down wall studs and around obstructions such as pipe and cables.	Expensive; needs separate vapor barrier.
Urea-formaldehyde foam (U-F)	High R value; fire-resistant; applied as liquid.	High price; uncertain shrinkage behavior.
Polystyrene foam (Styrofoam)	Useful in board form (tongue-and-groove); can be easily combined with mineral wool in any wall.	Not fire-resistant; needs gypsum wallboard for fire safety.
Urethane foam	Highest R value/thickness ratio; useful in board form.	Burns and releases toxic fumes when burning; needs gypsum wallboard for fire safety.

0.060 and 0.064 respectively. High moisture on exterior wood siding and sheathing were observed at the urea-formaldehyde wall section. This caused some blistering of the oil-based paint that was operating as a vapor barrier. During the summer the moisture dissipated.

The wall sections on the urea-formaldehyde were inspected periodically and the shrinkage away from the studs was measured. At three months shrinkage was 2.6 percent, at fifteen months it was 5.0 percent, and at twenty months 7.3 percent. Thus, shrinkage was considerable and still increasing when the study ended. In contrast, no settling of the loose-fill materials was observed over an eighteen-month period.

Thus, although further tests are needed and the results cannot be generalized too far beyond standard-sized and constructed walls, cellulose and fiber glass appear to be better-lasting materials and hence provide better insulation even though the urea-formaldehyde may have better initial specifications and be easier to use in certain areas. Cellulose materials (particularly old newspaper) are made from renewable sources and could form the backbone of the overall insulation and weatherization process going on in this

Table 4-8. Cost Estimates for Insulation in the Home

NOTE: Be sure to read this material before using the table:

In order to compute the various cost estimates that will be useful to you certain general assumptions had to be made. Make sure you remember them:

1. All costs are computed on the assumption that there is no existing insulation on the house; if there is some your cost will be lower.

2. All total cost estimates use the following house dimensions and characteristics:

- The floor area is 1000 square feet.
- The wall area is 750 square feet.
- The heating ducts are 25 feet long and 2 feet around, for an area of 50 square feet.
- There are twelve windows: Four have a surface area of 15 ft^2 each, three have a surface of 12 ft^2 each, two have a surface area of 9 ft^2, and three at 6 ft^2 each.
- There are two doors to the outside.

3. All total costs are computed on the assumption that $8.00, double-plastic-film temporary storm windows are used.

4. Cost of wall insulation where included is for materials only and is computed at 12 cents per square foot.

Heating Index	Cost per Ft^2 of All Insulating Materials*	Cost per Ft^2 of Attic and Floor Insulation†	Total Cost of Materials‡	Total Cost of Materials, Excluding Wall Insulation‡
1–3	.16	.0	$ .12	$ 12
4–6	.39	.11	212	122
7–10	.50	.22	322	232
11–12	.58	.30	434	344
13–15	.58	.30	458	368
16–19	.93	.49	676	586
20–27	.93	.49	706	616
28–35	.96	.52	760	670
36–45	1.20	.60	882	792
46–60	1.26	.66	942	852
61–85	1.47	.71	1004	914
86–105	1.55	.79	1084	994
106–130	1.58	.82	1114	1024
131–	1.80	.88	1186	1096

REMEMBER! *These estimates do not include cost of stopping infiltration!* Infiltration should be stopped before *any other* major effort to reduce heat losses is made

*Gives the total cost per ft^2 for all insulating materials for the attic, walls, floors, and ducts.
† It is appropriate to use this column if you do not have the capability to insulate the wall, and if there are no exposed heating ducts.
‡ Calculated for a 1000–square-foot house.

Source: Adapted from Community Services Administration, *A Community Planning Guide to Weatherization.*

country. Where choices exist between materials derived from fossil fuels and renewable supplies, if other factors are nearly equal, the renewable sources should be used.

Cost Estimates: Table 4-8 provides some cost estimates that will help you to figure out which balanced combination is best for a limited budget. Be sure to read and understand the notes before you try to use the table; otherwise, you may get confused. Basically, the table gives various cost estimates by heating index. When you find a cost estimate you can afford, read back horizontally across the page to see what heating index it applies to. Then go back to Table 4-4 and find the balanced combination that goes with that heating index. Even though this may not be the optimal combination for your area, it will be the balanced combination that you can afford. Note that you are not attempting to change your heating index; you are simply finding the least expensive balanced combination you can afford this year.

There may be structural limitations on the building that make it impossible or impractical to achieve optimal levels of conservation techniques. For instance, insulation cannot be added under floors in houses built on concrete slabs. In such cases, the other recommended improvements should still be added to the extent indicated on Table 4-4. Similarly, R–30 insulation may be recommended for an attic, but only R–19 may fit at the eaves or where the attic is floored. In this case make recommended improvements insofar as possible, but when structural constraints intervene come as close as you can on that improvement and be sure to maintain the balance on other recommended levels.

Moisture Control: Insulation batts can be purchased with or without a vapor barrier—the paper or foil covering on one side of the batt. The barrier retards water vapor, normally present in the house, from passing through or condensing in the insulation. The vapor barrier should face the living quarters of the house unless a competent air-conditioning specialist advises you otherwise.

Before you install insulation in closed cavities (such as wall spaces) it may be useful to consult an insulation specialist about possible moisture problems. If water vapor is allowed to condense in the insulated space it will lower the performance of the insulation and could damage the structure. In general, moisture problems can be prevented with proper installation of vapor barriers and adequate ventilation.

Insulation in Attics and Crawl Spaces: Two basic kinds of insulation are available for floors of unheated attics. Both will do the job if they are properly installed. One type is preformed mineral fiber (glass fiber or rock wool) batts or blankets; the other is cellulose or mineral fiber in loose-fill form.

When installing insulation in attics, you do not have to stop at the ceiling joists if the attic has no flooring, but insulation should not touch the roof at the eaves. Preformed insulation batts may be more economical than loose-fill materials in an unobstructed attic area without flooring if they fit snugly between the joists. They can be laid out easily and there is no need to staple them down.

The density of loose-fill insulation is extremely important in assuring the proper resistance to heat flow. The manufacturer will generally specify the number of bags of loose-fill materials needed to achieve a given R value over a specific area. If a contractor is insulating the attic, you should verify that the proper number of bags has been used. Get the verification in writing, too!

A well-insulated attic should also be well-ventilated to prevent moisture-accumulation problems. Never block ventilation ports and always provide at least two vent openings, located in such a way that air can flow in one vent and out the other. A good rule of thumb is to provide at least 1 square foot of opening for each 300 square feet of attic floor area. Ventilation ports should be tightly screened to prevent entrance of undesired pest wildlife (for example, rats, squirrels, bats, or birds).

Once the area between the joists is fully insulated the greatest source of heat loss in the attic is through the joists themselves, which may cover as much as 10 percent of the attic. For this reason, when adding insulation batts above the level of the ceiling joists, cover the joists completely, if possible.

If you want to add R–19 or R–22 insulation to existing insulation, it is usually best to add R–11 batts up to the level of the joists and cover the entire area with another layer of R–11 batts. Place the batts as close together as possible to prevent air from circulating between them.

Loose-fill insulation may be better if the access to your attic is difficult or if the attic has a floor. If flooring is present in an otherwise unfinished attic, you may have to remove some of it temporarily to allow insulation to be blown in. Loose insulation is usually blown into the attic through flexible tubing attached to a small machine that puffs up the insulation as it pushes it through the tube. This puffing action may cause some settling after the insulation is in place, so you should take that into account when measuring the depth. Small holes should be drilled into tight-fitting flooring at one-foot intervals to allow passage of any water vapor that may rise from the rooms below.

Crawl spaces beneath the house can be closed off in the winter but must be well-ventilated in summer to prevent the build-up of moisture from the rooms above. In many areas it is a good idea to cover the ground under a crawl space with plastic sheeting to reduce the moisture level in this area.

Floors over unheated areas, such as crawl spaces, garages, or basements, can be a major source of heat loss in an otherwise well-insulated house. Everyone knows that hot air rises, but, remember, heat flows to cold areas through solid surfaces in any direction: up, down, or sideways. Water pipes in unheated areas should also be insulated if there is danger of freezing after the floor insulation has been installed.

Information About Specific Materials: It has not been one of the purposes of this section to provide you with complete information about the various materials available on the market. It is best if you can speak with a local contractor who is informed on this subject, in order to make choices based on the particular factors of importance in your area.

The Home Economics of Weatherization: If your total energy bill for space heating is $500 per year, and if you can invest $200 to save $250 of this, then you will make money on weatherizing in the first year. Assuming, for example, that an attic and wall insulation job will last the life of the house, then savings actually will accrue each year during the life of the house. Storm windows will also continue providing savings beyond the pay-back period. Calculating the savings in this fashion is actually more realistic than calculating pay-back periods for any habitat change. Still, from an investment standpoint a pay-back period of three years, for example, or 33 percent each year, is one of the best around. A ten-year pay-back period, roughly 10 percent each year, is also a very good investment. Table 4-9 lists some cost estimates and yearly savings from which pay-back periods can be calculated. (Be careful in your reasoning about pay-back periods. Remember, there is no pay-back period on your existing systems, only pay periods, and *they* last forever. A solar heating system, for example, may pay for itself in ten years, but afterward, you become your own producer!) This table clearly shows that turning down the thermostat and putting on extra clothing, the practice in many countries of the world to save energy, offers the greatest money savings for the least cost. Changing one's habits is the most cost-effective, and probably the most health-effective, technique.

Space Heating

Your heating or electric bills or Table 4-10, which provides general averages for the whole country, will show that space heating is the most significant use of energy in the home. Two approaches are possible to affect this cost. One is reducing your uses or needs, while the other is using the heat more efficiently. It is important to remember that the original purpose for space heating is to prevent heat loss from the body. The factors that affect heat loss from the body are metabolism, circulation, diet, activity, clothing, shelter, and climate. Thus, a wholistic plan to affect the space heating situation should account for all these aspects of the problem.

In the 1920s, the indoor temperature used in house designs was 70°F (21.1°C). By the 1970s this had been increased to 75°F (23.9°C). The American idea of a comfortable indoor temperature has increased about one degree each decade. Obviously, one's ideas or beliefs about what is the right temperature can have a substantial impact on energy use.

Table 4-9. Costs & Pay-Back for Weatherization Improvements

Action	Initial Cost	Yearly Savings
Turn down thermostat*	zero	$20–65
Put on plastic storm windows	$5–7	$20–55
Service oil furnace	$25	$25–65
Caulk and weatherstrip	$75–105	$30–75
Insulate attic	$160–290	$35–120
Total	$265–427	$130–380

Source: U.S. Department of Housing and Urban Development, *In the Bank or Up the Chimney?*

*With thermostat put six degrees below usual setting; up to 35 percent of a heating bill can be saved by putting thermostat eight degrees below usual setting.

Table 4-10. **Residential Energy Consumption**

End Use	1960 Consumption (10^{12} Btu)	Percent of Total*	1968 Consumption (10^{12} Btu)	Percent of Total*
Space heating	4848	61	6675	57
Water heating	1159	15	1736	15
Cooking	556	7	637	6
Clothes drying	93	1	208	2
Refrigeration	369	5	692	6
Air conditioning	134	3	427	4
Other	809	10	1241	11
Total:	7968		11,616	

*Percent totals do not add up to 100 due to rounding off error.

Source: Adapted from Crawley, *Energy*.

The food we eat generates heat through metabolic processes. The body maintains a steady body temperature in order to avoid being damaged by too much or too little heat. Heat generation depends upon type of activities performed and their duration. For example, metabolic energy generation can vary from about 350 Btu per hour at rest (equivalent to the energy output of a 100-watt bulb) to over 1500 Btu per hour (equivalent to that of four 100-watt bulbs) when heavy work is being done. Light work can use 800 Btu per hour. A chilled person shivers, the heart beats faster, blood flow to arms and legs is restricted, and every effort is made to conserve heat for the vital organs. Foot-stomping, hand-waving, and maintaining a compact body posture are automatic responses to excessive cold. The opposite occurs in hot periods. Muscles relax, lungs operate faster to ventilate and carry heat away, capillaries rise closer to the skin and more perspiration occurs, increasing evaporative cooling. Body movements are slowed. Again, the automatic controls make these changes (Figure 4-1).

The obvious approach to these changes is to vary your clothing according to the season. In hot weather, lighter clothing is required, while in winter more layers of cloth are helpful since air will be trapped between each layer and act as insulation. Natural materials such as wool, cotton and fur are particularly good for insulating the body from the cold because of the air trapped between the fibers. Garments stuffed with feathers or the cocoons of caterpillars such as silkworms are choice: not only do they combine light weight with good insulation, but they originate from renewable sources as well. (At the Integral Urban House, we have started a hedge of mulberries to use as food for silkworms, the cocoons of which will be used as insulation material. Our first experiment with silkworms taught us that they are relatively easy to raise. Thirty silkworms kept in a roaster pan produced a nice handful of cocoons and plenty of eggs for the next generation.

Alterations of space temperatures in the home so that they fluctuate somewhat according to the outside conditions but still stay within the ranges for physiological adaptation, plus changes in adaptive clothing can result in substantial savings in energy normally used for space heating. We are also convinced that a moderate degree of physiological adaptation in the long term is actually healthier.

Nervous impulses and body temperature affect the hypothalamus, which stimulates the blood vessels, sweat glands, muscles, and metabolic processes. Constricted blood vessels decrease blood flow to the skin surface, resulting in less heat loss. Reduced heat loss occurs from less evaporation of water due to less sweat secretion. Body heat is augmented by increased muscle tone or shivering and more work. In very cold climates there is a tendency to voluntarily increase dietary proteins, thus stimulating metabolism. Conversely, dilated blood vessels, more sweating, reduced muscular heat production, and less protein intake increase heat loss when environmental conditions become too warm. Food temperatures and type of clothing are also compensating mechanisms useful in regulating body temperatures.

Figure 4-1. **Heat Homeostasis in the Body**

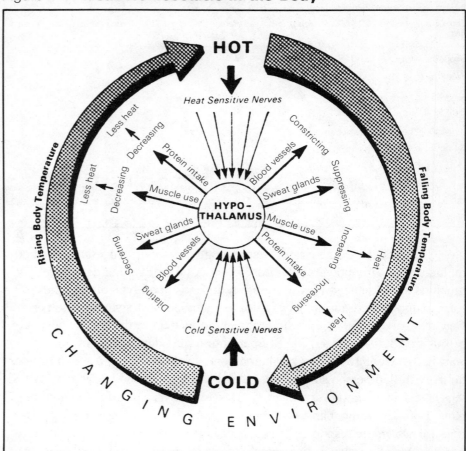

Thermostat Settings: The rate at which a house loses heat is a function of the difference between outside and inside temperatures. As this difference increases more heat is lost. The cooler the indoor temperature the less heat will be lost to the outside. A 1-degree reduction can reduce heat loss between 2 and 3 percent. A reduction of 7 degrees (for example, from 75 to 68 degrees) will result in a 15 to 20 percent reduction in fuel needs.

A morning thermostat setting of 60 degrees can be comfortable if a person is physically active. In the evening, after chores, a 68 setting is welcome, particularly if residents are sedentary then. Of course, if you cannot be physically active because of illness, extra clothing, hats, blankets, or hot water bottles can help.

Thermostat settings shouldn't be "jiggled." When changing settings, do not raise the thermostat to 80 degrees or so with the belief that the room will get warm faster. The fuel input to the furnace is fixed, and higher settings do not affect the rate of heat generation; they merely determine how long the furnace will remain on or off. The danger in the higher settings is that the occupant will forget to return the setting to its normal position until the house is overheated. It is better to set the thermostat at the desired level and leave it be.

Thermostat Control and Set-back Devices: The Federal Energy Administration pamphlet "Energy Savings Through Automatic Thermostat Controls" states. *There is a myth that says you won't save energy by turning down your thermostat at night, because it takes so much energy to warm the building in the morning. But this is untrue. Setting the thermostat back for several hours at a stretch each day during the heating season (up during the cooling season) will, in a centrally-heated and cooled building, save energy. Depending on your geographical location, the amount of energy you can save will range from nine to fifteen percent of what you used before adopting this energy-conserving habit.*

There are two ways you can accomplish temperature set-back and set-up: by adjusting the thermostat manually at the proper times, or by installing a device that makes the adjustments automatically. The manual technique, of course, requires no special equipment, but it does demand a greater degree of time and attention than many people are willing to put forth day in and day out. An automatic control device, on the other hand, involves some initial investment, but the outlay is more than repaid in dependability and energy savings over a period of time.

How Much Will a Set-Back Device Save?: *The exact energy and cost savings from a set-back device are dependent on building design, amount of insulation, climate, temperature setting, and utility rate structures. Several studies have been conducted to estimate the fuel and cost savings that can be realized by using a set-back device during both the heating and cooling seasons.* [Table 4-11 lists the approximate percentage of heating costs that can be saved in various cities throughout the country for an 8-hour night-time thermostat set-back of 5 degrees and 10 degrees.] *A replacement unit may range from seventy-five dollars to over one hundred dollars, depending on the model and the type and extent of installation labor required.*

How to Estimate Cost Savings: *From the table, you can estimate what you are likely to save by automatically setting back your thermostat during the heating season, from either 65°F [18.3°C] to either 60°F [15.6°C] or 55°F [12.8°C] at night. For example, if you live in or around Detroit, and your heating bills amount to approximately three hundred dollars for the heating season, by lowering your thermostat temperature at night from 65°F to 55°F [18.3 to 12.8°C], you could save as much as 11 percent, or thirty-three dollars a heating season. These estimated figures are based on an assumed daytime setting of 65°F [18.3°C].*

Types of Automatic Controls: *Two types of automatic controls are now available on the commercial market. One is a device that works with a conventional thermostat. The other type requires replacing the existing thermostat.*

The Converter Set-Back: *This type of control converts any existing thermostat to a timed device. Several variations are available. One is a two-component system in which a temperature control is mounted below the existing thermostat, and is connected by wires to a separate time unit plugged into a wall outlet. If the wires carry low-voltage current, they can be concealed in the wall if desired. (110-volt power cords cannot be so concealed.) Another is a single-unit device that is attached to the wall below the thermostat, and is either plugged into a nearby wall outlet, or operated by self-contained batteries.*

Replacement Set-Back *type of control replaces the conventional thermostat entirely and is generally wired to the building's electrical system and heating/cooling system. Several types are available, but this type of device is usually* more expensive to buy and costly to install, since it usually requires the additional wiring in existing walls. Its main advantage is that, having all wires hidden, it gives a neater appearance.

Automatic set-back devices are sold in many hardware and department stores, as well as in building material outlets. In general, converter types sell for less than replacement types, and can be installed by a do-it-yourselfer.

Note: A No-Cost Alternative to the Automatic Set-Back Device: Of course, you can continue to adjust your thermostat by hand, morning and evening, or whenever leaving your home or business for an extended period of time, and still achieve the same energy savings as with an automatic set-back device. Manual setting costs you nothing. However, since the automatic setback device pays for itself rather quickly, and will continue to return savings for years to come, you might prefer the regularity and convenience of an automatic control.

Energy Consumption from Activities in the Home: The use of appliances is one of the major factors inside the dwelling affecting energy consumption, directly by using electricity and gas and indirectly through heat production. Table 4-12, again using the "characteristic" house in the Baltimore/Washington, D.C. area, shows the energy used by various appliances.

This table clearly shows that hot water heaters use the most energy of all the appliances except space heating units. Indoor lighting ranks second in energy use. Although it would be best to know precisely how much energy you use in each category in order to help arrange priorities in your own approach to energy conservation, this model home and the data derived from it will probably suffice in most cases. The miscellaneous category, of course, includes appliances such as fans, pumps, stereos, radios, machines and so on. If you are interested in conserving energy, the questions you need to ask are: Do I need to purchase this appliance? Do I need to use this appliance? Can I get the work done by other means than purchase or use of an appliance?

(Incidentally, an excellent little book, *Pedal Power,* suggests ways of

Table 4-11. Heating Costs Saved With Night-Time Set-Back

City	5°F	10°F
	Approximate Percentage of Heating Costs Saved with 8-Hour Night-Time Set-Back of:	
Atlanta, Georgia	11	15
Boston, Massachusetts	7	11
Buffalo, New York	6	10
Chicago, Illinois	7	11
Cincinnati, Ohio	8	12
Cleveland, Ohio	8	12
Columbus, Ohio	7	11
Dallas, Texas	11	15
Denver, Colorado	7	11
Des Moines, Iowa	7	11
Detroit, Michigan	7	11
Kansas City, Missouri	8	12
Los Angeles, California	12	16
Louisville, Kentucky	9	13
Madison, Wisconsin	5	9
Miami, Florida	12	18
Milwaukee, Wisconsin	6	10
Minneapolis, Minnesota	5	9
New York, New York	8	12
Omaha, Nebraska	7	11
Philadelphia, Pennsylvania	8	12
Pittsburgh, Pennsylvania	7	11
Portland, Oregon	9	13
Salt Lake City, Utah	7	11
San Francisco, California	10	14
Seattle, Washington	8	12
St. Louis, Missouri	8	12
Syracuse, New York	7	11
Washington, D.C.	9	13

Source: ERDA, *Energy Savings Through Automatic Thermostat Controls.*

Source: HUD, *Residential Energy Consumption.*

Table 4-12. Annual Primary Energy Consumption in a Typical House, N.E. Region

Rank	Component	Energy (Therms)*	Percent of Total use
1	Hot water (gas)	270	23
2	Lights	218	19
3	Refrigerator/Freezer	200	17
4	Outside light	90	8
5	Color television	54	5
6	Range (gas)	50	4
7	Furnace fan	43	4
8	Clothes dryer (gas)	40	3
8	Dishwasher	40	3
9	Iron	16	1
10	Clothes washer	11	1
10	Coffee maker	11	1
11	Miscellaneous appliances	131	11
	Total	1174	100

Note: All are electric appliances except where indicated. *A therm is 10^5 Btu (100,000 Btu), and is used by utilities in billing. One therm is approximately equivalent to 30 kilowatt-hours of electricity. Appendix provides kilowatt ratings for most home appliances

adapting bicycle power to run various kitchen and other appliances.)

The hidden aspect of all these questions that does not show up in your monthly utility bill is the energy expended in extracting, manufacturing, and transporting the materials used to build the item. Still, as Table 4-11 shows, using certain appliances requires relatively little energy.

Because of increasing pressure by public interest groups and environmental lobbyists, over the next few years we expect to see a major transformation in the way appliances are constructed and used. One of the main areas will be in water heating appliances, but also affected will be refrigerators, freezers, air conditioners, stoves, ovens, and the rest. Hopefully, some of the changes that will appear will be advantageous to both consumer and the society at large because of better initial design, longer lifetimes, easier service, less noise, greater safety, and cheaper operation. Hot water heaters, for example, will have much more insulation. The same could be true of refrigerators, dryers, freezers, and ovens. More labeling and instructions for care and repair will accompany each appliance. Energy efficiency figures will also be part of the label, as with those on air conditioners now (the re-

Box 4-2. **Heating with Wood in the City**

Several factors make wood a practical and ecological form of fuel for supplemental heating and cooking in the city. Wood heating and cooking can play an important role in recycling the tremendous volumes of wastes that our cities produce. According to the United States Forest Service, as much as 30 percent of the debris headed for the typical city dump consists of combustible wood material. Certainly, many sources of wood fuel exist around and within many homes—for example, branches from pruned trees, newspapers and magazines that can be rolled into logs, and scrap wood from local lumber yards, cabinet shops, or construction sites. Wood fuel is a renewable source of energy derived from the direct energy income from the sun rather than from the capital of fossil fuel resources.

There is as much variation in the types of wood stoves as in the kinds of wood fuels available. Because most of the recycled wood products you will find in the city are relatively low in heating value, it is important to invest in a highly efficient wood heater for converting the low-grade fuels into usable heat. Heavy, cast-iron box stoves, such as the Scandinavian imports, burn wood and other combustible products very efficiently. Their interior-baffle construction and heavy cast-iron bodies allow for more thorough combustion and radiation of heat into the living space than do the lighter American models.

One disadvantage of using wood and trash as heating and cooking fuels in the urban environment is the potential threat to air quality resulting from smoke and particulate matter produced by poorly operated and maintained stoves and heaters. Still, this threat can be reduced to a minimum through the use of an efficient stove, the installation of screens at the top of the smokestack, and careful regulation of the amount of loose paper debris burnt. In fact, the use of an efficient wood-burning heater instead of a fireplace, which is notorious as an energy waster, is most likely to result in fuel-wood savings and reduced air pollution.

The economics of wood heating is most favorable when combustible waste products are used. In some areas even commercial firewood, if obtained at a reasonable price, is as cheap or cheaper than electricity or fuel oil, though it is seldom as inexpensive as gas. The table below compares several sources of heating fuels for their cost to provide one million Btu of usable heat.

See the bibliography for sources of more information on wood heat.

Fuel Source	Unit Cost*	Energy Value Btu per Unit	Quantity Needed to Provide One Million Btu of Usable Heat†	Cost to Provide One Million Btu of Usable Heat
White oak	$90 per cord	30,800,000	.065 cords	$ 5.85
Eastern white pine	$75 per cord	15,800,000	.1266 cords	$ 9.49
Douglas fir	$75 per cord	21,400,000	.0934 cords	$ 7.01
Gas	20¢ per therm	100,000	15.38 therms‡	$ 3.08
Electricity	4¢ per kilowatt-hour	3414	366.14 kilowatt-hours	$14.65
Heating oil	50¢ per gallon	140,000	10.99 gallons	$ 5.50

*Prices for Richmond, California, December, 1977.
† Assumes the following efficiencies: wood stove: 50 percent; gas furnace: 65 percent; electric furnace: 80 percent; oil furnace: 65 percent.
‡ Approximately 100 cubic feet per therm.

sult of a voluntary program organized by the Department of Commerce). New legislation will make annual costs of operation and a measure of energy performance part of the information available when the appliance is purchased. Almost any good service- or fix-it-yourself person could offer dozens of ideas about improvement in design that would extend the lifetime and repairability of most household appliances. A visit to the local dump in any city would result in a great many ideas as well.

Altering Heat-Delivery Systems: Getting the furnace inspected for leaks and overall efficiency is a good idea. Check to see if heating ducts are insulated. Long uninsulated lengths of pipe can reduce furnace efficiency by up to 25 percent. Fiber glass furnace duct insulation can be purchased (1.5-inch width by 100' length costs about $10) at local hardware stores. Closing ducts to unheated rooms as well as keeping the door closed can save $10 to $20 per month during the winter in some areas. The pilot light usually burns all year, but it is a good idea to shut it off if the furnace will not be used during the summer months. Turning pilot flames off and on is simple, but if done improperly it can be dangerous. Directions are usually provided on the furnace itself. Contact your local utility company for help if no directions are available. The National Center for Appropriate Technology has a good guide on maintaining furnace efficiency.

An Energy-Conserving Tour Around the Integral Urban House

Taking an imaginary tour around the ideal integral urban house is a helpful way to visualize the modifications that might be used to reduce energy consumption. While some of these ideas have been mentioned earlier, there is certain utility to gathering them here, all together, in an overview.

House Structure: We have discussed weatherizing already, but some additional things might be considered—for example, windbreaks for doors. The wind-chill factor goes up considerably as wind speed increases. A vestibule or air lock for all doors to the outside, or at least the front one, can reduce large intermittent heat losses. Installing a good storm or second door in the place where the screen door will be in the summer can also save considerable heat (see Box 4-3). Fences, berms (banks of soil), or hedges can help deflect winds around home.

Window shades, or shutters outside, can greatly affect the cooling needs of a home by reducing incoming radiation. Shade trees strategically planted can shade not only windows but also large portions of the roof area, and reduce overall infiltration rates, since they reduce the rate of air flow against the house. Where there is a crawl space beneath the house, a vapor barrier on the surface of the soil can reduce access of moisture to the house structures. Excess moisture will contribute to heat loss, since it is a better conductor than most building materials. Installing pipe and duct insulation is another measure that can result in significant savings (see Box 4-3).

There is a serious defect in the house design where heat is being lost from the lower levels of the home. Heat is always being generated in cooking areas, for example. If this heat can be trapped and held in the kitchen or in rooms immediately adjacent to it, those areas can serve as the main living spaces on cold days, reducing the need to heat the rest of the house. Stairways or room arrangements where heat can rise up and away from occupants create a situation where large amounts of fuel are used essentially to heat a mass of air that no one can use. Old Victorian houses, with their high ceilings, do this to some extent, but modern ranch-style houses, in which few rooms can be closed off from one another and the staircase is open to the entire house, have the same heat-loss effect.

The Kitchen: Two big energy users in the kitchen are the refrigerator and stove. When the oven is on the refrigerator has to work harder. It is best to keep all major heat sources as far from the refrigerator as possible. The refrigerator draws more electricity than anything in the house (about 25 percent of daily needs). Opening the refrigerator as little as possible will conserve energy, as well as keep the waistline down. If the interior of the refrigerator is well organized, with items such as sandwich fixings all collected together in a container that can be taken out for inspection, the length of time it needs to be open can be minimized. After watching members of our household open the refrigerator and stare thoughtfully into the interior for many minutes before even beginning to rummage around for pieces of cheese and so on, we began using labeled plastic bins for storing many items of a similar nature. Now these can be slipped out easily onto a table and investigated with the refrigerator closed.

Box 4-3. Install Combination Storm Doors and Duct Insulation

Combination (windows and screen) storm doors are designed for installation over exterior doors. They are sold almost everywhere, with or without the cost of installation.

Installation

You can save a few dollars (10% to 15% of the purchase price) by installing doors yourself. But you'll need some tools: hammer, drill, screwdriver, and weatherstripping. In most cases, it will be easier to have the supplier install your doors himself.

The supplier will first measure all the doors where you want storm doors installed. It will take anywhere from several days to a few weeks to make up your order before the supplier returns to install them. Installation should take less than one-half day.

Before the installer leaves, be sure the doors operate smoothly and close tightly. Check for cracks around the jamb and make sure the seal is as air-tight as possible. Also, remove and replace the exchangeable panels (window and screen) to make sure they fit properly and with a weather tight seal.

Selection: Judging Quality

Door finish: A mill finish (plain aluminum) will oxidize, reducing ease of operation and degrading appearance. An anodized or baked enamel finish is better.

Corner joints: Quality of construction affects the strength and effectiveness of storm doors. Corners are a good place to check construction. They should be strong and air tight. If you can see through the joints, they will leak air.

Weatherstripping: Storm doors are supposed to reduce air leakage around your doors. Weatherstripping quality makes a big difference in how well storm doors can do this. Compare several types before deciding.

Hardware quality: The quality of locks, hinges and catches should be evaluated since it can have a direct effect on durability and is a good indicator of overall construction quality.

Construction material: Storm doors of wood or steel can also be purchased within the same price range as the aluminum variety. They have the same quality differences and should be similarly evaluated. The choice between doors of similar quality but different material is primarily up to your own personal taste.

Duct Insulation

If the ducts for either your heating or your air conditioning system run exposed through your attic or garage (or any other space that is not heated or cooled) they should be insulated. Duct insulation comes generally in blankets 1 or 2″ thick. Get the thicker variety, particularly if you've got rectangular ducts. If you're doing this job at all, it's worth it to do it right. For air conditioning ducts, make sure you get the kind of insulation that has a vapor barrier (the vapor barrier goes on the outside). Seal the joints of the insulation tightly with tape to avoid condensation.
Note: Check for leaks in the duct and tape them tightly before insulating.
Source: HUD, *In the Bank or Up the Chimney?*

The Hot Water Heater: Since hot water heaters frequently break down and have to be replaced, servicing them often can be extremely worthwhile. Once or twice a year drain a bucket's worth of water out of the bottom of the hot water heater. This reduces the sediment that builds up and insulates the water in the tank from the burner flame. Next, use as low a setting as possible for the hot water heater. The lower setting will make reheating a new batch of water a little slower but will save energy. Setting the temperature ten degrees lower can save about $8 per year. Using less hot water, of course, is another way to conserve energy.

Showering instead of bathing also saves energy. Try it yourself as an experiment. Take a shower but close off the drain to the bathtub. When you have finished, observe how much water is in the tub and consider whether that amount would have been sufficient if you had been taking a bath.

You can also insulate the hot water heater by purchasing a fiber glass water heater insulation jacket for about $20. A minimal yearly savings of $4 to $6 is possible with this improvement. Also, all water pipes in crawl spaces should be insulated. Insulating cold-water pipes reduces the chance of freezing in winter and warming of water in summer. Hot water can be saved by washing most clothing in lukewarm or cold water. For most laundry, a cold-water wash and drying in the sun will do very well. Using cold water in a washing machine at twenty-two gallons per load can save about five cents per wash, or about ten dollars per year, depending on the rate of use.

Lighting: Eliminate all ornamental lights. A recent estimate of the energy that could be saved by eliminating just the outdoor gas lamps in the state of Virginia indicated that enough fuel would be saved to heat thousands of homes for a day. Getting into the habit of shutting lights off when you leave a room can help a great deal. In general, Americans use more light in many areas of the home than they really need to see with at night. Substantial reduction in wattage of light bulbs in certain places is possible with no difficulty. Hall and porch lights can be as low as fifteen watts. Task lighting or the use of a special lamp when doing precision work can provide more light directly where it is needed than can large overhead fixtures. Painting the interior of the home with light colors improves lighting in areas that rely on indirect light.

Fluorescent lights can cut electrical use by over 60 percent while still providing the same light output. "Warm white" tubes provide a pleasant color preferable to many people. Some manufacturers even provide full-spectrum light, if you are concerned about possible health hazards that may be associated with these devices. For more on this subject, see John Ott's book *Light and Health.* Ott suggests that because artificial lights do not cover the full spectrum of natural light they probably affect health adversely. He discusses many possible effects and his book raises basic environmental questions of sweeping import.

Although fluorescents are more expensive, if used more than four to five hours a day they will pay for themselves over a few years. Fluorescent retrofits for incandescent sockets are available in many hardware stores. The best known is the "Killerwatt" fixture. Fluorescent lights require extra energy to start up. If you leave the room for more than ten minutes shut them off; if you plan to return in just a few minutes leave them on.

The Bathroom: Since water conservation as it applies to the bathroom, particularly in regard to modifications of the shower and toilet, is discussed in detail in the next chapter, we will not cover the same material here.

In regard to other uses of energy, heat is the important factor in the bathroom. Efforts to warm the bathroom as well as dress it up are expressed in recent trends to cover with cloth more of the bathroom floor and fixtures such as the toilet seat, so that they feel warmer to the touch. A spot heater or heat lamp in the bathroom can provide the extra few degrees desirable for the brief period in which you step out of the shower to dry yourself, without requiring that you heat up the entire house to achieve this. But use caution with these appliances. Wherever electricity is used near water it must be safely grounded, since accidents can easily be fatal. Check a current consumer report issued by Consumers Union for information on which heating units are reliable for bathroom use.

The Bedroom: Electric blankets use about 175 to 200 watts on an intermittent basis, and using them—as opposed to heating the entire house for the purpose of keeping the bed warm—can save a great deal of energy. A relatively low house temperature setting of, say, 60 degrees can be made tolerable by an electric blanket with a lightweight insulated cover. The idea is to get the heat to where it is needed. If you are going to purchase one of these appliances, get the best model available. (Check the ratings given by consumer testing services such as Consumers Union.) Safety is an important consideration in selecting any electrical appliance, and careful shopping is therefore vital.

The shock of getting out of bed into the cold to go to the bathroom can be offset by keeping a potty or watering can near the bed or by the use of spot heaters where needed. Again, the strategy is to focus on the heat needs rather than to heat the entire house.

Extra blankets, feather beds, or curtains around the bed reduce loss of body heat. Specially designed and insulated cubicles or sleeping lofts can also help. Thermal underwear will reduce the need to heat the whole room on specially cold nights. In extremely cold temperatures, extra fatty meals may also help by providing more metabolic heat. Of course, sleeping with someone and receiving the other person's body heat is another way to keep warm. In fact, sleeping separately, each person in a separate bed, during cold weather is definitely a luxury of the modern industrial, energy-consuming lifestyle. In many cultures people have always slept together in cold weather to gain warmth from each other, sometimes whole families sharing a single sleeping space. Bedrooms should be located over heat sources on the south or west sides of homes so that sunlight can be captured to heat them prior to sleep. Windows can be covered during the night with insulated curtains or specially constructed panels. Extra rugs and false ceilings of recycled parachutes can help keep hot air lower in the room.

The Living Room: The American living room, with its fireplace and television, uses its share of energy primarily for entertainment. Much of the fare offered on television leaves so much to be desired that other types of family entertainment popular years ago (reading, games, music, and so on) are far better ways to use the energy much of the time. Board games are far superior to electronic ones in terms of energy conservation. The "instant-on" TV draws power even when the set is off because the internal instruments must be kept warm. Pulling the plug after use or installing a switch on the cord are ways to save this energy, worth about one dollar per month.

Fireplaces lose lots of heat, primarily because the damper on the flue is usually left open even after the fire is out. Closing the damper when the fireplace is not in use or putting an insulated panel over it can reduce this loss. Properly constructed fires will burn evenly, particularly if the fuel is elevated on a grate of some sort. All sorts of fireplace modifications are possible, from replacement with a stove to elaborate air-circulation and heat-storage systems.

Fans and evaporative coolers are useful in summer's hottest periods, especially in dry climates. If you do purchase an air conditioner buy the most efficient model. Every air conditioner is required to have an EER (Energy Efficiency Ratio) printed right on the unit. Do not purchase one with an EER below 8.5. The cost may be greater but will often be justified during the first summer. Raising the thermostat and thereby allowing the air temperature to remain high will reduce air conditioning costs. Timers can be used to avoid cooling an empty house. Don't cool empty rooms and avoid generating excessive heat from stoves, fireplaces, and so on while using the air conditioner. Use shades to prevent heating the room by sunlight while the air conditioner is running. In general, use the air conditioner as little as possible. Save it for the hottest periods. Use lighter clothing and make lighter meals in hot weather.

The Porch: Porches vary from small extensions off the kitchen to elaborate enclosed terraces for expanding the living areas. Where they are placed in relation to both the sun and the indoor living spaces will determine how much they can contribute to energy conservation.

A porch may be an excellent area for an herb garden, since frequently it gives easy access to the kitchen. Window greenhouses (see plans, page Appendix 2) built on a south-facing window provide added light and warmth for the interior of the home while offering a sunny place to raise some container vegetables and herbs. Open, sunny porches are good places for solar stills and ovens (see Chapter 12), even in the winter.

Be sure that you take advantage of a solar dryer (clothesline) whenever possible for hanging out your clothes. If one end is attached to the utility porch and another to a tree, pole, the edge of the garage, or the like, access from the house will be easy. The less you have to carry a heavy laundry basket, the more likely you will be to hang out the clothes instead of using a high-energy-consuming dryer.

The Basement: Basements, with their even, cool temperatures, are good places for storing canned goods and other foods, for example, potatoes and onions. Walls above and slightly below ground level should be insulated. Doors to stairs leading to uninsulated basements should be closed and weatherstripped. Basement vents should be closed unless moisture build-up is a possibility.

The Garage: Doors opening onto uninsulated garage space should be kept closed. If the garage is used frequently as a workspace it should be insulated, particularly if you heat it when working. Painting interior surfaces white will help to reflect light, requiring smaller lamps. For many homes the garage is also the workshop and is stocked with a great array of electric tools. Use hand tools when you can, reserving power tools for heavy-duty work and where their precision helps in constructing something that lasts longer and functions better. Service and store such tools so they will last as long as possible. Retain specifications and parts lists in a safe location so the tools can be repaired more easily.

The Vehicle: The private automobile is perhaps the worst offender in terms of extravagant fuel consumption. Our lifestyles, homes, and cities appear to be dominated by this form of transportation. To save energy, keep your car in good working order (have oil, spark plugs, breaker points, and so on replaced at appropriate intervals); outfit it with good tires; use the right fuels (ideally without lead); and minimize fuel consumption and wear by driving it only when necessary. Another good design hint is to place bike racks conveniently to help encourage bicycle use, since easy, safe storage and access is one of the major limiting factors in bicycle utilization, particularly in urban areas. As simple as all this advice may sound, we appreciate that for many people changing their transportation habits represents a major life change and reorganization they have not planned. Thus, some study time may be necessary. See the bibliography for suggested reading in this area.

5. WATER CONSERVATION

Figure 5-1. **Total Fresh Water Consumed in United States***

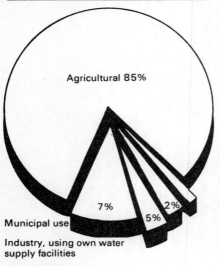

Agricultural 85%

7%   2%

5%

Municipal use

Industry, using own water supply facilities

Rural domestic

Steam-electric industry 1%

*Refers specifically to water consumed, not just withdrawn from water supplies and then immediately returned, such as is the practice in the steam-electric industry, which accounts for 45 percent of total U.S. water drawn, but only 1 percent actually consumed.

Source: Water Resources Council, *The Nation's Water Resources.*

In most areas of the country water is not a scarce commodity and conserving it is more significant as a means of conserving energy than preserving a disappearing resource. In the West, however, water is relatively scarce, so not only energy but the substance itself should be conserved. Some of the methods of water conservation practiced in the western parts of the United States therefore may help to show those in other regions of the country what is possible.

Residential water conservation has many desirable effects. Reduced water consumption in the home, and in the cities in general, means a reduced need for new dam construction, which itself causes untold environmental problems. Less water consumed also means less sewage produced, which in turn results in a reduced need for additional expensive treatment plants. As the urban population grows, which it is most likely to do, the best way to control the corresponding environmental impact is to implement comprehensive programs of resource conservation—of water, energy, and materials in general. Hopefully, a reduction in per capita use of water would offset the increase in demand produced by a growing population.

Figure 5-1 shows how the nation's fresh water is used. Clearly, agriculture uses the greatest amount of water. (It is important to note, however, that in a city such as Los Angeles, residential water use may account for as much as 54 percent of the total municipal use, according to a report by the California Water Resource Center.) Our contention is that, as with energy, water can be conserved by changing the design of the household. Residential groups producing supplementary food supplies near the home where intensive care and different cultivation methods are more feasible than in commercial operations will use proportionately less water. To support this idea we show in this chapter how relatively easy it is to use recycled water for food production.

At the Integral Urban House in Berkeley, we have made a great effort to minimize consumption within the house, both by educating ourselves in ways to conserve and by modifying our appliances and plumbing. Compare our consumption as shown in Figure 5-2 with that of the more typical household represented in Figure 5-3. The most striking difference in water consumption patterns between the two is the magnitude of use. Per capita water consumption in the Integral Urban House is hardly 40 percent that of the national average, even though a large vegetable garden and livestock are maintained at the site. An important factor in the water-conservation scheme at the Integral Urban House is the use of a waterless compost toilet. This fixture saves about thirty-two gallons of water per person per day—water that would otherwise be used to flush human wastes into the sewer. Bathing water is reduced through the use of flow restrictors. And the amount of fresh water used in the garden is held to a minimum through the use of recycled wastewater from the house.

   Consumption in the home, the largest water use in the cities, can be seen as a function of income. Water figures are usually given in gallons per capita per day (GPCPD). A high-income neighborhood may use as much as 300 GPCPD as compared with, say, 25 GPCPD for a low-income neighborhood in the same city. This difference is partially due to the fact that homes with gardens consume more water than those without, and generally the higher the income the greater the amount of land a home sits on. In fact,

Source: Milne, "Residential Water Conservation."

Figure 5-2. **Per Capita Consumption of Water at the Integral Urban House (August)**

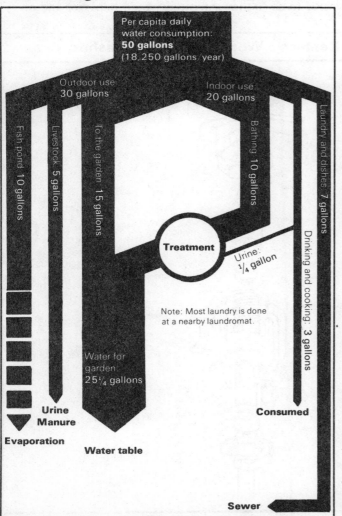

Figure 5-3. **Typical Water Consumption in a Suburban California House***

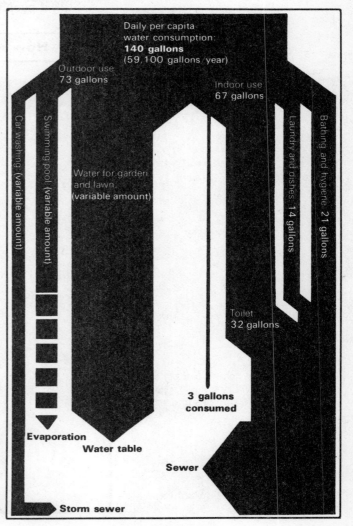

89

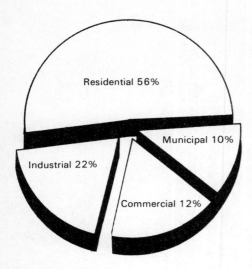

San Francisco East Bay Water Use by Sector, 1976

families with maintained grounds use up to 80 percent of their daily water expenditure on their outdoor vegetation.

Water wasting habits are widespread and appear almost ingrained. Some people regularly use a stream of water to clean sidewalks when a broom would suffice. Improper use and overuse of water in gardens here in the West result in great waste. The use of drinking water to move waste materials, as in the conventional toilet, seems almost criminal from an ecological viewpoint. And, worse, the practice seems to have convinced the last few generations that waste conveyance is a natural function of clean, fresh water.

High pressure in the lines also leads to unnecessary water use and waste, because wherever faucets are left on without being used (for example, for brushing teeth or letting water run to cold for drinking) a considerable amount of water is lost in a given amount of time. Where homes with flat rates are side by side with areas having metered water, the flat-rate homes use two to three times as much water as those where residents are charged by the amount used. The flat rate removes incentives to reduce use, or even to fix plumbing. Leaky faucets and faulty plumbing can also waste a tremendous amount of water. (Box 5-1 shows how to repair the most common plumbing problem, a worn-out washer.)

Still, if people decide to do so they can modify their behavior and re-

Box 5-1. **How to Replace a Worn-Out Faucet Washer**

handle

packing nut

ribbed end

packing
top washer

friction ring

valve stem

washer
bibb screw

faucet seat

cone washer

compression coupling nut

water supply

How to replace washers. Simply remove bibb screw. Pry out old washer. Replace with new one of same size.

Source: Consumers Cooperative of Berkeley, California

duce both use and waste. This was dramatically demonstrated during the California drought of 1976–77. Marin County, a wealthy suburb of San Francisco (median income $23,000) just north of the Bay along the Pacific Coast, used an average of 119 gallons per person per day prior to the drought. By the spring of 1977, after normal rain had failed to appear for two winters in a row, the reservoir on which most of the residents in the southern part of the county depended for water fell to 76 percent of normal. In response to the crisis (and to the threat of heavy penalties for exceeding imposed rations set by the county water district), residential users reduced their water consumption by 40 percent, to an average of 71 gallons per person per day. They made this change at the expense of lawns and landscaped yards, which were left to survive as best they could. During this same period, vegetable gardens were kept going by the use of mulches and windbreaks to reduce water loss from the soil surface, and by the recycling of wastewater.

Emotional reactions to the drought were varied, of course. But not uncommonly, people expressed a sense of accomplishment and improved self-image once they began to consciously conserve. It is also noteworthy that most residents consistently kept their use *below* their rationed allotment. Even when figures were released revealing that people could use more water if they chose to without being penalized, many did not do so.

Many of the drought-inspired conservation techniques were based on simple common sense. For instance, much water is wasted outdoors in the garden. Sprinkling by hand is particularly wasteful and a poor horticultural technique as well. The small amount of water delivered only wets the upper inches of the soil and encourages plant roots to rise to the surface where they are more subject to damage from traffic, temperature, and insects. The best strategy in garden watering is to water infrequently but as deeply as possible each time. Sprinklers should be positioned so that runoff does not go into the gutters. Use a broom rather than a hose to clean the sidewalk.

When watering ornamental plants, remember that a lot of water produces a lot of foliage. In the case of lawns or ivy, for example, this just means more material that must be cut and discarded. Reduce the amount of water used on these plants and you will save water and have less pruning to do as well. On the other hand, water used to produce foliage growth in the vegetable garden represents a source of food, not waste.

There are numerous other ways to reduce water use in the garden. Using mulch and windbreaks and avoiding unnecessary turning of the soil are examples. Planting methods can be modified under drought conditions and in some cases installation of drip-irrigation systems may be worthwhile. Many of these techniques are discussed in Chapter 8.

Conserving Water Indoors

Why bother to save water if you live in an area where supplies are plentiful? One reason is that it takes energy to move water from its source, through the treatment process, and into the home. To save water is to save energy, which is indeed a scarce resource. Unless you are getting your water from a well with wind energy or by gravity from a spring, fossil fuels, electricity, or nuclear energy is being used to pump the water to a height that will give adequate pressure for home appliance use and then deliver it to your home.

For each gallon of municipal water used in a San Francisco East Bay home, ten watt-hours of power are consumed to pump the water from its source in the Sierra Nevada through the matrix of pipes to the residence. This amount is equivalent to the energy consumed by a sixty-watt light bulb left on for ten minutes, or that required by an electric pump to lift ten gallons of water out of a well thirty feet deep. In major metropolitan areas such as Chicago and Dallas, where sources of water supply are polluted and require intensive purification before use, even greater amounts of energy are required in the delivery system.

Furthermore, over 50 percent of the nontoilet flush water consumed inside the home is hot water for the washing machine, dishwasher, bathtub, and so on. Shortened showers or rinse cycles for the washing machine would conserve the electricity or gas that heats the water as well as the water itself (see Table 5-1). Energy equivalent to a full gallon of oil is required to raise 120 gallons of water to 105°F. Therefore, such devices as water-saving shower nozzles pay for themselves much sooner by the savings in gas or electricity than by their savings of water alone.

A shower nozzle used at the Integral Urban House called "Min-use" reduces the amount of shower water from a conventional flow of five gallons of water per minute (at an average temperature of 105°F or 40.6°C) to one-half gallon per minute. Theoretically, therefore, in each five-minute shower with this device, 22.5 gallons of hot water are saved. Over the course of a year, a family of four taking four five-minute showers per day, could save some 32,850 gallons of heated water. That translates to an annual savings of $32.75 worth of water (computed at the nationwide average cost of water from a municipal supply sold to residences of 75¢ per 100 cubic feet of water [748 gallons] as of June, 1978) and $219.60 worth of electricity or $46.14 worth of gas (computed at the national average utility prices for 1978 of electricity sold to residences or 4¢ per kilowatt-hour of electricity and 20¢ per therm of gas). Accordingly, the Min-use shower device, which retails for $250, will pay for itself in twelve months if an electric water heater is used, or thirty-eight months if a gas heater is used.

More impressive in terms of pay-back period, are shower-head flow

Table 5-1. **Energy Savings by Reducing Use of Hot Water**

Use	Gal/Day per Person* (National Average)	Average Temperature of Use† (°F)	Energy Required to Heat Water to Desired Temperature‡ (Kilowatt-hours)	Annual Savings from 50 Percent Reduction in Water Use per Capita:§ Kilowatt-hours	Dollars
Dishwashing	4.0	140	0.98	356.2	14.20
Laundry	10.0	140	2.44	890.9	35.60
Bathing and hygiene	20.0	105	2.74	1001.9	40.60
Total	34.0	120 (average)	6.16	2249.0	90.44

*Average from various sources of information.
†Source of information: Keith Karnes, East Bay Municipal Utility District, Oakland, California.

‡Assuming that electric water heater is used, cold water supply is 60°F, and end-use efficiency, discounting losses due to fuel conversion and transmission, is 80 percent.

§Computed at 4 cents per kilowatt-hour (nationwide average cost of electricity sold to single-family residences in June, 1978).

restrictors, which are attached directly to an existing plumbing fixture. One unit in particular, the Nova, reduces flow from the shower to two gallons per minute. Annual savings from this unit for the same family taking four five-gallon showers each day, would be 21,900 gallons of heated water valued at $21.90, and 3660 kilowatt-hours of electricity valued at $146.40, or 153.8 therms of gas valued at $30.76. Such a shower device, which retails for $12 to $15, would pay for itself in a month and a half of use for the consumer of electricity, or three and a half months for the consumer of gas. This is quite a sound investment, environmentally as well as economically. In Table 5-2

Box 5-2. **Ecotopian Entrepreneurs: Inventor of the Sensible Urinal**

A couple of years ago, Clyde Chevrette of San Francisco was relieving himself in the usual manner, splashing away in several gallons of pristine Sierra runoff water. "What a messy way to go!" he mused, pulling the chain.

Chevrette began designing and improving designs, finally coming up with a simple-appearing funnel with a hose, which can easily be installed in any bathroom. Males can hold this "Sani-Saver" and urinate into it without splashing and without odor. It flushes with one cup of water. It costs $29. Chevrette invented some simple production machines which can be operated by two people.

Taking his invention to the American public, who could save great rivers full of water by adopting it, Chevrette has encountered an embarrassed wall of sales resistance. "People are very reluctant to discuss, let alone change, methods of bodily elimination," Chevrette explains. "It's like peeing in a bottle, which is hard for the American male to accept."

The few brave men who have taken the Sani-Saver in hand say it is absolutely wonderful. Chevrette believes that over time the psychological barrier against squirting in a funnel can be overcome. If you think you don't have such a hang-up, send your order to 766 Silver Ave., San Francisco, CA 94131, and let us know how it comes out.

Source: *North Country Star*, October 1977.

Table 5-2. **Low Water-Use Bathing and Personal Hygiene Fixtures**

Generic Classification	Manufactured Units	Water-Saving Mechanism	Percent Reduction in Flow	Average Yearly Savings		Purchase Price
				Water	Energy	
Faucets						
Flow control	American Standard *Aquamizer* Spearman *Autoflow*	Metal or plastic fitting inserted into pipe	50–75	$15–20	$50–75	75¢ to $20
Aerators	Chicago Faucet Ecological Water Products Wrightway	Produces bubbled water by introducing air into the faucet head	50–75	$15–20	$50–75	$1 to $5
Spray taps	Richard Fife Waller Crossweller Limited	Screen attached to faucet head delivers water in broad patterns or droplets	50–75	$15–20	$50–75	$1 to $5
Self-closing mixing valves	American Standard Chicago Faucet	Spring or pressure-closure device turns off faucet automatically	50–75	$15–20	$50–75	Same as conventional faucets
Thermostatically controlled mixing valves	Barber Colman Company	Sensitive bi-metal spring regulates hot and cold water supply to insure constant water temperature	50 of warm water	$15	$50	$60
Shower Heads						
Flow Restrictors	*Nova*	Reduces flow by reducing diameter of water pipe	50–80	At least $5	At least $50	$12 to $15
Air-assisted	*Min-use*	Compressor injects air into water stream	83–95	At least $15	At least $150	$250

several commercially available water restrictors are compared. Box 5-2 suggests another water-saving device, and indicates that waste management, particularly for toilet-related items, is difficult to sell to a public that considers the subject taboo.

While it is tempting to believe that a mechanical device will automatically solve your water-use problems, actually some thoughtful changes in behavior are required. Table 5-3 is a useful list of suggestions issued by a San Francisco Bay Area utility company. The right-hand column shows the behavior required to save the amounts of water listed in the adjacent column. Notice that no hardware, only behavior changes, are listed. Table 5-4, by contrast, is an analysis of the effects that various institutional changes might have on urban water conservation.

Table 5-3. **How to Save Water**

	Normal Use	Conservation	How to Do It
Shower	Water running 25 gallons	7 gallons	Wet down, soap up, rinse off. Install shower flow restricter
Brush Teeth	Tap running 3 gallons	1 pint	Use a glass, wet brush rinse briefly
Tub Bath	Full 35 Gallons	Partial 15–20 gallons	Minimal water level
Shaving	Tap running 10 gallons	1 gallon	Half fill basin and use stopper
Dishwashing	Tap running 30 Gallons	5 gallons	Wash and rinse in dishpans or sink
Automatic Dishwasher	2 cycles per day 14—30 gallons	1 cycle per day 7–15 gallons	Fully loaded, once per day and use short cycle
Washing Hands	Tap running 2 gallons	1 quart	Wet hands, shut water off, massage then rinse or use basin.
Toilet Flushing	Depending on tank size 4 to 7 gallons	1 to 6 gallons	Use tank displacement bottles or dams, or convert to manual flush.
Washing Machine	Full cycle, top water levle 50 gallons	25 gallons	Short cycle, minimal water level, full loads only
Outdoor Watering	Average hose 8 gallons per minute	Lower priority	Eliminate or maintain plants in stress condition only
Shampoo	12 gallons	8 gallons	Soap only once, and shampoo in the shower
Car Wash	6 gallons per minute	3–10 gallons per wash	Wash car using a bucket rinse only using hose.
Clean Sidewalks and Driveways	50–100 gallons	0	Sweep only

Source: Department of Water Resources, *Water Conservation in California*.

Note: This information, distributed by the Pacific Gas and Electric Company as a public service, helped encourage the public to conserve water.

Table 5-4. **Methods of Urban Water Conservation**

Means to Reduce Water Consumption	Implementation	Advantages	Disadvantages
Water saving plumbing fixtures in new and replacement construction.	Proscriptive	1. Mechanical devices render savings despite user habits. 2. Reduce waste water conveyance and treatment load.	1. Possible resistance to redesign and retooling to manufacture water conserving devices. 2. Drain pipe slope tolerances are more critical. 3. Initially, consumers may resist acceptance. 4. Initially, higher unit cost of water saving devices until demand increases and reduces cost. 5. May cause blockage problems in marginal sewage collection systems.
Modification (retrofit) of existing plumbing fixtures.	Proscriptive Voluntary Institutional	1. Many devices are nominal in cost. 2. Enables water and energy conservation in existing facilities and therefore has potential rapid, widespread savings. 3. Water savings mechanically effected. 4. Reduces waste water conveyance and treatment load.	1. Inconsistent effectiveness of retrofit devices because of variable design and construction of existing fixtures. 2. Consumer removal or tampering with retrofit devices because of suspected poor performance. 3. Some devices require skilled installation and/or follow-up adjustment. 4. May cause blockage problems in marginal sewage collection systems.
New technology.	Voluntary Institutional	1. Greater water and energy savings than conventional designed devices. 2. Reduce waste water conveyance and treatment load.	1. Uncertain long-term effectiveness. 2. Consumer and institutional resistance 3. Higher initial costs. 4. Conformance with existing codes and regulations; may require changes or variations.
Efficient irrigation using automatic devices	Voluntary	1. Healthier plants. 2. Decreased maintenance. 3. Mechanical type savings.	1. Periodic adjustments required. 2. Expensive initial cost.
Native and other low-water-using plants in landscaping.	Voluntary Institutional	1. Established native and other low-water-using plants need little or no irrigation. 2. Established plants need little care.	1. General preference for exotic plants. 2. Narrow selection of native plants in nurseries. 3. Difficult to establish some low-water-using plants and general lack of knowledge on care. 4. Somewhat higher costs because native and other low-water-using plants are not available.
Leak detection and repair of water agencies' distribution systems.	Institutional	1. Reduces unaccounted water losses. 2. Reduces undermining damage to streets, sidewalks, and other structures.	1. Because leaking water often percolates to usable ground water, water agencies sometimes ignore losses. 2. Low cost of lost water may not equal cost of detection and repair.
Leak detection and repair of consumers' systems.	Voluntary Institutional	1. Can reduce other home repair costs such as those from wood rot. 2. Many leaks simple and inexpensive to repair. 3. Reduces operational costs.	1. Difficult to induce flat-rate consumers and apartment dwellers to repair leaks. 2. Could be expensive to consumer if he needs professional service.
Metering	Institutional	1. Easier to implement than some of the other suggested methods. 2. May induce consumers to begin conserving water.	1. Consumer objection. 2. High capital cost. 3. Requires changes in rate structure and billing procedure.
Pricing	Institutional	1. May be relatively easy to implement. 2. Can affect all customers. 3. Can be strong inducement to effect consumer savings.	1. Consumer objection. 2. Requires well designed pricing structure to achieve effective, equitable pricing. 3. Often requires changes in rate structure, meter reading, and billing procedures.
Sewer service charges based on water consumption	Institutional	1. More equitable than flat-rate basis to pay operational cost of sewage treatment. 2. Achieve dual benefits of reduced water consumption and waste water flow.	1. Requires well designed rate structure. 2. Need to segregate inside and outside water consumption.
Education	Voluntary Proscriptive Institutional	1. Induces voluntary water conservation. 2. Changes long established, wasteful consumer habits. 3. Achieves long lasting results by influencing younger generation. 4. Ensures greater success and acceptance of other water saving means.	1. Effective program requires coordinated efforts of local and state agencies.

Reducing Sewage

Remember, whatever water is used in the home becomes sewage after it goes down the drain. Reducing water use in the house reduces sewage production. For a suburban family on an independent septic system, a reduction of water use could justify a smaller, less-expensive septic tank and shorter leaching lines. County health departments in many regions of the country are permitting reduced size septic systems for families that employ water conserving appliances. A smaller septic system can translate into significant monetary savings. Also, for the city-dweller hooked into the municipal sanitary lines, reduction in sewage production has equally important implications from the point of view of community conservation and ultimately the cost of municipal treatment facilities.

The toilet is the largest single consumer of water in the home, accounting for 40 percent of the water used indoors by a family. It is amazing to realize that for an American family of four, in a house equipped with conventional toilets, which use 5 to 8 gallons per flush, the average two flushes per person per day utilize about 40,000 gallons of fresh drinking water each year. This amount of water is used to flush into the sewer only 600 pounds of fecal waste. Even more remarkable is that one adult's yearly production of fecal wastes, once decomposed by microorganisms in a composting toilet such as the Clivus Multrum (see Chapter 6), will barely fill two five-gallon cans. Either by modifying your existing toilet for reduced flush or by acquiring a special "low flush" model, you can save water dramatically.

There are many gadgets on the market today for modifying the operation of your toilet so that it will use less water to flush. Placing bricks in the

Table 5-5. **Low-Water Flush Toilets and Water-Saving Toilet Attachments***

Generic Classification	Manufactured Units	Flushing Mechanisms	Gallons per Flush	Yearly Water Savings (gallons)	Purchase Price
Pressurized flush toilet	Microphor	Propulsion by air-pressure at 60 psi.; an air compressor is required	one-half	35,000	$360
Pressurized tank toilet	Flushmate	Propulsion by water-induced air-pressure tank attached to conventional tank	2.0–2.5	15–20,000	$40
Variable-flush attachment	Gold Ring Duo-Flush Flush Gard	Weight and/or flush mechanism that allows user to regulate flush volume	variable	10–30,000	$2.50 to $15
Dual flush	Econo-Flush Self-Skid	Special trip-lever allows choice of partial or full flush	variable	10–30,000	$16
Water-closet inserts		A device placed in the toilet tank to reduce the volume of water per flush	variable	10–30,000	$1 to $3.50

*For single family homes with municipal sewage hook-up.

Source: Milne, "Residential Water Conservation."

reservoir of the toilet is an old trick, but is not as effective as many of the other devices commercially available. One unit, called the Gold Ring, is a small lead weight that attaches to the lever mechanism inside the tank. The extra weight allows the user to regulate the amount of water used for flushing. Another unit, called a water dam, is composed of two pieces of plastic that fit inside the toilet tank and serve to decrease the effective reservoir area so less water is required to activate the flushing mechanism. A third type of unit modifies the operation of the ball-cock valve so that less water is released into the bowl with each flush. Most of these devices result in water savings of up to 75 percent, and pay for themselves within six months through reduced water consumption.

If you are building a new house and are making initial decisions about the type of toilet facilities you want (and don't wish to install a composting toilet of the kind described in the next chapter), you ought to consider the new types of low-flush toilets. (See Table 5-5 for a comparison of several of these.) A good example is the Microphor, which employs a pressurized vacuum system to aide in removing solids from the bowl. This unit requires only one-half gallon of water per flush, and represents a potential savings of nearly 35,000 gallons of water each year. This toilet, like many other comparable low-flush units, has the dimension of a conventional toilet and may be installed to an existing soil-pipe with only a few plumbing modifications.

Flushing less frequently is an obvious water-saving strategy, particularly in the disposal of urine. It is hard for people to accustom themselves to this, however. If you must flush after every use, consider flushing with wastewater that you have collected for such purposes. Run-off shower water can be caught in the tub or a container and scooped into plastic five-gallon buckets for storage near the toilet. To flush wastes, pour a bucket of bathtub water directly into the toilet bowl. (Do not fill the reservoir tank with soiled water, as the particulate matter will clog the mechanical flushing mechanisms.) The impacting force and level of the water poured into the bowl will activate the flushing mechanism. Theoretically, the daily shower of an individual (twenty gallons), if properly stored, ought to provide enough water to flush the toilet three or four times. Reusing shower water for toilet flushing is probably the most practical way to recycle greywater.

Recycling Greywater

The term *greywater* refers to all the wastewater from the *nontoilet* plumbing fixtures and appliances of the home. We originally became interested in it because we assumed that the phosphorus in many of the detergents used in dish- and clothes-washing ended up in the greywater, and would be a good complement to the nitrogen in human urine for use in the garden. Both nitrogen and phosphorus are essential plant nutrients needed in large amounts (see Chapter 8).

We made this assumption because phosphorus from detergents in wastewaters that emptied into lakes and ponds frequently accounted for algae blooms there. (The algae blooms are detrimental in natural bodies of water because the decomposition of the algae depletes the water of oxygen—needed for the decomposition process much as a fire requires it—killing many desirable fish species.) However, many of the detergent manufacturers have reduced or removed the phosphorus from their products. Furthermore, detergents contain a great many other ingredients supposedly useful in laundering or included to increase appeal to the customer, such as perfumes. Many of these ingredients are not necessarily beneficial to plants, and because manufacturers guard their formulas for fear of the competition, finding out just what is in such a product is difficult. Thus, our theory as to the beneficial effects of detergent in greywater was heartily disproved.

The wastes from a flush toilet are referred to as *blackwater*, and are *not* included in a greywater recycling system. However, in addition to hair and dead skin, small amounts of fecal matter, *Salmonella* bacteria, and other pathogenic organisms may be washed off the body in showers or baths or from clothing in the laundry, particularly if children's diapers or soiled bedding is included in the wash load. Added to this are the detergents, grease, oils, and food particles from the kitchen sink and the miscellaneous ingredients of various cosmetics and cleaning products, as well as other substances used in the household as part of everyday living and then washed away with water. Further, households that recycle their wastewater are also likely to be very conservative in their use of water generally. Thus, pollutants will be particularly concentrated in the wastewater there compared to those in less frugal homes where greater dilution of contaminants would be expected. From this you can begin to perceive that greywater, simply because it excludes toilet water, is not necessarily as safe and easy to use as one might first imagine.

The Farallones Institute has been experimenting with the use of greywater on a small-scale agricultural site (see the Farallones Institute Annual Report, 1977) and at the Integral Urban House in Berkeley. The following discussion is drawn from our experience with this system.*

A note of caution: Until recently the collection and reuse of greywater has been generally forbidden by health authorities. However, due to regional water shortages and as a result of widespread concern over conservation, local ordinances are being relaxed to permit selective use of homesite greywater recycling systems. In its strictest sense, wastewater is sewage and should be reused with extreme care. The following discussion provides recommendations for effecting the safe and sanitary reuse of household greywater. You are advised to check local health regulations before attempting the more extensive plumbing modifications.

How Much Greywater Can be Used in the Garden? Scale your wastewater recycling efforts to suit your garden's water requirement; collect and use only as much greywater as your garden requires. Excess wastewater should be discharged into the sewer in the conventional manner. A good, conservative rule is that a well-drained square foot of loamy garden soil, rich in organic matter, is capable of handling one-half gallon of wastewater per week. Sandy, lighter soils can absorb more water, and heavier soils (with a high clay content) absorb less. The absorption rate will be greater in the summer months when surface evaporation and plant transpiration is consid-

---

*These sections on greywater are adapted from a paper prepared by Tom Javits, Tom Fricke, Sheldon Leon and Scott Mathews. The first portion of the paper has been printed as a small pamphlet, *Grey-water Use in the Home Garden*, by the East Bay Municipal Utility District.

erable, and less during the winter when evaporation and transpiration is minimal. If the garden area suitable for greywater application is 500 square feet, then up to 250 gallons of water may be discharged to the garden each week during periods when rainfall is light (less than one inch of rain per week) or absent. Check soil moisture to determine precisely when the garden is in need of irrigation, so that the addition of greywater will not produce surface runoff.

As a general rule, soaps are less harmful than detergents to soils. But either may present problems over periods of sustained use of greywater. The common problem with most soaps and detergents is that they contain sodium salts, which, if present in irrigation water in excessive amounts, damage soil structure and create an alkaline condition and burn the leaves of plants as well. In general, soaps contain less sodium than do detergents. Gentle soaps, such as soap flakes, are preferred to those heavily laden with lanolin, perfumes, and other chemicals. When you must use detergents select ones that do not advertise their "softening powers" or claim to have "enzymatic action." Softeners and the like are high in sodium-based compounds, and water run through sodium-based water-softener filters should not be used in the recycling system. Soap sludge, the gelatinous mass that forms in greywater has heavy concentrations of soap, clogs soil pores, and should be filtered out.

If you plan on reusing washing machine water, minimize or eliminate bleach and absolutely avoid detergents or additives containing Boron. As mentioned earlier, phosphates in detergents are actually good for plant growth but unfortunately detergents highest in phosphates usually contain the greatest amount of sodium. Ammonia is preferable as a household cleaning and deodorizing agent to scouring products that contain chlorine.

The Danger of Disease: When the greywater is discharged onto the soil surface where organic matter is abundant, potentially harmful bacteria and viruses are broken down by the soil-decomposer organisms better suited to the soil environment. Those pathogens that may survive for short periods cannot be assimilated by plant roots or translocated internally to the edible portion of food plants. Nevertheless, it is safest to restrict use of greywater to irrigating ornamental plants and lawns.

Precautions Against Damage to the Soil: In soil that has been irrigated with greywater for an extended period sodium levels may build up, resulting in poor drainage and potential damage to plants. High levels of sodium may be detected by conducting a pH test of the soil with pH paper, commonly available from pharmacies or nurseries (see Chapter 8 for a more detailed discussion of soil pH). The ideal soil pH range for most common vegetable plants is 6.3 to 7.2. A pH of 7.5 or above indicates that the soil has become over-loaded with sodium. This problem can be corrected by spreading gypsum (calcium sulfate) over the soil at a rate of 2 pounds per 100 square feet per month. Treatment should be continued until the pH of the soil drops to 7.0. As a precaution against further sodium build-up, gypsum may be applied to the soil at a rate of three pounds per month for every 50 gallons per day of greywater to the area. Thus, if you are discharging wastewater to the garden at the rate of, say, 75 gallons per day, a monthly application of 4.5 pounds of gypsum is required to neutralize the detrimental effect of the sodium. Normal dilution of wastewater by rainfall or fresh-water irrigation also will help leach the soil of sodium and excess salts.

Transporting Greywater to the Garden: There are several easy and inexpensive methods for bringing basin, shower, and washing machine water to the garden. One obvious method is to scoop the waste water from the sinks and bathtub into pails and hand-carry it outside (see Figure 5-4). Siphoning the water from the bathtub or from deep basins to the yard through a garden hose is also a possibility. Siphoning aids for this purpose are available from hardware stores.

Better yet, the trap from the bathroom sink drain may be dislodged and rotated away from the drain pipe to permit collection of waste water in a

Applying Greywater to the Soil

Whether your wastewater is conveyed to the garden by hand-carried buckets or recycled through modifications in the household plumbing, use the following checklist for best results in irrigating with greywater.

1. Apply wastewater directly to the soil surface. Do not sprinkle from above or allow the recycled water to splash off the soil and contact the above-ground portion of your plants. Greywater can only be used for drip-irrigation if all solid matter is very carefully filtered out first; otherwise this material will clog the emitters in the pipe. (See the description of greywater use in greenhouses, Chapter 9.)

2. Distribute the greywater to flat garden areas; avoid steep slopes where surface runoff may be a problem.

3. Avoid concentrating wastewater on one particular site.

4. If rains are not frequent in your area during the growing season, use fresh water to aid in leaching the soil of contaminants.

5. Apply thick compost mulches (see page 139) to areas receiving greywater to facilitate natural decomposition of waste residues.

6. Greywater is alkaline. (The pH of greywater can be as high as 8.5, compared with the pH of rainwater, which is near 7. See the pH scale on page 205.) Do not use it on acid-loving plants such as rhododendrons, azaleas, and citrus trees. For lawns and deciduous fruit trees, rotate greywater with fresh water.

7. If you must irrigate food plants with wastewater use it only on plants whose above-ground parts are eaten, such as corn, tomatoes, or broccoli. *Do not* apply it to the soil around leafy vegetables or root crops. Ideally you should use greywater for your ornamental foliage only, using what fresh water is available for your vegetable garden.

8. Use the wastewater on well-established plants. Seedlings and houseplants may not be able to tolerate the impurities in household wastewater.

Figure 5-4. **Carrying Greywater to the Garden by Hand**

Figure 5-5. **Dislodging the Drainpipe to Collect Wastewater from the Sink**

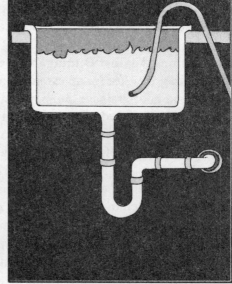

Figure 5-6 **Siphoning Washing-Machine Wastewater Directly to the Garden**

five-gallon bucket, as illustrated in Figure 5-5. The reclaimed water may be taken to the garden or used to flush the toilet by pouring the full bucket of water into the bowl. (As mentioned earlier, do not fill the toilet tank with greywater, as it may clog the flushing devices or create objectionable odors. Also, in the case of a temporary drop in water line pressure greywater could contaminate the water supply.)

If your washing machine discharges into a utility sink that is of sufficient height above the yard to permit gravity feed, the water may be collected in the basin and siphoned to the yard by way of a garden hose (Figure 5-6). Do not attach the garden hose directly to the discharge line of the washing machine, as the flow of water will be too great for even distribution over the soil. Water from the wash cycle is heavily polluted, and should only be used if it can be diluted with rinse water before garden application. Washing-machine wastewater from loads containing baby diapers or other clothes or bedding contaminated with fecal material should *not* be used in greywater recycling.

Possible Residential Greywater Recycling Installations: Simple techniques of recycling the wastewater by bucket and siphon are satisfactory on a temporary basis. However, they seldom allow for the degree of dilution, filtering, and ease of maintenance or the extent of distribution essential for a long-term use of greywater. A more permanent system of greywater recycling can be achieved through modification of the household plumbing so that greywater is channeled directly to the garden. What follows is an illustrated, step-by-step plan for a residential greywater recycling installation.

Figure 5-7. **Typical Home with Underfloor Plumbing**

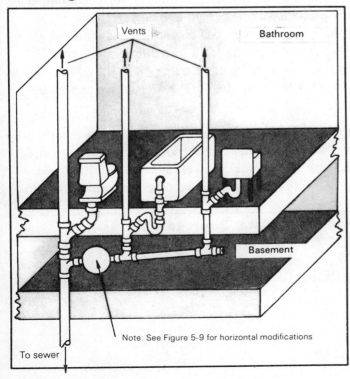

Figure 5-8. **Typical Home with Exterior Plumbing**

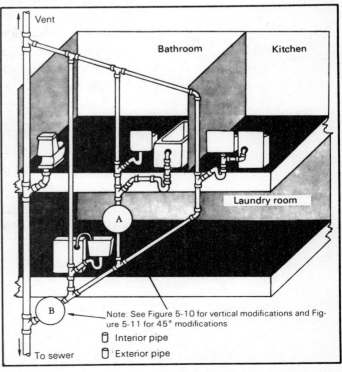

Initial Planning: Locate the wasteline plumbing in your home. Determine whether the plumbing arrangement is underfloor (Figure 5-7) or exterior (Figure 5-8). Underfloor plumbing will run either along a basement ceiling, as is commonly the case in a multistory home, or through a crawl space, usually true in a single-story home.

Identify the various wastelines as to their point of origin. Three- and four-inch waste pipes carry toilet sewage, and must *not* be altered. One-and-a-half inch or two-inch lines carry the wastewater from basins and appliances. Also distinguish between the drainpipes and the vents. It is a good idea to draw a sketch like Figure 5-7 or 5-8 of the wasteline plumbing system of your home. Refer to a plumbing manual for assistance.

Choose the wastelines from which you want to collect and reuse the wastewater. Base your choice on the comparative quality of the wastewater in regard to concentration of particulates, contaminants, and soaps, accessibility of wasteline pipes, and relative ease of plumbing modification.

Selective Use of Greywater: Drainage from the kitchen sink is the least desirable for recycling. The amount of wastewater generated here is relatively low, and the high concentration of food particles, grease, soaps, and so on impair flow to the garden. If your plumbing arrangement permits the selective use of household wastewater, follow this order of preferences: First choice should be water from shower and bathtubs; second, water from the bathroom sink; third, utility sink and washing machine; fourth, kitchen sink and dishwashers (Table 5-6).

In Figure 5-7, the plan of a two-story home with exterior wasteline plumbing, two possible points of interception of the wastewater are identified; point A or point B. In the case of point A, only the wastewater from the bath, shower, and bathroom sink would be diverted for garden irrigation. This is a good point for interception, since it allows for the reclaiming of a large fraction of the household wastewater but a small percentage of the total solids production. (In most homes, 60 percent of the nonflush wastewater discharged to the sewer originates from the bathroom fixtures.) Diverting wastewater at point B would be undesirable, since the additional solids and grease will impede the flow of the water to the garden and create objectionable residues.

Filtration: If drainpipes in your home converge in a manner which prohibits selective use of the wastewater (that is, if the kitchen drainage is combined with that of the bath and shower), then considerable care must be exercised in preventing solid matter, grease, and other impurities from en-

Table 5-6. **Preferred Greywater Sources**

Order of Preferred Use	Gallons of Waste Water Generated per Day	Percentage of Total Solids Production
Bath / shower	80	
Bathroom sink	8	27
Washing machine and utility sink	35	23
Kitchen sink	25	50

tering the drains. Install removable thin mesh plastic screens or metal grates at each basin to intercept food wastes, hair, and excess soap suds. These filters should be cleaned regularly and the material added to the compost. Reduce the amount of soaps and detergents used. *Do not use plumbing fixtures for disposing of wastes that can be composted, recycled, or discarded.* Sink-mounted garbage disposal units waste valuable organic resources and should not be used. If kitchen-sink water is recycled, then the disposal can't be used in any case, and only becomes a liability.

A filtration unit employing sand and gravel may be used to aid in removing solid matter before the greywater is discharged to the garden. Suit-

Figure 5-9. **Horizontal (Underfloor) Modifications**

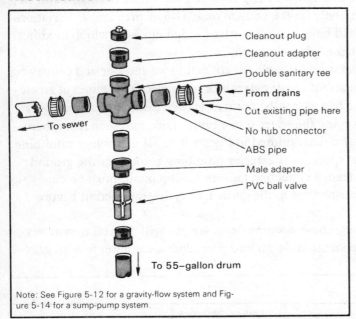

Cleanout plug
Cleanout adapter
Double sanitary tee
From drains
Cut existing pipe here
No hub connector
ABS pipe
Male adapter
PVC ball valve

To sewer

To 55–gallon drum

Note: See Figure 5-12 for a gravity-flow system and Figure 5-14 for a sump-pump system.

Figure 5-11. **Forty-Five-Degree Modifications**

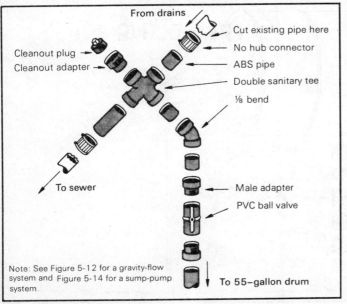

From drains
Cut existing pipe here
No hub connector
ABS pipe
Cleanout plug
Cleanout adapter
Double sanitary tee
⅛ bend

To sewer

Male adapter
PVC ball valve

Note: See Figure 5-12 for a gravity-flow system and Figure 5-14 for a sump-pump system.

To 55–gallon drum

Figure 5-10. **Vertical Modifications**

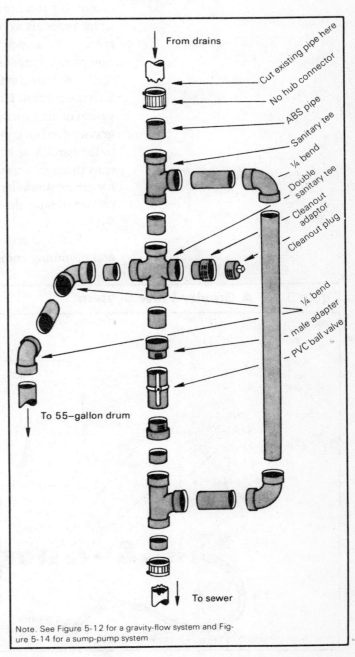

From drains
Cut existing pipe here
No hub connector
ABS pipe
Sanitary tee
¼ bend
Double sanitary tee
Cleanout adaptor
Cleanout plug
¼ bend
male adapter
PVC ball valve

To 55–gallon drum

To sewer

Note. See Figure 5-12 for a gravity-flow system and Figure 5-14 for a sump-pump system

able sand filters for filtering domestic wastewater have been developed at the Farallones Institute's rural center. (Technical plans may be obtained upon request. Write to the Farallones Institute, 15790 Coleman Valley Road, Occidental CA 95465.) Note, however, that filtration units add to the expense of and increase the maintenance required for a greywater recycling system. If the household residents are able to keep solids out of the water that is to be recycled, such a unit is unnecessary.

Modification Options: Once you have decided which wastelines will be the source of your wastewater, you are ready to plan the modification scheme appropriate for your plumbing situation. Three modification plans are diagrammed: Figure 5-9 shows a system for horizontal pipes; Figure 5-10 for vertical pipes; and Figure 5-11 for pipes at an angle. Underfloor wastelines commonly run horizontally with a slight slope for positive drainage, and exterior pipes are commonly on the vertical or at a 45-degree angle. Variations are infinite, so you will have to use your best judgment as to which modification plan is best suited to your situation.

Two basic systems are suitable for collecting wastewater and conveying it to the garden. Homes that have exterior or underfloor wastelines at an elevation of six or more feet above the point of garden discharge may employ gravity-feed in conveying the water into a buffer tank, and then from there to the garden, as shown diagrammed in Figure 5-12. If underfloor plumbing runs through a crawl space, or if exterior plumbing is too near the ground for efficient gravity feed, a collection tank and sump pump must be employed to push the wastewater to the garden, as is diagrammed in Figure 5-14.

Before discussing these systems, however, we will do well to note several plumbing components and standard procedures, common to both grav-

---

Figure 5-12. **A Gravity-Flow System**

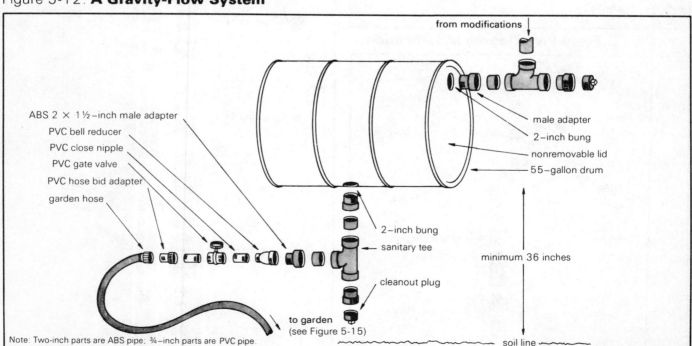

ABS 2 × 1½–inch male adapter
PVC bell reducer
PVC close nipple
PVC gate valve
PVC hose bid adapter
garden hose

from modifications

male adapter
2–inch bung
nonremovable lid
55–gallon drum

2–inch bung
sanitary tee

cleanout plug

minimum 36 inches

to garden
(see Figure 5-15)

Note: Two-inch parts are ABS pipe; ¾–inch parts are PVC pipe.

soil line

ity-feed and sump installation that will help establish a safe and reliable method of wastewater use.

First, wasteline modification should be made with ABS plastic pipe, which requires no special equipment to install and is less expensive and more versatile than iron pipe. Use "no-hub" connectors in joining existing cast-iron or galvanized iron drainpipes to the ABS modification.

Also, double sanitary tee fittings should be installed in the modified drainline to allow for diversion of the wastewater directly into a buffer tank, as in the gravity system, or into a sump collection tank.

Finally, install a threaded PVC ball or gate valve in the diversion line to permit regulation in the use or disposal of the greywater. The valve is opened during periods when the wastewater is desired for use as irrigation, and closed when you wish to direct the discharge of wastewater into the sewer. If modification is on a vertically oriented drainpipe (Figure 5-10), then the valve must be installed in the vertical portion of the ABS modification to permit wastewater to flow into the buffer tank or sump installation. The use of ball valves is preferred, as they have no ledges or cracks where suspended solids may lodge and affect valve operation.

Gravity-Flow System: In the gravity feed method (Figure 5-12), a buffer tank should receive the wastewater before it is conveyed to the garden. The tank may be a 55-gallon steel drum positioned horizontally on a stand elevated at a height sufficient to allow gravity flow to the garden, as illustrated in Figure 5-13.

Figure 5-13. **An Overhead Storage Drum**

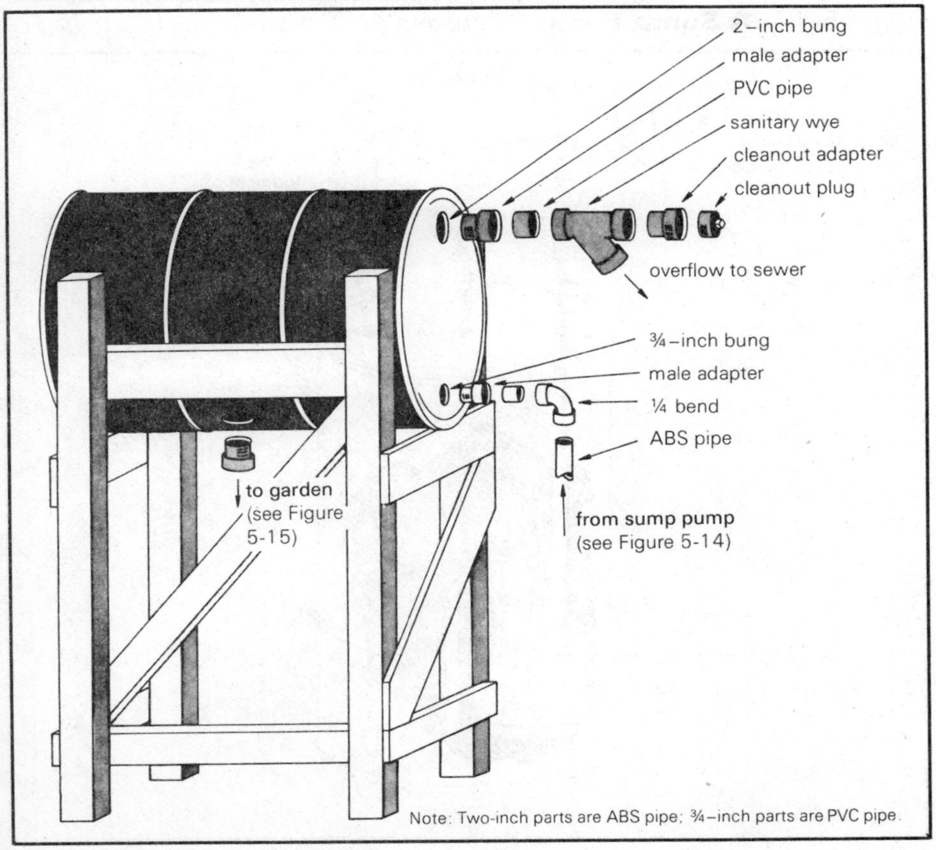

Note: Two-inch parts are ABS pipe; ¾-inch parts are PVC pipe.

A buffer tank is necessary to allow for cooling of hot wastewater. The tank shown in Figure 5-13 is equipped with two two-inch female threaded inlet ports (bungs). Wastewater enters the tank at the side bung and leaves from the bottom bung such that no sediments are allowed to collect in the tank and ferment. Water leaving the tank is directed by a sanitary tee and bell-reducer into one-inch PVC pipe which carries the water to the garden.

A gate valve is installed in the PVC line to permit regulation in the use of the greywater. To use this system, you would close it early in the morning to collect the water generated during morning use. Before leaving for the day, you would open the valve to drain the wastewater to the garden, and in the afternoon close it again to collect water generated during evening use. Before retiring for the night, you would open the valve once again, discharging the collected water to the garden. This short collection cycle discourages fermentation of the greywater within the tank.

If the gate valve is accidentally left closed for a full day and the tank fills to capacity, or if the outlet ports or hose connections get clogged, water will back up from the tank and overflow into the sewer as a safety precaution. The tank should be cleaned periodically. Do this by removing the cleanout fittings at either end of the tank and inserting a plumbing snake. If the recycling system is not to be used for several days, shut the ball or gate valve in the diversion line so that wastewater goes directly into the sewer (or open the valve, if yours is the vertical modification.).

Sump Installation and Pumping System: In many homes the gravity-

For effective and dependable operation, the submersible sump-pump should conform to these specifications:

1. The motor is low powered, around one-sixth horsepower, unless water has to be delivered great distances or to a high elevation.

2. The pump outlet design permits the installation of a flow restrictor, washer, or "glob" valve to moderate the flow output from the pump to the garden. Recommended pumping rates are between one and five gallons per minute at the point of discharge.

3. The pump is equipped with a screen or grate to prevent clogging of the pump mechanism by the solid matter in the wastewater.

4. The electrical connections are waterproofed.

Figure 5-14. **A Sump-Pump System**

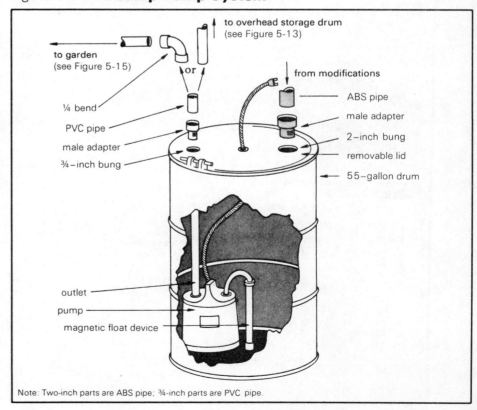

to garden (see Figure 5-15)
to overhead storage drum (see Figure 5-13)
or
from modifications
¼ bend
PVC pipe
male adapter
¾–inch bung
ABS pipe
male adapter
2–inch bung
removable lid
55–gallon drum
outlet
pump
magnetic float device

Note: Two-inch parts are ABS pipe; ¾-inch parts are PVC pipe.

flow system is not feasible, either because an elevated buffer tank is not practical or because the garden is located above the level of the house. In these cases, a collection tank and sump pump must be employed to move the water from house to garden, as illustrated in Figure 5-14.

A sump installation consists of a vertically oriented 55-gallon drum equipped with a removable tight-fitting lid. The drum is placed at a convenient location next to the foundation of the house. If the modification in your wastelines is low to the ground, then the sump tank may have to be sunk into the soil to permit gravity-flow into the top of the drum. The ABS pipe carrying the wastewater is fitted to the threaded entry port of the lid of the tank. Inside the lid, a male adapter fitting allows the pipe to extend to the bottom of the tank, where the wastewater is discharged.

A submersible sump pump placed on the bottom of the tank pumps water out of the sump through the exit port on the lid. The pump is controlled automatically by a float mechanism that activates the pump when the water level in the tank reaches a preset level and shuts it off when the tank is pumped dry (preferably at a height of ten inches or a volume of fifteen gallons). This pumping arrangement insures that wastewater will be dispatched quickly and not permitted to stand and ferment in the tank.

The wastewater may be pumped directly to the garden distribution lines or up to another drum elevated at a height sufficient to allow gravity flow to the garden. If technically possible, pumping to an overhead tank is preferred because it will provide for cooling and mixing of the wastewater as well as moderate distribution to the garden.

Figure 5-13 illustrates the overhead tank arrangement. Wastewater pumped out of the sump tank through PVC pipe enters a side bung of a sealed 55-gallon drum horizontally positioned on an elevated stand. The drum is equipped with three bungs or openings. The lower side bung is the inlet port, the bottom bung is the outlet port to the garden, and the higher side bung is an overflow port to the existing drainlines of the house. A plastic gate valve installed in the output line permits regulation in the discharge

Figure 5-15. **Applying Greywater to the Garden**

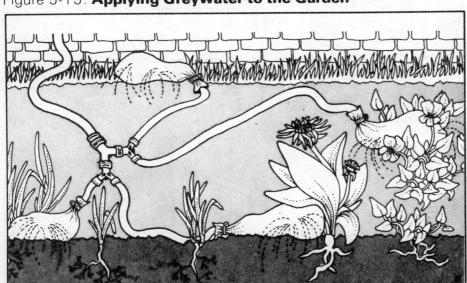

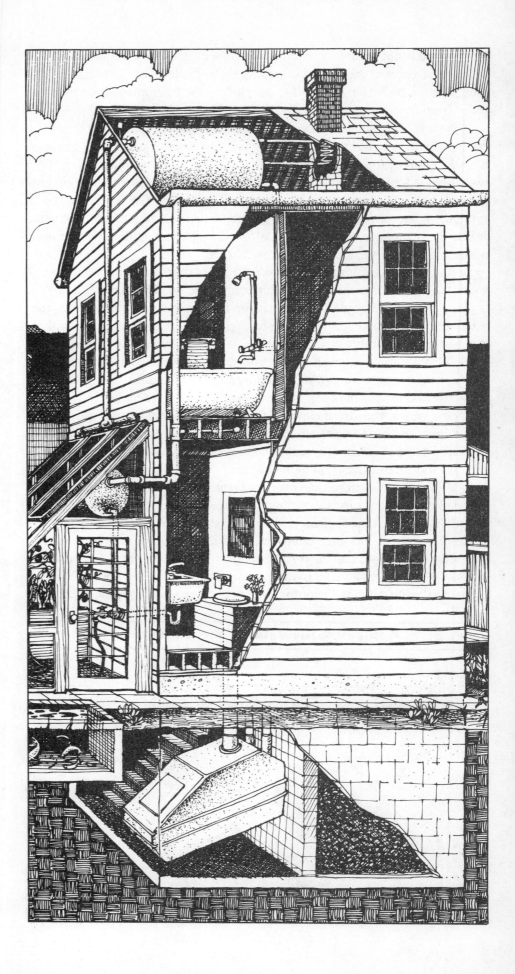

of water to the garden in the same manner described earlier. Cleanout plugs are installed in the exit and overflow ports to insure good sanitation.

Distribution to the Garden: Whether yours is a gravity-flow or sump-pump installation, the wastewater is best conveyed from the tank to the garden by either a ¾- or a 1-inch hose;—in fact, the bigger the better. A central hose may feed several lateral hoses connected by way of a Y-junction such that the wastewater is distributed over a large expanse of garden or lawn. The lateral arms should be rotated around the garden frequently to reduce the possibility of localized puddling or excessive residue build-up (Figure 5-15).

You can filter the water by attaching a cloth bag to the end of each lateral hose. The bag disperses the water outflow while intercepting particulates and soap residue. Such bags may be removed periodically, and waste residues dumped into a hot compost. Then they can be washed, sun-dried, and reused.

An essential objective of your greywater recycling system is to provide for maximum conformance to health regulations and minimal disturbance of your home's existing sanitary system. These design elements will insure that your system is safe and sanitary, but you are advised to check with local health officials and the municipal building department before making any modifications.

1. Do not alter or in any way modify the 3-inch and 4-inch wastelines; they carry the toilet wastes.

2. Direct drainage of all existing 1½-inch and 2-inch wastewater lines into the sewer must be maintained. The diversion lines are installed as an auxiliary system to the conventional sanitary system; not as its replacement.

3. To insure gravity flow into the buffer or sump tank, the 1½-inch or 2-inch horizontal pipes must be installed to slope at a rate of ¾-inch per running foot.

4. Cleanouts should be installed at the entrance and exit ports of the buffer drums and at all intersections of drainpipes to allow maintenance of the wastelines.

5. Do not collect wastewater in open tanks or reservoirs where children may gain access to the water or mosquitos may breed. The buffer and/or sump tank must have a tightly fitting lid.

6. Buffer tanks must have an accommodation for overflow into the sewer.

7. Do not allow any cross connections between supply lines and wasteline modification.

6. MANAGING ORGANIC AND INORGANIC WASTES

Many other material flows exist in the home besides water, and they all need to be considered when redesigning the habitat into an integrated system. One way to appreciate them is to trace the items now in the home back to their original sources in the earth or ecosystem. As you try this tracing exercise, you can observe what types of material flows blend together and are necessary to the production of a specific item, as well as what kind of energy sources and skills are needed in the manufacturing process. By merely casting your eyes around your room, the wonders of the modern industrial world and its interlaced nature become evident. One of the results of this exercise is the realization that we don't think much about many of the objects we buy and use in our homes beyond their basic composition. For example, we don't usually consider that a paper product is made from cellulose wood sources, nor do we think about its country of origin, for example, the United States, Japan, Europe, or South America. We also know very little about where these materials go after we are through with them and they have become "wastes."

All the materials carried into the house either stay there or are carried out again by sewer, by air, or by hand. The sewer takes away the disagreeable wastes we would rather not confront, but alas, there is always plenty of other refuse that must be dealt with directly. As anyone who carries out the household garbage knows, this can amount to a lot of material. Homeowners are usually charged for having it transported away from the house, usually by a public-supported garbage collection service. If you follow one of these specially constructed vehicles to their discharge point, you will see the material further processed, usually buried with considerable expense and energy to crush and otherwise reduce its volume. Some dumps burn refuse and then bury it. Some leave it in open piles where it becomes a habitat and food source for rats and flies, thus creating still other problems. If you are bothered by the sight of the materials you once bought for hard-earned money being smashed, buried, and otherwise destroyed, and if you dislike the idea that the energy and minerals that went into them are being wasted, then you may consider recycling alternatives as a first step toward redesigning your waste-management system.

It is useful to have an overall conception of how these materials, called wastes, fit into the larger resource-use patterns in the society. All the material flows of a home can be easily viewed as a series of cycles starting in the earth, going through the home, and then returning to the earth. Some of these cycles are long-term ones, as with steel, aluminum, or concrete structural members of the home. Such cycles are basically maintained by large energy and monetary inputs most evident when the home is purchased. Still, these relatively long-term material cycles have shorter cycles within them. Some of these subcycles are observable to us as items inside the home.

Although it seems logical that the tools and objects we use and the houses we live in be constructed so that they will last as long as possible, our economic system offers few rewards to those who take this point of view. In fact, the designer, manufacturer, architect, contractor, and builder have all to make their profits from the production process. That primary motivation drives all decision-making regarding materials, construction procedures, and functional life of the structures or objects. As a result, products are not made to last but to save the manufacturer the most money, and bring the most profits to the middle persons. Thus, much that might otherwise be saved and used for a long time is discarded as waste because of profit-oriented production.

It is convenient, in organizing our thinking about material wastes, to distinguish between organic and nonorganic materials, since their recycling pathways are quite different. Organic wastes can be further divided into human excrement (feces and wastes), garden debris, animal wastes, kitchen wastes, and paper.

Organic Wastes

Waste materials of plant or animal origin are referred to as *organic.* Such materials require special treatment because they provide valuable nutrients necessary for the growth of new plants and animals, but also because they often carry pathogenic organisms and thus potentially can transmit disease.

"One man's food is another man's poison." This common cliché can be applied to the use of organic wastes. One person discards something and another finds use in it. When our society was predominantly agricultural, the kitchen scraps naturally went to the chickens, rabbits, or pigs. When these animals were eaten, the kitchen scraps were literally eaten again. When animal and human wastes were used for fertilizer, they were basically eaten again by plants, which absorbed through their roots the minerals in the urine and feces. When the plants were eaten, the nutrients in the original wastes were used once more. The minerals in such wastes are essential to the cycle's continuation, yet the urban condition would remove this fact both from consciousness and from our behavior. When we planned the Integral Urban House in Berkeley, the facilitation of these recycling pathways was a major criteria in determining the design of our systems.

Figure 6-1 displays the pathways of organic-waste recycling at the House. The wastes are treated on the homesite through a series of biological and mechanical processes and reclaimed for their value as plant nutrients. This comprehensive reclamation and reuse of organic wastes results in a series of economic and environmental gains. First, significant reduction in water use results both from the use of a waterless toilet for composting human wastes and from the reuse of household wastewater for garden irrigation. Second, recycling of waste nutrients in the garden reduces the need for purchasing expensive commercial fertilizers and soil amendments. Third, large food yields resulting from fertile soil decrease food bills. Lastly, minimal discharge of organic wastes into the sewer and garbage dump results in a cleaner environment. An EPA study in 1973 determined that 36 percent of all municipal garbage was organic in nature and therefore recyclable at the homesite as described in this chapter. See Figure 6-2, which shows the composition of municipal wastes.

Recycling Human Body Wastes: Ultimately, the most dramatic tactic for reclaiming lost mineral nutrients and saving water in the house is to dispense with the use of a flush toilet and purchase or build a composting toilet. A composting toilet does not employ a water flush for carrying away wastes, but rather, by way of heat or biological processes, reduces the material to an unobjectionable form right in the toilet unit itself.

Several styles of waterless toilets are commercially available. Models range from large units that rely solely on the natural processes of decomposition to smaller ones that are aided by electricity. An excellent example of a compost toilet that is independent of an electrical source is the toilet used in

Figure 6-1. **Organic Wastes Recycling**

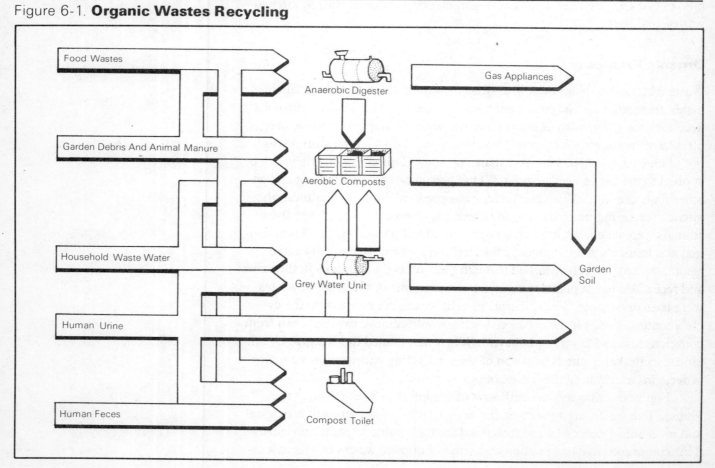

Figure 6-2. **Breakdown of Municipal Solid Waste Production**

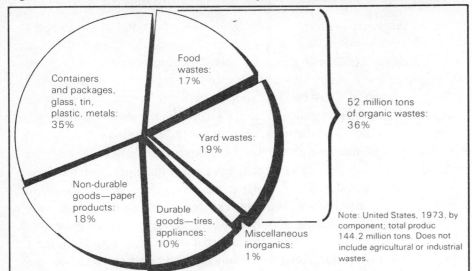

Containers and packages, glass, tin, plastic, metals: 35%

Food wastes: 17%

52 million tons of organic wastes: 36%

Yard wastes: 19%

Non-durable goods—paper products: 18%

Durable goods—tires, appliances: 10%

Miscellaneous inorganics: 1%

Note: United States, 1973, by component; total produc 144.2 million tons. Does not include agricultural or industrial wastes.

Source: Smith, Resource Recovery Division.

the Integral Urban House, a Clivus Multrum. As its name suggests, the toilet is of foreign origin, the concept first developed in Sweden in 1939. The literal translation means "inclined tank."

The active part of the Clivus Multrum is the large tank into which both human excrement from the bathroom and food wastes from the kitchen are deposited. The tank is positioned on an inclined rack under the floor in a crawl space, or in a basement beneath the bathroom. Excrement from the toilet seat above falls into the unit through a large portal. Another opening to the tank is set into the kitchen counter adjacent to the bathroom wall. Food wastes are discarded down this shoot into the tank below. The fecal material and food waste mixture composts in the chamber for a period of two to three years.

The vapors of decomposition leave the chamber through a third pipe that carries the gases through the roof of the house in the same way a conventional flush toilet is vented. Waste gases leaving the composting chamber through the vent pipe will not possess any objectionable odor if the compost is maintained properly. This upkeep includes adding at regular intervals kitchen wastes, leaves, sawdust, or other dry fibrous material to help prevent compaction of the fecal material and maintain aerobic conditions (conditions in which oxygen is present). The manufacturer claims that the potentially hazardous and offensive gases—hydrogen sulfide, ammonia, and methyl mercaptan emitted from the decomposition chamber are within the washroom safety limits established by the National Institute of Occupational Safety and Health. Given the added effect of dilution with the air around the vent, the potential for odors becoming an irritant is unlikely. As waste gases rise and leave the unit from the chimney, the draft induces fresh air to enter the composting chamber.

Air ducts run through the mass of decomposing material to promote aeration and allow circulation of gases within the unit. A system of baffles work in conjunction with the unit's thirty-degree incline to regulate the movement of the organic wastes. Feces enter at the uppermost chamber (refer to Figure 6-3). In our Clivus, after a varying length of time the partially decomposed wastes move beneath an inner baffle into a chamber that receives kitchen wastes. (We understand that the most recent models of the unit have dispensed with this first baffle.) There, the material mixes and more fully decomposes, as it slowly descends toward the front of the unit.

After a twenty-four to thirty-six-month detention period, varying according to ambient conditions and the specific composition of the organic wastes, the material slides beneath another baffle as it enters into the lowest chamber, where the process continues. Essentially, the incline of the unit promotes movement and the baffles prevent short-circuiting—that is, they keep the material that first enters the unit from tumbling over the old and entering the bottom chamber before it has been sufficiently composted. Table 6-1 compares the more popular composting toilets for their cost, size, capacity, power requirement, and relative advantages and disadvantages.

The large units such as the Clivus Multrum rely solely on the natural activity of microorganisms for stabilization of the wastes. The detention time of these units is quite long as a result their composting chambers are substantially larger than composting toilets that use auxillary heat to hasten the decomposition period. The Ecolet and Bio-Loo are examples of the latter. They have an electric element that runs throughout the decomposing mass of fecal and urine wastes. Detention time for these units rarely exceeds three months; therefore their composting chambers can be smaller. These

Figure 6-3. **A Cross-Section of a Clivus Multrum**

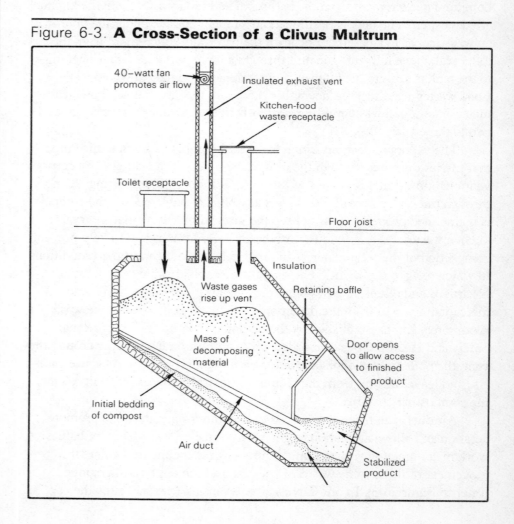

units fit quite easily into a bathroom in place of the conventional fixture. A small, compact, self-contained unit such as the Eco-let can be installed in a matter of hours. No sewer hook-up, no leach field, no water supply line for flushing are necessary. The Bio-Loo actually pasteurizes the material. A hand crank is used to move it into a separate heat chamber when a sufficient amount of fecal matter has accumulated. A small fan is used with many of these units to insure that no odors back up into the bathroom (see Figure 6-4).

Composting toilets have some very important advantages over conventional flush toilets. They conserve water, make good use of the nutrients in human wastes, and reduce the user's impact on the environment. Composting toilets also have some very important limitations. First, as their generic name implies, they only handle the solid portion of domestic sewage. A separate unit must be installed to treat wastewater from the house independently from human excrement. Second, the biological processes that go on within the tank of the composting toilet require maintenance. Attention must be given to the organisms' requirement for air, water and nutrients. These toilets create compost inside the house; their proximity to people's living quarters make their smooth functioning extremely crucial.

Third, composting toilets require that users make the psychological adjustment of becoming responsible for their own wastes. Gone is the carefree

Figure 6-4. **Exploded View of Bio-Loo Compost Toilet**

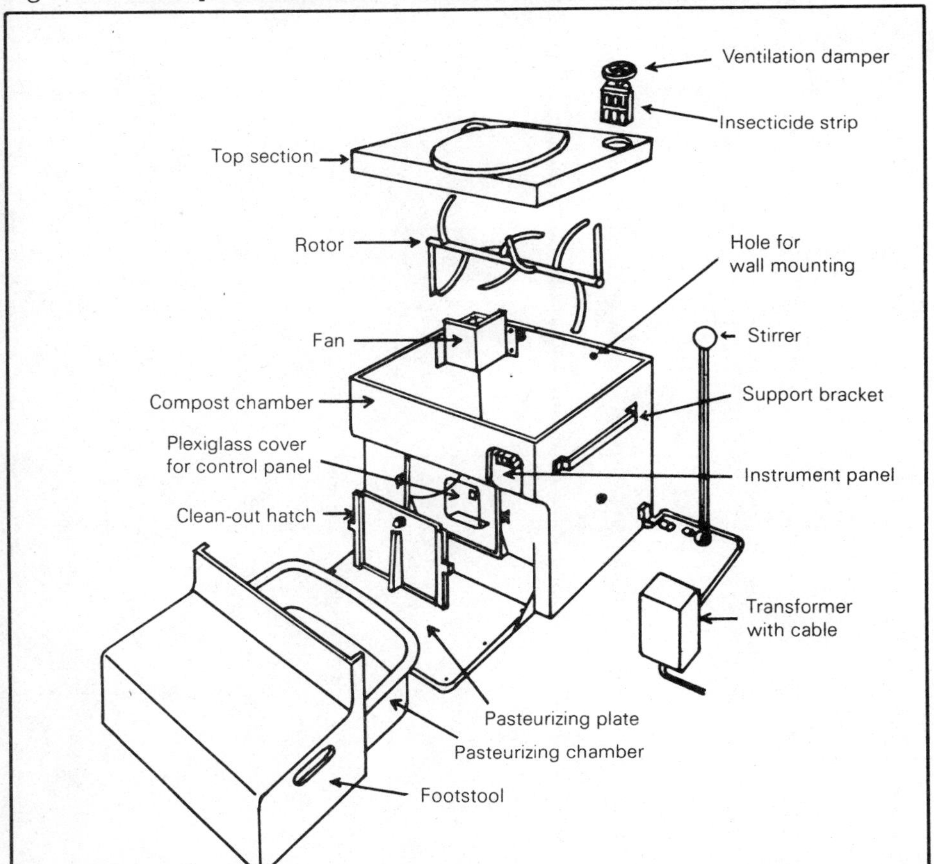

The Bio Loo is a compost toilet with a pasteurization tray whose heating element brings temperatures up high enough to render organic matter in the tray safe enough for full garden use.

Source: Stoner, *Goodbye to the Flush Toilet.*

attitude, "Out of sight, out of mind," that came in with the flush toilet. In fact, the smaller units give one a dramatic view of one's fecal material at close range. Although there is no odor, the sight alone may be disquieting to some. To others, of course, it is a challenge to overcome taboos and a pleasure to know that they are turning a problem into an asset. We like these toilets very much.

Finally, as of fall 1977, although such units have been installed in thirty-nine states, composting toilets had received sanction for residential use from health authorities in only four states. Other states, such as California, are permitting some composting toilets on an experimental basis for the purpose of gathering information on their operation and maintenance.

Table 6-1. **Comparison of Five Commercial Composting Toilets**

Toilet	Cost, as of Dec. 1977	External Dimensions and Volume	Capacity: Number of Persons That Can Comfortably Use Unit Without Overloading	Electrical Consumption
Clivus Multrum	$1685, inclusive, plus freight	45" wide 101" long 68" tall 6.61-cu. yd. composting tank	Four persons (eight for short periods)	40-watt fan exhausts waste gases, consuming 200–400 KWH annually, depending on use
Toa-Throne	$1190, inclusive	39" wide 66" long 51" tall 2.81-cu. yd. composting tank	Four persons (six for short periods)	20-watt fan exhausts waste gases, consuming 100–175 KWH annually
Ecolet	$750, including all accessories	24" wide 42" long 32" tall entire unit is .69 cu. yd.	Three persons (four for short periods)	21-watt fan and 140-watt heating coil consuming 1000–1400 KWH annually
Bio-Let	$795, including accessories	21" wide 30" long 28" tall entire unit is .38 cu. yd.	Two to three persons (four for short periods)	21-watt fan and two 25-watt heating elements consuming 1400–2100 KWH annually
Bio-Loo	$795, including accessories, but not including freight	25" wide 32" long 26" tall entire unit is .43 cu. yd.	Three persons (four for short periods)	23-watt fan, 100-watt heating coil, and 160-watt pasteurization unit consumes 800–1200 KWH annually

Health authorities are principally concerned over the question of pathogen and parasite contamination—reasonable concerns in light of the fact that many of society's most devastating diseases arise from fecal contamination of food and water. However, since many of these units have been used extensively in Sweden over the years and have passed tests for safety there, it is reasonable to assume that eventually models will be found acceptable for use in the United States and that they will become extremely common. Before you consider purchasing a compost toilet, consult your local county Department of Health to learn of the statutes and health regulations governing these units in your area.

Utilizing Compost from Human Fecal Waste: The quantity of the compost

Source: Adapted from Stoner, *Goodbye to the Flush Toilet.*

Restrictions in Use	Distinguishable Features	Advantages	Disadvantages
None; accepts most organic wastes	1. Large, insulated composting chamber under bathroom floor 2. Optional horizontal conveyor allows positioning elsewhere besides underneath bathroom	1. Uses little electricity 2. Has garbage chute for kitchen wastes 3. Large size allows for low-maintenance pile 4. Handles wide variety of organic wastes 5. Wastes kept farther from seat than in other units	1. Most expensive 2. Most difficult to install 3. Requires large area under floor of bathroom 4. Tendency for liquid build-up in bottom of tank 5. One year before good decomposition begins
None; accepts most organic wastes	1. Air-staircase promotes natural decomposition	1. Uses least electricity of all units described here 2. Less expensive and easier to install than Clivus 3. Air-staircase promotes natural heating and composting 4. Will handle variety of wastes	1. Tendency to heat and dry out 2. End-product not claimed to be pathogen-free without additional six-month holding period 3. Long start-up time before good decomposition begins
Urine input should be limited; accepts some kitchen food wastes but they must be chopped into small pieces	1. Manually operated rotor mixes and levels organic wastes	1. Easy installation; entire unit will fit in bathroom 2. Most widely sold unit of those described here 3. End-product has been extensively tested	1. Urine must be limited, especially during start-up period 2. Organic wastes get caught on electric coil 3. Subject to overload problems 4. Uses most electricity of units described here
Urine input should be limited; accepts some kitchen food wastes, but they must be chopped into small pieces	1. Fan-driven rotary arm automatically levels wastes 2. Thermostatically controlled air-recirculation system evaporates moisture and maintains aerobic conditions	1. Easy installation 2. Automatic leveling of wastes 3. Has greatest reduction in mass of material, giving it a higher capacity than for most small units	1. Easily overloaded 2. Urine must be limited to 4 liters per day for first three months 3. Lever must be moved manually to rake down material twice a week into collection box
Urine input should be limited; accepts some kitchen food wastes, but must be chopped into small pieces	1. Built-in heater maintains 95°F temperature within tank, promoting steady decomposition	1. Easy installation 2. End-product safest of all units described here	1. Frequent emptying—every two months with four persons using the unit 2. Uses considerable amount of electricity 3. Rotor can stick and break if pile dries out and compacts

produced and its physical and chemical characteristics will vary depending upon the type of compost toilet used. Generally, one person's yearly waste production will compost down to about one to two cubic feet of finished product. The smaller composting toilets, which rely on auxiliary heat, will yield less compost per year per person than the larger units, because the artificial heat more completely desiccates the material and reduces it to a dry, fibrous material. The percentages of nitrogen and other volatile elements will be smaller in the material produced in the electrified units also, since the higher internal temperatures promote volatilization of nutrient-rich gases. Texturally, the compost from the Clivus Multrum is like peat moss, while that from the Ecolet and similar units resembles dry, odorless coffee grounds. Only the end-product from the Bio-Loo, which has a built-in pasteurization unit, can be assumed to be relatively free of pathogenic organisms. See Table 6-2 for the composition of human excrement.

Regardless of the particular toilet from which a finished compost is derived, care in the handling and application of the product is essential.

Source: Gotaas, Composting—Sanitary Reclamation of Organic Wastes.

Table 6-2. **Composition of Human Excrement**[*]

	Approximate Quantity		Approximate Composition, Dry Basis							
	Per Capita per Day, Moist	Per Capita per Day, Dry	Moisture Content	Organic Matter, Dry	Nitrogen, Dry	Phosphorus (as P_2O_5)	Potassium (as K_2O)	Carbon	Calcium (as CaO)	C/N ratio
Human feces without urine	0.3–0.6 lb	0.08–0.16 lb	66.80%	88.97%	5.0–7.0%	3.0–5.4%	1.0–2.5%	40–55%	4–5%	5–10
Human urine	1¾–2¼ pints	0.12–0.16 lb	93.96%	65–85%	15–19%	2.5–5%	3.0–4.5%	11–17%	4.5–6%	–

[*]Feces and urine

Kitchen, Garden, and Animal (Nonhuman) Wastes: It is one of the paradoxes of our society that materials can change their value so quickly. The food on your plate, so desirable when first approached with a lively appetite—and having already been involved in an incredibly long chain of energy and resource expenditures in the processes of production and preparation for the table—may in one instant be turned into garbage by the satiated palate. What a moment ago was a chef's delight now is nasty stuff, at best a "leftover," consigned to the dog's dish or transferred from the plate to a little dish where it will mold in the back of the refrigerator. Most likely it is headed for the garbage can or sink disposal.

What an extraordinary value transformation, occurring entirely within the human mind! For, in reality the plate scrapings and vegetable and meat debris resulting from the preparation of the meal are still as complete with nutrients needed for life as when they were served from the kitchen. They offer a far more generous array of elements necessary for producing more food than can be found in any of the sacks of fertilizer at the store.

As a society, we put most of our attention on production processes and very little on decomposition. Yet it is the latter that must occur to make the former possible again. Anything that was once living can and will be decomposed, broken down by other living organisms into its simplest elements. A whole world of animals, plants, and microorganisms have evolved that derive their existence from this recycle pathway.

The final resolution into the basic constituents needed for plant growth is primarily the work of the true decomposer bacteria, actinomycetes, and fungi. Even the inorganic forms of such plant nutrients as phosphorus and potassium are released from their parent rock by the weathering action of the organic acids produced by the activities of the microorganisms. But the breaking up of the materials, which exposes many surfaces to the digestive action of the microorganisms, is largely the work of a host of detritivores, animals that are as common (such as earthworms, mites, beetles, etc.) around the house and garden as they are despised, unrecognized, or ignored by the human residents. (Detritivores will digest the microorganisms as well as the detritus on which they grow.)

The two most common pathways taken by the organic materials of the urban household both carry this potential plant fertilizer away, beyond the immediate boundaries of the home, which is a loss to the integral household system. And both pathways have other serious problems associated with them. Most common is that the material is removed through the municipal garbage collection system to a dump site. Organic wastes are about 36 percent of the nonpaper organic materials in the solid-waste stream (see Figure 6-2). (Because much waste paper in the household is contaminated with inks that should not go in to the compost, management of paper wastes is discussed separately. See pages 139–41.) Even with sanitary land-fills, there are attendant problems of rats, flies, smells, and undesired (because it is not usable) production of methane from underground decomposition, groundwater contamination by leaching, and loss of natural land contours and features. Under the present systems, the transporting and burying of organic materials, or their separation from nondecomposables through sophisticated mechanized sorting processes, involves considerable expenditures of fossil fuels and money.

Equally undesirable is using both energy and clean water to grind up the kitchen wastes in a sinkside sewage disposal machine and mixing it together with human fecal material from a flush toilet, sending both through the sewage system to be mixed with industrial wastes and then presented to the treatment plant for (partial) decontamination. Contamination of residential sewage with highly toxic industrial wastes will make the reclamation of sewage sludge increasingly difficult.

Ideally, kitchen wastes and other home organic refuse (excluding most paper) should be processed on the homesite to retrieve from them the valuable mineral components that will provide nutrients for growing plants once again. This treatment process is called composting.

Composting is the deliberate use and management of the biological processes of decomposition, in which primarily bacteria, fungi, and actinomycetes break down highly organized biochemical entities into smaller, simpler stable molecules that are then available to plants as nutrients. (See Box 6-1 for material on microorganisms found in compost.)

Many methods of homescale composting are recommended in the literature on this subject. They fall into three principal categories: anaerobic (without oxygen), aerobic (with oxygen), and a subset of the latter through the action of animals such as chickens and worms. Each method has its own

To reduce the chance for transmission of disease-causing organisms, follow these suggestions:

1. Before you use the material in the garden (with the exception of the end product of the Bio-Loo), process it through a hot, aerobic garden compost pile as specified in this chapter to insure thorough exposure to the high internal temperatures of the pile. Utilize the bin method (page 125) for processing human wastes to insure containment of the material. Use this method only if your garden compost pile produces internal temperatures above 145°F. A probe thermometer may be purchased for determining compost temperature. While this may sound like a nuisance, if you already have a bin composting system going, the addition of a few buckets of humus from the composting toilet once every three or four months is actually little trouble.

2. For safety, restrict the use of human waste-derived compost to ornamental foliage. Dig the material thoroughly into the soil, and cover the disturbed area with a thick layer of regular garden compost or leaves.

3. We do not recommend using human-waste-derived compost, even that which has gone through a pasteurization process, on food plants. Use it to fertilize shrubs, trees, and other ornamentals. Even though the yearly quantities of compost produced from the toilet are quite small, it would be foolish to take any chances.

4. If you use your wastes on food plants, though, wash your hands and cook your food thoroughly. From your own wastes you will not acquire pathogens that you don't already have, but you could increase the number of intestinal worms by reingesting their eggs. However, bacterial and viral pathogens can be transferred.

In summary, danger is relatively slight in eating from your own garden so fertilized—that is, judging from the existing occurrence of such pathogens.

The biochemical reaction of the anaerobic process of decomposition is:

$$(CH_2O)_x + H_2O \rightarrow CH_4 + CO_2$$

(organic compounds + water → methane + carbon dioxide)

The biochemical process of the aerobic compost is:

$$CH_2O + O_2 \rightarrow CO_2 + H_2O + 672 \text{ kcal/mole}$$

organic material + oxygen → carbon dioxide + water and heat

advantages, and, although we feel that the fast aerobic bin system is superior for the Integral Urban House, all the methods will be described briefly before we go into details on the recommended approach.

Anaerobic Composting

Some microorganisms do not need oxygen to decompose or oxidize complex organic matter. They can use carbon dioxide, partially oxidized organic compounds, sulfates, and nitrates. Often this process is referred to as *fermentation*. Fermenting materials are usually recognized by their strong smell. The characteristic odor of anaerobic processes is one of the reasons why they are not recommended for homesite composting.

Only an insignificant amount of heat is produced during the anaerobic process of decomposition, due to the fact that most of the energy of the process is stored as methane. This phenomenon has several consequences. The lack of heat means that decomposition of the materials may take much longer. The presence of some pesticides (residues of which are found on the outside leaves of commercially raised vegetables), certain virus-caused plant diseases (such as verticillium wilt of tomatoes), and many weed seeds, requires the higher temperatures of aerobic decomposition to render the compost safe for recycling back into the garden. Thus, materials must be held much longer in an anaerobic process to make sure all such pathogens and contaminants are broken down adequately.

Furthermore, the anaerobic process proceeds best at temperatures of 80°F to 105°F (25°C to 35°C). Summer temperatures may be sufficient to keep the material warm enough, but the action will slow down when the cool weather comes, and without supplemental heat a great length of time (frequently an entire year) may pass before the process is completed. Thus, anaerobic methods may be referred to as "slow" composting.

Pit or Trench Composting: Anaerobic composting is what takes place when a pit or trench is dug in the soil, the kitchen garbage dumped into it, and the soil thrown back on top. Sometimes the material is covered with a black plastic tarp to increase heat and to discourage fly production, but this technique is probably not effective for the latter. This method is a favorite for many people because it requires so little time or understanding of the process. It is acceptable where the householder has a great deal of ground space and the area does not need to be used again for a while, and where he

---

Box 6-1. **Microorganisms in Compost**

Three basic groups of microorganisms are responsible for decomposition in compost piles: bacteria, fungi, and actinomycetes. It is difficult to differentiate among the bacteria, fungi, and actinomycetes, because some forms have common intermediate characteristics. Fungi differ from bacteria in the way their genetic material is segregated and in their vegetative, branchlike growth, which is easily seen as threadlike white strands in decomposing material. Bacteria are not visible to the naked eye, and are generally single cells, though multicellular groupings are known. Some bacteria have photosynthetic capabilities, but no fungi or actinomycetes can fix sunlight. Actinomycetes are believed to be more closely related to bacteria; they have a similar genetic structure, though their ability to branch is limited, and thus they appear to be a transitional form between the two basic groups.

A list and review of the literature discussing microbial composition of compost is available in the paper by Poincelot, "The Biochemistry and Methodology of Composting" (see the bibliography).

or she is burying the material deeply enough so that dogs, rats, or other animals are unlikely to uncover it and toss it around. However, particularly because of the latter problem, as well as the likelihood of breeding flies, the pit method is not recommended.

One other note of caution regarding the burial method: The microbes that decompose the material need nitrogen, an element also needed in large amounts by plants. Microbes are also better at getting nitrogen out of the soil solution than are the plant roots. So, whenever plants are in direct competition with these decomposers, the plants may suffer a temporary nitrogen deficiency while the microorganisms use all of the locally available nitrogen for their decomposition activities. Only after their work is completed and the materials are thoroughly broken down and stabilized do the microbes die, releasing the nitrogen in their bodies for use by plants. That is the reason for not planting immediately in areas where substantial quantities of undecomposed organic matter has been buried. (For example, farmers often fertilize their fields in the autumn so they can plant in the spring after decomposition has been completed.) Thus, to use the trench method of composting, you need extra ground space. It should be noted that kitchen wastes or other very fresh plant or animal materials that are high in nitrogen are less likely to create this problem, but with them you risk the pest problems described above.

Methane Digesters: One of the by-products of anaerobic decomposition is methane, a flammable gas that can be used as a fuel like natural gas. (Natural gas contains between 70 and 95 percent methane.) Methane is one of the gases produced to some extent under all anaerobic circumstances, and usually dissipates harmlessly into the atmosphere. However, it can become a problem if buildings are situated on old dumpsites or sanitary land-fills. Many U.S. municipal governments are investigating the feasibility of mining the methane produced from their dumps, and are using the methane to augment their supply of natural gas.

The combination of methane and other gases is sometimes referred to as bio-gas (from biological gas), since it is essentially the same gas as that produced in swamps (marsh gas) and in the guts of animals (intestinal gas) where anaerobic conditions also exist. Bio-gas will rise, and can be collected separately and used to fuel a gas range for cooking or a gas mantle for lighting.

To deliberately achieve similar anaerobic conditions for the purposes of obtaining methane, one can place the organic wastes in a tightly closed tank designed for the purpose and referred to as a *methane digester*. When the action of the aerobic bacteria depletes whatever oxygen has been trapped inside, their activities cease, and those organisms that can live under anaerobic conditions begin their work. The bio-gas that they produce will be anywhere from 50 percent to 70 percent methane (depending on the material being decomposed), the remainder of the gas being primarily carbon dioxide with trace amounts of hydrogen sulphide and oxygen. Table 6-3 provides information on the gas-production figures for various types of digestible materials as well as the percent of methane of the gas evolved.

Table 6-3. **Bio-Gas Production from Sources of Digestible Organic Wastes**

Organic Wastes Put into Digester	Loading Proportions	Cubic Feet of Bio-Gas Produced per Pound of Volatile Solids Digested*	Percent Methane in Bio-Gas Produced
a. Chicken manure	100%	7.4	60
b. Chicken manure and paper pulp	33:67	10.2	60
c. Chicken manure and newspaper	50:50	9.1	66
d. Chicken manure and grass clippings	50:50	9.7	68
e. Steer manure	100%	5.0	65
f. Steer manure and grass clippings	50:50	9.2	51

*Volatile solids is the portion of the solid fraction of the waste which is capable of yielding bio-gas once digested by microorganisms. For most organic wastes, volatile solids are between 50 and 75 percent of the solid fraction. (The balance of the solid fraction is ash and other biologically inert material.) In the case of chicken manure, which is approximately 15 percent solid matter, 7.4 cubic feet of bio-gas was produced for every pound of volatile material actually digested by the microorganisms. The gas composition was 60 percent methane, the rest being primarily carbon dioxide.

Source: Sanitary Engineering Research Laboratory, Report Number 69-1.

Methane (CH_4) and carbon dioxide (CO_2) are composed of carbon, hydrogen, and oxygen; thus, you can see that whatever nitrogen might have been in the organic material originally will still be there after the bio-gas is produced. Because of the low temperature and anaerobic conditions within a methane digester, nitrogen does not volatilize as ammonia the way some small amount of nitrogen inevitably does, even in the best-made aerobic composts (see pages 128–30). Thus, in addition to providing a fuel, the methane-production process preserves nitrogen and other important nutrients needed for plant growth and originally present in the organic wastes to be decomposed. In fact, the final solid residue will have a higher percentage of nitrogen than the original material, because some carbonaceous matter will have been converted into CH_4 and CO_2, while the amount of nitrogenous material will have remained the same. When the methane bacteria have exhausted their use of the material, the slurry (wastes mixed with water remaining in the tank) can then be used as a fertilizer.

Since the anaerobic process is capable of producing both fuel and fertilizer from the same materials that produce only a fertilizer or soil amendment when composted aerobically, the questions naturally arise, Why isn't it done more often? and, How can the process be used in the integral urban house?

Methane is frequently produced in this country in sewage treatment plants, where it is sometimes used to provide heat to enhance the treatment process itself, and occasionally also to warm the buildings. It is also largely wasted in these operations, burned off to the sky, primarily because fossil fuels have been so cheap, and neither ethic nor expediency have encouraged the useful rechanneling of methane energy into our society. There are, however, several promising examples in the United States of municipalities selling sewage-derived bio-gas to the local power companies. Company officials estimate that the amount of bio-gas evolved from the sewage treatment facilities of the East Bay Municipal treatment plant in the San Francisco Bay Area would be comparable to the total annual energy requirement of one thousand homes in the area.

China is reported to be using methane extensively, and India and England also use it to some extent. Publications by Ram Bux Singh from the Gobar Gas Research Station in India excited interest among environmentalists in the U.S. in the early seventies, and this was followed by such eye-catching media items as the film on an Englishman, Harold Bates, and "His Wonderful Methane Machine," a car run entirely on compressed methane made from hog manure.

The authors have had firsthand experience with small-scale methane digesters, and have given a lot of thought to the theory behind their operation. We conclude that producing methane is not practical for the average urban household, because of the volume of materials needed to produce usable amounts of fuel. (Of course, this answer is somewhat simplified. For more details on methane, see recommended readings in the bibliography). The authors participated in developing a digester in which a pound of chicken manure produced about a cubic foot of bio-gas, of which approximately 70 percent was methane. The methane yielded roughly 700 Btu of energy—enough fuel to bring seven cups of water to a boil. To dramatize the point, consider that in order to generate enough gas to supply cooking fuel for an average family of four, the equivalent

Source: Golueke, *et al.*, *Final Report, Photosynthetic Reclamation of Agricultural Solid and Liquid Wastes.*

Figure 6-5. **Poultry Sanitation/Waste Materials Recycling System**

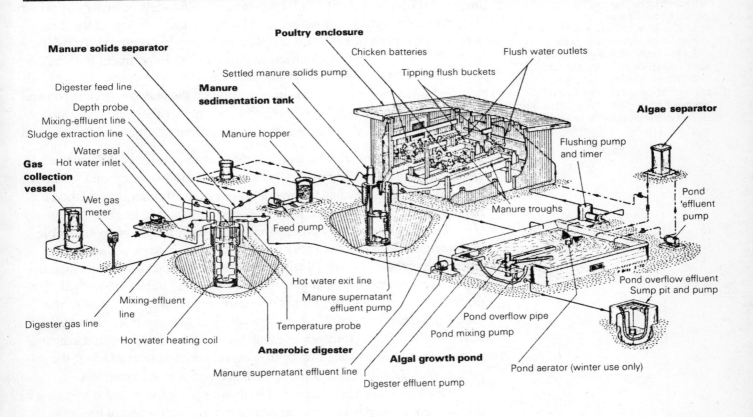

of five hundred pounds of chicken manure, or similar organic wastes, would have to be collected and digested each month.

However, where sufficient amounts of organic waste materials are available with the proper carbon-nitrogen ratio (see page 128), for example on dairy farms, feed-lots, chicken and hog farms, or canneries that generate fish wastes, unquestionably methane can have a role to play in producing cooking and heating fuel and, if compressed, automobile fuel as well. A bio-gas plant makes particularly good sense when it can be integrated into a diversified farm system that includes a network of food production, waste recycling, and energy-generation components. The bio-gas from the manure and other organic wastes can be used for cooking and lighting, and the effluent from the digester can be added to the crop irrigation water or for supplying nutrients to algae production ponds. The algae, in turn, will convert the nutrients of the effluent into proteinaceous material that can be mixed with a carbohydrate, such as oats, for use as fish food or hen mash. A process such as this was tested in 1974 at the Sanitary Engineering Laboratory of the University of California by Professors William Oswald and Clarence Goleuke. See Figure 6-5 for a diagram of their experimental poultry operation.

Aerobic Composting

Composting in the presence of oxygen is sometimes referred to as the "Indore" process, after the state in India where the British agronomist Sir Albert Howard developed and popularized a method of layering organic materials in a pile and turning it periodically for the dual purpose of managing local wastes and producing plant nutrients. An excellent history, detailed discussion of the microbial action in the process, and a review of the literature from the perspective of municipal composting has been written by Raymond P. Poincelot for the Connecticut Agricultural Experiment Station, New Haven, "The Biochemistry and Methodology of Composting."

Approaches vary between simply piling up the material in the open and confining it to some container, and also as to whether the "pile," as it is often called, is turned and mixed during the decomposition process.

Piles and Windrows: The simplest method and probably the one used most frequently, is to pile materials on the ground somewhere and let them decompose in their own good time. This is a perfectly adequate method for handling a mixture of garden weeds, grass clippings, and leaves.

Thus, many such compost heaps are really variations of an anaerobic slow method. This is satisfactory as long as kitchen wastes are *not* used, since the putrescible material will breed flies and attract rats unless high internal temperatures can be maintained. A pile with kitchen wastes will give off the characteristic rotting smell of anaerobic processes. To prevent this odor from developing, soil is sometimes heaped over the pile, or the pile is covered with a tarp. However, as mentioned earlier, a tarp will not keep a certain amount of fly-breeding from occurring around the surface of the pile, particularly if there is a lot of fresh green matter such as grass.

Dry leaves and coarse, dry materials from the garden added to such a pile prevent it from becoming too compact in the center and, with oxygen excluded due to a lack of air circulation, going anaerobic. In fact, however,

When composting the following points should be noted:
1. The best piles are made with a variety of compostable materials.
2. The smaller the pieces, the faster the pile will decompose.
3. When the pile is built, the materials must be combined so that the proper balance of carbon and nitrogen is preserved for optimum decomposition.

anaerobic conditions usually do prevail in the interior of many such piles, although oxygen is not deliberately excluded from the pile as in anaerobic digesters. This is particularly the case where the material particles are fine, as in piles that contain mainly grass clippings. Other materials that become water-logged through exposure to the weather will also create anaerobic conditions within the center of the pile.

Unturned piles are most successful where enough dry matter is in the mix to permit some air circulation and insure aerobic conditions (this is why building the pile in layers is frequently recommended) and the climate is sufficiently humid to permit decomposition to proceed slowly. In the most common variant of this method with which the authors are familiar, dry leaves from deciduous trees are raked up in the fall and, together with grass clippings, are left in a pile over the winter and used during the following summer. In such piles, decomposition proceeds largely by the action of fungi that operate at low temperatures, and the material often has a recognizable mushroom-like smell as it is decomposing.

If there is too much material for a single pile, a row of smaller heaps, called a *windrow*, may be constructed. In municipal composting, where volumes are high, long windrows are created and manipulated with machinery. (See Chapter 15 for a discussion of windrows in municipal "leaf banks" or garden compost centers.)

To insure that aerobic decomposition takes place and high temperatures for creating the desired end-product are maintained in the pile, and to insure that the material is available for use in a shorter period than under anaerobic conditions, the pile must be turned periodically (every month or six weeks, for example). Sometimes, in an effort to avoid turning the pile, ingenious means are employed to get the oxygen into the center. Methods include building the pile around poles that are removed when the pile is completed, leaving air holes going down through the layers, or using perforated pipes or similar inventions for the same purpose (see Figure 6-6). While these are harmless techniques if used with piles of dry leaves or garden debris that contains a high percent of dry matter, they defeat the pur-

Figure 6-6. **Windrow Method of Composting Using Wire Air Tubes**

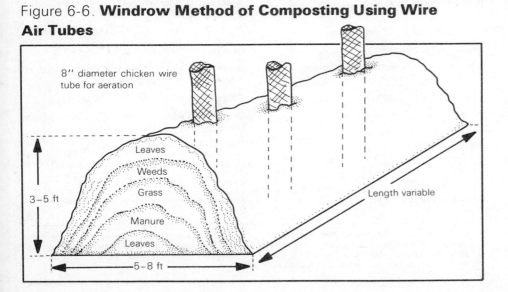

8'' diameter chicken wire tube for aeration

Leaves
Weeds
Grass
Manure
Leaves

3–5 ft

5–8 ft

Length variable

pose of constructing an aerobic pile somewhat—to contain the pile so that the temperatures within will rise sufficiently. Not only do such air holes cool the pile, they expose more surface to possible breeding of flies.

It must be emphasized again that in urban areas, kitchen garbage and manure should not be added to such uncontained piles and windrows because of the large number of flies that will breed and the real danger of enhancing the neighborhood rat population.

Contained Aerobic Methods: Since it is essential to make sure that enough oxygen is available to keep the process aerobic, and the aesthetic demands of some householders require that the heap not spill haphazardly about in the spot alloted to it, various types of containers have been devised to contain compost piles. The simplest are circles of mesh fencing to hold the materials in a column, but a great range of imaginative designs are available, many of them attempting to ensure that oxygen enters the pile with a minimum of turning or none at all.

Once again, because of the pest problem, kitchen garbage or manure cannot be used in mesh containers (although signs that pests are being attracted may not be recognized by an untrained person). Since it is important that the integral urban house inhabitants recycle their kitchen garbage

Table 6-4. **Temperature & Time of Exposure Required to Destroy Common Pathogens and Parasites**

Organism	Observations
Salmonella typhosa	No growth beyond 46°C; death within 30 minutes at 55°–60°C and within 20 minutes at 60°C; destroyed in a short time in compost environment.
Salmonella sp.	Death within 1 hour at 55°C and within 15–20 minutes at 60°C.
Shigella sp.	Death within 1 hour at 55°C
Escherichia coli	Most die within 1 hour at 55°C and within 15–20 minutes at 60°C.
Brucella abortus or B. suis	Death within 3 minutes at 62°–63°C and within 1 hour at 55°C.
Micrococcus pyogenes var. aureus	Death within 10 minutes at 50°C.
Streptococcus pyogenes	Death within 10 minutes at 54°C.
Mycobacterium tuberculosis var. hominis	Death within 15–20 minutes at 66°C or after momentary heating at 67°C.
Corynebacterium diphtheriae	Death within 45 minutes at 55°C.
Entamoeba histolytica cysts	Death within a few minutes at 45°C and within a few seconds at 55°C.
Taenia saginata	Death within a few minutes at 55°C.
Trichinella spiralis larvae	Quickly killed at 55°C; instantly killed at 60°C.
Necator americanus	Death within 50 minutes at 45°C.
Ascaris lumbricoides eggs	Death in less than 1 hour at temperatures over 50°C.

Source: Stoner, and Nesbitt, *Goodbye to the Flush Toilet.* Original Source: Golueke and McGauhey, *Reclamation of Municipal Refuse.*

Note: Although valuable as a guide to the relative effect of temperatures on pathogens and parasites, this chart should not be taken as gospel. According to Dr. Golueke, the temperatures represent wet heat, and the chart assumes that the bacteria are dispersed uniformly throughout the pile so that each is exposed to the high heat; this is rarely the case. Actual kills seldom reach 100 percent.

through the compost, we recommend a closed-bin method in which the materials to be composted are stored until a batch is made, and then a pile is assembled that is turned periodically. We will discuss this method in some detail.

Aerobic, Closed-Bin, Batch Composting—A Fast Method: The closed-bin batch composting method is the most successful we know of for treating household organic wastes because of the wide variety of materials that can be used and the excellence of the final product. The closed-bin method is also ideal from the public-health point of view, since it allows for good pest management.

When this aerobic composting method is followed, the materials will be subjected to a high heat through the action of the decomposing organisms themselves (see Box 6-1 above for information on the microorganisms active in such a compost). Under ideal conditions temperatures of approximately 160°F (71°C) are maintained for a period of a week or so. The population of microorganisms changes constantly as it fluctuates, each species performing its own function in breaking down the organic matter. The closed bin holds the temperature in, and the occasional turning of the pile not only assures that oxygen is available for these thermophilic (heat-producing) microorganisms, but also mixes the material at the sides and top of the pile, which is cooler, into the hot center.

With all parts of the batch eventually exposed to high heat, the weed seeds, pathogens (organisms that may cause plant disease), and pesticides are quickly broken down. In fact, the temperatures are sufficient to kill most human parasites and pathogens (see Table 6-4). Furthermore, fly eggs that might be laid on the top or sides, or larvae burrowing there while the material is still fresh, are also killed by the heat. The temperatures and speed with which the materials are broken down are also a deterrent to rats or other animals that might be tempted to go after the kitchen garbage in the pile.

There are many advantages to this means of producing compost, one of which is the time factor. The process is called a "fast" method, because the material is ready to use in a matter of a few weeks. By that time, the plant nutrients are present as stable, odorless compounds; through further microbial decomposition in the soil, these compounds will slowly release nutrients to the plants. Materials that would otherwise take a long time to decompose and would occupy considerable space in the garden, such as dried stalks of vegetables or weeds, are rendered useful in a short time through this process. Compared with anaerobic composting, aerobic methods are less odorous and more readily accepted in urban settings.

The major disadvantages are that aerobic closed-bin batch composting methods require a certain amount of maintenance. It has been our experience that a three-bin composting system can be satisfactorily maintained on one to two hours of work per week. Containers for storing and then composting the materials must be bought or built. The materials must be turned every few days for best results, and they should be examined for indications of how the process is going while doing so. However, we believe that because of the variety of wastes that can be composted, the desirable end-product, and the pest management achieved while creating it, the process is worth the effort.

What Can Be Composted?   All kitchen wastes can be composted: meat, fats, grains, banana peels, coffee grounds, bones, the outside leaves from all fruits and vegetables, and even spoiled food. The bits of paper that accumulate in the kitchen can go right along as additions of carbon (the end of the teabag, miscellaneous bits of paper napkins and towels, and so forth). Manure from cats, dogs, and other pets, human urine, the contents of vacuum cleaner bags, ashes from the fireplace (but see pages 139–41 regarding newspaper and magazine recycling), and, of course, all the leaves, grass clippings, weeds, and other garden debris that would normally go into a slow, partially aerobic pile. In short, any material derived from something previously alive that can be gathered from the household or the community may be added to this type of pile.

We are frequently asked if there are some specific types of leaves that should not be added to the pile. It is our experience that a little of anything can be added without any problem. This includes pine needles, eucalyptus, walnut, bamboo, and so on. Some leaves—for example, pine needles and eucalyptus leaves—break down very slowly, and others, such as walnut and bamboo leaves, may contain materials that inhibit the growth of other plants. Conceivably, composts made largely with these or similar leaves could exhibit these undesirable effects. It is also possible that the heat and microbial action of a hot compost could have a beneficial effect upon these leaves, cancelling their negative effects. We do not know of any published studies that have dealt with this subject specifically. Our experience and recommendation is this: Everything in moderation. Pine needles, eucalyptus leaves, and any other materials that you may have doubts about probably will compost well and yield a satisfactory product if they do not exceed 30 percent of the pile.

The Ratio of Carbon to Nitrogen: When organic matter is decomposed, the microorganisms that do the work use the carbon in the material to build their cells and as a source of energy. In the processes of their normal meta-

Table 6-5. **Carbon/Nitrogen Ratios and Nitrogen Content of Compost Materials**

Material	Percent Nitrogen (Dry Basis)	C/N Ratio	Percent Moist (Fresh Basis)
Human urine	15–18	0.8	97
Fish scraps	6.5–10	4	80
Poultry manure	6.3	4	75
Human feces	5.5–6.5	6–10	66–80
Meat scraps	5.1	6	65
Fresh grass clippings	4.0	12	95
Sun-dried grass clippings	2.4	19	40
Raw garbage	2.15	25	90
Mixed fresh garden debris	2.0	20	80
Cow manure	1.7	27	80
Seaweed	1.9	19	90
Fresh leaves	1.5	30	80
Oat straw	1.05	48	25
Dry leaves	1.0	45	40
Raw sawdust	0.25	208	5

Source: Adapted from Gotaas, World Health Organization Monograph #31.

bolic activities some carbon is released back into the air as carbon dioxide (CO_2) through respiration. Of each 30 parts of carbon used by the microorganisms, 10 parts are incorporated into their own cells and 20 parts go off as carbon dioxide. And, for each 10 parts of carbon that they use for cell-building, they use 1 part nitrogen. So, overall, these decomposers use carbon and nitrogen in the ratio of 30 to 1.

If an excess of nitrogen is present, the microorganisms will release it into the air as ammonia (NH_3) along with the carbon dioxide. Ammonia is the "soiled diaper" smell that comes from the nitrogen in urine. When there is too much nitrogen in a compost pile, this odor will be noticeable, especially during turning. Flies are also attracted to ammonia.

If there is too little nitrogen present, the pile will not be hot enough and decomposition will proceed very slowly. The only source of added nitrogen allowing the decomposition to continue will be that released from the bodies of microorganisms that die. Several stages of microbial activity are required to decompose the carbonaceous material under these conditions, and the process may go on for several months before it is completed. Thus, it is very important that the materials collected for use in the compost pile have the right proportions of carbon and nitrogen.

A general rule to follow is: Materials that are still green are high in nitrogen—for example, grass clippings and green weeds. Table scraps, particularly meat, are also high in nitrogen. On the other hand, dry materials—for example, sawdust, paper, dried grass and weeds—are high in carbon. Animal manures vary greatly in the amount of nitrogen they contain (see page 247, in the section on small livestock), and animal urine is always high in nitrogen (see page 246). Table 6-5 shows carbon to nitrogen ratios of

---

Box 6-2. **Determining the Carbon / Nitrogen Ratio of Your Compost**

Characteristic Ingredient	Lbs Fresh Weight	Percent Moisture	Percent Nitrogen, Dry Basis	C/N Ratio
Chicken manure	50	50	6.00	4
Sawdust	50	5	0.11	511
Food garbage	50	80	2.15	25
Dry leaves	75	25	1.00	45
Grass clippings	50	95	4.00	12
Total	275.0			

1. List the various ingredients in your compost and site the approximate weight for each. Using the data from Table 6-5 list for each ingredient the fresh weight, percent moisture, percent nitrogen, and the C/N ratio. If the specific material you are using does not appear on the table estimate the characteristics by comparing it to similar material. See above example.

2. Determine from the assembled data the following quantities for each ingredient.
a. the pounds dry weight by subtracting from the fresh weight the percentage of moisture
b. the pounds nitrogen by multiplying the dry weight by the percent nitrogen contained on a dry-weight basis
c. the pounds carbon by multiplying the pounds nitrogen by the carbon/nitrogen ratio.
See example lower left.

	Lbs Dry Matter	Lbs Nitrogen	Lbs Carbon
Chicken manure	25.0	1.50	6.0
Sawdust	47.5	.05	25.0
Food garbage	10.0	.22	5.4
Dry leaves	56.0	.56	25.2
Grass clippings	2.5		1.2
Totals	141.0	2.33	62.8

3. Compute for the total compost the cumulative moisture content by dividing the total dry weight by the total fresh weight.
Example: $\frac{144.5}{275.0} = 53\%$

4. Compute for the total compost the cumulative carbon to nitrogen ratio by dividing the total pounds carbon by total pounds nitrogen.
Example: $\frac{62.8}{2.33} = 27\%$

common materials that might be used in the compost. If you want to make an estimate regarding the carbon to nitrogen ratio of the materials you have available for making a compost, see Box 6-2.

It is not essential to use animal manure in order to have enough nitrogen for the pile. A high proportion of kitchen wastes may provide the nitrogen you need, and the problem may be more one of adding sufficient coarse carbonaceous material (such as dried straw) to prevent the pile from going anaerobic due to excessive moisture.

Human urine can be sprinkled on the pile as it is composting or when it is finished to supply additional nitrogen (see page 211 for a discussion of using human urine). Commercial sources such as blood meal, or nitrogen fertilizers such as ammonium sulphate (see pages 216–18 for a discussion of nitrogen fertilizers) can be used. However, because the latter requires fossil fuel to make and an outlay of money to buy, it is always better if you can find enough nitrogen for the pile through waste.

Collecting and Storing Materials: With this method of composting, the material is decomposed in batches. It is necessary to store materials for the compost until enough has been accumulated to make a pile.

Storage of highly carbonaceous materials is simple. They contain so little nitrogen that they will not start to rot by themselves. The main thing is to keep them dry. (If leaves are gathered from the neighborhood, be sure to select them from relatively untravelled streets to avoid excessive lead contamination. See pages 429–35 for a discussion of the lead pollution problem in urban areas.) Cardboard boxes, bins, bags, or piles covered with tarps will do for storing these materials.

One of the most valuable high-carbon materials available in some communities is sawdust. In the northwestern, north-central, and southern states, a great deal of sawdust is produced by the lumber industry, which destroys it by burning or allows it to remain unused where it accumulates. By becoming sensitive to where saws are being used, you can find sawdust in many places throughout a town. Lumber yards, cabinet shops, school woodworking classrooms, and home workshops are examples of places where this material is usually generated and then wasted.

You will find many uses for sawdust around your homestead. You can use it directly as a mulch (see page 164), beneath the animals to absorb urine and odors (see pages 263 and 282, on chickens and rabbits), as a nontoxic herbicide on the garden paths (see page 164), and for storage of high-nitrogen organic kitchen wastes (see Figure 6-7).

Materials high in nitrogen are much harder to store without creating smells and breeding flies, as almost everyone knows from experience with kitchen garbage. Since the flies are attracted to the materials because of their smells, decreasing the smells largely takes care of the flies. By placing sawdust beneath animal cages to absorb the urine, odors will be minimized in the manure beds. With respect to manure, the drier it is the less it will smell, so every effort should be made to store animal manure in such a way that it is out of the rain, irrigation water, or the path of plumbing leaks from the watering system. Wet manure also loses nitrogen.

Other high-carbon, absorbent materials can be used for the same pur-

Sawdust

Biochemically, sawdust consists of cellulose (50 percent), lignin (20 percent), and pentosans (15 percent), with slight variations depending upon the type of parent wood. The ultimate elemental composition of sawdust varies as follows:

Carbon 48 to 54 percent
Hydrogen 5.8 to 6.3 percent
Oxygen 39 to 45 percent
Nitrogen .1 to .6 percent

After aerobic composting, lignin and lignin degradation products, along with residues of microorganisms, tend to remain as constituents of soil humus. You should be careful to obtain sawdust from sources where you can be sure the wood was not previously treated with wood preservatives or pesticides.

Dog and cat manure can be stored for the compost if it is sufficiently dried out so that it doesn't produce odors and attract pests. A neighbor of ours gathers his dog's manure and dries it out behind his tool shed. Once dry, he chops it into small pieces and stores it in a bucket covered with a layer of sawdust until he is ready to make a compost.

pose as sawdust. Straw, pine shavings, rice hulls or other similar waste products specific to various regions of the country can all be used to absorb moisture and smells from high-nitrogen wastes that are in storage prior to being used in the compost.

A family of four will need to fill from eight to twelve small buckets with kitchen wastes to make a three-quarter cubic yard compost of the kind we are recommending below, if the kitchen wastes are to be the primary high-nitrogen additions. This much can usually be accumulated in a month or so, and therefore, a new compost pile can be made each month. If a great deal of animal manure is available, however, composts can be made more often. Of course, seasonal activities such as canning or household melon feasts will temporarily increase the amount of food wastes, and can also necessitate more frequent composts. A small family having an average sized yard will probably generate sufficient household and garden wastes to make one three-quarter cubic yard compost per month. Over a year's time this will result in the production of six cubic yards of finished compost, or enough mulch to supply a two-inch layer of compost over roughly one thousand square feet of garden area.

Many high-nitrogen materials that ordinarily go to waste in the community can be scavenged if the household is not generating enough of its own. Overripe fruits and vegetables, as well as outer leaves of the same, can be found in bins behind many grocery stores. Residue from restaurant juicing machines, manure from race tracks or riding stables, and grass clippings from commercial gardeners are all examples of materials that have been imported at one time or another by the authors into the Integral Urban House for the purpose of obtaining additional nitrogenous materials for the compost.

In most households, there is rarely enough space on the premises to store home-generated wastes plus the imported materials without creating a problem, so it is best to import the bulkier materials on the day the compost is made. However, when you construct the compost bins, you can build some covered storage containers for bulkier wastes as well. This will facilitate the composting process greatly, since you will be able to pick up materials when you happen to see them discarded, rather than having to ferret them out on the composting day when they may not be readily available.

Storing Kitchen Garbage in Sawdust

At the Integral Urban House in Berkeley, we devised the following method for handling table scraps and other food-related wastes from the kitchen:

1. During preparation for and clean-up after meals, the materials for the compost are left in a collander in the sink to drain off excess liquid.

2. Whenever the collander is full, it is emptied into a small five-gallon bucket that has a tight-fitting lid.

3. Each addition of kitchen waste to the five-gallon bucket is followed by a thick (one- to two-inch) layer of sawdust, dipped out of an adjacent sawdust-holding bucket. (See drawing.)

4. Periodically, the sawdust dipper is pressed down upon the surface of the material in the bucket, compacting it evenly. If necessary, more sawdust is added to keep smells from leaking out.

5. When the bucket is almost full, it is topped with an extra inch or so of sawdust, covered with its lid, and moved to a storage spot outside the kitchen. An empty bucket is brought in to take its place. When all the buckets are full, it is time to make another compost pile.

6. Once every couple of months, the sawdust bucket is hauled to a nearby cabinet shop (or other sawdust source) for refilling.

Figure 6-7. **Three Wooden Compost Bins Arranged in a Row**

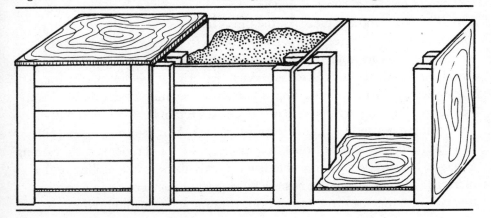

131

One note on scavenging grass clippings: Make sure that the grass you collect was not treated with fungicides, herbicides, or insecticides. These poisons are sometimes incorporated into the fertilizers sold for lawns and sometimes applied separately, and there is always a possibility of drift from nearby garden-spraying operations. It's best to know the gardeners from whom you are receiving such donations.

Siting and Constructing the Bins: While you are accumulating materials for the compost, you need to plan out and construct the bins in which the decomposing process will take place. Choose a site on your property where no precious sun exposure will be lost for growing plants. A shady place is ideal, since piles will not dry out too quickly there. Plan for at least two bins, since the compost will have to be turned from the first into the second in order to aerate it during decomposition. Three bins are better yet, since the third can be used for storing finished compost for gradual distribution, while another pile is made and turned; or two piles can be made and turned at the same time. A three-bin system is shown in Figure 6-7.

Allow space for storage of materials nearby, if possible. By siting the composting operations properly, work you expend in unnecessary transport, particularly with heavy loads of manure, can be saved. On the north side of the house or under a shady tree next to animal quarters and near the garden are good locations. Close access to the street is also desirable, since initially at least you may have to bring materials into the yard.

Although slow compost operations should be sited as far from the house as possible, largely because of attendant odor problems, this is not necessary with fast piles, although at the initiation of a pile and thereafter for two to three days some odors may be detected. These will never be as offensive as those from anaerobic piles, however. The experienced composter will make an effort to manage a pile so that few odors are noticeable, because smells usually represent loss of valuable nutrients.

The compost bins can be constructed of many possible materials; brick, cinderblock, or wood are all commonly used. Wooden bins have the advantage of being portable, so their location can be changed if necessary. They can certainly be made with scrap wood, although that is usually harder to build with. The floor and back receive the hardest wear, so the material needs to be sturdiest there. See Box 6-3 for plans for wooden compost bins.

The dimensions and characteristics of the compost bins provide optimal conditions for decomposition and promote economy in construction. The side, floor, and top pieces of the bins each have 32 inches as one of their dimensions, so that three panels may be sawn from each 4' x 8' sheet of plywood. The bins are approximately one cubic yard in size, a volume which when filled to the brim will accommodate the critical amount of organic wastes essential for rapid decomposition and generation of hot internal temperatures. The bins are boarded on all sides to retain heat within the decomposing mass and to minimize moisture loss. A tight-fitting hinged lid and careful construction of the bin itself keeps flies and rodents from gaining access to the compost. Removable front boards allow easy handling of the material. The three bins are positioned adjacent to each other in a row so that compost may be turned from bin to bin for aeration and mixing.

Compost Bin Construction

The four essential requirements for the construction of composting bins:

1. They must have fronts that can be removed to allow easy access to contents that are low in the bin;

2. They must be tight on all sides and have a close-fitting top to keep in the heat and discourage egg-laying by flies;

3. They must be of sufficient size so that the mass of the compost is able to retain the heat of decomposition, yet not so large that the pile becomes too big to turn easily;

4. And each bin must sit closely against its neighbor so that undecomposed organic matter cannot drop into the crack between the bins and breed flies there. In cases where the sides of the bins cannot be fitted sufficiently close together, one of the boards used in the front can be laid over the crack to catch anything that might drop from the pitchfork in the turning process.

Box 6-3. **Plans for Three Wooden Compost Bins**

Construction Material

Amount	Type of Material
5 sheets	½'' plywood CDX
16	10' 2'' × 4'' Douglas fir
8	12' 2'' × 6'' Douglas fir
3 lbs	16-penny galvanized nails
2 lbs	6-penny galvanized nails
3 pair	3'' butt hinges
3 gallons	Redwood stain log oil

Framing Procedures

1. Cut framing lumber according to following schedule:

No. of Pieces	Type of Material	Lengths	Code to Diagrams
6	2 × 6	34''	A
6	2 × 6	31½''	B
3	2 × 6	28½''	C
12	2 × 4	37½''	D & E
6	2 × 4	37½'' (notch)	F
14	2 × 4	34''	G & H
6	2 × 4	32''	I
6	2 × 4	24''	J
18	2 × 6	30''	K

2. Assemble 2 × 6 platform frame. End nail pieces B to pieces A and insert piece C halfway between pieces B.

3. Nail 2 × 4 upright members to platform frame. First attach pieces F after notching to fit around pieces A. Next, nail uprights E to platform. Cross members G are nailed between uprights E and F. Rear cross supports J are toe-nailed between rear uprights E. Front uprights D are nailed to front piece B.

Note: Care must be taken to ensure that upright members are square and perpendicular to the platform.

Sheathing Procedures

1. Cut ½'' CDX plywood according to the following schedule:

No. of Pieces	Size	Member Type
6	40'' × 32''	sides
3	31½'' × 31''	backs
3	38½'' × 31''	floor
3	41'' × 32''	tops

2. Nail floor panel with 6-penny nails to inside surface of platform, notching front corners to fit around upright pieces F and D. The gap between F and D can be filled with plywood scrap. Best side of plywood faces the inside of bin.

3. Nail side panels to outside of framework, aligning carefully to square framework. Bottom edge must be toe-nailed through flooring into piece A. A 40'' × 5½'' plywood strip can be added along base to complete sheathing.

4. Nail back panels to inside of framework, notching upper corners to fit around cross members G.

5. Construct top, reinforcing plywood with a 2 × 4 frame made with two 32'' 2 × 4's and two 34'' 2 × 4's. Hinge top to crosspiece J, recessing hinge for a flush fit.

6. For bin front use 30'' 2 × 6 boards. Plane ⅛'' from sides on both ends to allow easy movement through channel. Rip top board to fit flush with lid.

7. Fill all exposed cracks with construction grade caulking compound. Apply two coats of redwood stain log oil to entire surface.

8. Position bins on the north side of a shed or in a shady location. Ground must be level or sloped slightly towards the front of bin. Support bins on bricks to raise off of ground.

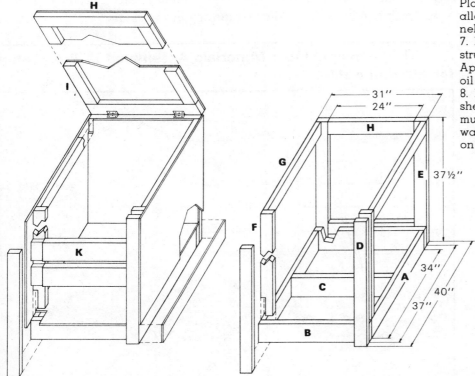

Where winters are very cold, kitchen wastes can be stored outside in a frozen condition until a thaw permits composting, or bins can be insulated with earth or sawdust within a basement, shed, or other protected area.

Making and Turning the Pile: When enough materials have been accumulated (it is best to accumulate enough materials to make compost all at once, rather than adding new materials as they are generated to an existing compost), they can be brought to the bins to start a new pile (see Figure 6-8). In general, the smaller the pieces of the organic material, the faster decomposition will proceed, since the microorganisms have more surface area on which to work. This has been interpreted by many people to mean that a compost grinder or shredder should be used or a power mower run over the material before using it. Our experience is that this is not necessary. Long vines that will tangle up in the pitchfork when you are trying to turn the pile, or tough weed stalks and chunky materials, such as the thick juicy pads of *Opuntia* cactus, can be chopped up into two- to four-inch lengths by hand with a cleaver. A piece of wood to be used as a chopping block can be kept near the bins. Chopping into smaller pieces is not necessary as long as there is some fine material in the pile along with these coarser pieces. Using a cleaver is a lot quieter than a machine, and saves on gasoline. (Another way to have garden debris shredded is to feed it to rabbits. They will quickly reduce it to pieces small enough to drop through the wire of their cages, and it can then be retrieved with the manure. Chickens will peck and trample garden wastes into the litter of their floor if given a chance.)

Instructions on how to build a compost pile usually suggest putting the materials down in layers. Layering is advised because it makes keeping track of the carbon/nitrogen ratio of the material easier. There is nothing sacred about the order of the layers or the content of each one; they will be thoroughly mixed during the first turning in any case.

Figure 6-8. **Compostable Materials Assembled in Preparation for Making a Pile**

Begin composting by placing an initial layer of dry, absorbent material in the bottom of the compost bin.

134

The first layer put down should be some absorbent material to prevent juices from running out the bottom of the bin. Sawdust, rice hulls, or crushed dried leaves are good for this. After this, add some green materials and then continue to alternate layers of materials high in carbon with those high in nitrogen. If you are using urine or another supplemental nitrogen source, you can sprinkle it over the layers as you make them.

Do not add any lime to the pile. This will cause a loss of nitrogen through volatilization as ammonia. No commercial compost starters are needed either. The spores of the decomposer microorganisms are everywhere, and will start to work as soon as the proper mix of moisture, oxygen, carbon, and nitrogen are available.

Some literature on composting also recommends adding rock phosphate to the pile. Not every soil needs phosphorus in addition to what is naturally available through the decomposed organic material. There is no need to add more phosphorus unless you know that your soil is deficient in it. (Methods for determining nutrient deficiencies are described in Chapter 8.) If it is deficient, the phosphate rock will not decompose fast enough to be useful the first season anyway (see page 219, on phosphorus fertilizers). However, the organic acids in the compost pile may initiate the process of weathering the phosphate rock so that it eventually becomes available to plants. If your garden is in need of a fertilizer as determined by a soil test (see Chapter 7), add it to the compost first. The fertilizer will hasten the decomposition process and the microbial action will convert the fertilizer to a form that will last longer in the soil. It is also both undesirable and unnecessary to add soil to the pile. Soil will make the composting material heavier to turn and is not needed to supply decomposer organisms.

The last layer in the pile should be dried grass, weeds, sawdust, or some other carbonaceous material. This will inhibit the kitchen garbage from giving out smells during the period between the start of the pile and when it begins to heat up.

When the pile is finished, the bin should be full, or even slightly higher than the top of the bin. If there is much less than three-quarters of a cubic

---

Figure 6-9. A Possible Layering Scheme for a "Fast" Compost

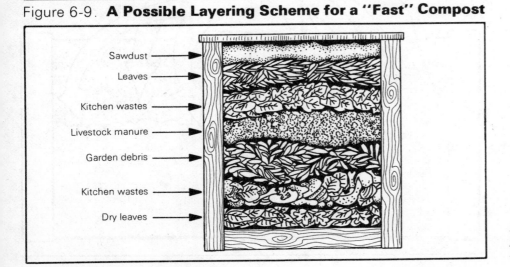

Sawdust
Leaves
Kitchen wastes
Livestock manure
Garden debris
Kitchen wastes
Dry leaves

In order to determine proper mixing proportions for an aerobic pile, begin by layering.

yard of material, there will not be enough mass to heat up properly (the bins in Figure 6-7 have a one-cubic-yard capacity). Apply water to the compost only if the majority of materials used were dry. It is difficult to tell how moist the pile is when you first build it. After it is turned the first time, you can make any necessary adjustments.

After the pile has had a chance to sit for a day or two, it should be turned into the adjoining bin with a pitchfork. An effort should be made to turn the top and edges into the interior, and this must be repeated each time it is turned, so that all parts of the pile pass through the center where the heat is the highest. (See Figure 6-10, on how to turn the pile.)

If moisture has begun to seep out from under the pile, lay down fresh sawdust or other absorbent material on the floor of the second bin before turning the pile onto it. The liquid in the pile contains nutrients and should not be lost. Each time you turn the material over, check it for moisture and odor. The material should be wet enough to squeeze together and look damp, but dry enough that a squeezed mass crumbles apart easily when released from pressure (the ideal moisture is about 50 percent). The smell of ammonia coming out of the pile is a sign that there is too much nitrogen, and more carbonaceous material, such as sawdust, should be added. If the pile smells foul, it has probably gone anaerobic and needs to be turned more frequently to get oxygen into it (perhaps every day for a few days). Or it may be too wet and could use the addition of dry leaves or sawdust plus the extra turning. If it does not heat up by the third day, it may need more nitrogen (try urine) or water, or both.

The pile should be turned every three or four days while you check its progress. A well-made compost will yield steam as it is being turned. This is an indication of high internal temperatures resulting from intensive biolog-

Figure 6-10. **Proper Distribution of Material When Turning Compost**

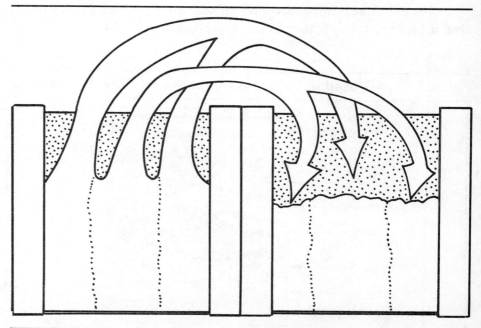

ical activity. Turning will cool it down for a few hours, but it will quickly heat up again if the pile is well made. Each time you empty the bin, clean it out thoroughly, using a broom and a shovel, so that no undecomposed pieces are left to cool in the corners and attract flies or rats.

Once the compost has been made, you may add more material for the first six or seven days in order to bring the level of the subsiding material to the top of the bin. However, after the first week, all additional material should be withheld and stored for the next compost so that the degree of decomposition of the material remains uniform.

Gradually, the material in the pile will turn dark brown and most of the various constituents will lose their recognizable individuality. After fifteen to twenty days, the temperature will begin to come down also. In approximately four weeks, the compost will be cool. At this point, assuming that it is still moist and did not lose its temperature because it dried out, the compost will be stabilized and ready to use. The length of time required for

Figure 6-11. **Composting Variables in Relation to Time and Temperature**

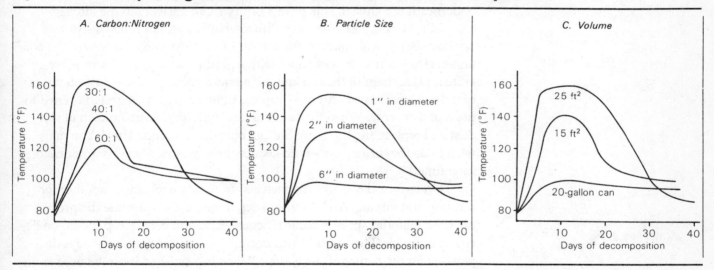

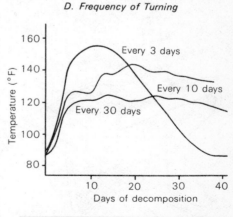

D. Frequency of Turning

decomposition varies from compost to compost, depending upon its volume, the carbon/nitrogen ratio, the particle size of the material, and how frequently the pile is turned. Figure 6-11 shows the relative temperature curves of compost as related to various other compost characteristics.

Do not expect all the contents of the pile to be equally decomposed. Some materials contain resins or lignins that take a long while to break down. These will be still recognizable at the end of this process unless they have been chopped up very fine. This does not matter, as they will continue to decompose out in the garden slowly enough so as not to rob the plants of nitrogen.

Reading about how to make a good compost is no substitute for actually making one. Acquiring the technique is very much like learning to cook or bake a new dish. The product may be fantastic the first time or it may not, but only practice will insure that it comes out just right every time. Once you have learned how to do it, making a compost pile shouldn't take more than an hour if all the materials have been conveniently stored near the bins (unless you are adding a great deal of materials that require hand chopping). Allow fifteen minutes for each turning. This is not very much time and labor to create nutrients for growing plants out of waste products you were probably paying to have carted away.

Bucket Composting for Apartment Dwellers: This method can be used if the family only generates small amounts of material, or when you wish to compost in an apartment with limited outdoor access.

The first step is to establish a compost container and sawdust supply. It is difficult to estimate here how many containers will be needed, since this will depend on the number of people living in the apartment, how often they eat at home, how much kitchen garbage they generate, and how often they turn the material from one can to another. Probably, at least five or six cans, however, will be needed, since composting will take over a month in these small containers. The larger the container, the hotter the process will be, but the larger containers are hard to lift and empty. Thus it is best to use eight-gallon plastic garbage cans with tight-fitting lids. Sawdust is stored separately in another plastic garbage can or a paper bag. Situate the containers underneath the kitchen sink or in a utility room adjacent to the kitchen.

Fill the compost container with alternate layers of food wastes and sawdust. Begin with an inch-thick layer of sawdust in the bottom of the container. (Do not line the container with a plastic bag.) As food scraps are generated, place them in the can and put a one-inch layer of sawdust on top of each food-waste layer. Always keep the tight-fitting lid securely fastened to prevent fly access. When the can is almost full, finish with an inch of sawdust and replace the lid. Store the can outside for composting. (You may wish to do the turning on a porch, since there may be some odor noticeable each time.)

Every four days, turn the material from one bucket into another for aeration and mixing. Add water to keep it moist, and continue the process until the material appears homogeneous, dark, and cool. Keep the lid on between turnings. The material will decompose in twenty to forty days depending on the nature of the wastes. When it is finished it can be used as any other compost, but will probably require the addition of nitrogen for vegetable growing.

Using the Finished Compost: *As a Growing Medium in Containers:* Compost made in the closed-bin batch method described above will contain all of the nutrients needed to grow new plants. If the compost structure is suitable, it can be used by itself—without soil—as a complete growing medium from which to produce more food for the household. The authors and many others have used compost alone to raise plants in containers on rooftops, patios, and in greenhouses.

The compost structure must be fine enough, however. That is, at least 50 percent of the bulk must be made up of pieces small enough to pass through a sieve with holes one-quarter inch in diameter, such as can be made with a piece of hardware cloth that size (see drawing). If the structure is too coarse, the material will contain air spaces so large that water will not be adequately retained within the mass when the compost is watered, and the containers will dry out too quickly. If this happens you may either

Sifting to provide a fine organic material useful for potting mixes or for starting seedlings.

sift the material, as described above to obtain a denser medium, or mix it with various amounts of soil to achieve a sufficiently even-textured dense material.

If you use the compost by itself as the sole growing medium in a container, you will need to replenish it regularly by adding fresh material to the top. It will be obvious when additional material is needed, since the surface level will sink away into the container. The simplest way to maintain the fertility of the container is to bring it back up to the original level by adding fresh compost each time a harvest is made and a new planting started. Occasional watering of the medium with a urine-water mixture may be desirable to boost production with nitrogen-demanding crops such as described in Chapters 7 and 8.

The excess irrigation water that runs out of a container filled with compost will be dark-colored and may contain a substantial amount of dissolved or suspended nutrients. If possible, use this leachate by letting it drain by gravity into soil areas where other plants grow. Porches or rooftops supporting compost-filled planter boxes should be modified so that they drain into terraced beds of plants below. (Drains, ideally, should be made of wood to avoid excess metal input; usually zinc and cadmium run off from galvanized gutters.)

Using the Finished Compost: *In the Garden:* Spread the finished compost around shrubs, use it as mulch for trees, or incorporate it into the top inches of the soil (where there is sufficient oxygen to complete the compost's decomposition). If it is used as a mulch (a layer on the surface of the ground) many highly desirable soil organisms will feed upon it, multiply, and carry it down into the soil, thus mixing it in for you. Organic matter in the soil increases the soil's water- and nutrient-holding capacities. The organisms that feed on it improve the structure and aeration of the soil (see page 198).

Incidentally, composting is a way of managing your organic wastes whether or not you are raising a garden. If you aren't growing plants, give your compost to a gardening friend or a community garden where doubtless there is never enough. Most gardeners we know cannot produce as much compost as they need and would welcome any you can spare.

Paper Recycling

Paper is an organic material. Except for very high quality paper made from rice or cloth (cotton), most of the paper we use comes from trees. In effect, we cut down our forests and throw the product in the dump. As an ingredient in municipal refuse, paper is nearly a third of the total (see Table 6-6, which shows the composition of municipal solid wastes). Thus, a substantial reduction in the municipal solid waste problem would result if the paper portion could be reused on-site or sent back through industrial pathways.

Creative Paper Recycling: In small amounts, well-shredded paper can be sent through a regular aerobic compost. If it is unprinted, paper can also be burned and the ashes added to the pile. But newspapers and magazines, which often make up most of the household paper wastes, are printed upon,

Creative Paper Recycling

Paper can be made into papier-mache, an excellent material for making masks and puppets—and a very small amount can be reused in this way in some households. The durability of the finished product is dependent on the type of glue used to bind together the pulp (paper softened to a mush in water) or strips of wet paper, as well as the quality of the paper itself. For example, with strips of used bond paper (from business envelopes and letters) and a "white glue," very durable Halloween masks or other papier mache products can be made by shaping the paper over balloons, bottles, or forms sculptured out of oil clay, and so on.

Paper can also be made into more paper by mashing it into a pulp with a stick, in a bucket of warm water, then using a roller to squeeze the water out of a thin layer of pulp spread over a screen, and letting the product dry in the sun. Some very practical small-scale paper-making machines have been designed and built by Anthony Hopkinson. The simplest hand-cranked model is practical for home use; the slightly larger, automatic one could form the basis for a cottage industry.

and the inks contain toxic materials, complicating their reuse. Among the toxic components of some inks are PCBs (polychlorinated biphenyls). In Box 6-4 the symptoms that can result from ingesting this toxicant are described and some of the many products are listed in which PCBs are found. Clearly, PCBs, via inked paper, should not go into the garden through ashes and/or compost. We recommend recycling it.

Table 6-6. **The Composition of Municipal Solid Wastes (US)**

Composition of Materials	Newspapers, Books, Magazines*	Containers, Packaging	Major Household Appliances	Furniture, Furnishings	Clothing, Footwear	Food, Food Products	Other Products	Other	Millions of Tons*	Percentage of Total Wastes
Paper	7.5%	14.9%	—	trace	trace	—	6.1%	—	39.1	28.6%
Glass	—	8.1	trace	trace	—	—	.7	—	12.1	8.9
Metals	—	4.5	1.4%	.1%	trace	—	2.8	—	11.9	8.7
ferrous	—	4.0	1.2	trace	—	—	2.6	—	10.6	7.8
aluminum	—	.4	.1	trace	—	—	.1	—	.8	.6
other nonferrous	—	.1	.1	trace	—	—	.2	—	.4	.3
Plastics	trace	1.8	—	.1	.2%	—	1.0	—	4.2	3.1
Rubber/Leather	—	trace	—	trace	.4	—	2.0	—	3.3	2.4
Textiles	trace	trace	—	.4	.4	—	.5	—	1.8	1.3
Wood	—	1.3	—	1.7	trace	—	.4	—	4.6	3.4
Food wastes	—	—	—	—	—	16.1%	—	—	22.0	16.1
Yard wastes	—	—	—	—	—	—	—	17.6%	24.1	17.6
Miscellaneous inorganics	—	—	—	—	—	—	—	1.2	1.8	1.2
Total (10^6 tons)	10.3	48.0	3.9	3.1	1.2	22.0	22.2	25.9	136.7†	
Percentage of Total wastes	7.5	35.1	2.9	2.3	1.0	16.1	16.4	18.8		100†

Source: Adapted from Lowe, *Energy Conservation Theory in Improved Solid Waste Mangement.*

Note: The data in this table includes wastes generated in households, commercial places and institutions, but excludes industrial, agricultural, animal wastes, abandoned autos, ashes, street sweepings, construction and demolition debris, and sewage sludges.
* As generated at the source.
† Rounding makes for slight errors in table.

Box 6-4. **PCBs: Polychlorinated Biphenyls**

The first widespread human epidemic of "*Yusho* disease" (Japanese for rice-oil disease) occurred in 1968 in southern Japan, when about a thousand people developed darkened skin, brownish pigmentation in the nails, lips, and gums, and severe acne. Other symptoms were more severe: numbness and neuralgic pains, swelling in joints—especially the heels—edema of the eyelids, transient visual and hearing disturbances, jaundice, and general weakness. Eleven live and two still-born babies exhibited the same symptoms. In many cases the disease persisted for more than three years. It was traced to food cooked with rice oil contaminated with Kanechlor 400, the main component of which is tetrachlorobiphenyl (a polychlorinated biphenyl [PCB]), which had leaked from a heat exchanger. Some patients consumed an average of two grams of the PCB. Minimum dose producing symptoms is one-half gram. Numerous cases of PCB-contaminated food have also occurred in the United States.

PCBs were first introduced in the United States in 1930. By 1970, thirty-four thousand tons a year were sold. PCBs are manufactured in Europe, Japan, and the USSR. PCBs as air pollutants are comparable to DDT: they degrade slowly, are stored in body tissue (one third of six hundred human samples had residues of at least one part per million), and are widely distributed around the earth (for example, in shrimp, nonmigratory Arctic bears, Great Lakes fishes, fish-eating birds, and human breast milk). In 1972, the Swedish government prohibited the use, importation, manufacture, and sale of PCBs.

PCBs are noninflammable and have high plasticizing ability. They are used in industrial transformers and capacitors, as hydraulic and heat-transfer fluids, as plasticizers and solvents in adhesives, as sealants, inorganic solvents, and electric wire coatings. They are used in asphalt protective coatings, rubber, floor tile, inks, brake linings, and certain carbonless reproducing paper. About four thousand tons enter our waterways through sewage annually, and up to two thousand tons escape into the air from plasticized materials.

Source: Waldbott, *Health Effects of Environmental Pollutants.*

Making the job easy for yourself is the name of the game. One way to do this with newspapers is to keep a pile going where it can be wrapped with cord for easy transport. Set up a cardboard or wooden box with the cords laid in place first, and then pile up the newspapers until the bundle is a size that can be easily carried. The cords can be tied quickly and easily, the newspapers removed, and new cords laid down for the next pile. Tied bundles can be stored until recycling time comes. In lieu of going to a recycling center, the newspapers can be given to community groups that make house pickups, sold to "junk" dealers, or taken directly to paper companies.

Only about 20 percent of all newspapers in this country are recycled. The reasons for this small percentage are various: in part a lack of consumer acceptance of recycling, and in part public health concerns over the dangers of using recycled paper for food packaging, a major use for paper. Another factor is the manipulation of the paper market by large industries. For example, newsprint users (such as newspapers), which often own their own lumber companies and/or forests, prefer to use virgin materials. Recycled papers usually have a slight tint (grey, pink, green) due to traces of the inks used previously, and this makes them less desirable for many uses. These same ink residues prevent used paper from being utilized to feed cattle, a logical reuse, since the microorganisms in the cow's stomach can digest the cellulose in paper very efficiently. Obviously, the development of nontoxic inks and/or improved de-inking processes would greatly enhance possibilities for paper recycling.

Currently, municipal recycling appears headed toward using paper and other organic wastes as a fuel substitute for power plants, since these materials have a relatively high Btu content (4500 btu per pound, or nine million Btu per ton) and low amounts of sulfur (compared to coal, for example). However, an ecological view or a net-energy analysis would probably suggest that virgin wood supplies made into paper should continue to cycle and recycle as paper as long as possible, since manufacturing paper takes so much energy in the first place. After several reuses, when fiber length is reduced and the value of the paper drops, the material should be fed to cattle or be burned. Burning of course represents an end-use point. Where the choices are equal, using residue paper as cattle feed would be better than burning, since the former use would provide food and feces, both recyclable. Once paper is burned, however, only ashes remain.

The principle involved here—that a high-quality product should be used as is for as long as possible, and then in as many degraded states as possible—is one that should govern all recycling activities. Although we have been discussing paper, the same concept should be applied to other products, for example, glass (see Chapter 15).

Managing Nonorganic Wastes in the Home

The way in which the home is constructed actually sets up certain buying and processing systems. For example, solid wastes are traditionally handled by using small containers (wastebaskets) that are repeatedly dumped into larger containers (garbage cans) that are dumped into a special wheeled container (garbage truck) that transports them to a place called a dump where the wastes are left all together in a vast heap.

The categories into which the household waste should be separated are:

1. *Organic materials to be composted* (discussed above)

2. *Organic materials to be burned* (paper, wood)

3. *Metal* (you will have to decide if there are enough beer and soft-drink consumers in your household to justify a division here into aluminum and steel or bi-metal containers)

4. *Glass*

5. *Nonrecyclables* (the materials that cannot be easily recycled by the time they are thrown away by the household)

Once the materials have all been mixed together, sorting them out again takes much more energy and time than would have been spent in separating them at their source. The obvious solution is to establish some sort of management center in the home where sorting can be done conveniently. Our experience has shown that the ease with which this separation of materials is accomplished and the accessibility and attractiveness of the location where it is done are important factors in making this effort a successful one. Earlier we discussed the Olkowskis' experiences in modifying their household to incorporate recycling activities. Here we make some detailed recommendations for creating a waste-sorting system.

The Home Recycling Center: Choose a location that family members are already using to dispose of most of the nonpaper items they are presently throwing away. For many households, this is the kitchen, but it is essential to determine what is the best location for your specific home. If residents are now in the habit of throwing all kinds of materials into the various baskets located throughout the house, then a general conference may have to be called to discuss the implementation of the new policy, and an agreement reached on a convenient central location for handling nonpaper items. If the house is large or has more than one story, it may be desirable to develop a secondary waste-sorting station upstairs where only paper and nonrecyclables can be handled. This would insure (as it did in our house) that the various types of wastes will not get mixed together just because people are too lazy or busy to walk downstairs. The last category consists of items that contain ceramics, plastics, or a mixture of materials bonded together and difficult to separate. Since plastics come in so many formulations, usually only their original manufacturers know how to take them apart again. In addition, plastics frequently give off toxic vapors when they are burned, and when added to the dump they take a very long time to decompose.

One beneficial result of beginning a household waste-sorting system is that residents will become conscious of just how much nonrecyclable material passes through their fingers. Hopefully, the next step will be their decision to discontinue buying products that generate such waste in the first place. Of course, avoidance is not always possible, since many necessary items may not be packaged in any other form, but at least there will be some conscious consumer decision-making going on in relation to this problem.

When you choose the containers for your recycling venture, keep several considerations in mind. Ideally, they should be as attractive as possible. Even if they are hidden away in a cupboard, closet, or other inconspicuous place, it is highly desirable that they be pleasant to look at and use. The whole idea behind this effort is to get the household residents to move away from the "out of sight, out of mind" approach to their wastes and to confront them directly. Thus, attractive, well-labeled containers in a place that is visible to both residents and visitors would be ideal.

The containers should also be chosen for durability and weight, since they will have to be emptied periodically. Baskets are good for the non-kitchen wastes, particularly if they are long and deep. One way to avoid having to lift the containers themselves, if they are heavy, is to line them with the large used paper grocery bags. Using liners also reduces the need for

cleaning the insides of the containers frequently and solves the problem of
miscellaneous small items, such as broken glass, getting scattered inside the
larger container where they have to be picked up by hand. After a couple of
trips to the recycling centers, the bags themselves should be recycled with
the paper. If you are among the few households that have managed to avoid
constantly importing paper bags by carrying cloth or fiber sacks or baskets to
market, as in many more frugal economies (Mexico and Europe, for example), reusable cloth bags can be fashioned to serve the same purpose.

Before separating glass, metal tins, or plastics that previously contained
food into the proper recycling receptacle, be sure to rinse them out and let
them drain. This will eliminate the problem of odors coming from the containers, which might make them attractive to flies or unpleasant for residents. Pull the plastic outer skins from paper containers that can be burned.
Small pieces of paper (approximately twenty square inches or less) can be
put in with the organic materials to be composted, or into the composting
toilet.

If possible, the in-house recycling center should be supplemented by
another storage area where the materials can accumulate in large amounts
before being recycled. This can be a back porch, garage, basement, shed, or
the like. The point is to make as few trips out to recycle the materials as
possible. It is ridiculous to use up in gasoline what you are saving in recycling materials.

Once you've worked out a system for sorting your nonorganic materials—glass, metals, and plastics—what then? So many cities in the country
already have one or more recycling centers that the next step may be a simple matter of waiting until you have a full load for the vehicle to which you
have access, and then taking all the material over to the recycling center
some Saturday morning. You may be more fortunate yet, and have some sort
of curbside recycling pick-up service available, as has been developed as private commercial enterprises or by municipal services in numerous communities across the nation. If no such center or service is available, you may
have to start one. We did. Our specific recommendations on this subject are
included in Chapter 15, about urban community.

Part Three:
Using The Sun's Energy

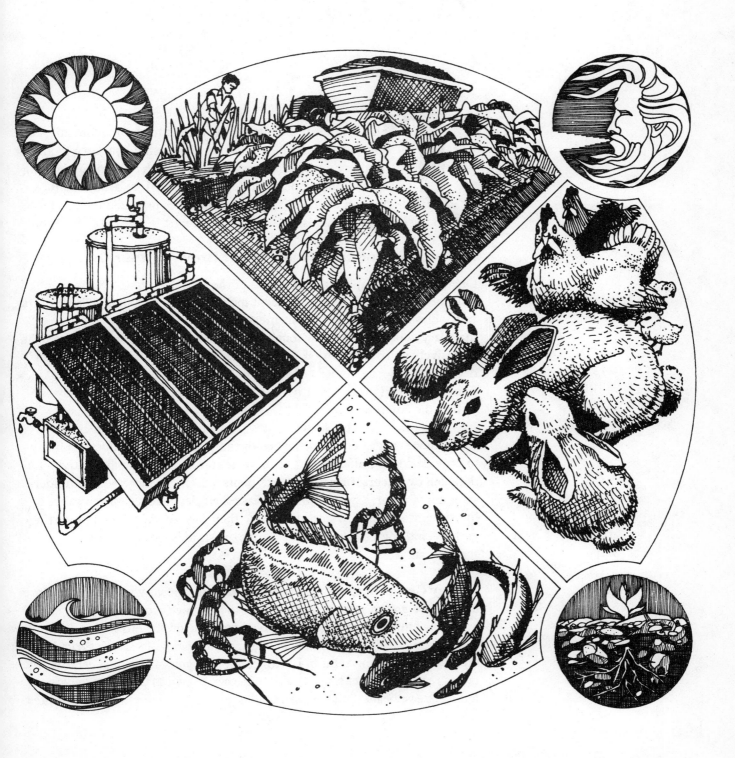

7. GROWING FOOD IN URBAN AREAS

This chapter is intended in part to set forth the economic, ecological, and social justifications for raising your own food. Its primary purpose, however, is to guide the reader in planning a food-raising program for the home. More detailed information on the raising of vegetables is provided in Chapter 8, and the raising of livestock is covered in Chapter 10.

Advantages and Disadvantages of Growing Your Own

One of the most important direct uses of the sun's energy is to raise plants; thus the integral urban house concept includes the production of some of the vegetables and fruits eaten by its inhabitants (see Figure 7-1). The amount may vary widely, from a few tomatoes grown in a five-gallon container to an intensively cultivated garden that produces surplus for the winter through drying, canning, and other types of storage. In either case, the home production of food will make a positive contribution to the health of the body as well as the environment.

The question often arises, Is it worthwhile to raise vegetables and fruits under urban constraints, when the amount of food produced is likely to provide an insignificant part of the year-round diet? No other activity undertaken by integral urban house residents is likely to increase their understanding of natural systems and decrease their dependence on centralized life systems so much as starting to raise their own food (unless it be sorting garbage and composting wastes), so this question is worth considering in some detail.

Energy Consumption: Interestingly enough, the very vegetables that are likely to be grown around the home are those which require the most energy-consuming agribusiness technology to raise on the farm. (See Table 3-3, page 57, which shows the net energy efficiencies of various agricultural crops. By comparing column B with column A, you can see that certain vegetables require more energy to raise than they provide.) Consider tomatoes, lettuce, peas, beans, and similar popular garden vegetables. Under our present commercial agricultural system, getting these foods to the table takes enormous amounts of fossil-fuel inputs in the form of gasoline, pesticides, and commercially manufactured fertilizers. Tractors prepare the soil with fertilizers and/or herbicides. Machinery is used again during crop growth in cultivation for weed-control, spraying (if chemical control of pests is used), and harvesting. Then follows sorting, loading onto trucks, transporting to the distributors (frequently with added energy costs of refrigeration), cleaning, and shipping to the retailer. Finally, the groceries are conveyed home by the consumer.

In fact, most striking in a visit to a tomato harvest operation is the roar and clamor of the machines and the smell of diesel fuel. Empty bins are driven up alongside the tomato harvester as it works its way through the field. The monster tears up the plants at its front end and tosses the tomatoes onto a conveyer belt along its spine. This bounces the fruit along in front of some twelve to fifteen persons who are riding on the machine on each side of the tumbling tomatoes (which are still green and of a variety having especially thick skins in order to survive this handling). The people work under a sunshade, bundled up in the 110°F (43.3°C) heat because of the irritating hairs on the plants and in the dust. Full bins are driven to the edge of the field where jitneys stack and load them onto huge double trailer trucks at regular intervals. The trucks rumble off with each full load and reappear with empty boxes. (The foreman, with his time chart, stands next to the

Figure 7-1. **Use of Available Energy for Food Production**

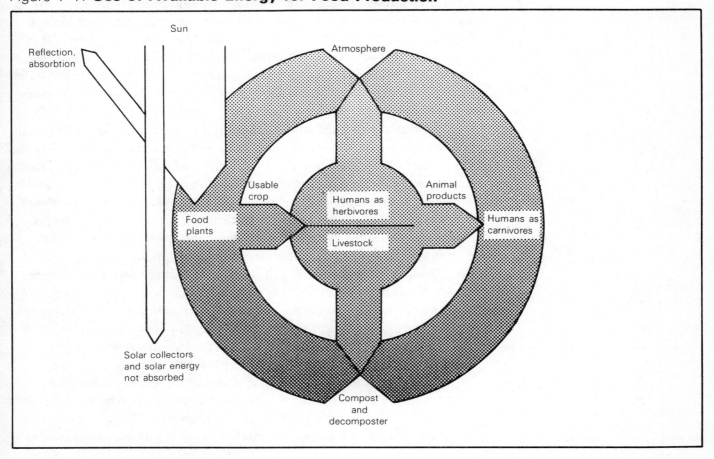

water cooler under a nearby tree, checking on worker performance, completing a picture that is similar to that of the assembly-line factories in the automobile and other industries.)

Furthermore, harvesting, culling, cleaning, and transporting operations produce an enormous amount of waste. Very little of such waste is treated as a resource, finding its way back to the land through decomposition. Much is transported to and burned in land-fills adjacent to the various processing stations along the way.

By contrast, compared with these common garden vegetables other foods raised on the farm consume relatively little fossil-fuel energy per calorie of food produced. Grains are the best example of this. Therefore, as we briefly discussed in Chapter 3, the foods you are least likely to raise in small spaces are also the very ones that are most suitably grown on the farm. For this reason raising your own vegetables can represent real savings in fuel energy for the nation as a whole. This energy-conservation factor is greatly increased when residents of cold-winter areas produce some of their vegetables during the winter months in solar greenhouses that use little or no auxiliary heat. In some areas, vegetables eaten during the winter may represent the greatest energy investment, given the energy use involved in long-distance shipping from the farms in the West to the country's northern and eastern cities.

Pesticide Residues: Quite aside from the energy questions related to pesticides derived from fossil fuels, pesticides are *poisons*. Vegetables produced and stored through major commercial agricultural channels are likely to have small residues remaining on them when they reach the home kitchen. Samples taken by the Food and Drug Administration at yearly intervals in "market-basket surveys" of supermarkets in thirty cities across the nation show these residues on a regular basis. Data from such a report are shown in Table 7-1. The results of these surveys are commonly reported in the *Pesticides Monitoring Journal.*

Disregarding for the moment the effects of these agricultural chemicals on the workers who come in direct contact with these materials as well as the effects they have on increasing pest problems and their possible long-term impact on the larger environment, what do these residues mean to you, the consumer of these poisons? No one really knows. As long as the amounts of residues are below certain government-defined "tolerance levels," the produce may be sold and eaten. However, those levels are set through a tug-of-war between government agencies and industry spokespeople, and are often based on data provided by the pesticide industry itself. Furthermore, various foods in a single meal may contain residue from many different poisons. No one has ever tested these chemicals in combination with each other, or with other contaminants that might be present—for example, lead, when the vegetables have been grown in fields in the lee of freeways (see pages 429-35 on lead contamination), or factory fallout.

Very little information is available to answer these questions: Who consumes these poisons? During what part of their lives? Which poisons are consumed in what quantities? What are the long-range effects of this consumption? People differ from one another metabolically and change individually at different stages—that is, in utero, when sick or elderly, and so on. What *is* known is that as antibiotics and improved sanitary conditions gradually reduced illness and death from the contagious diseases that were the scourges of humankind in the past, degenerative diseases—those that cause the breakdown of body functions, such as cancer and heart disease—took their place (see Table 1-1).

The rising mortality rates cannot be fully explained by the longer life-span of some of today's population, since these degenerative diseases are attacking young people also. Six to seven times more people die of cancer each year than died in the Vietnam War during its entire six-year duration (see Table 1-2). Experts now estimate that up to 90 percent of all cancer may

Table 7-1. Chemical Contaminants in Foods from Supermarkets*

Compound, in Order of Prevalence in Food Sampled	Type of Compound (CH = Chlorinated Hydrocarbon; OP = Organophosphate; C = Carbamate; I = Inorganic Compound)	Lethal Dose Necessary to Kill 50% of Test Animals (Mg/kg of Body Wt)	Range of Concentrations Found in Samples (Parts per Million, Mg Poison/Kg Food)
1. Dieldrin (C)	insecticide (CH)	40–188	0.0006–0.0330
2. DDE	insecticide (CH)†	N/A	0.0006–0.0330
3. BHC (C)	insecticide (CH)†	600–1250	0.0004–0.0070
4. DDT (C)	insecticide (CH)	113	0.002 –0.020
5. Malathion	insecticide (OP)	2800	0.003 –0.115
6. Lindane (M,C)	insecticide (CH)	88	0.003 –0.0120
7. Diazinon (T)	insecticide (OP)	300–850	0.0007–0.0270
8. Heptachlor Epoxide	insecticide (CH)†	N/A	0.0005–0.0040
9. TDE	insecticide (CH)	3400	0.001 –0.005
10. Arsenic (As$_2$O$_3$) (C)	insecticide (I)	20	0.03 –0.60
11. Endosulfan	insecticide (CH)	80–110	0.003 –0.012
12. HCB	fungicide (CH)	10	0.0003–0.0070
13. Parathion (M,T)	insecticide (OP)	13	0.003 –0.022
14. PCB	not a biocide, but a contaminant nonetheless	N/A	0.050
15. CIPC	herbicide (CH)	5000–7500	0.005 –0.467
16. PCA	herbicide (CH)	3300	0.004 –0.05
17. PCP	insecticide and herbicide (CH)	N/A	0.010 –0.033
18. Carbaryl (M,T)	insecticide (C)	800	0.05 –0.50
19. TCNB	fungicide (CH)	N/A	0.001 –0.284
20. Methoxychlor	insecticide (CH)	6000	0.004 –0.009
21. Methyl Parathion	insecticide (OP)	9–42	0.008
22. PCNB (C,T)	fungicide (CH)	1200	0.002 –0.005
23. Ethion	miticide (OP)-kills mites	24	0.003 –0.012
24. O-phenylphenol	fungicide	2480	0.050 –0.020
25. Leptophos	insecticide (CH)	50	0.013 –0.090
26. Perthane	insecticide (CH)†	8170	0.030 –2.28
27. Botran (M)	fungicide	1500–4000	0.006 –0.067
28. Toxaphene	insecticide (CH)	90	0.163
29. DCPA (Dacthal)	herbicide (CH)	above 3000	0.003 –0.013
30. Dicofol (Kelthane)	miticide (CH)-kills mites	809 ± 33	0.010
31. Aldrin (C)	insecticide	67	0.001
32. Captan (T)	fungicide	9000	0.178
33. Chlordane (C)	insecticide (CH)†	457–590	trace
34. Heptachlor (C)	insecticide (CH)†	40–188	0.004
35. Phosalone	molluscicide (CH)-kills snails	120	0.171
36. Ronnel	insecticide (OP)	1740	0.001
37. Nitrofen	herbicide (CH)	3050 ± 505	0.039

*From a Food and Drug Administration "Market-Basket Survey," August 1973 to July 1974.
†Certain of the compounds are so similar to others that they can be taken as the compound, or certain compounds are degradation products of other compounds, therefore should be understood as arising from that source. DDE and TDE are breakdown products of DDT. DDE is more toxic than DDT. Perthane is similar to DDT. Dieldrin is really a mixture of chlordane and heptachlor. Heptachlor epoxide is a degradation product of heptachlor (which is more toxic than heptachlor). Lindane is the gamma isomer of BHC.

Common abbreviations stand for:
DDE: 1,1'-dichloroethenylidene bis (4-chlorobenzene)
BHC: benzene hexachloride
DDT: 1,1'-(2,2,2-trichloroethylidene) bis (4-chlorobenzene)
TDE: 1,1'-(2,2-dichloroethylidene) bis (4-chlorobenzene)
HCB: hexachlorobenzene
PCB: polychlorinated biphenyl
CIPC: chlorprobam
PCA: pyrazon
PCP: pentachlorophenol
TCNB: tecnazene
PCNB: quintozene
DCPA: dimethyl 2,3,5,6-tetrachloro-1,4-benzenedicarboxylate
(M) = Mutagens: can cause genetic defects
(C) = Carcinogens: can cause cancer
(T) = Teratogens: can cause birth defects

Source: Manske and Johnson. "Pesticide and Other Chemical Residues in Total Diet Samples."

Lettuce

Scientific Name: Lactuca sativa
Place of Origin: Uncertain (perhaps Near East, Siberia, or the Mediterranean region)
Garden Varieties: Loosehead: "Oakleaf" (45–50 days); Romaine: "Paris White" (80–90 days); Looseleaf: "Butterhead" (75–80 days); Crisphead: "Great Lakes" (80–90 days).
Cultivation: Sow seed indoors to provide a continuous source of seedlings for garden transplanting. Best grown in cool weather or during summer under partial shade. Outer leaves of loosehead varieties may be collected gradually to extend harvest of single plant.

have an environmental cause. Even certain circulatory diseases may have an environmentally induced component, if recent studies on development of arteriosclerosis are any indication. So many of the toxic substances deliberately or accidentally introduced into the environment through human activities have been shown to be carcinogens (cancer-causing agents), that it is reasonable to assume many more will eventually be implicated. (But, lest you shrug your shoulders hopelessly and say that soon everything will be discovered to cause cancer, it is useful to realize that only 10 percent of the substances suspected of being carcinogens have actually been shown to cause cancer when tested, according to Dr. Samuel Epstein, from Chicago Medical Center, an authority in this field.)

Chemicals found to affect cell structure and processes may do so in ways that induce genetic abnormalities, including mutations and birth defects as well as cancer. Many scientists feel that evidence of any such cell damage, particularly if it involves DNA, should be considered a warning of all three possibilities. Basic cellular processes and reactions of all organisms—plant, animal, or bacteria—are very much alike. Mutagenic effects of chemicals can be discovered through relatively simple tests upon one-celled organisms or certain plant cells, although of course greater weight is attached to evidence of genetic damage in mammalian systems. It has been shown that any chemical that is mutagenic in certain bacterial tests is likely to be carcinogenic as well. By performing mutagen tests on the vast array of chemicals in our environment we could conceivably determine which need further testing. Very few pesticides have been tested adequately for any of these effects. The list in Table 7-2 is not complete, but gives representative examples. Where chemicals tested appear as residues in the Market-Basket survey, indicating the presence of the chemicals in U.S. diets, their range of

Table 7-2. **Pesticides Known to Be Carcinogens, Mutagens, and Teratogens, 1970**

Poison Used	Type of Compound	Dose Necessary to Kill 50-Percent of Test Animals (Rats; Mg/kg of Body Wt)	Range of Concentrations Found in Food Sampled (Parts per Million; Mg Poison/Kg Food)
Carcinogens:			
Aldrin	insecticide	6.7	0.001
Aminotriazole	herbicide	1100–2500	
Antu	rodenticide	(carcinogenic naphthylomines present as impurities)	
Aramite	acaricide	2000	
Arsenic	insecticide	20	0.03 –0.60
BHC	insecticide	600–1250	0.0004–0.0070
CDEC (sulfallate)	herbicide	850	
Chlordane	insecticide	457–590	
Chlorobenzilate	acaricide	916	
DDT	insecticide	113	0.0020–0.020
Diallate (avadex)	herbicide	395	
Dieldrin	insecticide	40–188	0.0006–0.0330
Ferbam	fungicide	17	
Griseofulvin	fungicide	non-toxic	
Heptachlor	insecticide	40-188	
Hydroxyethyl hydrozine	plant growth regulator, used as herbicide		

Table 7-2. **Pesticides Known to Be Carcinogens, Mutagens, and Teratogens, 1970 (Continued)**

Poison Used	Type of Compound	Dose Necessary to Kill 50-Percent of Test Animals (Rats; Mg/kg of Body Wt)	Range of Concentrations Found in Food Sampled (Parts per Million; Mg Poison/Kg Food)
Lindane	insecticide	88	0.0003–0.0120
Mancozeb	fungicide	8	
Maneb	fungicide	6750	
Mirex	insecticide	306 ± 71	
Nabam	fungicide	395	
PCNB (pentachloro-nitrobenzene)	fungicide	1200	0.0020–0.005
IPC (propham)	herbicide	5	
SMDC (vapam)	fungicide, nematocide, and herbicide	820	
Thiram	fungicide	375–865	
Zineb	fungicide	5200	
Ziram	fungicide	1400	
Mutagens:			
Acrilonitrile	insect fumigant	90	
Alanap		8400	
Aramite	acaricide	2000	
Atrazine	herbicide	3080	
Captan	fungicide	9000	
Carbaryl (sevin)	insecticide	800	0.05 –0.050
Chloroform	insect fumigant		
2,4-D	herbicide	370–1200	
DDT	insecticide	113	0.002 –0.020
Dichloran (botran)	fungicide	1500–4000	0.006 –0.067
Dichlorvos (DDVP)	insecticide with fumigant action	80	
Dicamba (banvel)	herbicide	290–800	
Endothall	herbicide	51	
Ethylmercuric chloride	fungicide	(chronic exposure has caused brain damage)	
Ferbam	fungicide	17	
Isocil	herbicide	3400	
Lindane	insecticide	88	0.0003–0.0120
Linuron (lorox)	herbicide	4000	
Maleic hydrazide	plant growth regulator, herbicide	6950	
Monuron	herbicide	3600	
Parathion	insecticide	13	0.003 –0.022
Pentachlorophenol	insecticide		
Phosphamidon	insecticide	28.3	
Potassium cyanide (KOCN)		841 (mice)	
Propham (IPC)	herbicide	5	
Teratogens:			
bidrin (dicrotophos)	acaricide, insecticide	16.5–22	
Captan	fungicide	9000	0.178
Carbaryl (sevin)	insecticide	800	0.05 –0.50
2,4-D	herbicide		
Diazinon	insecticide	66–600	0.0007–0. –270
Falpet		10	
Guthion (azinphos methyl)	acaricide, insecticide	16.4	
Mercurials	fungicides		
Parathion	insecticide	13	0.003 –0.022
PCNB	fungicide	1200	0.002 –0.005
Propham (IPC)	herbicide	5	
2,4,5-T	herbicide	500	
Trithion (carbophenothion)	acaricide, insecticide	32.2	

Carcinogen: causes cancer in the present generation
Mutagen: can affect many generations
Teratogen: causes birth defects in the next generation
Insecticide: used for killing insects
Acaricide: used for killing mites
Herbicide: used for killing plants
Fungicide: used for killing fungi
Rodenticide: used for killing rats
Nematocide: kills nematodes (roundworms)

Sources: Compiled by the Rachel Carson Trust using HCW, *Report of the Secretary's Commission on Pesticides;* Sutton and Harris, *Mutagenic Effects of Environmental Contaminants; Farm Chemical Handbook;* British Crop Protection Council, *Pesticide Manual,* and *Merck Index.*

concentrations is entered in the right-hand column. This list was compiled by the Rachel Carson Trust, a nonprofit organization that gathers research on human health and the environmental hazards of pesticides on a world-wide basis.

The fact that home gardeners have the opportunity to refrain from using pesticides in the garden is one of the great advantages in raising your own vegetables. Plants raised around the home will not necessarily have fewer insect and soil pests or suffer less competition from weeds than these same species grown commercially, although they may do better due to variety in planting and environmental differences. But on a small scale, these problems can be managed through a multitude of ingenious, often labor-intensive approaches that simply are not feasible when the ratio of area cultivated versus labor available is very large.

A Greater Variety of Vegetables: A first look at a good plant nursery catalogue (see Box 7-1 for a list of nurseries) may be quite a revelation to

Box 7-1. **Nurseries Featuring Vegetable Seeds**

Nichols Garden Nursery
1190 North Pacific Highway
Albany, OR 97321

Armstrong Nursery
Ontario, CA 91764

Omaha Plant Farms (25¢)
Route 7870G
Omaha, TX 75571

Breck's of Boston
200 Breck Boulevard
Boston, MA 02210

Burgess Seed & Plant Company
Galesburg, MI 49053

W. Atlee Burpee Company
Riverside, CA 92502

Burrell's Seeds
Rocky Ford, CO 81067

California Nursery Company
Niles, CA 94536

Johnny's Selected Seeds
N. Dixmont, ME 04932

Farmer Seed & Nursery Company
Faribault, MN 55021

Henry Field Seed &
Nursery Company
Shenandoah, IA 51601

Joseph Harris Company
Rochester, NY 14624

Ferndale Gardens
702 Nursery Lane
Faribault, MN 55021

Hemlock Hill Herb Farm
Litchfield, CT 06759

Inter-State Nurseries
14116 E. Street
Hamburg, IA 51640

J.W. Jung Seed Co.
Randolph, WI 53956

Royal Dutch Gardens
23 Walden Street
Dept. 408
Concord, MA 01742

Vermont Bean Seed Company
1 Way's Lane
Manchester, VT 05255

Henry Leuthardt Nurseries
E. Moriches
Long Island, NY 11940

J.L. Hudson Seed Company
Box 1058
Redwood City, CA 94064

Stribling's Nurseries
Box 793
Merced, CA 95340

Thompson & Morgan Inc.
c/o Box 24
401 Kennedy Boulevard
Somerdale, NJ 08083

Gurney Seeds
1148F Page Street
Yankton, SD 57078

Tsang & Ma International
P.O. Box 294
Belmont, CA 94002

Stark's Bros. Nursery
Louisiana, MO 63353

R.H. Shumway Seedsman
628 Cedar Street
Rockford, IL 61101

Geo. W. Park Seed Co.
Box 31
Greenwood, SC 29646

John Oster
L.L. Olds Seed Company
Box 1069
Madison, WI 53701

N.Y. State Fruit
Testing Coop Association
Geneva, NY 14456

Mellinger's
2310 W. South Range Rd.
North Lima, OH 45801

Van Bourgondien Brothers
Box A
245 Farmingdale Road
Pte. 109
Babylon, NY 11702

Stokes Seeds Inc.
Box 548
Main Post Office
Buffalo, NY 14240

Worldwide Herbs Ltd.
11 St. Catherine Street E
Montreal, 129 Ontario
Canada

De Giorgi Company, Inc.
Council Bluffs, IA 51501

Lakeland Nursery Sale
Hanover, PA 17331

Clyde Robin Seed Company
P.O. Box 2855
Castro Valley, CA 94546

Wapumne Native Plant
Nursery Company
8305 Cedar Crest Way
Sacramento, CA 95826

people used to getting all their vegetables at the corner store. Many more kinds of vegetables are available as seeds than will ever find their way to the grocery shelves. Some varieties, such as fava beans, chayote, and Jerusalem artichokes, are not popular enough to make growing and stocking them regularly economically worthwhile (except in certain areas where specific ethnic foods are in demand); and others do not ship or store well. In addition, for every two or three common varieties found in the store the seed catalogues sometimes make available three or four times that many. (In a recent national catalogue, thirty-nine varieties of tomatoes were counted. An Asian seed catalogue offered eight varieties of Chinese cabbage.) It is the great diversity in the choice of vegetable seeds to plant that enhances one's diet from a nutritional standpoint and one's garden from a cultural and aesthetic standpoint. Currently, a national organization is forming to test unexplored and unusual plant species and varieties. If you are interested in learning more about this subject, write to Paul Jackson, Box 599, Lynwood, California 90262. For information on the international research being done, write the Henry Doubleday Research Institute, Convent Lane, Braintree, Essex, England.

A few tomato varieties have been bred for the traits so desirable in the harvest operations described earlier: thick skins that permit rough handling during harvesting and shipping, uniform size and shape, ability to turn a ripe color after being picked unripe and stored for various lengths of time, and the likelihood of producing its main crop all in synchrony. These qualities are desirable when produce is to be harvested by machine. Commercial varieties will often be distinguished in the catalogues by such a term as "market" or "main crop." But the many other varieties of the same vegetable can provide good taste and nutritional value just not available through commercial channels. When the ethnic-specialty seed catalogues are taken into consideration, the variety of home-grown vegetables available compared with commercially obtainable ones is very great indeed.

Recreation and Self-Reliance: Two other advantages of raising one's own food are primarily psychological. For many people, the contact with living plants and the soil is pleasurable and relaxing. Pride in producing something to sustain oneself is interwoven with an increased sense of self-reliance—an important aspect of what the integral urban house is all about. The pleasure derived by many from gardening is available even to apartment dwellers who have only a windowsill or the corner of the room for raising plants. The recent growth of the house-plant industry in the United States indicates a new appreciation of the fact that plants in the home improve the livability of the urban environment.

Disadvantages: The most obvious disadvantages of raising one's own vegetables, or even of supporting a modest indoor plant collection, are the time and effort required. Many people are loathe even to give it a try because of the work they assume gardening will take. Often childhood drudgery, doing chores on the farm, or helping out in large family gardens accounts for the distaste. Sometimes aversion is due to some previous attempts

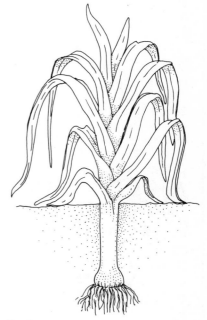

Leek

Scientific Name: Allium ampeloprasum
Place of Origin: Eastern Mediterranean or the Near East
Garden Varieties: "Broad London" (130 days).
Cultivation: Planted by seedling throughout the year where winters are mild. To produce high-quality leeks it is necessary to blanch the lower part of the plant by planting the seedlings in trenches or furrows and drawing up the soil around the maturing bulb to exclude light.

which, because of ignorance regarding the basic requirements of plants, indoors or out, ended in disaster. "Never again. I just don't have a green thumb." In other cases, reluctant gardeners are just extremely busy, urban people who can't figure out how to squeeze the activity into an already overcrowded life. For this reason in this book we have focused on methods that take as little time as possible and that are particularly suited to the schedules of urban people.

Further, we strongly emphasize the importance of starting small. A too-ambitious beginning can dampen the enthusiasm of even the most determined beginning gardener. When you are new to an activity you may take twice as long to accomplish your goals as when you are experienced.

One answer to the complaint of boredom and the sense of drudgery that may stem from a memory of endless farm chores is that an integral urban house system provides endless diversity in the work to be done. There are so many different tasks that the variety helps residents to enjoy the work. There is no denying, however, that harvesting and preparing fresh garden vegetables for cooking is more time-consuming than wielding a can opener or opening a package of frozen food. Though we are extremely busy ourselves, we have solved this problem either by taking time at intervals to prepare big stews or similar dishes that can be reheated on the run or, at the other extreme, by preparing Chinese stir-fried dishes that can be put together from garden odds and ends in a few moments. We decided generally that the flavor and nutrition of fresh vegetables is worth the time.

A final consideration is the problem of urban contaminants, primarily lead, that may coat the exposed portions of vegetables grown in these areas. This problem is likely to be far worse in the front of the house, along busy streets. In any case, lead contamination should be regarded as a community health problem and is covered in some detail in Chapter 14, on the interface of the integral urban house and the community.

Variables to Consider in Planning the Garden

How much can the integral urban house vegetable-growing efforts be expected to contribute to the residents' diet? This is a question of both productivity and nutrition. When working with plants, the determining factors are having enough *space* with (1) a growing medium containing nutrients required for plant growth, (2) light for photosynthesis, and (3) a temperature and humidity range tolerated by plants to be raised.

In addition, prospective gardeners must ask themselves how much time they can spend on the activity. Some high yields, very well-publicized and supposedly the result of certain gardening techniques and formulae, may actually have been achieved only by very high inputs of human labor. Unlimited amounts of time and effort can obtain equal yields using almost any methods. The challenge is to achieve a reasonable productivity *without* having to spend so much time in gardening; otherwise the time required is greater than that average working people can spare to integrate this component into their lives.

The final consideration, in addition to those of light, space, and time, is the problem of diet. The nutrition question involves two factors: *quantity*, or

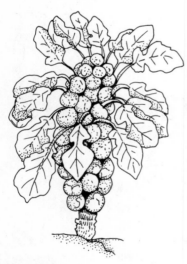

Brussels Sprouts

Scientific Name: Brassica oleracea
Place of Origin: Southern England, Wales, and the Adriatic Coast
Garden Varieties: "Jane Cross Hybrid" (90 days); "Long Island Improved" (100 days).
Cultivation: Seedlings are transplanted into the garden in early June for fall harvest. Do not plant on soil where members of the cabbage family grew the year before.

amount of food calories, and *quality*—that is, the proportions of necessary protein, fats, carbohydrates, vitamins, and minerals that can be supplied by the garden.

Light: Some light with the approximate spectrum of sunlight is necessary for the growth of all vegetable foods except mushrooms. (A discussion of light for indoor plants is discussed on page 223.) Finding a bit of space outside with adequate sunlight may be the biggest problem the would-be urban food gardener has to face.

Painting fences, house walls, and other structures white may help to reflect light into shady corners. However, because of the proximity of other buildings and/or shade trees, many urban food gardeners may be forced to use sunny areas where no usable soil is available. Compost, made by the closed-bin method described in Chapter 6, can be used as a growing medium in such areas, in homebuilt or scavenged containers adapted to sit upon cement driveways and parking areas, rooftops, porches, and so on.

When you become interested in growing plants, the position of the sun at different times of the day and year becomes important, just as it does when you build a structure that will be heated and cooled by the sun's energy. You must study the placement of the plants in relation to the sun's position as it moves across the sky. The same is true within the garden itself. Tall plants such as corn and Jerusalem artichokes, and staked vegetables such as tomatoes, beans, peas, cucumbers, and other squashes, must be placed along the north edge of the plot where they will not shade small plants behind them. Lettuce, radishes, beets, carrots, and other low vegetables should be planted to the south.

As a general rule, those plants from which you eat the leaves tolerate the most shade. Examples are lettuce, chard, spinach, mustard, collards, kale, and coriander. Where summer temperatures are high and light intensities are great because of low humidity, these greens are best grown in the open in spring and fall. To produce them during the summer months, filtered light, such as may be found under trees or a constructed lath-house, may be necessary.

Where neither outdoor nor indoor space is available around the house or apartment, we recommend that instead of using artificial lights you either find an acquaintance who will share a backyard with you or search out or start a community garden within walking distance of your house. Many communities have sunny vacant lots, parks, institutional grounds, as well as unused private backyards (which for one reason or another residents are not using for food production but which they may be willing to share in exchange for surplus vegetables or just garden maintenance). Some of these can be turned into food-producing areas through a little united action by community residents. Such efforts have now been initiated in many cities throughout the United States. See our suggestions on community gardens in Chapter 15.

Using Space Intensively: Once space with sufficient sunlight has been located, it is important to use it wisely. Few urban gardeners have as much area as they would like; therefore, they have to adopt various intensive

Spinach

Scientific Name: Spinacea oleracea
Place of origin: Uncertain
Garden Varieties: "Bloomsdale Long-Standing" (48 days); "Winter Bloomsdale" (45 days).
Cultivation: Sow seed or transplant seedlings in early spring for harvest before the heat of summer. For later sowing select varieties that resist bolting. For early spring use where winters are mild, sow in early fall, and mulch with a few inches of straw.

Bush Beans

Scientific Name: Phaseolus species
Place of Origin: South America
Garden Varieties: "Royal Purple" (51 days); "Golden Wax" (50 days); "Pinto" (85 days).
Cultivation: Sow seed directly into soil. Bush varieties are best for the interior of the garden. Choose shell bush beans for late season harvest. Beans make a good rotational crop with corn or cabbage.

155

methods of using the space they do have. For example, use a minimum of area in pathways. Planting in rows, as recommended by the typical USDA pamphlet, was designed to accommodate a horse or a tractor passing through the field for purposes of cultivating out the weeds and harvesting. Planting in beds is more appropriate for gardens where human labor is employed exclusively. Community gardens will require somewhat more concession to traffic than a private one, but in all cases leave as little ground-space as possible uncovered by plants. Seedlings should be spaced closely enough together so that when mature the leaves of the plants just touch. In general, high inputs of nutrients through large amounts of compost will permit this type of planting without decreasing yields through competition. But soil and types of plants vary, and the ideal placement for the varieties you choose will be best learned through experience. All growing vegetables prefer full, unobstructed sunlight. However, some plants are more tolerant of shade than others. Table 7-3 will help you place your vegetable plants in the garden depending upon the amount of light that falls upon a specific area.

Table 7-3. **Relative Light Requirements for Vegetable Plants**

Requires Maximum Light	Slightly Tolerant of Shade	Moderately Tolerant of Shade
Tomatoes	Cabbage	Lettuce, endive
Corn	Broccoli	Endive
Squash	Kale	Spinach
Peppers	Collard greens	Sorrell
Cucumbers	Beets	Mint
Beans	Turnips	Herbs
Eggplant	Radishes	
	Onions	
	Carrots	

Records that monitor the relative growth of vegetables with respect to how far apart the individual plants are spaced are useful in formulating garden management plans. See Table 7-4 for spacing requirements of common vegetables.

Starting seedlings indoors on windowsills or in greenhouses and cold-frames can save garden space wherever season length permits planting more than one crop. Well-started plants can be set in where others have been harvested, thus, waiting for the second crop to begin from seed in the newly vacated ground will be eliminated. Interplanting fast-growing plants such as radishes, turnips, mustard, and loose-leaf lettuce between cabbages and squashes, which mature more slowly, is another way of making efficient use of small spaces. Space is saved by training sprawling, vinelike plants up on trellises and fences or along the sides of homes, rather than letting them spread out over the ground.

Particularly useful to the urban gardener with limited space are those vegetables that naturally climb, can be repeatedly harvested from the same plant, or have been purposely bred for compactness. For example, climbing beans yield more beans in a given space than bush beans do. Loose-leaf lettuce can be harvested repeatedly; just take off the outer leaves and let the

Cucumber

Scientific Name: Cucumis sativus
Place of Origin: Southern Asia
Garden Varieties: "Lemon" (65 days), for salads; "Sunny Brook" (60 days), for slicing; "Burpee Pickler" (53 days), for pickling; "Jampanes climbing."
Cultivation: Warm season crop sown directly into soil. Plant several varieties to provide for various uses. Use bush varieties in the middle of the garden and climbing varieties along the perimeter fence.

plant continue producing for several weeks beyond the initial time of maturity. Another example is "sprouting broccoli." Characteristically unique from the single-headed broccoli grown for commercial productions, "sprouting broccoli" produces lateral heads after the primary head is cut. Although successive heads grow smaller, they will produce more food in the same space that season than if you pull out the whole plant and start over with a new one of the "heading" variety.

Since the choice of varieties of vegetables that will do well in your yard is dependent upon local soil and weather conditions the best guides for plant selection are your neighbors' gardens—where you can learn what is most successful in your area—and seed catalogues, which give information on the seeds they offer.

Temperature, Humidity, and Wind: Active plant growth is usually confined to a temperature range of 50 to 104°F (10 to 40°C). Temperature influences all aspects of plant germination, growth, flowering, and fruiting. Beyond making that observation, it is extremely difficult to generalize, since plants vary enormously in the temperature extremes that they will tolerate. Furthermore, the same plant may favor different temperatures at different stages of its growth. Sometimes night temperatures may be the crucial ones. Tomatoes, for example, set fruit when the days are warm but the nights cool:

Table 7-4. **Optimal Distance Between Plants in Beds**

Plants	Beds
Artichoke	36''
Asparagus	12''
Beans, broad	8''
Beans, bush	4''
Beans, lima bush	6''
Beans, lima pole	8''
Beans, pole	6''
Beets	3''
Broccoli	12''/15''
Brussels sprouts	18''
Cabbage	12''/15''
Cantaloupe	12''/18''
Carrots	1''/2''
Cauliflower	12''/15''
Celery	6''
Chard	8''
Chinese cabbage	10''
Chives	12''
Collards	12''
Corn	12''/18''
Cress	3''
Cucumbers	12''
Dandelion	3''
Eggplant	18''
Endive	8''
Garlic	2''/3''
Horseradish	12''
Jerusalem artichoke	15''
Kale	15''
Kohlrabi	4''
Leeks	3''
Lettuce, head	12''
Lettuce, leaf	8''
Mustard	6''
Okra	12''
Onions	2''/3''
Parsley	4''
Parsnips	3''
Peas, bush	3''
Peas, pole	4''
Peppers	12''
Potatoes	12''
Pumpkin	30''
Radishes	1''
Rhubarb	24''
Rutabagas	6''
Salsify	2''
Scallions	1''
Shallots	6''
Spinach	2''
Squash, summer	12''/18''
Squash, winter	30''
Tomatoes	24''
Turnips	3''
Watermelon	18''/24''

Note: Beds may be three to six feet wide and as long as desired.

Source: Adapted from USDA *Agricultural Statistics, 1972.*

Table 7-5. **Cool-Season and Warm-Season Crops**

Vegetable crops can be divided roughly into two broad groups. The cool-season vegetables are those of which the vegetative parts—roots, stems, leaves, and buds or immature flower parts—are eaten. There are two exceptions to this rule that are warm-season crops—sweet potato (root used) and New Zealand spinach (leaf and stem used). Those vegetables of which the immature or mature fruits are eaten are warm-season crops. Pea and broad bean are exceptions, being cool-season crops.

Cool-season crops generally differ from warm-season crops in the following respects:
1. They are hardy or frost tolerant.
2. Seeds germinate at cooler soil temperatures.
3. Root systems are shallower.
4. Plant size is smaller.
5. They respond more to nitrogen.
6. More attention must be paid to irrigation—usually plants must be irrigated more frequently.
7. Some, the biennials, are susceptible to premature seed stalk development from exposure to prolonged cool weather.
8. They are stored at close to 32°F., except the white potato. Sweet corn is the only warm-season crop held at 32°F. after harvest.
9. Harvested product is not subject to chilling injury at temperatures between 32 and 50°F. as is the case with some of the warm-season vegetables.

*Cool-Season Vegetables**

Artichoke	Carrot	Corn salad	Jerusalem	Parsley	Scorzonera
Asparagus	Cauliflower	Cress, garden	artichoke	Parsnip	Sea kale
Bean, broad	Celery	and upland	Kale	Pea	Shallot
Beet	Celeriac	Dandelion	Kohlrabi	Potato	Sorrel
Broccoli	Chard, Swiss	Endive	Leek	Radish	Spinach
Brussels	Chicory	Florence fennel	Lettuce	Rhubarb	Spinach dock
sprouts	Chinese cabbage	Garlic	Mustard	Rutabaga	Turnip
Cabbage	Chive	Horse-radish	Onion	Salsify	Watercress
Cardoon	Collard		Pak-choi	Scolymus	

Warm-Season Vegetables†

Bean	Cowpea	Martynia	Okra	Soybean	Tomato
Bean lima	(Southern pea)	Muskmelon	Pepper	Summer	Watermelon
Chayote	Cucumber	New Zealand	Pumpkin	squash	Winter
Corn	Eggplant	spinach	Roselle	Sweet potato	squash

*Minimum daily average temperature 50°F., maximum daily average temperature 85°F.

†Minimum daily average temperature 75°F., maximum daily average temperature 115°F.

59 to 64.4°F (15 to 18°C), while potatoes require night temperatures of 50 to 59°F (10 to 15°C) to form tubers. (See Table 7-5 on temperature requirements of different plants.) For other plants, variation between night and day is not as crucial. With melons, hotter temperatures mean increasing sweetness, and melon growers count degree-days to determine when they should harvest (see page 68 on calculating degree-days).

The heat energy available to plants comes either directly from the sun or by radiation from the earth or other surfaces the sun has warmed. A large part of the heat absorbed by a plant is reradiated from the plant surface. The remainder is transferred out of the leaf in the water vapor that is passed out through the stoma. (Stoma are openings in the leaf surface through which respiration takes place; see Figure 7-2.) This loss of water vapor, important in cooling the plant, is dependent on the amount of humidity in the air surrounding the leaf. The drier the air, the more water the leaf will transpire, and that in turn is partially a function of how much wind passes over the leaf, blowing the most humid air away.

Although every species has its preferred range of temperature, sudden changes in temperature at either extreme are the most damaging. Thus, sprinkling cold water on the hot leaves of plants under direct midday summer sunlight can easily cause sunscald or death of those cells where the temperature change is experienced in its extreme. The symptoms will be spot-

Figure 7-2. **The Structure of a Leaf, Showing Position of Stoma**

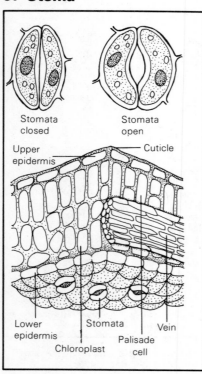

Figure 7-3. **Small Greenhouse and Cold Frame Designs**

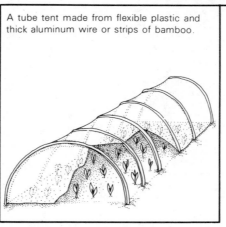

A tube tent made from flexible plastic and thick aluminum wire or strips of bamboo.

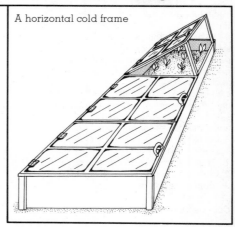

A horizontal cold frame

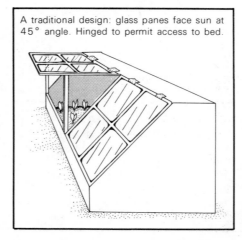

A traditional design: glass panes face sun at 45° angle. Hinged to permit access to bed.

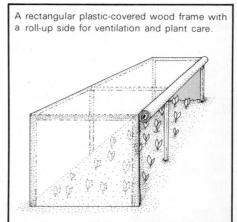

A rectangular plastic-covered wood frame with a roll-up side for ventilation and plant care.

ting on the leaves.

Particularly critical are sudden cold spells or frosts when plants are in an active growing state. This is the reason for withholding heavy pruning and nitrogen fertilization of shrubs and trees as the autumn approaches. It is essential that they "harden off" (prepare for a drop in air temperature) and not be caught with fresh young growing branchlets.

Frosts experienced during the growing season are often referred to as radiation frosts. They are likely to occur when there is no cloud cover to reflect back towards the earth the heat stored there during the day and radiated skyward at night. In areas where such frosts occur, any kind of removable roof—on at night and off during the day—that reflects this earth-stored heat back to the tender plants, rather than letting it radiate away to outer space, will prevent damage. Cardboard boxes, for example, can protect plants very nicely, as long as they are large enough so that the leaves of the plant do not touch the top and sides. If tender plants are in movable containers, they can be set under trees or under porch roofs or eaves for the night.

In the northern central states and in mountain areas where the days are sunny, the air is dry, and the nights often cloudless, radiation frosts can occur at almost any time during the growing season. The best method of dealing with this problem in places where frosts occur frequently is to use greenhouses in which containers of water store the heat while the sun is shining. This heat is then lost slowly during the night, preventing damage by low temperatures. Next best is to construct low frames of plastic, glass, or fly-screening over plant beds in the garden. If a frost is expected, the frames can be covered over with burlap, cardboard or even straw or hay.

In the northern states where the late spring frosts may be a problem, a wide variety of ingenious cold frames can be constructed. On extra cold nights, the beds can be covered as described above. Examples of such structures are shown in Figure 7-3.

The theory behind the design in all of these structures is that the sun's heat will build up inside as in a greenhouse, because the heat rays generated inside will pass less easily back through the glass or plastic than the light rays that came through originally. However, care must be taken to permit adequate ventilation, since as a part of their metabolic activities (including cooling) the plants will be transpiring water. If the humidity is allowed to build up, fungus and other diseases may become a problem.

Some general guides on first and last frosts and suggested planting dates for various vegetables are shown in Figures 7-4 and 7-5 and Tables 7-6 and 7-7. This material must be taken as generalization only, however, since local topography will have particular requirements. For example, proximity to large bodies of water will have a moderating influence; the water functions as a large heat-storage facility absorbing heat by day and reradiating it to the surrounding areas by night. Higher altitudes and more northern latitudes generally mean a decrease in temperature. But on the minitopographical level the higher altitudes may be warmer, since cold air is heavy and flows downhill, so narrow valleys and smaller depressions may contain pockets of cold air. Thus, hillsides may be preferable to the valley areas below for growing tender plants.

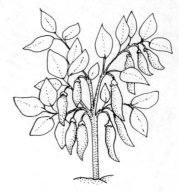

Red Pepper (Perennial)

Scientific Name: Capsicum frutescens
Place of Origin: West Indies
Garden Varieties: "Hungarian Wax" (65 days); "Long Red Cayenne" (72 days).
Cultivation: Cultivation is the same as for sweet varieties (see below). Plants will perenniate for several seasons if protected by shelter from winter cold.

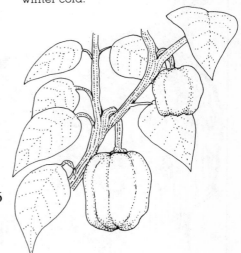

Sweet Pepper (Annual)

Scientific Name: Capsicum annum
Place of Origin: Central America
Garden Varieties: "California Wonder" (75 days).
Cultivation: Seeds are best sown indoors 8 to 10 weeks before outdoor planting in the spring. Very warm weather is required for high yield.

Figure 7-4. **Average Dates of the Last Killing Spring Frosts, 1899 to 1938**

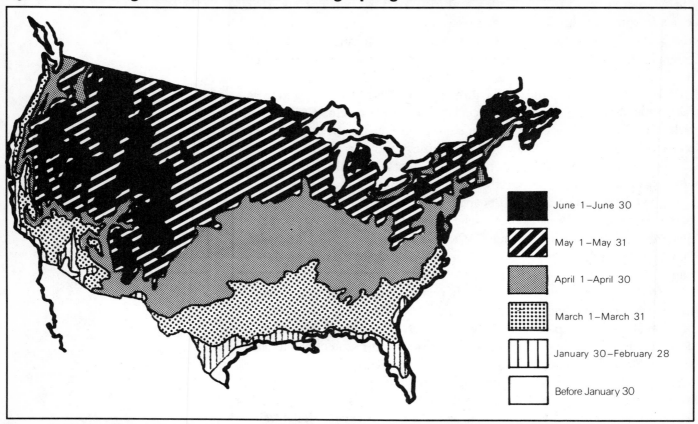

June 1–June 30

May 1–May 31

April 1–April 30

March 1–March 31

January 30–February 28

Before January 30

Figure 7-5. **Average Dates of the First Killing Fall Frosts, 1899 to 1938**

Source: USDA, *Suburban & Farm Vegetable Gardens.*

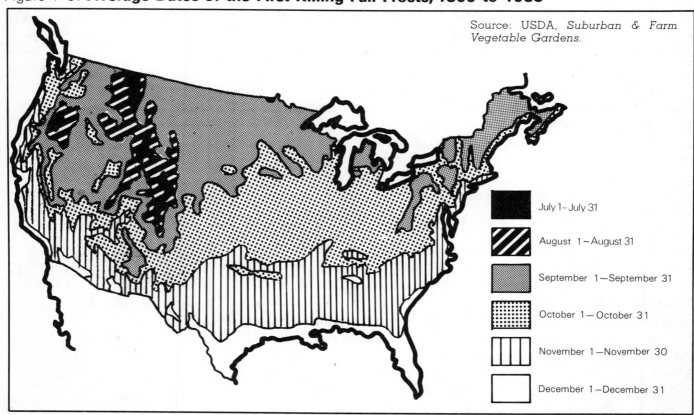

July 1– July 31

August 1–August 31

September 1—September 31

October 1— October 31

November 1—November 30

December 1—December 31

Hedges, walls, and other windbreaks can be designed to direct the flow of cold air away from the garden or the house, as well as to reduce the cooling and drying winds that blow across it. In general, to have a useful windbreak effect a structure should be about 30 to 50 percent permeable. A too-solid barrier frequently creates intolerable turbulence on the lee side. Windbreaks will give effective protection for eight to twelve times their height on the lee side, and for two to five times their height on the windward side. For example, an eight-foot hedge of vegetation will provide good wind protection for sixty-four to ninety-six feet behind it, and sixteen to forty feet in front.

Many plants have adapted to cold winter climates so well that they require a certain period of prior chilling before spring germination of seeds and/or proper plant growth can take place. Fruit trees, such as apples, apricots, and peaches require these low temperatures and will not do well in areas that are not cold for a sufficient length of time. Since the microclimates of all regions vary greatly, useful guides in the selection of varieties (particularly with respect to fruit trees and other perennials that require a substantial investment on the part of the landscaper) are local agricultural extension offices, university agronomy departments, garden clubs, and commercial nurseries. Best of all are close neighbors who have successful gardens and can give you cuttings or vegetative parts of plants that do well under conditions similar or identical to the ones around your own house.

The most satisfactory long-term solution of all for annual garden vegetables is to save the seeds year by year of those nonhybrid plants that do well in your own locality. Although the weather fluctuates from year to year, over a period of time you can develop strains of vegetables that are likely to be superior for growth in your area to those you might buy.

Urban dwellers tend to become insensitive to the microclimate variations of their habitat in a way that farmers can never afford to do. When you begin to raise some of your own plants, particularly when these plants are to produce food that will sustain you, you become aware of your outdoor living

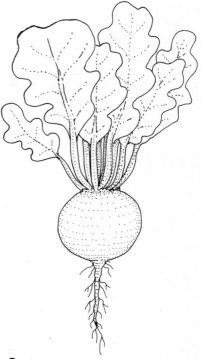

Beet

Scientific: Beta vulgaris
Place of Origin: Uncertain
Garden Varieties: "Red Ball" (60 days); "Golden Beet" (55 days).
Cultivation: Sow directly into garden in early spring. Stagger planting for a continuous supply through summer. May be grown during the winter in the South and Pacific Southwest.

Table 7-6. **Planting Times and Weather Requirements**

Cold-Hardy Plants for Early-Spring Planting		Cold-Tender or Heat-Hardy Plants for Late-Spring or Early-Summer Planting			Hardy Plants for Late-Summer or Fall Planting except in the North (*plant 6 to 8 weeks before first fall freeze*)
Very hardy (*plant 4 to 6 weeks before frost-free date*)	Hardy (*plant 2 to 4 weeks before frost-free date*)	Not cold-hardy (*plant on frost-free date*)	Requiring hot weather (*plant 1 week or more after frost-free date*)	Medium heat-tolerant (*good for summer planting*)	
Broccoli	Beets	Beans, snap	Beans, lima	Beans, all	Beets
Cabbage	Carrot	Okra	Eggplant	Chard	Collard
Lettuce	Chard	New Zealand spinach	Peppers	Soybean	Kale
Onions	Mustard	Soybean	Sweetpotato	New Zealand spinach	Lettuce
Peas	Parsnip	Squash	Cucumber	Squash	Mustard
Potato	Radish	Sweet corn	Melons	Sweet corn	Spinach
Spinach		Tomato			Turnip
Turnip					

Source: USDA, "Suburban and Farm Vegetable Gardens."

spaces in a new way. How the sunlight and shade move and the winds blow are once again significant. Small, warm, protected areas are cherished. It becomes a challenge to make productive use of cool, shady, or otherwise "waste" spaces. Compost bins and dry-leaf storage areas may fit with the rabbits on the north side. A mat for sunbathing can share a windbreak in the corner of a sunny balcony with containers of tomatoes. Because of the small scale involved, you will discover a great many ingenious methods for modifying temperature, humidity, and wind that would require far too much labor and too many materials for the farmer.

With the physical variables of light, space, and climate attended to, the more subjective considerations must come into play as one plans a food-

Table 7-7. **Dates for Spring Planting in the Open**

Planting Dates for Localities in Which Average Date of Last Freeze Is—

Crop	Jan. 30	Feb. 8	Feb. 18	Feb. 28	Mar. 10	Mar. 20	Mar. 30
Asparagus					Jan. 1–Mar. 1	Feb. 1–Mar. 10	Feb. 15–Mar. 20.
Beans, lima	Feb. 1–Apr. 15	Feb. 10–May 1	Mar. 1–May 1	Mar. 15–June 1	Mar. 20–June 1	Apr. 1–June 15	Apr. 15–June 20.
Beans, snap	Feb. 1–Apr. 1	Feb. 1–May 1	do	Mar. 10–May 15	Mar. 15–May 15	Mar. 15–May 25	Apr. 1–June 1.
Beet	Jan. 1–Mar. 15	Jan. 10–Mar. 15	Jan. 20–Apr. 1	Feb. 1–Apr. 15	Feb. 15–June 1	Feb. 15–May 15	Mar. 1–June 1.
Broccoli, sprouting	Jan. 1–30	Jan. 1–30	Jan. 15–Feb. 15	Feb. 1–Mar. 1	Feb. 15–Mar. 15	Feb. 15–Mar. 15	Mar. 1–20.
Brussels sprouts	do	do	do	do	do	do	do
Cabbage	Jan. 1–15	Jan. 1–Feb. 10	Jan. 1–Feb. 25	Jan. 15–Feb. 25	Jan. 25–Mar. 1	Feb. 1–Mar. 1	Feb. 15–Mar. 10.
Cabbage, Chinese							
Carrot	Jan. 1–Mar. 1	Jan. 1–Mar. 1	Jan. 15–Mar. 1	Feb. 1–Mar. 1	Feb. 10–Mar. 15	Feb. 15–Mar. 20	Mar. 1–Apr. 10.
Cauliflower	Jan. 1–Feb. 1	Jan. 1–Feb. 1	Jan. 10–Feb. 10	Jan. 20–Feb. 20	Feb. 1–Mar. 1	Feb. 10–Mar. 10	Feb. 20–Mar. 20.
Celery and celeriac	do	Jan. 10–Feb. 10	Jan. 20–Feb. 20	Feb. 1–Mar. 1	Feb. 20–Mar. 20	Mar. 1–Apr. 1	Mar. 15–Apr. 15.
Chard	Jan. 1–Apr. 1	Jan. 10–Apr. 1	Jan. 20–Apr. 15	Feb. 1–May 1	Feb. 15–May 15	Feb. 20–May 15	Mar. 1–May 25.
Chervil and chives	Jan. 1–Feb. 1	Jan. 1–Feb. 1	Jan. 1–Feb. 1	Jan. 15–Feb. 15	Feb. 1–Mar. 1	Feb. 10–Mar. 10	Feb. 15–Mar. 15.
Chicory, witloof					June 1–July 1	June 1–July 1	June 1–July 1.
Collards	Jan. 1–Feb. 15	Jan. 1–Feb. 15	Jan. 1–Mar. 15	Jan. 15–Mar. 15	Feb. 1–Apr. 1	Feb. 15–May 1	Mar. 1–June 1.
Cornsalad	do	do	do	Jan. 1–Mar. 1	Jan. 1–Mar. 15	Jan. 1–Mar. 15	Jan. 15–Mar. 15.
Corn, sweet	Feb. 1–Mar. 15	Feb. 10–Apr. 1	Feb. 20–Apr. 15	Mar. 1–Apr. 15	Mar. 10–Apr. 15	Mar. 15–May 1	Mar. 25–May 15.
Cress, upland	Jan. 1–Feb. 1	Jan. 1–Feb. 1	Jan. 15–Feb. 15	Feb. 1–Mar. 1	Feb. 10–Mar. 15	Feb. 20–Mar. 15	Mar. 1–Apr. 1.
Cucumber	Feb. 15–Mar. 15	Feb. 15–Apr. 1	Feb. 15–Apr. 15	Mar. 1–Apr. 15	Mar. 15–Apr. 15	Apr. 1–May 1	Apr. 10–May 15.
Dandelion	Jan. 1–Feb. 1	Jan. 1–Feb. 1	Jan. 15–Feb. 15	Jan. 15–Mar. 1	Feb. 1–Mar. 1	Feb. 10–Mar. 10	Feb. 20–Mar. 20.
Eggplant	Feb. 1–Mar. 1	Feb. 10–Mar. 15	Feb. 20–Apr. 1	Mar. 10–Apr. 15	Mar. 15–Apr. 15	Apr. 1–May 1	Apr. 15–May 15.
Endive	Jan. 1–Mar. 1	Jan. 1–Mar. 1	Jan. 15–Mar. 1	Feb. 1–Mar. 1	Feb. 15–Mar. 15	Mar. 1–Apr. 1	Mar. 10–Apr. 10.
Fennel, Florence	do	do	do	do	do	do	do
Garlic						Feb. 1–Mar. 1	Feb. 10–Mar. 10.
Horseradish							Mar. 1–Apr. 1.
Kale	Jan. 1–Feb. 1	Jan. 10–Feb. 1	Jan. 20–Feb. 10	Feb. 1–20	Feb. 10–Mar. 1	Feb. 20–Mar. 10	Mar. 1–20.
Kohlrabi	do	do	do	do	do	do	Mar. 1–Apr. 1.
Leek	do	Jan. 1–Feb. 1	Jan. 1–Feb. 15	Jan. 15–Feb. 15	Jan. 25–Mar. 1	Feb. 1–Mar. 1	Feb. 15–Mar. 15.
Lettuce, head	do	do	Jan. 1–Feb. 1	do	Feb. 1–20	Feb. 15–Mar. 10	Mar. 1–20.
Lettuce, leaf	do	do	Jan. 1–Mar. 15	Jan. 1–Mar. 15	Jan. 15–Apr. 1	Feb. 1–Apr. 1	Feb. 15–Apr. 15.
Muskmelon	Feb. 15–Mar. 15	Feb. 15–Apr. 1	Feb. 15–Apr. 15	Mar. 1–Apr. 15	Mar. 15–Apr. 15	Apr. 1–May 1	Apr. 10–May 15.
Mustard	Jan. 1–Mar. 1	Jan. 1–Mar. 1	Feb. 1–Mar. 1	Feb. 1–Mar. 1	Feb. 10–Mar. 15	Feb. 20–Apr. 1	Mar. 1–Apr. 15.
Okra	Feb. 15–Apr. 1	Feb. 15–Apr. 15	Mar. 1–June 1	Mar. 10–June 1	Mar. 20–June 1	Apr. 1–June 15	Apr. 10–June 15.
Onion	Jan. 1–15	Jan. 1–15	Jan. 1–15	Jan. 1–Feb. 1	Jan. 15–Feb. 15	Feb. 10–Mar. 10	Feb. 15–Mar. 15.
Onion, seed	do	do	do	Jan. 1–Feb. 15	Feb. 1–Mar. 1	do	Feb. 20–Mar. 15.
Onion, sets	do	do	do	Jan. 1–Mar. 1	Jan. 15–Mar. 10	Feb. 1–Mar. 20	Feb. 15–Mar. 20.
Parsley	Jan. 1–30	Jan. 1–30	Jan. 1–30	Jan. 15–Mar. 1	Feb. 1–Mar. 10	Feb. 15–Mar. 15	Mar. 1–Apr. 1.
Parsnip		Jan. 1–Feb. 1	Jan. 15–Feb. 15	Jan. 15–Mar. 1	Feb. 15–Mar. 1	do	do
Peas, garden	Jan. 1–Feb. 15	Jan. 1–Feb. 15	Jan. 1–Mar. 1	Jan. 15–Mar. 1	Jan. 15–Mar. 15	Feb. 1–Mar. 15	Feb. 10–Mar. 20.
Peas, black-eye	Feb. 15–May 1	Feb. 15–May 15	Mar. 1–June 15	Mar. 10–June 20	Mar. 15–July 1	Apr. 1–July 1	Apr. 15–July 1.
Pepper	Feb. 1–Apr. 1	Feb. 15–Apr. 15	Mar. 1–May 1	Mar. 15–May 1	Apr. 1–June 1	Apr. 10–June 1	Apr. 15–June 1.
Potato	Jan. 1–Feb. 15	Jan. 1–Feb. 15	Jan. 15–Mar. 1	Jan. 15–Mar. 1	Feb. 1–Mar. 1	Feb. 10–Mar. 15	Feb. 20–Mar. 20.
Radish	Jan. 1–Apr. 1	Jan. 1–Apr. 1	Jan. 1–Apr. 1	Jan. 1–Apr. 1	Jan. 1–Apr. 15	Jan. 20–May 1	Feb. 15–May 1.
Rhubarb							
Rutabaga				Jan. 1–Feb. 1	Jan. 15–Feb. 15	Jan. 15–Mar. 1	Feb. 1–Mar. 1.
Salsify	Jan. 1–Feb. 1	Jan. 10–Feb. 10	Jan. 15–Feb. 20	Jan. 15–Mar. 1	Feb. 1–Mar. 1	Feb. 15–Mar. 1	Mar. 1–15.
Shallot	do	Jan. 10–Feb. 10	Jan. 1–Feb. 20	Jan. 1–Mar. 1	Feb. 1–Mar. 1	Feb. 10–Mar. 10	Feb. 15–Mar. 15.
Sorrel	Jan. 1–Mar. 1	Jan. 1–Mar. 1	Jan. 15–Mar. 1	Feb. 1–Mar. 10	Feb. 10–Mar. 15	Feb. 10–Mar. 20	Feb. 20–Mar. 1.
Soybean	Mar. 1–June 30	Mar. 1–June 30	Mar. 10–June 30	Mar. 20–June 30	Apr. 10–June 30	Apr. 10–June 30	Apr. 20–June 30.
Spinach	Jan. 1–Feb. 15	Jan. 1–Feb. 15	Jan. 1–Mar. 1	Jan. 1–Mar. 1	Jan. 15–Mar. 10	Jan. 15–Mar. 15	Feb. 1–Mar. 20.
Spinach, New Zealand	Feb. 1–Apr. 15	Feb. 15–Apr. 15	Mar. 1–Apr. 15	Mar. 15–May 15	Mar. 20–May 15	Apr. 1–May 15	Apr. 10–June 1.
Squash, summer	do	do	do	do	Mar. 15–May 1	do	do
Sweetpotato	Feb. 15–May 15	Mar. 1–May 15	Mar. 20–June 1	Mar. 20–June 1	Apr. 1–June 1	Apr. 10–June 1	Apr. 20–June 1.
Tomato	Feb. 1–Apr. 1	Feb. 20–Apr. 10	Mar. 1–Apr. 20	Mar. 10–May 1	Mar. 20–May 10	Apr. 1–May 20	Apr. 10–June 1.
Turnip	Jan. 1–Mar. 1	Jan. 1–Mar. 1	Jan. 10–Mar. 1	Jan. 20–Mar. 1	Feb. 1–Mar. 1	Feb. 10–Mar. 10	Feb. 20–Mar. 20.
Watermelon	Feb. 15–Mar. 15	Feb. 15–Apr. 1	Feb. 15–Apr. 15	Mar. 1–Apr. 15	Mar. 15–Apr. 15	Apr. 1–May 1	Apr. 10–May 15.

raising program. A key element is *time,* one of the most limiting constraints for an urban person.

How Much Time Will It Take?   One of the ideas behind the integral urban house is that food production, organic-waste management, and energy and resource conservation are all easier, less time-consuming, and more attractive than in a traditional home where these systems are not designed into the flow of daily life. Since we are assuming that the residents will be following more or less urban lifestyles, it is taken for granted that they will be earning all or the major portion of their cash income outside the home. The challenge of incorporating some home-scale food production into the normal

Source: USDA, *Suburban & Farm Vegetable Gardens.*

Crop	Planting Dates for Localities in Which Average Date of Last Freeze Is—						
	Apr. 10	Apr. 20	Apr. 30	May 10	May 20	May 30	June 10
Asparagus	Mar. 10–Apr. 10	Mar. 15–Apr. 15	Mar. 20–Apr. 15	Apr. 10–Apr. 30	Apr. 20–May 15	May 1–June 1	May 15–June 1.
Beans, lima	Apr. 1–June 30	May 1–June 20	May 15–June 15	May 25–June 15			
Beans, snap	Apr. 10–June 30	Apr 25–June 30	May 10–June 30	May 10–June 30	May 15–June 30	May 25–June 15	
Beet	Mar. 10–June 1	Mar. 20–June 1	Apr. 1–June 15	Apr. 15–June 15	Apr. 25–June 15	May 1–June 15	May 15–June 15.
Broccoli, sprouting	Mar. 15–Apr. 15	Mar. 25–Apr. 20	Apr. 1–May 1	Apr. 15–June 1	May 1–June 15	May 10–June 10	May 20–June 10.
Brussels sprouts	do	do	do	do	do	do	do
Cabbage	Mar. 1–Apr. 1	Mar. 1–Apr. 1	Mar. 15–Apr. 10	Apr. 1–May 15	do	May 10–June 15	May 20–June 10.
Cabbage, Chinese				do	do	do	do
Carrot	Mar. 10–Apr. 20	Apr. 1–May 15	Apr. 10–June 1	Apr. 20–June 15	May 1–June 1	May 10–June 1	do
Cauliflower	Mar. 1–Mar. 20	Mar. 15–Apr. 20	Apr. 10–May 10	Apr. 15–May 15	May 10–June 15	May 20–June 1	June 1–June 15.
Celery and celeriac	Apr. 1–Apr. 20	Apr. 10–May 1	Apr. 15–May 1	Apr. 20–June 15	do	do	do
Chard	Mar. 15–June 15	Apr. 1–June 15	Apr. 15–June 15	do	do	do	do
Chervil and chives	Mar. 1–Apr. 1	Mar. 10–Apr. 10	Mar. 20–Apr. 20	Apr. 1–May 1	Apr. 15–May 15	May 1–June 1	May 15–June 1.
Chicory, witloof	June 10–July 1	June 15–July 1	June 15–July 1	June 1–20	June 1–15	June 1–15	June 1–15
Collards	Mar. 1–June 1	Mar. 10–June 1	Apr. 1–June 1	Apr. 15–June 1	May 1–June 1	May 10–June 1	May 20–June 1.
Cornsalad	Feb. 1–Apr. 1	Feb. 15–Apr. 15	Mar. 1–May 1	Apr. 1–June 1	Apr. 15–June 1	May 1–June 15	May 15–June 15.
Corn, sweet	Apr. 10–June 1	Apr. 25–June 15	May 10–June 15	May 10–June 15	May 15–June 1	May 20–June 1	
Cress, upland	Mar. 10–Apr. 15	Mar. 20–May 1	Apr. 10–May 10	Apr. 20–May 20	May 1–June 1	May 15–June 1	May 15–June 15.
Cucumber	Apr. 20–June 1	May 1–June 15	May 15–June 15	May 20–June 15	June 1–15		
Dandelion	Mar. 1–Apr. 1	Mar. 10–Apr. 10	Mar. 20–Apr. 20	Apr. 1–May 1	Apr. 15–May 15	May 1–30	May 1–30.
Eggplant	May 1–June 1	May 10–June 1	May 15–June 10	May 20–June 15	June 1–15		
Endive	Mar. 15–Apr. 15	Mar. 25–Apr. 15	Apr. 1–May 1	Apr. 15–May 15	May 1–30	May 1–30	May 15–June 1.
Fennel, Florence	do	do	do	do	do	do	do
Garlic	Feb. 20–Mar. 20	Mar. 10–Apr. 1	Mar. 15–Apr. 15	Apr. 1–May 1	Apr. 15–May 15	do	do
Horseradish	Mar. 10–Apr. 10	Mar. 20–Apr. 20	Apr. 1–30	Apr. 15–May 15	Apr. 20–May 20	do	do
Kale	Mar. 10–Apr. 1	Mar. 20–Apr. 10	Apr. 1–20	Apr. 10–May 1	Apr. 20–May 10	do	do
Kohlrabi	Mar. 10–Apr. 10	Mar. 20–May 1	Apr. 1–May 10	Apr. 10–May 15	Apr. 20–May 20	do	do
Leek	Mar. 1–Apr. 1	Mar. 15–Apr. 15	Apr. 1–May 1	Apr. 15–May 15	May 1–May 20	May 1–15	May 1–15
Lettuce, head	Mar. 10–Apr. 1	Mar. 20–Apr. 15	do	do	May 1–June 30	May 10–June 30	May 20–June 30
Lettuce, leaf	Mar. 15–May 15	Mar. 20–May 15	Apr. 1–June 1	Apr. 15–June 15	do	do	do
Muskmelon	Apr. 20–June 1	May 1–June 15	May 15–June 15	June 1–June 15			
Mustard	Mar. 10–Apr. 20	Mar. 20–May 1	Apr. 1–May 10	Apr. 15–June 1	June 1–20	May 10–June 30	May 20–June 30.
Okra	Apr. 20–June 15	May 1–June 1	May 10–June 1	May 20–June 10	June 1–20		
Onion	Mar. 1–Apr. 1	Mar. 15–Apr. 10	Apr. 1–May 1	Apr. 10–May 1	Apr. 20–May 15	May 1–30	May 10–June 10.
Onion, seed	do	Mar. 15–Apr. 1	Mar. 15–Apr. 15	Apr. 1–May 1	do	do	do
Onion, sets	do	Mar. 10–Apr. 1	Mar. 10–Apr. 10	Apr. 10–May 1	do	do	do
Parsley	Mar. 10–Apr. 10	Mar. 20–Apr. 20	Apr. 1–May 1	Apr. 15–May 15	May 1–20	May 10–June 1	May 20–June 10.
Parsnip	do	do	do	do	do	do	do
Peas, garden	Feb. 20–Mar. 20	Mar. 10–Apr. 10	Mar. 20–May 1	Apr. 1–May 15	Apr. 15–June 1	May 1–June 15	May 10–June 15.
Peas, black-eye	May 1–July 1	May 10–June 15	May 15–June 1				
Pepper	May 1–June 1	May 10–June 1	May 15–June 10	May 20–June 10	May 25–June 15	June 1–15	
Potato	Mar. 10–Apr. 1	Mar. 15–Apr. 10	Mar. 20–May 10	Apr. 1–June 1	Apr. 15–June 15	May 1–June 15	May 15–June 1.
Radish	Mar. 1–May 1	Mar. 10–May 10	do	do	Apr. 15–May 10	May 1–20	do
Rhubarb	Mar. 1–Apr. 1	Mar. 10–Apr. 1					do
Rutabaga		May 1–June 1	May 1–June 1	May 1–20	May 10–20	May 20–June 1.	
Salsify	Mar. 10–Apr. 15	Mar. 20–May 1	Apr. 1–May 15	Apr. 15–June 1	May 1–June 1	May 10–June 1	do
Shallot	Mar. 1–Apr. 1	Mar. 15–Apr. 15	Apr. 1–May 1	Apr. 10–May 1	Apr. 20–May 10	May 1–June 1	May 10–June 1.
Sorrel	Mar. 1–Apr. 1	Mar. 15–May 1	Apr. 1–May 15	Apr. 15–June 1	May 1–June 1	May 10–June 10	May 20–June 10.
Soybean	May 1–June 30	May 10–June 20	May 15–June 15	May 25–June 10			
Spinach	Feb. 15–Apr. 1	Mar. 1–Apr. 15	Mar. 20–Apr. 20	Apr. 1–June 15	Apr. 10–June 15	Apr. 20–June 15	May 1–June 15.
Spinach, New Zealand	Apr. 20–June 1	May 1–June 15	May 1–June 15	May 10–June 15	May 20–June 15	June 1–15	
Squash, summer	do	do	May 1–30	May 10–June 10	do	June 1–20	June 10–20.
Sweetpotato	May 1–June 1	May 10–June 10	May 20–June 10				
Tomato	Apr. 20–June 1	May 5–June 10	May 10–June 15	May 15–June 10	May 25–June 15	June 5–20	June 15–30.
Turnip	Mar. 1–Apr. 1	Mar. 10–Apr. 1	Mar. 20–May 1	Apr. 1–June 1	Apr. 15–June 1	May 1–June 15	May 15–June 15.
Watermelon	Apr. 20–June 1	May 1–June 15	May 15–June 15	June 1–June 15	June 15–July 1		

Rhubarb

Scientific Name: Rheum rhaponticum
Place of Origin: Siberia
Garden Varieties: "Victoria"; "Mac-Donald."
Cultivation: Rhubarb may be propagated by seed or root division. Plant seedlings or root divisions in early spring. Seeds will produce a crop in two years; root will produce crop one year after plants are divided. Eat the stems, *not* the leaves.

Broccoli

Scientific Name: Brassica oleracea
Place of Origin: Southern England
Garden Varieties: "Green Comet" (55 days); "De Cicco" (60 days); "Italian Green Sprouting" (65 days).
Cultivation: Transplant seedlings in early spring for first crop and in late midsummer for fall crop. Many varieties produce lateral buds when main head is cut.

work schedule is one we think can be met by overall design and planning of the systems and the adoption or invention of time-saving techniques.

A great time saver in the garden is the planting of seedlings rather than seeds outdoors. Traditionally, certain vegetables have been considered difficult to transplant: beans, carrots, beets, and peas, for example. However, if these vegetables are raised indoors in containers open at both ends, as described on page 175, the transplanting shock will be minimal, since the roots hardly need be disturbed at all. We have successfully transplanted every common garden vegetable after raising them indoors in the manner recommended. However, some plants, such as corn and carrots, are best started outdoors simply because of the numbers of plants that are normally used. Seeds that are planted in the ground directly can be soaked overnight first to speed germination. If the seeds are tiny, as with carrots, they may be mixed with sand for easy, even sowing.

Where vegetable gardening is popular, seedlings of common food plants and herbs are often available in plant nurseries around the time they are usually set into the ground locally. The advantage of buying these started plants is that you may obtain varieties that are known to do well in your area. However, this advantage is offset by the fact the variety selection is extremely limited. So, in general, we advise starting your own seedlings when you can, and starting them indoors to avoid problems of keeping the seedbed moist and fending off insects and other wildlife during the first critical weeks.

Another important time-saver is keeping the ground covered with a thick mulch of organic materials to whatever extent you can. Mulch keeps down weeds and by maintaining a friable ground-surface makes it easy to pull out those that might get a root hold (see the discussion of weeds in Chapter 12). Mulch can be of many materials, both organic and inorganic. Best are those that will gradually decompose and provide plant nutrients—hay and straw (although these may have much grass seed in them), dried leaves and, most important, compost. Newspapers have been used in many areas, but they may cause problems in places where snails and slugs lay eggs beneath them. (Snails often lay eggs under boards lying on the earth also.) Furthermore, as mentioned in the previous chapter, the inks of newspapers may contain heavy metals and PCBs, and these should be kept out of the garden.

Sawdust makes an excellent mulch in pathways where no plant growth is desired. Because of its high carbon content, nitrogen will be taken from the top inches of the soil by the decomposer organisms where sawdust is placed, retarding weed growth; thus the sawdust acts as a natural herbicide. However, sawdust should not be used as a mulch on the beds close to the shallow-rooted plants unless it has been composted first, because there the decomposer bacteria will rob the plants of the nitrogen they need. This phenomenon is further explained in Chapter 8.

When summer irrigation is necessary, designing your system to reduce hand-watering is another important time-saving strategy. Where overhead watering is preferred, this can be handled by setting up sprinklers on timers to cover the entire area at regular intervals for the period necessary to deliver the amount of water needed. Plants in containers can be linked up to a drip-watering system, which also can be attached to a timer and fully automated, saving both time and water. Management of the water in the garden is intimately linked to an appreciation for soil texture and structure; for this reason, it is discussed in the next chapter, following an introduction to some of the characteristics of soils.

Another time-saver for mild-winter areas is letting certain vegetables seed themselves in. The many seedlings that pop up in the spring can then be thinned out as if they were weeds. At the Berkeley house we have done this with *nonhybrid* carrots, parsley, coriander, upland cress, New Zealand spinach, chard, onions, fava, beans and leeks. The seeds blow about (lettuce), or the plant topples over (chard, leeks), and eventually, seedlings emerge wherever the seeds landed on the mulch. These can then be transplanted or used for food to thin them out. "Nonhybrid" is stressed here because hybrid plants produce seeds with the various characteristics of their mixed parentage, and thus may not result in the kind of plant you desire.

A caution about methods that save time: you may find that environmentally safe techniques take more time than those in vogue in the larger society. Managing wildlife by nonpesticide means is a perfect example. One of the appeals of pesticides is that they appear, at least at first, to take care of things quickly. Any method substituted will probably take more time and attention in the short-run. Eventually, however, by establishing a better balance of natural controls in the garden, nonpesticide methods may reduce the overall time that needs to be spent in pest management (see Chapter 13).

Globe Artichoke

Scientific Name: Cynara scolymus
Place of Origin: Mediterranean region
Cultivation: Common varieties must be propagated from suckers, which are cut off from base of parent plant, in early spring and planted in their permanent position. New plants often produce heads in their first year and continue to do so for four years.

Table 7-8. **Daily Dietary Allowances to Maintain Good Nutrition**

	Age (years)	Weight (kg.)	Weight (lbs.)	Height (cm.)	Height (in.)	kcal.	Protein (gm.)	Vitamin A Activity§ (I.U.)	Vitamin D (I.U.)	Vitamin E Activity (I.U.)
Infants	0–1/6	4	9	55	22	kg. × 120	kg. × 2.2	1500	400	5
	1/6–1/2	7	15	63	25	kg. × 110	kg. × 2.0	1500	400	5
	1/2–1	9	20	72	28	kg. × 100	kg. × 1.8	1500	400	5
Children	1–2	12	26	81	32	1.100	25	2000	400	10
	2–3	14	31	91	36	1.250	25	2000	400	10
	3–4	16	35	100	39	1.400	30	2500	400	10
	4–6	19	42	110	43	1.600	30	2500	400	10
	6–8	23	51	121	48	2.000	35	3500	400	15
	8–10	28	62	131	52	2.200	40	3500	400	15
Males	10–12	35	77	140	55	2.500	45	4500	400	20
	12–14	43	95	151	59	2.700	50	5000	400	20
	14–18	59	130	170	67	3.000	60	5000	400	25
	18–22	67	147	175	69	2.800	60	5000	400	30
	22–35	70	154	175	69	2.800	65	5000	—	30
	35–55	70	154	173	68	2.600	65	5000	—	30
	55–75+	70	154	171	67	2.400	65	5000	—	30
Females	10–12	35	77	142	56	2.250	50	4500	400	20
	12–14	44	97	154	61	2.300	50	5000	400	20
	14–16	52	114	157	62	2.400	55	5000	400	25
	16–18	54	119	160	63	2.300	55	5000	400	25
	18–22	58	128	163	64	2.000	55	5000	400	25
	22–35	58	128	163	64	2.000	55	5000	—	25
	35–55	58	128	160	63	1.850	55	5000	—	25
	55–75+	58	128	157	62	1.700	55	5000	—	25
Pregnancy						+200	65	6000	400	30
Lactation						+1.000	75	8000	400	30

Food and Nutrition Board: Recommended dietary allowances, ed. 7, Publication No. 1694, Washington, D.C. revised 1968, National Academy of Sciences–National Research Council.

The allowance levels are intended to cover individual variations among most normal persons as they live in the United States under usual environmental stresses. The recommended allowances can be attained with a variety of common foods, providing other nutrients for which human requirements have been less well defined.

Entries on lines for age range 22–35 years represent the reference man and woman at 22 years of age. All other entries represent allowances for the midpoint of the specified age range.

§ I.U. is an abbreviation for International Units.

Source: Guthrie, *Introductory Nutrition.*

Human Nutrition

In addition to the constraints of space, light, and time, nutrition must be considered in relation to how much of the diet can be supplied by the home vegetable garden. "How much" of one's diet, is a deceptively simple inquiry, since the answer must include not just the quantity of food (calories) that can be produced, but also the quality of nutrition those calories offer. What is a nutritionally good diet?

We live in a society that produces food for profit rather than for good nutrition, as Lappé and Collins have ably pointed out in their book, *Food First*. Adequate nutrition is generally described as that providing the recommended daily allowances (see Table 7-8). However, using this as a standard for good or excellent nutrition leaves much to be desired. We ourselves have come to the conclusion that a nutritionally good diet is one that keeps the individual healthy. Our ideal is an active, enjoyable living pattern that is socially constructive. This includes freedom from pain and misery due to disease. So, a good life includes an excellent diet, for diet is directly related to modern death and disease patterns.

Table 7-9 shows the changes in life expectancy in the United States between 1900 and 1968. For the infant life expectancy in 1968 was much better by about ten years, but for those forty-five or older there has been relatively little change. Thus, the overall average life expectancy has increased, but this is largely attributable to changes in life expectancy of early childhood.

In Chapter 1 (Table 1-1) we saw how the causes of death in overall mortality patterns have shifted toward the degenerative diseases: heart disease, stroke, and cancer. Forty-nine percent of all deaths in 1970 were related to cardiovascular difficulties. Study over the last twenty years has still not resolved the question about the role of fats in hardening of the arteries (atherosclerosis). The subject is controversial, but many researchers seem to feel that restriction of dietary cholesterol is extremely important in preventing this disease. Other factors besides nutrition are also involved (see Box 7-2), but nutritional factors are very significant. Eggs contain the highest source of cholesterol although they are one of the best sources of amino-acid

Carrot

Scientific Name: Daucus carota
Place of Origin: Southern Europe
Garden Varieties: "Chantenay Red-Cored" (70 days); "Nantes Half-Long" (70 days).
Cultivation: Sow seeds in spring for main harvest in summer and again in late summer for winter use. Short varieties are used for gardens with heavy or shallow soils.

Table 7-9. **Expectation of Life-Span in America, 1900–1968**

(Expressed as number of additional years to live, at a certain age)

Males

At Age:	1900	1930	1957	1968
0	46.3	58	66.3	66.6
45	25.6	————	27.5	25.8
65	11.5	11.7	12.6	12.8

Females

At Age:	1900	1930	1957	1968
0	48.3	61.6	72.5	74.0
45	31.7	————	36.8	32.5
65	12.2	12.8	15.3	16.3

balanced protein, and they also contain lecithin. Thus, a controversy exists over the importance of limiting egg intake as well.

Sodium is a factor about which there is agreement among nutritionists: Excesses of sodium chloride (salt) are related to hypertension (high blood pressure), which in turn is a key risk factor in various vascular pathologies such as heart disease. Methods of reducing sodium consumption include eating foods that have potassium as a substitute for sodium, such as potassium chloride salt substitute. Vegetables and fruits as a group of foods are low in sodium, as Table 7-10 indicates. Potassium can substitute in part for sodium in the body.

Researchers have had success in lowering blood pressure and generally alleviating cardiovascular problems by lowering total fat intake. One such approach to selection of foods with which the authors have had some favorable first-hand experience is outlined in Leonard, Hofer, and Pritikin, *Live*

Box 7-2. **An Atherosclerosis Prevention Plan**

1. **Adjust total caloric supply.** The energy derived from the food ingested should not exceed the body's needs. Overweight people will need to reduce their caloric intake below the maintenance level in order to make this readjustment.

2. **Reduce total dietary fat** to no more than 30 percent of the total caloric intake. Total fat intake is related to coronary death rates: the greater the fat intake, the greater risk of death from heart disease. If you are overweight, you may want to restrict fat intake further.

3. **Reduce saturated fatty acid intake** to no more than 10 percent of total calories, with a commensurate increase in unsaturated fatty acids.* In practice, the elimination of highly saturated animal fats, lard, butter, high-fat cheeses, highly hydrogenated (through an artificial saturation process) oils and shortening, high-fat meat, cream, is recommended. Increasing the intake of warm-water fish, lean meat, skim meat, skim milk, soft margarines, cot-

tage cheese, and olive and seed oil (excluding palm and coconut oil, which are rich in saturated fats), will reduce saturated-fat, as well as total fat, intake.

4. **Restrict dietary cholesterol.** Cholesterol intake should be less than 300 milligrams per day, excluding foods such as egg yolks, which are high in cholesterol. A one-quarter pound hamburger (about 100 grams) has about 70 milligrams of cholesterol.

5. **Limit simple-sugar and alcohol intake.** Substitute with complex carbohydrate present in cereals and vegetables.

6. **Maintain protein intake** in required ranges (see Table 7-8), with a balance between animal and vegetable proteins, along with an assured intake of vitamins and minerals.

7. **Limit salt (sodium chloride) intake** to less than 5 grams per day.

8. **Tend to distribute daily food intake** over as many meals as possible.

9. **Maintain adequate physical activity.**

10. **Increase consumption of unrefined foods** such as fruits, vegetables, potatoes, lean meat, and lean fish.

*Fatty acids are straight-chain carbon compounds, usually with even numbers of carbon atoms and a methyl group (—CH₃) and a carboxyl group (—COOH) at opposite ends of the chain. The general formula for any fatty acid is

$$CH_3 - (CH_2)_n - COOH$$

where n can be any even number from 2 to 25. With saturated fatty acids, each carbon has two attached hydrogen atoms. In monosaturated fatty acids, two adjacent carbons will each lack a hydrogen atom. Since each carbon atom has an unattached bond, they attach to each other, and the linkage is called a "double bond", written —C=C—. If double bonds occur in two or more places, the fatty acid is called a polyunsaturated fatty acid.

Source: Adapted from Angelico and Sonogy, "Prevention of Atherosclerosis by Diet," and from recommendations of the American Heart Association and Italian nutritional scientists.

Table 7-10. **Some Foods with Excessively High Levels of Sodium**

Food	Sodium Content (Mg/100 Gms Food)
Baby foods (all foods except fruit)	200–600
Canadian bacon, cooked, broiled, fried, and drained	2,555
Baking powders (home use) (contains sodium aluminum sulfate)	10,000
Bouillon cubes or powder	24,000
Caviar	2,200
Cheese, pasteurized process spread American	1,625
Cod, dehydrated, lightly salted	8,100
Cornflakes	1,005
Cornmeal, self-rising	1,380
Mustard, prepared	1,307
Olives, pickled, canned, bottled	2,400
Pickles, dill	1,428
Pretzels	1,628
Renin tablet	22,300
Salad dressing, Italian	2,092
Salt, table	38,758
Soy sauce	7,325
Beef	60
Vegetables	1–125

Source: USDA, *Composition of Foods, Agriculture Handbook.*

Source: Mount, *The Food and Health of Western Man.*

Longer Now. Fortunately, the vegetables that are the most efficient home-grown crops have very little fat. Notice in Table 7-11 that some insects are low in fat but relatively high in protein. Bee larvae appear to be particularly rich in Vitamins A and D.

Proportionally, increased vegetable intake can help reduce the risks of cardiovascular disease. Home-raised vegetables can also reduce the intake of toxicants, since small-scale food production methods can enable one to avoid or reduce the use of pesticides. Vegetables and whole grains also contribute fiber to the diet, another factor that has been correlated with lowering blood-fat levels and reducing risk of cancer of the intestine. Last but not least, the most highly appreciated contribution vegetables make to the diet are the vitamins and minerals they offer, see Box 7-3. You can be most confident that you are getting the benefit of these when you eat the vegetables as close as possible to the fresh raw state, or, when cooking them, make use of any liquid into which those nutrients may have leached.

If one begins to depend more on vegetables and less on meat to provide the essential nutrients the body needs, is it still possible to obtain enough

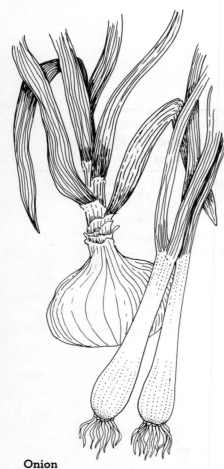

Onion

Scientific Name: Allium cepa
Place of Origin: Egypt
Garden Varieties: Bunching: "White Lisbon" (60 days); Red: "Red Bermuda" (110 days); Yellow: "Ebenezer" (95 days); Sweet Spanish: "Yellow Utah" (110 days).
Cultivation: May be planted by seed, seedling, or set. Sets are the most dependable method of propagation but also the most expensive, also, if not planted at proper time of year they will bolt early. Once bulbs are mature bend tops over to hasten ripening before harvest.

Source: Adapted from Taylor, *Butterflies in My Stomach.*

Table 7-11. **Nutrient Characteristics of Meat, Fish, Dairy Products & Insects***

Organism	Kilocalories	Percent Water	Percent Protein	Percent Fat	Percent Carbohydrates	Units of Vitamin A	Mg Vitamin B_1	Mg Vitamin B_2	Mg Niacin	Units of Vitamin D
Beef (retail, raw)	263	60	18	20	0	40	0.08	0.16	4.4	——
Pork (composite of cuts, raw)	311	56	16	27	0	——	0.76	0.18	4.1	—
Chicken (all classes, raw)	124	74	22	3.3	0	105	0.07	0.15	8.0	
Fish (lake trout, raw)	168	71	18	10	0	——	——	——	——	——
(halibut, raw)	100	77	21	1.2	0	440	0.09	0.12	2.7	——
Milk (whole)	66	87	3.5	3.7	4.9	150	0.07	0.07	8.3	41
Eggs (chicken, raw, whole)	163	74	13	12	0.9	1180	0.11	0.30	0.1	——
Bees (mature larvae of *Apis, mellifera*	——	77	15	3.7	0.4	10,500	——	——	——	700,000
Houseflies (pupae of *Musca domestica*)	265	3.9	63	16.0	——	——	——	——	——	——
Silkworm (*Bombyx mori*—pupae)	207	61.0	23.0	14.0	——	ample	——	——	——	——
Termite (living, unnamed)	347	45	23.0	28	——	——	——	——	——	——
Grasshoppers (Dried, mixed species)	——	5	63	14	11.0	——	——	1.75	7.5	——
(Living, mixed species	——	41	62	6	7.2	——	——	——	——	——

*Per 100 grams of tissue.

protein? The best discussion of this topic of which we are aware is found in *Diet for a Small Planet,* by Frances Moore Lappé. She points out that there are eight amino acids (amino acids are the so-called building blocks of proteins) that our bodies cannot make and must get from our food. Furthermore, all eight must be present at the same time and in a certain proportion. The proportion in which they are used is most closely approximated by a chicken egg, and so the proteins in other foods can be rated against the egg.

Since grains, nuts, and vegetables all vary in their proportions of these essential amino acids, it becomes a challenge to mix and match these foods so that the weaknesses of one are complemented by the strengths of the others. Traditional cultures discovered how to use foods in this way through thousands of years of trial and error, and many ethnic cuisines, if followed faithfully, offer excellent examples of ingredients balanced to achieve the greatest amounts of usable protein.

However, once you become familiar with the amino acid configuration of the common foods you like to eat, it is relatively easy to improvise endless original combinations, and the genius of Lappé's book is that it starts you off on doing just that. If you become interested in reducing your meat input for whatever reason, we highly recommend that you use her book as a guide.

This has been a relatively simple discussion of the food quality issue as it relates to garden-produced food. For more detail on nutrition and diet, see the books listed as sources for this discussion in the bibliography at the end of this chapter.

Selecting Food Plants to Grow

Climate will be the dominating influence in your choice of which plants to grow. For example, peanuts thrive in hot and humid weather, so they would

Table 7-12. **Comparative Cost of Protein and Calories for Selected Foods**

Product	Kcal per 100 Gm	Percent Protein	Percent Fat	Cost per Lb*	Cost per 100 Gm Protein	Cost per 1000 Kcal
Meat						
Beef—medium hamburger	268	17.9	21.2	.89	1.10	.73
Beef—porterhouse choice	390	14.8	36.2	2.29	3.41	1.29
Ham—medium fat	308	15.9	26.6	1.99	2.75	1.42
Chicken—fryer, flesh only	107	19.3	2.7	.65	.74	1.33
Turkey—flesh only	162	24.0	6.6	.69	.63	.94
Lamb—choice grade loin	293	16.3	24.8	2.69	3.73	3.66
Rabbit—domestic	162	21.	8.	1.79	7.87	2.43
Fish						
Trout—rainbow	195	21.5	11.4	2.79	2.92	3.15
Scallop—bay sea, muscle only	81	15.3	.2	3.98	5.72	10.82
Butterfish—northern, flesh only	169	18.1	10.2	1.25	1.52	1.62
Salmon—Chinook, flesh only	222	19.1	15.6	3.39	3.90	3.36
Tuna—water and solid	127	28.0	.0	2.26	1.77	3.91
Tuna—oil, drained solids	197	28.8	8.2	1.85	1.41	2.06

Growing Food in Urban Areas

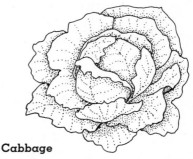

Cabbage

Scientific Name: Brassica oleracea
Place of Origin: Southern England, Wales, and the Adriatic Coast
Garden Varieties: Early: "Early Jersey Wakefield" (63 days); Midseason: "Copenhagen Market" (72 Days); Late fall or winter: "Late Flat Dutch" (105 days); Savoyed (wrinkled or curly leaved) "Savoy King" (90 Days).
Cultivation: Abundant varieties allow a full spectrum of types and planting dates to choose from. Mild climates can support year-round production of cabbage. Sow seeds in greenhouses six weeks before outdoor planting.

Tomato

Scientific Name: Lycopersicon esculentum
Place of Origin: South America
Garden Varieties: Fresh Use: "VF Hybrid" (72 days); Cherry: "Tiny Tim" (52 days); Paste: "Plum" (76 days).
Cultivation: Sown in greenhouse six to eight weeks before garden planting. Choose VF varieties for soils that have a history of disease. Paste varieties have meaty interiors, which are good for sauces. Cherry tomatoes are suitable for early spring greenhouse production.

Table 7-12. **(Continued)**

Product	Kcal per 100 Gm	Percent Protein	Percent Fat	Cost per Lb*	Cost per 100 Gm Protein	Cost per 1000 Kcal
Dairy Products						
Whole milk	65	3.5	3.5	.17	1.06	.57
Buttermilk—from skim milk	35	3.6	.1	.18	1.10	1.10
Swiss cheese	370	27.5	28.0	1.89	1.50	1.15
Cottage cheese, creamed—large or small	106	13.6	4.2	.67	1.09	1.38
Eggs	163	12.9	11.15	.42	.72	.57
Yogurt—plain, whole milk	62	3.0	3.4	.50	3.67	1.77
Vegetables						
Lettuce—romaine	18	1.3	.3	.25	4.23	3.05
Broccoli—cooked spears	32	3.6	.3	.39	2.38	2.68
Beets (raw)	43	.6	.1	.49	18.00	2.50
Potatoes (baked)	93	2.1	.1	.10	1.04	.23
Chard (cooked)	18	1.8	.2	.40	4.90	4.89
Spinach (cooked)	26	3.2	.3	.40	2.75	3.38
Carrots (raw)	42	1.1	.2	.29	5.80	1.52
Onions (boiled)	38	1.5	.1	.29	4.25	1.68
Sweet corn (cooked)	83	3.2	.1	.15	1.03	.40
Squash (summer)	14	.9	.1	.15	3.30	2.35
Tomatoes (raw)	22	1.1	.2	.39	7.80	3.90
Cabbage (raw)	24	1.3	12	.25	4.23	2.30
Green beans	32	1.9	12	.69	8.00	4.75
Avocado	167	21	16.4	.65	6.81	.85
Jerusalem artichokes	(7–75)‡	2.3	.1	.80	7.66	highly variable
Grains						
Wheat flour	333	13.3	2.0	.14	.23	.09
Barley (raw)	349	3.2	1.0	.39	1.04	.25
Soybeans (raw)	403	34.1	17.7	.59	.38	.32
Rice, brown	363	6.7	.4	.33	1.08	.20
Corn meal	355	9.2	3.9	.32	.76	.20
Lentils (raw)	340	24.7	1.1	1.05	.93	.68
Split dry peas (raw)	348	24.2	1.0	.60	.54	.38
Nuts						
Peanuts (raw)	564	26.0	47.5	1.60	1.35	.62
Cashews	561	17.2	45.7	2.79–5.00	3.57–6.40	1.09–1.96
Almonds	593	18.6	54.2	2.60	3.07	.95
White beans	340	22.3	1.6	.64	.63	.41
Pinto beans	349	22.9	1.2	.55	.53	.34
Pasta						
Spaghetti, enriched dry	369	12.5	1.2	.46	.81	.27
Peanut butter, no added fat	601	20.3	52.1	1.00	1.08	.36

‡Jerusalem artichokes change their caloric value as their major starch, inulin, is converted to glucose in storage.

Fava Bean

Scientific Name: Vicia faba
Place of Origin: Southern Europe
Cultivation: Large-seeded bean can be planted in late fall for spring harvest in regions with mild climates. Small pods can be picked early for fresh use. Matured pods are shelled and beans consumed as the dry crop.

be a good selection for Georgia and a poor one for Montana. With each species selected, say lettuce or tomato, there will also be some varieties that are better suited to your area. As mentioned earlier in making this selection use neighbors, plant nurseries, Agricultural Extension information, and nursery catalogues as guides. And, remember, if you construct a solar greenhouse (see Chapter 9, pages 235–40), your possibilities are greatly expanded in the direction of raising heat-loving plants from fall through spring, though some food plants may give poor returns under these conditions because of space limitations.

Among the many choices open to you, what plants should you select? Our belief is that, dietary needs aside, you should begin with those you like to eat and look at. For all its abundance of minerals and vitamins, a rutabaga will contribute little to the diet if it is rejected at the table.

Let us assume that your tastes are broad and you like most vegetables. What should determine your choice then? You might wish to select on the basis of economy—that is, grow the foods that would cost the most in the store, and buy the less expensive ones. Protein costs more in the store than starches. The comparative costs of foods can be computed based on the price for one hundred grams of protein. Table 7-12 shows the cost of protein and the total calories for common meat, fish, dairy products, vegetables, grains, nuts, and pasta. (Although the prices quoted on the chart are taken from a market in Berkeley, California, they are representative for the entire nation in terms of relative cost of foods.) Foods will cost more when they require high labor to harvest (an example would be snowpeas or whole-pod peas), when they do not ship and store well (as with Jerusalem artichokes), or when the demand is low because the food is unfamiliar or restricted to the cuisine of one particular ethnic or social group (fresh coriander, ginger, chayote, and many other excellent vegetables and fruits fall into this category). Although the unfamiliar vegetables are often those which do not grow in the local climate, this is not always the case. Many delicious varieties of Chinese and Japanese cabbage and mustard will grow almost anywhere in the United States, but are found in only a few markets. So, along with cost, you might wish to grow a plant just because it is hard to buy when you want it.

Preparing for the Growing Season

In areas with mild winters, one does not think in terms of once-a-year garden preparation. As one month follows the other around the seasons, garden preparation means a continuous process of making compost, spreading it thickly over the beds, and planting seedlings in it. On the West Coast, where a warm, dry summer is usually followed by a cool, wet winter, many people do relatively little winter growing, simply because the frequent rains and short days make the garden less attractive to them, at least from November through March. The best preparation for the spring in such cases is to heap the garden high with compost, fallen dry leaves, and grass clippings in the autumn, and let the winter rains, earthworms, and other soil organisms do their work.

This plan is also a good one for areas with cold winters, since early spring in those places corresponds in quality with West Coast winters. If you

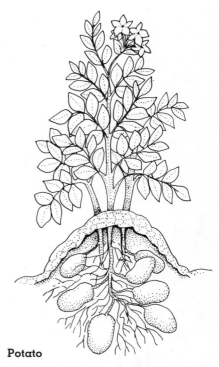

Potato

Scientific Name: Solanum tuberosum
Place of Origin: South America
Garden Varieties: "Queen Victoria"; "Russet."
Cultivation: Planted by tubers in spring. Tubers are cut into small sections and allowed to form callous surfaces in the open air. These sections are then placed on cultivated soil, eyes up, and covered with eight inches of mulch. Sprouts penetrate mulch and form the aerial portion of plant as tubers are formed under the straw, for easy harvest.

171

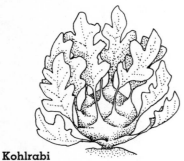

Kohlrabi

Scientific Name: Brassica oleracea
*Place of Origin: South England,
Wales, and the Adriatic Coast.*
Garden Varieties: "Early White
Vienna" (55 days); "Early Purple
Vienna" (60 days).
Cultivation: Seedlings are planted
from early spring through late sum-
mer for continuous harvest. The tur-
niplike swollen stem can be eaten
raw or cooked.

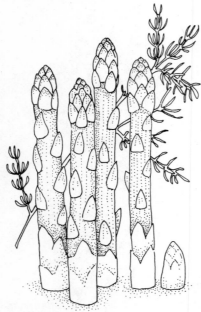

Asparagus

*Scientific Name: Asparagus offici-
nalis*
Place of Origin: Europe
Garden Varieties: "Mary Washington."
Cultivation: Root divisions are
planted early spring in manure-filled
trenches. Spears are uncut first year
to allow establishment of plant.
Young spears are harvested thereafter for many years.

have had an outdoor garden in the summer and your area gets cold enough in the winter to freeze the ground, with plenty of snow to insulate it, a num-ber of root crops (beets, carrots, parsnips) can be left in the ground and cov-ered with heaped-up straw or hay at the first hard freeze.

If the ground you wish to plant is either highly compacted from foot or other traffic or has been planted in lawn, you must spade it in order to incor-porate substantial amounts of compost into the top four to six inches of soil. (Avoid using a rototiller, if possible, since this destroys soil structure.) After spading, cover the spaded area with more compost and mulch, if you can make or find it. It is best to do this in the fall, so that it will not be necessary to disturb the wet soil in the early spring. Then, planting time the first com-post of the season can be spread out and the seedlings planted directly in it.

In regions where the springs are late and the soil stays cold until May, you can use some techniques to warm the soil and make it ready for trans-porting seedlings or being directly sown with seeds. If mulch has been cov-ering the soil through the winter, remove it in the early spring for two to three weeks in order to allow the soil beneath it to warm up. You might also spread black plastic sheets over the soil so as to accelerate the warming of the soil. Preferred soil temperatures for seed germination are between 50°F and 70°F.

Raised beds have become the vogue with some gardening groups, and where rains are frequent and the soil is heavy (containing a lot of clay) such beds offer the advantage of good drainage. They also clearly distinguish the planting areas from the paths. This is a decided advantage in community gardens, where there is a lot of traffic from the public, though as mentioned earlier, paths are a waste of space in a one-household garden.

One way to raise the beds is to scoop out the top few inches of the pathways and incorporate that soil with the compost into the topsoil of the planting area. Then some highly carbonaceous material can be placed in the pathways to prevent compaction, discourage weeds, and make it obvious to people where they should walk. If you use woodchips on the paths, you may need to construct borders around the beds, since woodchips tend to migrate into the planted areas. Sawdust is best for paths if you can get it, since not only does it smother some weeds if it is thick enough (one to two inches), but also it readily decomposes so that the pathways it covers can be used for planting at another time.

One should not adhere slavishly to raised beds if they are not suited to your area, however. Wherever water is scarce, soils are sandy, or drying winds are a problem, using a depressed bed for planting is preferable to planting on the level, and raised beds should be avoided. See Box 8-4, page 197, for a description of one technique of conservation gardening making use of a depression.

Propagating Seedlings Indoors

Advantages: The most common reason for starting seedlings indoors is to get a jump on the season. By the time danger from late frosts is past, the plants will be several inches high and ready to set out in the garden. If only a small number of plants are to be started, this can be accomplished very conveniently on the sill of a sunny window or on a shelf or table just in front of it. The most common vegetables started this way are those that transplant easily and are most likely to be harmed by cold nighttime temperatures, for example, tomatoes, peppers, squashes, and melons. However, over the years the authors have used this windowsill method to start every common garden vegetable grown from seed, and all were successful (although some were far too much trouble to start this way regularly, such as carrots and corn).

The map in Figure 7-4 showing last frosts across the United States may be useful to you in planning when to start seedlings. Consult it to see after what dates seedlings can be safely set into the ground or moved to the porch or terrace. Generally, seeds may be sown indoors or under a protective greenhouselike covering outdoors three to five weeks before the last expected frost. Our motives for starting seedlings indoors have been to reduce insect and bird damage and to maintain the young plants while they are most vulnerable.

Also, starting seedlings indoors is a space-saving method making possible an increase in productivity in small gardens. Normally, when seeds are sown directly outdoors large areas are consumed in seedbeds. By starting seeds indoors the seed bed areas are reduced to small flats, thus reserving the garden space for plants that are advanced in their development. We have calculated that 1 square foot of seed flats planked will provide seedlings for 150 square feet of garden area. As soon as one crop is pulled, say tomatoes in the fall, seedlings of broccoli, perhaps, can be planked in its place, saving time and space. The stronger the seedlings the better they will be able to withstand the rigors of competition in the garden when transplanted, assuming that they are not allowed to become pot-bound (meaning their roots grow too large for their container).

Besides reducing the amount of effort required to fend off wildlife, growing seedlings on the windowsill during the first weeks reduces the amount of care required in other respects. Germinating seedlings must be kept moist. If they are allowed to dry out during this process, they will not survive. While keeping them moist may be easy during a cool, moist spring, this becomes difficult during hot, sunny spells or periods of drying winds. Using a thin organic mulch over seedlings or stretching muslin or burlap over the beds may help. Nevertheless, seeds germinating outdoors must get at least a daily sprinkling when the weather is hot and dry.

Indoors, if the planting mix contains one-third or more of sifted compost, the seedlings can go for days or even more than a week without attention. Exactly how long they can last will also depend on the size of the container they are in—those in larger ones lasting longer—and how hot and dry the house is. This indoor method of starting plants is attractive, particularly if you work full time and do not relish having to do garden chores at the end of a long day.

Transplanting seedlings rather than starting with seeds directly in the garden is also a very useful technique where the outdoor growing area is limited. In some areas of the country, growing seedlings inside may permit the growing of a second or even a third crop in the same spot. Early spring vegetables make way for a main summer crop. In the south and coastal west, an early fall planting will provide peas and other cool-weather crops at

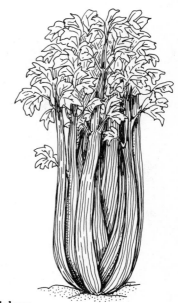

Celery

Scientific Name: Apium graveolens
Place of Origin: Central and Southern Europe
Garden Varieties: "Tendercrisp" (105 days); "Giant Pascal" (135 days).
Cultivation: Seeds are sown indoors six to eight weeks before spring planting outdoors. Heavy and frequent irrigation is required to keep celery sweet. A winter crop is possible in the South and Pacific Southwest. Tie stalks together several weeks before harvest to keep white and tender.

173

Cauliflower

Scientific Name: Brassica oleracea
Place of Origin: Southern England,
Wales, and the Adriatic Coast
Garden Varieties: "Snow Crown Hybrid" (53 days).
Cultivation: Cauliflower grows best
as a fall crop in most areas, planted
by seedling in late summer. In the
South and Pacific Southwest seedlings are planted later in the fall for
winter harvest or late in winter for
spring harvest. Outer leaves can be
tied over the maturing head to maintain whiteness of buds.

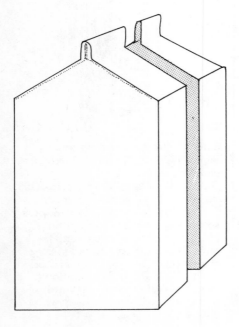

Christmas time. Each time a mature plant is harvested, a seedling that is already six to eight weeks old is planted in the same spot, using what space one does have very productively.

Starting seedlings indoors is also a very thrifty way of using seeds, since in most cases far fewer are needed than when the plants are started directly outdoors. With fresh seeds, one needs to start only two for each plant you wish to raise. (Older seed may require the planting of four or five, since percent of seeds germinated is likely to be lower.) Thinning is easy, few plants are unwanted, and when transplanting time comes the seedlings can be set out in the garden exactly where desired.

Materials: Seedlings can be started in almost anything that will contain a growing medium and permit drainage. Commercial peat pots, some already impregnated with fertilizer, are sold for this purpose. The containers used by successful gardeners are as varied as their users are creative. In our opinion, it is essential that there be enough root space for the plants to grow for many weeks so that transplanting at a precise time is not so crucial. Unexpected work or family demands may make it difficult to do the garden work on schedule. Thus, eggshells and other very tiny containers promoted by some garden literature are not desirable.

If you are actually relying upon the windowsill rather than a broader surface, it is also important to have containers that fit the space and permit watering without spillage or floor damage. An ideal solution is the use of half-gallon and quart milk containers. These are a waste product in many households and may be recycled in this way before being discarded. In place of the half-gallon containers, which are split in half lengthwise to make trays, one can use old aluminum ice trays with removable cube compartments, though, as discussed in the next section, there are some distinct advantages to using milk cartons for this purpose. Large size (twelve fluid ounces) frozen orange juice containers or small soup cans can also be pressed into service, used in the trays to hold the growing medium and seeds.

One-third soil, one-third sand, and one-third peat moss or sifted compost is a good mixture in which to plant the seeds. Actually, if your soil is very sandy, one-half soil and one-half compost will be fine, while a clay soil requires more sand for adequate drainage (see Boxes 8-2 and 8-3, pages 193–94). Sifted compost (see Chapter 6) is far superior to peat, because it will provide nutrients as well as improve the soil's water-holding capacity. Peat contributes little besides this water-retaining ability and is harder to use because it must be kneaded with water before you can be certain that it is moist throughout. Composed sawdust, fir bark, and vermiculite are also possible substitutes for peat, though compost is best.

It is desirable to prepare some markers to identify what you have planted. Toothpicks stuck through little strips of paper are adequate, the sticks from ice cream or sherbet bars are fine, and of course wooden and plastic markers are sold for this purpose also. Write labels in pencil so they will not run when wet or fade in the sunlight.

Procedure: We feel that there are certain advantages to using the milk carton cubes as containers, because their open end and flexible sides make them particularly easy to transplant from. Thus we will describe how to use them in detail.

A combination of sharp knife and big scissors are useful for cutting up the cartons. The half-gallon should be cut in half lengthwise. One half is then ready to use as a tray as it is. If you wish to use the other side, you must fold and staple the spout end closed so it will not leak when water runs out of the containers of seedlings. The quart cartons can be cut in thirds or halves, depending on how large a seed you wish to plant, or how long you anticipate having to leave the seedling in its container before transplanting.

The open-ended cubes are then filled with the soil mix. The ingredients of this should be blended thoroughly ahead of time, and if the soil component is heavy clay, it should be dry when blended to ensure that all the handling does not compact it. This dry, well-mixed material is then pressed into the cubes from the quart containers as they are sitting in the trays made of the half-gallons. A large funnel such as the plastic top of a drip coffee-maker and a small flexible plastic bowl make the job of filling easy. Pack the mixture down with the back of your knuckles, leaving one-half to an inch space at the top to retain water.

Then pour water into the containers and allow it to soak in. For this first time you can fill the trays repeatedly until the top of the soil mix is completely wet. Test the soil by pressing down on the surface with a fingertip. If a layer of soil breaks away and clings to your finger, leaving a dry spot beneath, the mixture is not thoroughly wet. Extra water standing in the trays this first time is not a problem; generally it will be absorbed by the next day, and in any case it does not hurt the seeds to be soaked overnight when they are started. After this first watering, however, it is very important to be sparing of the water, only wetting the surface when it seems dry in the beginning, and watering progressively more deeply as the seedling grows and extends its root down into the soil mix.

The number of seedlings you can raise per container will depend on several factors. Usually four, one in each corner, is a maximum. Obviously, the size of the seed and the container, and length of time you might wish to wait before transplanting will all affect the number per carton. In addition, you need to decide if you will wish to remove the seedling from the container when setting it into the ground or simply set the entire container down firmly in a spot in the garden that has been watered thoroughly to receive it, without removing the seedling at all. The latter is recommended when you are working with children or others not confident of their ability to handle baby plants. Since the cube is open at the bottom, the roots will grow directly into the soil. While the plant is young and none of its leaves touch the ground, this method of transplanting may also furnish some minimal discouragement to certain ground-crawling herbivores such as cutworm, snails, and others. If you intend to use this method of transplanting, only one seedling per cube should be grown.

To plant a seed in the cube, make a small depression with your finger where you wish to place a seed, drop the seed into it, and press it gently into the soil mix. Then cover it lightly with a layer of sand no deeper than the seed is large. The exception is lettuce, which can be left to germinate in the light. The reason for not covering the seeds as deeply as may be recom-

Making Planting Containers from a Quart Milk Carton

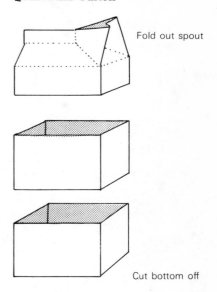

Fold out spout

Cut bottom off

The bottomless middle section is set in the trays made from half-gallon cartons.

Removing the Milk Carton Container from Soil

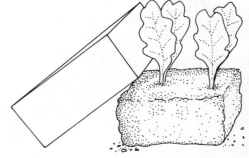

175

mended by the directions on the seed package is that in the darker and more simplified environment of the house the seeds may be more susceptible to the water molds and other "damping-off" fungi. (*Pythium* species and *Rhizoctonia* species are soil fungi that may harm germinating seedlings.) Symptoms are thinning and darkening stems of the new seedlings prior to their collapse, or their failure to appear at all.

Should you pasteurize the soil to avoid problems of damping-off? This can be done by placing the soil mix in an open roaster pan in the oven and heating it to 180°F (82.2°C) for thirty minutes before filling the containers. You may wish to do this if you do not have compost to add to the mix or if you have had previous experience with seedlings damping-off in your soil mixture. We use a sifted compost in the planting medium and rely on a complex living soil community to keep plant pathogens in check, with uniformly good results. In general there are two opposing points of view on how to manage problems inherent in oversimplified ecosystems. We tend to favor approaches that would increase complexity, but this is not always possible, nor does it always lead to the desired stability. We will return to this question again in discussing plants indoors and managing wildlife.

When the seeds have all been planted and covered, set the trays on a sunny windowsill and await the appearance of the seedlings. Actually, until they do appear the sun is of no special benefit, but afterward it is essential that they have as much light as possible. If the house is very warm, the trays may be slipped into plastic bags to aid in retaining moisture at the soil surface, but usually this is not necessary. If bags are used, remove them as soon as the seedlings show above the soil or the excess moisture will cause fungus problems.

Nothing further needs to be done until the seedlings are ready to be thinned. Make sure they have plenty of light and stay just damp enough to keep growing. Seedlings grown in a place that is too dark become weak and spindly. After they have grown their true leaves, if more than one seed has germinated in each depression, snip out the unwanted seedlings with a scissors—carefully, leaving only the strongest seedlings in each individual depression. Normal thinning should leave a one-inch space between seedlings for most vegetable plants. At this time, you can select the plant that looks the strongest or appeals to you in other ways (such as an especially colorful red-lettuce seedling).

Transplanting Seedlings

Any time after the seedlings have put out their second or true leaves, they may be moved to an outdoor planting area, either in the ground or in a container. Before they are actually replanted they must be "hardened off"—that is, given a chance to become accustomed to the outdoor temperatures. To do this, set the entire tray in a shady sheltered spot for a day or two. The less difference there is between the indoor and outdoor environment the less shock to the young seedling in being moved from one place to the other.

Choose a cool, windless time to transplant. Early evening is good. Soak the area where the seedling will be placed, and make a little depression with an elevated center to hold water around the new plant. Slip the container off

Summer, or Pole, Bean

Scientific Name: Phaseolus species
Place of Origin: South America
Garden Varieties: "Scarlet Runner" (70 days); "Kentucky Wonder" (65 days); "Romano" (60 days).
Cultivation: Sow seed directly into soil. Plant along existing fence or trellis to take advantage of vertical space. Choose rust-resistant varieties where damp evenings favor fungus.

of the plant and gently work the seedling's soil into the depression. The elevated center will allow water to drain away from the stem but soak in around the roots. An ideal planting is shown in the margin.

If you do not plan to remove the plant from its container, simply press the little cube with seedling firmly into the center of the depression so that it sinks in an inch or so, not more, into the wet earth or compost mulch. Water once again, and if the weather is hot and/or windy you may wish to cover the seedling with an upside-down clay flower pot for the day so that it has a chance to adjust to the new location without losing too much water.

This problem of water loss is critical during transplanting. Plants take in water through fragile hairs one cell wide that grow in a region just behind the elongating root tip as it expands through the soil. These hairs may be damaged during the transplanting process (see Figure 7-6). Plants lose water through pores in the surface of the leaf, called stoma. How much they lose is greatly influenced by how moist the air is outside the leaf. The drier and hotter the air is, the faster the moist air directly adjacent to the leaf surface is blown away by the winds, and the quicker the plant loses water. If the little root hairs have been damaged and are unable to take in water as before, the plant may wilt irretrievably.

Covering the transplanted seedling for a short period is one solution to this problem. This allows a build-up of humidity directly around the plant, thus reducing water transpiration for a short period while new root hairs grow. The clay flower pot, mentioned above, is ideal for this purpose because it has an air hole at the top to permit some gas exchange. It is opaque so the little seedling won't cook in the sun, and it is heavy enough so that the winds or passing animals are unlikely to knock it over.

Another way to reduce water loss temporarily is to pinch off a large leaf (or more, if the plant has quite a few). This will permit the seedling to regrow its water-absorbing root hairs without losing too much fluid. With larger plants, it is always a good idea to cut back the top in proportion to the amount of damage you think may have occurred to the root system.

To separate several plants growing in one container, hold the container half an inch or so above the ground (not more) and move the sides gently to that the entire cube slips out. Then, with two hands, you can easily break the soil cube apart into halves and then again into quarters. If the soil should fall away from the seedlings in the process, handle the plants by the stem, not the roots. Be sure to keep the other seedlings protected from the sun and wind so that they do not dry out while you are planting their companion. Make a little depression in the moist earth or compost, set the seedling in, and press the soil back firmly around it. In cases where the roots have become exposed, it is particularly important to protect the seedling from drying out by one or both of the methods suggested above. Of course, should you be transplanting on a cool, moist, overcast day, additional precautions may not be necessary.

Raising Food on the Roof or Porch

Rooftop or porch gardening means growing plants in containers, and it shares various advantages and disadvantages with patio and indoor garden-

Figure 7-6. **Detail of a Root Hair**

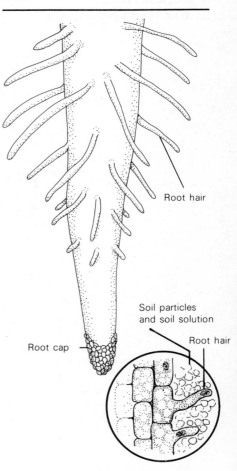

Root hair

Soil particles and soil solution

Root hair

Root cap

Close up shows root hairs in contact with the soil particles and soil solution from which the root obtains essential elements for growth and reproduction.

An Ideal Planting

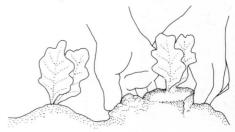

ing. The principal advantages are several: having less overall area to weed, water, and maintain; having the plants elevated off the ground, which makes them available for inspection with less stopping; having each plant, or group of plants, stand out as a separate specimen; and often having your plants closer to the kitchen than an outdoor garden might be.

The difficulties include providing enough root space, adequate mineral nutrition, water and drainage, and an environment diverse enough to keep plant pests and diseases under natural control (although rooftop plants are insulated from some of the crawling pests, such as slugs and snails). Three additional problems unique to roof gardens are controlling the weight of the garden, preventing damage to the plants from wind, and preventing root damage from foot traffic.

It is obvious that there is a limit to how much weight a rooftop can bear. Pure water weighs 62.5 pounds per cubic foot, and moist soil roughly 80 pounds per cubic foot. That means a 5-gallon container weighs over 62 pounds when moist. One means of decreasing this weight may be to use lightweight soil mixes (see Table 7-13 for a wet and dry comparison of common ingredients of growing media). Unfortunately, though mixes containing peat moss or other materials may give good structure to the soil and often increase its water-holding capacity, they do not provide any nutrients. The clay component of a good loam provides plant nutrients, but it is heavy and disposed to shrink as it dries out, pulling the soil mix away from the sides of the container.

This problem can be solved in two ways. One is to make or buy a light soil mix, incorporating plenty of the porous commercial material manufactured expressly for this purpose (for example, vermiculite or perlite). Then the plant nutrients are added as fertilizer, mixed in water or sprinkled on top of the soil and watered in. This is probably the best method for those who have no space for making compost. A number of planter-box soil mixtures are sold. If they are marked "for house plants" they may be too acid for vegetables. The addition of a small sprinkling of dolomite lime to the mixture will make the medium more palatable for them.

If you have access to soil, you can make your own mix using one-third soil, one-third sand, and one-third peat moss; or you can make a soilless mix using just sand and peat moss. Either way, be sure to wet the peat moss a day or two in advance, and mix the ingredients thoroughly so that they are evenly distributed in the mixture. If you are using soil, sift it through a screen first if necessary to break up hard clumps and remove stones. Vermiculite, perlite, or similar commercial products may be substituted for peat moss.

While plants, unlike humans and other animals, can make their own food in the presence of sunlight through the process of photosynthesis, they must pick up certain nutrients from their environment—primarily through their roots (see Chapter 8). The problem of providing nutrients in a container presents a special dilemma. The essential nutrients are usually found attached to the clay particles in the soil. The clay itself contributes some potassium. So, generally, the more clay in the soil mix, the more nutrients for the plants. But a mix with more clay is not only heavier and likely to shrink, it also has less pore space for oxygen to reach the roots. On the other hand,

Table 7-13. Density of Soil, Compost, and Other Planting Media

Material	Pounds per Cubic Foot, Dry	Pounds per Cubic Foot, at Field Capacity*
Sand	78	95
Loam	85	105
Clay	100	120
Compost	20	60
Peat moss	10	45

*Field capacity is the amount of water held after the excess is drained away.

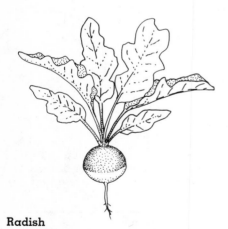

Radish

Scientific Name: Raphanus sativus
Place of Origin: Egypt
Garden Varieties: "French Breakfast" (23 days); "Scarlet Globe" (24 days).
Cultivation: Does best in the cool weather of spring and fall, when growth is quick and steady. May be sown from fall to late spring in regions where winters are mild.

the greater the proportion of additives such as peat moss and perlite used to lighten the mix, the less you can depend on having enough plant nutrients present. In such a case, you must be prepared to add them when needed.

If, for purposes of achieving a very light-growing medium, you use no soil at all, then you will need to provide all the nutrients commonly required by plants and will have to supply more than a basic N-P-K fertilizer. A complete fertilizer, which is necessary in any hydroponic gardening where plants are grown in sand, gravel, sawdust, or pure water, will naturally be far more expensive than the conventional varieties.

Our solution to the problem of keeping weight to a minimum and still providing adequate plant nutrients has been to grow container plants in a mixture of one-half compost and one-half soil. This medium is lighter than pure soil, provides all the nutrients the plants need, holds water well but drains easily so there is oxygen for the plant roots, and has less of a tendency to shrink away from the sides of the container. All you need is the knowledge and willingness to make a good compost. (See Chapter 6, on recycling organic wastes.)

Bins for compost-making can be constructed on the roof and can function to recycle the organic wastes of a household into a growing medium for plants just as they would in the garden. We developed such a rooftop system on top of an old warehouse occupied by Antioch College/West in downtown San Francisco a couple of years ago. We started by building two compost bins and began to accumulate materials for the pile. A nearby cabinet shop produced a daily supply of sawdust that we used as a carbon source. For nitrogen, we used left-over kitchen wastes from the school pot-lucks and student bag lunches (stored in sawdust until composted, so the material wouldn't smell and attract flies) and restaurant wastes from the immediate area. Particularly useful were the vegetable and fruit residues from a juicer used in a cafeteria we visited nearby. If you use a high proportion of these wastes, however, you will need plenty of sawdust to absorb the moisture and keep the pile from going anaerobic.

While the first batch of compost was maturing, we built long wooden containers about two feet deep and eighteen inches wide. We also started seedlings in milk cartons in the sunny windows of one of the classrooms. By the time the first compost batch was cooled down and ready to use, the seedlings were up and had their second (true) pair of leaves, all ready to transplant outside.

In filling the boxes, we left six inches between the level of the compost and the top of the container so that the seedlings sat well down inside, protected from wind during the period when they were small. A friend discovered an old discarded window frame nearby with glass intact, and we laid this across a portion of one box to create a sort of greenhouse. This was a very successful experiment—the seedlings under the glass quickly responded to the increased warmth by growing faster than their companions out under the open sky. Of course, this was in San Francisco, which remains cool and windy all summer long.

Besides the obvious physical effects of the wind on a rooftop garden in whipping the plants about, one has to consider the drying power of the moving air as it removes the moisture from the leaves and soil surface. There are

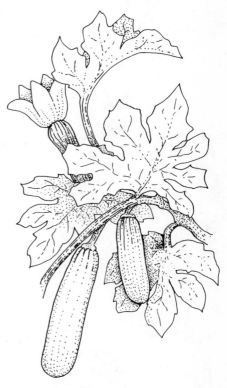

Squash

Scientific Names: Summer varieties: *Cucurbita pepo;* Winter varieties: *Cucurbita maxima.*
Place of Origin: America
Garden Varieties: Summer Squash: "Zucchini" (48–57 days); "Yellow Crookneck" (53 days); "White Bush Scallop" (54 days). Fall and Winter Squash: "Banana" (95 days); "Acorn" (85 days); "Hubbard" (85 days).
Cultivation: Summer varieties may be started indoors and transplanted for an extra-early crop. Bush varieties should be selected to economize on space. Winter and fall varieties produce hard-shelled fruit in late summer that will store indoors for winter consumption. Vines of banana and hubbard squash can be trained along fences.

Corn

Scientific Name: Zea mays
Place of Origin: North America
Garden Varieties: "Early Sunglow Hybrid" (63 days); "Golden Cross Bantam" (85 days); "Silver Queen" (92 days).
Cultivation: Plant several varieties by seed in the garden simultaneously to insure a long harvest of fresh corn. Late varieties should provide crop for canning. If popcorn or ornamental corn is planted, keep at considerable distance from eating varieties to prevent cross-fertilization.

two obvious ways of dealing with excessive air movements. One is to build some barriers to slow down the wind; the other is to keep the soil surface covered with a mulch and at a level six to eight inches below the top of the container as we did in the garden described above.

As mentioned earlier, the important thing to remember about a barrier is that it should be partially permeable if it is to improve the situation rather than make it worse. If the barrier is solid, turbulent gusts of wind will churn the air on the leeward (away from the wind) side. However, if some air can flow through the barrier—about 60 percent permeability seems best—these drafts can be prevented and the overall effect will be to create a calmer climate for the rooftop garden. Appropriate windbreak materials for roof gardens are a lath fence with 60 percent spacing between the boards, a 4-foot-high hedge, or some shade netting tacked onto a support framework.

One advantage of using compost as a growing medium is that it is porous and holds water well, and although the surface may dry out, the deeper portions of the container do not quickly lose moisture through the capillary action. If drying is a problem for you, it is important that the compost not be a coarse one, or if it is that it be mixed with a bit of soil. However, in very windy areas, it still may be desirable to cover the surface of the soil around the plants with a piece of cloth, such as burlap, held down with some attractive stones.

It is important to ensure that the water in the containers can drain freely. If you are drilling or punching drainage holes into a solid container, make them at the very bottom of the sides rather than on the bottom itself, so that the surface on which the container rests will not slow the drainage from the pot.

Many roofs that are sturdy enough to support the weight of a container garden are not surfaced to handle the foot traffic usually required for culturing plants. Tar covered with gravel, for instance, will soon wear through. The result can be costly damage to the roof beneath from the rain and water running from the plants. One solution is to build a wooden deck that will raise the traffic and containers several inches off the roof. In some cases, it may be desirable to anchor the supports for the deck to the roof itself with an adhesive roofing compound. This is the method we applied on the old warehouse roof in San Francisco.

The variety of plants that can be grown on rooftops and porches is enormous, and varies as much as your capacity to create sheltered spots and various types of containers. Shallow containers, eight inches to a foot deep (the soil, of course, would be one or more inches shallower), will grow lettuce, radishes, turnips, green onions, beets, chives, cabbage, chard, herbs, medium-sized carrots such as Danvers Half-Long, and a variety of other shallow-rooted vegetables or flowering plants. With tomatoes, green peppers, beans, cucumbers, zucchini, and other squash, the more root space you can provide, the more fruit the plants will yield, and it is hardly worthwhile to use less growing space than is provided in a five-gallon can. As you consider planting larger permanent shrubs or dwarf trees, the containers must be correspondingly larger, and it may be desirable to stake or use wires to provide additional support against the buffeting of the wind.

Our first rooftop garden was on a porch roof to which we had access from the second floor of the residence. A hose connection was fitted to the pipes below the bathroom sink, and a garden hose kept coiled up there when not used to water the rooftop. Again, we built a deck to keep the traffic from harming the roof surface. In this case we built a few containers, but scavenged for many others. We found 5-gallon cans thrown away by bakeries and restaurants and 55-gallon drums that we torched in half to make large containers. We experimented with growing just about every vegetable you can think of (except corn) in that motley assemblage of boxes and cans, and none failed to give us food. Some, such as bush beans and Chinese cabbage, are amazingly productive under those circumstances.

A similar rooftop garden is now open to the public at the Integral Urban House of the Farallones Institute. Figure 7-7 is an illustration of a section of the Integral Urban House porch garden. A drip irrigation system periodically delivers water to the container plants. Wire screen is positioned over seedlings to protect against bird damage.

Figure 7-7. **Porch Container Garden with Automatic Watering System**

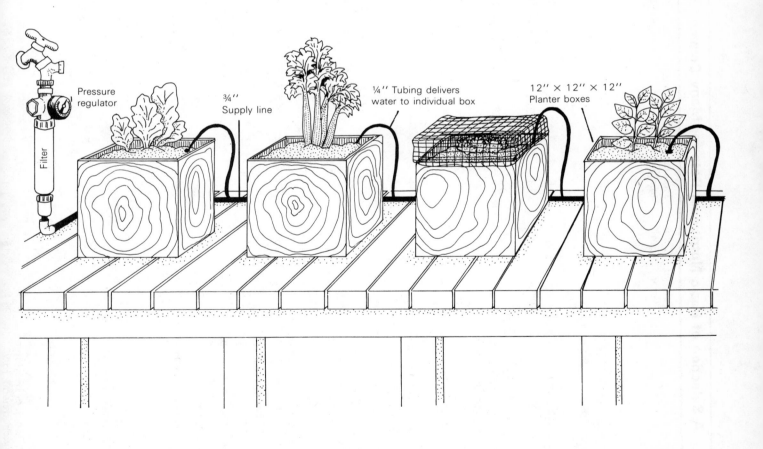

Box 7-3. **A Selection of Basic Nutritional Data for Many Common Vegetables**

	Percent Water	Calories (gm)	Protein (gm)	Fat (gm)	Carbohydrate Total (gm)	Fiber (gm)	Ca (mg)	P (mg)	Fe (mg)	Na (mg)	K (mg)	A (units)	Thiamine (mg)	Riboflavin (mg)	Niacin (mg)	C Ascorbic acid (mg)
Artichokes: boiled and drained	86.5	8–44*	2.8	.2	9.9*	2.4	51	69	1.1	30	301	150	.07	.04	.7	8
Asparagus, spears: boiled and drained	93.6	20	2.2	.2	3.6	.7	21	50	.6	1	183	900	.16	.18	1.4	26
Bamboo shoots: raw	91.0	27	2.6	.3	5.2	.7	13	59	.5	—	533	20	.15	.07	.6	4
Beans, white: cooked	69.0	118	7.8	.6	21.2	1.5	50	148	2.7	7	416	—	.14	.07	.7	—
Beans, lima: boiled and drained	71.1	111	7.6	.5	19.8	1.8	47	121	2.5	1	650	290	.24	.12	1.4	29
Beans, mung: sprouted seeds, uncooked	88.8	35	3.8	.2	6.6	.7	19	64	1.3	5	223	20	.13	.13	.8	19
Beans, green, snap: boiled and drained	92.4	25	1.6	.2	5.4	1.0	50	37	.6	5	151	540	.07	.09	.5	12
Beets, red: boiled and drained	90.9	32	1.1	.1	7.2	.8	14	23	.5	43	208	20	.03	.04	.3	6
Beet greens: boiled and drained	93.6	18	1.7	.2	3.3	1.1	99	25	1.9	76	332	5100	.07	.15	.3	15
Broccoli, spears: boiled and drained	91.3	26	3.1	.3	4.5	1.5	88	62	.8	10	267	2500	.09	.20	.8	90
Brussels sprouts: boiled and drained	88.2	36	4.2	.4	6.4	1.6	32	72	1.1	10	273	520	.08	.14	.8	87
Cabbage, common: boiled until tender, drained	94.3	18	1.0	.2	4.0	.8	42	17	.3	13	151	120	.02	.02	.1	24
Cabbage, Chinese: compact, heading-type raw	95.0	14	1.2	.1	3.0	.6	43	40	.6	23	253	150	.05	.04	.6	25
Cabbage, spoon (bok choy) nonheading green-leaf type: boiled and drained	95.2	14	1.4	.2	2.4	.6	148	33	.6	18	214	3100	.04	.08	.7	15
Carrots: boiled and drained	91.2	31	.9	.2	7.1	1.0	33	31	.6	33	222	10,500	.05	.05	.5	6
Cauliflower: boiled and drained	92.8	22	2.3	.2	4.1	1.0	21	42	.7	9	206	60	.09	.08	.6	55
Celery, raw	94.1	17	.9	.1	3.9	.6	39	28	.3	126	341	290	.03	.03	.3	9
Chard, Swiss: boiled and drained	93.7	18	1.8	.2	3.3	.7	73	24	1.8	86	321	5400	.04	.11	.4	16
Chayote, raw	91.8	28	.6	.1	7.1	.7	13	26	.5	5	102	20	.03	.03	.4	19
Chick peas (garbanzos): dry, raw	10.7	360	20.5	4.8	61.0	5.0	150	331	6.9	26	797	50	.31	.15	2.0	—
Chicory (French or Belgian endive): bleached head, raw	95.1	15	1.0	.1	3.2		18	21	.5	7	182	trace	—	—		

Food	Water															
Chicory greens, raw	92.8	20	1.8	.3	3.8	.8	86	40	.9	—	420	4000	.06	.10	.5	22
Chives, raw	91.3	28	1.8	.3	5.8	1.1	69	44	1.7	—	250	5800	.08	.13	.5	56
Collards: boiled and drained	90.8	29	2.7	.6	4.9	.8	152	39	.6	25	234	5400	.14	.20	1.2	46
Corn, sweet: kernels cooked on cob	74.1	91	3.3	1.0	21.0	.7	3	89	.6	trace	196	400	.12	.10	1.4	9
Cowpeas, blackeye peas: cooked, boiled, drained	71.8	108	8.1	.8	18.1	1.8	24	146	2.1	1	379	350	.30	.11	1.4	17
Cress, garden: cooked, boiled, drained	92.5	23	1.9	.6	3.8	.9	61	48	.8	8	353	7700	.06	.16	.8	34
Cucumbers: raw, pared	95.7	14	.6	.1	3.2	.3	17	18	.3	6	160	trace	.03	.04	.2	11
Dandelion greens: boiled and drained	89.8	33	2.0	.6	6.4	1.3	140	42	1.8	44	232	11,700	.13	.16	—	18
Dock: boiled and drained	93.6	19	1.6	.2	3.9	.7	55	26	.9	3	198	10,800	.06	.13	.4	54
Eggplant: boiled and drained	94.3	19	1.0	.2	4.1	.9	11	21	.6	1	150	10	.05	.04	.5	3
Endive (curly endive, escarole): raw	93.1	20	1.7	.1	4.1	.9	81	54	1.7	14	294	3300	.07	.14	.5	10
Fennel: leaves, raw	90.1	28	2.8	.4	5.1	.5	100	51	2.7	—	397	3500	—	—	—	31
Garlic, cloves: raw	61.3	137	6.2	.2	30.8	1.5	29	202	1.5	19	529	trace	.25	.08	.5	15
Horseradish: raw	74.6	87	3.2	.3	19.7	2.4	140	64	1.4	8	564	—	.07	—	—	81
Kale, leaves, stems: boiled and drained	91.2	28	3.2	.7	4.0	1.1	134	46	1.2	43	221	7400	—	—	—	62
Kohlrabi: boiled and drained	92.2	24	1.7	.1	5.3	1.0	33	41	.3	6	260	20	.06	.03	.2	43
Leek, bulbs and lower leaf portion: raw	85.4	52	2.2	.3	11.2	1.3	52	50	1.1	5	347	40	.11	.06	.5	17
Lettuce, looseleaf and bunched varieties: raw	94.1	18	1.3	.3	3.5	.7	68	25	1.4	9	264	1900	.05	.08	.4	18
Mushroom: raw	90.4	28	2.7	.3	4.4	.8	6	116	.8	15	414	trace	.10	.46	4.2	3
Mustard greens: boiled and drained	92.6	23	2.2	.4	4.0	.9	138	32	1.8	18	220	5800	.08	.14	.6	48
Okra: boiled and drained	91.1	29	2.0	.3	6.0	1.0	92	41	.5	2	174	490	(.13)	(.18)	(.9)	20
Onions, yellow-flesh varieties, mature (dry): raw	89.1	38	1.5	.1	8.7	.6	27	36	.5	10	157	40	.03	.04	.2	10
Onions, yellow-flesh varieties, mature (dry): boiled and drained	91.8	29	1.2	.1	6.5	.6	24	29	.4	7	110	40	.03	.03	.2	7
Onions, young, green (bunching variety): raw, bulb and entire top	89.4	36	1.5	.2	8.2	(1.2)	51	39	1.0	5	231	(2000)	.05	.05	.4	32
Onions, young, green (bunching variety): raw, tops only (green portion)	91.8	27	1.6	.4	5.5	1.3	56	39	2.2	5	231	4000	.07	.10	.6	51

Box 7-3. A Selection of Basic Nutritional Data for Many Common Vegetables (Continued)

	Percent Water	Calories (gm)	Protein (gm)	Fat (gm)	Carbohydrate Total (gm)	Fiber (gm)	Ca (mg)	P (mg)	Fe (mg)	Na (mg)	K (mg)	A (units)	Thiamine (mg)	Riboflavin (mg)	Niacin (mg)	C Ascorbic acid (mg)
Parsley, plain, curled leaf	85.1	44	3.6	.6	8.5	1.5	203	63	6.2	45	727	8500	.12	.26	1.2	172
Parsnips: boiled and drained	82.2	66	1.5	.5	14.9	2.0	45	62	.6	8	379	30	.07	.08	.1	10
Peas, edible, podded: boiled and drained:	86.6	43	2.9	.2	9.5	1.2	56	76	.5	—	119	(610)	.22	.11	—	14
Peas, green, immature: boiled and drained:	81.5	71	5.4	.4	12.1	2.0	23	99	1.8	1	196	540	.28	.11	2.3	20
Peas, mature seeds, dry: cooked	70.0	115	8.0	.3	20.8	.4	11	89	1.7	13	296	40	.15	.09	.9	—
Peppers, hot chile, immature green: raw pods, excluding seeds	88.8	37	1.3	.2	9.1	1.8	10	25	.7	—	—	770	.09	.06	1.7	235
Peppers, raw, mature red: pods including seeds	74.3	93	3.7	2.3	18.1	9.0	29	78	1.2	—	—	21,600	.22	.36	4.4	369
Peppers, raw, mature red: pods excluding seeds	80.3	65	2.3	.4	15.8	2.3	16	49	1.4	25	564	21,600	.10	.20	2.9	369
Peppers, sweet, garden varieties: immature green, raw	93.4	22	1.2	.2	4.8	1.4	9	22	.7	13	213	420	.08	.08	.5	128
Peppers, sweet, garden varieties: immature green, cooked, boiled, drained	94.7	18	1.0	.2	3.8	1.4	9	16	.5	9	149	420	.06	.07	.5	96
Potatoes: cooked, baked in skin	75.1	93	2.6	.1	21.1	.6	9	65	.7	4	503	trace	.10	.04	1.7	20
Potatoes: cooked, boiled in skin	79.8	76	2.1	.1	17.1	.5	7	53	.6	3	407	trace	.09	.04	1.5	16
Potatoes: boiled, pared before cooking	82.2	65	1.9	.1	14.5	.5	6	42	.5	2	285	trace	.09	.03	1.2	16
Purslane, leaves, including stems: boiled and drained	94.7	15	1.2	.3	2.8	.8	86	24	1.2	—	—	2100	.02	.06	.4	12
Radishes, common: raw	94.5	17	1.0	.1	3.6	.7	30	31	1.0	18	322	10	.03	.03	.3	26
Rutabagas: boiled and drained	90.2	35	.9	.1	8.2	1.1	59	31	.3	4	167	550	.06	.06	.8	26
Salsify: boiled and drained	81.0	12–70	2.6	.6	15.1	1.8	42	53	1.3	—	266	10	.03	.04	.2	7
Spinach: raw	90.7	26	3.2	.3	4.3	.6	93	51	3.1	71	470	8100	.10	.20	.6	51
Spinach: boiled and drained	92.0	23	3.0	.3	3.6	.6	93	38	2.2	50	324	8100	.07	.14	.5	28
Squash, summer: boiled and drained	94.5	14	.9	.1	3.1	.6	25	25	.4	1	141	390	.05	.08	.8	10
Squash, winter: baked	81.4	63	1.8	.4	15.4	1.8	28	48	.8	1	461	4200	.05	.13	.7	13
Squash, winter: boiled and mashed	88.8	38	1.1	.3	9.2	1.4	20	32	.5	1	258	3500	.04	.10	.4	8

Squash, acorn: baked	82.9	55	1.9	.1	14.0	39	29	1.1	1	480	1400	.05	.13	.7	13
Squash, butternut: baked	79.6	68	1.8	.1	17.5	40	72	1.0	1	609	6400	.05	.13	.7	8
Squash, hubbard: baked	85.1	50	1.8	.4	11.7	24	39	.8	1	271	4800	.05	.13	.7	10
Sweet potatoes: baked in skin	63.7	141	2.1	.5	32.5	40	58	.9	12	300	8100	.09	.07	.7	22
Turnips: boiled and drained	93.6	23	.8	.2	4.9	35	24	.4	34	188	trace	.04	.05	.3	22
Turnip greens, leaves, including stems: boiled and drained	93.2	20	2.2	.2	3.6	184	37	1.1	—	—	6300	.15	.24	.6	69
Watercress, leaves, including stems: raw	93.3	19	2.2	.3	3.0	151	54	1.7	52	282	4900	.08	.16	.9	79

Sweet Pea

Scientific Name: Pisum sativum
Place of Origin: Near East
Garden Varieties: "Dwarf Gray Sugar" (65 days): edible pod; "Blue Bantam" (64 days); "Wando" (68 days): good summer variety.
Cultivation: Planting the seedlings of the edible pod variety into the soil in late winter will provide an early spring harvest when weather permits. Later, warm weather varieties produce shelled pea crop. Best planted along a fence or supported by a trellis.

8. WHAT PLANTS NEED TO GROW

The basic partnership between incoming solar energy and the minerals of the earth creates the substance of life in every plant and animal. We are what we eat, and we eat plants or other animals that have fed on plants. Thus, we are basically what plants absorb through their roots, plus what they can manufacture from the gases of the air in the presence of sunlight through photosynthesis. Understanding how plants take up nutrients, and from what materials nutrients are available to us is essential to the creation of a lasting civilization. Urban peoples cannot safely continue to ignore this fundamental information, since, gardeners or not, each of us is ultimately affected by plant nutrition, and it in turn governs world food production and the public policy of distribution.

Nearly three quarters of the earth's surface is covered by water. Of the exposed land area only a fraction is presently or potentially arable. The vast majority of land surface is either too extreme in latitude, elevation, or climate to permit agricultural activity. The availability of soil as well as its preservation and maintenance are basic limiting factors around which humans must cooperate. The purpose of this section is to explore the relationship between human beings and the soil, and to provide basic information on preserving and working with soils around the urban home.

The Functions of Soil

The soil functions to support plants mechanically, provide nutrients and water necessary for plant growth, and permit the gas exchanges necessary for root respiration. (That roots do breathe, in a sense, is one of the basic facts of life that the urban dweller may not be aware of, but this has certain definite consequences for the management of plants under urban constraints.)

One of the ironic aspects of the urban condition is that cities are frequently built upon soils that originally were agriculturally the most desirable in the area. California is very interesting with respect to soil quality and land use. California's deep, productive soils have always been one of the great attractions of the state. In 1976, the state still supplied 40 percent of the nation's fruits and vegetables. Yet, from World War II to the present, this cropland was rapidly overtaken by urban sprawl. Such expansion of the urban carpet over what once was very fertile agricultural land is evident throughout much of the country, and indeed the entire world. The trend seems to be one that will continue given the fact of increased population growth.

Level stretches of deep, well-drained soil, easy to plow and harvest, were naturally chosen first for cultivation by our pioneer ancestors. Just as naturally, the growing population from the earliest settlements nearby spread over those same accessible and easily utilized areas. Yet, by the time the urban structures—that is, houses, sidewalks, roads, utility fixtures, and so on—were completed, most of the agriculturally valuable qualities of the soil were lost due to compaction and contamination from human activity. Thus, the growing areas immediately adjacent to the urban house and most accessible for plant raising may be in poor condition and require improvement before they are capable of supporting plant growth.

A "good" soil has certain specific characteristics and takes a very long time to develop. In fact, it may take as long as a thousand years for one inch of it to be created. After air and water, soil is the most basic of resources needed to sustain life, and it can easily be lost through erosion related to human activities. In many instances the knowledge of how to prevent soil erosion has not been sufficiently clear even to the farmer. Thus, it is not surprising that many urbanites, dangerously out of touch with their own life-support systems, should be uninformed as to the nature and properties of soil and the qualities that make it desirable as a medium for growing plants.

Soil science is a complex subject, and it is not the intention of the authors to provide an introductory course here. However, understanding cer-

Notice how little land area exists in comparison to the whole.

Source: Van Ripen, *Man's Physical World.*

Figure 8-1. **A Comparison of the Surface Area of the Earth at Various Elevations**

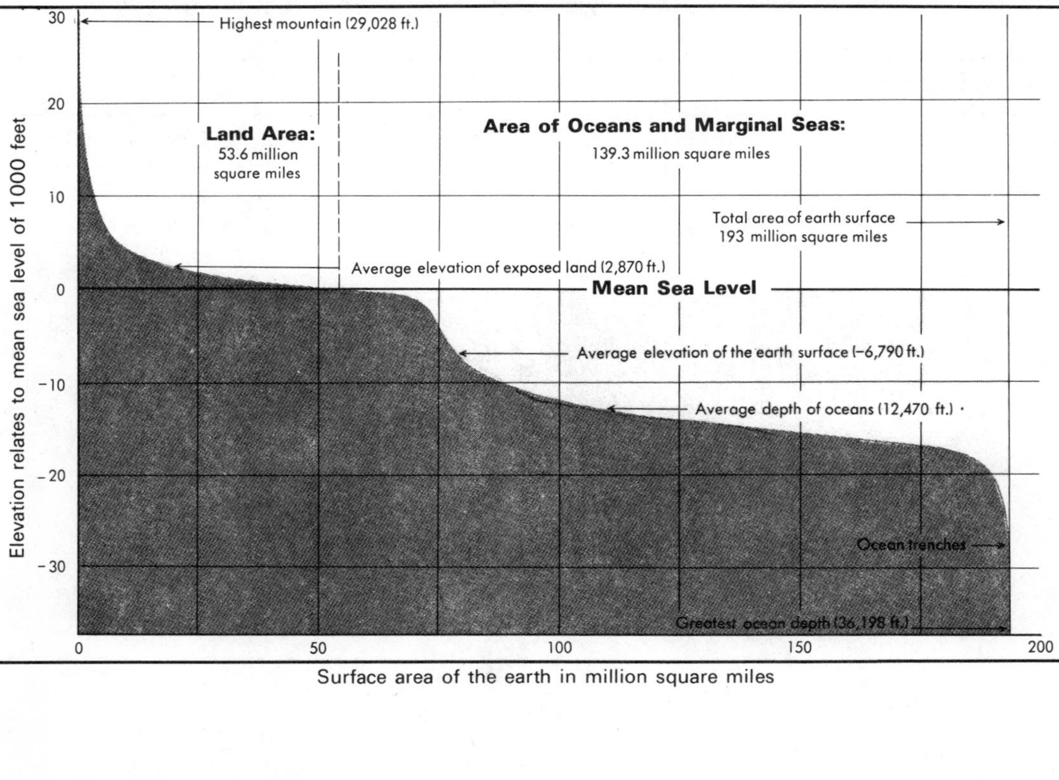

tain elementary aspects of the nature of soils is necessary to the intelligent use of the earth surrounding the integral urban house. At least a basic knowledge is also necessary for the decision making regarding national and local land use in which urban inhabitants are increasingly involved. These basic characteristics of soils may be examined under the headings of origin, texture, structure, chemistry, and biological components or soil life.

Soil Origin: The rocks that make up the continents are the parent material of all soil. Rocks are made up of mineral compounds, and these in turn are composed of basic elements. Rocks may be soft or hard, dense or relatively permeable, and the mineral compounds of which they are composed vary enormously. In part these differences among rocks determine the characteristics of the soils that are derived from them.

Excluding meteorites, which originate outside our atmosphere, most of the rocks currently found on this planet presumably started out as cooled *magmas,* or molten materials, that welled up from beneath the surface of the earth. These rocks, referred to as *igneous* (from *igni,* the Latin for fire; the root is seen in such words as ignition and ignite), are subject to transformation by erosion, sedimentation, pressure, heat, and chemical action.

Igneous rocks may be roughly divided into those that contain quartz and those that do not. These, in turn, can be categorized as fine-grained or coarse-grained, according to whether they cooled slowly (allowing large crystals to form) or extra quickly. The most extreme examples of the latter would be glassy rocks, such as obsidian (prized by Indians for making arrowheads) in which no crystal structure can be discerned at all. The overall classification of these igneous rocks is given in Table 8-1.

These original igneous materials are broken down through a process usually referred to as *weathering.* The heating and cooling of the earth's surface through daily and seasonal temperature changes causes expansion and shrinking, which in turn result in cracking and a breaking away of the surface. Wind and water cause direct physical erosion. Rain mixes with the car-

Source: Van Riper, *Man's Physical World.*

Table 8-1. **Classification of Igneous Rocks**

Textural Class	Sialic (acidic)*	Intermediate	Sima or Mafic (basic)†
	Maximum ←	Silica content →	Minimum
	Minimum ←	Base content →	Maximum
	Potassium Sodium	Calcium Magnesium Iron	
	Light ←	Color →	Dark
	Low ←	Melting point →	High
	Maximum ←	Feldspar content →	Min.
	Minimum ←	Content of hornblende, olivene, pyroxene and amphiboles →	Maximum
Granitic	GRANITE (with quartz) SYENITE (without quartz)	DIORITE	GABBRO; AUGITE; PERIDOTITE
Aphanitic	RHYOLITE (with quartz) TRACHYTE (without quartz)	ANDESITE	DIABASE BASALT
Vesicular (with gas holes)	PUMICE		SCORIA

*Sialic (si = silica; al = aluminum) rocks are lighter density portions of the earth's crust. Sialic rocks are relatively lightweight, predominantly pink, light gray, and white. Constituent minerals are high in silicon, oxygen, aluminum, potassium, and sodium. The most common sialic rock is granite, which forms the body of the continent. It floats on a world layer of denser basalt forming the basis of ocean floors.

† Sima (si = silica; ma = magnesium) rocks are a continuous crust or outer shell of the earth; they are darker and their minerals are lower in silica content than sialic rocks. The most common sima rock is basalt.

bon dioxide of the air to form carbonic acid (in the reaction $CO_2 + H_2O \rightarrow H_2CO_3$), and the weak acid dissolves the mineral constituents of the rocks. Acid excretions of plant roots erode the rock as well. All these actions break the rocks down into progressively smaller and smaller pieces.

The smaller rock pieces accumulate through the action of gravity, wind, and water as loose sediment. Deposits of sediment are found wherever running water, blowing wind, or moving glaciers have left the material they carried. The sediments accumulate along the edges of streams and rivers where these waterways enter lakes or oceans. Or they spread out on valley floors beneath steep slopes or in sand dunes and other accumulations and fine dust particles. Sediments are also found where glacier snows melt and deposit the materials plucked from the mountains by the action of the ice. (Similarly, sediments composed of the skeletons of marine organisms develop beneath the oceans.) As these materials accumulate, the deepest layers are compressed into *sedimentary rocks.* These may be loosely classified as to particle size, mineral composition, and origin (see Table 8-2).

Depending on earth movements, these sedimentary rocks may be either elevated above sea level (becoming subject to the forces of weathering, as were their igneous parents, and creating entirely new sedimentary rocks eventually) or buried still more deeply in the earth. In the latter case, extreme pressure and heat will transform them once more into *metamorphic rocks* (from "metamorphose," to change). Metamorphic rocks exhibit a characteristic hardness, density, and mineral arrangement (see Table 8-3).

These three rock types compose the substance of the land, whether exposed at the surface or at varying depths beneath it. And from this original material soil is created by a complex interaction of climate, plants, animals, and topography.

Table 8-2. **Sedimentary Rocks: Characteristics and Sediments**

Sedimentary Rock	Characteristics	Sediments Derived from Rocks
Conglomerates, breccias	Mixtures of fine and coarse cemented fragmented particles	Gravels, pebbles, cobbles
Sandstones	Sand turned to stone, mostly by cementation and pressure	Sands
Shales, siltstones, graywackes	Shales are compacted clays and muds; silts are compacted into siltstones or graywackes	Clays, muds, and silts
Limestones	Solidified masses of calcium carbonate ($CaCO_3$)	Lime oozes, marine shells, chalk, marl, etc.
Flint	Microcrystalline forms of silica, occur mainly as nodules or lumps in limestones or chalks	Precipitated silica gels
Chert	Microcrystalline silica occurs in large formation	Skeletons of radiolarians
Bituminous coal	Formed by accumulation of plant debris; 5 percent moisture, 80 percent carbon; precursor to anthracite	Peat, lignite

Table 8-3. **Rock Types & Metamorphic Equivalents**

Original Rock	Metamorphic Equivalent
Sandstone	Quartzite
Limestone	Marble
Shale	Slate, phyllite, schist
Bituminous coal	Anthracite
Granite, slate, shale	Gneiss, schist

Source: Van Riper, *Man's Physical World.*

Source: Adapted from: Van Riper, *Man's Physical World.*

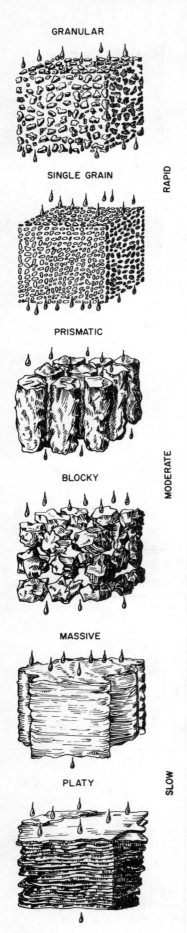

GRANULAR

SINGLE GRAIN

RAPID

PRISMATIC

BLOCKY

MODERATE

MASSIVE

PLATY

SLOW

Building Soil: Nowhere is the coevolution of life and environment more clearly demonstrated than in the soil-building process. Because an area of the planet experiences a certain climate and its local expression (the daily weather), and also because the land has a certain slope and the underlying rocks contain constituent materials that provide many of the nutrients needed for plant growth, specific kinds of plants can grow in that place. And because those particular plants can grow there, specific animals and microorganisms can survive. The growth activities of these interdependent life forms together with the physical effects of the environment create the soil type that will determine the further possibilities for plant and animal survival. For example, rainfall is one of the important limiting factors determining whether an area can support forests or only grasses.

Trees and grasses tend to extract from the soil different quantities of the various minerals needed for plant growth. Grasses, for instance, accumulate substantial amounts of the "bases" from the soil such as calcium and magnesium (actually, as oxides). By contrast, trees (conifers particularly) "mine" fewer of these bases from the soil, and in addition accumulate acidic resins in their needles. Further, pines favor fungi, and these produce biochemicals that lower the soil pH. The resultant debris accumulating beneath conifers is therefore far more acidic than that in a grassland. The makeup of the debris in turn influences the kinds of microorganisms that flourish there to decompose it. Fungi can survive under a wide range of conditions from quite acidic to fairly alkaline. Bacteria and actinomycetes need a more neutral medium in which to grow. The end products of decomposition will vary also, depending on the decomposers—fungi produces compounds that are easily soluble in water while bacteria and actinomycetes produce more resistant compounds.

At least one additional factor must be mentioned: grasses produce a great deal of new organic material each year in the form of large, fibrous root systems and above-ground tissues that die back and become available for decomposition. Conifers, by contrast, produce relatively little such dead material yearly, either above or below ground. Much of what they cast off may be in the form of twigs and other plant tissues impregnated with resins and other compounds that can only be broken down slowly.

Given this information we can begin to form a generalization about the soils found in grasslands versus naturally forested areas. In soils under grasses, the amount of organic material may be considerable, the soils will be neutral in reaction (meaning the acidity and alkalinity will be balanced), and they will probably be high in the products of decomposition, which are the nutrients necessary for plant growth. Conversely, we would expect the soil under conifers to be poor in organic material, acidic, and low in plant nutrients.

The complexity of contributing factors is increased by temperature and slope. In high temperatures organic matter decomposes quickly. Where rainfall is sufficient the organic debris may decompose and be leached away as quickly as it accumulates; as a result the soil will be impoverished, as in many tropical areas. Where the slope is steep, the action of wind, water, and gravity may constantly erode the soil so that soil never accumulates to a sufficient depth to support plant growth.

190

Soil Profile: As a soil develops, distinct layers becomes discernible, starting with the surface, where organic debris accumulates, and going downward to the unchanged bedrock. These layers are often strikingly visible in roadway cuts or building excavations. They are referred to as *soil horizons,* the uppermost being the *O horizon,* and the lowest the *R layer.* (See Figure 8-2, for a summary of soil horizon nomenclature.) Not all soils have all horizons, and the thickness of each layer present can vary greatly.

The A horizon is often the darkest, because here *humus,* which is decomposed organic material, coats the soil particles. It is also the layer of the soil from which minerals are washed through, or *eluviated;* older soils have lost most of these minerals and are thus less fertile. As the compounds are weathered out of the A horizon, they are deposited (*illuviated*) in the B horizon, where a layer of clay and various iron compounds may accumulate. Eventually this layer (called a *pan,* or *hard-pan*) may become so dense that it restricts the drainage of water or the entry of roots and the gas exchanges they require.

Urban soils often show the effects of human activities, and such activities may modify the profile that originally formed in the area. In street leveling, foundation digging, or wrecking and rebuilding, and similar soil-moving efforts, the original profile may become deeply buried and new material brought in upon the intact or destroyed A horizon. Previous agricultural activities may also have affected the soil. The mechanical action of repeated plowing to the same depth can make a clay hard-pan in the B horizon as dense as one formed by natural weathering processes. Other agricultural activities can also seriously affect the soil. An example is the long-term use of lead-arsenic insecticides in the early period of this century, which created serious heavy-metal contamination of some soils in areas of the eastern United States. These areas were originally apple orchards but are now suburban housing tracts.

Urban Soil Profile Modifications

The most serious modifications of the soil profile around urban dwellings are likely to be
  1. Removal of the fertile A horizon during grading for house siting
  2. The mixing of the A horizon and/or underlying layers with construction debris
  3. Accumulation and incorporation of inorganic trash, such as broken glass, into the top layers (commonly seen in inner-city empty lots)
  4. Compaction from heavy machinery used in house construction
  5. The addition of a supposedly more fertile topsoil, superimposed over whatever soil surface was left exposed after construction was completed. In the latter case, if the added layer of material is not partially mixed with the level beneath a drainage problem will occur at the interface, resulting in poor growing conditions. Frequently the new homeowner's first indication that something is wrong is when plants repeatedly and mysteriously die from what appear to be root-related disease problems. Excessive water accumulates in such poor interface areas and root respiration is then reduced. This effect in turn encourages pathogens and saprophytes (mushrooms and toadstools) to invade and destroy root tissue.

Figure 8-2. **Soil Horizons**

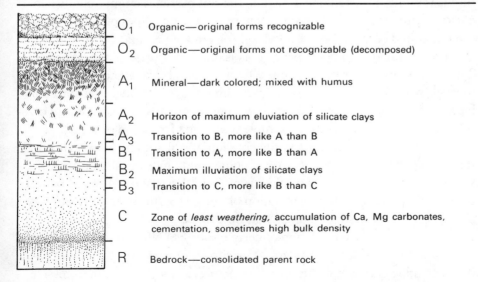

O₁	Organic—original forms recognizable
O₂	Organic—original forms not recognizable (decomposed)
A₁	Mineral—dark colored; mixed with humus
A₂	Horizon of maximum eluviation of silicate clays
A₃	Transition to B, more like A than B
B₁	Transition to A, more like B than A
B₂	Maximum illuviation of silicate clays
B₃	Transition to C, more like B than C
C	Zone of *least weathering,* accumulation of Ca, Mg carbonates, cementation, sometimes high bulk density
R	Bedrock—consolidated parent rock

Note: *Eluviation* is the process by which nutrients are leached from one soil zone to another, *illuviation* is the concentration of nutrients in one zone as a result of eluviation.

How to improve the structure of soil

1. **Add organic matter:** well-made compost is the best. In clay soils, this will increase aggregation and the pore spaces needed for gas exchanges. In sandy soils, it will increase water- and nutrient-holding capacity. In all soils, it will provide nutrient materials for varied soil flora and fauna, the activities of which aid in forming and maintaining soil pores necessary for gas exchanges, and provide nutrients necessary for plant growth.

2. **Till the soil as little as possible** once you have established your garden area (once a year, or not at all—only to add organic matter, if necessary). Tillage is usually done to remove weeds. The weed problem is better handled by mulching (placing material, preferably compost, on *top* of the soil). Mulches have a number of beneficial effects. They (a) smother weed seedlings, (b) make large weeds easier to pull by keeping the ground surface soft and moist, (c) improve water penetration when it rains or when you irrigate, (d) reduce erosion of the soil surface, (e) eliminate rain compaction and mud splattering (the latter is sometimes an important factor in transmission of plant disease), (f) add organic matter to the area where most of the microorganisms are that can decompose it, and (g) maintain even temperatures at the soil surface.

3. **Do not rototill.** This destroys soil aggregates! If you must turn the soil, use a digging fork. (In large areas, use a disc harrow.)

4. **Do not walk on growing areas.** Sawdust on paths will reduce compaction.

5. **Never disturb the soil when it is wet!** Soils saturated with water, particularly soils which have high concentrations of clay particles, are easily compacted and are difficult to cultivate. The best time to work a soil is when it is in a moist to dry condition.

Soil Texture: The rock or mineral portion of a soil is classified by particle size. Particle size as one of the key indicators of potential soil productivity. After stones and pebbles are removed, the largest particles visible to the eye are sand. The sand and silt (the next largest particles) are derived primarily from the physical weathering of rocks and are important to the structure of the soil because of the physical qualities they give it. The larger the particles, the larger the spaces between them. The spaces are important for the passage of water and of gases such as oxygen and carbon dioxide.

The smallest particles in the soil are platelets of clay. These are microscopic bits shaped rather like razor blades, and their surfaces are covered with negative electrical charges. The clay particles result primarily from chemical alterations of the original parent rock material. They are important in the chemistry of the soil because their charged surfaces attract and hold the plant nutrients as well as water molecules. The sand, silt, and clay particles vary in their proportions in different soils. Consequently soils vary in their characteristic water- and nutrient-holding abilities. These qualities, in turn, affect horticultural practices and plant growth.

Knowing the proportions of the sand, silt, and clay particles in one's soil is useful for calculating liming (adjusting the soil pH using lime) and watering rates, and in generally understanding the behavior of the soil. A very rough field test of a soil texture can be done using only one's hands and a little bit of water, as described in Box 8-2. A more accurate laboratory method requires a graduated cylinder and a soil hydrometer, and is described in Box 8-3. Once the relative percentage of sand, silt, and clay particles of a soil is determined, the soil's textural classification can be identified by using a soil texture triangle, shown in the margin on page 195.

Soil Structure: The arrangement of the soil particles is referred to as *structure*. It is highly desirable that there be pore spaces within the soil so that water may drain through it and gas exchanges occur. These pore spaces should vary somewhat in size and be well distributed. The ideal soil structure is thus a granulated one, in which the soil particles clump together in clusters with air spaces between. Some of the various types of soil structure are illustrated on page 190. A good soil for growing plants is half-hollow, that is, half-filled with pore space. This is often a surprise to the layperson. This pore space/soil ratio explains why it is desirable to avoid compacting the soil by walking or driving heavy machinery over it. Since wet soils collapse under weight more easily than dry ones, one must be particularly careful not to disturb wet soil (for example, following irrigation or rains).

Many factors contribute to the creation of soil structure. Freezing and thawing of the water in the soil, the amounts and kinds of salts in the soil water, the growth and death of plant roots, and the action of the soil life all contribute to the resulting distribution of the soil particles and the stability of the aggregates or small clumps that may form.

An excessive accumulation of certain salts can effect soil chemistry and make a soil too alkaline (see pages 203–08 on soil pH). Sodium has a particularly undesirable effect upon soil structure, as its presence in excessive amounts causes the clay particles to disperse evenly throughout the mass of soil. A crust may form, the permeability of the soil decreases, and the soil

(see pages 97–98 on greywater systems)

Box 8-1. **Soil Erosion**

The importance of soil erosion is not fully appreciated, yet this factor alone is probably one of the most serious problems facing agriculture, our basic life-support system. The most fertile and the lightest, finest soil fractions—the clay and organic matter—are usually the first to erode. One way to measure the loss of fertility due to water run-off is to assess the nutrients carried in the waters of major rivers. The following table documents such an analysis for the Ohio and Mississippi Rivers.

Amount of Nutrients Carried in Solution Annually

Element	Ohio (tons)	Mississippi (tons)
Phosphorus	17,199	62,188
Sodium	119,446	630,720
Potassium	396,521	1,626,312
Calcium	6,752,222	22,446,379
Magnesium	1,629,319	5,179,788
Sulphur	2,229,544	6,732,936

Good documentation exists on fertility losses due to wind action, especially for particular areas and years. The dust storms of the 1930s are a classic example. Such losses are still sustained. For good discussions of erosion management consult Stallings, *Soil Conservation;* and the Soil Conservation Society, *Conservation Tillage.*

structure deteriorates. (A soil can become so salty that plants actually have difficulty absorbing water from it.) Thus it is important that laundry and wash water (see pages 97–98 on greywater systems) that has passed through sodium water softeners not be used in irrigation.

Box 8-2. **The Touch Test for Your Soil**

Is your soil light (sandy) or heavy (lots of clay)? Learning to tell the texture—or the proportion of sand, silt, and clay—of your soil by this method takes practice. It is like training your ear to recognize different notes of the musical scale—a comparison with other notes is helpful. Try this touch test with *many* soils and see how they differ. Wherever you go, take a bit of soil into your hand and try it out, while remembering the soils you've worked before.

Take a bit of soil into the palm of one hand—a tablespoonful or a little less. Add a little water (you can even use saliva). With the fingers of the other hand, work the water into the soil so that it is thoroughly wet, but don't use so much water that the mixture is runny; it should be quite firm. Now try two tests:

1. Rub the mixture out thinly against your palm. What do you feel and see?

Clay gives the soil a shine when you press down firmly and spread it out. It feels slippery and may stick to your fingers as you work it.

If the soil is *sandy*, there will be no shine. It will feel gritty, and you may be able to feel individual sand grains.

Take the time to mix and knead the soil thoroughly, because clay takes a while to wet through. You can be deceived into thinking you are feeling sand particles, when really they are

hard clay lumps that haven't yet softened.

If the soil contains a high percentage of *silt*, it will have a greasy quality and will easily slip through your fingers as you work it, but it will not have the plastic quality of a soil with high clay content.

2. Roll the wet soil into a ball and then into a snake as long and thin as possible (see the accompanying drawing). Let the last inch or so of the snake stick out over the edge of your palm. If you can, pick up the snake-roll by one end. The sandier the soil,

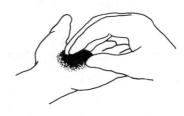

the harder it will be to roll into a ball, and any snake you manage to shape will quickly fall apart. As the percent of clay increases, you will be able to roll a thick snake that keeps its shape, but if the end protrudes beyond the edge of your hand, it will be apt to crack and break off. The ability of moistened soil to maintain a shape is referred to as its *plasticity.* The easier it can be molded, the more plastic it is said to be. The more clay, the thinner the snake you can roll, until, with a high-percent-clay soil you can roll a very thin strip that will hold together when you pick up one end. (When the amount of clay in the soil reaches approximately 35 percent or more, a snake one-quarter of an inch in diameter can be picked up by one end without breaking.) A silty soil will maintain its shape better than a sandy soil, but not as well as a soil having a high percentage of clay.

Here is something else to try: Mix a small amount of sifted compost in with the soil sample before it is moistened. Once the mixture is moistened, you'll be able to sense the influence of the organic matter. The sample will require more water to become wet through, since organic matter is so absorbent. If your soil is sandy the organic matter will help the soil adhere to a shape, and if it is high in clay the organic matter will help prevent it from becoming too sticky and unworkable in your palm.

193

Box 8-3. Determining Soil Texture by the Bouyoucus Hydrometer Method

The Bouyoucus (boy-yu-cus) hydrometer method of textural analysis provides a precise reading of the percentage of sand, silt, and clay of your soil. The extra expense of equipment and time involved in this method is offset by the precision of the results and the educational experience derived from the process. The test is particularly suitable as a classroom experiment.

This method is based on the fact that the rate at which soil particles settle out of a water solution is dependent upon their relative densities. The most dense soil particles are the sands, and they will settle first. Next are the silts, and finally the clay. Using selective sedimentation rates of the soil constituents, a test may be constructed to determine the exact proportions of sand, silt, and clay in the soil.

Materials and Equipment

For each sample tested:
1. 50 grams of oven-dried soil that has been pulverized (for instance, in a hand-cranked coffee grinder)
2. 5 grams of Calgon dispersing agent (water softener)
3. 1000 milliliters (0.9 quart) water
4. One large (2-quart or greater) wide-mouth jar with a tight-fitting lid
5. A gram scale
6. A soil hydrometer calibrated in units of grams per liter
7. A 100-milliliter (or larger) graduated cylinder

Procedure

Collect a half-pound sample of the garden soil you desire to test. Dry it in the oven at a moderate heat until all the moisture has been driven off. Pulverize it with a coffee grinder, mortar and pestle, or some other comparable device.

Weigh out a 50-gram sample of the soil and place it in the wide-mouth jar. Prepare a solution of 5 grams of Calgon and 50 milliliters of water. Add the Calgon solution and an additional 600 milliliters of water to the soil. Let stand for 1 hour, and then mix vigorously for 5 minutes. (A second person might help with this, for the stirring is tiring.) Add enough water to increase the volume of the suspension to 1000 milliliters (0.91 quarts) exactly.

Place the lid on the jar and shake vigorously for an additional 30 seconds. Place the jar on a countertop, remove the lid, and at exactly 20 seconds after the shaking has stopped lower the hydrometer into the suspension. Gently balance the hydrometer in the solution to obtain an accurate reading. At the end of 40 seconds from the time the shaking ceased take a reading on the hydrometer. This reading records the amount of silt and clay still in suspension; the sand fraction will have already settled out.

Do not disturb the hydrometer or suspension. In 2 hours take a second reading. This one will record the amount of clay still in suspension; by this time the silt will have settled out and joined the sand on the bottom of the jar.

Interpreting the Results:

Record the readings as follows:

1. *The 40-second reading:*
_____ grams/liter minus 5 grams/liter Calgon equals _____ grams/liter silt and clay (A)

2. *The 2-hour reading:*
_____ grams/liter minus 5 grams/liter Calgon equals _____ grams/liter clay (B)

3. The 40-second reading (A) minus the 2-hour reading (B) equals the grams/liter silt (C)

(A) _____ − (B) _____
= (C) _____ grams/liter silt

4. The grams/liter of silt and clay (A) subtracted from the total concentration of solids in the solution (which was 50 grams/liter) equals the grams/liter of sand (D)

50 grams/liter − (A) _____
= (D) _____ grams/liter sand

5. Multiply each of these concentrations (B, C, and D) by 2, to get the percentage of each fraction in the original soil sample. For instance, if (B) is 25, then the sample had 2 × 25, or 50 percent clay.

Water softeners chemically replace heavy base elements in water, such as calcium and magnesium, with sodium. Unfortunately, the base elements, which are a menace to the cleaning power of the detergent, are extremely important in preserving good soil structure. So from a standpoint of soil fertility, water softeners take good things out and put harmful things into the water. Detergents with large amounts of sodium in them should also be avoided (particularly those containing water softeners). It is also essential that rock salt, used in winter for ice management, be kept from draining into garden areas. Ashes, sawdust, or sand should be used as antislip materials wherever possible.

Particularly valuable in creating good soil structure are the actions of soil animals that feed upon the organic matter in the soil, and on its surface (see pages 198–200). These organisms mix and aerate the soil, and secrete complex slimes that hold open soil passageways by gluing the soil particles together. No mechanical turning and breaking up of the soil by humans or machinery can equal the beneficial action of these animals. In fact, numerous studies have shown that repeated human cultivation of the soil is more likely to decrease the amount of pore space in the soil than improve it. The more thorough the disturbance to the soil the lower the porosity—or, the fewer the soil pores—after the first soaking. Rototillers and similar machines have the worst effect because of their eggbeater-like operation; disks are least offensive because they only open the soil surface. Spading, particularly if the soil is moist and sticky, can also be detrimental.

Management for Good Soil Structure: This information translates into practical garden soil management. Since soil animals are so important in creating good soil structure, and since they in turn depend upon organic material in the soil, this latter must be regularly supplied through the addition of compost or other organic mulches. These can be either applied to the surface of the soil to simulate the accumulation of plant litter under nonhuman-manipulated conditions, or else incorporated into the top layer, where there is sufficient oxygen to facilitate decomposition.

In general, disturb the soil as little as possible. Permit the soil animals to do the turning and to incorporate the organic material. An exception is where a garden is started over an underlying hard-pan, which might need to be broken up initially, or where sod (a mat of lawn) is being turned into a garden. (To reiterate, a *hard-pan* is a layer of impervious soil, sometimes produced as a result of repeated plowing to the same depth, and in other cases due to natural deposition of minerals in a layer beneath the surface.) Sufficient seed-bed preparation can generally be achieved by a light mixing of compost into the top inches of the soil surface. If deeper aeration is desired in a heavy clay soil, a digging fork can be plunged in vertically every four to six inches and worked back and forth to break open the underlying soil, allowing some organic matter from the surface to fall into the cracks, but not turning the soil completely over.

The authors have used a minimum-tillage approach for many years similar to the method first popularized in this country by Ruth Stout, author of the classic *How to Have a Green Thumb Without an Aching Back*. Preliminary studies of such methods conducted in England by the Henry Doubleday Research Association showed that good yields can be maintained for three to seven years on various soils prepared in this way. Depending on the soil, however, there came a period in each plot studied where yields declined and some cultivation was needed to bring them up to previous levels of production once again. This is probably due to small particles migrating down in the soil profile. What one can generalize from these studies is limited. Still, the conclusion we derive from these as well as our own studies is that much back-breaking cultivation practiced by home gardeners is totally unnecessary and may actually have detrimental effects. Mulching with compost for weed suppression can substitute for cultivation in many situations, and the end result will be a soft, friable soil filled with earthworms, and of an excellent structure for growing vegetables. The list in the margin (page 192) summarizes techniques for improving soil structure.

An additional note about mulches: a thick (four-inch) layer of compost on top of the soil may be desirable most of the year, but it could prevent the soil from warming up quickly in the early spring. Therefore, rake the mulch back from those areas where you wish to plant heat-loving seedlings such as

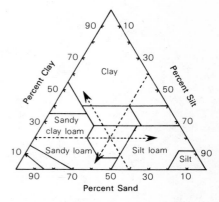

The composition of the textural classes of soils used by the United States Soil Survey. (Sand 2-0·05 mm., silt 0·05-0·002 mm., clay below 0·002 mm.)

How to Use the Textural Diagram of Soil Classification

Imagine that you learned from the Bouyoucus hydrometer test that your soil is composed of 40 percent sand, 40 percent silt, and 20 percent clay. Locate the 40 percent mark along the *percent sand* axis. From that point draw a line into the pyramid, running parallel to the *percent silt* axis. Locate the 40 percent mark along the *percent silt* axis. From that point draw a line into the pyramid parallel to the *percent clay* axis. The two lines intersect in the quadrant that describes the soil textural classification, in this case loam. Although the diagram has three sides, one for each soil fraction, only two coordinates are required to determine the texture of a soil. The third coordinate will confirm what is established by the previous two. (Locate the 20 percent mark along the *percent clay* axis, and draw a line from that point, into the triangle, parallel to the sand axis.)

tomatoes. Once the soil has warmed, the mulch can be tucked back around the plants. Do not permit the mulch to fall within the center of such low-growing plants as lettuce and strawberries, as this will promote the growth of organisms that can cause plant disease.

Watering: Water can be in the soil and yet still inaccessible to the plants. Water molecules closest to the clay particles are held there tightly by hydrogen bonding—that is, the electrical attraction of positive hydrogen ions for the negative charges on the clay. As explained later in this chapter (pages 200–01) both clay and organic matter are covered with these negative electric charges, and thus both can hold great quantities of water.

How the soil particles are arranged—the soil structure—is also extremely important to the water-holding (and -releasing) qualities of a soil. In a clay soil, for example, the water will be held in tiny pores by surface tension and not drain easily. Furthermore, soils with a high percentage of clay will swell as they absorb moisture, preventing the further penetration of water.

Two or three days after a rain or irrigation, when the water has drained downward from all the larger pores under the influence of gravity, the moisture content of the soil will have reached what is referred to as *field capacity*. The *wilting point* is that moisture content below which the water is no longer available and useful to plants. The water may be there, but is held so tightly that the plant roots cannot pull it out.

Various devices exist to measure the amount of moisture in the soil. For example, sometimes the varying electrical resistances of gypsum blocks are monitored as they gain or lose water. Field capacity is calibrated to record a value of 100, and a wilting point of 0 (zero). The blocks are buried in the soil at various depths, and a portable meter (potentiometer) can be connected to them when a reading is needed. More sophisticated devices, called tensiometers, are available in different lengths, and are used for the same purpose. They are not exorbitantly expensive, and under some circumstances may be well worth the investment. Such moisture meters can be set to turn on a sprinkler when the soil dries out beyond a certain point.

The water-holding capacity of a soil depends largely on the texture, or the amount of sand, silt, and clay in the soil. Since clay minerals are highly water-absorbent, the degree to which soils will hold water against the force of gravity (their field capacity) is a function of their clay content. The greater its concentration of clay, the more the soil will absorb and retain water.

The depth at which the water is stored is also very important, since evaporation is greatest from the soil surface. Thus it is always better to water a great deal at one time rather than a little bit many times, assuming that you do not exceed the capacity of the soil to absorb the water at any particular moment, causing surface run-off and erosion. In sandy soils, because of their coarse texture, water is quick to drain to a depth beneath the root zone of vegetable plants, and therefore is easily lost through evaporation. Soils with a higher percentage of clay minerals will hold more water on the top few inches and will require considerably more irrigation or rainfall than lighter soils for water to penetrate to greater depths. Therefore, clay soils must be watered for longer periods but less frequently than sandy soils.

Incorporation of organic matter into a soil will significantly modify its water-holding or drainage capacity. In a clay soil, organic matter tends to reform soil particles into tiny clumps called aggregates, allowing water to drain more readily. For a sandy soil, addition of organic matter will help bind the minerals together so that the soil holds water.

Under drought conditions, plenty of nitrogen must be available to plants so that they can grow long roots in search for water. However, this also means that they will exhaust the soil moisture to a greater degree. If a second dry year follows, so may a poor crop. Still, drought is less of a problem to the householder than to the farmer, since even under the worst conditions enough wastewater is usually created by the human activities in the house to provide some for the plants too.

To calculate roughly how often you need to water with a sprinkler, you need to figure in the texture of your soil (this can be approximate, as determined by the hand test in Box 8-2); the average temperature, humidity, and amount of wind in your garden; the amount of water delivered by your sprinkler (it is worthwhile testing how evenly your sprinkler delivers water by placing empty coffee cans or measuring cups out at various distances from the center); and the transpiration and root-depth characteristics of the

Box 8-4. **Water-Conservation Gardening**

1. Start seeds indoors or in a garden coldframe whenever possible. The absence of wind and the moderate temperature conditions within the house, plus the ability to easily confine the watering to just the area surrounding the seedling's roots, means water use will be reduced during the first weeks of the seedling's life.

2. Incorporate as much organic material into the soil as possible. This will increase the water-holding capacity. Compost is the best material for this.

3. Mulch the plant beds heavily with compost, dry leaves, or straw to prevent water loss through evaporation from the bare ground.

4. Construct windbreaks to the windward side of the garden, or grow in the lee side of protecting structures (wherever such windbreaks will not shade the garden).

5. Whenever possible, plant seedlings in depressions rather than in raised beds, using the berm around the sides of the plant to reduce wind and restrict irrigation water to the area immediately surrounding the plant roots. We suggest the following planting method:

a. Shape a depression on the ground in the form of a trench, narrow enough so that you can reach to the center of it easily, and as long as you need for the number of plants you will grow.

b. Using a digging fork, mix the soil in the bottom of the trench with compost, so it is part soil and one-fourth to one-half compost. (If possible, this compost-soil mixture should be at least one foot deep.)

c. Thoroughly soak the depression by flooding it with water.

d. Set the young seedlings into the trench, pressing the soil down firmly around them and adding a little water around each seedling so that it is thoroughly wet.

e. Pile compost, straw, or other organic mulch around the seedlings four to six inches deep; add mulch as seedlings grow larger.

f. Put your fingers into the soil under the mulch to test the degree of dryness before adding more water; with soils containing a moderate to heavy proportion of clay, and with plenty of organic matter and thick mulch, you may be able to go for many weeks, even when outdoor temperatures are in the nineties or higher, without needing to add any water at all.

g. When water is needed, let it run slowly under the mulch from a hose, and fill the depression once.

6. Corn, melons, and celery are three vegetables that require large amounts of water for the amount of edible material returned, and probably should not be attempted when water is in short supply. It is likely that traditional Hopi corn strains may be more productive under drought conditions than the commercial varieties available; however, we have not tested this.

7. Carrots, among the few vegetables that need to be seeded directly in the ground, should have their seeds soaked overnight and mixed with sand for broadcasting over the prepared bed. The bed should have large amounts of organic matter incorporated into the soil and should be thoroughly soaked before the seeds are scattered over it. Seeds scattered over the bed should be covered with a fine, thin mulch (sifted compost is best). If parallel boards are staked on each side of the carrot bed, with a line of projecting nails along the top edge, burlap or other cloth can be stretched across the bed two or three inches above the emerging seedlings to shade them during the first ten days or so and reduce the chances of their drying out.

plants you are growing. Calculating your water needs is difficult to do often but attempting to figure it out once is worthwhile. If you have a good-sized growing area, this calculation is likely to save you much water over the years, as well as the energy it takes to pump it to your house. Many urban people waste a great deal of water on their lawns and gardens because they have no sense of how much they should be, or are, applying. Water that soaks beneath the root depths of the plants will be of little use to them.

Economizing on Water: Many homemade and commercial systems have been devised for economizing on water where that resource is in short supply. Where dew-fall is heavy, plants can be placed in the center of depressions that lead the water toward the stems. Soaker hoses have long been employed to apply water just where it is needed, rather than sprinkling the whole garden. Sophisticated drip-irrigation equipment is now available whereby a series of pipes or tubes are fitted with emitters that meter out the water in each spot in a specific number of gallons per minute. These can be obtained to fit container gardens also, a small tube leading from the main hose, bringing water to each individual container (see Figure 7-7). A simple method of drought gardening is described in Box 8-4.

Soil Life and Organic Matter: A good soil is teeming with life, at least in the upper inches where oxygen is available for metabolic activity. The living part of the soil consists of plant roots, microorganisms (some of which may be classed as plants and others as animals), and macroorganisms (such as insects, mites, and other arthropods, earthworms, pot worms, nematodes, and larger animals such as moles, rodents, and so on). Many of these organisms are very small and may be present in incredible numbers.

The organisms in these soil communities may be classified as decomposers and detritivores. The latter have a primarily physical effect upon organic matter, tearing it into smaller pieces and exposing more surface to attack by the decomposers, which actually effect a chemical change. The decomposers are chiefly bacteria and fungi. The detritivores feed both on organic matter and decomposer microorganisms. Some of these soil food chains are shown in Figure 8-3. As can be seen in that figure, the organisms in the soil interact with each other to form a maze of food chains. Soil food chains begin with microorganisms, such as bacteria and fungi, and herbivorous animals, such as snails and mites, feeding on organic residues. In the case of the soil food chain pictured in Figure 8-3, food wastes are the primary source of energy for the microorganisms and herbivorous soil animals. In turn, these organisms are consumed by the first-order carnivores, such as predatory mites, springtails, and flat worms. These animals are fed upon by yet another level of soil organisms, the second order of predators—beetles and centipedes for example. Each level of feeding activity is termed a trophic level, in reference to the place the organism occupies in the food web.

Ultimately these organisms not only help to create a good structure in the soil by mixing and aerating it and secreting slimes that help to hold the soil crumbs together, but also break down the materials into their chemical constituents so that they are available to plants.

The fuel for this highly desirable activity by microorganisms is organic matter—the dead remains of other plants and animals. In areas undisturbed by humans, this organic matter is supplied by the natural death of the plants and animals themselves. Under favorable conditions, where soils are deep, rainfall adequate, and growing season temperatures moderate, large amounts of organic matter may accumulate as dead plant roots and plant debris at the soil surface. However, wherever humans harvest plant materials from the soil, less remains there at the end of each growing season than grew there earlier. In addition, when the soil is disturbed with plows or other implements the decomposition of organic matter present is greatly speeded up through exposure to more oxygen and heat than would have occurred naturally, and thus the loss of organic matter from the soil is hastened.

It is essential that wherever humans do disturb the soil through agriculture and wish to continue to harvest crops in that same place, the lost or-

Follow arrows to trace food chains.

Figure 8-3. **Food Web of Organisms in Mulch or Soil**

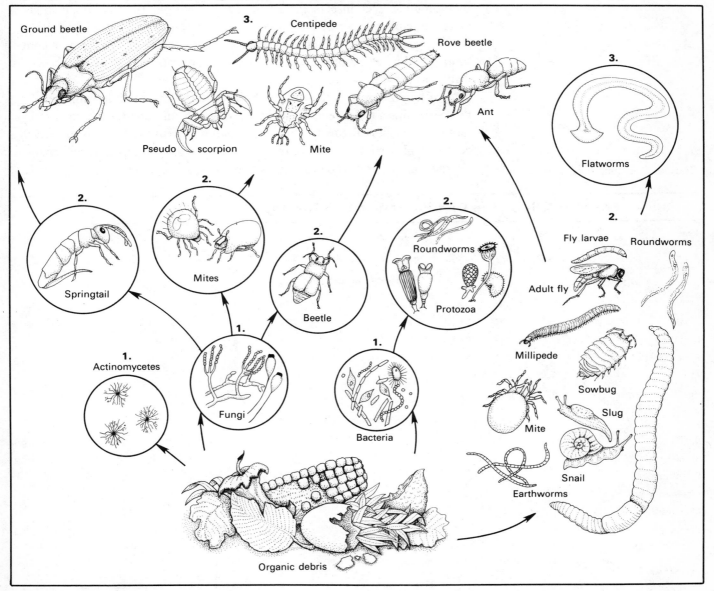

ganic matter be replaced to feed the soil organisms so they can survive and continue their valuable activities. The farmer can do this by plowing under crop residues left after harvest, adding manure, rotating crops, and growing green manure (crops turned under to provide the nitrogen they have fixed in their tissues—legume crops are an example). Crops that leave very little organic matter behind, such as corn, should be followed with those that have a deep and extensive root system and leave much organic material in and on the soil when harvested. Wheat, oats, and alfalfa are examples of the latter.

The intensive home gardener is in a more fortunate position. He or she need only maintain a small area with adequate amounts of organic matter. By utilizing all the organic waste matter of the household through composting, and by adding whatever organic waste matter can be scavenged, providing enough organic matter to support an adequate soil community in the backyard plot is not too difficult.

It is also important not to contaminate or kill off a part of these soil communities through applications of pesticides. Since soil organisms—including bacteria, insects, mites, and fungi—are plants and animals, there is always a danger that materials used to control plant pests will fall or wash into the soil, causing depletion, imbalances, or contamination of these communities. The effect of the soil sterilant carbon disulphide (CS_2) is shown in Table 8-4, as an example.

When the bulk of the fresh organic material has been decomposed, there remains a fully decomposed fraction of organic matter which is resistant to further breakdown. This is called *humus*. Humus remains in the soil coating soil particles, and like the clay it is covered with negative electric charges that permit it to attract positively charged chemical particles, called

Source: From: Schaller, *Soil Animals.*

Table 8-4. **Effect of CS_2 on the Distribution of Soil Arthropods***

Year						1957							1958		Total
Month	Feb.	Mar.	Apr.	May	June	July	Aug.	Sept.	Oct.	Nov.	Dec.	Jan.	Feb.		
Control field, untreated															
Springtails	61	72	225	55	76	133	189	164	219	175	118	149	84		1,720
Mites	103	113	118	63	63	139	191	133	186	187	123	139	123		1,810
Symphyla	4	3	1	1	1	3	6	8	6	1	2	3	4		43
Dipterous larvae	2	1	—	2	5	—	—	—	2	1	—	—	3		16
Millipedes	—	—	—	—	—	—	1	2	—	—	1	—	2		6
Beetles (+ larvae)	—	2	—	—	—	—	6	—	1	—	1	—	—		10
Poisoned field															
Springtails	3	15	78	513	75	47	161	103	282	508	207	147	448		2,499
Mites	6	1	12	38	167	107	112	52	86	152	45	35	85		898
Symphyla	—	—	—	—	—	—	—	—	—	—	—	—	—		—
Dipterous larvae	—	—	—	3	1	—	—	1	—	15	1	2	—		23
Millipedes	—	—	—	—	—	—	—	—	—	—	—	—	—		—
Beetles (+ larvae)	2	—	—	—	4	—	—	—	—	2	—	—	2		10

*From a Bavarian vineyard, 400 gm per square meter applied May 12, 1956.

Note: Carbon disulphide (CS_2) is a fumigant widely used against soil insects.

cations (cāt-i-ons). (A good way to remember that cations are positive is to visualize the "t" in cation as being a "+.") The chemical nutrients needed by plants for growth and released from rocks and organic material by weathering and the action of soil life in the soil are primarily in the form of these charged particles, or cations. The importance of humus and clay in the soil should be obvious, since they operate like negatively charged magnets attracting the positive cations. This ability to retain and let go of the charged particles is called *cation-exchange capacity.* Sand and silt, the other major soil constituents, have none of this capacity at all. Of the three basic nonorganic soil fractions, clay alone has exchange capacity. Thus, if plant nutrients are added to sand or silt, they will leach right through with water. That is why sandy soils, though easy to dig in and containing plenty of air spaces for the growth of plant roots and the drainage of water, are relatively infertile in their natural state. Large amounts of organic matter must be added to them to increase their cation-exchange capacity.

On the other hand, the potential fertility of clay soils is very great. Clay, varying considerably with the type, has a high exchange capacity. But because their particles are so fine, clay soils may present problems with water drainage and adequate gas exchanges. The addition of organic matter to clay soils increases those desirable structural characteristics.

On the scale on which this cation-exchange capacity is rated, clay may vary from 3 to 100, while humus may have a capacity as high as 300.

Plant Nutrients and the Chemistry of the Soil

When water falls through the air it picks up carbon dioxide and becomes a weak acid, capable of leaching certain minerals from the rock fragments. Rainwater may also pick up sulphur from industrial pollutants in the air. The roots of the plants exude weak organic acids. The metabolic activities of the soil organisms and the results of their activities in breaking down organic matter, including the decomposition of their own bodies, all contribute to the freeing of certain specific elements within the soil that become available to plants. These elements in their ionic form are exchanged by the clay and humus particles with the soil water and the plant roots. They provide most of the necessary nutrients needed for plant growth and ultimately human survival.

Specifically, the elements needed for plant growth are oxygen, hydrogen, carbon, nitrogen, phosphorus, potassium, sulfur, calcium, magnesium, iron, manganese, molybdenum, copper, zinc, boron, chlorine, and sodium. The first nine are thought of as *macronutrients,* since large amounts are needed by crops. The remaining ones, *micronutrients,* are needed in only very small amounts. Table 8-5 shows the elements, their symbols, the principal ions in which they occur, and their functions.

Even the elements that are needed in tiny amounts are still essential, and the plant will show obvious deficiencies and not grow adequately in their absence. It is interesting that the elements essential to plants are not the same as those needed by animals. Luckily, in some cases plants will pick up from the soil and incorporate into their tissues elements nonessential to their

Table 8-5. **Plant Nutrition at a Glance**

Chemical Symbol	Element	Chemical Form in Which Element Is Assimilated by Plant Roots	Physiological Function Performed in the Plant
Macronutrients			
N	Nitrogen	NO_3^- (nitrate) and NH_4^+ (ammonium)	Formation of amino acids, chlorophyll, DNA, RNA
P	Phosphorus	H_2PO_4 (phosphoric acid)	Constituent of DNA, RNA, functions in metabolism reactions; respiration (ATP)
K	Potassium	K^+	Activator for many enzymes; required for protein synthesis
Ca	Calcium	Ca^{++}	Nitrogen metabolism; holds plant cell walls together
S	Sulfur	SO_4^{--} (sulfate)	Well-distributed throughout tissues and organs; constituent in hormones; functions in protein production, holds polypeptide strains together in proteins
Mg	Magnesium	Mg^{++}	Essential part of chlorophyll molecule; activates numerous essential enzymes for work
Micronutrients			
Fe	Iron	Fe^{++} (ferrous) Fe^{+++} (ferric)	Essential activator for some enzymes involved in chlorophyll synthesis; essential part of pigment molecules that act as electron carriers in photosynthesis and respiration
Mn	Manganese	Mn^{++}	Activates many enzymes; structural role in the chloroplast-membrane system
Mo	Molybdenum	MoO_4^{--} (molybdate)	Electron carrier in conversion of nitrates to ammonium ions; essential to process of nitrogen fixation
Zn	Zinc	Zn^{++}	Participates in chlorophyll formation; produces a hormone involved in stem growth
Cu	Copper	Cu^{++}	Electron carrier; may also be a catalyst for nitrogen fixation
Cl	Chlorine	Cl^-	Stimulation of photosynthesis
B	Boron	Bo_3^{---} (borate)	Involved in sugar transport through phloem

$$H_2O + CO_2 \longrightarrow H_2CO_3$$
Water + carbon dioxide $\longrightarrow$ carbonic acid

$$H_2O + SO_3 \longrightarrow H_2SO_4$$
Water + sulfate $\longrightarrow$ sulfuric acid

When a water solution contains more hydrogen cations (H^+) than hydroxyl anions (OH^-), the solution is said to be *acid*. When there are more OH^- anions in the solution, it is referred to as *alkaline*, or *basic*. pH (pronounced pēē-ā'ch) is a measurement used to express acidity and alkalinity on a scale whose values run from 0 to 14 (see Table 8-7). pH stands for "power of hydrogen." The pH scale is a logarithmic one, and refers to the logarithm of the reciprocal of the hydrogen ion concentration, or more precisely:

pH = the negative logarithm of the hydrogen ion concentration (in moles per liter), or

$$pH = \frac{1}{(H^+)}$$

$$= \log \frac{1}{\text{hydrogen ion concentration}}$$

own growth. The best-known example from human diets is iodine. This element, essential to the proper functioning of our thyroid gland, is not needed by plants. Still plants will take it up where it is present in the soil along the coast of continents (iodine is found in seawater and sea foods such as seaweed). Humans eating those plants cannot fail to pick up the iodine they need. In the interior of continents, iodine is not found in the soil, and thus is not taken up by plants. Consequently, goiter, an abnormality of the thyroid gland the symptom of which is a visible enlargement in the neck, occurred frequently in those areas before the common use of iodized salt.

Plants may also pick up elements nonessential but nonharmful to themselves that are dangerous to animals. Good examples are the heavy metals and pesticides.

Uptake of Heavy Metals and Pesticides: The fact that heavy metals are absorbed by plant roots is well-established. The Market Basket Survey, discussed in Chapter 7 in relation to pesticides, also reports on the concentrations of zinc, cadmium, lead, mercury, arsenic, and selenium (some of the heavy metals) in plants. ("Heavy" refers to the atomic weights.) Some of the pesticides known to be absorbed and translocated in food plants are aldrin, dieldrin, heptachlor, heptachlor epoxide, amiben, EPN, BHC, and chlordane. Thus, soils polluted with these compounds and elements may cause food contamination through plant uptake. Heavy metals do not break down. Therefore, unless they are changed in form (as in methylation, or other biochemical processes), or are moved by erosion, run-off, leaching, bio-magnification, or other such processes, they will persist in the soil indefinitely.

Methylation makes some heavy metals—for example, mercury—much more dangerous. Pesticides degrade but the rate of decomposition varies widely. Chlordane, for example, will persist for twelve years, dieldrin for six years, *BHC* for more than eleven years, heptachlor for more than nine years, pentachlorophenol (*PCP*) for more than five years, toxaphene for more than six years, and other chlorinated hydrocarbons will persist for decades in the soil. (For a more detailed discussion and listing of pesticides see the UNESCO book *Soil Biology*.)

For home food producers, the persistence of these materials means that you need to know the history of a soil in order to be assured that these types of compounds are not entering your diet, even if you are producing your own food without using toxicants. The home producer who wants to avoid toxic levels of zinc and cadmium will have a difficult time in certain cases because galvanized rain gutters are so widespread. Galvanizing means adding a coat of zinc, and the extremely toxic heavy metal cadmium is a contaminant with zinc. Also, until arsenical poisons are removed from the marketplace, arsenic too will continue to be introduced into soils.

The Role Played by Plant Nutrients

Oxygen: is one of the important plant macronutrients. It constitutes 21 percent of the air (see Table 8-6 showing percent of gases in the air). It is taken in directly by plants during the process of respiration, through their stomata, or pores, which dot the (primarily upper) surface of the leaves, as well as through the root cells. Oxygen is abundantly present in the soil; it makes up the bulk of water molecules, and is extremely important in forming organic and inorganic compounds with the other elements.

Hydrogen: is a key element in soil chemistry, as well as being essential for plant growth. It is a very small cation (positive ion) that apparently can slip in close to the negatively charged clay and organic matter so that it balances the electric charges of water, minerals, and complex compounds.

The degree of acidity or alkalinity (pH) of a solution is determined by the relative number of hydrogen and hydroxyl (OH^-) ions in the water (see margin). The difference between an acid or basic condition in the soil solution is great.

Plant growth is not directly affected by pH, but the plant nutrients and the kinds of compounds in which they are present and their availability for use by the plants are affected. Thus pH ultimately influences what plants

Table 8-6. **Composition of the Clean Atmosphere Near Sea Level**

Constituent	Chemical Formula	Percent by Volume	Parts per Million by Volume
Permanent gases			
Nitrogen	N_2	78.084	
Oxygen	O_2	20.946	
Argon	Ar	0.934	
Neon	Ne		18.2
Helium	He		5.2
Krypton	Kr		1.1
Hydrogen	H_2		0.5
Nitrous oxide	N_2O		0.3
Xenon	Xe		0.09
Variable gases			
Water vapor	H_2O	0–7	
Carbon dioxide	CO_2	0.032	
Methane	CH_4		1.5
Carbon monoxide	CO		0.1
Ozone	O_3		0.02
Ammonia	NH_3		0.01
Nitrogen dioxide	NO_2		0.001
Sulfur dioxide	SO_2		0.0002
Hydrogen sulfide	H_2S		0.0002

Source: Williamson, *Fundamentals of Air Pollution*.

can grow in a given soil. Acidity also affects the cation-exchange capacity, or the potential fertility, of a soil, since the hydrogen ions may attach to so many of the negative-charged sites on the clay and organic matter that few are left open to hold cations of the other elements needed for plant growth.

When the H^+ and OH^- ions balance each other, the solution is referred to as *neutral*. In the logarithmic scale used to measure pH, 7.0 is neutral. A soil close to neutral is preferred by many common food plants, as well as by the bacteria important in decomposing organic material and developing good soil structure. (See Figure 8-4, showing suitable pH ranges for various crops.)

In areas such as the eastern United States, where there is adequate water to grow large crops without irrigation, the soils have become somewhat acid. This is both because the hydrogen ions are abundantly available from the frequent rainfall, and because the water has leached away much of the calcium compounds and other bases. In areas of low rainfall, on the other hand, such as the semiarid valleys of the West and Southwest, these bases will not have leached away and the soils may be alkaline. In many cases, one can improve such alkaline soils by creating better drainage (often by setting in subsoil drainage tiles) and then just leaching the salts away with irrigation water. Where soils are acidic, lime is added periodically to bring them back toward neutral.

The base that is most helpful in creating a good soil structure is calcium (Ca^{++}). Ground limestone rock, high in calcium, is the most commonly used material for amending an acid soil. If dolomite lime is used, some magnesium is present also. Because raising the soil pH toward neutral will increase the bacterial activity, the addition of lime will speed up the decomposition of organic matter. Therefore, it is important for the grower to add either manure or other organic material, such as crop residues, when lime is used. Otherwise, the first years' good yields will be followed by

Figure 8-4. **Suitable pH Ranges for Selected Crops**

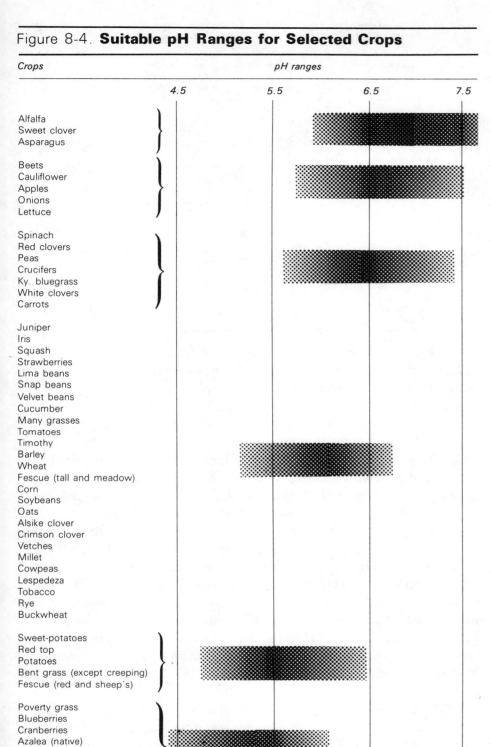

Crops — pH ranges

Source: Janick, Schery, Woods, and Ruttan, *Plant Science.*

poorer crops in subsequent years. Where organic wastes are regularly turned back to the soil in the form of mulch, this is not a problem.

How can you tell the pH of your soil? A reliable, inexpensive method is with the use of "pHydrion papers" (one of several available brands). A pH paper should be ordered that contains the full pH range from 4.0 to 9.0.

Table 8-7. pH Values of Hydrogen + Hydroxyl

	pH		Hydrogen Ion Concentration (Moles/Liter)*	Hydroxyl Ion Concentration (Moles/Liter)*	Acidity of Common Solutions
	0		10^0	10^{-14}	
	1		10^{-1}	10^{-13}	
	2		10^{-2}	10^{-12}	
Acid	3		10^{-3}	10^{-11}	lemon juice
	4		10^{-4}	10^{-10}	beer
	5	Normal	10^{-5}	10^{-9}	boric acid
	6	soil	10^{-6}	10^{-8}	milk
Neutral	7	or	10^{-7}†	10^{-7}	pure water
	8	plant	10^{-8}	10^{-6}	sea water
	9	range	10^{-9}	10^{-5}	soap solution
Basic	10		10^{-10}	10^{-4}	milk of magnesia
	11		10^{-11}	10^{-3}	ammonia
	12		10^{-12}	10^{-2}	trisodium phosphate
	13		10^{-13}	10^{-1}	lye
	14		10^{-14}	10^0	

*One mole of any substance is a quantity of grams equal in number to its molecular weight, and is equivalent to 6×10^{23} molecules of that substance.

† 10^{-7} is a notation for $\frac{1}{10^7}$, or $\frac{1}{10,000,000}$, or 0.000,000,1.

Source: Donahue, Shickluna, and Robertson, *Soils: An Introduction to Soils and Plant Growth.*

(The address for ordering is Micro-Essential Laboratory, Brooklyn, N.Y. 11210.) A tablespoon of mineral soil from the top few inches beneath the mulch is mixed with a little water, and the tip of the pH paper strip is immersed in it. By comparing the color the paper turns with the color key that comes with the paper, you can get a reasonably accurate reading. Mixing distilled water rather than tap water with the soil will improve the accuracy. By testing the soil from different parts of the garden and from different depths, and by repeating the tests each year at different seasons, you should get a reasonable picture of how acid or alkaline your soil is at any time, and this will help you determine if any special treatment is needed.

Adding organic matter to the soil has a buffering effect (creates a stable condition in which the pH does not change easily) because it increases the cation-exchange capacity (by increasing the number of sites where cations can be attached to the clay or organic material). It also may move the soil gradually toward the acid side, because decomposition of the material gradually releases organic acids anto the soil. Thus additions of lime may be needed occasionally even in California and southwest gardens that do not receive regular summer growing-season rainfall, since these are artificially irrigated regularly, and have large amounts of organic matter added in the form of compost.

Table 8-8 is offered as a guide for computing how much lime should be used to raise the pH, if necessary. Notice that it takes more to move the pH from 5 to 6 than from 4 to 5. It takes more lime to change soils high in clay and/or organic matter because of their higher cation-exchange capacity. This is one of the operable buffer systems in the soil; organic matter is another. Table 8-9 shows soil conditioning materials most commonly used to treat acid soils. When an acid soil is limed, the lime should be mixed with the top inches of the soil whenever possible to increase the rate of its availability.

Too much lime may cause the soil to develop an overly alkaline reaction and may result in as much of a problem as too little. When the soil becomes too alkaline—that is, has a pH above 7.5—nutrients such as iron, phosphorus, manganese, boron, zinc, and potassium become tied up in compounds which are not soluble in water and thus are unavailable to plants even though they are present in the soil. The chief symptom noticeable when acid-loving plants such as azaleas and rhododendrons are grown in too-alkaline soil is an abnormal light green color, or *chlorosis,* of the leaves due to the lack of iron. (See Box 8-7, page 220, on how to tell nutrient deficiencies in plants.) These plants are often used as foundation plantings around homes with stucco finishes. Although iron is plentiful in the soil, a little of the calcium in the stucco washes off onto the ground, raising the pH to the point where the iron forms insoluble compounds. Similar problems may result with the other essential plant nutrients.

In cases where the soil is too alkaline for the plants you plan to grow, it is possible to acidify the soil by adding sulfur. Sulfur-loving bacteria in the soil will gradually convert this to sulfuric acid, and lower the pH. Ferrosulphate is often used for this purpose, since it also supplies iron. Table 8-10 shows how to determine the amount of sulphur needed for acidifying a particular soil. The cost of several sources of sulfur are compared on Table

Table 8-8. **Liming**

To Change pH	Pounds of Limestone, per 100 Square Feet of Ground, Required to Raise the pH of Various Soils, as Indicated					
	Sand	Sandy Loam	Loam	Silt Loam	Clay Loam	Muck*
from 4.0 to 6.5	6.0	11.5	16.1	19.3	23.0	43.6
from 4.5 to 6.5	5.1	9.6	13.3	16.1	19.3	37.2
from 5.0 to 6.5	4.1	7.8	10.6	12.9	15.2	28.9
from 5.5 to 6.5	2.8	6.0	7.8	9.2	10.6	19.7
from 6.0 to 6.5	1.4	3.2	4.1	5.1	5.5	10.1

*Muck is soil with very high organic matter concentration.

Source: Adapted from Knott, *Handbook for Vegetable Growers.*

Table 8-9. **Liming Materials Most Commonly Used to Treat Acid Soils**

Name	Chemical	Equivalent* CaCO₃	Source
Shell meal	$CaCO_2$	95%	Natural shell deposits
Limestone	$CaCO_3$	95%	Natural limestone deposits
Hydrated lime	$Ca(OH)_2$	120%	Limestone burned with steam
Burned lime	CaO	150%	Limestone burned in kiln
Dolomite	$CaCO_3MgCO_3$	110%	Natural mineral deposit
Sugar beet lime	$CaCO_3$†	80–90%	By-product lime from sugar beet refineries

*That is, its relative strength in correcting soil acidity compared to pure calcium carbonate.

† 4 to 10% may be organic matter.

Source: Bogart, Briggs, and Calloway, *Nutrition and Physical Fitness.*

207

Table 8-10. **Sulfur Required to Acidify 100 Square Feet**

To change pH	Pounds of Sulfur Required for Various Soil Types		
	Sandy	Loamy	Clayey
from 8.5 to 7.0	1.65	4.96	11.57
from 8.0 to 7.0	1.10	3.30	7.71
from 7.5 to 7.0	.55	1.65	3.86

Source: adapted from *Hellige Soil Handbook.*

Table 8-11 **Sources of Sulfur for Adjusting pH**

Sources	$ per Lb* (As Purchased)	Percent Sulfur	$ per Lb Sulfur*
$CaSO_4$	$ .06/lb	23.5	$ .26
$FeSO_4$	$ .40/lb	21.4	$1.87
Flowers of sulfur	$1.98/lb	100	$1.98

*Typical prices of major commercial sources of agricultural products.

8-11. Of course, the addition of abundant organic matter to the soil will eventually have an acidifying effect, as mentioned before, and the soil can become too acid. If this happens, aluminum and other elements may become so soluble that they are available in amounts toxic to the plants.

Nitrogen: The three macronutrients sold in "complete" fertilizers are nitrogen (N), phosphorus (P), and potassium (K). *Nitrogen,* needed by food plants at an average of 100 to 300 pounds per acre, comprises about 78 percent of the atmosphere, but is unavailable to higher plants in this form because it exists as inert nitrogen gas, N_2. Certain bacteria and also lightning can combine this gas with hydrogen, carbon, or oxygen into compounds, some of which the plants can use. The process is called *nitrogen fixation.* The nitrogen fixed by lightning may be carried to the soil by rainwater. It must have originally been the only source of soil nitrogen, since igneous rocks contain little or none of that element. Some nitrogen is still supplied to the soils from this source, but the amount is minimal and will not support much plant growth.

Certain free-living bacteria in the soil, Nitrosomas, *Azotobacter,* and *Clostridium* species, are able to use atmospheric nitrogen, if the amount available to them in the material they are decomposing is not adequate. When they die, the nitrogen they have fixed in their bodies is available for plants. Because these bacteria are only active in fairly neutral soils (above pH 6.5), and have a low conversion efficiency (approximately one hundred pounds of carbon is used up in respiration for every pound of nitrogen used), their addition of nitrogen to the soil is not highly significant from the agricultural point of view. Blue-green algae can also fix nitrogen. They live in ponds or wet soils and are very important in fixing nitrogen in rice paddies and aquaculture ponds (for example, *Anabaena* species, *Nostoc* species, and other members of the algal order Nostocales).

The most important organisms for fixing nitrogen are the *Rhizobium* species of bacteria that live in a mutually beneficial relationship with the roots of higher plants. They use the carbohydrates produced by the plant in photosynthesis and fix nitrogen, some of which is available to the plant host. (Examples of the amounts of nitrogen fixed by these organisms is given in Table 8-12.) Table 8-13 shows the nitrogen changes occurring after different crops in a rotation scheme. As mentioned earlier, crop rotation is a method used to essentially grow fertilizer (primarily nitrogen supplies) with one crop which is usually not harvested. The crops that follow then feed from the first which was plowed under.

The best-known examples of nitrogen fixers are the legumes (the family of plants whose members are distinguished by being able to support nitrogen-fixing symbiants on their roots—for example, beans, peas, and clover). In legumes the *Rhizobia* live in nodules along the roots of the plant. These bacteria are highly specific, and the same species that infects clover will not help, for example, beans. Furthermore, the proper strain of *Rhizobia* may not already be present in the soil where a particular crop is to be grown. To ensure the presence of the right *Rhizobia* species for the legume you are planting, it is wise to buy an inoculant, sold commercially by nurseries and seed suppliers. Before planting, the dark bacterial spores are shaken onto the mass of legume seeds, which are then stirred or rotated for even coating. Soil where inoculated legumes have been grown before can be used to reinfect the following year's seeds if they are of the same species. You may wish to develop a *Rhizobia* bank in your garden by mulching your

Table 8-12. **Relative Rates of Biological Nitrogen Fixation**

Organism or System	N_2 Fixed*	
	Kilogram per Hectare per Year	Pounds per Acre per Year
Legumes		
soybeans	57–94	51–84
cowpeas	84	406
clover	104–160	93–142
alfalfa	128–600	114–534
lupins	150–169	137–151
Nodulated nonlegumes		
Alivus	40–300	36–267
Hippophae	2–179	2–159
Coenothus	60	53
Coriaria	150	134
Plant algal associations		
Gunnera	12–21	11–19
Azollas	313	279
lichens	39–84	35–75
Free-living microorganisms		
Blue-green algae	25	22
Azotobacter	0.3	.26
Clostridium pasteurianum	0.1–0.5	.09–.44

Source: Evans, and Barber. "Biological Nitrogen Fixation for Food and Fiber Production."

*To convert kilograms/hectare to pounds per acre multiply by the following equivalents:

$$\frac{2.2\ lbs}{kg} \times \frac{hectare}{2.47\ acres} \times \frac{kg}{hectare}$$

Table 8-13. **Amount of Nitrogen Fixed by Leguminous Crops**

Crops	Total Nitrogen Fixed by Legumes (lbs/ac)	Nitrogen Harvested by Legume (lbs/ac)	by Cereal (lbs/ac)	Nitrogen Gain or Loss per Rotation (lbs/ac)	Following Yield of Cereal Grain (lbs/ac)
Legumes					
lucerne	450	299	66	122	2320
clover	260	125	51	115	1940
sweet clover	270	170	51	84	1890
soy beans	160	176	29	−8	1180
field beans	70	103	25	−20	1060
Cereal (every year)	———	———	22	−10	870

Source: *Soil Conditions and Plant Growth.*

old legumes in one particular area. Then each planting period you can return to the "bank" for some inoculated soil to add to the soil mix when desired.

Some organisms in the soil convert soil nitrogen into a gas and release it back into the atmosphere. This is referred to as *denitrification,* and it occurs primarily in very wet soils. Losses from this process can be very high. Thus, good drainage is as essential to preserving nitrogen in the soil as the addition of organic material and rotation with nitrogen-fixing crops. (See Figure 8-5 for a full picture of the nitrogen cycle.)

Nitrogen is often one of the important factors limiting plant growth. Plants need large amounts of it, and when they remove it from the soil to build their tissues and are subsequently harvested for food the soil is depleted by that amount. Even if only the seeds of legumes are eaten and the rest returned to the soil as compost, a large percentage of the nitrogen has been lost to the system. It is then incorporated into human tissue, or excreted and flushed away. In order to reinstate the natural cycling that modern systems of agriculture have disrupted, an effort should be made to return to the soil the plant nutrients that have been removed. Of considerable importance is the recycling of nutrients present in human sewage.

Furthermore, nitrate (NO_3), one of the most common forms that nitro-

Source: Redrawn from Berry, Osgood, and St. John, *Chemical Villains.*

Figure 8-5. **Nitrogen Cycling**

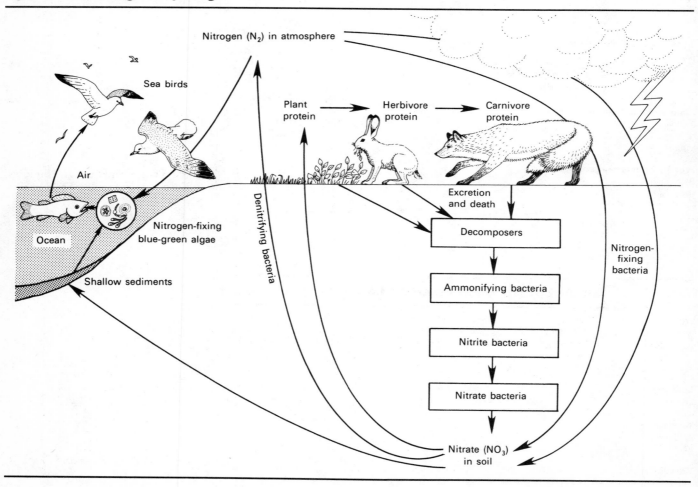

gen takes in the soil and a product of the *Rhizobia* bacteria, is negatively charged. Thus, it is not attracted to the negative charges on the clay and organic matter. Therefore, every time it rains or the plants are irrigated, some nitrogen is leached out of the soil into the groundwater. This is a problem where nitrate fertilizers are used also.

Plants that are deficient in nitrogen grow slowly and appear pale because they are also deficient in chlorophyll, the green pigment present in the leaves. Nitrogen is a mobile nutrient in a plant; it can be moved from the older to the younger parts of the plant or leaves as needed. In a plant suffering from nitrogen deficiency paleness will be most pronounced along the veins of the older leaves, indicating that the plant's nitrogen supply has moved into the younger regions of the leaf.

You can test your soil for nitrogen as well as the other macronutrients, phosphorus and potassium. The inexpensive soil test kit, sold for this purpose, is very unreliable, but home methods are available, if you are willing to obtain the necessary ingredients and take the trouble to perform the test. The method called pot *testing* is one of the most reliable, since you use a food plant that you would probably actually be growing in your garden (usually tomatoes) to measure the necessary nutrients in the soil. See Box 8-5 for instructions on pot testing your soil.

Commercial laboratories and some state agricultural experiment stations will also test your soils. It is important to select the soil to be tested from the various different parts of the area in which you intend to plant to obtain a representative sample. It is also desirable to furnish information to the laboratory on the planned use for the soil, since you need to know not so much what nutrients are present as which are available for your purpose.

Compost or manure add a small amount of nitrogen to the soil but these sources are never really high in nitrogen. (See pages 128–30 on nitrogen in typical fast compost and common manures.) Most of the nitrogen excreted by mammals is in the urine. Chicken manure—as with all birds, a combination of feces and urine—is an exception, being a good source of nitrogen. Horse and steer manure is often combined with large amounts of high-carbon bedding, and frequently sits around exposed to the weather, losing nutrients through leaching. Thus, manure may not substantially add nitrogen to the soil (though, of course, it will always be useful in terms of improving soil structure).

Using Human Urine: Human urine is also high in nitrogen. In fact, the average adult produces enough nitrogen in his or her urine to fertilize approximately fifteen hundred square feet of soil (a garden about forty by forty feet) at the annual rate of three hundred pounds of nitrogen per acre or .7 pounds per 1.00 square feet—truly a substantial amount.

Sodium buildup in the soil can be prevented by the application of lime or gypsum to the garden areas fertilized with urine. Lime and gypsum contain calcium, an element that replaces sodium on soil particles and causes it to leach away from the root zone of plants. This process is another example of cation exchange. The amount of lime or gypsum required to supply enough calcium to replace the sodium in urine can be calculated using simple chemistry.

Box 8-5. **Pot Testing to Measure Soil Fertility**

Description

Pot testing is a biological method of testing the soil. It uses plant growth as the actual indicator of soil fertility. By visually diagnosing the height, breadth, and vigor of the plants grown in a specially prepared soil, you can determine fertilizer requirements. This test is suitable for the home garden, since it does not require elaborate laboratory equipment.

When to Conduct the Test

A pot test is best conducted in early spring. This will allow you to determine fertilizer practices in time for late spring planting of summer vegetables. Seedlings in the test take six to eight weeks to grow large enough to show nutrient deficiencies in a climate with a long, cold winter, so the test is best conducted under the shelter of a coldframe, in a greenhouse, or on a table in front of a sunny window. If the garden soil will be frozen or too wet to test in early spring, enough soil for the purpose should be brought in and stored in a basement or similar area over the winter.

Collecting the Soil

The pot test should be conducted with the soil from the part or parts of the yard where you will actually be raising a garden. If you suspect that your property is not uniform in soil type because of landscape alterations, you may wish to run a separate test for each different area. About 40 pounds of soil are needed for the test (a 5-gallon can's-worth). Sweep away the surface cover of leaves or compost, dig the soil to a depth of 8 inches, and collect it in a burlap sack. If you wish to analyze the subsoil of your lot as well, collect a sample at a depth of 12 to 18 inches below the surface. Do not mix the samples from the top- and sublevels; rather, conduct a separate test for each. You must sift the soil through a half-inch mesh screen to make it suitable and lay it out in the sun or under a heat lamp to dry before testing.

Setting Up the Equipment

You will need 12 5-inch clay pots for the experiment. Clay pots are preferred to plastic or glazed ceramic pots, because they are permeable, thus allowing the plant roots to breathe. This permeability will reduce the incidence of root diseases that could confuse the results. Do not insert pieces of crockery or any other materials in the base of the pots in an attempt to prevent soil loss through hold. Set the pot on small pebbles contained in a clay saucer. Weigh 2 1200-gram portions of the test soil, and pour into each of 2 pots (approximately 3.5 pound). If no scale is available, fill the pots to within an inch of the top.

These 2 pots will remain unfertilized and serve as checks on the effects of fertilizers in the other pots as well as indicators of the natural fertility of the soil. Two check pots and 2 pots for each of the 5 fertilizer treatments are used as a measurement of variability in the soil and to improve the validity of the test.

The Fertilizer Treatment

Soil scientists and farmers generally use mineral fertilizers as their testing agents because the chemical certainty of the fertilizers allows them to conduct precise analyses. The standard chemicals and the nutrients for which they test, are as follows: ammonium nitrate, for nitrogen (N); treble super-phosphate, or calcium phosphate, for phosphorus (P); potassium sulfate for potassium (K); and sulfur (S).

For the home gardener who does not intend to fertilize with commercial, synthetic chemical fertilizers, nonsynthetic sources of nutrients may be substituted as the testing agents. However, because of the relative uncertainty regarding their exact chemical compositions, results will be less precise. Still, in our experience, results obtained with natural testing agents are quite satisfactory for the small grower. The nonsynthetic materials we suggest and the nutrients for which they test, are as follows: bloodmeal (N); bonemeal (P); kelp meal (K); and flowers of sulfur (S). These products are common at most retail nurseries.

The treatments to be compared to the two unfertilized control pots are as follows: nitrogen alone (N), phosphate alone (P), the two together (N-P), the two combined with potassium (N-P-K), and the four together (N-P-K-S). These comparisons will account for any major nutrient deficiencies that a soil might have. The amount of the testing agent used in the treatments is determined by the percentage that each contains of the principle element, and the per-acre equivalent of nutrient application chosen as the rate commonly used in the fertilization of field crops. Generally, per-acre application of nitrogen is 300 pounds; of phosphorus, 150 pounds; and of potassium and sulfur, 100 pounds each. Obviously these rates are enormous and must be adjusted to amounts which are appropriate to a small-scale soil test. In order to approximate a 300-pound nitrogen equivalent per acre, 0.180 grams of nitrogen is added to the 5-inch pot. This amount, 0.180 grams of nitrogen, is represented by .514

Test	Number of pots	Treatment rate (in lb/acre)	Amount of synthetic material per 5-inch pot	Amount of nonsynthetic material per 5-inch pot
(A) Control	2	Remains untreated	0	0
(B) Nitrogen only	2	300 N	.514 g (⅛ tsp) ammonium nitrate	1.38 g (⅓ tsp) bloodmeal
(C) Phosphorus only	2	150 P	.366 g (⅛ tsp) primary calcium phosphate	0.76 g (¼ tsp) bonemeal
(D) Nitrogen and phosphorus	2	300 N 150 P	Amount measured for (A) and for (B) together	Amount measured for (A) and for (B) together
(E) Nitrogen, phosphorus, and potassium	2	300 N 150 P 100 K	Amounts measured for (A) and (B) plus .11 gram (⅛ tsp) of potassium chloride	Amounts measured for (A) and (B), plus .95 gram (¼ tsp) of kelp meal
(F) Nitrogen, phosphorus, potassium, and sulfur	2	300 N 150 P 100 K 100 S	The amounts for (E), plus .24 g (⅛ tsp) potassium sulfate	The amounts for (E), plus .96 g (¼ tsp) flowers of sulfur

grams of ammonium nitrate, at 28.6 percent nitrogen, or 1.38 grams of bloodmeal, at 13 percent nitrogen. Precision in weighing out materials to the one-hundredth gram is impossible on any but the most exact laboratory scales. Converting the theoretical amounts to teaspoon equivalents at the rate of 4.7 grams per one level teaspoon, will yield a more practical unit of measurement. The chart below provides a schedule for the amount of chemical or organic materials needed for conducting the test:

Once you have obtained the test fertilizers, you are ready to prepare the test pots. For each test, use the same size sample of soil (1200 grams). As you measure each quantity of soil, spread it on its own piece of wrapping paper on a workbench or table. Sprinkle the carefully measured quantity of fertilizer specified in the chart over the soil sample, and mix it thoroughly into the soil by running your hands through the mixture. Using the paper as a spout, pour the soil into a pot. For each test, duplicate the procedure in a second pot. If you choose to conduct the complete test, you should have twelve pots full of the soil and fertilizer mixture. Using a pencil, label each pot with the specific test, the date, and the crop used.

Selecting the Crop

The choice of plants to use as indicators of the soil fertility depends both on the crop(s) you plan on raising during the growing season and on what will grow during the testing period. Tomatoes are a good choice, since they are commonly raised in home vegetable gardens, will grow at a satisfactory rate during the spring if provided with a warm environment, and readily exhibit nutrient deficiencies in their leaves. Barley is another good choice, because of its rapid growth, resistance to disease and insect damage, and sensitivity to nutrient deficiencies. If you plan on testing more than one crop, an entire pot test must be conducted for each species.

Planting the Crop

Plant 7 seeds in each pot in a concentric pattern around the pot's perimeter. The seeds should be planted at a depth of approximately 6 times their width. For tomatoes, that is one-quarter inch, for barley, one-half inch. Press the seeds firmly into place

and cover with soil. Taking care to disturb the soil as little as possible, moisten each pot with about one-half cup of water, using a watering can.

Subsequent watering must be done on a regular basis. Since you are trying to provide optimum growing conditions, the plants must not be allowed to wilt, nor should they be overwatered to the extent that water drains from the pot, carrying away important nutrients.

Growing the Plants

Place the pots where they will receive full sunlight for a good part of the day, and where the plants will be protected from insects, birds, and rodents. As mentioned above, if the test is conducted in very early spring a coldframe or a greenhouse structure may have to be used in order to protect the plants from low temperatures.

A week after the seeds have germinated and the plants break the soil, thin the plants to 5 seedlings for barley or 3 for tomatoes. Favor those seedlings which are equal in size, strongest, and most evenly spaced throughout the pot. Weekly, as the plants are growing, record relative size, color, and vigor.

Harvesting

Allow the plants to grow for at least 6 weeks after planting, or up to the point when it appears that definite differences are measurable. When the growth period is finished, record your final visual observations. Harvest the plants by clipping each at the soil level with a scissors. Place the plants from each pot in a separate, labeled paper bag, and allow the contents to dry for several days under the heat of a pilot lamp or heat lamp. After the plants have been sufficiently dried out to the point that they are easily crumbled, weigh them. A postage scale will do nicely.

Analyzing the Tests

Each treatment should have 2 oven-dried weights, 1 for each pot. Each pair should be averaged to arrive at 1 oven-dried weight per treatment. Construct a data table for purposes of analysis, such as the one below, recording the pot test of your soil.

Crop: Tomatoes
Planted: 3/12
Harvested: 5/1

Treatment	Dry Weight
control	1.1 grams
N	4.3 grams
P	2.8 grams
N-P	5.4 grams
N-P-K	5.6 grams
N-P-K-S	5.6 grams

The results of the example test clearly shows a deficiency of nitrogen and phosphorus in the soil, because both the nitrogen and phosphorus treatment produced higher yields than the check. The table also reveals that there is not a significant deficiency of potassium nor sulfur, because neither the N-P-K, nor the N-P-K-S treatments faired appreciably better than the N-P treatment. The relative difference between fresh and dry weights of the different treatments as well as the color of the foliage will also assist you in determining the vigor of the plants.

Interpreting the Results

The results from the pot test will serve as a guide for general practices in the garden. It is not possible to determine quantitatively the exact nutrient deficiencies of a soil using the pot test, only qualitative relationships. From the pot test we conducted for the Integral Urban House garden, we learned that our soil was in need of nitrogen; how much was a matter of judgment on our part. We decided to increase the supply of nitrogen to the garden by increasing the nitrogen content of the compost as well as by applying diluted urine directly to the soil. So far, our results have been favorable.

The pot test may also be used to determine proper methods for correcting acidity, alkalinity, or salt toxicity in the soil, by devising an appropriate treatment procedure, based on the methods described here. For instance, to determine the best method for correcting an acid soil, various rates of lime or other sources of carbonate would be applied to test pots in which plants were grown. Visual diagnoses of the plant would reveal the best method.

Box 8-6. **Calculating the Amount of Lime or Gypsum to Replace Sodium**

Calculate the amount of sodium going into the soil in units of *moles* (one mole is the weight in grams of 6.02×10^{23} molecules of any particular element, ion, or compound, depending on its atomic or molecular weight). Then the equivalent counteracting amount of calcium is found. The computations are as follows:

1. Assume that a 120–pound woman applies 1000 cc (= 1 liter = 1.06 quarts) of urine to the garden each day (diluted with water, as discussed below). From Table 8-14, we know that 1000 cc of urine (undiluted) contains 10 grams of sodium chloride (NaCl), which is 40 percent sodium (Na^+).

2. The amount of sodium in 10 grams of sodium chloride is derived thusly:

10 grams NaCl

$\times \dfrac{23 \text{ grams per mole } Na^+}{53 \text{ grams per mole } NaCl}$

$= 4.0$ grams Na^+

(the molecular kit of sodium chloride is 53 grams per mole)

3. The number of moles of sodium which 4.0 grams represents is derived:

$\dfrac{4.0 \text{ grams sodium}}{23 \text{ grams per mole}}$

$= .17$ moles of sodium

4. One atom of calcium forms two bonds while sodium forms one and therefore is twice as reactive (because calcium exists as a divalent ion—Ca^{++}). Therefore, .17 moles of sodium can be theoretically replaced by one-half that, or .085 moles of calcium.

5. The grams of calcium contained in .085 moles is:

.085 moles $\times$ 40 grams per mole

$= 3.4$ grams calcium

6. Lime ($CaCO_3$) contains 40 percent calcium, by weight. The amount of lime required to obtain 3.4 grams of Ca^{++}, is derived thusly:

3.4 grams $CA^{++} \times \dfrac{1 \text{ gram lime}}{.40 \text{ grams } Ca^{++}}$

$= 8.5$ grams lime

Application Rates of Lime and Gypsum

Daily urine application to garden:	Pounds of lime to add per month		Pounds of gypsum to add per month
1 pint	.5		.75
1 quart	1.0		1.5
1.5 quarts	1.5	or	2.3
2 quarts	2.0		3.0
3 quarts	3.0		4.5
1 gallon	4.0		6.0

7. Gypsum ($CaSO_4 \cdot 2H_2O$) contains 23 percent Ca^{++}. The amount of gypsum required to obtain 3.4 grams of Ca^{++} is similarly derived:

3.4 grams $Ca^{++} \times \dfrac{1 \text{ gram gypsum}}{.23 \text{ grams } Ca^{++}}$

$= 14.78$ grams gypsum

The weights of lime and gypsum calculated as shown here should be increased by 50 percent, to insure that sufficient calcium is applied to the soil. Application of calcium is best done on a monthly basis. After a month of using urine at a rate of one liter per day, apply one pound of lime or one and a half pounds of gypsum to the top of the soil receiving urine. Lime is the better source of calcium, where soils are acid and it is advantageous to raise the pH. Gypsum should be used where no change in pH is desired, or where soils are deficient in sulfur. Use the chart below to determine application rates of lime or gypsum quickly.

Table 8-14 shows the percentage of nitrogen contained in the various chemical components of urine, and indicates the total weight of nitrogen excreted on a daily basis from the urine of a 180–pound man. A man who produces 1500 cc (1.5 quarts) of urine each day, over a year's time excretes 12.25 pounds of nitrogen. At an application rate equivalent to 300 pounds of nitrogen per acre, which is comparable to the rates applied on farms, one man's annual production is sufficient to fertilize over 2000 square feet of vegetable garden. If the value of 12.25 pounds nitrogen is computed at the cost per pound of bloodmeal, which is $3.50, then a man's annual nitrogen production is worth $43.75.

The trick is in applying the nitrogenous urine to the garden soil at an even and well-regulated rate. Figure that each square foot of garden requires, over a year's time, 3.13 grams nitrogen. In terms of sound fertilization practice, it is best to apply one-half of the yearly requirement twice a year, rather than all at once, since the latter might result in nutrient toxicity, or undesirable leaching. At one-half that rate, or 1.63 grams per square foot (.50 $\times$ 3.13 grams), 6.5 square feet of garden area could be fertilized each day by the urine production of a 120–pound woman (see the margin note, this page). After one-half year of daily application, a total of 1,136 square feet of garden soil could be fertilized. The urine application would be repeated on the same amount of land during the second half of the year to reach the desired annual fertilization rate of 300 pounds per acre.

In order to use urine in this way wisely, you must consider its chemical composition. Although the nitrogen content of urine is beneficial to plant growth, the high concentration of sodium salts in urine is detrimental both to the soil and to the plants. The application rate of urine, therefore, must be carefully regulated to obtain the greatest benefit from the nitrogen, and to avoid problems from the sodium salts.

Collecting Human Urine: Collecting your own urine for use in supplying nitrogen to the garden provides satisfactory results inexpensively as long as certain procedures are followed.

It is advisable to dilute the urine with water before it is used in the garden, so that it can be spread around more evenly. A ratio of five parts water to one part urine is desirable, although the urine can certainly be diluted more. Occasionally more concentrated applications will not hurt most plants. Men can collect their urine directly in a watering can, filling it just far enough to leave room for the necessary amount of water. Then water can be added and the diluted urine applied directly to the garden. It is best to use a watering can that is not zinc-coated to avoid leaching the zinc ions into the urine. A sturdy plastic watering can will last for many years, if cared for properly.

Women may find it easier to use a chair made to hold the container that will catch the urine. A number of wide-mouth teakettles of stainless steel,

Compute your own daily urine output on the basis of 1000 cc (which equals exactly 1.06 quarts) produced per each 120 pounds of body weight. For example, if her drinking and eating habits were normal, a 120-pound woman would probably produce 1000 cc (1.06 quarts) of urine per day. That much urine would contain 10.15 grams of nitrogen calculated thusly:

$$\frac{15.23 \text{ N}}{1500 \text{ cc urine}} \times 1000 \text{ cc} = 10.15 \text{ N}$$

Table 8-14. **Nitrogen Manufacture in Urine, by Homo Sapiens**

(chemical composition of urine from a 180-pound man, producing 1500 cc urine)

Salts	Dry Weight (in Grams)	Percent Nitrogen	Amount of Nitrogen Produced per liter urine (in Grams)
Urea	30.0	46.7	14.0
Sodium chloride	15.0	——	——
Potassium	3.3	——	——
Phosphoric acid	2.5	——	——
Sulfuric acid	2.5	——	——
Creatinne	1.0	37.0	0.37
Ammonia	0.7	78.0	0.58
Uric acid	0.7	33.3	0.23
Hippuric acid	0.7	7.8	0.05
Magnesium	0.6	——	——
Calcium	0.3	——	——
Others	2.8	——	——
			Total: 15.23 g/day; 12.25 lb/yr

Note: The average daily output of urine:
Volume: 1.75 to 2.875 pints (1 to 1.5 liters)*
Dry weight: .09 to .13 lbs (40 to 50 grams; calculated from 96 percent moisture)

*One liter = 1000 cc = 1.06 quarts = 33.8 fluid ounces

Note: A 25-pound bag of ammonium sulfate, at 21 percent nitrogen (5.25 pounds of nitrogen), consumes 42,000 kilocalories, or 1.7×10^5 Btu in the production of nitrogen. That is equivalent to the amount of food-energy calories consumed by an average adult male during an entire two-week period.

Sources: Carlson and Johnson, *The Machinery of the Body*, and World Health Organization, *Composting.*

enameled metal, or glass are available commercially that do nicely for the purpose. They should have a close-fitting cover to prevent objectionable odors. (Note that urea from the urine, if allowed to stand, will be converted to ammonia by bacteria.) The entire chair can sit in the corner of the bedroom, very close and convenient for use on chilly nights. When full, this kettle can be emptied into a watering can, along with rinse water, and the diluted mixture can then be used. When empty, the kettle can sit for a few hours open in the midday sun to be completely deodorized; all trace of ammonia smells will be removed and the kettle can then be returned to the bedroom once again.

Is Human Urine Safe to Use?: The most serious disease spread by human urine worldwide is schistosomiasis. A parasitic schistosome (blood fluke) follows a complex life cycle; it starts as an aquatic snail common in irrigation ditches and as an adult lives in the veins of the urinary bladder or the large intestine of humans. The cercariae (or immature schistosome) penetrates the skin of people wading in snail-infested water. Urine or feces, depending on the species of schistosome, from infected people reaches the same water and transmits the parasite's eggs. This is a problem in various tropical areas of Africa, South America, Asia, and the Middle East, but it does not occur in the United States, where the cultural milieu is totally different.

In this country, infectious hepatitis is a possible problem, as far as disease transmission through urine is concerned. Therefore, it is best to confine urine use in your own backyard to that of family members, and only when the individuals contributing are in good health. (Ironically, the urine from the sick, rejected from the garden, will then join the municipal waste stream, in some communities without adequate treatment facilities, conceivably creating problems in local bodies of water.)

In persons without specific bladder infections, urine, unlike human feces, is generally sterile and safe to use. To be safe, avoid splashing urine on parts of vegetables you tend to eat raw. (Hopefully, you will be washing vegetables carefully before use in any case to remove the lead. See Chapter 14, on lead in the garden.) The urine, diluted with water, is best sprinkled out on the compost mulch around the plants where most pathogenic microorganisms will not long survive. There, the complex communities of microorganisms will quickly decompose or kill any pathogens that may be deposited with the urine.

Commercial Nitrogen Fertilizers: Nitrogen fertilizers are available commercially (see Table 8-15.) The most commonly supplied for home gardens are ammonium sulphate—$(NH_4)_2SO_4$—which contains 21 percent nitrogen; ammonium nitrate—NH_4NO_3—33.5 percent nitrogen; mono-ammonium phosphate—$NH_4H_2PO_4$—11 percent nitrogen; and diammonium phosphate—$(NH_4)_2HPO_4$—16 to 18 percent nitrogen. The price of these synthetic fertilizers, as well as fertilizer derived from organic materials varies according to the concentrations of the chief ingredient, in this case, nitrogen. Not surprisingly, some fertilizers are better buys than others. To learn the relative costs of chief ingredients in several fertilizers, as well as how to calculate their price per pound, see margin note opposite.

Table 8-15. **Fertilizers at a Glance**

Product	Percent of Chief Ingredient Contained in Product	Cost, as Purchased	Cost, per Pound, of Chief Ingredient
Nitrogen			
fish emulsion	6	$ 7.00 / gal	$ 15.56
cottonseed meal	6.5	$ 8.50 / 25 lb	$ 5.23
citrus food	10	$ 5.95 / 25 lb	$ 2.38
hoof and horn	10	$ 17.50 / 20 lb	$ 8.75
blood meal	13	$ 11.00 / 25 lb	$ 3.38
mono ammonium phosphate	11	$ 7.85 / 25 lb	$ 1.96
ammonia sulfate	21	$ 4.75 / 25 lb	$ .90
kelp, powdered	41*	$ 30.00 / 50 lb	
urea	46	$ 8.00 / 20 lb	$ .87
Phosphorus			
hoof and horn	2	$ 17.50 / 20 lb	$ 44.00
kelp, powdered	2	$ 30.00 / 50 lb	
fish meal	4	$ 35.00 / 60 lb	$ 14.58
0-10-10	10	$ 5.85 / 25 lb	$ 2.34
bone meal	12	$ 9.50 / 25 lb	$ 3.17
citrus food	12	$ 5.95 / 25 lb	$ 1.98
ammonium phosphate	16	$ 7.85 / 25 lb	$ 1.96
super-phosphate	18	$ 5.50 / 25 lb	$ 1.22
Potassium			
fish meal	4	$ 35.00 / 60 lb	$ 14.58
kelp, powdered	6	$ 30.00 / 50 lb	
0-10-10	10	$ 5.85 / 25 lb	$ 2.34
citurs food	14	$ 5.45 / 25 lb	$ 1.56
sulphate of potash	53	$ 4.65 / 25 lb.	$ .35
potassium sulphate	62		
Sulfur			
aluminum sulphate	51	$ 2.50 / 5 lb	$ .98
Iron			
iron sulphate	20	$ 2.10 / 5 lb	$ 2.10

Note: Costs are common retail prices, Berkeley, California, December 1977.

*37% of the nitrogen in kelp is not water soluble, and is a long term soil enrichment

In an article in *Science* David Pimentel indicated that commercial sources of nitrogen, phosphorus, and potassium require energy expenditures of 800, 1450, and 1000 kilocalories per pound. Although conceivably the same processes could be fueled by solar furnaces, this is not presently the case. Thus, using commercial fertilizers when organic sources (compost, urine, manure, rotation with legumes) will do the job, is a waste of dwindling nonrenewable forms of energy.

Second, commercial fertilizers, no matter how potent, only contain a few of the many nutrients needed for plant growth. For this reason, as well as the need to modify soil structure to improve water-holding and gas-exchange qualities, commercial fertilizer can never be a substitute for adding organic matter to the soil.

It is the singular use of chemical fertilizers by agribusiness farmers that is subject to criticism by the organic or biological farmer. Furthermore, commercial fertilizers are frequently far more soluble than their organic, or "natural," counterparts. Thus, they provide a quick "jolt" for the plants, but may, like the nitrates, be leached equally quickly by rainfall or irrigation water. When the fertilizers move out of the topsoil, they may contaminate

To calculate the price per pound of chief ingredients for any fertilizer, multiply the price per pound of the product by 100, and divide by the percent of the chief ingredient in the product. For example, to calculate the cost per pound of nitrogen in ammonium sulfate, which costs 19¢ per pound, as purchased, and having a nitrogen content of 21 percent:

$$19¢/lb \times \frac{100}{21\ N}$$

$$= 90¢ \text{ per pound of nitrogen}$$

The calculation is complicated to a degree by the fact that for some fertilizers the chief ingredients are reported as chemical radicals (compounds with positive or negative charges) rather than as discrete elements. Such is often the case with potassium, which is commonly represented on the label of the fertilizer bag as potash (K_2O). The percentage of elemental potassium contained in potash can be calculated by dividing twice the atomic weight of potassium (because two atoms of potassium are represented in the molecule K_2O) by the molecular weight of potash. Thus,

atomic weight of potassium
$$= 39; \text{ so } 39 \times 2 = 78$$
atomic weight of oxygen = 16;
78 + 16
$$= \text{atomic weight of potash, } 94;$$
$$\text{percentage potassium} = \frac{78}{94} = 83\%$$

If potash is 83 percent potassium, then, to derive the percent of potassium in a fertilizer, the percent of potash would have to be multiplied by .83.

groundwater supplies. At any event they are no longer available to the plants they were supposed to benefit. This leaching of nitrogen can be a problem with run-off from manure in feedlots as well. Improperly stored manure may be leached by rains and ultimately contaminate wells or irrigation water. However, the problem is particularly likely to occur where overzealous farmers, encouraged by fertilizer sales promotions, figure, "If a little is good, a lot will be much better," and overfertilize with easily leached commercial products. Water containing more than forty-five parts per million of nitrate is regarded as unsafe for babies; there have been cases of children being poisoned by pureed spinach baby food made from plants excessively high in nitrate. Plants that receive too much nitrogen, usually become very dark green, and the stems may become weak and succulent. The vegetative or leafy parts of the plant grows luxuriantly at the expense of the fruit, and fruit setting is delayed. For example, tomato plants will grow lush and green but produce few tomatoes. Potatoes may be watery. Shrubs and trees may maintain succulent growth late into the year, making them more susceptible to frost damage.

If too much nitrogen is used by mistake, the effects can sometimes be counteracted by the addition of more phosphorus and potassium, since these elements generally have the opposite effects on plants (encouraging fruiting, stocky growth, and so on). But the best solution is to obtain the nitrogen you need as much as possible from organic materials that release it slowly. Use the energy-expensive commercial materials as sparingly as possible.

Phosphorus: One of the key elements in life processes that comes originally from rocks. In this form is rather insoluble, except under very acid

Figure 8-6. **The Phosphorus Cycle**

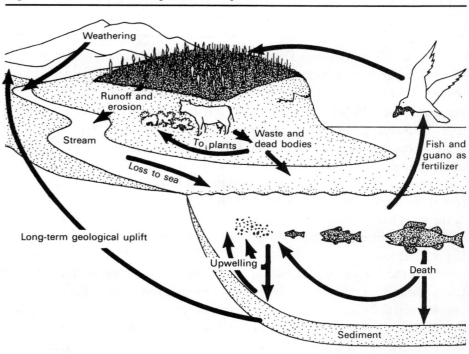

Source: Berry, Osgood, and St. John, *Chemical Villains.*

conditions. The phosphorus cycle is shown in Figure 8-6. Small crystals of phosphorus are scattered through most igneous rocks, and they slowly dissolve out as the rock weathers. The only concentrated deposits of phosphate in the world are guano and fossil guano (phosphate rock), and these are mined for fertilizer. It will be interesting to see how world political relationships form and decompose as phosphorus supplies become scarcer in the manner of fossil fuels.

The use of untreated crushed phosphate rock has been popular with some gardeners for a long time, so it is worthwhile understanding the problems associated with using it. The extremely slow release makes crushed rock useless for treating phosphorus deficiencies in the soil during the current season. However, if sufficient organic material and nitrogen is present in the soil, there will be enough organic acids produced to acidify the soil and slowly release phosphorus ions into it over a period of years. Because of this extremely slow release of phosphorus, modern methods of treating rock powder with acid to produce superphosphate were developed. By stimulating and accelerating the natural process of the soil, such treatment renders the phosphorus immediately available to the plants where it is placed. Phosphorus is incorporated into most living tissues. Bones and shells contain a particularly high percentage of it. A compost derived from food wastes containing bones and shells will probably have an ample supply of phosphorus for most garden needs.

Phosphorus is very important in the fruiting processes of plants. Deficiencies are noticeable by a delayed production of fruits or seeds (where high concentrations are normally present to aid in the development of the next generation). Phosphorus is absent from chlorophyll, so plants that lack phosphorus but are relatively high in nitrogen will be an abnormally dark green with a purplish coat. This condition is easy to recognize on tomato seedlings used in pot testing the soil (see Box 8-5).

Many soils in the southern, eastern and a few areas an the midwestern states are low in phosphorus, partly because those soils are older and more weathered than those of the West and Northwest. When soils show, through plant-deficiency symptoms or other tests, that they are low in phosphorus, the addition of compost and manure may be sufficient to correct the situation. The organic material contributes some phosphorus of its own, and the acids from it help to dissolve the additional amounts from the soil particles. As noted, bone meal is another good source, and commercial superphosphate, available in several formulae—monocalcium phosphate, $Ca(H_2PO_4)_2$; dicalcium phosphate, Ca_2HPO_4, or diammonium phosphate, $(NH_4)_2HPO_4$ —can be used. However, the same reservations regarding the energy costs of using commercial nitrogen applies to phosphorus (see note, page 217).

Since phosphorus does not leach as readily as nitrogen from the soil, the problems with its application result primarily with its potential for becoming fixed in relatively insoluble compounds. Under alkaline conditions, phosphorus combines with calcium; when the soil is acid it forms compounds with iron and aluminum, so it is most available in neutral soils.

To reduce losses by fixation, soluble phosphorus fertilizers should be placed in a concentrated band, deep enough in the soil to be near the plant roots, or beneath the seed if it is being used as a seed starter. Rock phosphate becomes available so slowly that it can be thoroughly mixed with the soil along with manure or organic matter.

Potassium: The third macronutrient is usually available in commercially "complete" plant fertilizers. It weathers slowly out of rocks, originating primarily from mica and orthoclase feldspar (both constituents of granite), as they are slowly turned to clay. Potassium is also available from organic matter. The large, positive ions move easily into the soil water, and some losses occur through leaching. Potassium deficiencies are experienced primarily in the eastern half of the United States, with its higher rainfall, rather than in the West (with the exception of western areas that have been irrigated for many years). Highly weathered soils are also likely to be more acid, and have more H^+, and less K^+, on their exchange sites and in the soil solution.

Potassium is absorbed by very young roots. They require well-aerated soils to make possible the respiration to provide the energy for potassium uptake. By improving soil structure, encouraging adequate water drainage, and adding organic matter in the soil, uptake of this nutrient can be increased. The soil can be home-tested for available potassium, along with nitrogen and phosphorus, in a pot test, as described in Box 8-5.

Potassium deficiency symptoms show first in the older leaves, since potassium, like nitrogen, can be moved by the plant from old to new growth if it is in short supply. Potassium is more concentrated in the veins than elsewhere. In potassium deficiency, the veins will remain green while the edges and areas between the veins in the old leaves will turn yellow, then brown, and then dead spots will appear (see Box 8-7).

Wood ashes were originally used to supply potassium, and the term potash (pot ash) is still used to refer to potassium fertilizers. Commercial

---

Box 8-7. **Key to Nutrient Deficiency Symptoms of Higher Plants**

Symptoms appearing first or most severely on youngest leaves

1. *Interveinal chlorosis (yellowing) on young leaves*
   a. Black spots adjacent to veins; smallest veins remain green (mosaic pattern of chlorosis); grey specks on grasses: **Manganese.**
   b. Black spots absent; small veins do not remain green: **Iron.**
   c. New leaves are very small (little-leaf): **Zinc.**

2. *Interveinal chlorosis absent; young leaves remain rolled, appear needlelike in grasses; failure of growing points.*
   a. Necrotic spots sharply delimited and sunken: **Copper.**
   b. Tissues brittle, especially stems; saw-tooth edges on leaves of grasses: **Boron.**

Symptoms appearing uniformly throughout plant or most severely on oldest leaves

1. *Chlorosis general, no interveinal chlorosis*
   a. Veins of lower leaf surface purple; petioles tend to be more vertical: **Sulfur.**
   b. First symptoms show yellowing of oldest leaves, spreading to entire plant; the growing point may remain green in less severe cases; oldest leaves drop off: **Nitrogen.**

2. *Chlorosis interveinal, first appearing on oldest leaves*
   a. Chlorotic areas are bright yellow or orange; turning brown; becoming necrotic; oldest leaves affected most: **Magnesium.**
   b. Chlorotic areas pale-yellow, affecting whole plant; leaf edges curl upward: **Molybdenum.**

3. *Chlorosis absent*
   a. Oldest leaves of corn, wheat, barley severely scorched at edges; sunken spots on edges of old leaves of tomato, clover, alfalfa: **Potassium.**
   b. Purpling in veins and interveins (i-v) of lower leaf surfaces, also stems of tomato; in corn, purple color on leaf edges and lower stalk of plant: **Phosphorus**
   c. Bronze-colored necrosis of leaves; plants prone to wilt: **Chlorine**

Source: Information obtained, courtesy of Dr. James Vlamis, Department of Soils and Plant Nutrition, University of California, Berkeley, California.

fertilizers supply potassium in compounds with chlorine, sulphur, and nitrogen. The same problem of energy consumption used in processing and transporting exists with these potassium fertilizers as it does with nitrogen. Potassium chloride (KCl) probably represents the least energy investment, since it is mined and used more or less directly from old lake deposits. However, excess chlorine may have adverse effects on the growth of some crops, such as potatoes. A good source of potassium is seaweed, commonly available from nurseries as kelp meal. Since potassium is held tightly by clay and will not move much in the soil, if concentrated sources of potassium are needed, the fertilizer should be placed in bands at root depth, when possible.

Other Plant Nutrients: The remaining plant nutrients will not be discussed in detail individually. Additions to the soil of sulfur and calcium when needed has been discussed on pages 204 – 8 Magnesium deficiencies are only rarely encountered, usually on well-weathered soils formed from rocks that were originally poor in that element. Along with calcium, it can be supplied through use of dolomite limestone.

The micronutrients, iron, boron, manganese, copper, zinc, molybdenum, sodium and chlorine, are all as essential to the growth of plants as the macronutrients, but they are needed in only trace amounts. For example, boron deficiencies may be corrected with the addition of as little as one pound per acre (.01 grams per square foot). While soils deficient in one or more nutrients are occasionally found throughout the United States, the amounts needed to correct the condition is so small as to be handled adequately on a small scale with the addition of organic matter from compost made from kitchen wastes, manure, and so on.

Since some nutrients are easily moved within plants and others are not, a key for recognizing the symptoms of plant nutrient deficiencies can be constructed according to whether the signs appear first in the old or the young portions of the plant. Box 8-7 gives a summary of plant nutrients, and the key may be useful in helping the beginner learn the symptoms of nutrient deficiencies.

A literary device for remembering the essential plant nutrients is "*See Hopkins Cafe, Mighty Good Club, Cousin Moman,*" which translates to:

C	carbon
H	hydrogen
O	oxygen
P	phosphorus
K	potassium
N	nitrogen
S	sulfur
Ca	calcium
Fe	iron
Mg	magnesium
Cl	chlorine
Cu	copper
Zn	zinc
Mn	manganese

9. RAISING PLANTS INDOORS

We believe that raising plants indoors is only the start of the integration of outdoor and indoor environments that is sweeping the country. We expect that eventually indoor vegetable growing beds, dwarf fruit trees, and plants operating as air filters will be commonplace. Indoor herb gardens and even small-scale commercial homescale crops are other possibilities. In support of these predictions, householders throughout the country are beginning to attach greenhouses for food and heat production to their homes. Such greenhouses can also be used as small-scale nurseries for specialized plants, as intensive food-production sources for animal feeds (for example, alfalfa for rabbits) and as plant sources for small insectaries, producing predatory insects for mail order sales. But indoor growing is not limited to a greenhouse. If you have a south-facing or sunny window you can begin growing plants indoors.

The phenomenal growth of the house-plant industry points to an increased appreciation of the importance growing plants can have for the psychic health of urban people. From downtown Manhattan to central San Francisco, apartments sprout with more verdure than has been seen since Victorian conservatories were in fashion. Office buildings and restaurants contract for plant maintenance services that routinely water, treat with pesticides, and replace plants that have overgrown their containers or languish because of improper care. Yearnings for a bit of green in a forest of concrete and plastic have created a very big business, from which the enterprising home-scale producer might be able to profit.

Green plants hold a promise of renewal when the landscape outside is clothed in the chilly, lifeless garment of ice and snow. The fancy of the apartment-bound occupant can wander freely through the peaceful forest supported by a six-inch clay pot, and momentarily shut out the clamor and industrial grime of the street below. An African violet or philodendron may not contribute directly to the family diet, but just being able to grow *something* provides a boost for the human spirit. Also, plants indoors can contribute directly to human physiological comfort by humidifying the air and absorbing some gases while releasing others. And although greening the interior of the home is simply a good idea for some, if you are an apartment or city dweller without a yard, gardening indoors may be all that is possible.

For many of us, the degree to which our experiments with potted plants indoors or on porches and patios succeed contributes significantly to our self-image. We think of ourselves as "having a green thumb" or as "no good with plants," depending on the results of our more or less informed efforts to insure the survival of a series of container plants that we have selected or received as gifts. When all goes well, often through a happy combination of environmental circumstances, we gain confidence. Government bureaucrats in downtown Washington graduate from caring for philodendrons and Boston ferns to composting on the roof and growing cherry tomatoes in a sunny window. But when repeated disaster strikes, which it frequently does through ignorance of plant care, disease, or insect invasion, one may be discouraged from further horticultural efforts. In desperation, one even may be tempted to use toxic materials inside the house to attempt to kill off some "pest" attacking a cherished window tomato plant.

Certain useful generalizations can be made with respect to the similarities and differences between food plants and ornamental plants grown in containers, both indoors and out. Because growing ornamental plants in containers may be the only opportunity some urban people have for learning about plant growth—and ultimately all animal, including human, life—considering the subject of indoor plants in some detail will be worthwhile. Certainly the ideal integral urban house would include an abundance of indoor house plants, as well as cut flowers from the garden. This chapter is meant as a source of information for those with or planning indoor plant-raising systems.

The Indoor Environment

When raising plants in a home or specially constructed greenhouse, one has to deal with the same constraints that confront urban dwellers outdoors. In the home, however, these constraints are present in their most extreme state. The limiting factors are light, humidity, temperature, and reduced ecosystem diversification.

Light: A foot candle is the amount of light cast on a surface one foot away from a candle. Outdoors, the light-intensity range during the day tends to vary around ten- to twelve-thousand foot candles. Indoors, in a sunny window, the range may be four- to five-thousand foot candles. Just a few feet back from the window the light intensity may be as low as two hundred foot candles, while farther inside, it may measure only ten to a hundred. (A book can be read comfortably at fifty foot candles or slightly less.) Skylights may raise the intensities inside a room significantly, of course.

Should one boost indoor light conditions by adding artificial light? In general, unless you are energy-rich with renewable, nonpolluting sources, such as solar, wind, methane or hydroelectric power, our answer would be an emphatic "no!" However, some situations might warrant use of supplemental lights—for example, where the winter nights are so long or the days so dark because of clouds and rain that food plants such as windowsill tomatoes or lettuce will not grow, or where the spring days are so dark and rainy that starting vegetable seedlings indoors is otherwise impossible.

Neither the ordinary light bulb or fluorescent lights begin to approximate the full spectrum of the sun. To some extent they complement each other, and thus are usually used together (one watt of incandescent lamp for every two of fluorescent). While the seeds are germinating no extra light is necessary, but once they show above ground, a light fixture connected to a timer (set to provide spring day-length) can be suspended above them. (Figure 9-1, page 228, shows window, shelf, seedlings in cartons, and a fluorescent fixture above them.)

Humidity: While within a greenhouse, with its great concentration of plants and moist growing medium, the humidity may become too great, in the house quite the opposite is true. Of course, there are exceptions—for example, when it is raining or very humid outdoors and the house is unheated. But generally the environment inside a house is very dry, ranging commonly between 10 and 30 percent humidity. The drier extreme is experienced not only in desert and semiarid regions, but also at certain times in some high-altitude areas such as Denver.

Low humidity in a house can be unpleasant for the human occupants. Particularly annoying may be the charge of static electricity that quickly accumulates when one walks across a rug and suddenly discharges itself when he or she touches a doorknob or elevator button. Thus, those who design homes in dry areas—solar architect Richard Crowther, for example, a leader in the solar energy field who has done some very imaginative and advanced home designs, and his associates—often build in bays and skylights expressly to accommodate large indoor foliage plants as well as attached greenhouses for the precise purpose of humidifying the air and improving human comfort within the house.

The low humidity indoors that results from many home heating systems during the winter is thought to influence susceptibility to colds in humans. The mucus membranes of the nasal passages may be dried and irritated by the dry air, making them more vulnerable to virus invasion. Presumably, until the invention of centralized forced-air heating, humans endured indoor humidities that were more similar to natural environments outdoors and fairly damp during rainy or cold periods.

The dry conditions that cause difficulties for humans may put even more stress on many house plants. With the exception of cactus and other true desert dwellers, most commonly grown house plants prefer humidity from 70 to 90 percent.

Temperature: The general range of indoor temperatures can also cause plants some difficulty. The comfort zone for humans ranges between 60°F and 75°F (15.6 to 32.9°C). The common house plants, with very few exceptions, do best in a range of between 70°F and 90°F (21.1 to 32.2°C). (See the discussion of greenhouse temperatures, page 240.) One can conclude from these differences in ideal humidity and temperature ranges that plants in the house will give a less-than-optimum performance regardless of how much tender loving care they receive, although one may use various strategies to compensate for each of the constraints indoors.

The Simplified Environment: A house plant living in splendid isolation in its little flower pot experiences an extremely simplified environment compared with those in any natural habitat. Consider for example the reduced physical microclimate range, and the reduced plant, insect, and microbial competitors in the soil indoors. The indoor environment is even more simplified than that in a greenhouse setting. The quality of the environment may aggravate the possible consequent pest and disease problems. The natural enemies of many plant pests, for example, are frequently excluded indoors. Furthermore, inside a house the management techniques that deal effectively with pest and disease problems may be more difficult in the slightly more detached greenhouse setting. The relative lack of animal, fungal, and microbial life inside means that much natural biological control of insects and plant pathogens will be eliminated. Pest and disease problems will be most extreme for house plants that remain indoors all year because they are too big to take outdoors or too tender for the outside climate. Apartment dwellers may have no place outdoors where they can move house plants temporarily. Many people have no time to give such care in any case.

Raising Food Plants in the House

In general, plants that produce food for human use require more light than can be found in the average room indoors, except next to a sunny window or under a large sunny skylight. However, with either of those conditions one can grow some good additions to the salad or stew. The authors have grown sweet (bell) and hot peppers, Chinese garlics and numerous other herbs, and Tiny Tim and "patio" tomatoes indoors on sunny windowsills. Greenhouse cucumbers were less successful in our experience, perhaps because maintaining adequate humidity in the house itself was difficult. The peppers and tomatoes produce fruit proportionate to the root space they are given. The most productive were grown in compost in five-gallon cans standing in a galvanized tray on the floor.

A number of citrus varieties can also be grown indoors successfully, if given containers of a substantial size. We have had particular success with raising dwarf lemons, limes, and mandarin oranges in containers. You may wish to consult *Dwarf Fruit Trees, Indoors and Outdoors,* by Robert E. Atkinson for an expanded discussion of this subject.

Typical Ornamental House Plants

When devising managment strategies in caring for house plants, it helps to know something about the native environments in which they originated. One might ask this question: given the constraints imposed by the house interior, where in the world could one go to find plants that could survive under those conditions?

Understory Plants: With respect to the reduced light inside a house, many house plants developed originally on the forest floor or in the shade of other plants, so their natural habitat is shaded. Even most species of cactus get

225

their start in the protection of rocks or vegetation, and some will survive only in those conditions. If such understory plants are moved outdoors for a time, they should be placed where the light is filtered by trees or lath, or where they are shaded from midday on. (Since cactus can sunburn easily but grows sun tolerant after exposure, mark the side of the pot that is facing the sun so that if it is moved you can maintain the same orientation.)

Surrounded by other vegetation and close to the ground, these plants may have developed under circumstances of even high humidity. To create similar conditions indoors, group plants together and use special watering and potting techniques (see pages 226–33).

Tropical and Subtropical Plants: A large number of house plants, in addition to developing in understory microclimates, come from tropical and subtropical areas. It is interesting to note that most house plants are produced commercially in Florida. Many were discovered originally in such places as Ceylon or the West Indies (for example, the philodendron). In addition to the reduced light and high humidity mentioned above, these areas have a number of specific characteristics which helped to develop plants that can survive indoor conditions, for example, even temperature. Many house plants cannot take sudden chills, and should even be watered with water that has been allowed to come to room temperature. Drops of cold water falling on the leaves may cause them to spot. African violets are an example. When you move such plants outdoors, make sure that all danger of a cold spell is past. Place them in a location outdoors that is sheltered from chilling winds. Move them back inside when outdoor and indoor temperatures are still nearly the same; that is, do not wait too long in the fall to bring them back inside. Cooler outdoor temperatures will force the plant to adapt to some degree by slowing its growth. At that point, returning the plant to a warm environment will cause a flush of growth just as the days are growing shorter, when the plant should be resting.

Although the tropical or subtropical environment may have had high humidities, this is usually accompanied by good drainage. As a result, few house plants can survive with their roots sitting in water. Roots need to breathe, taking in oxygen and giving off carbon dioxide. In low-oxygen environments, such as water-logged soils, they will smother and succumb to plant pathogens. When deciding on potting and watering techniques (see pages 226–33) you must take these factors into account.

Another characteristic of the original environment is that the native soils are leached of nutrients from heavy and frequent rains. The high ground temperatures cause rapid decomposition of whatever organic matter might otherwise have accumulated there, and the rainwater mixed with the organic acids resulting from this rapid decomposition in turn create fairly acid soils. Consequently, most common house plants (again, some cacti are an exception) have a very low tolerance for salts. In the house environment, the salt such plants are most likely to come in contact with is chlorine, since most municipal water supplies are chlorinated. Chlorine salts are often seen as small white crystals encrusting the soil surface and sides of clay pots containing house plants. These salts frequently accumulate because the plants are set on saucers onto which the excess water is allowed to drain. This water reenters the pot and evaporates from the surface of the porous container and from the soil, leaving the salt behind. In due time, depending upon the species, the plant will show brown dry tips and leaf margins, and eventually it will die. Allowing chlorine salts to gather is a popular method of killing ferns, for instance.

Other harmful salts in the water may be sodium (NaCl), found in some water softeners, as well as a variety of detergent ingredients often found in greywater. Of course, the same kind of burn injury may be a result of over-fertilizing. The problem of low salt tolerance must be handled through watering and fertilizing techniques (see pages 228–30).

Plants from Arid and Semiarid Environments: In contrast, some house plants such as cacti, euphorbias, and other succulents may have originated in arid or semiarid environments. These areas are characterized by long periods of dryness between rains, or a wet season followed by dry, and plants native to them respond best to a similar treatment indoors. In fact, cacti may not flower unless they are allowed to dry out thoroughly for at least one to two months once a year. Consequently, owners of many windowsill cactus gardens have never seen their plants bloom. They may not realize that the flowers are frequently the most spectacular aspect of these unusual plants.

Plant Size: There is one final point to mention in summing up these generalizations on the nature of house plants and their environments. Many of the plants commonly grown for years in six- or eight-inch pots, can, when growing naturally under ideal conditions, reach what are truly gigantic proportions in comparison. Some, such as Draceana, are capable of becoming trees, while many others easily assume large shrublike growth totally inappropriate for the average indoor setting. Thus, it is apparent that the real trick in raising house plants is to keep them healthy but stunted, or they will quickly outgrow their containers and require constant pruning and other maintenance.

An acquaintance of ours tells of how his lawn-growing strategy differs from that of his son. When the son is home on vacation he waters and fertilizes the lawn optimally, rapidly creating a lush green growth. This in turn, means he must tend to it constantly with regular mowing and trimming. When the son returns to college, the father, with a sigh of relief, reverts to a less demanding maintenance regime, providing just the minimal water and fertilizer needed to keep the lawn surviving adequately, but reducing the need for all that energy expenditure and maintenance. The lesson to be learned here for house plant owners is unless you have lots of extra time to spend in repotting, cutting back, and fighting off the bugs, such as aphids, that flourish from the high nitrogen of the rapidly growing succulent foliage, learn something about the basic environment required by each particular species you are raising and then maintain the plant so it grows as slowly as possible and stays healthy. There are a number of good encyclopedias of house plants, some with pictures that will help you recognize plants whose scientific names you don't know. These books will give you tips on the ideal conditions.

House Plant Management: The following sections translate the general information above into explicit advice on plant care.

Selection and Siting: For best results select plants that do well in the environments you can provide easily (without fossil-fuel energy). This means that you should not acquire unfamiliar species on impulse and at random, since you may not be able to provide the indoor conditions necessary for them to survive. If you buy such plants and they languish and die you might conclude, quite incorrectly, that you have no aptitude for raising plants.

A good method for selecting plants is to take a house plant encyclopedia (see the bibliography) with you on a trip to a large house-plant store or nursery. Each time you see a plant you find attractive, learn its name and check it out in the book to see if you can provide the care and environment the plant will need. Store clerks can rarely provide you with the time, attention, and expert information you need.

To site your newly acquired plants in your home, place those plants needing the most direct sun in south windows or under large skylights. East windows or northern-facing spots are best for plants that require less light. White or light interior walls and furnishings will help reflect light to those plants set back within a room. You may wish to check out your home environment from this perspective before you make that trip to the plant store.

Assess your house interior for temperature variations as well as humidity. West windows are often hot spots. Bathrooms and kitchens may be more humid. Rooms on the north side and north walls may stay cool most evenly.

Figure 9-1. Seedlings Underneath Fluorescent Light Fixture

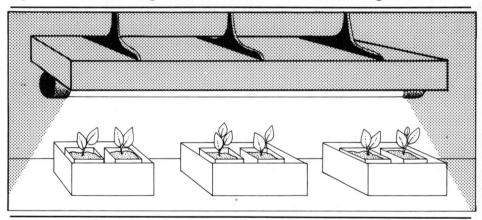

Amass plants together when possible so that they can provide some humidity for each other through their normal transpiration.

And, finally, if even growth is desired (it is not always), rotate the plants regularly so that all sides are exposed to the light.

Watering: The most important rule here is, do not overwater! Symptoms of overwatering are yellowing of leaves and the shedding of a lot of leaves at once. Use your plant encyclopedia to learn which of your plants may need a slight drying out of the soil between waterings and which prefer an even, moist growing medium. Test the soil with your finger to see if more watering is needed, instead of dousing the plants whenever you might feel the urge.

In general, water from the top down whenever possible. Place the flowerpot on pebbles or crushed rock so that water can drain out of the container into the saucer but cannot reenter the pot. Extra water standing below the pot can be syringed out with a baster if the plant is not a lover of high humidity (see Figure 9-2).

Do not use pottery bits in the bottom of the pot either to permit drainage or to cover the hole to keep the soil from running out. Although many gardening books may suggest doing so, this is bad advice, as plant pathologists will confirm. It is extremely important that the water be able to drain freely away from the plant roots. When pieces of crockery or other similar materials are used in the bottom of the pot, the water will fill up all the spaces between them before it begins to drain. Water standing in the pot in this fashion invites fungal growth, root-rot, and other soil-related plant disease.

Crown-rot is a disease that affects some plants, such as African violets, at the point where the leaves or roots meet. If your plants show evidence of this disease and you are afraid that top-down watering will wet the center, let the plant stand in a basin of water for no longer than one-half hour and then set it where the excess can freely drain. Crown rot produces decomposed tissues at the crown level resulting in wilting and plant death.

Whenever possible, remove the chlorine from the water for plants by letting it stand overnight before using it or by boiling it and letting it cool. (Since boiling takes energy, it is better to plan ahead by keeping a filled pail somewhere in a corner out of which you can dip your water when the house plants need it.)

Figure 9-2. **Proper Method of Watering Indoor Plants**

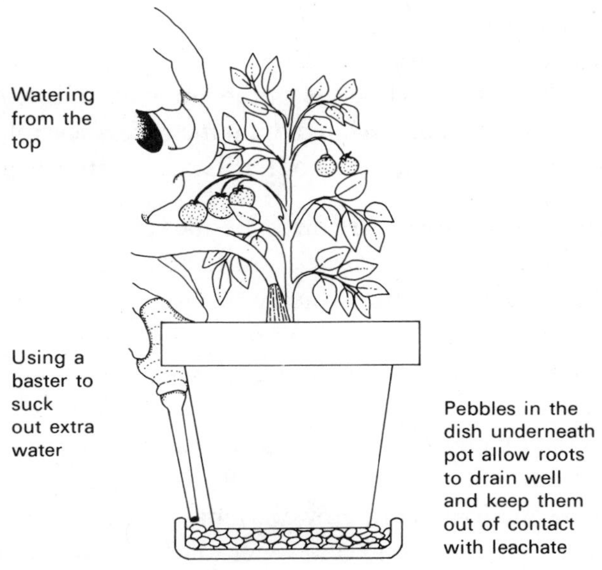

Watering from the top

Using a baster to suck out extra water

Pebbles in the dish underneath pot allow roots to drain well and keep them out of contact with leachate

For tropical plants and others that spot when cold water touches their leaves, bring the water to room temperature before using it.

For plants that like a high humidity, in addition to massing them together in one area, try (1) misting with an atomizer, (2) setting the plant on pebbles in a tray filled with water so that the evaporating water adds to the humidity around the plants, and (3) placing the clay pot containing the plant on pebbles within a much larger glazed pot and lining the space between the two with spagnum moss so that the mass around the pot can be kept wet, maintaining an even moisture around the pot without drowning the roots. Spagnum moss can usually be purchased in nurseries or house plant stores.

Watering When You Are Away: You can keep your plants from drying out if you are to be gone a short period by covering the plant and pot with a large plastic bag and setting it out of the sun for the duration of your absence. For absences of several weeks, it is best to have a friend come in and check them regularly. If you do take them to a neighbor's for care while you are away, be sure your instructions are explicit, since it is as as easy (or easier) to kill plants with kindness as with neglect, through overwatering by well-meaning plantsitters.

Fertilizing: As in the garden, compost is ideal for providing house plants with nutrients by releasing them slowly over a long period of time, making available to the plants a selection far greater than the ordinary commercial fertilizer, and providing a wealth of soil organisms to combat plant pathogens. However, if you do use commercial fertilizer, in general it is wisest to choose one that provides N-P-K (nitrogen-phosphorus-potassium) in the ratio of 1:2:1. This is because you don't wish the plants to grow too fast, encouraging weakness in the stems as well as aphids and mealybugs. High nitrogen to phosphorus and potassium ratios can cause such excessive growth rates. Also, with commercial products it is best to fertilize indoor plants infrequently unless no nutrients at all are provided by the growing medium (see page 179). Fertilize at most every four months, and not at all during the dark short days of winter or during other times (such as dry periods) when the plants are growing slowly.

As mentioned earlier, overfertilizing can kill a plant through salt build-up. If you think this has become a problem with a plant of yours, repot the plant in fresh soil or soak and drain the excess several times at the sink. For a more complete discussion of fertilizing plants, see pages 201–19.

Cleaning: Urban environments are dirty. Besides collecting in your lungs, the particulate products of our industrial world will coat the leaves of your plants, covering the pores through which water is transpired and gases exchanged. (For a discussion of lead fallout on outdoor vegetables, see pages 429–35. For a description of the breathing apparatus of plants, see page 158, Figure 7-2.)

Because indoor plants do not receive the benefit of rain or sprinklers, it is a good idea to wash their leaves occasionally. The simplest way is to move the plant outdoors and hose it off. However, many plants are too large to move or too fragile or sensitive to cold water to withstand that treatment. An alternative is to wipe off smooth-leaved plants gently with a damp cloth. Hairy-leaved plants can be either inverted and sloshed through a pan of mild soapy water and then rinsed with clear water or rinsed off with a gentle stream of warm water with a faucet hose in the bathtub.

Do not attempt to shine the leaves with salad or other oil, as was done by a friend of ours. This will block the stoma (breathing pores) and smother the plant. One of the advantages of a leaf-by-leaf wipe with water is that this close attention to the plant will help you spot any incipient insect or other problem, which can then be managed before it becomes too great.

Pruning: Many house plants that lengthen gradually, with the growing tip moving ever further away from the main stem, benefit from occasional pruning. If the stems are soft and succulent, pruning can be done simply with thumb and forefinger. If not, then pruning shears should be used. The reason for pruning is to encourage the foliage to become more dense. The top bud of each stem produces a chemical inhibitor that prevents or restrains the growth of all the buds on its stalk between it and the base. Removal of that top bud will temporarily release the lower buds from that restraining influence and they will promptly begin to grow, giving the plant a less leggy, more bushy appearance. By pinching off some side buds and leaving others, you can gradually shape the plant to your fancy.

Since a number of house plants reproduce easily from cuttings, you can sometimes begin new plants and prune the old at the same time. Early spring is the best time for both activities, since the days are lengthening then and the plants are entering an active growth phase once again.

Repotting: Some plants like to be crowded in their pots and some do not. How can you tell when a particular specimen needs repotting? Some signs are the production of smaller and smaller leaves as the plant ages, the appearance of roots on the top of the soil and from the hole at the base of the pot, and frequent wilting, so that the plant must be watered more and more often.

As with pruning and fertilizing, repotting is best done in the spring, when the plant begins its more vigorous growth. Plan to use an unglazed clay pot or natural wood container about two inches wider and deeper than the old pot. Neither plastic nor glazed ceramic material permits sufficient exchange of gases and evaporation of excess moisture from the soil. The un-

Figure 9-3. **Good Potting Arrangement Using a Glazed Pot**

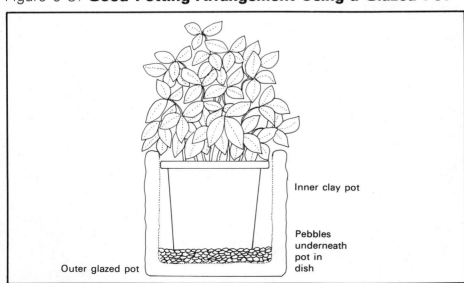

Inner clay pot

Pebbles underneath pot in dish

Outer glazed pot

glazed pot may be set into any kind of more ornamental container you might choose, providing that the inner pot is raised above the bottom of the outer one by pebbles or something similar, so that water draining out of one cannot reenter once again (see Figure 9-3). The new potting medium should extend clear down into the base of the pot, tamped firmly across the bottom. A very small amount will drain out with the first watering, but after that the contents will hold firm.

A general potting mix often recommended for house plants is one part garden loam (see page 178), one part organic material, and one part sand. The sand will permit good drainage. Peat moss is frequently used as the organic component, but it contributes little in the way of plant nutrients. We prefer sifted compost. As you might guess, we do not sterilize the soil, since we want to keep as much life within it as possible. If you wish to use a more sterile medium, you can heat the mix in open pans in the oven at 180°F (82.2°C) for thirty minutes. (See pages 198–201 for a discussion of soil life and its function.)

For plants that like a mixture richer in organic matter—philodendrons are an example—you can use one part compost to one part soil. In any case, whatever the potting mix, it should be as dry as possible so that you can tamp it down without compacting it.

Before attempting to remove the plant from its pot, soak it thoroughly and let it drain. Then, working over newspapers spread to catch the soil that will fall away in the process, turn the plant on its side or upside down and tap firmly around the edges of the pot until the soil loosens and can be eased out. If the plant is stuck, strike the pot against a counter or table to free it (see Figure 9-4).

Any roots that were coming out the bottom should be pruned off, and the entire ball of roots should be set into the new pot upon two inches of new potting mix that has been pressed down firmly. Then, working round and round the pot, add new soil bit by bit and tamp it down with something appropriately long and thin, such as the handle of a trowel or screwdriver.

Figure 9-4. **Repotting of House Plants**

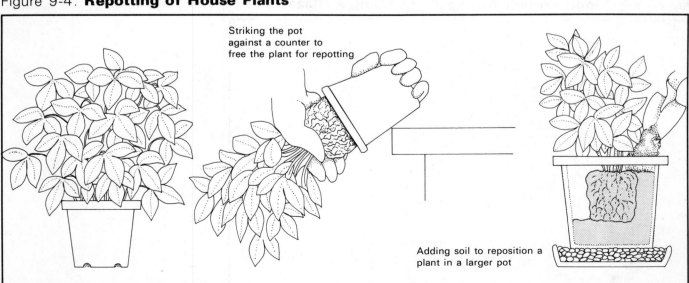

Striking the pot against a counter to free the plant for repotting

Adding soil to reposition a plant in a larger pot

It is important not to place the new potting mix over the old soil surface. This could produce a boundary layer where moisture collects. The stem should join the roots so that air can circulate around the juncture. This will prevent crown rot. Be sure to leave an inch or so of space for watering.

When the plant has been repotted, pinch it back in rough proportion to the amount of damage you feel the roots may have sustained during transplanting. Then soak the pot thoroughly by immersing it in a pan of water until water rises to the top and bubbles stop forming. Let the plant drain and move it to its place on a pebble-laden saucer large enough to accommodate the new pot. An exception to this general procedure is repotting cactus.

Cactus should not be soaked after moving. Let it sit in the new dry soil for several weeks at least, allowing any damage to its roots to heal before giving the first good watering.

Insect Management: Because of the extremely simplified ecosystem, indoor plants may suffer from the lack of biological controls, that is, the predators that would keep plant pests in check in a more biologically complex environment. Insect pests may be even more difficult to control in the house than in the greenhouse, where lacewings and predatory mites can sometimes be maintained on a year-round basis (see pages 378–80).

The major pests indoors are aphids, scales, whiteflies, mealybugs, and mites. (These first four are all closely related Homoptera, producing honeydew; see pages 381 and 387–88.) The pest insects usually enter the home on the houseplant itself or are brought in with other garden materials and find their way to the house plants.

The first strategy you might wish to use when a few bugs appear is physical: handpick, squash, or rub them off. Cotton swabs or a small brush dipped in alcohol may help you to get into hard-to-reach nooks and crannies where the insects may be found. Washing the plant off in a mild soapy water may also help.

During late spring and summer, when plenty of general insect predators and parasites are found in the garden, putting the afflicted plant outdoors for several weeks may take care of the problem. Either the pests will be consumed, or, as with migratory aphids, the summer generation may fly away to another host.

Twice a small hot pepper plant that grows indoors on our kitchen windowsill and provides us spices for chili and beans has been infested in the early spring with an aphid (*Myzus persicae*). Infestation became obvious because the aphids' honeydew (the sweet, sticky sugar protein excreted by many plant-sucking insects) began to shine on the leaves. We usually squished the first few aphids by hand, but invariably the aphid population escaped this control measure and began to spread. Usually by this time, the weather had become so mild that the plant could be set outside in a protected sunny spot on the porch. However, the aphid parasites and predators had not arrived in the area yet, so the pepper plant had to be hosed off vigorously each week. If this was not done, the plant began to turn yellow and drop its leaves. As the season progressed the biological controls appeared. First we would notice parasitized aphids among the colonies (see page 383); then we would see syrphid fly larvae and adult lady beetles consuming their share. By early summer not an aphid was to be seen. Apparently all had

233

either been eaten by insects or flown off to other hosts. The plant was then promptly moved back into the kitchen, where it lived without apparent insect companions until another spring. How did the aphids get there each year? Since there are a couple of early spring aphids in our area that can live on more than one species of plant, it is easy to see how a winged one might fly or be blown in through an open window or door.

Several years ago, aphids got started on this same plant quite late in the spring, and soon after we noticed their presence parasitized individuals (see Figure 13-10) became apparent. Not only had the aphid found its way into the house, but its parasites had too. Since none of the parasites' parasites found the plant, the parasite proceeded to wipe out every last aphid, ending the problem for that year without our having to move the plant outdoors. But that event has not been repeated, perhaps because we are reluctant to leave the kitchen window open without screens because of house flies.

When moving plants infested with honeydew producers outside, you might wish to place them on stands with ant-excluders around the legs so that ants don't prevent the aphid predators and parasites from doing a good job (see page 311).

For bug-infested plants that are too large to move, handpick, or hose off, you can import predatory lacewings or mites just as in greenhouse pest management. After cleaning up the pest insects the predators will die off from lack of food, so for each new outbreak new predators will have to be imported (see pages 378–80). An excellent book on using biological controls on houseplants is *Windowsill Ecology,* by William Jorden.

What about using synthetic commercial poisons on house plant bug problems? We have expressed our thoughts on pesticides elsewhere (see pages 368–77). If you feel that a plant is so valuable that it must be saved at all costs, and have exhausted all safer methods of insect management, then be sure to select the least toxic material that will do the job (see pages 376–77). Move the plant outdoors, and wear a mask and gloves while handling the poison and treating the plant, washing yourself and your clothes afterwards. Remember, the house plants are supposedly being kept to increase your pleasure and health, not to add one more touch of poison to an urban environment already burdened with substances toxic to humans. (For illustrations of the insects described in this section and an expanded discussion of insect management see Chapter 13.)

Disease Management: When plants look sick, and no insect can be found, the usual assumption is that it is being attacked by a pathogen. Plant diseases are harder to cure than either insect infestations or salt build-up. (Another occasional threat to house plants—guests surreptitiously dumping unwanted alcoholic drinks into the nearest greenery—will not be dealt with here.) The checklist in the margin may be useful in preventing disease.

A last thought on maintaining house plants: they do grow best with attention. Whether this is a response to increased carbon dioxide from human respiration, to the caretaker's alertness with respect to watering, bug management, and repotting needs, or to some relationship between humans and plants not yet satisfactorily explained, the authors are not prepared to guess.

Preventing Plant Disease

1. Do not overwater.
2. Do not overfertilize. (Excess nitrogen may encourage aphid infestations indoors as well as out, in addition to creating weak, oversucculent plants more susceptible to disease.)
3. If you or experts you are able to ask for advice cannot diagnose the ailment, try repotting the plant in fresh material.
4. Leaves infested with mold or fungus leaf-spots can be cut off and composted. Necrotic (black) areas on cactus can be cut out with a sharp knife. The cut area should be dusted with sulfur and the entire plant left to dry, out of direct sun, in a light, well-ventilated place until the wound has calyxed over.
5. Where crown-, stem-, or root-rot is the problem, it is best to destroy the plants. Avoid the problem in the future by not overwatering or overfertilizing, and by keeping water off susceptible plants.

Since the indoor environment of the house is usually too dark and often too dry for the satisfactory growth of many plants, glasshouses or greenhouses have been devised to provide adequate light along with protection from the outdoor climate. Because conventional greenhouses heat up excessively during warm seasons and become too cold during winter, a great deal of energy is usually expended in attempting to cool and heat these structures. Recently, extensive attempts have been made to adapt energy-saving techniques to these systems.

At the time of this writing, we are not aware of any large-scale commercial greenhouse operators attempting to reduce what have become enormous burdens in operating costs by more perfectly solarizing their structures. However, the number of small home-scale attached solar greenhouses of various designs is now extensive, particularly in the mountainous West and Southwest, where clear, sunny, dry days are coupled with short growing seasons and cold winters. The very satisfactory operation of many of these smaller greenhouses means that the large-scale application of these principles cannot be far behind.

Greenhouses attached to homes and other structures essentially operate as solar collectors gathering heat for the home or structure. Without a way to store the excess heat collected during the hotter portions of the day, supplementary heating at night and cooling/ventilation systems during the day will be required to stabilize temperatures. All new greenhouses, especially the free-standing ones, should have sufficient heat storage capability as well as multiple glazing to reduce heat losses, particularly at night. This is particularly true of the smaller greenhouses because the costs of installing such storage systems will be recovered faster. New greenhouses should also be integrated into existing or new structures to create situations where normally wasted heat either from the structures (for example, bakeries, laundries, large commercial furnaces) or the greenhouse operations (for example, nurseries, florists) can be utilized.

Compared with more traditional structures, most solar greenhouses, whether free-standing or attached to the side of a building, combine some or all of the following special features:

1. Reduced glass (or plastic) on the north side, where heat loss is the greatest. This reduction may be accomplished by attaching the greenhouse to the house itself, so that the side of the larger house forms the north wall of the greenhouse, as in a lean-to. Obviously, such a design is particularly suitable for urban areas. It makes for a compact greenhouse, and in some cases excess heat from the basement furnace can be vented into the structure. In free-standing structures, the north wall may be insulated with a mass of earth or some other material heaped up against it. In addition to the insulation, the north wall may be lined inside with rows of black fifty-gallon drums filled with water or other water-storage containers.

2. Regardless of whether it is used along the north wall, water is used somewhere in the house for heat storage. In the aesthetically appealing structures of the New Alchemists (a widely known appropriate-technology group located outside Woods Hole, Massachusetts), open ponds, used for

235

summer fish-raising, also moderate the greenhouse temperature (see the *Journal of the New Alchemists,* listed in the bibliography). Sometimes the greenhouse itself is designed primarily for aquacultural purposes. Water stored in the greenhouse will help to moderate the extremes of both heat and cold.

3. In many cases, mass, in the form of rocks, earth, cinder blocks, or other dense building materials is exposed within the house to receive the direct rays of the sun.

4. The greenhouse is sited to make maximum use of prevailing winds, which permits ventilation in summer. When additional cooling is needed shading may be provided through hanging sun-screens or by raising annual vines or other tall plants.

5. Particularly in areas where nighttime and winter temperatures regularly drop below 45°F (7.2°C), the transparent surfaces of the greenhouse have two or even three layers of glazing material to help prevent undesirable heat loss. Typically, the outer layer of glazing is either glass or some sort of rigid fiber glass material that is resistant to the degrading effect of ultraviolet rays. "Tedlar"-coated fiber glass is such a material, and comes either as a roll (Filon is its trademark) for use on vertical or near-vertical walls or as corrugated roofing (trademarked Lascolite). The interior glazing is commonly greenhouse quality 6–mil polyethylene. In many solar greenhouse designs, insulated panels are hinged to the south, glazed wall to permit regulation of heat gain into, and heat loss out of, the greenhouse. The panels are lowered in the morning, exposing the bottom portion of the clear south-facing wall to the sun. The panels' white surfaces reflect additional light into the greenhouse. Black-painted drums filled with water are positioned underneath the seedling table inside to collect the sun's heat. At dusk, the insulated panels are raised to shield the portion of the wall they cover against heat loss. The warmth absorbed by the drums during the day radiates into the greenhouse at night.

Another strategy for reducing heat loss is to use a plastic tube tent (see Figure 7-3) inside the greenhouse, either over benches or over rows for low-growing vegetation. This strategy and the internal panel idea should be combined where possible. Bench growing systems can utilize still another concept—that of water storage beneath the benches. Barrels or even more innovative constructions should be utilized where water is the heat-storage medium to help decrease temperature differences between day and night. These and other concepts are reviewed in Jensen's "Energy Alternatives and Conservation for Greenhouses."

6. The solid walls of the greenhouse are insulated, and careful attention is given to the plugging of cracks and crevices anywhere in the structure that could permit heat loss through infiltration. Foam or other insulation is used on the ground along the inside perimeter of the structure to prevent loss of heat into the earth.

As the costs of heating greenhouses continues to spiral upward, many large-scale existing systems will probably reduce the size of their operations and still others will go out of business. The consequences for the urban dweller will be winter vegetable scarcity, higher prices for vegetables grown in nearby greenhouses, or more importing of vegetables from warmer areas such as southern regions of the United States or Mexico. The cut-flower and floral industry will be most severely curbed by the rise in heating costs. An alternative is integrating greenhouse systems into homes and developing home-scale food production possibilities and smaller commercial operations focused on high cash crops in industrial areas. Innovative designs for such systems will undoubtedly become commonplace.

The smallest and most "integral" greenhouse the authors have visited personally is one constructed by Abby Rockefeller along the outside of her living room wall in Cambridge, Massachusetts. This structure is impressive because it has been so well integrated into the living systems of the house. The plants in Abby's greenhouse are watered entirely by greywater, and they are grown in a leaf compost made in the backyard. Abby has written down for us the following detailed description of what she regards to be the interesting features of this greenhouse. Note that in her mind it is as valuable as a treatment system for the household greywater (wastewater) as for its abundant vegetable productivity:

"The greenhouse has a three-foot-deep rock bed underneath the concrete slab floor, which is six feet by twelve feet—the dimensions of the greenhouse itself. This serves to moderate the temperature, cutting down both highs and lows. A thermostatically controlled fan draws the hottest air near the peak down a tube, and into the stone storage. An opening in the slab at the other end permits the cool ground air to be blown into the greenhouse.

"The washwater from the house, after passing through a stone roughing filter, is automatically pumped into 1½-inch leachlines, four inches below the soil surface in the soil boxes. This washwater, hence, is the irrigation source for the greenhouse.

This experimental house system integrates food production, solar heat collection, and waste recycling.

Figure 9-5. **Cross-section of the Clivus Multrum Wastewater System**

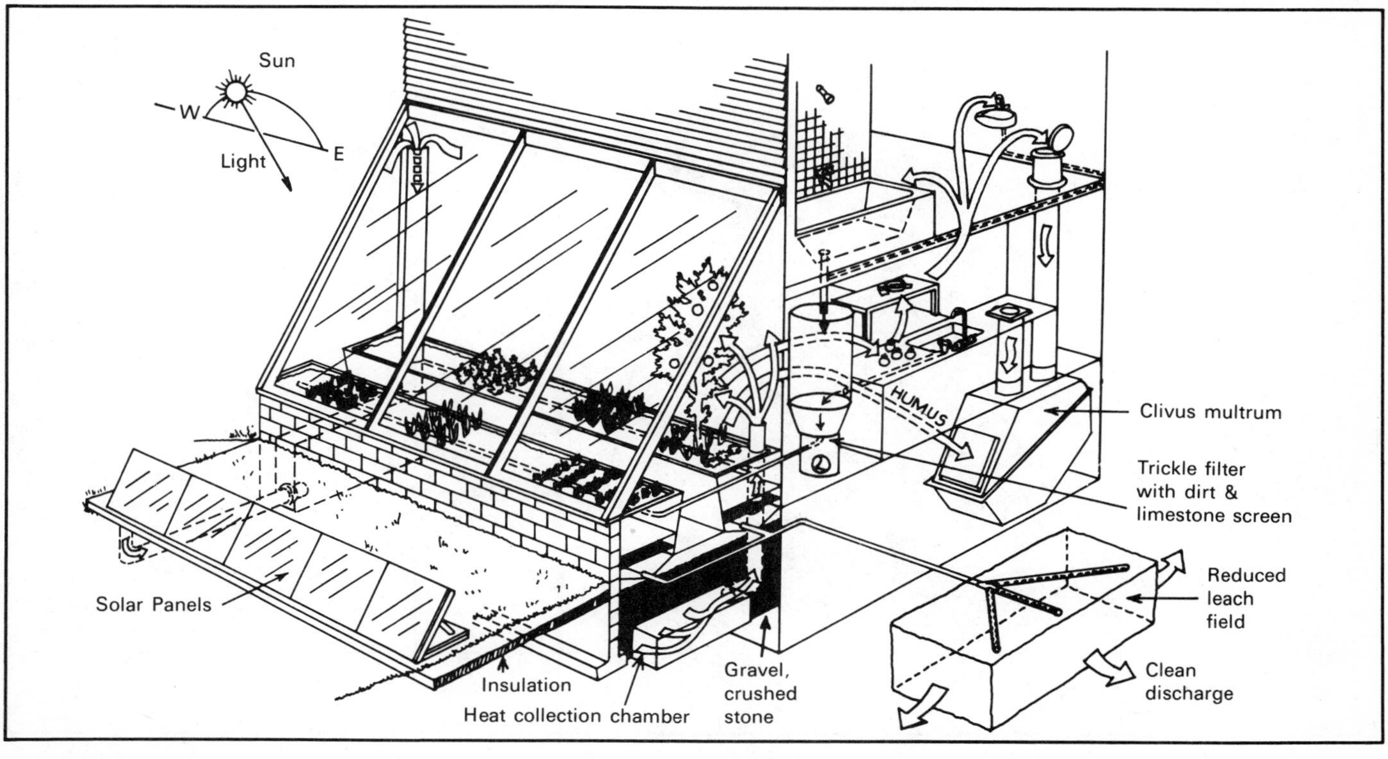

237

"The soil boxes, unlike the standard shallow benches, are four feet deep. The soil in them, which is organically rich to allow for good drainage (it is half topsoil, half leaf compost), serves as the major purification medium for the wash water. The wastewater is by no means even significantly absorbed and utilized by the soil and plants; rather, the greater part will pass straight down, as in a standard leaching field, to receive its final treatment in the soil below the greenhouse (or rock storage). The soil boxes are then, in effect, raised leaching beds; these improve greatly the chances of the water being pure before it hits groundwater level. The growing vegetables will serve the important function of recapturing the nutrients in the washwater. The large soil mass in these boxes has the added advantage of helping to maintain a more stable temperature and moisture content, and of supporting a more heterogeneous soil ecosystem (for example, mites, beetles, earthworms) than is possible with shallow benches. The richness of the deep soil also encourages the activity of the invertebrates even to the bottom, thus insuring that the soil will not become plugged by bacterial slime."

A cross-section of this greywater filter, greenhouse, and compost system is shown in Figure 9-5.

The easiest to understand, detailed, step-by-step description of how to plan and build a lean-to solar greenhouse is to be found in a book by Rick Fisher and Bill Yanda (see the bibliography at the end of the book). They include a survey of some twenty-seven large and small lean-to and free-standing solar greenhouses of differing designs from around the United

Figure 9-6. **A Yanda-style Greenhouse**

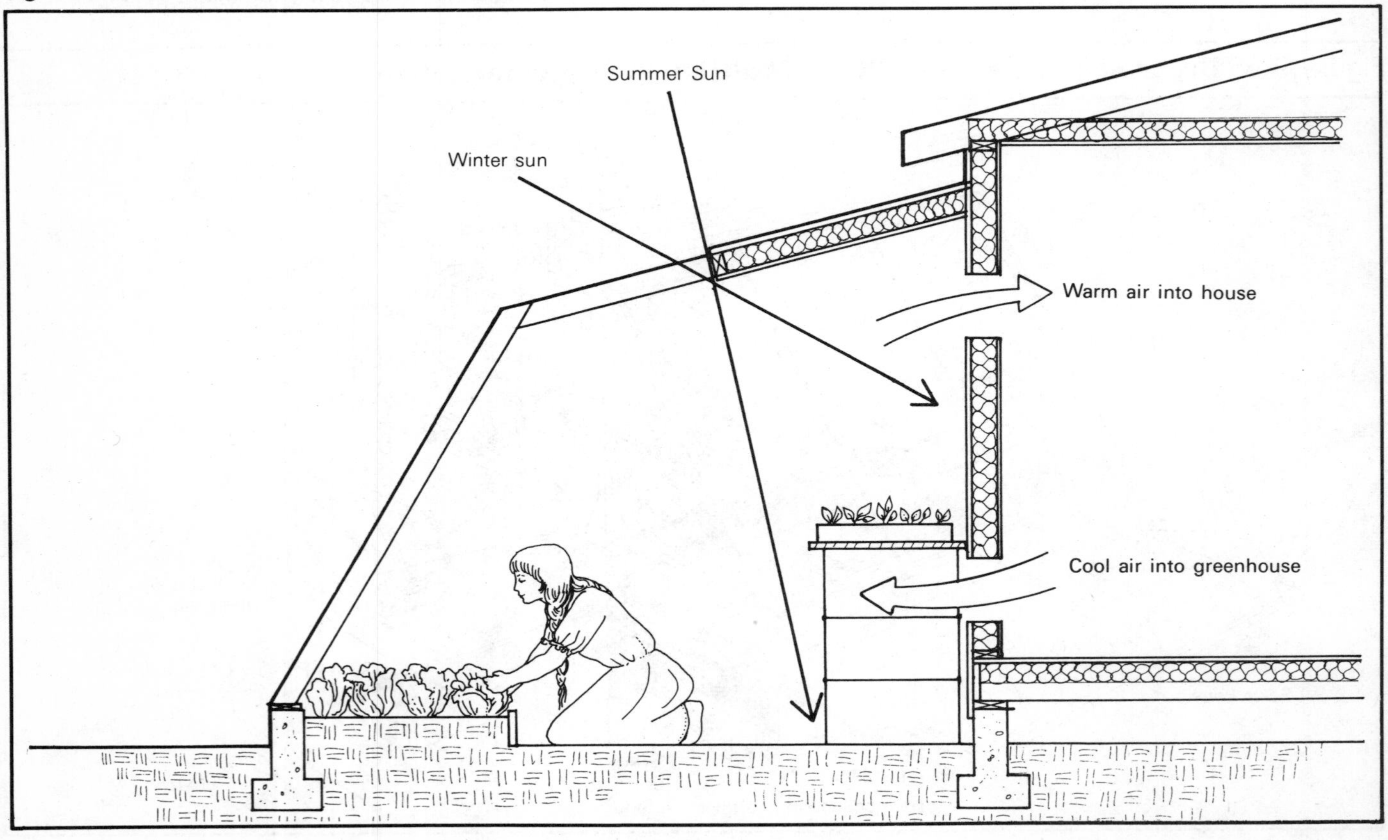

Figure 9-7. **Framing Isometric of Solar Propagation Greenhouse**

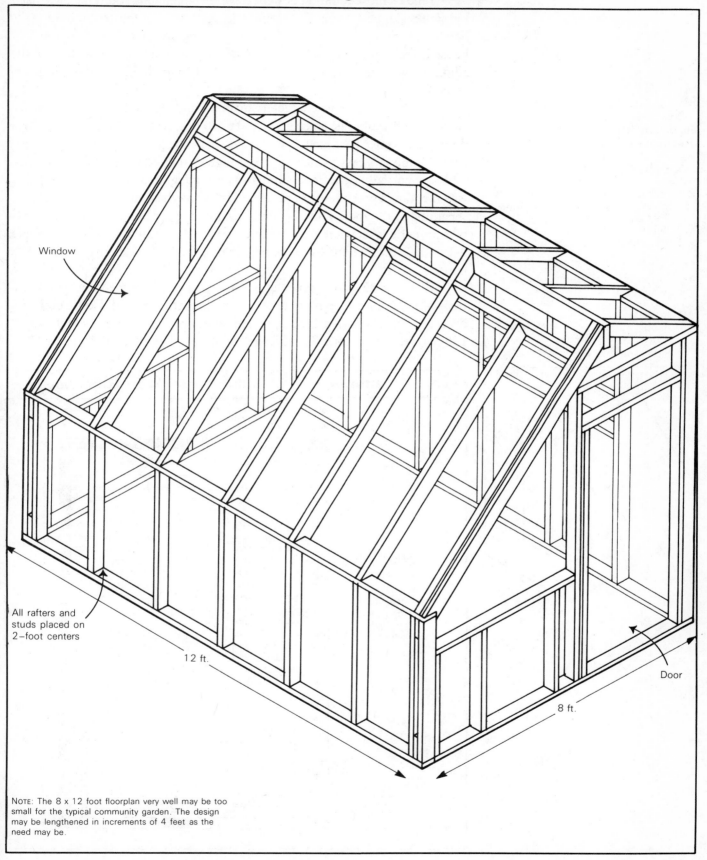

Window

All rafters and
studs placed on
2–foot centers

12 ft.

8 ft.

Door

NOTE: The 8 x 12 foot floorplan very well may be too
small for the typical community garden. The design
may be lengthened in increments of 4 feet as the
need may be.

States with photographs and instructive comments about each.

Yanda's most common designs have the greenhouse built off the existing south wall of a home. Vents along the wall connect the greenhouse to the house and allow the warm air to enter the living area. Cool air from the house is recirculated into the greenhouse through vents along the base of the adjoining wall. Figure 9-6 is a generalized schematic of a Yanda-style greenhouse.

Another distinctive characteristic of a Yanda greenhouse is the sharply angled south wall. The steep angle (60 to 70 degrees) maximizes heat gain during the winter because the sun's rays strike the glass at nearly a 90-degree angle. Summer's rays, which originate higher in the sky—shown in Figure 9-6—are partially deflected, helping to keep the greenhouse cool. Another way the Yanda greenhouse is protected from overheating is by the partial sheathing of the roof. This sheathing technique prevents some penetration by summer's rays, while permitting complete penetration by winter's. Table 9-1 in the next section is a guide for planting in the Yanda-Fisher greenhouse.

Free-standing solar greenhouses are designed with the same considerations of temperature regulation as are attached greenhouses. Construction drawings for free-standing solar greenhouses are available from Malcolm Lillywhite, of Domestic Technology Institute in Colorado, PO Box 2043,

Sheathing Schedule for Solar Greenhouse

CODE	EXTERIOR	MIDDLE	INTERIOR
A.	Filon	Air space	6-mil polyethylene
B.	½″ A-C plywood	R-11 insulation	6-mil polyethylene
C.	½″ C-DX plywood with roofing	R-11 insulation	6-mil polyethylene
D.	6-mil polyethylene	1″ styrofoam	4″ gravel

Note: Letters on the diagram refer to letters at right.

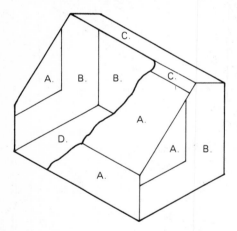

Figure 9-8. **Interior Plan of Solar Propagation Greenhouse**

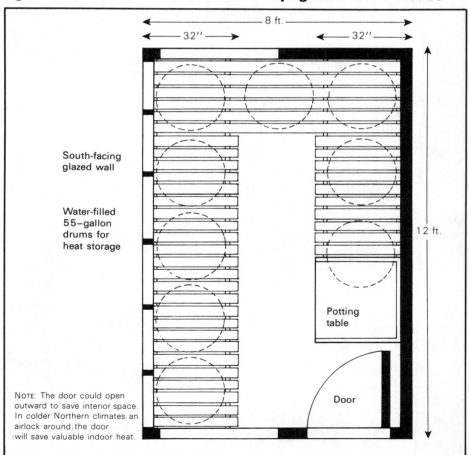

South-facing glazed wall

Water-filled 55–gallon drums for heat storage

8 ft.

32″   32″

12 ft.

Potting table

Door

NOTE: The door could open outward to save interior space. In colder Northern climates an airlock around the door will save valuable indoor heat.

Evergreen Colorado 80439 (see bibliography) and from the Integral Urban House, 1516 5th Street, Berkeley, California 94706.

The construction for an 8 by 12-foot greenhouse for propagating seedings in flats is shown in Figure 9-7. Such a greenhouse is particularly useful for community gardens, where a ready supply of seedlings will contribute to accelerated production and sustained yields. The 8 x 12-foot floorplan is concededly small. The design can be lengthened by increments of 4 feet (corresponding to the size of plywood sheets). A sheathing and glazing schedule plus interior plans and some construction details for this greenhouse are given in Figures 9-8 and 9-9.

While plants in small containers could be grown on the benches, for substantial winter production of vegetables modifications would have to be made to permit growing directly in or on the ground in raised beds.

Planting the Greenhouse

In many traditional greenhouses, the plants are grown in pots, flats, or other containers on tables. The advantages of this design factor are that you don't have to bend over to care for plants and excluding ants is easy (ants may become a pest by protecting plant-eating insects such as aphids and mealybugs from their natural enemies; see description of ant excluder, page 309). Also, in a solar greenhouse the space under the tables can contain drums of water to moderate the temperature. However, the disadvantages of using tables are also great, since it is difficult to have a soil medium of sufficient depth for large yields with many plants (such as tomatoes and cucumbers). And if climbing plants are grown, the ceiling would have to be higher than is optimum for heat conservation. The best plan is probably a mixture: the major food production going on in the ground beds, and some table or shelf space, with water drums as table supports, where seedlings can be started.

In Abby's greenhouse described above, the deep beds of soil and com-

Figure 9-9. **Detail of Potting Table for Solar Propagation Greenhouse**

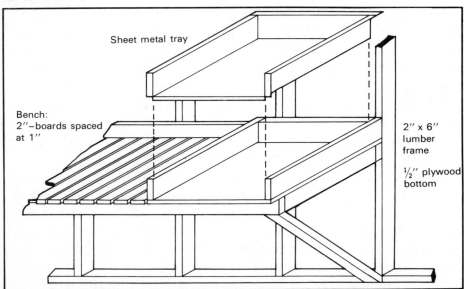

Sheet metal tray

Bench:
2″–boards spaced
at 1″

2″ x 6″
lumber
frame

½″ plywood
bottom

post are laid over screen with rocks below to permit good drainage. In a very succesful home greenhouse built by Glen Scriven (of the Riverside, California, Division of Biological Control, University of California) for the raising of predatory mites to control pest mites, the planting media are laid on sheets of plastic directly on the cinder block floor, sloped for drainage. Under the cinder blocks are ducts for hot air, which is collected at the top of the north (drum) wall, and blown under the floor by small fans, heating the plants from below.

Where possible, plants such as tomatoes, cucumbers, squash, melons, beans, and peas should be trained on trellises or strings, and plans must be made for this in the planting design. Do not be afraid to trim off foliage as older leaves become large and start to turn yellow. Trimming will increase air circulation and help inhibit plant diseases, which thrive on excess humidity. Trimming will also let more light through. (Trimming is important for an intensively planted outdoor garden also.)

Unless enough insects such as bees and flies can get into the greenhouse, you will need to pollinate the flowers of peppers, cucumbers, tomatoes, and eggplants by hand, using a small brush and knocking the pollen from the stamens onto the pistils. For recommended varieties for greenhouse growing, planting seasons, preferred locations in the greenhouse, and growing instructions see Table 9-1.

Abby used compost mixed with soil for her plant beds. This mixture is appealing, because with it food production is linked directly with household waste management. Since not all households produce enough compost for a large greenhouse, a good alternative is one-third good topsoil, one-third sand, and one-third perlite, to which is added as much compost as possible. A fir bark addition is another possibility. As in the garden, one can add nitrogen by watering (on the growing medium itself, without splashing the plants) with a mixture of human urine and water. (See pages 211–16. Note the necessity for adding lime periodically.)

If the greenhouse is watered with a subsurface drip system, additional watering is required only when new seedlings are added and only until their roots have reached the water level.

Hydroponic gardening (using nutrients dissolved in water) has a certain fascination to it, and some people believe the method results in higher yields. The authors are by no means convinced of this for small-scale greenhouses, and tend not to recommend the hydroponic approach for a number of reasons:

1. Because the plants depend on nutrients delivered to them rather than seeking them out on their own as needed from the soil or compost, a hydroponic system is far more fragile and subject to upset. In other words, it takes more management to keep it in balance.

2. If commercial fertilizers are used a considerable energy investment is involved. The same is true if pumps are needed to move the fluids around.

3. Good pest management without using poisons often requires the build-up at the soil surface of a complex material, such as compost, to provide a habitat for some of the predatory insects and spiders that control plant pests.

4. A hydroponic system would not integrate easily into the waste-

management or other systems of the house.

In an attempt to avoid the energy use involved in using commercial hydroponic nutrient solutions, Miranda Smith of the Institute for Local Self-Reliance, developed some nutrient solutions for use in the institute's hydroponic greenhouse on a rooftop in Washington, D.C. To avoid the use of pumps, she fills containers with the liquid mixture by hand, using the

Table 9-1. **Planting Chart for Greenhouse Growing**

Plant	Varieties	Location	Time of Year to Plant	Special Instructions
Tomato	Earliana Big boy Marglobe Michigan ohio Early girl Any small variety Patio, cherry, pear Cold set for winter	Front of greenhouse in spring. On back wall in winter	Early spring Mid-August	Need full photoperiod. Pollinate by lightly tapping open blossoms or shake plant vigorously. Train plants up strings. Trim foliage severely when infested with insects and in fall to prevent shading of greenhouse. Do not cut top growth until you are ready for plant to stop growing. Tomatoes are perennials and will produce for a long time. Pull suckers (found in crotch of limbs) off. They can be rooted: start in sand or vermiculite.
Cucumber	Any type will do, but European forcing types which produce fruit without artificial pollination are easier.	Clear side of greenhouse in spring. Back wall in winter. Can stand some shading.	Early spring Mid-August	Need full photoperiod. Pollinate with a small brush or let the bees in. Pull off first several feet of blossoms for better fruit set. Train on string or twine. Can be trained to climb all over the sides and roof of greenhouse.
Peppers	Red chile Any green, bell Wax	Full light area	Early spring Mid-August	Adapt well to small container or beds. Pollinate with small brush. Be careful not to overwater. Chile peppers do not seem to get as hot as they do outdoors; still delicious, however.
Melons and squash	Watermelon Cantaloupe Pumpkin Honeydew Crookneck Zucchini Acorn	Need light and lots of room. Front of greenhouse.	Early spring	Trim vegetation. Grow out the vents—summer. Will cross pollinate: try to separate varieties by distance.
Leafy greens	Leaf lettuce Endive Kale Spinach Mustard greens Cress Chard Collards Chicory Celtuce	Medium light. Cool.	Any time—makes the most sense in late fall, winter, early spring	Dependable winter producers. Head lettuce does not head well in greenhouse. Plant densely, thin as you eat. Leafy greens will grow in pots, on vertical surfaces, almost anywhere. Plant under trimmed tomatoes or cucumbers. Can be cut many times while growing. Will go to seed if temperatures get too hot.
Carrots	Smaller varieties	Sunny	Fall Winter Early spring	Plant thickly and thin out. Slow maturers. Interplant with tomatoes.
Beets Turnips	Any	Medium light	Fall Winter	Do well in shallow boxes. Plant thickly, but thin to allow root to become large. Foliage when small makes good edibles.
Radishes	Any	Any place	Anytime	Don't plant more than you can eat. Excellent indicator of soil viability: should sprout in 3–5 days.
Broccoli Cauliflower	Calabrese, Italian Snowball	Medium light. Cool	Late summer—early fall for winter heading	Spatially consuming crops. Do well in pots. Transplant well into garden.

Table 9-1. **Planting Chart for Greenhouse Growing (Continued)**

Plant	Varieties	Location	Time of Year to Plant	Special Instructions
Cabbage Brussel sprouts	Golden acre, Chinese Jade cross			
Beans	Pole Burpee golden Blue lake	Medium light. Up walls.	Early spring. Late summer.	Great on north wall of greenhouse. Train on trellises. Climbers can be used on greenhouse exterior for shade (red pole beans).
Eggplant	Black beauty Early beauty	Sunny	Early spring through summer	Pollinate with small brush or fingertip. Transplant from garden back to greenhouse in fall.
Peas	Burpeeana early Blue bantam Snow Sugar	Shady areas. Cool.	Fall Winter Early spring	Used to replenish nitrogen in soil. Four poles in corners, string lattices across.
Onions Scallions Garlic	Any	Medium light.	Fall Winter	Keep soil moist. Fresh tops are great in salads, trim regularly. Start seeds in greenhouse for garden sets. Garlic is an insect fighter, either growing or ground into water solution.
Strawberries	Everbearing	Shade. Under tables	Fall	Like more water than vegetables.
Herbs	Most	Medium light	Early spring	Do well in cold weather.

Transplants Out

Tomatoes Peppers Melons Broccoli Eggplant Sunflowers Celery Cucumbers Squash Corn	Best for transplant from greenhouse to garden. Don't be deceived. Start 6–8 weeks before anticipated last frost. They grow fast. Try not to disturb root system any more than possible; melon and cucumber roots are easily damaged. Harden off by exposing to outdoor temperatures two weeks before transplanting. Grow in small containers when you can: we have used jiffy pots (these need to be cut before being put into the ground, they do not disintegrate quickly enough and the plant can become root bound), expanding	peat pellets, styrofoam cups, milk cartons, Macdonalds' quarter pounder containers, tin cans. If possible, transplant on a cloudy day, shade and water well after transplanting. Do not forget that all of these seedlings plus flower and herb starts are big sellers in the spring. A small (160 square foot) solar greenhouse I built in Idaho sold $273.00 worth of seedlings its first spring. That was over half the cost of the greenhouse.

Transplants In

Tomatoes Peppers Eggplant Melons Onions Broccoli Petunias Pansies Marigolds Nasturtiums Geraniums	If you are careful, you can transplant healthy garden crops back into the greenhouse in the fall. Be sure to check for insects and disease first. Get all the root system you can, shade and water them in their new home.

Source: Fisher and Yanda. *The Food and Heat Producing Solar Greenhouse.*

water pressure in the water line, and then suspends them over the beds with hoses dangling down to particular plants. When watering is necessary, the nutrients are supplied to the plants by gravity flow.

In *Self Reliance*, the magazine published by the institute, Smith describes her recipe for a homemade nutrient solution:

One can either use a tea made from a high quality compost, or one can mix a basic solution of one tablespoon fish emulsion, one tablespoon liquid seaweed and a tablespoon of bloodmeal to each gallon of water. The mix varies, depend-

ing upon the type of plant being grown. Less bloodmeal should be used with flowering and fruiting produce than with leafy crops. Other nutrients can also be added; blended eggshells, for example, might be helpful when added to a cabbage crop. There is room for variation and for more experimentation; the basic mix is meant to be a starting point rather than a proven end-product.

10. RAISING SMALL STOCK

At the integral urban house there are several pathways for the utilization of waste products. The organic wastes from growing, preparing, and consuming human food may go into the waterless toilet to provide additional carbonaceous material, as well as promote superior aeration, for the process of decomposing the human fecal wastes. Or, it may be stored in sawdust or crushed dry leaves until it is combined with other materials in a batch in the compost bins. In either case, the end product, compost, ultimately goes to the garden. Here food is raised, not only for human consumption, but for small stock—chickens and rabbits—as well. However, where there is a choice, kitchen and garden scraps are a better source of animal feed, since this pathway conserves more energy and nitrogen. Where chickens are on the ground, or raised in wire cages above the ground, organic kitchen wastes may be fed to them directly, and garden wastes (weeds, tough outer portions of garden vegetables, pruning from ornamental plants) may be fed to the rabbits. Additional food from commercial sources is imported—alfalfa for the rabbits and grains for the chickens. Insects, principally flies, may be trapped or raised on wastes and also fed to the chickens. The manure from the animals is then used in the compost, which helps to grow the plants, or in the case of rabbit manure, may go directly to the soil around the plants as fertilizer. See Figure 10-1 and refer back to Chapter 2, Figure 2-5, which shows these material flows.

Why Raise Small Stock in the City?

The principal reasons for raising small stock are to obtain high-quality protein for human consumption in the form of meat and eggs, and manure to use in composting and ultimately in the garden as fertilizer, as well as for pleasure or recreation. Additional benefits are obtaining rabbit pelts or wool (the latter from the Angora breed), and the satisfaction of knowing that the meat you eat is relatively free of the pesticides and hormones frequently used in commercial livestock production.

Under some circumstances, the cost of producing these products compares favorably with their price in the store. In any case, both animals, but chickens particularly, can recycle the family organic waste effectively. Let us examine each of these advantages in detail.

The major considerations in raising livestock in the city are outlined in Table 10-1. Several types of animals are compared on the basis of production efficiencies, feed and housing requirements, level of husbandry skills demanded, and legal and social codes that may impinge upon the raising of the particular animal. The dog is included in the table for the purpose of providing a comparison between an animal urban people are likely to be acquainted with and livestock with which they are less familiar.

Human Diet: The authors' own original motive for raising their own animal protein was the desire to avoid consuming hormone residues, particularly that of diethylstilbestrol (DES). This hormone was used routinely in animal feeds up until a few years ago, and is still implanted in steers to increase weight gain. It was also used in humans as a "morning after" pill and

Developed at the Integral Urban House depicting imported and home-derived feed sources.

Figure 10-1. **Home-Based Protein Production Schematic**

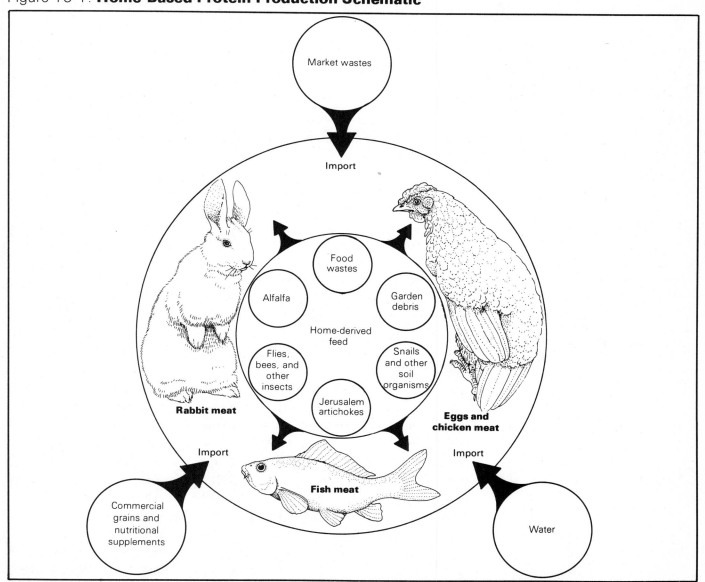

Table 10-1. **Comparison of Various Animals for Urban Small-Stock Production**

Animal	Products	Food Production	Odor	Management of Manure	Noise Generation	Space Requirement	Type of Feed	Husbandry Skills	Slaughtering Skills	Typical Municipal Ordinances	Social Acceptance as Urban Livestock
Rabbit	Meat, pelts, wool	52 lb meat, 12 lb protein yr/doe	Minor	Easy	None	8′ × 6′ × 4′ (1 buck, 4 does)	Garden debris, hay, pellets, broad leaf crops	Simple	Relatively easy to kill	25′ from neighbor's window	High
Chicken	Eggs	200 eggs/yr/hen = 3 lb protein/hen/yr	Moderate	Moderate	Moderate	8′ × 8′ (8 hens) yard and house	Garden debris, insects, snails, grains	Easy to moderate to raise	Easy to moderate to kill	25′ from neighbor's window	Moderate
Pig	Meat, hide	100 lb/6 mo. per pig = 20 lb protein/6 mo	Extreme	Difficult	Moderate	8′ × 8′ × 5′ (1 hog)	Garbage, grains, comfrey	Difficult to raise	Difficult to kill	Usually prohibited	Poor
Goat	Milk, meat, hide	4 quarts milk/day/doe = 35 lb protein/doe/yr	Moderate	Easy	Moderate to extreme	200 sq ft (1 doe)	Garden debris, alfalfa, hay, grains	Difficult to raise	Moderate to kill	By special permit	Low to poor
Dog	Hair	——	Moderate to extreme	Difficult	Moderate to extreme	——	Garbage, meat	Moderate to raise	Moderate to kill	None	Poor

It is recommended that you consult your local health authorities in regard to specific ordinances in your town.

to prevent miscarriages. Recently, evidence has shown that DES has caused vaginal cancer in daughters of women who took it during pregnancy twenty years ago. Theoretically, the hormone is supposed to be removed from the animals' food a certain number of days before slaughtering. But familiarity with the volume and automation of the modern feedlot has left us skeptical regarding the reliability of the uninspected meat, at least as far as contamination by this hormone is concerned. With homesite raising of livestock, the contamination of meat and eggs by hazardous chemicals is largely avoided.

Manure: Since few pathogens or parasites of chickens and rabbits can cause disease in humans, use of their manure as fertilizer in the vegetable garden is generally regarded as safer than using human fecal matter. Birds, unlike mammals, excrete urine and feces together as a single mixture. Since it is the urine that contains most of the nitrogen, chicken manure is much higher in this plant nutrient than manure from rabbits. (Actually, rabbit manure is usually tested for nitrogen separately from the bedding beneath, since the bedding absorbs the urine. Because in our systems, we use both manure and bedding together in the compost, we are actually getting the benefit of more of the total nitrogen excreted by the rabbits than an analysis of the manure would suggest.) In fact, chicken manure is so high in nitrogen that it is best composted prior to being placed in the garden, as the ammonia may actually sterilize the soil of its microflora and fauna, and "burn" the plants when the manure is used fresh, or "hot." Rabbit manure is usually referred to as a "cool" manure, meaning that it is low enough in nitrogen to be quite safe for use directly around the plants, and many gardeners with a rabbitry do so. However, because of the likelihood that the uncomposted rabbit manure will breed flies, and possibly even attract into the garden *Hylemia brassicae,* a fly pest of brassicas (cabbage family vegetables) and a close relative of certain manure flies, it is probably desirable to compost the rabbit manure as well. For a comparison of the nitrogen content and annual production of various animal manures, see Table 10-2.

Table 10-2. **Nitrogen Content of Various Manures**

Animal	Pounds Excrement (wet weight) Produced per 100 lbs Live Weight of Animal/Year	Percent Nitrogen in Feces and Urine Mixture on Dry Weight Basis
Rabbit	1000	2.5
Chicken	860	6.3
Horse	1800	2.3
Cow	2700	1.7
Pig	3160	3.8
Sheep	1260	3.8
Human urine	730	15.9
Human feces	165	5.7

Source: Gotass, *Composting and Sanitary Reclamation of Organic Wastes.*

As nitrogen is usually the nutrient in shortest supply in a composting (unless green succulent material such as grass clipping and fresh weeds are the only or major constituents of the pile), the manure from these animals is highly desirable. Furthermore, both chickens and rabbits do such a good job of grinding up a wide variety of bulky or tough and fibrous materials (particularly rabbits on these), that passing most of the kitchen and garden wastes through the feeding troughs of these animals largely eliminates the need for the compost grinder or cleaver in compost production.

Economics: Only if you can raise (or trap, in the case of insects) a substantial amount of your own feed, can home chicken-raising produce eggs or meat competitive with 1977 commercial prices. However, in the future, the cost of commercial poultry products may reflect the scarcity of fossil fuel for mechanized production, transportation, refrigeration, and distribution, throwing the advantage more and more to the homescale system. In any case, one-half to three-fourths of a chicken's diet can be made up of grass clippings, weeds, and insects. The home-scale approach, which utilizes waste products as a supplementary source of feed, yields a more favorable economic estimate. The cost of producing a dozen eggs using various mixtures of home-produced and commercial feed is shown in Table 10-8, page 283, in the section on raising chickens.

Rabbit meat is usually cheaper to raise than to buy in urban supermarkets, if it can be obtained at all. According to personal accounts of long-time California residents, during the Depression, rabbits were apparently a common source of inexpensive, city-raised meat. Since more affluent times have arrived (though possibly they are transient), rabbit has largely lost its following, the exceptions being in large metropolitan areas where good French or other European restaurants flourish and rabbit meat is appreciated for the gourmet food that it is. An estimate of the cost of producing rabbit meat under three different regimes, ranging from all commercial feed to all home-raised, is shown in Table 10-4, page 268, in the discussion on feeding rabbits.

Our limited experience with the economics of Angora rabbit production is reported in Box 10-1. This experience is included here to suggest a potential home-scale cottage industry.

Pleasure: The pleasure of raising chickens and rabbits is considerable. The antics of the young animals of both species are as amusing as those of kittens or puppies. When fully grown, chickens can be extremely cruel to each other, but rabbits are very passive. Still, the adult behavior in both species is also extremely interesting, and great is the pride that one can experience in successfully raising one's own meat and eggs. Generations of former 4–H participants will testify to the educational value of these activities.

A common response of novices to the art of small-stock raising is, "But they're so cute, I could never bear to kill them." Perhaps. We refer to this as the "Bambi syndrome." It results from the fact that urban children grow up unaware of what it takes for life to survive; they are exposed to countless sentimental stories of anthropomorphized, "cute" little animals, and their limited experience leads them to believe that meat and eggs originate in the store in sanitary-looking plastic containers.

In fact, through a simple demonstration of how quick, painless, and aesthetically acceptable the butchering of these animals is when done prop-

---

Box 10-1. **Economics of Angora Rabbit Production**

One Angora rabbit, weighing five to six pounds, will yield an average of twenty-one ounces of wool each year. In the San Francisco Bay area, Angora rabbit wool sold for $1.50 an ounce in 1977. That is somewhere in the neighborhood of $31.50 worth of wool per rabbit each year. Better yet is the price that can be obtained from homespun Angora rabbit wool; it has a market value of four times that of unspun wool. Given these economics, a herd of ten Angora rabbits could potentially produce $1260 worth of spun wool in one year.

Maintaining a healthy and productive herd of Angora is a real challenge. This special breed, because of its inbred lineage and long, awkward coat, is more delicate than meat rabbits. It is particularly important to keep the Angoras warm after plucking, as they are susceptible to chill at that time. If you plan to establish a small herd, keeping them inside a shed or a garage where they are protected from drafts would be ideal.

A student of ours tried her hand at raising a male and female Angora at the student gardens at the University of California. She wrote in her report that hand-plucking of an Angora required thirty minutes every three months. (A wide-toothed comb or special brush might have been useful here.) Shearing the wool with mechanical clippers is faster, but produces a shorter, less-valuable product. Carding and spinning the wool, she estimated, would require an additional four hours per Angora each year. Housing, feed, and care of the animals must also be considered in the economic analysis of wool production. Apparently there is economy of scale when more than two rabbits are raised. A reasonable size herd might be ten—not requiring too much work and providing some profit, assuming that a market can be found to warrant the endeavor.

The following is a rough estimate of the possible profit derived from such a system in the first year. The

productive life of an Angora rabbit should be about three years. Once you have purchased your breeding stock, of course, the cost would go down, since your herd would replenish itself. Angoras may also be desired by some people as pets, as are Angora cats, and the sale of live pet rabbits could also doubtless bring in substantial additional income.

Theoretical Economic Analysis of Production of Ten Angora Rabbits for One Year (based on 1977 prices in Berkeley, California)

Cost of stock (ten @ $20 ea)	$ 67*
Cost of cage and equipment	80*
Feed	180
	$ 327
Value of spun yarn	1300
Profit	$ 973

*These expenses are averaged over a three-year period.

Note: the above calculations do not take into consideration your labor.

erly, we have, between us, taught hundreds of meat-eating people to do an adequate job of it and find satisfaction in accomplishing the task. Our feeling is that if you do eat meat, confronting directly the fact that someone must butcher it might be desirable. Rather than confining someone to a slaughterhouse for eight hours a day as an occupation, you might better handle the job yourself.

Should One Eat Meat?

Committed vegetarianism is a perspective that we respect though do not share. It is quite possible, by careful attention to the nutritional contents of vegetables and fruits, to create a diet in which the necessary complement of amino acids is obtained. This is easier to accomplish if dairy products and eggs are included, however, and more difficult for pregnant women to achieve. As noted earlier, the best guide we know of, *Diet for a Small Planet* by Frances Moore Lappé, gives detailed recipes on how to get the most out of vegetables, grains, and nuts. However, the basic reasoning—that vegetarianism is a desirable way for everyone to go, because of the very real population pressures on the world food supply—may be a little faulty. Worldwide, there is approximately twice as much permanent grassland as land used for growing crops that humans can eat directly. For reasons of soil type, slope, or climate, and the energy input required, it is unlikely that most of these grasslands will ever be converted into croplands. Thus, the only way these ranges can be put to the service of feeding humans at all is by passing their high cellulose forages, undigestible by humans, through the stomachs of such ruminants as sheep, goats and cows (and many less familiar domestic and wild animals), where it will be converted into meat and milk that humans can consume. When raised completely on forage or high cellulose agricultural wastes, a cow or sheep is uncompetitive with people, so beef and lamb may be around for quite some time yet.

Religious reasons for avoiding meat are obviously a private matter. It is hard to accept the fact that staying alive means taking life, and hard to draw a line in the continuum of life between microbes, plants, and animals. One can eat a carrot alive, kill a cucumber cell by cell in brine while transforming it into a pickle, consume microscopic life every time one swallows, yet have the desire to refuse a leg of chicken. It seems as if awe and respect for the human intellect can lead a person to one of two paths: either to avoid deliberately taking the life of any animal that seems to show obvious kinship with our species and a consciousness similar to our own, or, on the other hand, to conclude that life and death are but two sides of the same coin, each needing the other to exist. The latter course permits one to be a fully conscious and responsible carnivore. For those, like us, who choose this course, raising some of your own meat may be an exciting spiritual as well as physical adventure, if certain constraints can be managed.

Analyzing Your Living Situation

As with deciding to raise a dog, cat, tropical fish, or myna bird, you need to ask yourself whether rabbits and/or chickens will fit into your life. Obviously, the management of animals is more complicated than that of plants.

Angora Rabbit Breeders

Chueys Bunny Patch
67 North Price Street
Hubbard, OH, 44425

Gordons Rabbit Hutch
P.O. Box 506
Rosebury, OR, 97470

Guckerts Angoras
136 Acme Street
Marietta, OH, 45750

Bunnyhaven
Laural Dasch
115 N. Main
Penacook, NH, 03301

A & C Rabbit Farms
Box 6086
Rohrerstown, PA, 17603

Betty Lettenmaier
Kendrick, ID, 83537

Peter Harchula
Swan Road
Lewiston, NY, 14092

Robert Hauert
1028 San Lorenzo NW
Albuquerque, NM, 87107

Riverside Acres
Rt. 1
Rice Lake, WI, 54868

Tryggestad Rabbitries
Route 2
South Haven, MN, 55382

They must be contained in some sort of enclosure, and restrained from foraging for themselves. They require more regular attention than the plants in the garden. Automatic animal feed- and water-delivery systems are excellent devices, and they do free one from anxiety when your work schedule does not permit you to hover over the cages. Still, weekly care is almost a necessity for chickens; and rabbits must be tended to yet more frequently, since they may overeat if left to their own devices with hoppers full of food.

Do You Have Enough of the Right Kind of Space? Both chickens and rabbits need an area that can be protected from dogs, teasing children, rain, winter winds and snow, and the heat of the summer sun. They must be located where the cackles of chickens or an occasional whiff of rabbit urine will not send the neighbors to telephone the police. Some cities have ordinances specifying the distance animals must be from the property line, others will not permit more than a specified number of certain animals, and some municipalities forbid the raising of stock altogether. In any case, the unwritten law seems to be, Don't annoy the neighbors. Many of the ideas we share with you in this chapter are ways of reducing or by-passing problems that might otherwise get you into trouble.

Most municipal ordinances restricting livestock were made to protect urbanites from the smell, noise, flies, and general nuisance-causing behavior associated with farm animals in the city that are managed as if they were still on the farm. Systems must be constructed that allow small livestock to be raised compatibly with urban sensibilities. This requires some special technology, but first adequate space must be available for the job.

Both chickens and rabbits can be raised on porches and rooftops; we have done both in several different environments. The flat warehouse roofs of many inner-city neighborhoods lend themselves well to housing small stock if there is adequate space for construction of manure disposal systems and access to nearby restaurant or supermarket wastes to supplement the animal's diet. However, a chicken house we built on the porch of the Integral Urban House in Berkeley was a disaster. Hordes of flies, already thriving on the garbage and pet manure in the neighborhood and attracted to the chicken pen, were regularly blown by the prevailing winds into the kitchen, which opens out onto the porch through unscreened double doors. The pens that now exist on the north side of the House do not present this problem, since the side door was easily fitted with a screened door. The rabbit and chicken pens are located only a few feet from the house, so it is clear that if the systems are properly designed and maintained they will not produce problems with smells, noise or flies.

Do You Have Enough Time? The amount of time the various animal systems will take depends on several factors: how large or small the systems are, how well-designed and automated you make them, how experienced you are in working with the animals, and how leisurely or efficiently you approach the process. Naturally, putting the system together will take more time than managing it when it is running, and the more you learn, the easier and quicker it becomes.

At the Integral Urban House in Berkeley, we have found that rabbit

Some examples of alternative feeds we have used:

1. Kitchen scraps. These are for chickens primarily, although rabbits will eat some uncooked vegetable trimmings. In general, chickens are good at consuming all kinds of garbage, including meat and the rinds of fruits. How much they eat is determined by how small the pieces are. For example, if a quarter section of an orange is given to them, they will clean it out and leave the half-moon of rind. However, if you chop the orange section into small pieces, they will consume it entirely. Rabbits are more restricted in their diet; for example, they will not eat meat. They are also less skilled at eating from a hopper, and will let small pieces fall through their cage grating.

2. Garden trimmings. Rabbits will eat a great variety of raw vegetable matter, and they like to chew on fibrous material to wear down their teeth. (This is one of the two good reasons for not making their cages out of wood, the other being smell from the absorption of urine.) Trimmings from a number of ornamental plants can be used, but it is wise to learn which are poisonous, since some common garden plants (for example, oleander) are toxic. Chickens are very fond of grass clippings, and both animals like a variety of feeds and vegetable discards.

management takes approximately two hours per week. That includes feeding, slaughtering, and general husbandry, but not tanning the pelts or playing with the young. Cleaning the manure out is part of the composting process (see pages 255–56). The chicken system takes approximately one hour per week. One should add to this any extra time spent in the garden to raise alfalfa for the rabbits or to trap flies for the chickens.

Feed to Supplement Commercial Grains and Food Products:

Homesite-derived feed will affect both the amount of time and the cost of these systems. Of course, providing alternative feed sources will increase the amount of time you spend dealing with the system, but it is likely to decrease the cost. In general, if the animals are fed solely on commercial feed rations without any supplement, their meat or eggs probably won't be any less expensive than products purchased in the market, though of course you will still have the manure for fertilizer in the garden as a bonus. The more alternative feeds you can raise, trap, or scrounge, the cheaper the system.

Managing the Manure

When we first started raising animals in the city, the purpose was as much to obtain nitrogen for the compost pile as it was to provide food for ourselves. In other words, fast aerobic bin composting came first (see pages 127–38, and Olkowski and Olkowski *City People's Book of Raising Food*). Think through ahead of time the manure-management approach you will use. Otherwise, within a short time after acquiring the animals, you will have an odor and fly problem that your neighbors may well consider to be the kind of nuisance many city ordinances were created to prohibit. In keeping with this advice, we will discuss the possible methods of manure management suitable for an urban environment before discussing the raising of the stock.

Chicken Manure: *The Deep Litter System*—The simplest approach with chickens is to use a *deep litter system*. Dan Clancy, a friend and former instructor at a local college, designed and once marketed a self-contained chicken house that incorporates such a system. This chicken house, which we used on the porch of the Berkeley Integral Urban House, is illustrated in Figure 10-2. In the deep litter system, the ground of the chicken house and, if the chickens are given access to the outdoors, the surrounding pen in which they are confined, is "seeded" with eight to twelve inches of compost, leaves, straw, grass clippings, and weeds. With this method it is essential that the chickens have access to all areas in which their manure falls. Then the chickens themselves will consistently pick through this material, over and over, eating any fly larvae that develops. Their thorough scratching will expose all debris and manure to the drying action of the air so that odors will not develop. The regular addition of weeds, debris, and kitchen wastes will gradually build up on the floor, and at intervals of a half a year or so a portion can be removed and used in the garden as compost.

The advantage of the deep litter system for waste management is its simplicity. The chickens have access to a number of insects that may start to live in the material. Being able to give themselves dust-baths periodically

3. Crops intentionally raised for animal feed. Some vegetable and ornamental crops may be grown specifically to feed your animals. Examples are alfalfa, comfrey, and Jerusalem artichokes. Raising feed, of course, refers back to the space problem. It is true that areas used to grow feed for animals cannot be used for raising human food. However, some spaces might be most suitable for this use. For example, Jerusalem artichokes require little care, and can provide a high hedge for privacy during the growing season. At the Integral Urban House, we planted both chrysanthemums and alfalfa to provide greenery to the house entrance, and we use the cuttings to feed the rabbits. (Note: see the discussion in Chapter 14, on heavy-metal problems associated with front-yard plantings.)

4. Snails, slugs, flies and other insects for chickens. Any insect is a possible chicken food, if it is numerous enough to be a pest (frequently meaning that it has escaped the control of its natural enemies either temporarily or permanently, as when an insect invades from another country, leaving its predators and parasites behind—see Chapter 13). In general, insects are high in protein, and chickens are well-adapted to digesting them, although there are some they do not eat, either because of taste or digestibility. The problem is in devising methods of harvesting or raising the insects and other small garden pests, such as snails, that chickens like.

5. Food wastes from vegetable and fruit markets. Chickens readily eat lettuce, chard, and beet tops. Rabbits are especially fond of carrot tops and cabbage family plants. The coarse outer leaves of all these vegetables often make up the bulk of the vegetable garbage thrown away at supermarkets. These wastes may provide an ideal free source of greens for your animals. The only concern you might have is that the outer leaves of these vegetables may be carrying undesirable pesticide residues. One way around that is to use wastes from organic food stores and restaurants only. Frequently such stores will throw away spilled grain, which can be used for chickens as well.

253

Figure 10-2. **A Deep-Litter Self-Contained Chicken House**

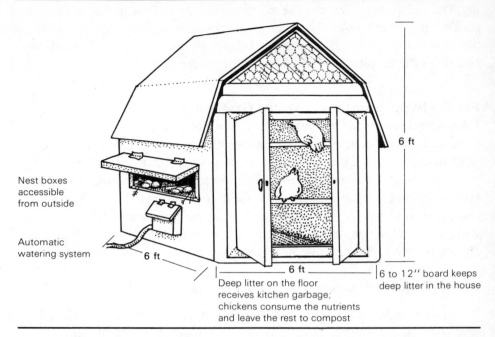

Nest boxes
accessible
from outside

Automatic
watering system

6 ft

6 ft

6 ft

6 to 12″ board keeps
deep litter in the house

Deep litter on the floor
receives kitchen garbage;
chickens consume the nutrients
and leave the rest to compost

undoubtedly helps to control external parasites such as lice, unlike chickens raised in wire cages, not having access to their litter. This system works as a management approach for kitchen as well as animal wastes. As mentioned before, chickens will eat almost anything, including meat. Instead of being stored to be used later in making a batch compost, the leftover materials from preparing, cooking, and eating meals can just be taken out to the chickens daily. With a deep litter system the uneaten leftovers from the chickens will help form the litter. Feeding scraps to chickens on wire is sometimes difficult because scraps fall through the cage, and the residue of leftovers in their feeding trough needs to be removed.

The disadvantages of this system are the loss of nitrogen, greater needs for space and climate protection, and the greater chance of cannibalism among the chickens. Let's take these points one by one.

The constant turning and exposure to the air (and any rain or other water that may fall on the material, if there is an outdoor pen), will cause nitrogen in the manure to move into the air as ammonia or be leached down into the soil. The latter may be prevented to some degree if there is a cement floor beneath the litter, but a soggy mass, which may develop if any excess water accumulates and cannot drain away through the soil, is undesirable also. Nitrogen that is lost from the chicken pen in this way is not available to the plants in the garden.

Chickens that are running about freely require more space per bird (about three square feet of room per hen) than confined chickens, and use up more of their food energy in physical activity, rather than putting it into producing eggs, which is why commercial growers keep layers on wire in separate cages. The larger space encompassed by the deep litter system must be adequately protected from rain and snow if compost is to be provided for the garden at a later date. The entire area must also be securely enclosed to

The methods of manure management most applicable to urban situations are these:

1. Apply directly to the garden (rabbit manure only).

2. Use in compost pile or bins.

3. Allow chickens to pick over deep litter.

4. Use manure as worm culture (ideal for rabbit manure, but the process requires special care).

5. Use in an anaerobic digester, with or without algae ponds (more complex to establish, and not really suitable for small-scale systems).

keep out dogs, coyotes, raccoons, possums, and rats, the most common predators on chickens and their food and eggs in urban areas. Obviously, this protection should be provided in any case, but is more of a problem when the chickens themselves have a larger area in which to roam.

Finally, chickens are very aggressive; they compete fiercely for food and even kill and eat each other. Therefore, if they are confined to a small pen where they can get at each other freely, it may be necessary to clip their beaks. A chicken beak is made of the same type of horny material that composes human fingernails. Similarly, since it contains no blood vessels or nerve endings where it protrudes beyond the flesh, the beak can be cut off without causing pain or blood loss. This is easiest done with a young chicken, since the beak is soft and the small bird is easier to restrain, but it can be done at any age. One person should hold the bird steady; it is best to tuck the bird under an arm. The other person holds the bird's head firmly, so that the end of the beak that protrudes beyond the flesh can be plainly seen against the light, and trims off the very tip with a pair of sharp kitchen shears.

Tray System and Composting: If the chickens are kept in cages and their manure falls into a tray or storage area that is not accessible to the chickens, then special attention must be given to the system to avoid the breeding of flies and generation of odors. Two basic principles are involved in successful manure management under these conditions: (1) keeping the manure as dry as possible, and (2) removing only part of the manure at a time, so that the fly predators and parasites have an opportunity to build up in the manure piles and to escape being totally wiped out when the trays are cleaned.

Keeping the manure dry means protecting it not only from rain, but also from leaks or spills from the watering system. Wherever the manure is wet fly breeding will occur. An inch or so of sawdust placed on the trays where the manure has just been cleaned out, and a sprinkling over the pile occasionally between emptyings if the weather is hot and humid, may help to keep the piles dried out. Good ventilation in the chicken house is also essential.

Manure flies can be managed by the introduction of parasites and the encouragement of local predators in the piles under the chickens. Three parasites are available commercially from several sources at the time of this writing. Doubtless more of such small businesses will start up as more and more people decide to use primarily biological and physical control for pest management rather than relying exclusively on the chemical pesticide approach. See page 414, Chapter 13 for a list of insectaries that sell parasites of flies.

Control of manure flies through the introduction of parasites works best if the parasites are bought and released at intervals. A portion of the manure should be removed periodically also. Ideally, manure removal should coincide with the making of a new compost batch using a bin system (see pages 127–38). In most cases, this will be every two to three weeks, depending primarily on how much other materials for the compost are accumulated by the household, how often time can be spared to make a fresh compost, and how many bins have been constructed for this purpose.

When a section of the manure tray is scraped clean, dry sawdust is

Fannia canicularis

This fly is most common around rabbit systems, but also develops in garbage and in pet manures. The adult males can be commonly seen slowly circling in semi-lighted situations, indoors or outdoors.

spread over the clean area and some of the nearby old compost is raked over the sawdust so that the new manure falls upon the old. In very dry climates, or during dry periods of the year, this last procedure may be sufficient to keep the system going without the addition of any sawdust.

Along with the management of the manure, some trapping of adult flies is desirable during warm weather. This is because many garbage-can flies are likely to be drawn into an area from the neighborhood. Luckily, the flies that are attracted to the odor of the chicken manure are those that can be caught fairly easily in variations of the standard public-health fly trap. Furthermore, trapped flies can be used as a supplemental feed for the chickens, as mentioned earlier. (For a full description of fly-trap construction and use, see pages 283–86 and Appendix 2).

Tray System: Anaerobic Digestion and Algae Ponds: In 1969, we visited a very intensive automated alternative system for manure removal being demonstrated at the Richmond Field Station of the University of California under the direction of Dr. W. Oswald. Although it was being investigated by University researchers as a prototype for implementation on large-scale commercial chicken farms, such a system actually might be more usefully integrated into an urban homestead chicken-fish-garden system.

The demonstration project consisted of one hundred laying hens (White Leghorns), two to a standard commercial-sized cage, in a small chicken house the size of a one-car garage. There was a noticeable absence of odor and flies in the area, doubtless due to the speedy manure removal and the tight, well-screened building. Between each double row of chicken cages, where the chickens could just stretch out their necks to take a drink, was a narrow, slightly slanted trough containing a constant thin trickle of fresh water, which ran down and off the end into a "tipping bucket." The bucket was constructed so it would tip over whenever the liquid reached a certain depth, pouring the contents down upon the slanted manure trays beneath the chickens. After tipping, the empty bucket would flip back to receive the trickle of water once again, while its former contents would wash down the manure trays, carrying into a settling tank any fecal material that had accumulated since the last flooding.

In the settling (sedimentation) tank, the heavy materials sank to the bottom and were periodically pumped into a digester where a culture of anaerobic microorganisms produced methane (CH_4). (In some situations, a Savonius rotor using wind power could be used, as described in the next chapter, to pump the solids into the digester.) The methane was burned off and the solids were removed and dried to be used as a fairly high protein supplement for various ruminant animals. However, if a gas-collecting and pressurizing system were added to such a system, the methane might be usable as fuel for providing supplemental heat to the chicken house in the winter. Certainly, there would be enough gas to heat the digester itself if it were well-insulated. This would be essential in cold weather, since the anaerobic bacteria producing methane do not function well at low temperatures. In the process of making methane, none of the original nitrogen is lost from the manure. For this reason, slurry from the digester could be added to a compost or directly to the garden as fertilizer, rather than being dried for animal feed.

In the demonstration system, the lighter liquid from the sedimentation tank passed through a filter that removed any feathers. It was then pumped into a large pond to grow algae. The algae was dried and fed back to the chickens as a protein supplement. Up to 25 percent of the chickens' feed could be replaced with this algae without affecting egg yields. However, after the addition of 15 percent algae, some flecks appeared in the egg shells. While the spots were harmless, the investigators assumed that they would decrease consumer acceptance. Figure 10-3 depicts the protein pathway as demonstrated at the Richmond Field Station. It seems to us that the algae pond would provide an excellent environment for the raising of either native algae-eating fish, such as the blackfish being raised at the Integral Urban House (see Chapter 11), or several species of the exotic genus *Tilapia*, which the New Alchemy Institute in Woods Hole, Massachusetts, is researching.

As with the more solid material in the settling tank, in some areas and situations the algae-laden water could also be pumped and aerated by a Savonius rotor (a system like this is described in Chapter 11).

Figure 10-3. **Feed Protein Pathway in Experimental Algal Conversion Process**

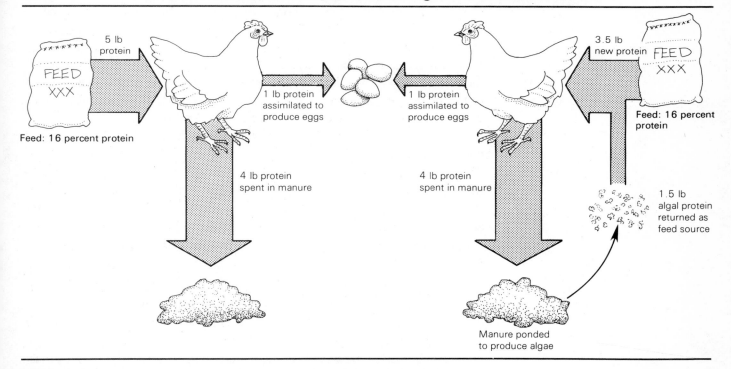

Rabbit Manure: *Directly to the Garden*—As suggested before, the simplest method of handling rabbit manure is to put it straight out into the garden around the plants. One system for doing this is with free-standing cages above slanted cement floors. The slant allows the pellets of manure to roll down to a collecting area from which they can be easily scraped together and shoveled out as a mulch around the vegetables. The cages are set outdoors and the sun and wind help to evaporate the urine.

Obviously, the success of such an arrangement would depend to some extent on dry, warm, and sunny weather where evaporation would occur efficiently. However, such a system would not conserve nitrogen because it would be lost as ammonia along with the evaporating moisture. The crucial question in managing rabbit wastes is therefore whether the urine can be recycled or absorbed into some material and/or dried up, since the urine, not the manure, of rabbits is the high-nitrogen component that provides the ammonia odor objectionable to many people and attractive to flies.

Besides the warm, dry weather, another factor necessary for the success of this system is that manure be collected and shoveled out among the plants almost daily. Once the manure is in contact with the soil organisms, with each new shovelful being spread out thinly over the ground, it quickly decomposes to the point where it no longer breeds flies.

However, if the manure is allowed to build up beneath the rabbits, and remains moist from the addition of urine, the mass will soon become fairly pungent and attract dog flies, *Fannia canicularis*. The males of this species circle around and around near the cages and are difficult to catch in a trap. Occasionally, they will alight on flypaper, and early in the morning or in the evening they may be killed with a fly swatter on vertical surfaces where they rest for the night. But these methods of killing them will not make much of a dent in the population if you have a serious problem.

Compost Bin or Pile: One method of managing rabbit manure is to place thick sawdust in pans beneath the rabbits. Each time the pans are cleaned out, the sawdust is replaced. The pans are emptied every two to three weeks when a new batch of compost is started. The microbial action and heat of the pile quickly breaks down the manure. All things considered, we judge this to be the best disposal method of rabbit wastes for an urban situation where chickens are not free to roam beneath the rabbits.

A critical point to consider in hutch construction is that all urine-wood contact must be avoided. No matter how frequently the pens are emptied, a distinctive, and to some, repellent, odor results from permitting the rabbit urine to soak into the wood frame of the cages. Male rabbits use their urine to mark their territories, and they are quite adept at shooting it out sideways and behind them. Thus, all areas that are likely to become splashed in this fashion should be made of metal or other nonabsorbent materials.

Manure Worms: It is possible to raise manure worms beneath the rabbits. If this system is carefully managed, it may be possible to reduce fly breeding in the manure trays. However, this activity adds a whole dimension of complexity to the waste-management process, since you are then actually having to manage two animal systems rather than one.

If you wish to use worms in the manure trays beneath the rabbits, these boxes must be deep—at least a foot is desirable. The boxes are prepared with a bed of compost or peat moss three to six inches deep. The manure, or "red worms," are seeded into this and the rabbit manure allowed to fall on top. The red or hybrid worms available from commercial sources are ideal for such systems because they have been selected over many generations for their ability to live in high-nitrogen environments. Once every week a light sprinkling of dolomite lime should be spread over the beds to keep the mixture from becoming too acid. If manure tends to build up more in some areas than others, it is best to rake it out across the worm bed so that flies are less likely to build up in the wet accumulations. An alternative approach is to use separate wormboxes and transfer rabbit droppings to them. This avoids the adverse pH effects of rabbit urine.

Success in keeping the manure worms going and creating a minimum of fly breeding seems to depend on having the right amount of bedding, level of alkalinity and moisture, and concentration of worms. The beds must also be well protected from rain, since too much moisture may encourage the worms to migrate out of the boxes, much as garden worms do, traveling over the lawn surface after a heavy rain. An excellent book on raising earthworms is *The Earthworm Book* by Jerry Minnish.

Manure, or red, worms are not garden worms, however; they need a higher nitrogen concentration and richer organic mix than their hardier cousins. This means that contrary to what many have been led to believe by clever advertising pitches, manure worms cannot be used to enrich the garden, as they will not survive there. What about their castings, or "waste" products? These, indeed, are valuable as compost, more so than the rabbit manure from which the worms were raised because by their metabolic activity they release carbon dioxide and thus make the CIN ratio more favorable to plant growth.

What about harvesting worms for fish food? For feeding fish, the worms must be separated from the bedding and manure by hand or with a small garden fork. We recommend worm cultures as a manure-management method only if you have the interest in giving them the time and attention they will require.

Rabbit Manure Managed by Chickens: The rabbit hutches may be opened up below to the chicken pen, giving the hens free rein to scratch and poke through the rabbit manure and eat any maggots (fly larvae) that may get started. (This is really a version of the deep litter system!) This design will work well if the chickens can get access to every nook and cranny where

Figure 10-4. **Possible Plan for a Rabbit-Chicken Integrated Housing System**

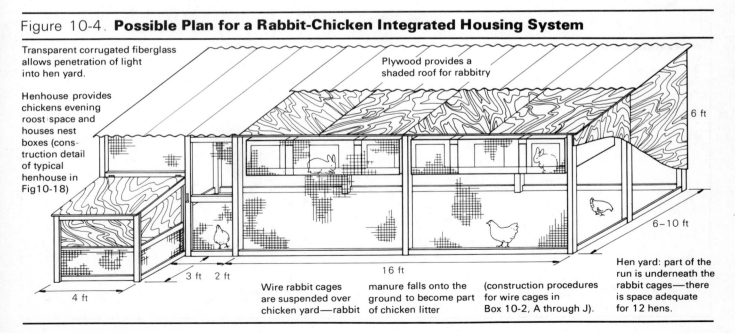

Transparent corrugated fiberglass allows penetration of light into hen yard.

Plywood provides a shaded roof for rabbitry

Henhouse provides chickens evening roost space and houses nest boxes (construction detail of typical henhouse in Fig 10-18)

6 ft

6–10 ft

4 ft

3 ft   2 ft

16 ft

Wire rabbit cages are suspended over chicken yard—rabbit

manure falls onto the ground to become part of chicken litter

(construction procedures for wire cages in Box 10-2, A through J).

Hen yard: part of the run is underneath the rabbit cages—there is space adequate for 12 hens.

259

rabbit feces and urine might fall, and if the chickens are not able to perch up above the rabbit cages, fouling the rabbits and their mangers or water with their own droppings. The rabbit cages should also be far enough off the ground so the chickens cannot peck at the rabbits' feet through the cage floors (see Figure 10-4). If more rabbit manure accumulates than can be used comfortably in the compost (or if the compost is made infrequently), then the hutches can be constructed so that the top layer of cages accumulates the manure in trays for use in the compost, and the lower tier drops the manure into the deep litter area available to the chickens. Of course, the same disadvantages, primarily the loss of nitrogen, apply to this system as to the deep litter management of chicken manure alone (see pages 253–54).

Raising Rabbits

Rabbits are a very desirable meat animal for urban areas because they are quiet and relatively easy to maintain. Their space requirements are also naturally very small, and they may be housed in cages located in small otherwise wasted spaces around the yard. In a study of wild rabbits done in Eng-

Figure 10-5. **Some Common Breeds of Rabbit Stock**

Silver Martin
Meat, pelts
8–9.5 lbs mature
Black body, white chest

Red Satin
Meat, pelts
7.5–8.5 lbs mature
Red body with white chest

French Angora
Wool
5–6 lbs mature
All white; pink eyes and inner ears

New Zealand White
Meat
9.5–10 lbs mature
Pure white; pink inner ear and eyes

Californian
Meat
9–9.5 lbs mature
White body; black markings on paws, tips of ears, and tail

land, it was found that not only are their territories quite restricted in nature, but they spend the better part of their time sitting quietly in their burrows—just as they do in their cages in the home rabbitry.

Breeding Stock: The most common breeds of rabbits raised for meat are New Zealand, Californian, and Silver Martin. Some rabbit breeds are pictured in Figure 10-5. Decisions on which to keep seem to be based mainly on aesthetics. If the pelts are to be used with the hair on, color and appearance of the fur will be important. Rabbits can be obtained from pet stores, rabbitries, 4-H members (who often exhibit their stock at state and county fairs) as well as from friends who are already raising rabbits for meat or pets. If you do not buy a rabbit from registered breeders, you run the risk of getting one with undesirable characteristics. However, since rabbits have so many litters per year, by careful selection (eliminating those that are poor mothers—for example, who neglect their young, have small litters, are nervous, hostile, or hard to breed), you can soon build up a good stock of your own.

Determining the Size of Your Herd: How large a stock of breeding animals you decide to keep depends on the amount of meat you wish to have per week, and how much space and time you can devote to the project. We usually recommend starting with one buck and four does (females). Such a herd is small enough to fit into waste spaces around the house. Under intensive management, a doe can have four litters a year, each averaging eight young per litter. This four-doe—one-buck system will yield roughly five pounds of dressed meat each week. (See Tables 10-5 and 10-6 below). If a rabbit meal is desired more than once a week, does can be added. Each one will provide an additional twenty ounces of meat per week.

Rabbitry Design: *Location:* You may have to give highest priority to local legal requirements that indicate how far from the neighbors' property your animals have to be. Another consideration is prevailing winds, which are likely to waft undesirable smells into your neighbors' (or your own) kitchen or bedroom window. If possible, select a site that does not reduce your planting area—for example, one that does not receive direct sun or where plants in the ground would compete with tree roots, and so on. Rabbits can take very cold weather if they are protected from rain and wind, but they cannot stand high temperatures. In California's Central Valley, where temperatures regularly rise to 110°F in July and August, a rabbitry we are familiar with was located under some large oak trees. A very satisfactory cooling system was devised by piling straw on top of the hutches, with burlap bags hanging down the sides. The thatch and bags were kept wet with a sprinkler set on the roof during the hottest hours. Figure 10-6 illustrates this system. On small city lots, the north side of the house or garage is often an ideal location for the rabbitry.

Cage Size: Mature rabbits must be housed separately in order to insure dependable breeding. Each buck and dry doe (doe without litters) must have 4 to 5 square feet of floor space. Cages 32 inches deep are satisfactory to permit easy access to the animals and provide sufficient depth for accommodat-

Figure 10-6. **Cooling System for Rabbit Cages**

Figure 10-7. **A Double-Tier Rabbitry**

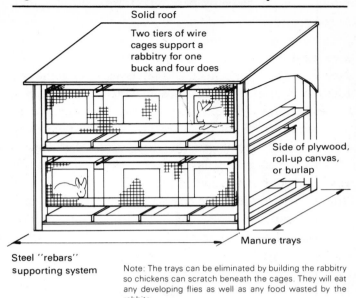

Solid roof

Two tiers of wire cages support a rabbitry for one buck and four does

Side of plywood, roll-up canvas, or burlap

Manure trays

Steel "rebars" supporting system

Note: The trays can be eliminated by building the rabbitry so chickens can scratch beneath the cages. They will eat any developing flies as well as any food wasted by the rabbits.

The cooling system is composed of a straw and burlap cover wet by a sprinkler above.

ing large rabbits. A rabbitry housing a breeding stock of 1 buck and 4 does plus progeny should have 4 small compartments, each twenty-two inches by thirty-two inches, and 2 large compartments, each thirty-six inches by thirty-two inches. The smaller units will accommodate the buck, dry and pregnant does, and weaned fryer rabbits. The larger units will accommodate the does and their litters.

Two separate cages should be constructed to provide housing for the 4-doe—1-buck rabbitry. Each cage is comprised of 1 large compartment, bordered on each side by 2 smaller compartments. The individual compartments can be divided from each other by a manger from which the rabbits may draw fresh alfalfa and leafy greens. Total yard area consumed by a 1 buck and 4 doe rabbitry can be as small as 36 inches wide by 8 feet long, if the 2 separate cages are mounted, one over the other, in a double tier system, as described in Figure 10-7. If the tier system is not desired and the cages are positioned side by side, or back to back, then an area 3 feet by 16 feet, or 6 feet by 8 feet is required, respectively.

Cage Construction: Regardless of the size of your rabbitry or its logistical arrangement, the cage components should be constructed completely of welded wire to promote unobstructed passage of manure and urine through the hutches into manure trays, worm beds, or a chicken yard below. This characteristic should be emphasized, because rabbit diseases are most commonly transmitted in the feces that accumulate on wooden floors of rabbit hutches. All-wire surfaces stay clean and dry, helping to prevent the rabbits from developing sore hocks.

Equally important is preventing the rabbits' urine from fouling the wooden structure on which the cages are supported. Either provide a six-inch distance between the edge of the cage and the framework or nail metal wire guards of sheet wire to the surrounding wooden members, to prevent urine fouling and reduce potential odor generation.

While commercial all-wire cages can be purchased at pet stores or feed mills, it is better to make your own. Not only will it be cheaper, but you will be able to construct individual compartments with the correct dimensions and incorporate convenient manger divisions, not included in the commercial cages, into your design. See Box 10-2 for a detailed plan for constructing a 90-inch rabbit cage describing in detail the construction steps for a wire rabbit cage.

The wire cage is a discrete unit and can be incorporated into a variety of animal-shelter designs. If space is a major constraint, consider the double-tier design shown in Figure 10-7. This system employs a framework constructed of lumber from which the wire cages hang. The cages are suspended from the wooden superstructure by $3/8$-inch diameter reinforcement bars threaded through eyebolts screwed into the framework. This system allows for the complete distribution of weight of the rabbits (which can be as much as 75 pounds per cage) throughout the wooden framework, and also allows for easy removal of the cages for cleaning, repair, or transportation. The convenience of being able to move the lightweight wire cages independently from the wooden structure will be appreciated by rabbit raisers in the northeast, who prefer to house their stock in an enclosed shed during the winter and outdoors under a tree during the summer.

In the double-tier system, rabbit manure is collected in galvanized steel manure pans which are either built into or sit upon the wooden structure beneath the cage floor. You can construct your own manure pans, designing them so they can be cleaned by being scraped out with a short hoe into a bucket, or so that they can be lifted out and carried to the compost bins. In the latter case, they must be small enough so that they can be lifted out when they are full of heavy, urine-soaked manure. They should also fit tightly together, or have removable covers where they touch, to prevent urine and feces from dropping down below. If they are to be scraped out, then sufficient space beneath the cages must be provided in which to maneuver the scraping tool. Care should be taken to construct the corners of the pans so that they are leak-proof.

A bedding of sawdust or finished compost is placed in the bottom of the trays, two to three inches thick, to absorb the rabbit urine and to minimize odor.

Manure from the rabbits in the lower tier may be collected in another set of pans, or it may be allowed to fall into a worm bed (see pages 258-59) or onto a chicken yard below (pages 257-59).

If you have more space available and are seeking a system that requires a very low maintenance the arrangement shown earlier, in Figure 10-4, might be more appropriate. Here the cages are side by side and are suspended directly over a chicken yard, thus overcoming the need for manure collectors. The integration of rabbit and chicken housing has several important advantages. First, as previously stated, it reduces fly production because the chickens aggressively peck all insect eggs and larvae from the litter into which the rabbit manure falls. Second, all the greens that fall through the wire floor of the manger are consumed by the chickens below. Third, space is utilized intensively. Fourth, the proximity of the animals to each other reduces maintenance time.

Comfrey

Symphytum officinale
Spring-Fall.
Annual yield: 100 lbs/
100 ft², fresh weight

Box 10-2. **Construction Procedures for Wire Rabbit Cages**

Materials

26 feet of 1″ x 2″ welded wire, 72″ high
16 feet of ½″ x 1″ welded wire, 36″ high
2 pounds of "C" clips
30′ of heavy cage aluminum wire
4 6″ feeders
12 10″ feeders
8 4″ eyescrews with 1″ diameter head
12′ of ½″ steel reinforcement bar

Tools and Equipment

"C" clip crimper
Wire cutters and pliers
Steel file
Gloves

Construction Steps

1. Cut welded wire according to plan illustrated in Figures B, C, and D. These drawings are *not* in scale and the depicted spacing between welds does not reflect the reality. The dimensions given, however, are accurate, and they should be followed. The 72″ x 130″ piece of 1″ x 2″ welded wire is cut to use as top, front, back, and sides. Make sure that cuts are made at outer edge of dimension desired. Save scrap pieces for use as doors. A 90″ x 36″ piece of 1″ x ½″ wire is for the cage bottom (Figure C). For each cage, cut four 32″ x 20″ pieces of 1″ x 2″ wire for manger divisions (Figure D).

A. Dimensions of 90″ Cage*

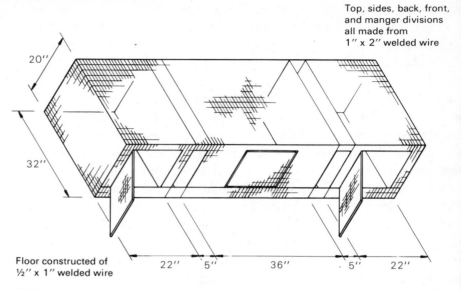

Top, sides, back, front, and manger divisions all made from 1″ x 2″ welded wire

20″

32″

Floor constructed of ½″ x 1″ welded wire

22″ 5″ 36″ 5″ 22″

B. Cutting and Folding Plan*

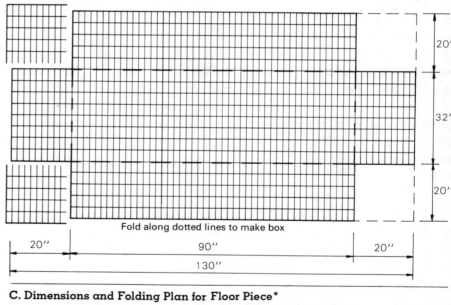

20″

32″

20″

Fold along dotted lines to make box

20″ 90″ 20″

130″

D. Dimensions for Manger Division, Four per Cage*

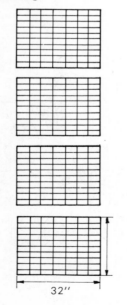

32″

C. Dimensions and Folding Plan for Floor Piece*

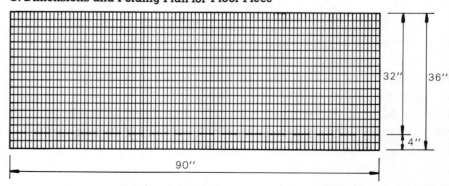

32″ 36″

4″

90″

*Note: Figures are not drawn to scale.

Make upright fold at 4″ mark to provide correct floor dimension and lip for front of cage

2. Fold and secure together separate pieces as shown in Figure E. First fold the large 1″ x 2″ wire piece to make the front, back, top, and sides. Next, set in place and secure the manger divisions to the inside of the body of the cage. Then fold the ½″ x 1″ wire floor piece 4 inches from the edge in order to provide an overlap on the front for the purpose of adding strength. Fit and secure this piece to the body of the cage. Take care in connecting the pieces to each other to insure that all edges line up accurately. Figure F illustrates the proper technique for making the connections using "C" clips. A "C" clip is secured at every third weld. If no "C" clips and "C" clip pliers are available in your area, then use small pieces of wire to make the connections.

F. Procedure for Making Connections with the "C" Clips*

"C" clips or other wire fasteners should be placed every 3rd weld

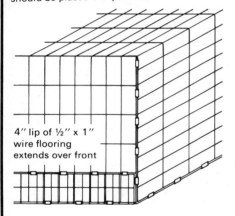

4″ lip of ½″ x 1″ wire flooring extends over front

3. Once the basic cage is constructed, make the holes for the doors and manger openings. Figure G shows the proper dimensions for the doors and manger openings. Do not cut the wire flush to the edge since this would leave a dangerously sharp edge. Leave ½ to 1 inch of wire for folding. See Figure H for detail of folded wire.

4. Doors are constructed from the small pieces cut from the 1″ x 2″ wire used for the top, back, front, and sides. Two 14″ x 14″ and one 14″ x 16″ doors are required per cage. A piece of heavy-gauge aluminum wire is fastened to the perimeter of each door except for the side from which the door is hinged to the cage. The aluminum wire adds strength and will keep the door from bending with use. (The doors are hinged to the out-

E. Exploded View of Assembly of Various Pieces*

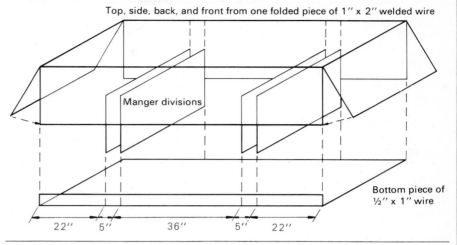

Top, side, back, and front from one folded piece of 1″ x 2″ welded wire

Manger divisions

Bottom piece of ½″ x 1″ wire

22″ 5″ 36″ 5″ 22″

G. Plan for Cutting Door and Openings*

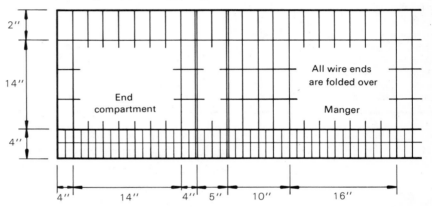

2″

14″

4″

End compartment

All wire ends are folded over

Manger

4″ 14″ 4″ 5″ 10″ 16″

H. Detail of Cage Openings*

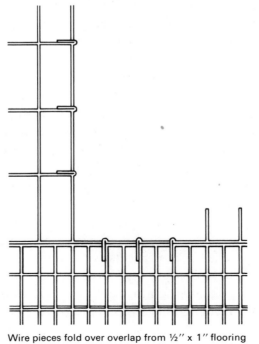

Wire pieces fold over overlap from ½″ x 1″ flooring

265

Box 10-2. **Continued**

side of the cage with ''C'' clips or with pieces of wire.) Another piece of pliable heavy-gauge aluminum, steel, or copper wire is used as a latch to keep the door closed, as shown in Figure I. No cover for the manger door is necessary.

5. Once complete with doors, the cage is ready to be hung into place. If a wooden frame is used for the supporting structure, eyescrews can be screwed into the wood support member as shown in Figure J. A piece of steel reinforcement bar or other comparable material is threaded through the eyebolts and the top welds of the cage. The cage is rested on the bar. Two pairs of eyescrews are needed for each cage. They are placed in line with the middle of the manger.

6. After the cage is properly supported, set the feeding and watering equipment in place. Cut holes in the wire for the metal feed hoppers. Place the hoppers 4 inches from the bottom of the cage and to the side of

I. Detail of Door Latch Made from Heavy-gauge Aluminum Wire*

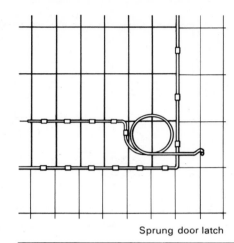

Sprung door latch

J. Cross View Showing Supporting Steel Rod

Eyescrew

Supporting frame

Steel bar threaded through eyebolts

Heavy gauge aluminum wire also used around perimeter of door piece to provide reinforcement

the doors. The hoppers should be accessible from the outside. If ceramic water bowls are used, place them inside the cage; if you prefer water bottles, hang them by wire from the out-

side of the cage. If you use an automatic watering system, run the piping behind the cage and place the water emitters so that they protrude through the wire.

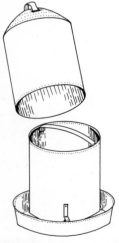

A Good Water Bowl

Although water bowls are easy to start with, automatic watering systems require less labor.

Feeding Devices: The rabbits will no doubt be eating a mixture of fresh greens, either grown or scavenged, and commercial feed. Thus, two types of feeding devices must be provided. The commercial feed is best fed in hoppers that allow pellets to fall into the tray as the old ones are consumed. If you make your own feeders, be sure to use metal rather than wood, as the rabbits will chew on the wood. The floor of the hopper should be perforated or made of screen to permit the powdery "fines" to fall out; otherwise the rabbits will be tempted to dig in the tray and waste a lot of food by scattering it about. Also, the "fines" will mold and could contaminate the good pellets.

The best feeding device is an automatic watering system in which these same ball-bearing dispensers are hooked up to a pipe that is connected to the house water supply (see Figure 10-8). Putting this system together requires some basic plumbing skill, but is worth it because it saves water and maintenance time, and the water remains as clean and sanitary as your general house water supply.

Rabbit Herd Management: *Feeding*—In general it is desirable to feed the animals just enough to keep them healthy, but not so much that they deposit fat on their bodies in excess of what is required to keep them warm. The bucks, particularly, should be kept on the lean side if they are to remain in satisfactory breeding condition. Since rabbits will overeat the commercial feed, it is best to meter this out to them on a daily basis, rather than allowing them unlimited access to a full hopper. The exception is a doe with a nursing litter—she should be allowed to eat as much as she wants. Suggested feeding amounts in a mild climate are shown in Table 10-3.

Estimated costs of producing a four-pound fryer rabbit under a variety of feeding programs are given in Table 10-4. Cost per pound of dressed meat produced will vary considerably depending upon the percentage of commercial pellets in the animal's diet. The optimal feeding program, in terms of reduction of cost and efficiency of feed handling and conversion into meat is program C on the table, where the total caloric intake of the rabbit is comprised of 50 percent commercial pellets, 25 percent alfalfa hay, and 25 percent weeds and waste greens. At 37¢ per pound of meat, the cost of production is roughly one-fifth that of store-bought rabbit using a cost of $1.85 per pound. However, as further savings in cost are sought through more extensive substitutions of greens for commercial pellets, the bulk of total feed required presents a problem. In the case of feeding programs where 50 percent of the calories in the animal's diet are derived from alfalfa hay and the other 50 percent from garden greens, a full 60 pounds of greens

Raising Small Stock

Pellet Feeder for Rabbits

The best feeders have a screen bottom which permits the fine pieces eroded from the pellets to fall into the manure trays, worm boxes, or chicken yard below.

Figure 10-8. **An Automatic Water System for Rabbits**

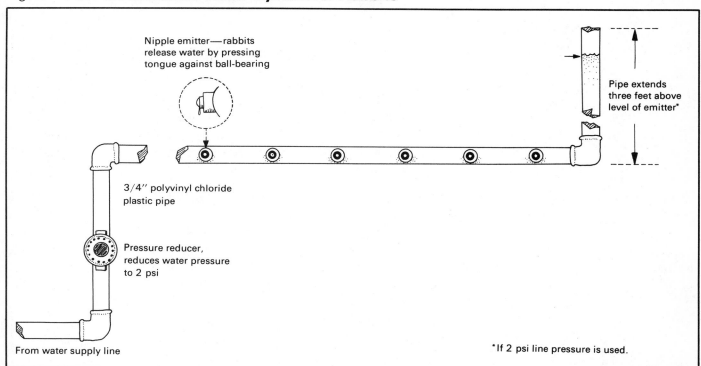

Nipple emitter—rabbits release water by pressing tongue against ball-bearing

Pipe extends three feet above level of emitter*

3/4″ polyvinyl chloride plastic pipe

Pressure reducer, reduces water pressure to 2 psi

From water supply line

*If 2 psi line pressure is used.

Table 10-3. **Suggested Daily Feeding Amounts for Common Meat Rabbits**

Animal	Amount of Complete Pellets, if No Supplement of Hay or Fresh Greens Is Used	Amount of Pellets if Animal Has Free Access to Hay or Greens
10 lb adult buck	6 ounces	2.5 ounces
10 lb dry adult doe	6 ounces	2.5 ounces
Pregnant doe	10 ounces	6 ounces
Doe with litter	free choice	free choice

Watering device for chickens. This unit, commercially available, may be raised off ground to keep the water free of grit.

Table 10-4. **Feed to Produce a Four-Pound Fryer Rabbit (Live Weight)**

Feeding Program*	Pounds of Complete Pellets**	+	Pounds of Fresh Greens†	+	Pounds of Alfalfa Hay‡	=	Total Pounds Required	@	Cost per Pound of Dressed Meat§
A. Complete pellets only	15.4	+	0	+	0	=	15.4	@	70¢
B. 75 percent pellets 25 percent alfalfa hay	8.8	+	0	+	3.72	=	12.52	@	49¢
C. 50 percent pellets 25 percent alfalfa hay 25 percent fresh greens	6.0	+	30	+	4.2	=	40.2	@	37¢
D. 50 percent alfalfa hay 50 percent fresh greens	0	+	60	+	9.0	=	69.0	@	27¢
E. 100 percent fresh greens	0	+	120	+	0	=	120.0	@	no cost

*Percentages refer to portion of total kilocalorie requirement provided by each feed.
**Complete pellets contain 1000 metabolizable kilocalories per pound; cost $9 per 100 lbs @ Berkeley, December, 1976.

† Fresh greens (garden debris, weeds, produce scraps) contain 100 metabolizable kilocalories per pound.
‡ Alfalfa hay, with a 70 percent moisture content, contains 700 metabolizable kilocalories per pound; at $5 per 100 lb @ Berkeley, December, 1976.
§ Dressed weight is approximately one-half live weight.

Source: Templeton, *Domestic Rabbit Production*, and National Academy of Sciences, *Nutrient Requirements of Poultry.*

Jerusalem Artichoke

Helianthus tuberosis
   Spring-Fall tuber harvested in winter.
   Annual yield: 500 lbs/ 100 ft², fresh weight

Alfalfa

Medicago sativa
   Spring-Fall.
   Annual yield: 150 lbs/ 100 ft², fresh weight

have to be collected from the garden or obtained from a produce market in order to provide sufficient calories to produce one four-pound, dressed rabbit. In addition, a less concentrated diet will undoubtedly slow down the rabbit's weight gain, because more bulk must be consumed to acquire the same amount of calories. The proper feeding program combines considerations of cost with that of sound nutrition.

Determining Sex: Very young rabbits are difficult to sex, but by eight weeks they can usually be distinguished. The older the rabbit, the more likely they are to struggle and attempt to avoid being turned over for the sexing process. Cradle the rabbit against your body, supporting its back with one hand while keeping the other hand free to inspect the animal's genitals. Use the middle finger to expose the genital area, pressing down on the lower abdomen with a finger on each side of the genital opening. The genitals of young female and male rabbits are similar, but the difference is discernible. The female genitals resemble a slit; the male has a small, round opening. Rabbits over the age of three months will have developed distinguishable genitalia. The penis of the more advanced male will protrude upon application of pressure to the area and the testicles will be readily visible. See Figure 10-9 for illustrations of male and female rabbit genitals, and Figure 10-10 for ways of handling rabbits.

Breeding Programs: Does may be bred from four to five times a year without stressing them unduly. However, they should not be bred so that they are pregnant during extremely hot weather, as you may lose both mother and babies.

   The does reach sexual maturity between five and six months of age. They have two fifteen-day estrus cycles each month and are capable of ovulating—that is, of being fertile—for thirteen days of each cycle. Female rabbits are *reflex ovulators*, meaning that eggs will be released from the ovaries and implanted in the uterus only in response to sexual stimulation, either from mating or mounting by another female. This makes for a very dependable conception when the female mates with a male, but a period of false pregnancy, resulting from mounting by another female, will cause the doe to be incapable of conception for seventeen days. False pregnancy is avoided by keeping the adult females in separate cages.

When you wish to mate a female, you can bring her to the buck's cage or take them both to a neutral area. The mating is usually very rapid. After sniffing about both the female and the cage, and often marking the area with his urine, the male will mount and copulate vigorously for two or three sec-

Figure 10-9. **Determining the Sex of Rabbits**

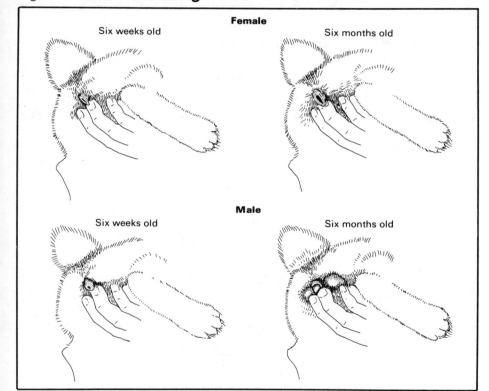

Female Rabbit

Genitals of young females resemble a slit.

Male Rabbit

Genitals of young males resemble a hole at the end of a very short shaft; penis and testicles are obvious on older males.

Figure 10-10. **Proper Techniques for Handling Rabbits**

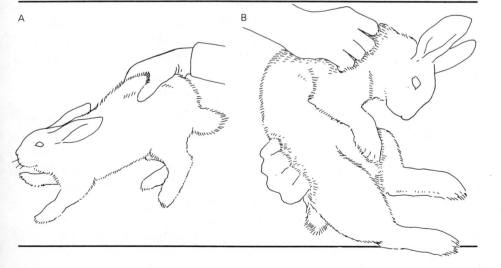

A. Rabbits twelve weeks and younger may be picked up by grasping at hips and carrying rabbit in a head-down position. B. Older, heavier rabbits are held with one hand behind the animal's neck and the other supporting the animal's hind legs.

269

Figure 10-11. **Palpation to Determine Pregnancy**

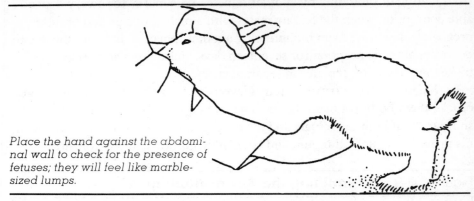

Place the hand against the abdominal wall to check for the presence of fetuses; they will feel like marble-sized lumps.

onds. The female shows she is willing by holding still and raising her rump. A successful mating is usually signaled by the male falling off to one side.

Gestation lasts thirty to thirty-one days. By the seventeenth day following the mating, the growing embryos can usually be felt within the mother's body by gentle palpation. Palpation, illustrated in Figure 10-11 involves restraining the doe and placing your hand under her abdominal wall to check for development of fetuses. These will feel like marble-sized lumps. For this reason, as well as others, it is desirable to stroke and otherwise handle the rabbits, both young and old, so that they become used to being touched by humans, and do not become frightened and struggle and hurt themselves when it is necessary that they be held. If the doe does not appear to be pregnant, you will need to remate her. This can often be tested two or three days after the first mating by seeing if she will accept the male again. If she is pregnant, she will not hold still so he can mount.

During her pregnancy, the doe should be kept as secluded as possible. Hanging a burlap bag over the front of the cage so that visitors or activities in the rabbitry do not disturb her may be a good idea. If she is seriously frightened or inadequately fed during this time the pregnancy may be aborted. Around the twenty-eighth day, a nest box should be placed in her cage. This is a wooden box so constructed that the entrance is several inches above floor level. Construction plans for a nest box are given in Box 10-3.

The nest box is made to have a raised entrance so that nursing babies will be brushed or fall off when the mother jumps out, rather than being dragged accidentally out into the cage. The nest box should be filled with straw, dried grass, fur from a box used for a previous litter, or any soft stuffing material that is not stringy, so the babies cannot become entangled in it. It is important to put the nest box into the mother's cage at just the right time (that is, twenty-eight days after mating), since, if she has access to it too early she will foul it with feces, but if you put it in too late, the litter might be born outside on the wire, where they may die from cold and lack of care. Sometimes babies either born or dragged outside the box onto the cage floor can be warmed up under a lamp, placed back with the mother in the nest box, and actually survive, but this is rare, since the mother often will not reaccept newborn babies that have been handled by humans. (Using clean gloves, if you must handle the newborn, is a good idea for this reason.)

Around the thirtieth day of the pregnancy, the doe's hair will loosen on

Box 10-3. Procedure for Constructing Rabbit Nest Box

1. Cut pieces of ½" plywood as follows:
Floor: 12" x 16"
2 sides: 11½" x 16", with angle cut out
Top: 12" x 16"
Front: 11" x 5"

2. Glue and nail sides together
3. Sand to smooth the corners. *Do not paint*, since rabbits will chew on box and ingest the paint. To prevent box-chewing, edge with metal.

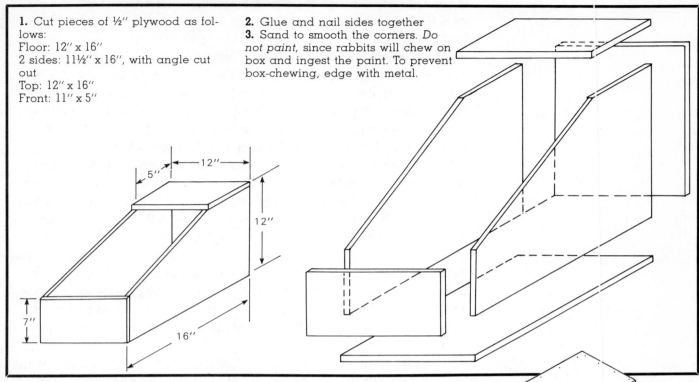

her chest, and she will begin to pull it out and use it to line her nest. Any loose hair blowing about the cage can be added to the box, and the whole mass saved and used for another litter after the young are mature enough not to need the box any longer.

Eight is an average size litter. Does that produce consistently less should probably be culled from the herd. The female young of those producing more than eight babies per litter should be selected out and kept as breeders for improving the herd.

Do not disturb the litter to view it immediately. If the babies are all safely within the nest box, let them be for at least a day or two. It is most convenient if the box is made so that the top lifts up, permitting a view of the interior. On the second or third day it is safe to explore gently through the litter and remove any dead babies. These will be still and cold to the touch, while the healthy live ones will bob about very vigorously, responding to your touch and the heat of your hand. Do any work in and around the cage very quietly and slowly so as not to alarm the mother. It is not at all uncommon for a doe to kill and eat or abandon her new babies if circumstances seem unsettling to her.

Around six days after birth, the young will develop their fur coats, and within ten days, they will be venturing out of the nest box. This box should be removed as soon as all the babies are seen to be spending most of their time both running about and sleeping outside the box, in approximately thirty days.

By the time they are two months old, the young males must be slaughtered or separated from each other or they will fight constantly, the most aggressive of the litter eventually castrating all the others. They will also mate

271

with their sisters and their mother. As soon as the babies are no longer nursing and are large enough to pester their mother excessively (eight to ten weeks) the doe should be removed from her litter and remated with the buck. After remating she must be put in a separate cage.

The wire-cage rabbitry described earlier, consists of a pair of 90-inch cages each having 3 separate compartments to accommodate a herd of one buck and four does and progeny if the breeding program is managed carefully. Figure 10-12 shows the arrangement of the breeders and their young that makes most efficient use of space. The buck has his own cage and is never moved. The does' breeding cycles are staggered three weeks apart from each other. Two does occupy small compartments: one doe that has recently been mated and another that is advanced in her pregnancy. The two other does occupy the large middle cages: one doe that has recently suckled a litter, and the other whose litter is nearly weaned. At weaning, which will occur anytime from eight to twelve weeks after birth, depending upon the growth rate of the litters, the male offspring are culled for slaughter and the females moved into the remaining unoccupied small cage for further growth. The doe is remated and moved to a small cage, changing places with another doe that is nearly ready to give birth to a litter. If this rotation is adhered to, some 128 rabbits will be produced each year for slaughter from the four does. (Refer to Table 10-5.)

Under more intensive breeding regimes, in which each doe has six litters per year, remating of the females occurs when their litters are hardly four and a half weeks of age. Three days after her previous litter is weaned, the doe gives birth again. We discourage such intensive breeding schedules because of the *strict* discipline it entails, and the fact that it exhausts the does before their time.

Culling—Choosing for Slaughter: During the next two weeks, the young males are culled from the litter. They are ready to use as fryers as soon as they reach a live weight of four pounds (between eight and twelve weeks). After the young males are slaughtered, the small or poor-colored females should also be taken. The finest-looking females should be considered for selling or replacing your breeding stock. The older the animal, the stringier and more strongly flavored the meat. However, domestic rabbits never seem to get very tough, and their taste always seems mild enough to take on the flavor of the sauce or condiments with which they are cooked.

Table 10-5. Breeding Programs for Domestic Rabbits

Number of Litters per Doe per Year	Age of Young at Time Mother Doe Is Remated	Number of Offspring per Year per Doe, Computed at Eight Young per Litter	Meat Production per Year, if Killed at 4 lb Live Weight	Expected Productive Life of Doe (Months)	Total Production of Meat, for Life of Doe
Three	12 weeks	24	48	36	144 lbs
Four (preferred)	8	32	64	36	192 lbs
Five	6.5	40	80	30	192 lbs
Six	4.5	48	96	18	144 lbs
Seven	3.5	56	112	12	112 lbs

Figure 10-12. **One-Buck, Four-Doe Breeder Arrangement**

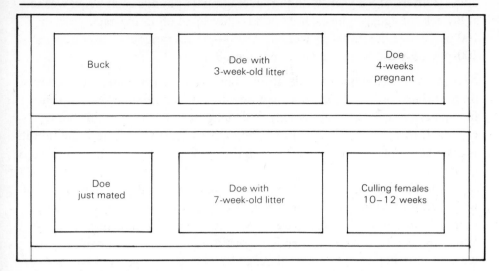

| Buck | Doe with 3-week-old litter | Doe 4-weeks pregnant |
| Doe just mated | Doe with 7-week-old litter | Culling females 10–12 weeks |

Each doe has four litters per year.

Meat Production: Approximately 65 percent of the live weight of a four-pound fryer rabbit is carcass. Of the carcass, 80 percent is edible meat (with a 25 percent protein content). That makes a meat production of two pounds, and protein production of one-half pound per rabbit. The most efficient weight at which to slaughter rabbits is four pounds. As the animals get larger, the cost of production of each additional pound of meat increases, as described in Table 10-6.

One of the outstanding characteristics of rabbits is the amount of meat that each breeding doe can produce relative to her own body weight. A 10-pound doe that bears 4 litters of 8 rabbits in one year, will produce 128 pounds of offspring at the time they are weaned and slaughtered. That represents an animal production of young nearly 1300 percent the doe's weight. That is a phenomenal rate of production, particularly when compared to

Table 10-6. **Weight Gain in Meat Rabbits versus Size and Age of Animal**

Change in Rabbit's Weight	Additional Number of Days Required to Put on That Additional Pound	Additional Pounds of Commercial Feed Required to Increase Rabbit's Weight One Additional Pound	Additional Cost to Produce One Additional Pound*
3.0 to 3.9	8	4.0	$ .36
4.0 to 4.9	9	4.5	$ .41
5.0 to 5.9	10	5.0	$ .45
6.0 to 6.9	12	5.5	$ .50
7.0 to 7.9	15	8.0	$ .72
8.0 to 8.9	21	11.5	$1.04
9.0 to 10.0	26	14.0	$1.26

*Cost computed at price of commercial feed: $9 per 100 pounds

The following is an example of how to read table 10-6. "If your rabbit weighs three pounds, it will take an additional eight days and four more pounds of feed (36 cents worth), to bring it up to 3.9 pounds, which is the usual fryer weight." Notice that as the rabbit gets larger, it costs more for you to produce each additional pound.

Source: Adapted from Templeton, *Domestic Rabbit Production.*

273

rates of other meat-producing livestock. A 400-pound brood sow that produces 2 litters of 8 a year, with pigs averaging 25 pounds each when weaned at 8 weeks of age, produces 400 pounds of weaned offspring each year, or 100 percent of the mother's weight. A 1000-pound range cow producing a 400-pound, weaned calf, gives a return of 40 percent.

Slaughtering: A major consideration when deciding upon an animal to raise under urban constraints is the ease with which it can be slaughtered. Finding an aesthetically tolerable method of slaughtering is essential if home-raising of meat is to be acceptable. The method we use for killing the rabbits is dislocation of the neck, which, when done correctly, results in a quick and bloodless death.

The first step is to prepare a rack and make ready the implements you will need for skinning and butchering. The rack can be a board, suspended vertically five feet above the ground, with two hooks or nails driven into it. When the dead animal is suspended by its hind feet, it should hang freely without obstruction. The internal organs, blood, and undesirable parts, when removed, should be able to fall cleanly into a bucket of absorbent material. The implements you will need are a sharp knife for skinning and butchering, and a metal hanger on which to place the pelt for drying.

Remove the animal from its hutch and place it on a table or on the ground. Calm the rabbit by petting it as you position it properly. If the rabbit is used to being handled, it will not panic and will die peacefully (see Figure 10-13). To position the animal for slaughter, grasp both hind legs with the left hand, place the thumb of your right hand on the neck just below the ears and curl four fingers under the animal's chin. As you assume this position, orient the animal in a vertical position alongside your right thigh. Push down on the neck with the right hand, stretching the animal. Press down with the thumb; then raise the animal's neck with a quick movement and dislocate the neck. The rabbit will lose consciousness instantly and will cease to struggle.

You can judge whether you have successfully dislocated the neck while you maintain the animal in the vertically stretched position. With the small finger of your right hand, touch the animal's eye to test for reflexes. If the eye is fully open and no reflex is observed, you can assume that the rabbit is dead and is ready for skinning. When prompt dislocation of the neck cannot be achieved, one can kill the animal quickly with a heavy blow of a stick at the base of the skull. Manual dislocation is preferred since no hemorrhaging and subsequent bleeding occurs.

Skinning: Hold the dead animal up against the skinning rack by one of its hind legs. Its abdomen should face you when you have pinned up both legs. Make an incision into a leg of the carcass between the tendon and bone just above the hock. Suspend the carcass by pressing the hook through the incision. Repeat the procedure with the other leg.

Using a well-sharpened knife, begin removing the pelt by cutting through the skin of one of the hind legs just below the point where it is hung. Run the knife down the leg to the crotch. Next, cut around the leg below the hock and free the skin from the body by pulling the pelt from the carcass and cutting through the thin connective tissue. After you have ex-

Figure 10-13. **Slaughtering, Skinning, and Butchering a Rabbit.**

A. Calming the animal in preparation for slaughtering.

B. Dislocating the neck by sharp twist of wrist.

C. Hanging the slaughtered animal by its hind feet from a nail mounted in the board.

D. Making the initial cut through the pelt along the animal's hind leg.

E. Continuing the skinning by cutting through connective tissue.

F. Removing the head by cutting along the top vertebrae.

G. Making an incision through the abdominal wall to expose internal organs.

H. Cutting the meat from the carcass.

posed the carcass of one leg down to the hindquarters, begin in the same fashion with the other hind leg. With both hindquarters exposed, cut around the crotch, leaving a portion of fur over the animal's genitals. Keeping the pelt in one entire piece, pull the skin away from the carcass with your free hand on the underside of the pelt as you cut through the connective tissue, working your way down the back and abdominal wall until you reach the forelegs (see Figure 10-13E). Begin cutting through the first foreleg as you press it up through the pelt, exposing the connective tissue. Skin the leg no further than the hock joint at which you cut through the pelt, freeing the entire foreleg. After the other foreleg is freed, remove the skin further until the back of the skull is reached. Take special care to leave all fat on the carcass as the skin is removed from the animal. Cut around the neck and free the pelt from the carcass. Quickly stretch the pelt over the piece of heavy wire and remove any remaining pieces of pelt from the carcass. Remove the head by making an incision around the jaw bone and cutting through the dislocated section of the neck. Allow the head to fall into a bucket of sawdust placed beneath the rabbit.

Taking care not to puncture the bladder, make a slit along the midline of the carcass down to the throat. By pulling with your free hand, remove the entrails and discard them into the absorbent material for composting, or give them to your chickens. The kidneys, heart, and liver may be eaten once the gall bladder has been carefully removed and recycled. (Incidentally, the percentage weight of liver to total body weight is twice that of the chicken and three times that of the cow.) Run the index finger of your free hand up the anal tube to clear out remaining manure pellets.

Butchering: With the skin and entrails thoroughly removed and the carcass still suspended on the rack, commence butchering. Begin by cutting off the two pieces of the abdominal wall. Next, cut off both forelegs at the top of the shoulder (see Figure 10-13H). Remove one side of the breast by using the knife to cut through the vertebrae along the backbone. Leave the other side of the breast attached to the backbone and remove in one piece by cutting them away from the two hind legs. The latter are each removed from the rack and the feet are cut off along the hock joints.

After the meat has soaked for one hour in salt water, drain and rinse off the pieces. They are now ready for cooking or freezing.

Casing and Tanning the Pelt: The rabbits' skins are an important by-product of the meat and manure production. They can be used to make clothing, blankets, pillow covers, or ornamental hangings for your home. To make them usable, they must be managed carefully after being removed from the animal. The pelts are not cut open after skinning, but should be stretched as one whole piece immediately. Stretchers are made from number 9 to 14-gauge aluminum rod shaped by three turns over a 2-inch pipe to provide a spiral spring in the middle, as shown in Figure 10-14. Draw the skin over the stretcher, flesh side out, leaving the holes from the two front legs both on the same side. The skin of the hind legs will then follow the wire down its length and may be held fast by ordinary spring clothes pins.

Figure 10-14. **Stretching a Freshly Skinned Rabbit Pelt over Wire**

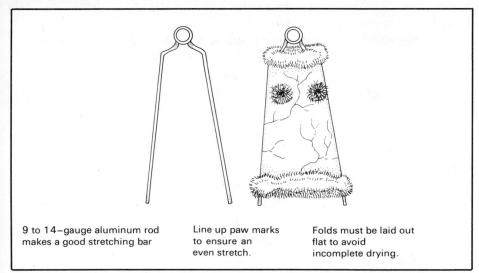

9 to 14–gauge aluminum rod makes a good stretching bar

Line up paw marks to ensure an even stretch.

Folds must be laid out flat to avoid incomplete drying.

Pull the skin down on the stretcher so as to give it full length, but do not make the error of stretching it too thin. Hang stretcher in the shade where the air circulates freely until the skin becomes bone dry. The "dewlap," or heavy fur at the neck, must be pulled up straight and the forelegs straightened out in order to dry thoroughly.

After the skin has been hanging for four to five days, you may remove it by compressing the ends of the stretcher and slipping it off. Keep flies from the wet skins, and see that the skins are thoroughly dry. Stretching a skin in this manner is termed *casing*. Do not salt the fresh skin in order to hasten the drying process. Salt will impair tannage and will result in a disposal problem. Since rabbit skins are so small, it is desirable to accumulate several before beginning the tanning process, and then tan them all at one time. We have found that six pelts is a good number to work with. Too few does not warrant the preparation time involved in the process, and too many presents a regrettable burden in terms of time.

After drying, slit the cased skins down the middle with a sharp knife and soak them in a weak solution of soda or borax (one ounce per gallon of water) in a five-gallon plastic bucket. Keep the pelts submerged under the water with a brick for a period of six hours.

Remove the skins from the solution and "flesh" them—that is, pull off the thin membrane and any clinging fat that might adhere to the inside of the skin. You should do this with a sharp skinning or jackknife, usually while holding the skin over the edge of a board. How well the skin comes out at the end of the tanning process depends on how thoroughly and skillfully the fleshing is done. It does take experience, since the skins are thin and it is all too easy to poke through the pelt accidentally. Fleshing each skin usually takes about fifteen to twenty minutes, but if you have never fleshed a pelt before, allow more time in the beginning. As soon as each pelt is fleshed, immediately return it to the cleaning solution, and make ready the tanning solution (see page 278). Leave the pelts in the air as little as possible.

Place the wet, fleshed pelts into the tanning solution and soak them for

A tanning solution

Commercial tanning companies have a variety of formulae for a tanning solution, usually kept secret, and many contain caustic chemicals. The materials we recommend are fairly easy to obtain. For tanning for six rabbit pelts prepare this solution:
- one pound of potassium alum, dissolved in one gallon of cold water
- eight ounces of salt and four ounces of washing soda, dissolved together in one-half gallon of water
- **Important!** First put the alum solution into a plastic bucket, porcelain crock, or glass container (do not use metal). *Then* add the soda-salt solution to the alum water.

four to seven days. Soaking, fleshing, and placing the pelts in the tanning solution should be done in quick succession. Keep the container in a cool, shaded place. Stir the tanning pelts at least twice a day. Keep them weighted down and submerged in solution at all times. After four to seven days, remove the pelts and rinse them thoroughly in cold water. In the next to last rinse, use one ounce of borax for every gallon of water, and leave skins in water for about five minutes, agitating them occasionally. Give them a final rinse in plain cold water and squeeze out excess water from the pelts gently. Do *not* wring the pelts—treat them as you would a fine woolen garment.

Stretch the pelts on a board to full size, fur side down, and pin down the edges with thumb tacks. Rub a bar of Ivory soap into the skin side, working up a good, thick lather with the moisture that remains in the skin. As the pelts are drying, rub in a little Neats foot oil and work the skin back and forth in your hands, gently stretching the hide until it turns an off-white color. This should be continued until the pelt is limp, soft, and dry.

The pelts may be sown into garments, either fur or skin side out depending on your desire. Mittens, vest, and bed spreads are all good possibilities for these useful, pretty skins. Ten to twelve skins from medium-sized rabbits, will make a man's large warm, wind- and drizzle-proof vest.

For some excellent booklets on the tanning process, including garment making, see *Tanning,* published by Fat Cabin Press. For an unusual article on tanning large and small skins in the Indian style, using animal brains and no other materials, see the bibliography entry for Carson.

Health Problems in Domestic Rabbits: Rabbit diseases can be largely prevented by keeping all hutches and hutch equipment clean, and by prompt disposal of all sick animals. In addition, rabbits that are slaughtered when young, as described above, are even less likely to incur health problems. Thus, the urban rabbit raiser is unlikely to see many of the diseases that the commercial breeder sees. In spite of this, a number of such "rare" diseases will be discussed.

You should clean hutches, boxes, and so on frequently and thoroughly by soaking them in some disinfectant such as an ammonia solution for five to ten minutes, and then allowing them to dry in the sun. Compost rabbit manure and bedding promptly to prevent the breeding of flies and other pests. Kill all sick animals immediately and compost or bury their whole carcass with pelt. Most noncommercial rabbit raisers do not have the time, expertise, or even the space to quarantine sick animals, diagnose their disease, treat them with the proper medication, and so on. In addition, many of the diseases of rabbits are highly contagious.

Wild rabbits and hares are susceptible to many viral diseases, but domestic animals get very few of these. Some of these viruses cause malignant and nonmalignant tumors, while others cause respiratory diseases. The most widely known of these diseases is *myxomatosis,* a highly specific disease of rabbits that was intentionally introduced into Australia just after World War II in an attempt to control the previously introduced European rabbits. All domestic rabbit strains are highly susceptible to this disease, which is transmitted by mosquitos. A more likely occurrence is coccidiosis. Sitting in a hunched position, refusing to eat, with diarrhea, a swollen belly, "the staggers" (inability to maintain balance) are key signs for this protozoan-induced disease. The disease attacks the young, primarily, and can kill. Various medications are available but prevention should be the primary approach. Since the pathogen is spread through droppings, clean hutches with wire net floors can reduce transmission to healthy rabbits.

As with most other animals, rabbits harbor ectoparasites. These include mites, fleas, lice, ticks, ringworm (a fungus that is easily transmitted to humans), and warbles (the larval stage of flies). Ear mites are a particularly common parasite on domestic rabbits. A mite infestation is evidenced by scabby growth inside the base of the ear (see Table 10-7). An initial fungal growth results from unsanitary conditions; the mites feed on the fungal growth. Control is best obtained by treating infestations with liberal applications of sulphur powder dissolved in mineral oil, at the rate of one teaspoon of sulphur per cup of oil. Gently swab the infected area with the mixture. The cage should be cleaned and all manure and debris removed from the floor.

Sore hocks, which are inflamed and ulcerated areas of feet surfaces (Table 10-7), are also a frequent problem. The condition is caused by wet and dirty floors, particularly when the feet are bruised by being stamped during excited and active running. These bruised tissues are very susceptible to infection. This is one reason why uneaten greens should not be left on the floor of the rabbit cage to decompose and form a wet mat under the animal.

Table 10-7. **Diseases of Domestic Rabbits**

Disease	Symptom	Cause	Treatment
Ear mites	Mites evident on fungal growth in depth of ear	Initial fungal growth caused by unsanitary conditions; mites feed on fungal growth	Clean cage; get rid of all debris and manure from floor; apply sulphur powder/mineral oil solution to infected area
Sore hocks	Scabs on paws of hind feet	Animal resting on damp manure or greens; aggravated by stamping hind feet on wire floor	Clean cage floor; place board in cage for animal to sit on until paws heal.

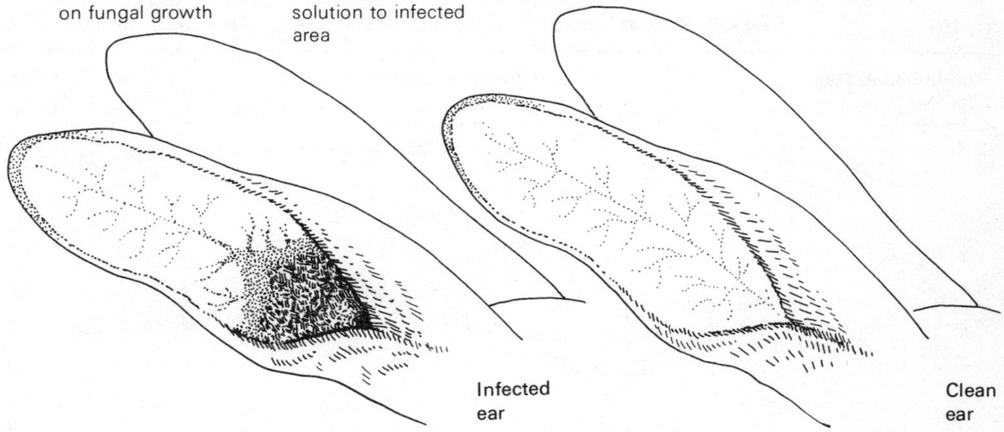

Infected ear

Clean ear

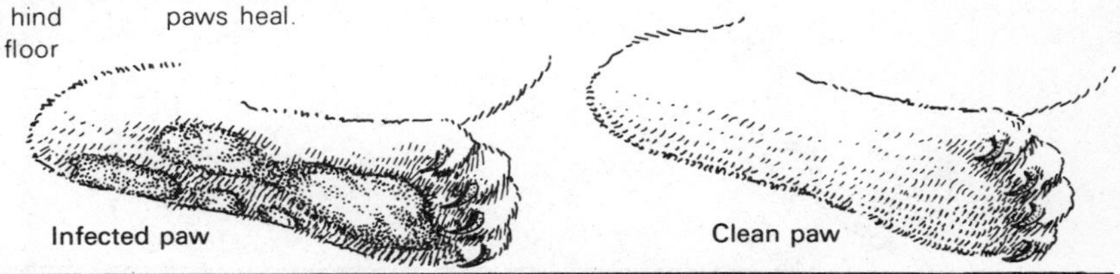

Infected paw

Clean paw

Mild cases can be treated by washing the infected areas with soap and warm water, and then applying a zinc or iodine ointment. The cage should be cleaned and a board placed inside for the animal to sit on until its paws heal, but rabbits with serious cases should be butchered.

Raising Chickens

Selecting a Breed: Chicken breeds vary with respect to temperament and egg and meat production. White Leghorns produce the most eggs for the amount of feed they consume, often in excess of 250 eggs per year. They can also withstand hot weather rather well. But they tend to be very nervous and aggressive toward each other, and they are a rather scrawny meat bird.

The White Cornish Cross is a relatively calm bird, with delicious tasting meat, but it is a poor layer. For the home producer, Rhode Island or New Hampshire Reds and Plymouth Rocks are good egg and meat producers. The first two lay brown-shelled eggs. Bantams are a small breed and are very hardy. They breed easily and may go semiwild if allowed to roam freely in suburban areas where undisturbed natural areas are still to be found. A wide variety of decorative chickens are also available. Some large heavy-set breeds, such as Plymouth Rocks, are well-adapted to cold climates. Such magazines as *Countryside* and *Organic Gardening and Farming* usually carry ads for hatcheries that will ship a variety of breeds, and both Sears Roebuck and Montgomery Ward carry the common types.

How Many Chickens Should You Keep? The size of your flock will depend on both the space you have for pens and the amount of meat and/or eggs you wish to produce. If you want to eat a chicken a week, you will need

Figure 10-15. **Three Varieties of Chicken Suitable for Domestic Production**

Rhode Island Red
Eggs, meat
4 lbs mature
Deep red body

White Leghorn
Eggs
2.5 lbs mature
All white body, lean profile

White Cornish Cross
Meat
6 lbs mature
White body, large profile

a standing crop of twelve meat birds. If you intend to harvest fryers between the ages of two and three months at weekly intervals, you will need to raise replacements just as regularly.

Should you choose to raise chickens solely for egg production, you will need to determine the number of eggs you wish to consume each week. (In deciding this, you may wish to consider the controversy over the role of cholesterol in cardiovascular disease, as eggs are extremely high in cholesterol.) A hen will lay on the average of 200 eggs per year. Chickens lay more in the late spring when the days are longest, and production drops off sharply during the short days of winter. To obtain approximately four eggs a day, you will need seven or eight hens. Thus, to have enough eggs all year, you may want to preserve some during periods of heavy production. An old-time method for doing so is to lower the extra fresh-laid eggs into a crock of sodium silicate, or "water glass."

"Water glass" is still sold in pharmacies and general stores occasionally, but usually for the purpose of sealing leaks in the radiator of a car than the older use of sealing the shells of an egg. It is obtained as a concentrate and must be diluted with water before being used. (Directions will be on the bottle.) Use a big crock, set it in a cool place, and keep it covered, adding water as it evaporates. Write the date on the shell in pencil before setting them away. If put away fresh, the eggs will still be good to eat after as long as ten months, although the white of the raw stored egg doesn't stand up in the pan the way it does when they are just laid. The other alternative is to burn electric lights to extend the daylight hours around the chickens during the winter. We would be inclined to discourage the additional use of energy for this purpose, unless of course you obtain the electricity from some non-polluting, nonfossil-fuel source, such as the wind.

Obtaining Stock: It is not necessary to keep a rooster to have eggs to eat, although some people believe fertile eggs provide superior nutrition. The crowing of roosters is very likely to cause complaints in urban areas. Although we have neighbors in Berkeley who do keep them we do not have roosters ourselves. It is possible to perform surgery on a rooster's vocal apparatus and reduce the noise he makes, but the procedure is tricky, and it isn't easy to find someone who knows how to do it.

An easier way to start your flock is to buy day-old chicks. Both mixed sexes and hens alone are sold. If you buy an unsexed batch, you run the risk of getting mostly roosters. These can be eaten when they reach crowing size, of course, but they will generally all mature at the same time, meaning a lot of sudden undesired crowing and mandatory slaughtering, not necessarily at the most convenient time for you. So for the first batch, at least, buying all hens may be the best plan, particularly if your main reason for raising chickens is to have eggs.

Care of Baby Chicks: For the first several weeks, while they are covered with down and do not yet have their true feathers, the baby chicks are fragile and must be protected. A simple brooder should be constructed with a light bulb inside to keep the chicks warm when they arrive. A 100-watt bulb will be just right to start with, about six inches above the floor. Hang a cloth over

Waterer and Feeder for Chicks

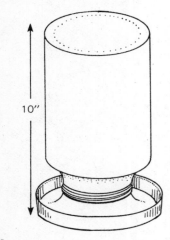

10″

Waterer

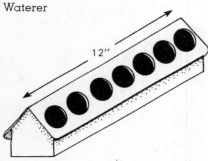

12″

Feeder

the front of the cage and lift and lower it according to the behavior of the chicks that is, depending on whether the chicks appear to be too warm or too cold (if they all huddle together near the bulb, lower the cloth, and if they flock to the sides away from the bulb, cool them off by raising the cloth). They like 90°F to 95°F (32.5°C to 35.3°C) the first week, and you can plan to reduce the heat by substituting a lower-watt bulb every two weeks (75-watts to 60 to 40) until they look well-feathered enough to go without extra heat.

Chicks raised during a summer hot spell may need supplementary heat only at night. Again, the best way to tell if the temperature is right for them is by watching their behavior. You can adjust the bulb wattage and cover-cloth according to how they react to the bulb.

The floor of the brooder should be covered with sawdust to absorb the chicks' droppings. If the manure is kept dry and the brooder is screened in, there will be a minimum of fly-breeding problems. The chicks need fresh water at all times, but it is necessary to keep them from fouling it with their manure or the sawdust. A jar waterer, such as is commonly sold in pet stores, is best to use, propped up on a chunk of wood or other support to raise it up off the floor. Young chicks can eat from a cardboard egg carton or other improvised container, but they tend to waste a lot. Best is a chick feeder, also obtainable from pet shops or some hardware stores. During the first month or so, they can be fed chick starter, and then gradually introduced to adult commercial mash and greens.

After two to three weeks, or as soon as the chicks have their mature feathers, they can be exposed to the normal temperatures of the chicken house, provided that they have a protected place where they can huddle together out of the wind and rain. A small covered wooden box with an entrance just big enough for the chickens, in the corner of the larger pen will give them a place to get away from the pecking of the larger birds and warm up their space with their body heat. Such special provisions must be made for the young chicks even if they are feathered enough to be added to a pen with other chickens. New additions to the flock will always be pecked by all the older hens, and the newcomers may be kept out of the main chicken house for a while. Thus, the little chicks need a place they can escape to, and sources of water and food of their own until they are big and old enough to fight back and establish their place in the pecking order.

Flock Management: Since the chicks are so delicate, it is desirable to obtain the day-olds after the weather has become really warm, unless you are prepared to give them plenty of attention and keep them indoors. Most hatcheries stop selling day-olds in the fall, and begin again in early spring. For layers, you may wish to reorder once a year, putting the older hens in the stew pot as they become less productive. Fryers need to be reordered more frequently.

The hens will not begin to lay until they are six months old, and will do their most efficient feed-to-egg conversion during the first year. Once they begin to lay, it is essential that calcium be added to their diet. Oyster shell is commonly used for this purpose. You can also feed them their own shells back, crushed up, but they will need more calcium than this will provide. (If you do use this system, be sure to crush their eggshells so the chickens do not get the idea of eating their own fully-formed eggs.) Table 10-8 shows the total pounds of feed required on four different feeding regimes using different proportions of commercially obtained chicken food (which is primarily grain), fresh greens, and trapped flies.

Table 10-8. **Pounds Feed Required to Produce 1 Dozen Eggs***

Feeding Program	Lbs Commercial Chicken Feed† at 1400 M kcals per Lb	+ Lbs Fresh Greens at 100 M kcals per Lb	+ Lbs Flies at 700 M kcals per Lb	= Total lbs Feed Required	Cost per Dozen Eggs§
Commercial chicken feed only	5.00	——	——	5.00	$ .50
75 percent commercial feed 25 percent fresh greens	3.75	17.50	——	21.25	.37.5
50 percent commercial feed 40 percent fresh greens 10 percent flies	2.50	28.00	1.00	31.50	.25.0
25 percent commercial feed 60 percent fresh greens 15 percent flies	1.25	42.00	1.50	44.75	.12.5

*Feeding proportions derived from percent caloric contribution to total diet of 7000 M kcals feed consumed by hen for 1 dozen eggs produced. (M kcals are metabolized kilocalories.)

† 2–lb white Leghorn hen
§ Price for commercial feed computed at $10/100 lbs; Berkeley, 1977.

Trapping Flies for Chickens: The common flies attracted to the ammonia smell of the chicken manure are *Musca domestica, Phoenicia* species, and *Ophyra leucostoma.* They can be easily trapped if you know something about their behavior. Since it is the smells that they are attracted to, any trap made to catch them must be properly baited (see the subsection below). After feeding at the bait, the flies will fly up to the light. Thus, by a little ingenious manipulation of flyscreen, they can be trapped. In the standard flytrap, a cone of screen is placed above the bait with a hole at its apex. The fly leaving the bait flies up toward the sky and lands on the inside of the screen cone. Seeing the light coming through the hole at the top of the cone, the fly then walks up the inside on the screen towards it. This cone is surrounded with another screened enclosure, which is cylindrical. Once through the hole of the inner cone, the fly is trapped inside the surrounding cylinder. It then circles about until it dies.

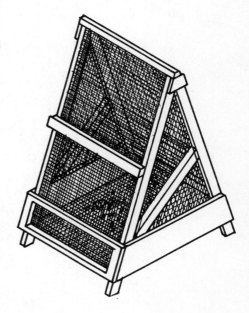

Making the standard flytrap requires some minor soldering skills. Furthermore, since the top lifts off for the removal of dead flies, the live ones still circling can escape at that time. To overcome this defect, we designed a large pup-tent-shaped trap in which the dead flies fall down to one side, where a trap door opens to let them drop out (into the chicken's feeding trough or pen, if the trap is above). Making this trap requires a little carpentry. (See Appendix B.)

With the idea of devising a trap that a relatively unskilled person could put together quickly with common household tools (a stapler and scissors), Gary Satrom, a Farallones-Antioch College West student, devised a trap made primarily of aluminum flyscreen (see Appendix 2). When devising flytraps of your own, keep in mind that the most important factor is to make the hole(s) through which the fly crawls the lightest point the fly will see after leaving the bait.

Baiting the A-frame Flytrap: Place any type of food or liquid that will attract the flies (buttermilk, molasses and syrups, sweet-smelling fermenting foods, meat, fish, kitchen scraps, animal manures, and so on) into a saucer or plate under the A-frame trap (see page 283). Position the dish in the middle. If it is too close to the edge, the flies will find it easy to feed at the outer edges and escape the trap altogether. The objective is to attract the flies into the lower area of the trap where the contrast between light and dark is greatest. You can elevate the dish on some bricks and/or boards in order to get the bait three to four inches up into the trapping area.

The secret of successful baiting is to keep the bait wet! Since flies have sponging mouthparts, and have to take in liquid nutriment, the baits become much less effective as they dry out. To keep your traps going, you may have to moisten the baits every day or so, depending on the type of bait you use. Or recharge the traps often with fresh materials. *Remember, the trap will work only as well as the bait you use!*

You may have to do some experimenting to see which baits work best for your fly species, location, and conditions. Not all flies are alike in their food preferences. Blow flies, or calliphorids (medium-to large-bodied shiny metallic-colored flies), feed primarily on carrion (dead tissue of animals, or meat scraps, and so on, as in garbage cans), whereas the typical house flies (the medium- to small-bodied greyish-brown flies with striped backs) are attracted to a wide variety of food wastes and animal manures.

To avoid "putting all your bait in one basket," so to speak, you might want to use a combination of baits. For instance, combine something sweet and smelly (fermenting) with meat scraps, or dead snails, or fish heads, or the like, *and* with some animal manure. Dog droppings are usually quite readily available, and chicken manure mixed with broken eggs works well, particularly for the blow flies.

Mixtures of cornmeal and molasses will ferment and attract house flies (*Musca domestica*), the common greenbottle flies (*Phoenicia seriata*), and others. The advantage of this mixture over others is that the flies cannot breed in it as they can in the other baits. The disadvantages of this bait is its cost. It also takes a while before it ferments and becomes attractive. Yeast can be added to speed up the process.

Placement of the Trap: Trap location is important because if you place the trap in an area where the bait in your trap will get heavy competition from some other nearby food source, you may not trap many flies at all. On the other hand, if your trap is baited adequately for your conditions, you will be catching flies by the hundreds every day in warm weather. If you must place your trap near competing food sources (an animal yard, for instance), then beef up your bait accordingly.

Ideal placement must be determined individually for each household, and will doubtless shift as the sun, prevailing winds, and household activities shift at different times of the year. Assuming that you are not producing flies on the property (because you are managing kitchen and animal wastes correctly), the ideal place for your flytrap is out near the property line, where they are drawn into your area by the animal smells. Finding this location will take some experimenting; you'll have to learn the air currents and directions from which most of your flies seem to be arriving.

If possible, place the trap in the sunshine; most flies are more active in sunlit areas. Or, if you notice cool-weather flies seeking shaded areas during hot weather, move your traps around accordingly. In general, try to become aware of how the fly activity varies during different times of day. This will help you place traps as well as sticky tapes (a good way to trap the swarms of adult male flies which hover around).

Place the traps away from areas where you do not want a lot of fly activity—away from doorways and entrances, for example. Once the traps are working well, there will be quite a few flies buzzing around them.

If you are concerned about children and pets, just build a shelf to elevate the trap, or place it on top of a drum or barrel to get it up off the ground.

Cleaning the Trap and Harvesting the Flies: Harvesting the dead flies from the trap is very easy using the lift-up panel. The dead flies can be used as food for chickens and other fowl. They are high in protein (as are the garbage and food wastes they feed upon).

The birds are naturally adapted to eating them. However, to avoid any possibility of infecting your chickens with disease organisms that may survive inside the adult flies, it is advisable to sterilize the flies before feeding them to your birds. (Most disease organisms don't survive from the fly's maggot stage to the adult stage, but a few do.) The flies can be sterilized by placing them in a glass jar with a lid and letting them "cook" in the hot sun for a few days. Or you can use a plastic bag. (Glass is better, however, as it does not release materials into the food when heated, while plastic does.) You can also put them in aluminum foil and roast them at high temperatures in the oven or in a fire for thirty minutes. If you are planning to harvest the dead flies for feeding your chickens or fish, and the ants are eating them up before you get to them, place the trap on an ant-exclusion stand (see page 311). If you have no other use for the dead flies, compost them or bury them.

Important! This trap will not work miracles! It will not, in all likelihood, solve the fly problems that are part of a much larger picture of inadequate or inappropriate waste management at a community level. However, this trap *does* enable you to take large quantities of flies out of egg-laying circulation without the use of pesticides, sprays, or pest-strips.

Effective, permanent fly control is possible without heavy reliance on pesticides. "Integrated fly management" combines special waste-management practices with the release of beneficial insects that prey only on flies. Establishment of these parasites and predators results in the biological control of fly populations to keep them well below intolerable levels. Integrated fly management is not an instant solution, but it is the only environmentally sound strategy.

For more information about this type of fly control program, see Chapter 13. You can also get information and purchase natural enemies from Beneficial Biosystems, 1523 63rd Street, Department N8, Emeryville, California 84608; Rincon-Vitova Insectaries, Inc., P.O. Box 95, Oakview, California 93022; Spaulding Laboratories, Route 2, Box 737, Printz Road, Arroyo Grande, California 93420.

Culling: Hens should be removed from the flock when they are no longer laying (see Figure 10-16 for ways to handle a chicken). You can ascertain that they have reached this stage by feeling the distance between the pubic bones with your fingers. If the bones are two fingers apart and feel flexible, and the comb and wattles of the hen appear pale the hen is still laying. The reverse means she is already, or becoming, unproductive. Since chickens, unlike rabbits, become very tough as they grow older, it is wise to butcher them as soon as they are no longer laying well. The other reason for culling from your flock (besides removing noisy roosters), is to remove sick chickens.

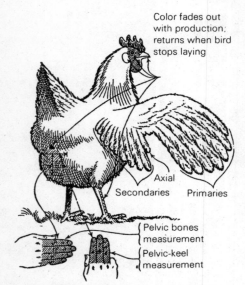

Color fades out with production; returns when bird stops laying

Axial

Secondaries   Primaries

Pelvic bones measurement

Pelvic-keel measurement

The three principal points to look for when culling: A space the width of two or more fingers between the pelvic bones and four or more fingers between the pelvic and keel bones indicates the hen is laying. Pigmentation tells how long she has been laying. If yellow color has faded out of vent, eye ring, ear lobes only, she has been laying only a few days; fading from entire beak indicates four to six weeks of production; bleached shanks indicate five to six months of laying. Good layers molt rapidly, losing two, three or more primary feathers at once. Poor hens lose their primaries one at a time.

Source: *From Chick to Layer—A Complete Guide Book for Poultry Raisers,* published by Poultry Tribune.

Figure 10-16. **Two Methods for Carrying a Large Hen**

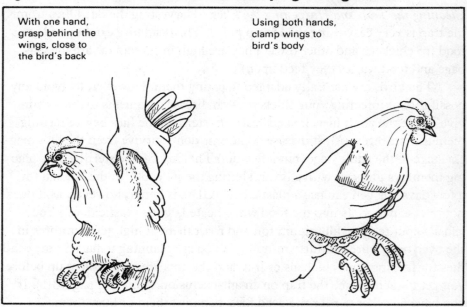

With one hand, grasp behind the wings, close to the bird's back

Using both hands, clamp wings to bird's body

Disease Prevention: Chickens are susceptible to a wide variety of pathogens and parasites. For a few diseases, such as Newcastle disease, you may wish to provide immunization. This will depend to a large extent on the amount of commercial chicken raising that goes on in your area. The newspapers generally report any disease outbreaks in the state, and that is the time to call your state public health department to find out what measures are being advised, and where you can go to obtain the necessary treatments for your flock. Since problems and procedures vary around the nation and from time to time, it is pointless to attempt to advise you in this book.

Slaughtering and Butchering: People who have memories of old-time farm homestead chicken slaughtering usually assume that this aspect of flock management must be a rather grim and bloody affair. Chickens were often beheaded with an axe and left to flop about the yard until all muscle reflex action ended. Our methods are not as spectacular, create far less of a mess, and are a more uplifting emotional experience.

The chicken to be slaughtered is carried by the feet to a tree branch or horizontal board from which a rope or strip of rag is strung. Chickens generally remain calm when carried upside down this way, and it is the common way of transporting them to market for trade or sale in most rural areas. The chicken is tied by the legs and suspended upside down (see Figure 10-17A). The wings can be restrained to prevent flapping and splattering of blood.

The head is then grasped with one hand, with a thumb under the beak as shown in Figure 10-17B. The neck is stretched down gently toward the ground, and with a very sharp knife a cut is made in the neck just above the point where the head joins it. The neck is *not* cut through, but cut deeply enough to let the blood flow freely onto the ground. (This is nitrogen fertilizer for the tree, as those who have bought blood meal in the store no doubt realize.) It is important to continue to hold the head firmly, because for two or three minutes after the chicken loses consciousness, the wings may flap reflexively. We have started to experiment with a bloodless, more humane process for killing chickens. It is also faster then using a knife. A chicken can be killed by squeezing with two hands around the backbone beneath the ribs. This increases the pressure in the abdominal cavity, which stops blood flow to the heart, causing the bird to die of a heart attack.

The following are some preventive measures to keep your flock healthy:

1. Make sure their water is kept clean.

2. Give the chickens a well-ventilated, dry area in which to live.

3. Provide them with a roost so they can perch above their manure.

4. Cull any chickens immediately if they appear sick. Ideally, you should have a separate cage to which you can confine for observation any chicken that is not behaving normally, away from the rest of the flock. When in doubt, kill, bury or compost the chicken. Through experience you will learn the appearance of the healthy chicken's internal organs. How the chicken looks when you are cleaning and preparing it for cooking will tell you a great deal about your flock's state of health. You can check the liver for spots which indicate pathogens, parasites, or tumors. A pale overall color suggests deneration or fatty infiltration. If the liver edge is not sharp, the liver is swollen, indicating presence of a toxic or disease process.

5. Chickens given occasional access to fine, dry dust, will give themselves baths in it to keep down external parasites.

Figure 10-17. **Slaughtering and Preparing a Chicken**

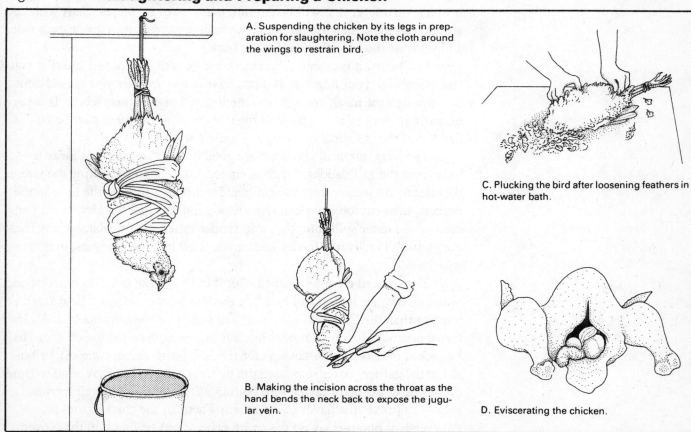

A. Suspending the chicken by its legs in preparation for slaughtering. Note the cloth around the wings to restrain bird.

B. Making the incision across the throat as the hand bends the neck back to expose the jugular vein.

C. Plucking the bird after loosening feathers in hot-water bath.

D. Eviscerating the chicken.

287

Once the bird is quiet it is ready to be plucked. Take it down and submerge it in a big pot of boiling water, holding it there for two or three minutes. (Use a towel or potholder to protect your hand from the steam.) This process will loosen the feathers, after which they can be pulled out by hand. The exceptions are some of the wing and tail-feathers on older birds, which may require the additional aid of a pair of pliers. Since plucking is a bit messy, you will want to spread some newspapers for this, or do it outdoors if the weather permits. If the skin is not desired for eating or flavoring a broth, the chicken may be skinned with its feathers still attached. Feathers and skin may be returned to the other chickens to be picked over, along with the dead chicken's head. Or this material may be placed in a bucket of sawdust to await the making of the next batch of hot compost, or buried in the garden. In the latter case, the burial must be deep enough and covered over well enough so that the material does not betray itself to rats, dogs, or other animals that would be interested in digging it up.

The next step is cleaning the chicken. For this, a sharp knife and poultry shears are best. If the chicken is to be left whole for roasting and/or stuffing, then cuts should be made with a knife around the neck, down to the bone, through the air passageway, and around the anus (see Figure 10-17D). Reach your hand inside, carefully disengage the internal organs from the body cavity, and slo-o-o-o-wly draw them out. A membrane (diaphragm) lies between these organs and the chest cavity and this is what one is feeling for in order to separate the two. With experience, the entire mass can be drawn out cleanly. Since it is easier to do this after you have seen a chicken's organs spread out, perhaps the first attempt at cleaning the chicken should be made on a fryer that will be cut into many separate pieces. Start with cuts around the anus, then use the shears or knife up across the ribs on each side, and separate the breastbone from the back.

In all cuts, it is essential that the knife be well-sharpened and that you feel along with your finger as you cut, so that you are sure you are only cutting through the meat, and not into the internal organs themselves. It is particularly important not to cut into the intestines, as the meat may be off-flavored if the intestinal contents are spilled upon it.

The liver, gizzard, and heart are good to eat. Carefully cut away the liver from the gallbladder, which is embedded in it. In separating the two, it is better to cut well around the gallbladder, losing a little of the liver in the process, than cut too close and risk nicking into the gall bladder. If the contents of the latter spills out, they will render bitter and unpalatable any meat they touch. The liver is tender and can be fried in a few minutes, in butter with onions.

The gizzard must be cleaned. Cut it in half, wash out the contents, and under cold water loosen and pull free the tough inner lining. The gizzard is tougher than the liver, and is best stewed slowly or pressure cooked. All internal organs that you do not wish to eat can be returned to the chickens to be picked over, stored in sawdust for the next batch of hot compost, or buried in the garden. After removing the internal organs, you may wish to rinse the inside of the body cavity with boiling water. (Some cooks claim this greatly improves the flavor of the meat.) Then cut the chicken into pieces. An excellent photo-essay on the entire process can be found in the November 1977 issue of *Countryside Magazine*.

Usually, when the feathers are removed, long "hairs" are left behind clinging to the skin. If these are objectionable they may be singed off over a candle or gas flame. This is easy to do after the chicken has been cut into serving-size pieces.

A note of caution: Chicken, like fish, spoils easily and should be cooled down and refrigerated or frozen quickly after slaughtering. All raw meats (and the shells of uncooked eggs) are likely to carry salmonella, an organism that can cause severe diarrhea and intestinal cramps if ingested. Thus, hands and all utensils that come into contact with raw meat should be washed carefully. Any wooden cutting board that has been used for raw meat should be salted down well after washing. The best precaution against salmonella poisoning is to use one board exclusively for raw meat and a separate one for vegetables and fruits that are to be eaten raw.

Space Requirements: Each chicken should have a minimum of four square feet (184 square centimeters) of living space and approximately seven inches (18 centimeters) of roost. They do not need direct sunlight, but good ventilation is important. Adequate protection from chilling winds and rain is essential. If the chicken house is placed in full sun, a shady retreat will be needed. As suggested on page 282, either a separate facility or a portion of the larger pen should be set aside for the young chicks to retreat into, unless all the chickens are kept separately, or by twos, in individual cages.

Layers that are not in individual cages need nest boxes to lay their eggs in. These should be approximately a foot (thirty centimeters) square, and situated in the darkest portion of the chicken house. Only one box is needed for every four or five chickens. It should have a low bar at its entrance to prevent the eggs from rolling out. If this lifts out, it will make the periodic cleaning of the nest boxes easier. This is necessary since they will eventually become contaminated with small amounts of manure and occasional broken eggs. There seems to be less egg breakage if the boxes are kept filled with soft nesting materials such as straw, dried grass, leaves, or weeds. This material will have to be renewed weekly.

Chickens that become used to pecking at their eggs are a real nuisance. Often this can be corrected by increasing the amount of calcium in the diet and making the nest boxes softer and stuffed more fully with dried vegetation. Where the hen persists in this behavior, she might best be killed and eaten, since the others may learn this habit from her by imitation.

There should be a perch in front of the nest boxes so that the chickens can get up to them easily. It is important to have easy access from the outside to the boxes, and to the indoor coop in general, for egg removal, cleaning, and checking of chickens. Chickens are very docile at night. This is the best time to lift them out to examine or transport them to another area.

The major factor influencing cage design is the manure-management system you have chosen to follow. The two basic systems—deep litter and tray accumulation—and variants of each, are discussed on pages 253–56. (Deep litter, with chickens under rabbit cages, is discussed on page 259.) Figure 10-18 shows a cut-away view of a hen house designed to be used in conjunction with an outdoor run area, as is illustrated in Figure 10-4, page

To save energy in cooking an old chicken, use a pressure cooker, adding onions, garlic or other spices at the beginning, so that the flavors become absorbed into the meat. It is difficult to gauge the time required, since toughness varies. The best plan is to use approximately ten pounds pressure and cool down and check the contents of the pot after twenty minutes, continuing the process until the meat is fork-tender and falls from the bones. Then, if possible, separate meat from broth and chill the latter until the fat is solid and can be removed easily. Old chickens make fine-flavored soup or broth. Since it is difficult to find such chicken in the market for this purpose, this is one of the real boons in raising your own.

Housing

In designing your chickens' system, you need to take into consideration the following factors:

1. Space requirements, both in terms of location within your yard area and of the chicken's needs
2. Manure management and other sanitation requirements
3. Feeding and watering systems, in regard to time and skills required for construction and maintenance
4. Other maintenance considerations, such as egg removal, new additions to the flock, and so on.

Figure 10-18. **Construction Drawing of Typical Henhouse**

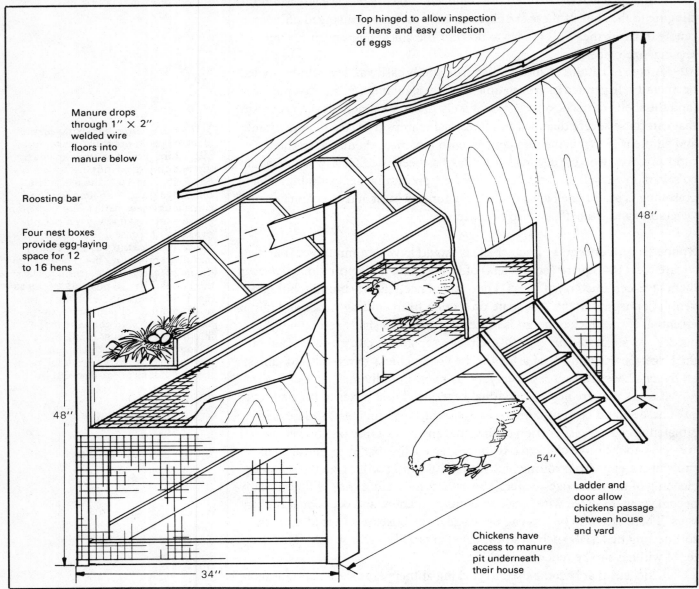

Top hinged to allow inspection of hens and easy collection of eggs

Manure drops through 1″ × 2″ welded wire floors into manure below

Roosting bar

Four nest boxes provide egg-laying space for 12 to 16 hens

48″

48″

48″

34″

54″

Ladder and door allow chickens passage between house and yard

Chickens have access to manure pit underneath their house

259. Manure from the house drops through welded wire floors into a portion of the chicken yard below. Chickens have access to the manure collection areas, so they can keep the fly problem under control.

Feeding and Watering Systems: Feeding regimes are discussed on page 283, and provisions for feeding and watering day-old chicks are discussed on page 281. With adults, the same basic concern should dominate design requirements as with the chicks: avoid wastage and contamination. Water that spills onto the manure will eventually create fly problems. Feed that spills where chickens cannot get it is costly. The latter is less of a problem with whole or cracked grains, which the chickens are expert at picking up off the ground, than it is with mash, which when spilled is essentially lost.

Both feed and water must be kept free of fecal materials and other debris. This can be accomplished both by design of the dispensing devices and

Figure 10-19. **A Wire Manger for Feeding Vegetable Material to Chickens**

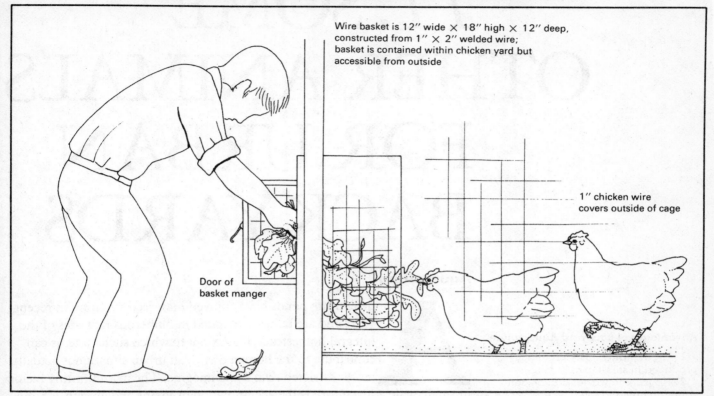

Wire basket is 12″ wide × 18″ high × 12″ deep, constructed from 1″ × 2″ welded wire; basket is contained within chicken yard but accessible from outside

1″ chicken wire covers outside of cage

Door of basket manger

by their placement in the chicken area. The drawing opposite is an example of a commercially available waterer.

A wire manger built into the side of a chicken yard and accessible from the outside is shown in Figure 10-19. A manger keeps vegetable material off the ground of the coop, and encourages the efficient and sanitary feeding of leafy greens and garden wastes to the chickens.

If you wish to set up a feeding system that allows the chickens to go for a week or two at a time without your attention, you will need to increase the numbers or sizes of your feeding and watering devices accordingly.

11. SOME OTHER ANIMALS FOR URBAN BACKYARDS

Aquaculture

Advantages of Backyard Aquaculture

1. High quality, tasty protein is produced in small increments.

2. Household wastes can be converted to human food. The energy by which this food is produced would have been lost as heat if the wastes were composted.

3. Macronutrients—especially nitrogen and phosphorus, present in fish excretions—as well as many micronutrients are available for garden plants if pond water is used for watering.

4. Aquatic plants can be grown for human and livestock food.

5. Invertebrate food animals can be cultured with wastes in very limited space and used as aquaculture feed or sold at premium prices in the aquarium pet trade.

6. Aquaculture animals are quiet and do not create odors when alive.

7. With good design aquaculture ponds can be very pleasing aesthetically, and can make a significant contribution to the human use of the backyard space.

8. With proper attention fish can be raised which are much less polluted than those sold in the market.

9. Good quality feed plus extreme freshness make for remarkably good flavor in backyard pond fish as compared with those otherwise available in the city.

10. Raising aquatic animals is extremely interesting to some people and is an excellent way to learn biological and ecological principles.

Aquaculture ponds have enjoyed increased attention in recent years and are naively included in numerous fantasies of the integral homestead. The extent to which such systems can contribute to the human diet in an urban situation is actually more restricted than some imagine. The main limiting factor in small-scale aquaculture is the accumulation of toxins and growth-inhibiting wastes and metabolites in the water. Terrestrial husbandry systems largely avoid this problem, because wastes are either carried off in the air, absorbed into the soil, or can be easily removed mechanically. When water quality problems are solved, the next limiting factor is the territorial behavior of the animals raised. Trophic (feeding level) limitations constitute the third factor.

The trophic limitations are a matter of ecosystem dynamics. Only 1 percent of the sun's energy falling upon typical vegetables is generally fixed as tissue under field situations, although higher efficiencies have been achieved with other plants under laboratory conditions (see the earlier discussion of the photosynthetic efficiency rate, page 28). Another way of expressing this rate is to say that 1000 kilocalories of light energy can produce ten kilocalories (2.5 grams) of plant matter. Animals eating those plants (in this instance, fish) can obtain only 10 percent of the energy originally utilized by the plants. And animals eating those animals (humans eating fish) can obtain only 1 percent of the energy originally utilized by the plants.

With these facts at our disposal, some aspects of aquaculture quickly become obvious. For example, one could get the most food energy (calories) out of a given pond area by eating the plants, not animals, grown in it directly. In fact, there are edible species of algae that can be consumed directly, such as *Chlorella* sp. Next best is to raise a plant-eating fish and eat that. The least amount of energy in a pond system would be derived from the raising of carnivorous fish exclusively. Figure 11-1 shows that by the time catfish, the carnivorous fish, are harvested, only 67 kcals per day of food energy would be derived from a daily algae production of 2700 kcal.

292

Significant losses of usable energy are sustained in the conversion of algae to zooplankton and then zooplankton to catfish.

Aquaculture systems, especially backyard ones, do not exactly fit the trophic model in Figure 11-1, however, because feed, kitchen wastes, and weeds from outside the pond can be used as food for the fish, or feed animals can be cultured from them. The backyard fish pond can thus be part of a detritivore system in which a very rich food source (garbage) supports several trophic levels. Here too each level receives 10 percent of the energy of the preceding level.

Nevertheless, number of calories alone is not the only reason for wanting to include animal protein such as fish in the diet. Fish protein is a high-*quality* protein, meaning that the number and balance of amino acids corresponds closely to that required in human nutrition. Most aquaculture animals are smaller than other livestock, which means that they can be conveniently harvested in increments proportional to the daily need for animal protein in the human diet.

Furthermore, fish or crayfish provide variety in the diet, an important factor if the household is subsisting on home-raised vegetables supplemented by grains. Such fare can grow monotonous for some, even when dairy products and eggs are added. And there is a certain fascination in raising aquatic animals, so maintaining an aquaculture system for the purposes of recreation alone and the information one can learn about biological systems should not be discounted. However, the reader is warned that such systems are complex and may take a great deal of attention.

The advantages and disadvantages of maintaining backyard aquaculture systems are summarized in the margins.

Figure 11-1. **Aquacultured Food Chain, Showing Trophic Levels**

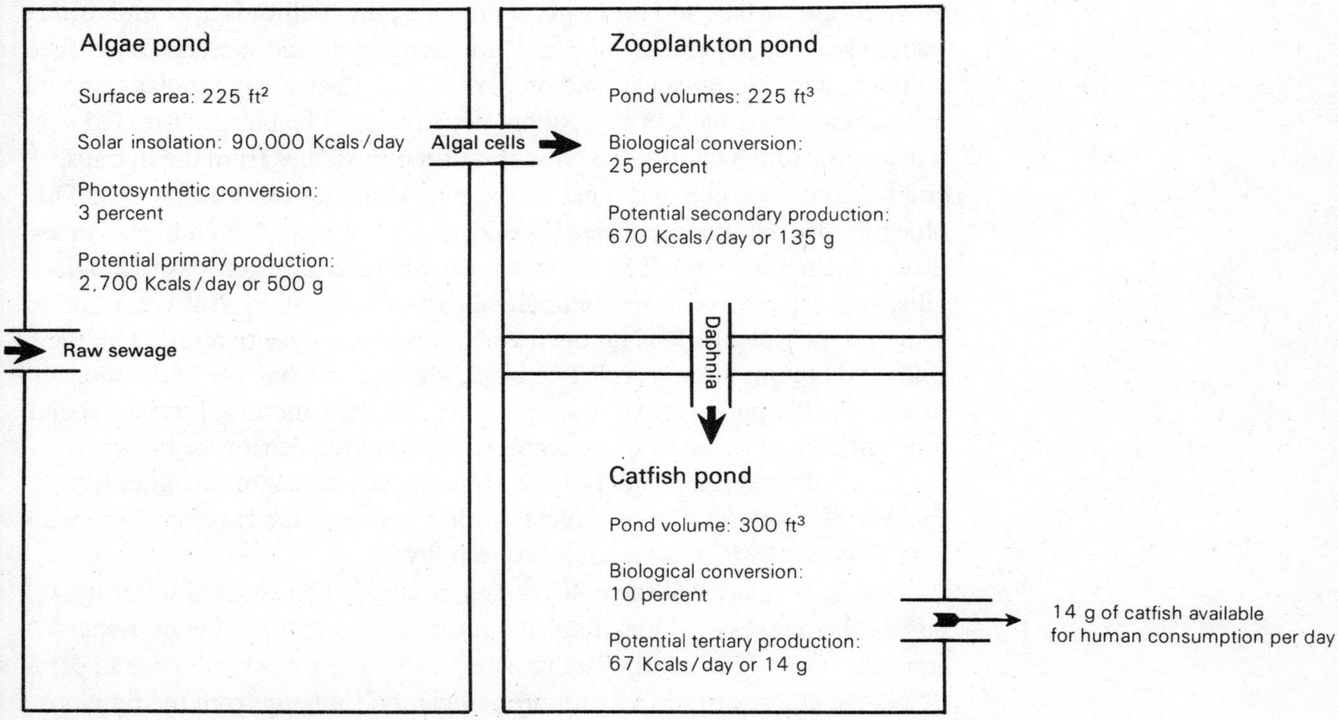

Algae pond

Surface area: 225 ft^2

Solar insolation: 90,000 Kcals/day

Photosynthetic conversion: 3 percent

Potential primary production: 2,700 Kcals/day or 500 g

Raw sewage

→ Algal cells →

Zooplankton pond

Pond volumes: 225 ft^3

Biological conversion: 25 percent

Potential secondary production: 670 Kcals/day or 135 g

Daphnia

Catfish pond

Pond volume: 300 ft^3

Biological conversion: 10 percent

Potential tertiary production: 67 Kcals/day or 14 g

→ 14 g of catfish available for human consumption per day

293

Polyculture in the Pond: Aquaculture has considerable theoretical appeal for those planning to implement the integral house concept. However, actually making a backyard system productive requires extensive knowledge of the biology and behavior of the species raised as well as the artful use of ecological principles in the design of the system. There is no valid cookbook formula for an aquacultural system that will work anywhere. One must always begin by carefully considering the local conditions, designing a system that has the possibility of meeting one's needs, and choosing species that fit that system and each other.

One way to increase the efficiency of backyard fishponds is by using the notion of polyculture skillfully, that is, simulating the development of a natural aquatic community by choosing species whose feeding modes and preferences differ in ways that are complementary. Better use is thus made of food inputs to the pond and, because less food is left over to promote the growth of bacteria and fungi, water quality is improved. At the experimental backyard pond at the Integral Urban House we have found several species combinations which appear to work in this way. For example, in the cooler season we grow *Pacifastacus* crayfish (Figure 11-2) together with rainbow trout. The trout are voracious omnivores that feed at all levels in the water, and the crayfish are bottom scavengers and detritivores. Both species have the same preferred temperature range. The crayfish eat whatever food is missed by the trout as well as coarse plant material that the trout do not eat, and they also consume the trout excrement, which would otherwise accumulate on the bottom. As detritivores, they live in large part on bacteria growing on decayed matter. Both trout and crayfish grow rapidly under these conditions, and water quality is much better than if the trout are raised alone.

In the warm season, from May to October, we have been using a combination of bluegills, black bullhead catfish, and Sacramento blackfish. The bluegills are surface and midwater omnivores, the bullheads are omnivorous bottom scavengers, and the blackfish are omnivorous feeders. The latter feed on the bottom, in midwater, and on the surface. They are phytoplankton and zooplankton filter feeders and bottom detritivores. The bluegills are fed redworms (from a culture fed on rabbit droppings), flies from the flytraps, and fresh corn kernels and other soft vegetable matter from the garden. The bluegills also get numerous dead bees, which are dropped from hives immediately facing the pond. The bullheads eat whatever fare gets past the bluegills, and also receive some commercial catfish feed pellets. Bullheads and to some extent bluegills feed on the filamentous green algae that grows on the sides and bottom of the pond. The blackfish feed on whatever of the food tossed into the pond is small enough to get into their mouths, but they spend much of their time vertically oriented as they gobble detritus or browse on the filamentous green algae. In feeding on the excrement of the other fish species the blackfish occupy a niche similar to that of the crayfish in the winter polyculture, and are growing very rapidly.

About a quarter of the pond surface is covered by a raft of water hyacinth, which gives the bluegills shady refuge and takes up some nutrients from the water. The pond water remains surprisingly clear, which is in part due to the efficacy of the polyculture association (judging from the previous

Figure 11-2. **Some Species for a Polycultural Fish Pond**

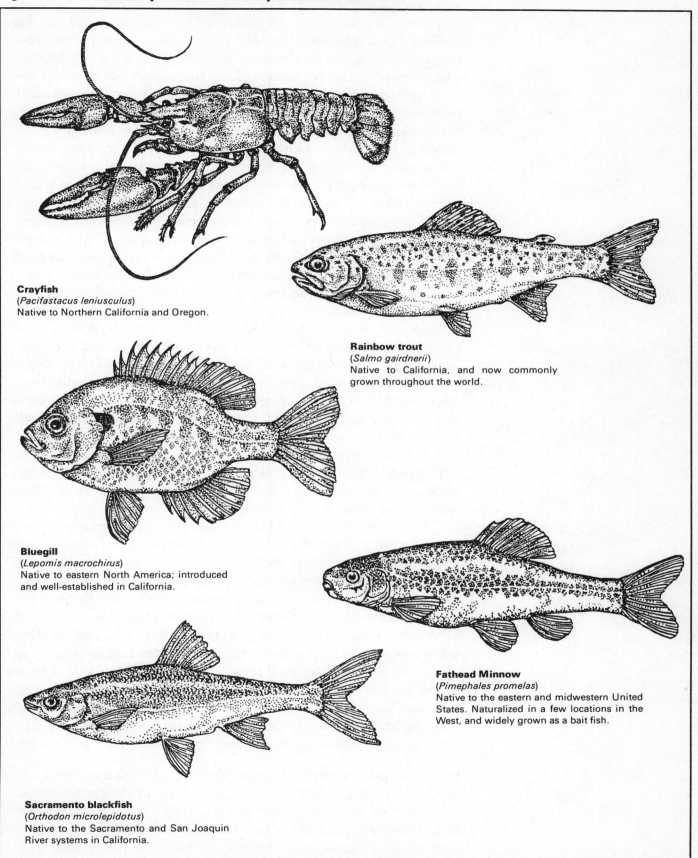

Crayfish
(*Pacifastacus leniusculus*)
Native to Northern California and Oregon.

Rainbow trout
(*Salmo gairdnerii*)
Native to California, and now commonly grown throughout the world.

Bluegill
(*Lepomis macrochirus*)
Native to eastern North America; introduced and well-established in California.

Fathead Minnow
(*Pimephales promelas*)
Native to the eastern and midwestern United States. Naturalized in a few locations in the West, and widely grown as a bait fish.

Sacramento blackfish
(*Orthodon microlepidotus*)
Native to the Sacramento and San Joaquin River systems in California.

year when biological filter and hyacinths were present as now but blackfish were raised alone).

We present these examples because we have had experience with them under backyard conditions. The variety of possible polyculture combinations is very great, and the likelihood of success depends not only upon a wise choice of species, but upon stocking ratios, size of fishes, types of food input, pond design, and other physical conditions. The most sophisticated polyculture described in the literature is the classical Chinese pond cultivation of several carp species with differing feeding niches. Another polyculture technique that is widely used is the stocking of a predatory fish to prevent overpopulation and stunting of the primary fish being raised. Examples of this approach are the use of pike or brown trout in carp ponds in Europe, and of snakeheads in Southeast Asian polyculture.

A more familiar application of this predator principle is the stocking of farm ponds with a bluegill-largemouth bass combination. The intention is to provide bluegill as forage for the bass. Unfortunately, sportsmen are much more interested in catching bass than bluegill. The bass are usually soon fished out, with the result that the bluegills overpopulate and become stunted. The few large bass that remain are unable to reproduce because their eggs are devoured by hordes of hungry little bluegills. However, if one harvests only bluegills and returns all bass caught, a farm pond initially stocked with the proper ratios will continue to produce good crops of large, edible-sized bluegills for many years with no supplementary feeding or other management required. Fertilization of the water will increase productivity as long as the pond is not overeutrophied (in which case microorganisms would compete with fish for oxygen).

For those fortunate enough to have a farm pond, this method of managing the bluegill-bass combination allows an annual harvest of more than two hundred pounds per acre with virtually no maintenance expense. With fertilization considerably higher yields can be realized.

If one is mainly interested in producing tasty and cheap animal protein for the human diet, a small farm pond can be used to grow fathead minnows (Figure 11-2). These little fish are mainly vegetarian (see Table 11-1), and increase very rapidly since they can go through two generations in a year. They are soft-rayed and can be eaten like sardines—bones, intestines, and all—even at the adult size of three to four inches. The gall bladder imparts a bitter taste and should best be snipped out of each fish with a pair of scissors, before cooking. Once this is done the fathead minnows are surprisingly tasty and make a good breakfast fried in patties or put into an omelette. They can also be dried and stored easily. The culinary properties of these little fish have been largely ignored because we think of them as bait minnows. In Asia small fishes are often eaten. Because the whole fish is eaten they are nutritionally superior to the large fillets of fish muscle prized in the West.

Intensive Aquaculture: If you are determined to raise fish in your urban backyard some degree of intensiveness will be required to increase per area productivity to the point where it can make a significant contribution to the family's diet. The rewards are likely to be educational, symbolic, and gustatory rather than economic. However, if water from the pond is used in the garden, the fertilizer equivalent of the nutrients supplied should be considered as an additional benefit. Since it will probably cost at least $100 to construct a 100 square foot pond and several hundred dollars more to build a pump and filter system, the initial costs are high, since if you can produce more than twenty-five pounds of fish a year from such a pond you will be in the forefront of America's backyard aquaculture innovators.

Intensive systems use artificial means to perform life-support functions that would be carried out by natural processes in more extensive systems. By the use of technological means of aeration, waste removal, and temperature control it is possible to reach truly phenomenal productivities, exceeding a pound of fish per cubic foot of water per year, but these techniques are extremely energy-intensive, and the cost of electricity keeps going up. Moreover, if one talks with people who have had experience in maintaining intensive aquaculture systems for several years, they will usually tell you about the time when they went away for the weekend and a power failure or some other mishap occurred, and when they came back on Monday all the fish were dead.

It is probably the course of wisdom for the backyard aquaculturalist to use artificial supports only to promote growth, not to sustain life. This means settling for a moderate degree of intensity and a moderate level of production. Wind- or solar-powered support systems are adequate for this level of intensity. Fish under conditions too severe to allow growth may survive for extended periods of time if they are not too crowded. In such intermittent situations a pond will fluctuate between maintenance and growth.

Although aeration may be critical for a backyard pond in extremely hot weather or when the water is eutrophic, the support function most in need of

Table 11-1. **Some Species for Polyculture**[*]

Common and Scientific Name	Preferred Temperature	Feeding Mode	Breeding Regime	Approximate Annual Yield
Rainbow trout (*Salmo gairdnerii*)	55–70°F (82°F lethal)	In nature, carnivorous (worms, insects, etc.); in culture, omnivorous (will eat wide variety of meat and grain preparations)	Hatchery spawning (artificial)	0.5 lb/ft^2 in intensive culture; 100 lb/acre in pond culture
Sacramento blackfish (*Orthodon microlepidotus*)	60–75°F	When under five inches long eats small aquatic animals; when larger, a bottom detritivore and filter-feeder on phytoplankton and zooplankton; also eats decaying weeds	Pond spawning in spring	800 lb/acre in pond culture
Fathead minnow (*Pimephales promelas*)	60–85°F (95°F lethal)	Omnivorous but primarily eats filamentous algae, decaying weeds, and small aquatic animals	Pond spawning in spring and summer	3000 lb/acre in pond culture w/supplemental feed; 1000 lb/acre without feed
Bluegill (*Lepomis macrochirus*)	60–77°F	Omnivorous, but primarily carnivorous; eats insects, isopods, amphipods, worms, etc., also filamentous algae and decaying weeds	Pond spawning in spring and summer	0.5 lb/ft^2 in intensive culture; 300 lb/acre in ponds
Pacific crayfish (*Pacifastacus leniusculus*)	60–72°F (inactive above 75°)	Omnivorous; eats wide variety of plant and animal matter and detritus	Winter spawning in fallow swimming pools or garden ponds	0.5 lb/ft^2 in intensive culture; 400 lb/acre in ponds

[*]Information courtesy of Sterling Bunnell, Farallones Institute, Berkeley, California.

assistance is waste removal. Most aquatic animals excrete nitrogen in the form of ammonia, which is quite toxic to them. In confined spaces it accumulates to levels that inhibit growth and then to slightly higher levels which cause death. Certain bacteria (*Nitrosomas*) oxidize ammonia (NH_3) to nitrite (NO_2), and other bacteria (*Nitrobacter*) oxidize nitrite to nitrate (NO_3). Since nitrate is hundreds of times less toxic to fish than ammonia, the aquaculturalist can greatly increase the carrying capacity and productivity of a recirculating aquatic system by promoting this conversion. This can be done by means of a biological filter. The water is pumped through a bed of gravel or other granular substance, such as crushed clam shells. The bacteria attach to the granular surfaces and to particles of detritus that accumulate in the interspaces. Water must pass through the filter bed uniformly and have sufficient dissolved oxygen, since the nitrifying bacteria require oxygen to do their work. With the energy derived from the oxidation of ammonia they convert carbon dioxide into carbohydrates for their own use. Nitrifying bacteria have been found to be 100 times more numerous in the filter bed than in the water of the tank.

Many species of freshwater fish secrete hormonelike substances that inhibit growth when they reach sufficient concentrations in the water. These substances are eventually broken down by bacteria. It seems likely that a biological filter may provide a substrate where breakdown of these substances could occur more rapidly, although this remains to be conclusively demonstrated.

If the supply of water is not limited to a certain slope, problems can be circumvented by use of a throughput system (a system which allows water to continuously enter and leave the pond at the same rate). With crowding-tolerant fish such as trout or catfish, extremely high productivities can be reached with intensive throughput systems.

The Wind-Powered Pump and Filter: The following description of the wind-powered pump and biological filter at the Integral House in Berkeley is adapted from one written by Tom Fricke for the Farallones Institute 1978 Report. Fricke, together with Peter Holloway, built the system pictured in Figure 11-3, largely out of scavenged parts from various automobile graveyards and dump sites.

The aquaculture system in the southwest corner of the Integral Urban House garden employs a unique device, called the Savonius Rotor, to prevent our pond from becoming stagnant and eutrophic. The rotor takes its name from J. Savonius, a Finnish engineer who studied the aerodynamic properties of S-shaped vertical (upright) axis turbines. The design is from the early 1930s.

The wind machine is constructed of three recycled 55-gallon drums that have been cut in half longitudinally. The halves are positioned on three tiers, clamped between plates of salvaged lumber, and offset at 60-degree angles around a 1-inch shaft of discarded steel.

The Savonius can catch winds from any direction, and a gust of seven-to-eight-miles per hour will start the machine moving. Rotation will continue until the windspeed dies down to below 3 miles per hour, since the thrust bearings on which the mill is mounted are quite frictionless. Although

Disadvantages of Backyard Aquaculture

1. Aquaculture is usually considerably more expensive than fishing. On the small backyard scale it is especially so.

2. Certain constraints to productivity, such as water quality and territoriality, are most critical for small-scale systems.

3. The limited pond space available in backyards mandates some degree of intensiveness in aquaculture. More attention and expertise is required to maintain intensive systems than extensive systems such as farm ponds.

4. Disease and parasites can spread rapidly through intensive ponds.

5. Intensive systems require high initial capital expenditures relative to the value of annual production.

6. A sufficient stock of young fish must be available. Breeding and caring for young often requires special conditions and expertise.

7. Aquacultural productivity is dependent on temperature.

8. Quality of available water may limit aquacultural possibilities.

9. Ponds can act as traps for airborne pollutants.

10. Damage to local natural ecosystems, often irreversible, can result from the escape or release of exotic aquaculture organisms.

Figure 11-3. **Wind Aquaculture Unit**

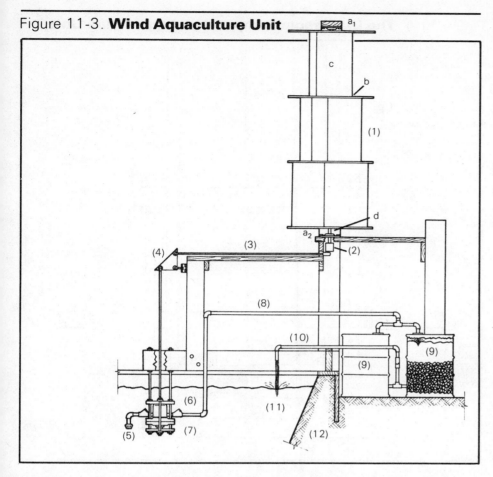

Key to Wind Aquaculture Units

(1) Savonius rotor vertical axis wind turbine
  - (a_1) flange-mounted bearing
  - (a_2) flange-mounted thrust bearing
  - (b) plywood end-caps, with 1" flange for mounting axial shaft
  - (c) bisected oil-drum (or aluminum, fiberglass, etc., sheet) impellers, offset 60°, bracket mounted
  - (d) 1" rolled steel bar, axial shaft

(2) Eccentric-mounted bushing
(3) Lightweight scrap aluminum linkage, pump rods
(4) Triangular bell crank
(5) Inlet pipe with strainer
(6) Pump stirrups
(7) Handmade diaphragm pump
(8) 1" water pipe, for delivery from pump to filtration unit
(9) Oil-drum biological filtration unit (one drum is shown in section)
(10) Filtered water delivery pipe
(11) Fish pond, lined with Hypalon and formboards
(12) Tamped earth

high torques are achieved with this device due to its enormous size, the Savonius rarely achieves high rpms (rotations per minute). Mechanical energy conversion seems to be an ideal use of the wind energy rather than electrical energy, which requires both high wind speeds and rpms. With linkage improvised from scrap metal and spare parts, we converted the rotational force to vertical strokes which activate a homemade diaphragm pump, submerged in the pond (details of construction are shown in Figure 11-4).

The pump raises water to a biological filtration unit which is housed in another steel drum, the top of which is five feet above the surface of the water. Primary filtration of large particles is achieved by a felt bag located on top of the drum, and secondary filtration consists of a bed of crushed oyster shells that fills the drum. The toxic ammonia and growth-inhibiting hormones excreted by the fish are removed by bacteria lodged in the oyster shell bed of the filter. Filtered water passes through a faucet aerator to restore oxygen to the pond to complete the cycle.

We have estimated that in a 15–mile-per-hour wind, the Savonius can cycle 1.5 gallons of water per minute through the filter. Though seemingly not a great amount of pumping power, 8 hours of pumping will circulate nearly 750 gallons of water, or one third of the pond's volume, which is our optimum design consideration.

Pond Construction: The pond should be constructed so that it is easy to net the fish out when they are to be harvested or examined. If the water is at

Figure 11-4. **The Diaphragm Pump on the Aquaculture Unit**

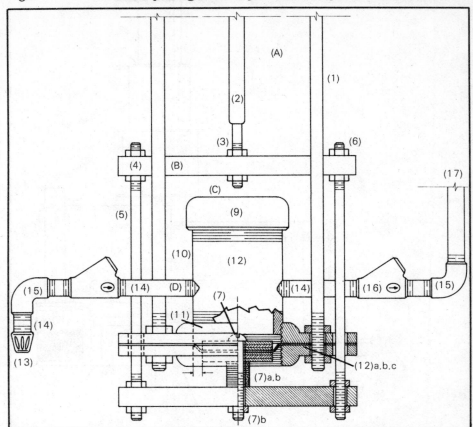

Key to the Diaphragm Pump

(A) *Linkage and support connectors:*
  (1) threaded ¾″ bar, to connect entire pump from support members above pond to submerged level-bars inserted into four of six 4″ flange holes.
  (2) lightweight aluminum pumprod, transfers vertical strokes from linkage to Savonius Rotor
  (3) adjustable mechanism
    (a) threaded ½″ bar, inserted into pumprod
    (b) ½″ machine nut

(B) *Stirrups:*
  (4) ¾″ × 1¼″ aluminum stock, drilled as shown
  (5) ¾″ bar, threaded on both ends
  (6) ⅜″ machine nuts
  (7) ⅜″ machine bolt, approximately 3¼″ long
    (a) metal spacers
    (b) ⅜″ machine nut

(C) *Pump chamber:*
  (9) 4″ threaded cap (metal or ABS plastic)
  (10) 4″ double nipple, tapped and drilled on sides to receive 1″ pipe nipples
  (11) 4″ pipe flange
  (12) Rubber diaphragm, approximately ³⁄₃₂″ thick (from discarded truck tire tube)
    (a) holes cut into the rubber at flange bolt holes
    (b) fit snugly flat to insure that there are no leaks
    (c) diaphragm, when flexed, during pump stroke

(D) *Delivery and supply pipe:*
  (13) simple strainer made of screen, affixed by crimped wire or hose clamp
  (14) 1″ pipe nipples
  (15) 1″ elbows
  (16) 1″ nonreturn valves
  (17) supply pipe to filter

least two feet deep in the shallowest part, raccoons (which can be a problem even in cities) may be frustrated in their attempts to catch fish. If the deepest part goes down four feet there will be a certain amount of temperature stability if the weather should suddenly turn extreme. If the pump intake is placed near the bottom of the deepest point circulation within the pond will be optimized.

Finding the right lining material for the pond can be a problem. An earth bottom can be sealed with bentonite (a fine clay powder) but this remains rather "goopy," is hard to clean, and some creatures do not like it although others may find it satisfactory. Heavy polyethylene (5 or 6 mil) is relatively inexpensive but is subject to damage and disintegrates spontaneously after a few months due to the action of the ultraviolet frequencies in sunlight. Black polyethylene lasts somewhat longer than clear, but it too must be replaced after a season. Hypalon is quite durable and is said to be nontoxic, but it is expensive. Other plastic and vinyl lining materials are to be regarded with caution, as they often emit plasticizers and other toxic substances that can kill fish and may not be very good for the people who consume them either. Concrete or ferrocement makes an esthetic and durable coating for a fishpond. It should be leached with several changes of water over a week or so to remove excess alkalinity before fish are introduced. A nontoxic sealer may be required to prevent seepage through the concrete. Although initially more expensive, concrete will last for many years and can be much more interestingly designed than the other materials. Its main disadvantage is that it makes it harder to move your pond if you decide to re-arrange your backyard.

Requirements of the Species Grown: The psychological requirements of fish must be considered in designing a backyard pond. Some fish, such as bluegills, feed better if they have a secluded shelter from which to forage. Food falling within a certain radius of their hiding place is more likely to be taken. Rafts of water hyacinths provide a good shelter of this kind, under which many fish can take refuge at the same time. Trout tend to establish feeding territories in the open water, which they cruise actively. The dominant trout become so voracious and aggressive that less dominant ones are frequently prevented from feeding and so the trout in a pond tend to grow at quite differing rates. This imbalance can be compensated for by periodically harvesting the dominant fish so that the others have a chance to grow faster, or by crowding the trout until they lose much of their territoriality. Bullhead catfish are quite gregarious and will eat more when crowded because they stimulate one another into a feeding frenzy. The territoriality of crayfish appears to be mostly horizontal. Vertically oriented structures such as bundles of weeds or the roots of water hyacinths markedly decrease combat and losses due to cannibalism.

While it makes good sense from the trophic standpoint to raise animals that are at least partially vegetarian, most aquatic animals, especially when young, require at least some animal protein for good growth. The list of invertebrates that can be cultured for fish food is extensive. We have cultured *Daphnia,* ostracods, amphipods, chironomid larvae, mosquito larvae, mayfly larvae, tubifex worms, redworms, and isopods. All were grown on wastes and weeds. Redworms and isopods are good food for larger fish and can be grown with very little effort and attention, whereas the others are mainly for smaller fish and require more care if they are to remain highly productive throughout the year.

The optimum conditions for breeding and rearing young fish are different from those in which the most rapid growth to large size occurs. When fish become reproductive most of their energy goes into behavior rather than growth. Therefore, good breeding situations are not desirable in grow-out ponds. It is advisable to separate breeding ponds from grow-out ponds in urban aquaculture. The best use of most backyard ponds is as grow-out ponds, for which fingerlings are obtained which are of the right size to eat the foods usually available.

Species Selection: Each species of fish or other aquatic animal has a preferred temperature range within which growth occurs most rapidly. Beyond this optimum in either direction growth slows markedly and at either extreme death occurs. The aspiring aquaculturalist would do well to consider raising species that are adapted to the local climate. Much has been written about the aquacultural promise of tropical creatures such as *Tilapia* or the giant freshwater prawn *Macrobrachium,* and many persons living in the temperate zone have been tempted to try them. However, these animals die when the water temperatures drop into the low fifties Fahrenheit. Even when the pond is enclosed in a greenhouse, expensive heating systems are

301

required to keep such species alive through a cold winter. Why not consider bluegills and crayfish, which occupy much the same niches but are adapted to a temperate climate?

The highest productivity can probably be obtained from backyard ponds by double-cropping—that is, growing cool-water species in the colder months and warm-water species in summer. Depending on local conditions, a portable greenhouse may be useful for moderating the climate during the cooler months.

Many state fish and game departments are justifiably concerned about enthusiastic aquaculturalists releasing exotic species into natural waters, and some species with aquacultural potential, such as grass carp, are banned from importation into some states. One need consider only the destruction wrought by the common carp, brought to America as "that most delicious of all fish" or more recently the *Clarias* catfish in Florida, to share their concern.

It is a good idea for aquaculturalists to look at their own region and, as much as possible, stock their ponds with native species or exotic species that are already harmoniously established in local waters. That way, if any individuals escape no great harm will be done. State fish and game departments can usually supply directories of breeders that have fingerling trout, warm-water game fish, and bait fish for sale. Permits from the same agency may be required to buy or transport them.

Keeping Bees in Urban Areas

The integral urban house concept can include beekeeping because of the pollination capabilities of bees and their production of honey and pollen. Beekeeping is one of those hobbies that can be self-supporting, at least to the degree that the household consumes home-produced honey instead of granulated cane or beet sugar bought at the store. Keeping hives in some metropolitan regions can be even more productive than in some rural locations because city people often maintain ornamental plants that bloom more frequently than farm crops, and thus provide nectar and pollen for a larger portion of the year. Although bees will travel a radius of two to five miles from their home seeking flowers, there is probably not enough pollen and nectar-producing foliage in the city to support a hive in every home. Still, it is unlikely that all households will want a beehive. We offer the following discussion for those who do.

The great importance of bees in pollinating crops is rarely understood by city dwellers, whose primary reaction to these insects is often fear of being stung. A number of cities have restrictive ordinances against beekeeping primarily to protect citizens from being stung. But the fact is, less than 1 percent of the population has an allergic reaction to insect stings. For people who do have extreme reactions, the best policy to follow is individual desensitization, a successful procedure available through allergy clinics and doctors who specialize in treating allergies. For the vast majority of people, the likelihood of being stung is slight, and the fear of the possibility is all out of proportion to the consequences.

Once, in our neighborhood, when a swarm of bees clustered on a shrub four feet above the sidewalk in front of a house near ours, a group of pan-icked housewives came over to ask advice, saying, "Please do something, be-cause the young children will be stung." It is true that there are quite a few toddlers on the block as well as some rather mischievous kindergartners. We suggested to the mothers that they relax and not scare the children, but rather encourage them to appreciate this relatively rare and fascinating sight. If the children could be induced to stop and watch quietly, they might learn something.

Since the children took their clues from the warning noises of the in-sects and stayed at a respectful distance, all went well. We proposed making a sign—not for the children, who didn't need it, having enough sense to ap-preciate such a special happening, but for the insect-fearing adults who might be passing by. It read, "See our beautiful bees. Enjoy watching them. Do not disturb them and they will not bother you." All too soon the bees moved on, leaving a number of adults wondering why they had been so frightened.

Such opportunities to observe bees close up can be very valuable in helping people to overcome their fear of them and lead to further tolerance of beekeeping within urban areas. This in turn can result in increased fruit and vegetable yields in home gardens and more honey for the integral urban house table.

The honey bee, unlike hornets and wasps, loses its life when it stings, for it fatally injures itself internally trying to free its stinger. At the entrance to the hive there are a few guard bees whose job it is to come to the defense of the nest. It is these bees that first attack someone walking in front of a hive. Away from the hive, it is difficult to get honey bees to sting at all. They seem reluctant to sting in self-defense; self-defense, in this case, would mean death.

Other factors threaten bees' lives that are less in their control.

Many of the commonly used insecticides are highly toxic to bees. Un-fortunately, a major use of these insecticides by home gardeners is directed toward producing a perfect rose or other flower, and the honeybee visiting the flower to obtain nectar is the unintended victim. In the revised edition of the classic *ABC and XYZ of Bee Culture,* A. I. Root states, "During the last twenty years . . . insect pollination of crops has become a more critical problem in the United States and in some other countries because . . . the use of insecticides is reducing the population of wild bees. . . . *Sevin* and the *arsenicals* are especially dangerous because they may be stored with pollen in the hive and later fed to the brood." Root's detailed chart on the effects of various poison sprays on bees rates pyrethrum as being low in toxicity in both laboratory and field trials.

In spite of occasional prohibitory ordinances many people do keep bees in urban and suburban areas. These beekeepers quickly learn to make their hives inconspicuous by keeping them hidden or painting them unobtrusive colors. Gifts of honey or beeswax candles may help to make neighbors friendly, as gifts of fresh eggs may do in regard to raising chickens. When a town near us reviewed their laws prohibiting beekeeping recently, some thirty residents who were already keeping hives appeared before the city council and had all the legal constraints repealed. One of the arguments they used was that every town needs to have some responsible beekeepers who will capture the inevitable wild swarms for the public, as well as for their own benefit. We know several urban beekeepers who charge a fee for this service and each spring make a supplemental income at it.

Honey and Other Products of the Hive: Honey is the nectar and sugary exudate of plants that has been gathered, processed, and stored in the cells within the combs of the hive. The comb itself is a waxy substance constructed for the purpose of holding the honey, pollen, nectar, and the young larvae of bees while they develop. To produce honey, worker bees gather nectar, sucking it from the plant into their stomach. Here, various enzymes mix with the nectar. When the stomach is full, the bee flies back to the hive and deposits what is now the honey into cells allotted for that purpose in the combs. The hive boxes holding these honey-laden combs are usually high in the hive; the room below is used for rearing young. Once the honey is deposited, the worker bee goes out again to find additional food sources.

When the honey is first placed in the hive by the worker bee, it has a watery consistency and would probably ferment if no further processing occurred. Hive bees, however, take the honey back out and air drops of it in their mouth parts so that water evaporates. The dehydrated honey is then returned to a cell in the comb and a wax cap is placed over it. Finished honey has an average moisture content of 17.2 percent.

The beekeeper inspects the hive to see what proportion of cells are capped. Capping indicates that the honey has the proper moisture content for harvesting and storing. Frames with all capped cells can be stored away until it is convenient to take the honey out. Various devices can be used to remove honey, the most common of which is a centrifuge. The small beekeeper can use a hand-operated centrifuge, or a solar extractor that uses sunlight to heat the wax comb so that the honey runs out of it.

The "average American" eats somewhere in excess of one hundred pounds of sugar each year. While undoubtedly a good part of this annual amount is consumed without the person's knowledge as additives to restaurant meals or processed foods (breakfast cereals, baked goods, soft drinks, sauces, and so on), a considerable amount of sugar is consciously added to various dishes and drinks in the home. For the latter, honey is a splendid, fine-flavored substitute. It is actually sweeter than sucrose, the sugar derived from cane and beets, so you may even find yourself using less overall sugar. It makes a fine spread just as it is, either in syrup form or partially crystallized, for toast and pancakes. It can be used in canning and baking, but less by half is required than sugar (liquid contents should be reduced accordingly), since honey is more fluid. For an analysis of the mineral content of honey see Table 11-2.

One colony of bees can provide as much as one hundred pounds or more of honey per year. In addition to honey, which is a carbohydrate, protein can be harvested from a beehive as well. The two protein sources are pollen and the bees themselves. Pollen traps, whether purchased or constructed at home, make its collection easy. Advertisers in bee journals—for example, *American Bee Journal, Gleanings in Bee Culture*—sell such devices. Be cautioned, however, that since the bees also utilize pollen as a protein

A hand-operated centrifuge is used to spin the honey-filled frames. The honey flows out of the gate at the bottom.

source to develop their young, you need to learn how much pollen to harvest, so as not to damage the hive's reproductive potential.

Pure pollen also can be purchased in certain health food stores. Unheated honey, comb honey, or honey from cappings will have some intact pollen mixed in. It has been suggested these sources have an excellent effect in reducing certain allergies. Presumably they work by exposing the sufferer to steady, low doses of particular allergens; desensitization occurs after a long period of this sort of exposure. Pure pollen might possibly be used in the same fashion, but it should be tried first in very small amounts. Too much at once may cause a severe reaction.

Although beekeepers are known to eat larvae of developing bees as a sort of special treat on occasion, the possibility of regular harvesting of this protein source as a supplement to human or domestic animal diets is a potential and unexplored protein supply. The yeasty-tasting larvae are best offered to neophytes in a milkshake or a similar beverage, preferably after blending to destroy any resemblance to the original organisms. However, they can also be eaten directly. Still, eating queen larvae directly may be too much of a good thing. The taste is very strong.

In general, people are conservative about food. If they weren't exposed to something as edible when they were children they usually resist eating it later. When you do try a new food, it is wise to go slowly in any case. Each individual has a slightly different physiology to which he or she has adapted mature food habits. A gradual adjustment to something new is always wise.

At the Berkeley Integral Urban House, preliminary experiments showed that fish would eat dead bees. To make this fact useful, a beehive was mounted over a pond so that when bees died they fell into the pond and thus became a supplementary protein source for the animals within. This arrangement takes advantage of the normal process of bees dying. A strong hive of sixty thousand bees will have an average daily mortality rate of 1.5 percent during the periods of peak activity. This means that as many as a thousand bees per day can die in heavy honey-flow periods in the spring. This bee-fish combination exemplifies the integration principle by which systems that may be net losers from an energy, labor, or economic point of view, when combined can provide a net gain.

A way to use the dead bees without having to mount the hive above a pond is to employ a dead bee trap to collect all the dead bees as they are removed from the hive, or as they try to fly away from the hive with their last dying effort. Although additional research will undoubtedly turn up more ways to use dead bees, the underlying concept will most likely be to make use of the protein they contain.

Beeswax is probably one of the more important hive products, judging from its range of uses. However, in the future, honey converted into alcohol through fermentation may become important as a fuel for running vehicles. Beeswax can also be utilized as a heat source by burning, as in a paraffin heater; by extension, it could conceivably be used to fuel an engine of some sort directly. Of course, the most obvious use of beeswax is for producing high-quality candles, though one rarely encounters beeswax candles anymore. They are easy to make and are excellent gifts.

Propolis is a hive product that even beekeepers generally fail to recog-

Table 11-2. **The Mineral Content of Honey**

Mineral	Ppm in Light Honey*	Ppm in Dark Honey*
Potassium	205	1676
Chlorine	52	113
Sulfur	58	100
Calcium	49	51
Sodium	18	76
Phosphorus	35	47
Magnesium	19	35
Silica	22	36
Iron	2.4	9.4
Manganese	.3	4.1
Copper	.29	.60

Total ash .02–1.0 percent
(average ash = .17 percent)

*Ppm is the abbreviation for parts per million; in this case, milligrams of mineral per kilogram of honey.

Note: If you compare honey and white sugar, you will notice that honey has small amounts of organic ingredients, and as the above shows, some inorganic minerals, while these have been removed from white sugar, in the process of "refining" it.

Source: *Beekeeping in the United States.*

nize as a potential crop. It is the resinous plant product gathered and utilized by bees as a home sealer or caulking compound. The bees use propolis wherever a gap occurs in the hive, and in various other places as well. Propolis does have an export market, particularly from the United States to Japan, where it is used in various products, one of which is thought to be an aphrodisiac. The fragrance and water-repelling properties of propolis could make the material useful as a waterproofing compound, for example in basket-making. This product could become more important in the future, particularly if collection methods were well worked out. Presumably, a hive could be designed that would increase the amount of caulking done by the bees, or a strain of bees developed that would be especially adept at producing propolis.

There is a ready market for royal jelly (see below) and pollen. (In Berkeley, California, at this writing health food stores are selling royal jelly for $9.95 per 100 milligrams, or $74.00 per ounce, and pollen sells for about 50 cents per ounce.) A market also exists for workers, queens, hives and equipment. Another possible marketable product is bee venom. Bee venom therapy for arthritis utilizes the secretions of the poison glands as a way to alter the sufferer's immune system. For those interested in this form of therapy, consult the two articles and short note on the subject in issues of *American Bee Journal* listed in the bibliography at the end of the book. The articles describe how to use bees to sting arthritic joints and the beneficial results obtained. They also indicate that a method exists for harvesting the venom without killing the insects.

The Bees: One needs to know something about the biology of bees in order to manage them successfully. Table 11-3 shows the developmental period for the three different castes of *Apis mellifera,* the common domestic honey bee derived from European strains. (A caste is the name given by bi-

Table 11-3. **The Development Period of the Three Hive Castes**

	Queen	Worker	Drone
		Days	
Egg	3	3	3
Larvae	5½	6	6.5
Pupa	7½	12	14.5

ologists to the respective hive groups: workers, drones, and queens. The word is useful because it designates that members are recruited into the group at birth.) A vigorous hive during its peak in the spring will have fifty to sixty thousand workers and about three thousand drones (males), but only one queen. A queen bee (larger than the others) and worker bees are shown in Figure 11-5.

A young healthy queen can lay up to two thousand eggs per day, and live up to five years. The average life-span of the worker bee varies with the season—about six weeks in the active spring period and up to six months through the winter if it lives all the way to spring. Drones are fairly specialized creatures; they do no work except in nuptial flights. They need to be

Figure 11-5. **A Queen and Workers in a Frame**

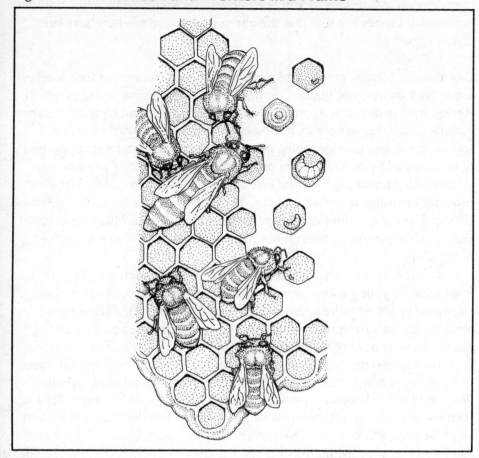

*Note the size and shape differences
of the bees.*

fed, as they do not forage for themselves, and they seldom live for more than
four months. Near the season's end when less honey is available the drones
are actually forced from the hive to die. Drones are easy to distinguish from
the workers because they are much bigger than the other bees and have large
eyes that almost entirely encompass the head. Also, they have no stinger.
They are stouter than the queen, and their abdomens are less pointed.

The queen determines the sex of the developing grub or larvae by
whether or not she fertilizes the eggs. Unfertilized eggs produce males
through a genetic mechanism common throughout the Hymenoptera (the insect order that contains the bees, ants, wasps, and many parasitic natural enemies of other insects). The queen keeps a supply of sperm from her first
and only mating, with which she inseminates all the fertilized eggs. How
this feat is accomplished has attracted researchers who are interested in reducing the cost of sperm storage in artificial insemination programs.

The workers determine whether a fertilized egg will develop into a
queen or a worker. They do this by selecting the food fed to the developing
larvae. All young are fed royal jelly and "bee bread" (honey and pollen
mixed together) for the first three days. The larva to become the queen
continues to receive the royal jelly; those larvae that do not become the
workers. Workers and drones are also fed more intermittently, and thus are
really "incomplete queens," since queens take longer to develop. They are
considered incomplete because they don't lay eggs. In extraordinary circum-

stances, workers in queenless colonies *do* lay eggs. These being infertile, they develop into drones. If you open up an overwintering hive, the unusual presence of drones is a sign that the queen is gone and workers have been laying eggs.

Bee Food: Nectar, pollen, and water are the three sources of food workers use to feed themselves, queens, drones, and the developing larvae or brood. Recent studies in South America also indicate that fats can be collected from various plants that secrete such substances. Nectar is the carbohydrate source, but it also provides some minerals, some water, and a small portion of enzymes and vitamins. Pollen provides the only source of protein especially needed for brood food and colony reproduction. In addition, pollen provides vitamins, minerals, and fats. Bees require water for energy production, dissolving and diluting honey, and maintaining water balance in blood and body tissues. Adult bees do not require pollen, and live on nectar or honey alone.

Royal jelly, so named because of its key role in developing the queen, is secreted by young nurse, or worker, bees aged five to fifteen days. This substance might be more appropriately called brood food, since it constitutes the larvae's basic food supply. Brood food is secreted by a pair of glands near the head of the worker bees and these glands extract materials from the blood stream. The secretion is passed down through special ducts to the mouth cavity at the base of the tongue. With additions of carbohydrates and possibly other secretions, the thick, creamy, milky white fluid is then fed to the larvae. A commercial process has been developed to harvest this hive product. As noted above, royal jelly can often be found in health food stores as a special human diet supplement.

The Seasonal Life of the Hive and Management Suggestions: The hive is basically a superorganism with the queen operating as a key control agent through chemical cues or phenomena. The queen produces a special chemical (9-oxo-dec-2-enoic acid) from her mandibular gland, and distributes it over her body during cleaning operations. Worker bees obtain it when licking the queen. This "queen substance" enables the bees to know when the queen is absent. As she gets older and produces less queen substance, the workers are stimulated to feed another developing larval queen. The workers who usually surround the queen distribute the queen substance to other bees in their normal process of sharing food.

In the winter, the queen stops laying eggs, and she places herself in the relative center of the hive, with a surrounding ball of workers as insulation and as a heat source. During this period, the bees live off the stored honey and pollen. This is one reason for leaving an ample supply of honey during harvesting operations. Otherwise, supplemental feeding will be needed to help the hive make it through the coldest periods.

Winter is a good time to plan the next year's activities and organize and construct new equipment. Spring is the period of greatest hive activity, for this the major period of nectar and pollen production.

It is instructive to observe bees as they pass into the hive at the landing board. Here, you can see the different-colored pollen balls attached to their

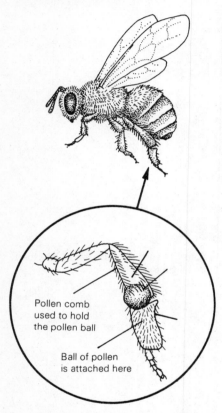

Figure 11-6. **The Pollen Basket and Comb**

Pollen comb used to hold the pollen ball

Ball of pollen is attached here

Pollen is held on the lower part of the expanded tibial leg segment by means of the regularly spaced spiny hairs on the first tarsal segment.

hind legs. If you can match the different colors with the predominant blooming flowers, you will know from which plants the bees are harvesting at a particular time. See Figure 11-6, which shows the so-called "pollen basket" on the worker bee. Spring is a busy season for the beekeeper as well as the bees, because harvesting and controlling swarms require extra time. (Swarms occur when a new queen and a group of workers fly off to start a new hive. This can reduce hive strength and productivity so it should be prevented.) These activities must be included in your schedule. Plan carefully and make regular assessments of hive conditions. In some areas, summer is like spring, and the bees will continue their foraging. In other places, summer may be drier and/or less flowers will bloom. You will have to learn which season is the busiest for your area and anticipate harvesting and swarm-control periods.

The fall period is highlighted by the expulsion of drones. This is a good time to open the hive and check out the remaining stores of honey and pollen, number of workers, age and amount of brood, egg-laying rate of the queen, and general condition of hive. One way to learn to judge for all these factors is to take out each frame (a frame is one of the nine vertical sections where the bees build their wax cells) and ask a helper to keep notes as you make percentage estimates for each one. By periodically making a thorough assessment you will begin to become sensitized to the key factors that keep the hive alive and thriving. In making the fall inspections, winter survival is the key factor to consider. Since it is difficult for the beginning beekeeper to judge if enough food will be available, either be sure to leave plenty or prepare to supplement the hive's food supply.

Starting Your Own System: Starting any new project requires motivation and resources as well as a general scheme. A design for developing a bee system for your home should be broken down into three phases: planning, construction, and management. During the planning process you may wish to educate yourself about bees and beekeeping from the extensive literature on the subject, and perhaps attend a class or make direct observations of beekeepers in action. Construction of the system requires assembling the materials (the hive and the bees). Management is the regular work of observing, operating, and readjusting the overall system.

Obtaining bees and equipment can be accomplished in several ways. It is possible to buy a full hive or a nucleus ("nuc"), which is a small hive with a few frames containing brood and a queen. Or you can purchase the components and assemble them yourself. When spring arrives, you then buy workers and queen(s) and watch the colony grow. The latter process is probably cheaper and will teach you more of the basics if you are starting alone. The former process is faster, and you will be a beekeeper as soon as the hives are yours. This kind of start may be a bit abrupt unless you are certain when you purchase your hive that a practicing beekeeper will advise you personally, and let you use equipment.

Starting with two or more hives is recommended. If you have only one and the queen dies, you will have lost everything. With more than one, dividing colonies and propagating from the other hives or combining two colonies becomes possible. Queenless colonies can be added to those with

Notebook for writing down records and special observations.

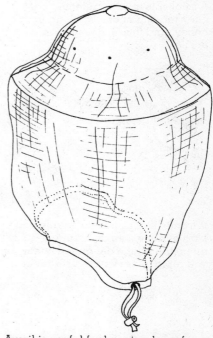

A veil is useful for keeping bees from stinging the face and neck.

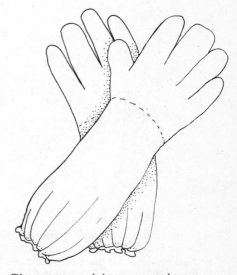

Gloves are useful to prevent bee-stings on the hands.

A smoker is used to quiet the bees. They react to smoke by filling up on honey, and this makes them more docile.

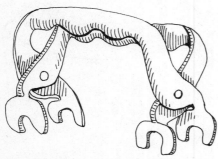

A frame lifter is used to enable you to hold a frame with one hand. It is useful in finding the old queen bee when you replace her with a new queen.

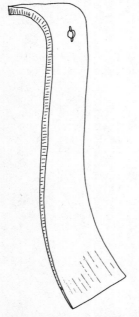

A hive tool is used to pry up the cover and the hive boxes, which often are sealed together by the sticky resinous material called propolis that the bees harvest from trees.

queens by stacking the supers (hive sections that hold combs), with a paper sheet between. By the time the bees have eaten through the paper, the queen substances will have mingled enough so that no fighting will occur between the two formerly distinct populations.

Building your own equipment is a definite possibility, particularly if you are skilled at carpentry. Good plans for assembly of hives and honey extractors are available from Garden Way Publishing, Charlotte, Vermont 05445, or can be obtained from various published sources in local libraries or by letter to agricultural experiment stations.

Essential tools needed to start are a veil, hive tool, smoker, gloves, possibly overalls and a notebook. These items can be purchased from bee supply houses listed in bee journals, or if they are unavailable, mail order departments of Sears or Montgomery Ward. The latter mail order firms distribute equipment, bees, and tools, and you can learn from their catalog and use it to plan the cost of the adventure.

Setting up your initial hives with an ant excluder platform may help protect your hives against certain ant species. Such a stand can be used instead of a chlordane treatment, which is the common practice. Chlordane is a chlorinated hydrocarbon that accumulates in food chains and it should be avoided wherever possible.

A New Type of Hive: Don Simoni of San Francisco, California, has invented a new kind of beehive that can be used indoors and that reduces the possibility that the beekeeper might be stung. Such a hive may encourage many more people to become involved in beekeeping, particularly urban people, since the hive can be kept indoors, even in the kitchen where few onlookers will notice. This hive is outfitted with plastic look-in sides that allow easy observation. Thus it is possible to view many hive mysteries—egg laying, the waggle dance (see Box 11-1), and honey processing.

The queen and worker bees are placed into the bottom of this hive. There the queen lays her eggs. As the bee population increases the sliding gate between the two chambers is opened and the bees move up into the honey chamber. In a few months, when the bees fill the honey chamber with honey, the sliding gate is closed to prevent more bees from entering the chamber. In the honey chamber are devices for removing the bees and making honey harvesting easier. A passage off to one side allows the bees to travel out of the chamber through a one-way exit and down into the brood chamber. The majority of the bees as a part of their regular movements will leave the honey chamber within six hours of closing the passage, but a few will remain. To encourage these stragglers to leave, a smoking system built into the honey chamber burns incense cones. The smoke irritates the remaining bees enough to cause them to leave. A few hours after the smoker is used the honey chamber can be opened and the honey removed.

This observatory hive is designed to be kept indoors on a table or secured to the wall. Normal shelf brackets sold in hardware stores provide a solid base when attached to 2×4s in the wall. The most important consideration when placing the hive is to point the exit tube away from people or pet traffic. These exit tubes can be mounted in a window so the bees can come and go easily while you watch. Bees normally bother no one, but to be

Box 11-1. **The Bee Waggle Dance**

If you watch a bee land on the platform of an observation hive and move up into the hive you will notice that it is wagging its tail vigorously and rapidly circling. Other bees appear to be attracted to this dance. By ingenious studies, Karl von Frisch discovered the significance of this behavioral routine. He found that two types of information are conveyed by the dance: distance to a food source (by the dance tempo) and direction from the hive (the angular deviation from the vertical path of the dance indicates the angular deviation of the food source from the hive-sun axis). This complex dance has stirred apiculturists and behaviorists to long discussions about bee language and the evolution of language in these social insects. Recently, sound vibrations have also been shown to be involved in information dissemination in the hive.

safe you should place the entrance to the hive away from a frequented sidewall or the front or back door of the house.

If you are interested in this hive, write to Don Simoni, 177 Pixley Street, San Francisco, California 94123. He is continually experimenting with new designs. He is in the process of patenting this idea and sells handcrafted versions for $150 each. He cautions that the idea still requires further experimentation. If you want to join in, you may find yourself participating in a beekeeping revolution.

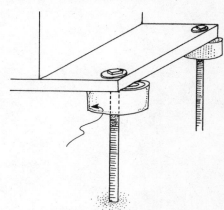

An Ant-Guard Hive Platform

Stickem (a brand name) is placed on the inside, where it is protected from rain, debris, and dust.

Figure 11-7. **The Indoor Observation Beehive**

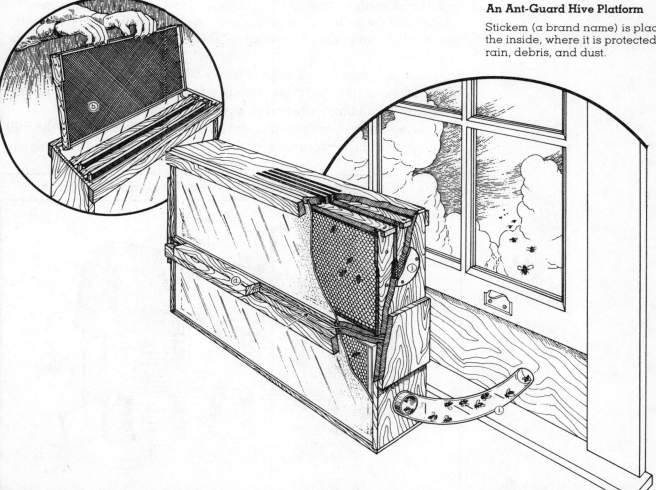

12. SOLAR TECHNOLOGY

The House and Climate

When a society begins to produce more value than is needed for its own subsistence, it develops the freedom to begin the evolution of its culture. One of the goals of Western civilization has been the development of human well-being by, among other factors, ever decreasing the influence of climate and weather on day-to-day activities. The invention of methods of modifying climate in and around buildings gave builders and the society at large great freedom—freedom to emphasize cultural symbols rather than the purpose of shelter as determinants of architectural form.

Although even in the design of homes Western architecture prior to the Industrial Revolution had evolved decisively away from the concept of simple shelter, a building's habitability was severely constrained by the marginal ability of open fireplaces, stoves, and warming pans to cut the chill of European and American winters. Consequently, buildings were generally

Figure 12-1. **Eighteenth Century New England Farmhouse**

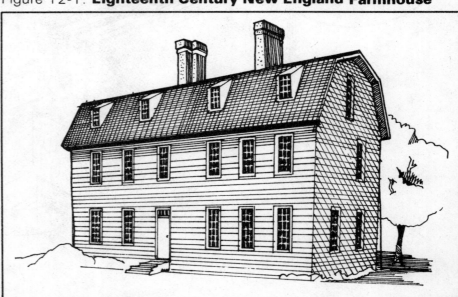

Shelter from winter cold and wind

built to be massive, with small openings, both for structural reasons and to dampen diurnal temperature fluctuations. In this country, this tradition is typified by the four-square, solid, New England farmhouse of the eighteenth century characterized by masonry or post-and-beam timber construction, small windows, and a siting that faces it away from winter north winds.

In warmer, humid climates the European influence was modified with the lighter structure, verandas, jalousied shutters, and breezeways found for example on older houses in the American South. Such houses encouraged the flow of cooling night breezes, but denied entrance to direct sunlight. The warm but dry climate of the Mediterranean, the American Southwest, and Spanish California encouraged the use of massive walls with carefully placed windows, which protected interiors from the fierce heat and glare of the semi-desert. After sunset, as the outside air temperature dropped rapidly, the day's heat was released from the massive walls, both warming the inhabitants and precooling the walls to accept the next day's heat.

Figure 12-2. **Eighteenth Century Southern Home**

Adapted to summer climate, admitting cooling breezes, excluding sun

Figure 12-3. **Southwest's Adobe Construction**

Moderates the temperature extremes of hot days and cold nights

313

Figure 12-4. **Victorian Row House**

Reaching for daylight and respectability

Even San Francisco's ubiquitous bay windows represented a response to the need for light in a climate often overcast with coastal fog, although the popularity of the Victorian row house itself was due more to the air of East Coast respectability it brought to the raffish Barbary Coast than to a response to the local climate.

Although from our present perspective we might ridicule such wholesale and climatically inappropriate transplants of culture as typified by the building of English bungalows in Delhi, American-style apartment blocks in Kuwait, or even the adoption of European dress in Central Africa, we have made the same mistakes in this country in embracing the evolution of universal architectural forms without regard for local climate, traditions, or available materials. For instance, it is common to find the same basic Cape Cod salt-box-style house marketed successfully in Texas, southern California, and the Pacific Northwest, as well as New England. We have learned to demand, and the building industry to gladly supply, structures that ignore local realities in imposing a homogenized design. The latter reflects an assumed cultural symbol and the real economies of mass marketing.

The promise of thermal comfort in any structure under any conditions has, until now, been guaranteed by the technological "explosion" started in the Industrial Revolution and fueled by an era of cheap energy and materials. The period between 1850 and 1925 saw the invention and commercial application of central heating and ventilation, electric lighting and power, evaporative cooling, dehumidification, and finally Willis Carrier's "man-made weather" (air conditioning). These developments provided us with the potential for the total control over a building's microclimate. Our ever increasing consumption of energy—first wood and coal, then electricity, gas, and oil—fueled these thermal processes and gave designers and builders the freedom to ignore almost all environmental constraints.

We in the United States have taken full advantage of this freedom, supporting our relative wealth in large measure with a per capita daily energy consumption six times the world average. Since 1973, however, it has become apparent that the era of cheap, abundant fossil energy is drawing to a close. Regardless of future successes in the development of alternative energy sources, no energy will be inexpensive in comparison with today's energy prices. Consequently, we must reduce our consumption if we are to avoid inflicting economic depression and great social hardship on ourselves and the rest of the world.

We know that we can substantially reduce our energy consumption *and* probably improve our national standard of living. We know this because several highly industrialized nations (for example, Sweden, West Germany, Switzerland) have as high or a higher quality of life than our own (measured in terms of per capita income, cost of services, education, and so on) while consuming only half the energy per capita of the United States.

Figure 12-5. **National Energy Use Per Capita**

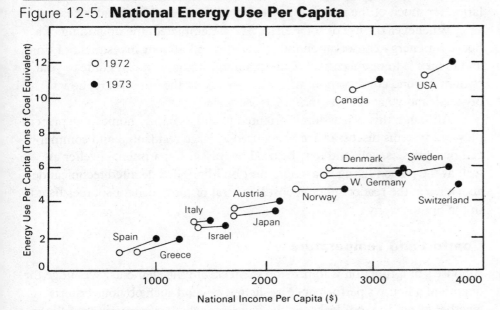

Several highly industrialized nations enjoy a quality of life comparable to that of the U.S., at half the energy cost

Change begins at home. The residential section of our economy is responsible for almost 20 percent of the nation's energy consumption, and almost three-quarters of that high-quality energy goes to the heating of water to 140°F and air to 70–75°F. A substantial portion of this energy is needlessly wasted. For instance, the residential building stock of Sweden, after accounting for the severe climate and different energy-source mix, uses fully

315

Table 12-1. Residential Heating Efficency by Climate Regions

	United States			Sweden		
	So. Calif.	Penna.	Minn.	Malmo	Stockholm	Norrbotten
Degree-Days (base 68°)	1900	5500	8500	7700	9200	13,000
BTU/Sq. Ft. Deg.-Day	34	20	15	9	8.5	8.2

33 percent less energy per capita than American housing. There is evidence that a severe climate fosters efficient design, but that factor would account for only a portion of Sweden's better performance. Table 12-1 shows the relative severity of microclimates in three regions of each country and the average energy consumption per unit floor area of the regions' housing stock. A "degree-day" is a measure of heating requirement. It represents the difference between each day's mean temperature and 65°F, the temperature below which houses are assumed to need heat. For example, if a winter day's mean temperature (highest + lowest ÷ 2) equals 45°, then its degree-day total for that day would be 20 degree-days. (See pages 69-71 for a further discussion of degree-days.)

The creation of an integral urban house involves maintaining climate comfort with as little imported energy as possible. In Chapter 4 we presented the most effective methods of upgrading both existing and new houses to reduce their need for heating and cooling. This chapter is concerned with modifying existing homes to use solar energy and natural ventilation for much of the remaining space conditioning and hot water heating.

Whenever the use of solar energy is contemplated, the upgrading of a house for energy conservation must be a "given," if your investment of time and money is to be successful. This chapter is a nontechnical guide to your options beyond conservation: where to start, what the options are, how to proceed, and what expectations are reasonable.

Although this discussion is oriented to single-family homes, the principles and systems discussed are being used in large residential and commercial buildings as well, and may be used by, say, the apartment-dweller as well as the person living in a single-unit building. For detailed technical design advice, the reader should consult several of the excellent sources listed in the bibliography.

Comfort and Temperature

A house's first function is to provide shelter from the elements. We judge the quality of a house's performance as shelter, beyond such obvious criteria as whether or not the roof leaks, by the degree to which it maintains our "comfort." Human comfort is a result of a delicate balance of several factors, including air temperature, air movement, temperature of surrounding surfaces, level of activity, amount of clothing, and even age and sex. It is almost always oversimplified to one parameter—air temperature. In general, if all the other variables are within certain limits, a certain air temperature will provide satisfaction to most people.

The defined comfort range for most Americans has changed since the invention of central heating (see margin). The change has been influenced by changes in diet, living patterns, and comfort expectations, and it has led to the increased wearing of light clothing year round. In practice, the trend toward a higher comfort range has resulted in most heating and cooling systems being designed to maintain 75°F in winter, and 72°F in summer. The maintenance of relatively high/low interior temperature has, in turn, increased the heat loss/gain from buildings and, consequently, their energy consumption.

The first post-oil-embargo reaction to this situation was a campaign to promote less restrictive conditions in buildings—to allow 68°F in winter and 78°F in summer. Reductions to these levels certainly conserve energy, but they have not been overly popular, because the resulting thermal environments were outside the range of our expectations. The simple alteration of air temperature does not promote comfort, only cold feet or sweaty lethargy. Rather, all the important factors affecting comfort should influence the design, or redesign, of spaces for people. Air temperature then becomes less influential and can be altered significantly without reducing comfort.

Our bodies exchange heat with our surroundings in several ways, primarily by

- *Radiation* (40 percent)—the direct exchange of heat with warm or

1900 65 to 75°F
1960 75 to 78°F
1972 76°—present ASHRAE[1] "comfort" temperature for sedentary adults

Figure 12-6. **Sources of Heat Transfer Affecting Human Comfort**

cool surfaces—for example, warming near a hot stove or cooling off near a window.

• *Convection* (40 percent)—the heating or cooling of skin by contact with a warmer or cooler air flow.

• *Evaporation* (20 percent)—the cooling of the skin by evaporation of perspiration.

Air temperature, which governs convection, accounts for only 40 percent of the thermal environment. An equal proportion is controlled by the mean radiant temperature of the environment's surfaces "seen" by its occupants. In practice, this means that the surface temperature of objects having a large area exposed to a room's occupants—such as windows, walls, floor, and ceiling—has a significant impact on their comfort. The remaining influence is air movement, which, in the form of chilling winter drafts and welcome summer breezes, determines 20 percent of an environment's comfort.

These variables governing comfort—mean radiant temperature, air temperature, and air movement—act interdependently. That is, the alteration of one variable's level requires compensation in the others if a steady state perception of "comfort" is to be felt. This phenomenon can be put to work in your house to provide, in many cases, an improved level of comfort while using less energy to do so. Consider these examples:

• If in winter you wish to maintain, say, a comfort level equivalent to 72°F, and are willing to wear warmer clothes than you do in July, and if (1) you can weatherstrip your home to prevent drafts, (2) insulate to lower heat loss, (3) curtain windows or double glaze to prevent radiant losses to the cold glass, and (4) alter your house to provide a large surface area in your living spaces (floor, wall, and the like) having a surface temperature approaching 80°, then you can lower air temperature to 65° without sacrificing comfort.

• During summer, after (1) dressing lightly for the season, (2) shading windows with blinds, shade trees, or awnings to prevent radiant discomfort from direct sunlight and glare, (3) insulating or shading the roof to reduce heat transmitted heat gain, and if you maintain that large surface in your living area at 68–70°F, then you can allow the air temperature to rise to 85–87°. The air temperature perceived by those in the room will be in the range 76–78°F. This would make air conditioning unnecessary on all but the hottest days, since your house, insulated and shaded from the sun, will maintain an interior temperature in the 80s even though outside the temperature soars above 100.

• We are all familiar with the cooling effect a breeze has on a fan on a hot day, but we do not generally make the connection between air flow and perceived air temperature. If, in our air conditioned houses and offices, we worked or sat in the breeze from a small fan, a building could be cooled only to 80–85°, while its occupants sensed a temperature of 74–78°F.

These examples illustrate the three rules of thumb (see margin) for the consideration of comfort expectations in an integral urban house. It is important to remember these considerations when deciding upon alterations to your house. In many cases a substantial amount of money can be saved if alterations, solar or otherwise, are designed to meet the needs of a 65/85° environment, rather than a narrowly defined 75° one.

Comfort in the integral urban house

1. Careful attention to improving a house's radiant environment in living spaces will allow the maintenance of lower/higher air temperatures, thus conserving heating and cooling energy and permitting the use of smaller conditioning equipment (solar or conventional).

2. Air movement must be encouraged during the cooling season but prevented during winter, since it increases heat loss from the body as well as from the house itself.

3. Expect to dress with the season if you are to be comfortable in a house adapted to its climate. For instance, if, using the first example above, you chose not to wear warmer clothes in winter, an 80° radiant temperature surface would allow you to reduce the air temperature only to 70°, if you wished to maintain a 72° comfort level—5° above that needed for comfort if you dress appropriately.

When planning for adaptations in your house for making better use of climate and sun, budget for conservation first. Almost all houses, regardless of their situation, can benefit from alterations that will help temper their daily temperature extremes. Conservation includes not only the "tightening up" of a house covered by Chapter 4, but also the investment in features that improve summer comfort as well as reduce energy consumption. For instance, a ceiling-mounted attic fan can provide that cooling breeze needed for hot weather comfort *and* reduce your air conditioning load by precooling your house's structure with cool night air. During the heat of the next day, part of the heat normally dissipated by your house's air conditioning system will be absorbed by the house's structure instead (radiant heat absorbed by cool surfaces).

Another energy conservation feature that provides multiple benefits is the shade tree. Although most species do not mature for twenty to forty years, your house may well have a lifetime of seventy-five to a hundred years. During its maturity, a well-placed deciduous tree will help clean and cool the air in its vicinity (by evapotranspiration), reduce the transmitted and radiant heat gain through walls, roof, and windows in its shade, and improve the appearance and value of your property. Planting a few well placed nursery stock trees in five-gallon containers (emphasize the protection of east- and west-facing walls and roofs from summer sun) will offer, over the long run, an extremely high return on their investment.

Figure 12-7. **Thermal Comfort From Trees and Shrubs**

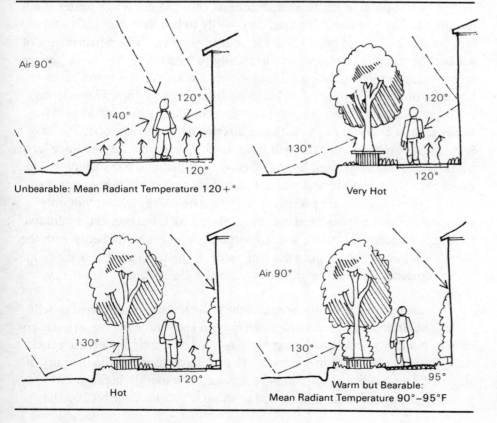

Unbearable: Mean Radiant Temperature 120+°

Very Hot

Hot

Warm but Bearable:
Mean Radiant Temperature 90°–95°F

Well placed trees and shrubs substantially improve thermal comfort in and around buildings

Investment in energy-conservation features will generally have a higher return than money spent on energy conversion, solar or otherwise. It is always easier to save a Btu than to generate one to take its place. However, at some level of investment, depending on climate and fuel cost, you will reach the point of diminishing return, where spending another dollar on, say, thicker insulation will save less in future fuel cost than a dollar spent on an alternate energy system that will save that fuel by providing heat from another source. Consult several sources in the bibliography for guidance as to the economic level of conservation spending. In general, after you have upgraded your house to a degree of "tightness" that recovers its cost in fuel savings within five to eight years, you are ready to consider alternate energy systems to provide the majority of the house's remaining requirements.

Prudent investment in solar technology for your home requires attention to these common-sense guidelines:

• Consider first the simple, traditional, and manually controlled design concepts. They are likely to provide the highest return on your investment, both in terms of dollars and conservation of resources.

• Choose the least complex design option that provides sufficient performance, control, and design integration to meet your needs. Remember, "out of sight, out of mind" control of a dynamic system that must respond to changes in sun, weather, and interior conditions will breed complexity, which is both expensive and prone to misjudgment. In most cases, the most sophisticated design will be simple and, with your assistance from time to time, self-regulating.

• Invest only to the point of economic and/or philosophical diminishing return.

The last point needs further attention. Your gas hot water heater is not required to pay you back its initial cost—only to last long enough for you to feel you have received good value for your investment. The performance of a solar hot water heater, however, is usually judged on its "payback," or the rate of return on its initial cost increase over a conventional system measured by the present value of its assumed future fuel savings. Considering paybacks is a sound business practice when comparing bulldozers or typewriters, but a case can be made that it discriminates against solar. We have a subsidized fuel economy, and will have for the forseeable future, since letting the cost of energy seek its true, free-market value to our society would cause massive economic and social dislocations for which neither our institutions nor politicians are prepared. An alternate energy system not only saves its owner the subsidized cost of displaced fuel, but conserves valuable high-grade energy for future use. Unfortunately, it is credited only with the subsidized cost reduction, not the true value of the fuel saved, nor the reduction in environmental stress due to the use of a clean, renewable energy source.

Consequently, several states and the federal government have or will undertake limited tax credit programs to both encourage the use of solar energy in buildings and to make a gesture toward offsetting the existing fuel subsidies. A great many investors, moreover, have accepted the inequity of standard economic analysis and have invested to a moral "break-even point," gaining the same satisfaction as those who "did their bit" on the

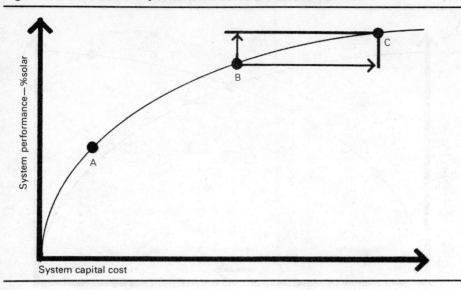

Figure 12-8. **Solar System Cost vs. Performance**

home front during World War II.

In either case, there is a level of investment beyond which a dollar spent does not result in a significant improvement in performance. Performance is usually quantified in terms of the percentage of a house's yearly thermal load supplied by the system (percent solar) or the yearly quantity of energy delivered to the house per dollar of system cost (Btu/dollar).

Figure 12-1 shows a typical relationship between system cost and performance. A modest, manually controlled system that supplies only a small portion of the house's load (represented by Point A) makes efficient use of its investor's dollars, since the full system capacity is used most of the time and little is spent on features not directly converting energy.

A larger system, providing perhaps three-quarters of the house's heating needs, requires additional capacity to collect and store heat that may or may not be needed on a daily basis, since the heating needs of the house vary with weather. Also, a larger system will require a means of control, whether automatic or manual (shutters, exterior shading, and the like). The control device adds to the system cost but does not directly convert energy; rather, it serves to prevent overheating during collection and meters heat flow out of storage as needed. Such a system (Point B) will show a lower rate of return on its investment but will reliably provide most of the house's heating needs.

Point C represents a system designed to totally solar heat a residence. In some cases, this is an appropriate level of investment, especially if the owner can take responsibility for system control, and if most of the system components do double duty as structure. However, in most American climate regions, the weather is sufficiently variable to require a system sized out of all proportion to the average daily loads, if 100 percent solar performance is to be guaranteed (with no auxiliary heating system installed). Therefore, the incremental cost increase between Point B and C is very large in proportion to the improvement in system performance.

Most investors should seek the middle path, balancing their level of

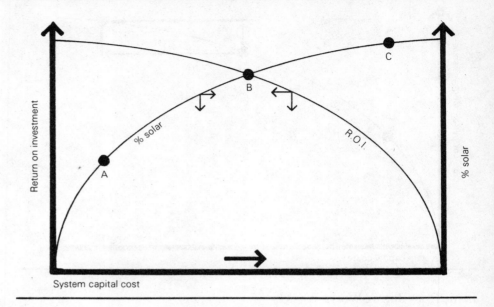

Figure 12-9. **Solar System Cost vs. Return on Investment**

investment with system performance and fuel cost savings. In practice, this approach has resulted in systems that meet between 50 and 75 percent of a house's heating or hot water needs. This "optimum" percentage may be somewhat higher in regions having sunny, cold winters (for instance, the Rocky Mountains), and, ironically, often lower in areas having mild but hazy winters (the Southeast, southern California).

The Window as Solar Collector

Your search for that optimum combination of simplicity, design sophistication, and respectable performance must start with your house's existing windows. Windows are usually cited as the primary cause of excessive heat loss in houses, responsible for a quarter of a house's annual heat loss. Even after refitting with weatherstripping, double glazing, and movable insulation, they will still cause a third or more of your house's heat loss, since the upgrading of performance of walls, roof, doors, and the like is more effective thermally than the opportunities available for windows. Consequently, you should concentrate on upgrading your windows to emphasize their benefits rather than limiting your efforts to reducing their liabilities.

Several computer and measured analyses in recent years have concluded that, even though residential windows in general are substantial net losers of energy on a yearly basis, properly managed south-facing windows can provide far more usable solar heat than they lose at night, and thus are net gainers. Weatherstripping and double glazing take full advantage of this benefit (see margin opposite).

Double glazing not only reduces a window's convected heat loss, but its radiation as well. The addition of an outer glazing raises the surface temperature of the window's inner light (by approximately 15° over that of a single glazed window to 58° if outside air is in high twenties) since it is no longer in direct contact with, nor does it "see," the cold exterior environment. A warmer glass-surface temperature reduces the radiation to it from surfaces inside the house, including people. This markedly improves comfort in rooms having large glass areas.

A word of caution. In winter, there is usually more water vapor in the air inside a house than outside, due to higher air temperature, cooking, watering of houseplants, and so on. Where double-glazed windows have air paths to the inside (poor or no caulking of inner light) condensation between the glazings is likely to occur whenever moist warm air contacts the cooler glass surfaces inside the window. Although more an annoyance than a problem, protracted condensation can rot wood frames. Therefore, unless the double-glazing assembly is hermetically sealed, you should ensure that inner lights are well sealed against air flow, and that the window's dead-air space is provided with a small "weep hole" drilled through the frame to the *outside*. These precautions will tend to maintain the air space at the same relative humidity as the cold outside air, thus preventing condensation.

Weatherstripping and double glazing will improve the thermal performance of a window to a respectable degree, but alone are not enough to keep your house comfortably heated. Remember the influence of radiation when sitting in view of a large, cold, surface on a winter night is distinctly uncomfortable, regardless of whether the window is double glazed or not. If you are to prevent uncomfortable radiant losses from all your house's windows and manage your south-facing windows for a net thermal gain, you will require a means of control: an operable thermal barrier.

Simple curtains or drapes will largely prevent radiant losses from warm room surfaces and from skin to cold windows. A curtain is surrounded by air and, not being a good conductor, it therefore has a radiant temperature much closer to that of the air than the cold window. Consequently, it is not seen as "cold" by warm room surfaces. A simple curtain, however, can actually *increase* the conducted/convected heat loss from a window. Air in

First things first

1. Weatherstrip all doors and windows. Regardless of climate, existing "leaky" houses lose over half of the energy used to heat them through cracks around doors, windows, and poorly constructed building joints. Beyond the heat loss, the presence of chilling drafts around doors and windows is distinctly uncomfortable. Use Chapter 4 and the technical references in the bibliography for ideas on techniques and products.

2. Double glaze or add storm windows and doors in regions having heating seasons of 2500 degree-days or more (see page 314 for a definition of degree-days). Glass is a good heat conductor. Consequently, even a well weatherstripped window will lose a great deal of heat through its glass area. Still air is a relatively poor conductor. If another glass layer is added to the window, trapping a dead air space between the glazing layers, the window's heat loss will be reduced by 50 percent. The still air space, as an insulator, will prevent the convection/conduction of heat from warm inner glass to cold outside air. The inner glass will now lose most of its heat by radiating directly to the outer layer, which is much cooler than the inner light since it is in direct contact with the cold outside air flow. The air space is the key to the performance of the window. It must be still—that is, it must be enclosed on all sides—since moving air *is* quite effective in transferring heat. It should also separate the glazing layers enough to prevent direct conduction of heat from glass to glass, but not far enough to allow room for air movement. The optimum glass to glass distance is $\frac{1}{2}$ to 1 inch, but the window's performance will benefit greatly from any separation between $\frac{3}{8}$ to 4 inches.

Figure 12-10. **The Non-Sealed Double Glazed Window**

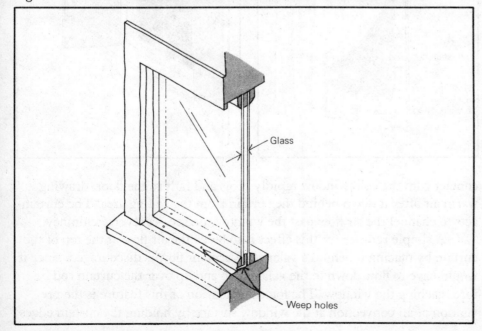

Glass

Weep holes

Double glazed windows not hermetically sealed require venting to the outside.

Figure 12-11. **Convection at a Curtained Window**

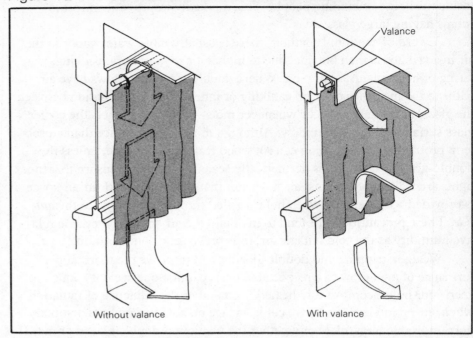

Without valance

With valance

Figure12-12.**Adding Insulation to a Conventional Curtain**

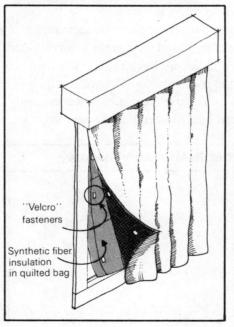

"Velcro" fasteners

Synthetic fiber insulation in quilted bag

Figure 12-13. **Insulating Shutter**

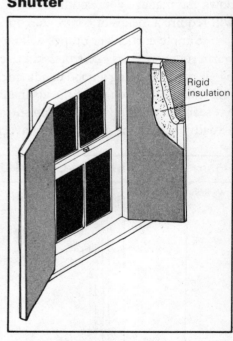

Rigid insulation

The thermal performance of a conventional curtain is substantially improved with the addition of insulation

contact with the cold window rapidly cools and falls to the floor, drawing warm air after it down behind the curtain from the ceiling area. The curtain acts to channel the air flow past the window surface—a reverse chimney.

A simple remedy for this effect is to block the air flow at the top of the curtain by placing it behind a valance. Warm air flow is discouraged, since it would have to flow down to the valance lip and up over the curtain rod before reaching the window. The logical extension of this feature is the prevention of all convection at the window surface by holding the curtain edges tightly to the window frame and sill, either with Velcro, staves of wood, or a hem weighted with sand. If these measures are contemplated, the curtain itself should be given some insulation value by using multiple layers of thick material or a quilt batting fill.

By far the most effective means of window thermal control is the insulating panel or shutter. In its simplest version, a piece of high-quality $\frac{3}{4}''$-thick polystyrene insulation board is cut to fit the window frame or the glass area itself. At night, the panel is taken out of a closet and either press-fitted into the window frame or held against the glass with permanently attached magnetic strips. Even this simple movable insulation will cut a double-glazed window's heat loss by 75 percent, bringing its insulation value to within half that of an insulated stud wall. Notes of caution: use only the best quality, closed-cell insulation board—not "beadboard," which lacks the strength to withstand daily handling. Painting the board with a high-quality epoxy paint will help protect its surface from degrading. Make sure the panel fits snugly against the window frame or glass to prevent convection losses.

A more permanent version of the movable panel is a hinged shutter, with a rigid wood frame and durable sheathing enclosing the insulation

Figure 12-14. "Rolladen"—Exterior Shading and Insulation

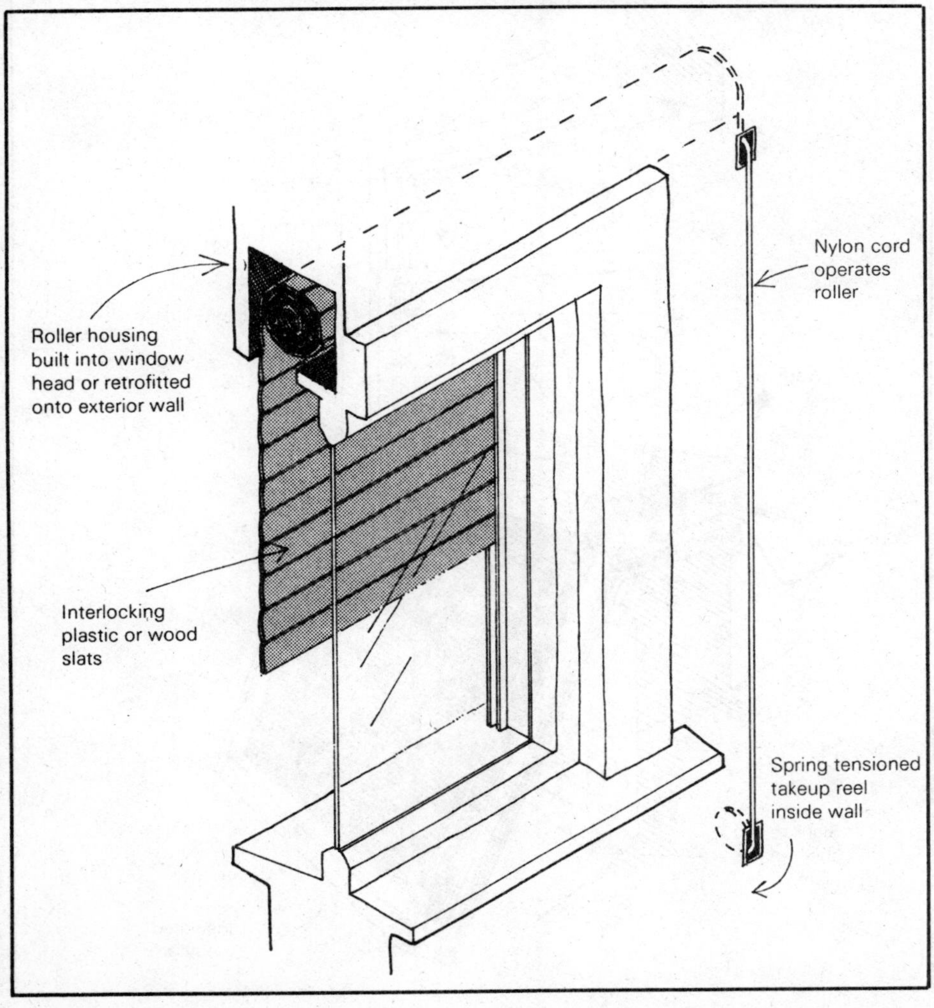

Roller housing built into window head or retrofitted onto exterior wall

Nylon cord operates roller

Interlocking plastic or wood slats

Spring tensioned takeup reel inside wall

board. This option combines durability with ease of operation, but requires a suitable window configuration if the opened insulating panels are not to appear awkward.

The most elegant, and most expensive, window shutter has been in common use in Europe for years. Generally called "Rolladen," it consists of interlocking wood, plastic, or foam-filled plastic slats, wound on a rolled housing mounted in the wall above a window. The shutter, when cranked or pulled by a cord from inside the house, descends to cover the outside of the window, guided by tracks on either side. The great virtue of this system is its exterior position. Although it cannot match an interior shutter in insulation value, it compensates by protecting the exterior glass surface from wind and radiant losses to the cold night environment. The use of Rolladen, double glazing, and an interior curtain will give as much comfort as an interior shutter, although the window assembly's heat loss will be slightly higher.

A secondary benefit of Rolladen is their ability to shade a window. When Rolladen are lowered but still hanging off the roller, the interlocking slats allow some light to pass through. In summer this feature is useful in

Figure 12-15. **Window Box Collector**

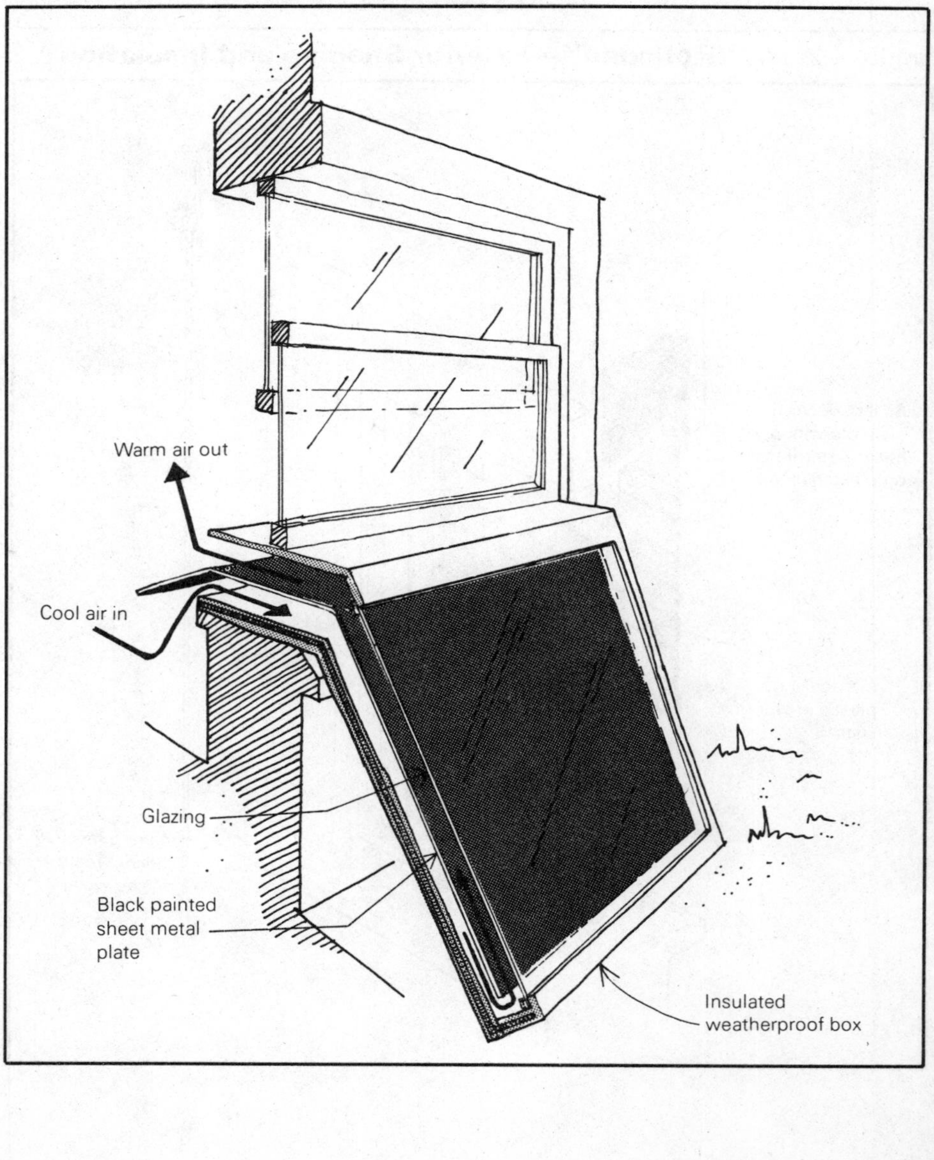

Warm air out

Cool air in

Glazing

Black painted sheet metal plate

Insulated weatherproof box

shading a window from direct sunlight while letting a diffuse, patterned light into the room.

Most manufacturers of Rolladen market kits suitable for the retrofit of existing windows, although you should expect to apply some ingenuity in adapting the kits to your situation. Also, expect to pay dearly for the product, at least for the near future, since most are imported. However, their multiple benefits, ease of operation, and thermal performance may make them an excellent investment when compared with the cost of exterior shading plus interior shutters.

The management of well-outfitted windows is a matter of simple and traditional common sense. In winter, open the house to the sun, and close it at night to retain as much heat as possible. In summer, do the reverse, closing the house against summer heat and glare, opening it wide at night to flush out the day's accumulated heat. The conscious management of your house's windows and doors will substantially reduce your heating and cooling costs, by 20 to 30 percent. Remember, however, that the manipulation of a window as an energy machine should run a poor third to its benefits in providing daylight and a psychologically important connection to the outside—it is not worth depriving yourself of daylight and view simply to reduce heat loss on a cloudy day, especially if you use electric light to compensate for the loss of daylight.

The Window Box Collector

If a managed south-facing window is a net energy gainer, then the larger the window the greater the benefit. Well, maybe. As those who experienced the large expanses of floor-to-ceiling glass in the "solar houses" of the fifties know, such a solution certainly provides a great deal of heat on a sunny winter day, but one also gets glare, extensive night heat loss, and chill convection drafts whenever the sun is not on the window.

A simple means of increasing the collection area of a window without increasing its glare or heat loss is the windowbox collector. It consists of an insulated sheet metal or plywood box with one side glazed. The box is divided by a flat black-painted metal or plywood sheet, and is connected to the space to be heated by fitting its manifold into the window frame. It operates by natural convection (see margin).

A word on orientation and tilt. The orientation of a collector (the direction it faces) and its tilt (its angle with the horizontal) affects performance, but not as much as intuition would indicate. The shadowing of a solar absorber (that black-painted plate) by the collector's structure and the reflection of light from its glazing reduces the percentage of sunlight converted to heat in proportion to the difference between actual and optimum tilt/orientation for that region. Generally, the optimum situation for a collector providing winter heat is this

• *Orientation:* Due south or slightly favoring the sun's position when the sky is clearest in midwinter. For instance, regions experiencing morning ground fog in winter may benefit from an orientation slightly west of south.

• *Tilt:* Perpendicular to the sun's average altitude at noon during the heating season. In practice, this results in two rules of thumb: tilt for winter

The window box collector

1. Sunlight passes through the glazing, striking the black-painted surface, where most of it is absorbed as heat.
2. The plate, heated by the sun, in turn heats the air surrounding it.
3. The warm air, becoming less dense as it expands with heat, rises in the collector, and passes into the room through the upper manifold; cool air is drawn out of the room down through the lower manifold.
4. This cycle continues as long as there is sufficient heat from the sun to power it.
5. In the absence of sunlight, the heat loss from the collector cools the air in the collector. The cool air, becoming more dense, forms a "plug" at the bottom of the collector, preventing any warm house air from circulating through the manifold. The collector is therefore self-regulating: it provides solar heat whenever available, and at all other times prevents the loss of heated air from the house through the collector so long as the house is warmer than the outside temperature.

Figure 12-16. **Nomenclature: Orientation and Tilt**

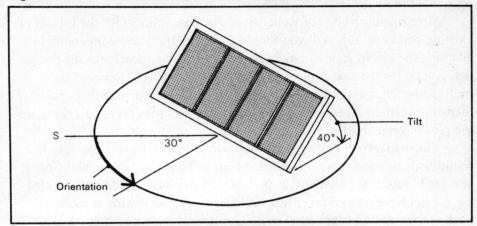

This collector's orientation is 30° east of south; its tilt is 40°

Figure 12-17. **Optimum Tilt for Winter Heating**

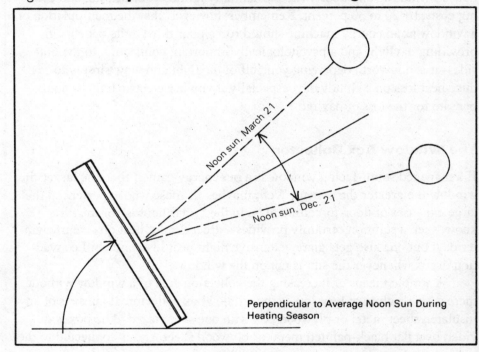

Noon sun, March 21

Noon sun, Dec. 21

Perpendicular to Average Noon Sun During Heating Season

heating: latitude + 10°; tilt for yearround heat: latitude.

If your house's southern windows do not face directly south, do not bother to try to make your windowbox collectors face due south. A collector oriented up to 45° east or west of south will still receive 75 percent of what it would collect if optimumly oriented. Furthermore, if for structural or aesthetic reasons you cannot tilt your collectors at the prescribed latitude + 10°, you will still receive approximately 75 percent of possible insulation with either a vertical or almost horizontal collector. In fact, if your region is in the northern part of the country or is blanketed with snow for much of the heating season, or both, a vertical collector will actually out-perform one placed at the "optimum" tilt. The combination of low-angle winter sunlight and reflection from the snow will increase its performance by 15 to 30 percent over one "correctly" tilted.

Do not expect a windowbox collector system to provide most of your house's heating. Even a collector system that effectively doubles your south-facing glass area will not provide more than 50 percent of your needs, since it has no means of storing heat collected during the day for use at night. This simple but efficient design option is, therefore, particularly well suited for regions having cold winter climates with heating deficits even on sunny days. The vertical windowbox version should be considered for those regions, since it combines superior performance with an opportunity to integrate the collector visually into the wall of the house.

The windowbox collector is inexpensive to build, and needs little or no "design." Consult several sources in the bibliography for illustrations of different versions, or invent your own. The only design requirements are that the collector box be airtight and that you provide a complete convection loop path (outlet higher than inlet).

Thermal Storage

Most well-insulated houses can heat themselves during the daytime using the sunlight entering the house through south-side windows. However, most of a house's heating load occurs at night. If the sun is to provide a significant portion of a house's heating energy, a means of storing heat collected during the day must be provided.

Heat can be stored in any dense material through heating it by radiation, convection, or direct conduction, insulating the heated mass during the storage period, and drawing out the stored heat by either exposing the heated mass to a cooler environment, or by convection or conduction to a cooler fluid (water, air, and so on).

Materials suitable for thermal storage must satisfy two requirements: 1. Be inexpensive, widely available, and easy to contain; and 2. Have a high heat capacity (the amount of energy stored per unit volume per degree temperature rise).

In practice, these requirements generally result in the use of water in tanks, rocks in bins or under floors, and masonry or concrete walls and floors. Your house already has some thermal storage in its most inexpensive form—the house's structure. For instance, if you have a concrete-slab floor in south-facing rooms, or even stud walls with gypsum board paneling, the thermal mass of the concrete or gypsum will absorb some of the heat collected by the south-facing windows during winter.

The influence of the thermal storage will tend to lengthen the period heated by the sun to as much as three or four hours after sunset, and will help reduce the overheating of a room flooded with winter sunlight by absorbing some of the heat gain directly.

From Managed Window to Natural System: A well-managed south window is a very effective means of helping your house heat itself, but even with the addition of a windowbox collector it is not a system. That is, the collector, storage, and heated space exist as a fortuitous combination with many imbalances that result in low overall performance and require careful attention to management.

The difference between a well-managed but fortuitous combination

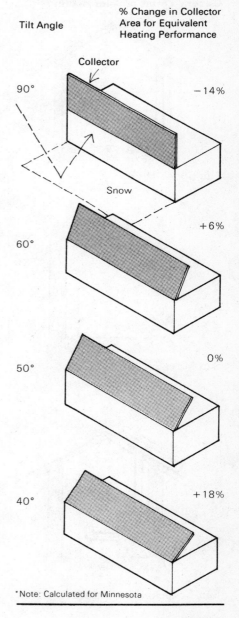

Figure 12-18. **Effect of Collector Tilt on System Performance***

Tilt Angle

% Change in Collector Area for Equivalent Heating Performance

Collector

90°   −14%

Snow

60°   +6%

50°   0%

40°   +18%

*Note: Calculated for Minnesota

329

Generic Forms of Solar Heating

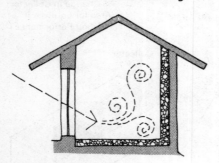

Sun-Space-Mass

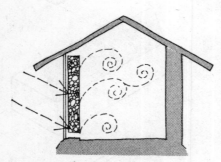

Sun-Mass-Space

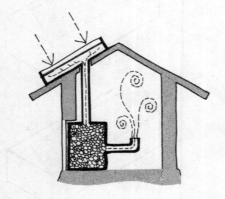

Sun-Collector-Mass-Space

and a solar system is one of the design and performance. A solar system's components are designed to perform together, and thus their performance is measured in terms of days, rather than hours, of thermal storage capacity, and the conventional heating system becomes an auxiliary, rather than a primary, source of heat.

It is often helpful to organize the various solar design options by the energy flow path through their components. All solar systems consist of at least three components and the heat transfer between them: Energy Source (Sun), Storage Medium (Mass), and the Heated Space (Space). In addition, systems collecting solar energy remote from the storage or heated space contain a fourth component (Collector). The margin shows several conceptual solar design configurations. For instance, the simple use of south glass and a room's structure as a solar system is illustrated as Option A "Sun-Space-Mass." At the other end of the scale is Option C "Sun-Collector-Mass-Space," which describes an active solar system with both collection and thermal storage remote from the heated space.

In between these extremes lie several options using various combinations of components. In this chapter they are presented roughly in order of increasing complexity, cost, and similarity in performance to conventional heating systems. Remember, in shopping for design options suitable for adaptation to your house, weigh their merits in light of the common-sense guidelines given in the section above headed First Things First.

Direct Solar Gain

Like many solar applications, the direct use of sunlight to heat houses is not a new development. Frank Lloyd Wright, in creating his "Usonian" houses during the thirties (a set of modest houses—priced between $7,000 and $10,000 in 1940—designed for middle class families of limited means and typified by radiant floor heating, novel construction methods, and open planning), relied heavily on extensive expanses of south-facing glass protected by roof overhangs to help temper living areas, aided by hot-water-fed radiant floor heating. His influence spread rapidly during the late forties and early fifties, and the "solar house," with its vast expanses of south-facing glass, extensive use of concrete and masonry floors and walls, and marked roof overhangs, became quite popular. Unfortunately, most designers and clients lacked Wright's understanding of the dynamics of sunlight and climate: glass areas became overlarge, overhangs were no longer designed for appearance and function, and glass areas expanded on east, west, and north facades. The results were houses that cooked in summer, froze in winter, and were very expensive to heat and cool, even during the energy-cheap sixties. Only recently, in the work of designers such as David Wright, has a renaissance of the "solar house" successfully combined architectural excellence with functional comfort and respectable solar performance. The lesson of this short history is clear: the direct-gain design concept is extremely simple, but its execution requires special care and understanding. Still, do not be afraid to investigate this option. Understanding grows out of study, and is not necessarily the province of design professionals.

A typical direct-gain solar system consists of a heated space—a living

Figure 12-19. **Direct Gain Solar Heating System**

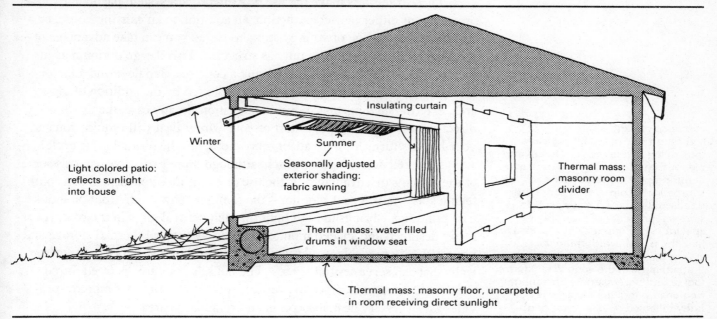

Winter

Insulating curtain

Summer

Light colored patio: reflects sunlight into house

Seasonally adjusted exterior shading: fabric awning

Thermal mass: masonry room divider

Thermal mass: water filled drums in window seat

Thermal mass: masonry floor, uncarpeted in room receiving direct sunlight

room, all south-facing rooms, and so on, that is largely glazed on the south-facing side, and equipped with the same conservation features that are used on standard windows, only to a greater degree, because the potential for heat loss is greater with a larger glass area. The heated space has a substantial area of thermal mass—concrete floor, masonry wall, water-filled window seats—in plain view of the window and preferably in the path of direct winter sunlight. The entrance of sunlight is controlled by manually closing blinds or drapes, venting by opening windows, and by the seasonal shading of the window by a roof overhang. The sequence of operation of the system is given in the margin.

The performance of a direct-gain system is primarily dependent on your house's configuration and your expectations. If you have masonry walls dividing the solar-heated space from other rooms, those rooms will receive some benefit from the radiation of heat stored in the wall, but later at night than the solar-heated room, again due to the resistance of the masonry to heat flow (referred to as "thermal lag," about which more later). If not, then expect little direct heating of other rooms, since the storage heats primarily by radiation. However, your system can easily provide well over 90 percent of the comfort heating for your living area, and keep the chill off the rest of the house.

The great advantages of a direct-gain system are its simplicity and integration with the house's structure. If you manually control the shading and movable insulation at the window line, and if you are able to amortize part of the added glass and masonry cost against savings in standard structural and heating equipment costs, the system will be quite inexpensive in relation to its performance.

However, you must be prepared to accept the possibility of fading of furnishings exposed to direct or reflected sunlight, and the necessity of conscientious daily management of your windows' shades and insulation, if the

Operating sequence of the direct-gain solar system

1. As the sun's path sinks lower in the sky during the heating season, direct sunlight is allowed to shine through the glass onto the concrete or masonry floor or the water-filled containers, and is diffused and reflected onto the space's masonry walls.

2. The light striking the floor or wall surface is either reflected to strike other surfaces in the room or absorbed by the surface as heat. A dark-colored floor surface is most effective in absorbing heat, but if other areas of thermal mass can be provided (walls, free-standing tubes of water) a light floor can be used to diffuse the solar energy evenly throughout the space. This approach may even be more efficient than trying to absorb most of the incoming energy on one surface. The rate at which thermal storage can accept heat is limited by its conductivity (for instance, silver conducts heat more efficiently than wood). Since most materials suitable for use as thermal storage have limited conductivity, your dark-painted floor will not be able to absorb much of the heat from the sun. It will radiate and convect the excess, quickly overheating the room if the space does not need the heat. Your system will perform more effectively (that is, store a greater percentage of the incoming solar energy) if you can "smear" the light over a large area of mass, thus preventing the "overloading" of its ac-

331

system is to maintain comfort rather than freeze and roast the heated space.

These trade-offs make the use of a direct-gain system particularly appropriate for either new construction, an addition to an existing house, or a significant renovation of your existing house, so you can take advantage of the thermal storage's double duty as structure. This design option may also be suitable for an existing house having a concrete-slab floor and a major southern exposure, which can be easily exploited by the addition of glass area, exterior shading, and movable insulation. In any case, the use of a direct-gain system to supply most of your winter heat will require you and your house's furnishings to adapt more closely to the diurnal solar cycle.

A related design option which, although more expensive, cancels some of the systems disadvantages, is the use of a roof monitor instead of a south-facing glass wall. A roof monitor—the familiar "saw tooth" roof on industrial buildings—brings in high light through vertical glass in the roof. A correctly designed and shaded monitor, backed by vertical thermal storage and provided with movable insulation, can direct the sun's energy onto storage walls that can serve several spaces. The house's floor area is freed for conventional furnishings, since the vertical walls under the roof monitor provides the necessary heat absorption and reradiation area.

In new construction this concept can be carried further by providing an interior atrium, lit by roof monitors and surrounded by thermal storage walls. In the morning, the walls fronting living spaces are heated. In the afternoon, as the sun moves to the west, the walls on the east side of the atrium, fronting the bedrooms, receive their share of sunlight. By this time, the heat collected on the west walls has traveled through the wall, and is warming the living spaces during the evening. By bedtime, the east walls have also begun to radiate heat into the bedrooms: an example of the planned integration of daily activities with the diurnal thermal cycle of the house.

Trombe Walls

The logical extension of the direct-gain concept is to move the thermal storage mass from the living area to the collector, thus avoiding the fading, glare, and overheating that occurs when you live in a solar collector. The thermal mass is then heated directly on one side by the sun, and a few hours later it radiates this heat from the other side of the wall, facing the room.

The practical application of this concept was developed first in France during the sixties by Felix Trombe (pronounced "Trōm"). A concrete wall is placed between a living space and a conventional, shaded, glazed window wall, as shown in Figure 12-21. The wall is held three to four inches behind the glass plane, and rectangular vents are provided at the top and bottom of the wall connecting the room to the air space between wall and collector. Dampers may also be provided to vent the air space to the outside. The system's operation is given in the margin on page 334.

A secondary benefit of the Trombe wall is its ability to help cool a house during summer. In summer, the wall's glazing is shaded by the roof overhang, but still transmits heat from reflected sunlight and air-temperature differential. Air in the space between glazing and mass wall is heated

ceptance of heat.

A rough rule of thumb suggests that, at the minimum, you should supply four square feet of floor area sunlit during part of the day for each square foot of glass area supplying direct sunlight, if your system is to store enough energy to supply respectable performance. If you wish to limit the risk of overheating the space, provide eight square feet of thermal mass in the space per square foot of glass area supplying sunlight, and ensure that the sunlight is partially reflected onto secondary absorption surfaces. Of course, the floor, wall, or free-standing glass area must not be obscured by carpet, wall hangings, or plants if it is to earn its keep as thermal storage.

3. At night, as the space begins to lose heat to other rooms in the house and to the outside as heat loss, the thermal storage begins to reradiate the heat it collected during the day. This process is essentially self-regulating, in that the mechanism regulating the rate of heat flow out of storage is the temperature differential between the surface of the storage and other surfaces in the room. As the room's temperature drops, the relatively light furniture, furnishings, and of course, the window area, cool off too, thus "drawing" heat out of storage. Since the rate of heat flow out of storage is as deliberate as its inflow, the room's thermal mass will generally maintain a comfortable environment throughout the night (a hearth is often still warm in the mornings, long after the night's fire is burned out).

4. The next day the process is repeated, as soon as direct, reflected, or even diffuse sunlight strikes the surface of the room's thermal storage, heating it enough to reverse the direction of heat flow.

Figure 12-20. **South Facing Roof Monitors and Central Atrium**

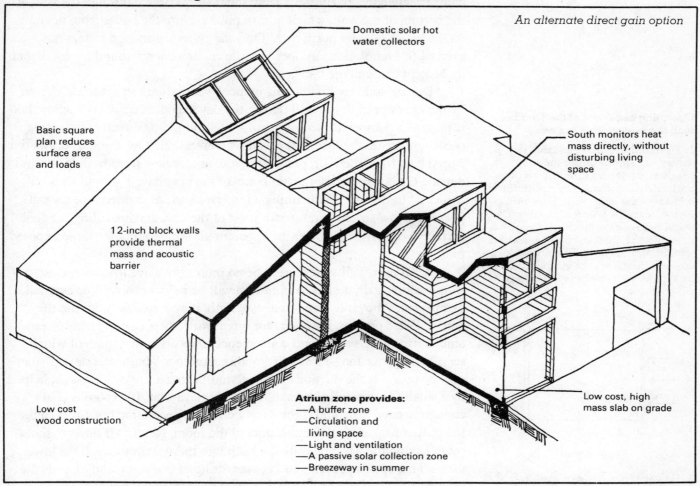

An alternate direct gain option

Domestic solar hot water collectors

Basic square plan reduces surface area and loads

South monitors heat mass directly, without disturbing living space

12-inch block walls provide thermal mass and acoustic barrier

Low cost wood construction

Low cost, high mass slab on grade

Atrium zone provides:
—A buffer zone
—Circulation and living space
—Light and ventilation
—A passive solar collection zone
—Breezeway in summer

Figure 12-21. **Trombe Wall**

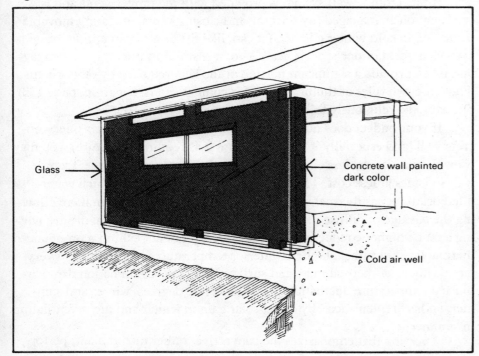

Glass

Concrete wall painted dark color

Cold air well

The Trombe wall

1. A 12-inch-thick Trombe wall in a well-insulated house, when operating under "normal" temperate-zone winter conditions, will provide sufficient storage carryover for 1 to 1.5 day's heat loss.

2. In planning for use of a Trombe wall as a house's primary heating source, allow for approximately 1 square foot of Trombe wall surface area for each 2 to 4 cubic feet of house volume to be directly or indirectly heated.

333

and rises to the top of the wall, where it is exhausted to the outside through a damper above the glazing. Air from the house is drawn through the vent at the bottom of the wall, which in turn pulls air into the house from openings on the house's cooler north side. Thus the system, although it does not precool the ventilation air, does provide enough energy to induce cooling air movement through the house.

During summer nights, this induced ventilation can continue, driven by the heat stored in the wall during the day. An alternative cooling method is to open a damper at the bottom of the glazing, thus directly circulating cool night air up the face of the wall by convection. The night air draws the stored heat from the wall, precooling it to accept heat from both inside and outside the house during the hot hours of the next day. The wall thus becomes a "heat sink," maintaining an interior surface temperature several degrees below air temperature for most of the day, and providing the cool surface area that helps lower the apparent air temperature for those exposed to it.

A Trombe wall system need be no more expensive to construct than a simple direct-gain design. A premium will be paid, however, for external dampers and movable insulation, especially if operable from within the house. These options, however, are often worth their cost in terms of extended use of the system and convenience in its operation, both of which serve to improve long-term performance. Another "extra-cost option" that may be useful is the ducting of convection-heated air to other rooms, helped by a small fan controlled by a differential thermostat. If a room is cool enough to need heat, and if the Trombe wall is generating hot air, then the fan pushes heated air through a duct to the room. Return air flows to the room having the Trombe wall and back into the system through the lower vents. This option prevents local overheating of one room and extends the influence of the Trombe wall to a greater portion of the house.

If the Trombe wall system is provided with the proper vents and is conscientiously managed (by opening and closing vents, operating movable insulation in cold winter climates) it can, like the direct-gain option, provide over 90 percent of one space's heat. Also, if assisted by ducting or room layout, it can provide a significant portion of the heat required by other rooms. There are two rules of thumb, useful for comparison (see margin, page 333) but not to be religiously followed for design.

If your budget does not allow for construction of a 12-inch-thick concrete wall (and especially if you cannot use it as required structure), you may want to consider the less elaborate options that retain most of the Trombe wall's virtues at less cost. The cheapest is the drum wall, in which water-filled drums act as thermal storage, with the interstices between them allowing the passage of diffuse daylight and convected heat. Water in drums, having a much higher conductivity than concrete, does not exhibit a pronounced thermal lag, but rather stabilizes interior temperatures by providing a very large amount of thermal mass and surface area. This combination dampens diurnal temperature fluctuations to within a few degrees, winter and summer, and is "replenished" by direct solar gain in winter and night ventilation in summer.

A version that emphasizes the convective, rather than radiant, perfor-

Operating sequence of the Trombe wall thermal storage system

1. During the heating season, low winter sun shines under the roof overhang, passing through the glass and striking the rough, black-painted surface of the mass wall. (The wall surface may be painted any dark, flat color, but black is the most absorptive.) Most of the sunlight is absorbed into the wall as heat. The surface of the wall heats, and begins to transmit heat through its mass to the colder side of the wall.

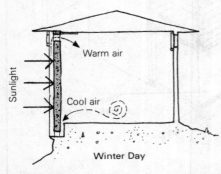

Winter Day

2. However, the hot surface (up to 150°) of the wall also convects heat to the air between it and the glass. Much of that heat is captured by providing a convection loop to the cooler room. The warm, solar-heated air rises to the top of the air space and passes into the room through the vents in the wall. Cool air is drawn into the collector space from the room's floor area through the lower vents. Thus, while the wall is heating itself for night reradiation, the system provides daytime convected heat by using energy that otherwise would be lost through the glass.

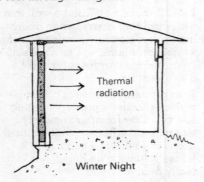

Winter Night

Figure 12-22. **Drum Wall**

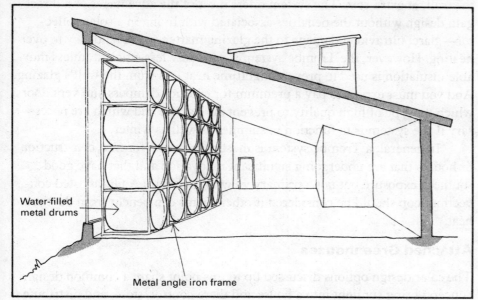

Water-filled metal drums

Metal angle iron frame

mance of the Trombe system is the tube wall, which consists of water-filled tubes of metal or plastic set in a house's wall, glazed in front and insulated behind. Here, the heat transfer is by convection only, but the option is very suitable for retrofit on existing wood-framed south walls.

The Trombe system, then, offers a potential improvement in comfort and is surely more forgiving of mismanagement than a direct-gain system, but at the cost of a substantial architectural intrusion, especially if your pri-

Figure 12-23. **Tube Wall**

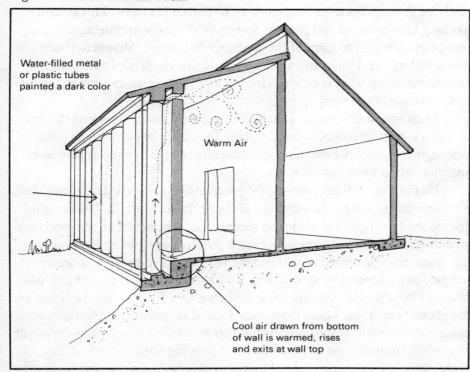

Water-filled metal or plastic tubes painted a dark color

Warm Air

Cool air drawn from bottom of wall is warmed, rises and exits at wall top

3. As the sun sets the convection slows, as the rate of heat loss through the glass begins to "catch up" with the rate of heat radiated and convected from the wall surface. At some point during the evening the convection cycle will reverse, drawing warm air from the room to feed the heat loss through the glass. To prevent this, the system is provided with a "well" at the bottom of the mass wall. The coldest and most dense air in the system collects here, and forms a "plug" to prevent air circulation, in that the energy driving the night convection loop is insufficient to overcome the weight of the cold air "plug." The air within the collector air space, therefore, remains still until the system absorbs sufficient energy from the sun the next day to warm the cold air and move it. If, for structural reasons, this well cannot be provided, manually operated vent doors or movable insulation doors over the front of the collector will perform the same function,

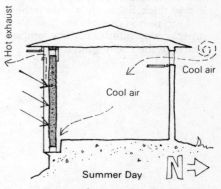

Hot exhaust

Cool air

Cool air

Summer Day

N

at a premium of manual operation twice a day. A fourth, very simple, option is the use of polyethylene flaps backed by hardware cloth on the inside of the upper vents and the outside of the lower ones. The flaps are opened and closed by the slightest air movement, thus forming a reasonably good barrier against air flowing in the wrong direction.

4. The primary heating mechanism for this system is the radiation of heat from the interior surface of the thermal-storage wall, and the key to its performance is its thickness. The thickness of the wall is governed by two criteria—its heat-storage capacity, and the length of time delay between the charging cycle on one side of the wall and the radiation cycle on the other—its "thermal lag." A thicker wall, having more mass per unit area, will store more heat than a thin wall, but beyond a certain thickness the thermal resistance of the wall itself will dissipate much of the heat, thus reducing the room's mean radiant temperature and, therefore, its comfort. The thermal lag of an overly thick wall will delay the passage of the day's heat through the wall, so that its added capacity will be wasted because its peak radiation period will not coincide with the space's need for heat. The design goal, therefore, is to strike a compromise between the optimum delay period, required heat capacity, and desired radiant surface temperature of the wall. In practice, Trombe walls built of standard concrete have usually been constructed eight to twelve inches thick. Such walls have a thermal lag period of six to ten hours, and develop interior surface temperatures in the mid-eighties.

mary view is to the south, although windows can be easily incorporated into the wall, at extra cost. The system offers most of the advantages of a direct-gain design without the penalties associated with living in a solar collector—glare, ultraviolet damage to the glazing matter, and a tendency to overheating. However, the Trombe system is generally less efficient unless movable insulation is used to prevent nighttime heat loss from the wall's glazing. And you must expect to pay a premium for exterior dampers and vent doors, which must be of high quality to prevent air leakage and which are necessary if the system is to function in summer as well as winter.

In general, a Trombe system is most appropriate for new construction or houses that are undergoing significant renovation and that have good southern exposure but not a primary view to the south. A fan-assisted convection loop should be considered if other rooms can benefit from daytime heat.

Attached Greenhouses

The solar design options discussed up to this point share a common design concept: bring sunlight into a house and there control, store, and distribute it as heat. Necessarily, these concepts demand structural and operational concessions from the house and its inhabitants. An alternate concept is used by another group of systems: collect sunlight as heat *outside* the house's envelope, while storing and distributing its heat inside the house. This concept avoids the problems associated with opening and closing your house to the outside environment conscientiously twice a day, but at the cost of greater system complexity.

The attached-greenhouse system is actually a transition between paths, in that it collects heat outside the house proper and yet offers the considerable amenity of a sun-warmed winter living and growing space, which can easily be shut off from the house proper to reduce heat loss. This amenity has long been a useful and popular feature of domestic architecture in Europe, especially in the form of the seventeenth-century "orangerie" or "wintering gallery" and the conservatory of Victorian England. In fact, the Dutch developed what is now referred to as a "solar greenhouse" in the early seventeenth century.

In its simplest form, an attached-greenhouse system involves the erection of a lean-to greenhouse backing onto the south, or even east or west, side of your house. A French door connecting the greenhouse is provided, and you have a source of solar heat.

Part of the sunlight entering the greenhouse is absorbed by plants, for photosynthesis, and by the structure of the greenhouse itself. The remainder goes to the heating of the air in the greenhouse. Since even on winter days a greenhouse will collect more heat than it requires to offset its daytime loss, the space must be vented or you run the risk of exceeding the maximum temperature tolerated by most plants. If that excess heat is vented into your house rather than out through the greenhouse's roof vent, both the house and the plants benefit: the house from solar-heated air having a high moisture content (from plant evapotranspiration) relative to the usually too-dry air of a centrally heated house in winter, thus improving human comfort; and the plants from a supply of tempered house air that prevents thermal shock from too-cold outside air flowing into the greenhouse.

At night, the house is closed off from the greenhouse by shutting the French doors and drawing heavy curtains across them. The greenhouse, with its glazing layer, volume of relatively still air, and radiation from its own structure, will help reduce heat loss from the house through the French door to a level below that of a comparable door equipped with movable insulation. In summer, the greenhouse must be shaded, both to control temperatures in the space and to prevent burning of the leaves of any seedlings you may want to propagate.

Of course, this level of greenhouse retrofit, like the windowbox collector, is not a system, but only a collector that requires close attention if it is to provide a net energy benefit to your house. If it is to become a solar heating system, you must improve the performance of the greenhouse itself, and provide a means of storing heat and controlling its movement from the greenhouse into the house.

Like any greenhouse, a simple lean-to must itself be retrofitted if it is not to lose so much heat at night during winter that your prize cherry tomatoes at best remain stunted and, more likely, freeze on the vine. You must reduce its heat loss by following the same techniques used on the house's windows: weatherstripping all openings, double glazing, and, if your plants' constitutions are delicate and your concern for their health strong enough, providing movable insulation.

A word on glazing materials for greenhouses: glass is the common building glazing material due to virtues of undistorted light transmission, wide availability, longevity, and tradition. Greenhouses, however, do not need transparent glazing. In fact, the use of translucent glazing often improves the growing environment due to the diffusion of light by the glazing, thus tending to more evenly light the entire space. Consequently, you should consider using one of the cheaper alternatives presently available for greenhouse glazing, and even for collector covers, skylights, and utility-room windows. These range from inexpensive UV-resistant polyethylene to thermally efficient but quite expensive double-wall acrylic plastic. Table 12-2 compares some of the qualities of the more commonly available options. You

Table 12-2. **Greenhouse Glazing Materials Comparison**

Single Glazing Material	Longwave Transmission, %	Daily Average Shortwave Trans., %	Cost Index (glass = 100)
Polyethylene, 4 mil	80	88.8	4
Flat Fiberglass, Regular, 25 mil	12	83.1	56
Flat Fiberglass, Premium, 40 mil	6	72.9	84
Polyester, weatherable, 5 mil (Mylar)	32	86.5	36
Corrugated Fiberglass, 40 mil	8	79.2	110
Corrugated Fiberglass, 40 mil	7	78.1	98
Glass, Double Strength, 1/8''	3	87.8	100
Polycarbonate, 1/16'' (Lexan)	6	84.4	500
Polyvinylfluoride, 3 mil (Tedlar)	43	91	34

should consider materials having the best combination of these qualities: low cost, high visible light transmission, low long-wave radiation transmission, and long life. Of course, for your situation, it may make more sense to replace cheap polyethylene glazing every two years than to invest in expensive glass or acrylic. This option has been so attractive to commercial growers that special glazing systems have been developed to allow the easy and inexpensive replacement of poly every two years.

You should also keep an eye out for the commercial introduction of selective-transmission thin film plastics, the first generation of which is now ending its R&D phase. These thin plastic films promise to provide various combinations of light and heat transmission and reflection that will allow your windows to very efficiently control the passage of light and heat and yet maintain visual clarity. For instance, one version will have qualities of very high light transmission and equally high heat reflection. Another will reflect both heat and light.

Next you must provide thermal storage. If your greenhouse will be used for winter planting, it will require a source of nighttime heat to maintain the space's temperature at least above freezing. A direct-gain thermal-storage wall at the back of the greenhouse, combined with additional mass in the floor (brick, concrete, gravel) and under growing benches (water drums) will in most cases provide enough thermal mass to allow the greenhouse to "coast" through the night using the heat stored during the day. Consult the several references on solar greenhouses for other ideas and design information.

If you plan to use the greenhouse solely as a solarium, with perhaps a few house plants, you will not need to provide separate thermal storage for the greenhouse itself. In either case, you will want to provide an efficient

Figure 12-24. **Convection Loop Heat Collection**

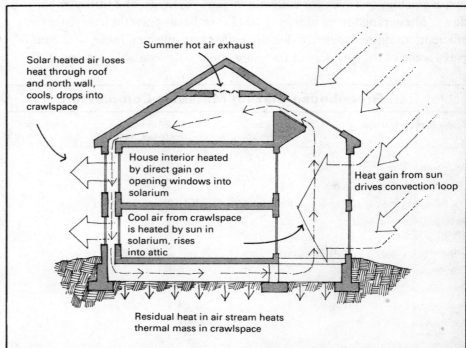

means of storing and distributing the greenhouse's excess heat. The simplest option, and the one most suitable for the retrofit of existing houses, is to re-place the existing stud wall between house and greenhouse with a relatively thin masonry one—thinner than a Trombe wall, since it will not store as much heat operating at the lower temperatures required by a greenhouse. However, its nighttime radiation into the house, coupled with the convected heat available from the top of the greenhouse, will give it a respectable per-formance.

Two other storage options offer superior performance but are more suitable for new construction. We turn first to Lee Porter Butler's concept of using the energy of natural convection to drive a circulation loop which, in effect, wraps a house in a blanket of solar-heated air.

Natural convection forces solar-heated air from the top of an attached greenhouse into a series of plenum spaces built into the structural spaces in and above a house's ceiling, inside its north wall, and under its floor. The air stream travels across the house, down the north side, and back under the floor to rise again into the greenhouse through a wood grating set in its floor. The operation of the convection loop depends both on the air stream being heated by the sun, and its losing enough heat during its loop to prevent the formation of a stagnant warm air mass in the attic, thereby blocking circula-tion. This necessary heat loss is the key to the ingenuity of the system. But-ler's concept is to "sacrifice" the heat collected in the greenhouse to fuel the heat loss from the majority of the building's surfaces, thus maintaining a nearly steady state thermal environment within the house. The difference is made up by heat from cooking, people, a small wood stove, and some con-vected and radiant heat from both the greenhouse itself and the gravel-covered earth beneath the house's floor (heated by whatever heat remains in

Figure 12-25. **Convection Loop Heat Loss**

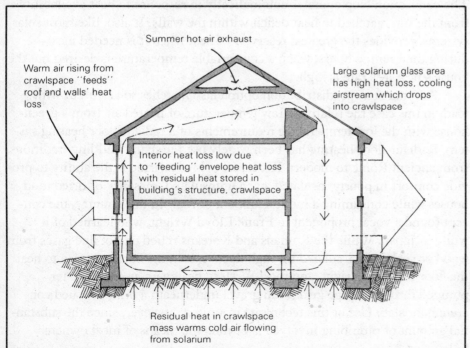

Summer hot air exhaust

Warm air rising from crawlspace "feeds" roof and walls' heat loss

Large solarium glass area has high heat loss, cooling airstream which drops into crawlspace

Interior heat loss low due to "feeding" envelope heat loss with residual heat stored in building's structure, crawlspace

Residual heat in crawlspace mass warms cold air flowing from solarium

Figure 12-26. **Greenhouse Coupled with Rockbed/Radiant Floor**

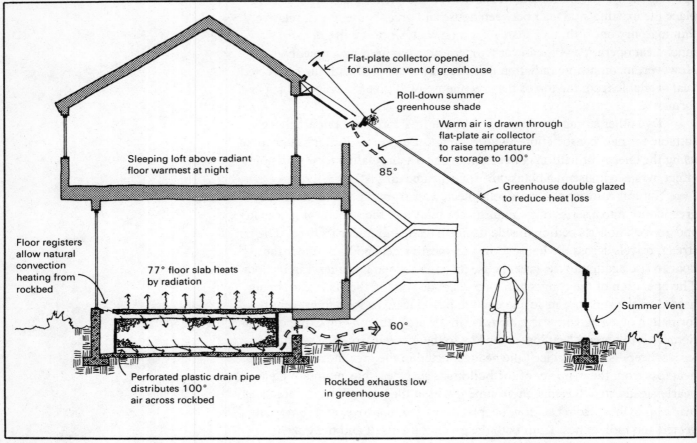

Flat-plate collector opened
for summer vent of greenhouse

Roll-down summer
greenhouse shade

Warm air is drawn through
flat-plate air collector
to raise temperature
for storage to 100°

85°

Greenhouse double glazed
to reduce heat loss

Sleeping loft above radiant
floor warmest at night

Floor registers
allow natural
convection
heating from
rockbed

77° floor slab heats
by radiation

Summer Vent

60°

Perforated plastic drain pipe
distributes 100°
air across rockbed

Rockbed exhausts low
in greenhouse

the convection loop's air stream).

An additional virtue of this concept is its tendency to regulate itself. The convection loop operates automatically in response to heat availability from the sun matched to heat deficit within the walls. It also, like most solar systems, provides the greatest reservoir of heat when it is needed most—during the evening hours, when a comfortable temperature is desired but the house's heat loss rate is high.

Another storage/distribution option also matches solar output with load, in this case the relatively low temperature of heated air from a greenhouse with the low temperature requirements of a radiant-floor heating system. Radiant-floor heating has been widely used in many building traditions, from ancient Rome to modern Korea. Its primary virtue is the ability to provide comfort in poorly insulated, even uninsulated, masonry or dried mud houses while consuming a modest amount of fuel. In this country, the concept found a vocal proponent in Frank Lloyd Wright, who learned of it while in Japan. While the Romans and Koreans relied on hot flue gases from wood or coal fires circulated through ducts cast in the floor masonry to heat the floor surface, Wright, and most Western designers, used hot water pumped through a pipe grid set in gravel underneath a thin, polished concrete floor slab. Use of this technique is limited, however, since the substantial amount of plumbing involved is beyond the means of most owners today.

What Wright noticed in Japan, the "climatic effect" of this sort of heating, is simply the result of providing a large surface area exposed to the view of a room's inhabitants, and which has a surface temperature warm enough to offset the chilling effect of a cool air temperature. A floor is an ideal surface to use, as it offers the desirable combination of "cool head—warm feet." For a room that is reasonably well insulated (ceiling insulation is most important, since the floor "sees" the ceiling best and therefore would tend to lose heat to an uninsulated ceiling much faster than to uninsulated walls or windows), the floor surface temperature need be only 78 to 85°F. This low surface temperature was particularly suited to the limitations of Roman and Korean use of flue gases from wood or coal fires directed through underfloor ducts. It is also particularly well-suited to the temperatures provided by a solar system.

The solar-heated radiant floor, an alternative developed by Peter Calthorpe, promises to substantially reduce a radiant floor's construction costs and provide multiple benefits. A rockbed is located within the footing walls of the portion of the house to be heated. It is filled with commonly available gravel or small stones, and is supplied with many small air ducts set in its upper and lower surfaces, in the form of perforated plastic drainage pipe connecting to larger plenums at opposite sides of the bed. A thin concrete slab is poured directly onto the rock surface, the rockbed itself supporting the weight of the floor. Any relatively conductive floor-finish material can be used, from tile to thin wood parquet directly applied to the slab surface.

Little structural changes are required (none if an existing door is used), and the house benefits from daytime solar heat without increasing its nighttime heat loss. If, for reasons of cost or lack of yard space, even this option is ruled out, consider a windowbox greenhouse. You can't sun yourself in it, but you can grow your winter tomatoes there and it will provide you with solar heat, in proportion to its size. At night, simply close the window and drapes to prevent losing heat through the windowbox.

Indirect Systems

The concept that architectural space be designed to help provide comfort for its inhabitants has been part of the mainstream of Western architectural thought since Vitruvius and his often quoted dictum outlining the proper qualities of architecture: "Firmness, commodity, delight." Unfortunately, this notion seems to have slipped our mind during the past few generations. Consequently, while we might wish otherwise, since the 1973 Mideast oil embargo by far the greatest national effort has been developing of technology for providing solar mechanical systems that are either comparable to or replace conventional heating and cooling machinery. It is now apparent that such mechanical systems are substantially more expensive than the architectural ones discussed earlier, for a similar level of performance. They have virtues, however, that may make investment in them quite attractive—*after* you have considered and invested in those architectural solar design features suitable for your situation.

Solar mechanical systems generally separate the collector, storage, and distribution of energy from significant dependence on a house's form, struc-

Figure 12-27. **Window Box Greenhouse**

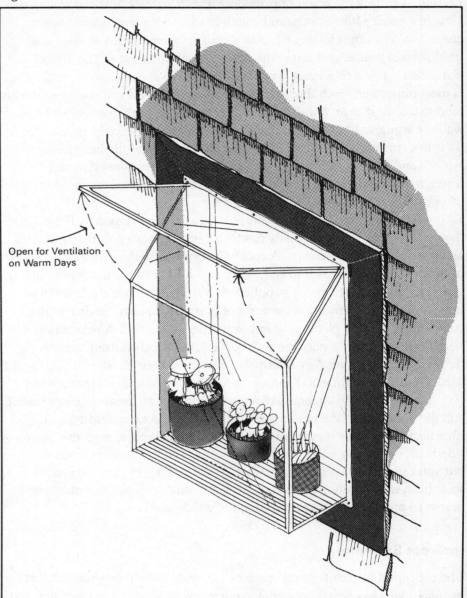

Open for Ventilation
on Warm Days

ture, orientation, and interior layout. This independence is one of their advantages, in that they can, within limits, be "bolted" onto most existing structures, including the very common "universal" house designs inveighed against earlier, without significantly disturbing the house or its owner's habits. They are also generally compatible with conventional heating and plumbing systems, thus making full use of your house's existing investment.

This compatibility offers a third advantage: it gives one a level of control over comfort coupled with a freedom from daily management very similar to that with conventional heating systems. That is, you would not know, or even have to care, whether your house or water was being heated by the sun or the conventional auxiliary heating system. The largely automatic control of solar mechanical systems ensures that the sun's heat will be used whenever possible to do the job. In any case, the hot air coming out of the wall register and the hot water from the tap maintains a temperature as constant as that from a conventional system alone. (Actually, your hot water heater's performance may be significantly improved in that it will be harder to run out of hot water since the system has a larger storage capacity.)

Solar Mechanical Heating Systems

Referring back to the classification of solar design options by the energy flow path through their components, solar mechanical systems form the "Sun-Collector-Mass-Space" option, with another component—"Control"—linking their interaction. Two standard systems will be described—"air" and "water"—classified by the fluid generally used to transport heat between components.

Figure 12-28. **Sun-Collector-Mass-Space**

The energy of the sun, although powerful, is widely distributed. (The earth receives each day only fifty billionths of the sun's daily energy output, yet even this miniscule amount is over two hundred times the total *annual* U.S. energy consumption.) In the systems described above, the sun's energy is largely used as received, as low-temperature heat derived from direct and diffuse sunlight. A solar mechanical system, however, must concentrate the sun's energy, for two reasons. First, compatibility with conventional heating equipment demands a high-temperature heat source, usually above 100°F. Second, since the system's thermal storage does not perform double duty as structure or amenity, its size must be reduced to conserve space and reduce cost. Reducing the volume of thermal storage requires that the heat be stored at a higher temperature, if the total amount of heat stored is to be

Figure 12-29. **A Simple Concentrating Collector**

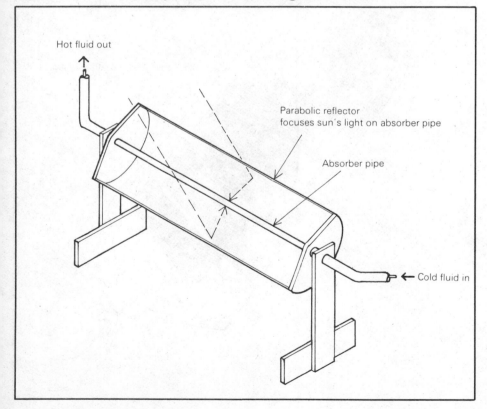

Hot fluid out

Parabolic reflector
focuses sun's light on absorber pipe

Absorber pipe

Cold fluid in

A collector that will provide high temperature heat but requires clear sky and direct sunlight for efficient operation

equivalent to that stored at low temperatures in structure.

The sun's energy can be optically concentrated at the collector, using reflectors or lenses to beam light collected over a large area onto a small one. This method, although quite efficient, is not commonly used on residential systems for several reasons: It requires seasonal to continuous adjustment to track the sun, depending on its degree of concentration of sunlight. Its usual output temperature range—180 to 250°F—is higher than that normally required for residential systems. But it will collect efficiently only under clear-sky, bright-sunlight conditions. Its *overall* efficiency is usually quite low for residential heating systems requiring medium temperatures during often hazy winters when the sun is low in the sky. Furthermore, its performance is very much reduced if its reflecting surfaces or lenses are allowed to become dirty. This means the collectors must be washed every few weeks, or even more often in regions having heavy air pollution.

Most residential solar mechanical systems use "flat-plate collectors," which, as the name implies, collect the sun's energy by the heating of a surface; then the system transfers that heat to storage. This method concen-

Figure 12-30. **Air Heating Collector**

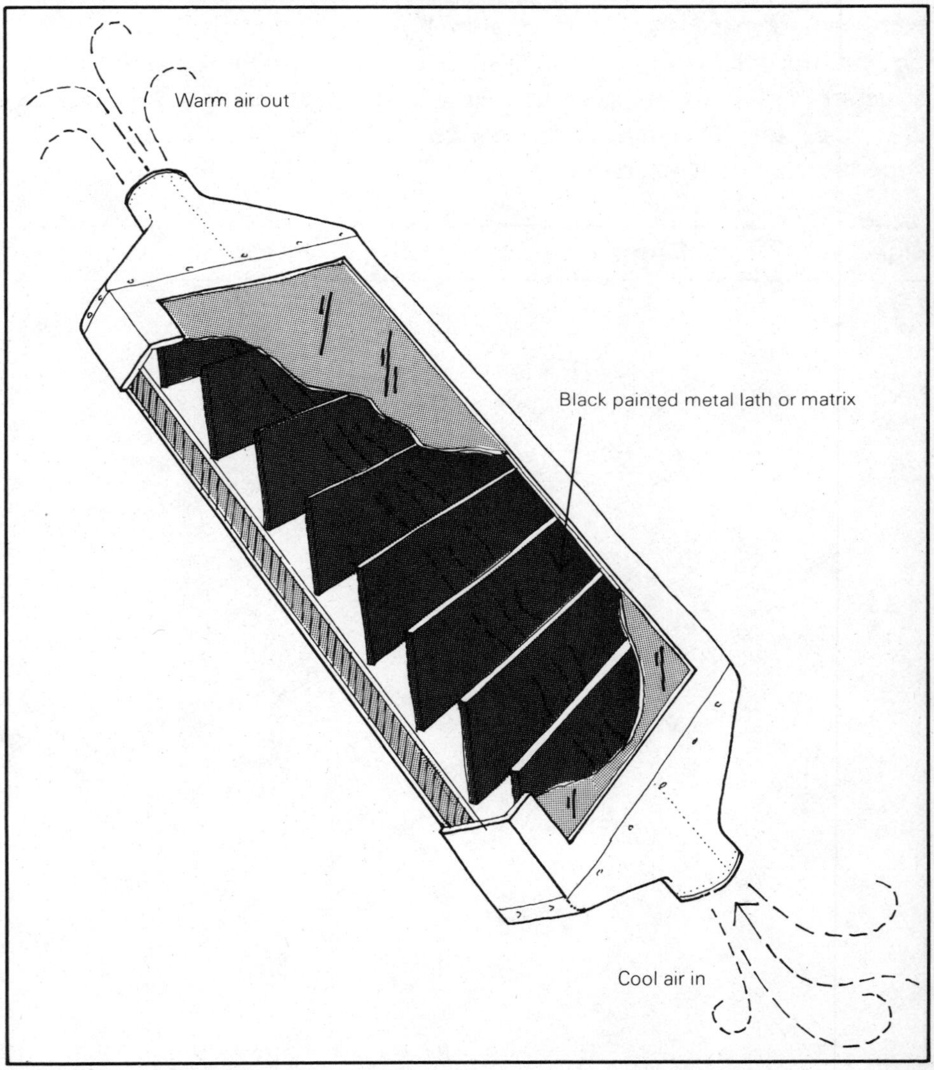

Warm air out

Black painted metal lath or matrix

Cool air in

trates the sun's heat by passing the heat-transfer fluid (water or air) through the collector many times during the day, increasing its temperature a few degrees each pass.

A flat-plate collector using air as its heat-transfer fluid is very similar in design to that used for the windowbox air heater. A flat, insulated box is glazed and provided with openings at top and bottom. A material having a high heat conductivity, large surface area, and light weight (expanded plaster lath, layers of metal screen cloth, strips of sheetmetal) is painted black and arranged inside the collector, ideally in such a manner that air passing through the collector is directed up towards the top of the collector but also away from the cover glazing in order to reduce heat loss out through the front of the collector. Direct or diffuse sunlight striking the mesh or metal strips inside the collector is almost totally absorbed as heat. Air, blown through the collector from bottom to top, is in turn heated by contact with the hot metal.

Water-type flat-plate collectors also use an insulated glazed box to contain the solar absorber. In this case the absorber consists of a series of $\frac{3}{8}$ to

Figure 12-31. **Fluid Heating Flat Plate Collector**

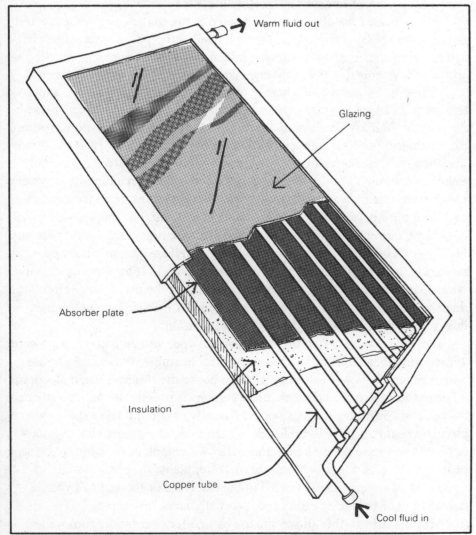

Warm fluid out

Glazing

Absorber plate

Insulation

Copper tube

Cool fluid in

½-inch diameter tubes, usually copper, arranged along the length of the collector box, spaced 4 to 6 inches apart, and connected to larger diameter distribution manifolds at top and bottom. The tubes are soldered or clamped to thin copper or aluminum sheets, or fins, which form the collector's absorber. Sunlight, striking the flat black-painted fins, is absorbed as heat and is immediately transferred by the high-conductivity metal of the fin and tube into the stream of water pumped through the tubes.

Individual collectors of both types are ganged together to form an array with enough absorber surface area to collect the desired daily amount of heat. In general, collector arrays large enough to provide 50 to 75 percent of a single family home's space heating needs will be between one hundred and five hundred square feet in area, and should be oriented and tilted using the same guidelines presented for windowbox air heaters. However, since the roof, rather than a south-facing wall, is often the practical mounting place for large collector arrays, you may have to give careful thought to the trade-off between mounting the array at the existing roof angle (usually between 18 and 45°) and spending extra money on a support structure to provide a higher tilt for winter heating (50 to 60°). Whereas a steep, or even a vertical, tilt is usually a good choice for a windowbox collector, the extra expense of such a tilt on a roof may not be worthwhile.

Solar-heated water or air is circulated between the collector array and thermal storage by pump or fan through insulated pipes or ducts. The characteristics of the circulation subsystem define several differences between air and water systems that may influence your choice of one over the other.

First, water has a much higher mass per unit volume than air, and therefore it can store and transport heat more efficiently. A stream of water flowing through a ¾-inch-diameter pipe, forced by a ¹⁄₂₀ horsepower pump, can transfer more heat than a stream of air blown through a 12-inch square duct by a ¼ horsepower fan. Next, a water-circulation system is generally easier to design and build, and is less prone to leaks than a lone-duct system. On the other hand, water can easily freeze and burst the collector tubes or manifold piping, causing expensive damage. The usual remedies—use of antifreeze, automatic night draining of collectors, night circulation of heated water—are either cumbersome, expensive, or reduce system efficiency. Consequently, water systems are usually favored in regions having milder winter climates, in cases where space limitations prevent the use of large circulation ducts and thermal-storage volumes, and by most mechanical contractors, due to their relative ease of design and installation.

An air system is often the best choice if your situation combines a cold winter climate, an existing forced-air central heating system, and a house with a generous garage or utility room to house the system's thermal storage. Thermal storage for solar mechanical systems is usually not located adjacent to collectors or heater space, since it is usually easier and less expensive to circulate heat relatively long distances than make the extensive alterations necessary to locate a very heavy and bulky water tank or rock bin in the attic or living room. A water system's thermal storage is, simply, a heavily insulated tank of water, usually buried in the backyard or located in a vacant corner of your garage or utility room (usually *much* less expensive).

If pressurized (this allows the use of smaller circulation pump) the

Figure 12-32. **Liquid Type Solar Heating System:**

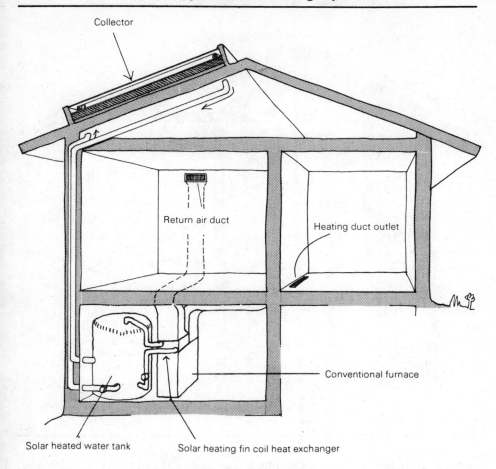

Collector

Return air duct

Heating duct outlet

Conventional furnace

Solar heated water tank

Solar heating fin coil heat exchanger

water system's thermal storage must be constructed of glass-lined steel. If not, then high-temperature gel-coated fiber glass is often quite economical. The volume will range from 1.5 to 3 gallons per square feet of collector area. A properly designed system will take advantage of the tendencies of heat to stratify in the tank. That is, natural convection will force the hottest water to the top of the tank, the coldest to the bottom. Circulation connections take advantage of this phenomenon. The pump draws the coldest water from the bottom of the tank, circulates it through the collectors, and returns it to the tank at a level approximately a third of the way down from its highest point. Heated water returning from the collector array will either sink or rise, depending on its temperature. The hottest water is drawn off to help heat the house, and returned at the bottom of the tank.

An air system uses the same thermal storage concept as Calthorpe's attached-greenhouse/radiant-floor system, but in a more compact form, permitted by the much higher temperature at which heat is stored (100 to 160°F). Like the floor-sized rockbed, this version has plenums above and below the rock mass, and will circulate heat down through the rockbed when charging, and up through the bed when extracting heat at night. The rocks are usually contained in a rectangular bin constructed of plywood reinforced with lumber framing and steel tension rods to counteract the outward pres-

Figure 12-33. **Air Heating System**

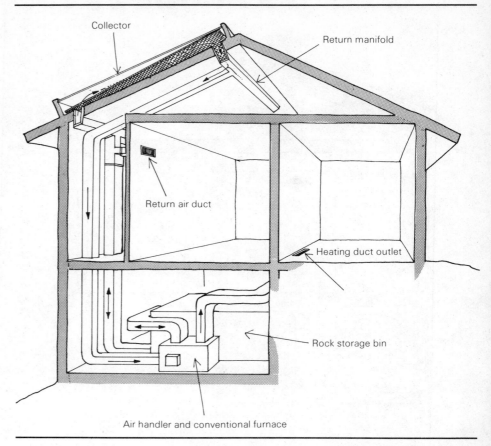

Air handler and conventional furnace

sure of six or seven feet of rock. The bin is insulated and provided with duct connections at each plenum.

The diameter of rock used will vary according to the length of air path through the bed. A short path, such as that for the greenhouse system, will allow the use of pea gravel. A long path, however, will need to develop less resistance to air flow so that the system's power consumption can be kept low; thus ¾ to 1½-inch-diameter rock is usually used in deeper beds. The volume of a rock-storage bin will be approximately three times that of a water tank to store the same amount of heat, due to both the lower heat capacity of rock, and voids occupying 34 to 50 percent of the bin's volume. However, a rock bin, once built, is maintenance-free and will not suffer from leaks or corrosion—an advantage that may offset the penalty of its size.

The most common and economical way of moving solar heat from remote thermal storage to the rooms requiring it is by way of your conventional forced-air or hot water-convection ("radiator") system. This connection is quite simple for a solar water system, requiring only a second pumped loop that takes water from the top of the solar storage tank, circulates it through a finned coil located in the forced-air furnace (very similar to coils used to add central air conditioning to furnaces), and returns it near the bottom of the tank. Solar-heated water can also be used to partially heat return water from a hot water convector system, or pumped directly into a radiant-floor piping grid.

A rockbed is more difficult to connect to a conventional heating system, in that multiple dampers are required to route air flow in different directions, depending on the system's mode of operation. Several self-contained units are now marketed, at handsome prices, which contain both automatic controls and dampers allowing the use of both furnace and collector loop fans to power several modes of operation (see margin). Of course the resetting of dampers to change the direction of heat flow can also be done manually. In relatively temperate regions not requiring much daytime heat this option may work quite well. However, manual control of a mechanical system will tend to reduce system efficiency, unless you are prepared to monitor it continuously.

The automatic control of a water system is also usually accomplished with a prepackaged unit that turns both collector circulation and furnace-cool circulation pumps on and off in response to sensor signals. These relatively inexpensive units ($40 to $200) operate the collector loop whenever solar heat can be collected, protect the system from freezing, and deliver solar heat to the furnace on call from its thermostat. There is really no need to consider manual controls since the automatic versions do the job well and inexpensively.

A word of caution: by far the most common cause of poor or no performance in solar mechanical systems is an inaccurate sensing of temperature by their automatic control units' sensors, which in turn is due to the use of uncalibrated sensors and, more commonly, sloppy installation. Sensors must have good thermal contact with the surface or fluid whose temperature is being monitored. Any separation at all, no matter how small, will result in a false reading, and a substantial penalty in performance. Although you will probably use professional design and construction services in building your solar mechanical system, you, as owner, should become thoroughly familiar with the control manufacturer's recommendations concerning proper placement of the sensors, require that the sensors be tested for accuracy, and inspect their installation. This personal attention will both guarantee peace of mind and prepare you to troubleshoot in case of malfunction. The situation is roughly analogous to being prepared to wiggle wires and change the fan belt in the family car.

The relative complexity of both air and water solar mechanical systems will generally result in their costing a good deal more than the architectural ones in terms of benefits received. That is, a solar mechanical system costing $20 to $40 per square feet of collector area will develop as much heat as an attached greenhouse system (cost: $15 to $25 per square feet of greenhouse area, including storage), but will not provide any other amenities, such as winter growing space or an increase in daytime living area. Also, the heat provided will be in the form of warm air, which will not help lower the house's heating requirements, since it has no influence over the radiant environment, but will only improve the conventional portion of that requirement (air temperature).

Of course, if your house cannot benefit from the architectural system's secondary virtues or it is not a simple matter to alter the house to do so, then a solar mechanical system may offer a much better investment. In that case, the choice between an air and water system is usually determined by your

- **Heat to storage from collector:** collection only, no heating
- **Heat to house from collector:** daytime solar heat
- **Heat to house from storage:** nighttime solar heat
- **Heat to house from furnace:** auxiliary heating

house's configuration (room for ducts?) and climate region (freeze protection required?). If the choice is still a toss-up, you should consider the long-term consequences of your choice: a water system is decidedly easier to design and install, but requires periodic maintenance—checking water quality, replenishing antifreeze and corrosion inhibitors, and replacing pump seals and anticorrosion anodes in the storage tank. An air system, once shoe-horned into your house, requires no more maintenance than your forced-air furnace—filter and fan belt replacement, oiling of motors.

The State of the Art

This chapter has described the generic solar heating options available now for use in your own house. The combinations of components described are certainly not exhaustive and your actual options are limited only by your ingenuity and/or pocketbook. For instance, you can install a special thin-slat Venetian blind between the glazing layers of a large south-facing double-glazed window and use the assembly as a solar collector in winter (sunlight absorbed by black-painted side of blinds, heat removed by air blown through the window's air space) and as a shading device in summer (light reflected back out through the window from the other, chrome-plated, side of the blinds). Also, if your house is built on a south-facing hillside, you can use a giant air collector, identical in design to the windowbox unit, to circulate solar-heated air through rockbed floor storage borrowed from the attached-greenhouse system.

Furthermore, even as this book goes to press, the state of the art of

Figure 12-34. **Thin-Slat Blind Collector Heating**

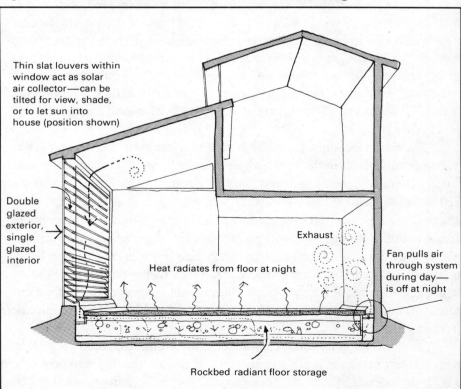

Thin slat louvers within window act as solar air collector—can be tilted for view, shade, or to let sun into house (position shown)

Double glazed exterior, single glazed interior

Exhaust

Fan pulls air through system during day—is off at night

Heat radiates from floor at night

Rockbed radiant floor storage

Figure 12-35. **Thermosiphon Air Heating System**   **Solar Technology**

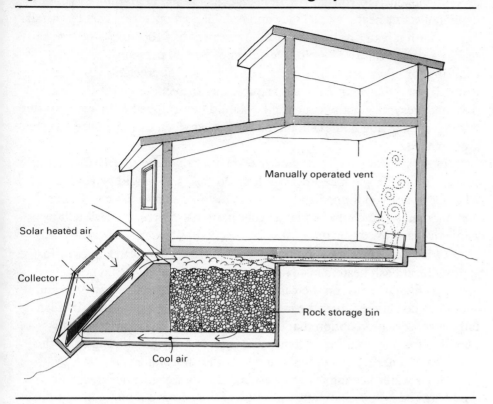

Manually operated vent

Solar heated air

Collector

Rock storage bin

Cool air

solar utilization is advancing rapidly. These advances, however, are technical in nature: inexpensive but efficient thermal storage compounds, "smart" glazing that can reflect heat into the building, simplified design methods, new products for system control and shading. They will not affect your decisions: 1) whether to invest now or wait until rising prices make the investment more attractive and until the technology becomes less of a novelty, and 2) to what degree to involve yourself in the day to day management of your own comfort.

As for the first decision, remember that, as energy prices rise, so does the price of the energy intensive materials used in the construction of solar systems: glass, metals, concrete. The present return on an investment today may be low, but it will improve radically in the future. If, however, you wait you may not be able to secure as high a return since the cost of construction generally inflates at a rate substantially faster than that for energy and general inflation.

This chapter has provided commonsense guidelines to help you make the second decision. Solar technology can help provide you with any level of comfort you desire (even air conditioning, at a substantial cost premium), but a decision to select an option which involves you and your house in responding to the diurnal solar cycle will reward you in both the pocketbook and in your house's comfort.

Heating Water with the Sun

Your hot water heater is responsible for a major portion of your utility bill,

Conserving heated water

1. Insulate your hot water heater. For an outlay of $15 to $20, you can more than double your heater's insulation by wrapping it in a plastic-covered, fitted, insulating shell. This ten-minute job will improve your heater's performance and pay for itself within a year.

2. Install efficient fixtures. Fixtures and faucets that use less water to do the job also save energy. This is especially true of shower heads, which vary from two to ten gallons per minute to do essentially the same job.

3. Reduce hot water temperature. Heating water to a higher temperature than required not only uses more energy but increases heat loss from the heater itself and hot-water piping.

second only to the cost of heating and air conditioning. One of the better investments open to you at present is investing in the upgrading of your existing hot water heater's efficiency and reducing its operating cost by installing a solar hot water heater. With an investment of $1000 to $2000 you can realize a pretax return of your investment of 7 to 20 percent—before accounting for other benefits, such as tax credits and appreciation of property value. In fact, the technology is so simple and the economic return so positive that every new house constructed should be equipped with a solar water heater, and existing homes should be retrofitted when their hot water heaters are replaced.

However, first you must conserve the water you heat, regardless of its source. Three simple measures will help do this, and should be adopted whether or not you immediately go on to install a solar hot water heater. If you do, then so much the better, as your system's "percent solar" will be markedly improved (see margin).

Other conservation options, such as insulating hot-water lines or installing local flash heaters instead of a central storage heater do not have nearly as high a return on their investment as the options emphasized and should be considered *after* the installation of a solar water heater. Incidentally, a conservation option that is quite effective in new construction is planning for the grouping of fixtures to shorten hot water piping runs: this saves water, energy, and time spent waiting for hot water.

Solar water heating is not a new concept, nor even a new technology. The Day and Night Company (now one of the nation's major conventional water heater manufacturers) was marketing solar water heaters in southern California at the turn of the century, and any G.I. who has taken a warm shower under a black-painted 55-gallon drum or discarded wing tank can attest to the effectiveness of solar water heating, even in a primitive form.

The advent of cheap natural gas and electricity, beginning in the twenties, caused the early demise of the infant industry, although Israel and Japan have maintained small but thriving solar industries, primarily due to the high cost of their almost totally imported energy. An early prediction of our present energy situation by several researchers in the late sixties caused a resurgence of solar research and product development, with the result that, once again, we have a fledgling solar industry, eager and ready to install solar hot water heaters anywhere in the country.

There are three generic design options for solar water heaters. Water heaters, like those for space heating, range from the simple, manually operated to the relatively complex, automatically controlled system. Unlike the space heating options, however, they all provide just one benefit—hot water—so there is a closer correlation between cost and performance than with options having multiple benefits.

Breadbox Water Heater

A breadbox system is simply an extension of the "G.I." shower to allow water to store heat after sundown. It derives its name from its usual finished appearance, and is most appropriate as a do-it-yourself project for those wishing to preheat water for a conventional hot water heater.

Figure 12-36. "Bread Box" Solar Water Heater

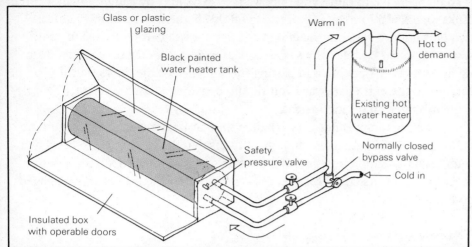

A discarded conventional glass-lined gas or electric hot-water heater is cannibalized for its tank. An insulated box is constructed to hold the tank, and is glazed on two of its long sides. A simple insulating cover system is provided to prevent heat loss out through the collector's glazing whenever the sun is not shining. The box and insulating doors must be weatherproof to prevent water damage to their insulation.

The breadbox is located where you can reach its doors, and oriented to the south. Its water tank is plumbed to the cold inlet line to your house's hot water heater so that the conventional heater draws its "cold" water from the breadbox collector. The collector's tank is plumbed so the line leading to the house's hot water heater tends to draw off the tank's warmest water, with the cold inlet located at the opposite end of the tank. The tank is painted flat black and the insides of the box are painted white or covered with foil, as are the inner faces of the insulating doors.

After sunrise, the insulating doors are manually opened to allow sunlight to strike the tank. The glazed sides of the box, facing the sky and south, allow sunlight into the box where it is absorbed by the tank as heat, thus heating the water in the tank. The box and glazing reduce heat loss from the tank, and the inner faces of the insulating doors, if properly tilted, reflect additional sunlight into the box. The box remains open until late afternoon, when it must be closed to prevent heat loss.

This very simple and inexpensive system is capable of heating the entire tank of water to well over 100°F on a good day, but its usefulness depends on its being able to retain that heat until your family's evening and next morning heavy water-use periods.

Your twice-daily management of the insulating doors is necessary. Breadboxes built with multiple glazing layers substituting for insulating doors have had poor success in most parts of the country: a triple-glazed window has less than half the insulating value of a door sandwiching a one-inch layer of rigid insulation between two sheets of thin plywood, and would perform even more poorly, since the hot, black tank would radiate heat very well to the glazing, thus heating it and aggravating the actual heat loss of the box.

Points to consider when planning a thermosiphon system:

1. Water weighs over eight pounds per gallon. When planning for installation of an elevated storage tank, consult a professional engineer on its proper bracing if you live in a region prone to earthquakes.

2. If in doubt, oversize the piping connecting collector to storage tank. The force of natural convection is so small that any flow obstruction can severely reduce the system's flow rate, which in turn reduces the amount of energy collected and stored, since lower flow rates result in hotter collector temperatures and greater daytime heat loss. Calculating an optimum pipe size is quite a chore. It is usually cheaper in the long run to use the next larger pipe size than you think you need.

3. Try to mount the storage tank as high as possible above the collector. Not only does this prevent back-siphoning, but it increases the system's flow rate, since, in effect, you are lengthening the two columns of water connecting collector and storage. The cooler column is denser than the column returning to the tank. So long as you heavily insulate both lines, the higher the columns of water, the greater the difference in weight between the two, and the greater the force of gravity acting to speed circulation. Of course, there is a practical limit to this effect—that length of pipe having a heat loss which robs as much energy from the system as increased water column height adds to it. However, that limit will probably not be reached in a house if you take care to heavily insulate both piping and storage tank.

4. Plan for a collector to storage tank ratio of 1.5 to 3 gallons per square foot of collector area.

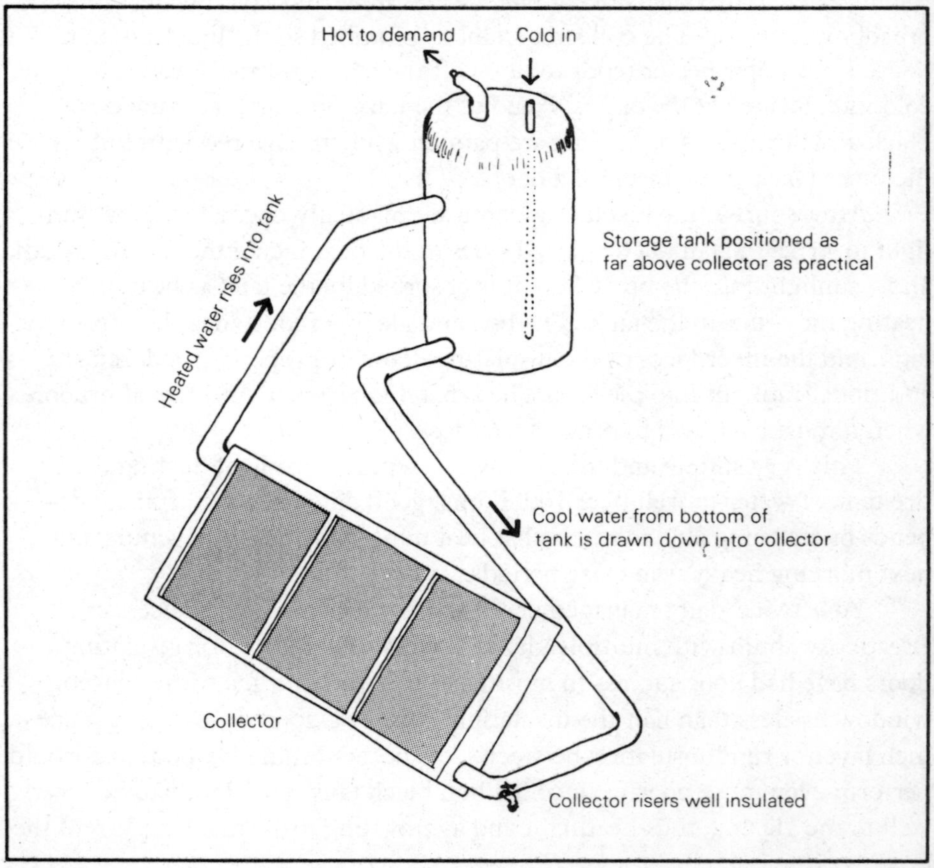

American Society of Heating, Refrigeration and Air Conditioning Engineers.

However, in consolation for its manual operation, the breadbox system is so inexpensive to build you may want to expand it by ganging two or three tanks together, plumbed in series. If you do so, then you will have at least two tanks of hot water at the end of the day for use before in-rushing cold water begins to "dilute" the system's heat output. Of course, you could rig up an automatic opening and closing mechanism for the doors, but if you can afford the extra hardware you should consider a more efficient, self-regulating design option instead.

The breadbox is not very efficient, in that its hot water is stored in the collector, which cannot be economically insulated well enough to prevent a high heat-loss rate. However, at a materials cost of under $300 for a two or three tank unit, its cost effectiveness is very high if the collector is managed conscientiously.

Thermosiphon System

The thermosiphon design option is, conceptually, the most elegant and efficient of solar water heaters. It is self-regulating, requires little maintenance, and has an efficiency equal to that of the more complex pumped systems. Unfortunately, it requires special structural considerations in its installation that are often difficult to meet in single-story houses.

A standard water-type flat-plate collector, or series of collectors, is mounted on your roof using the same orientation and tilt guidelines as for

Figure 12-37. Thermosiphon Solar Water Heater

Hot to demand

Cold in

Heated water rises into tank

Storage tank positioned as far above collector as practical

Cool water from bottom of tank is drawn down into collector

Collector

Collector risers well insulated

other flat-plate collectors. An insulated storage tank is shoe-horned into your house, usually in the attic, so that its bottom is at least one to two feet *above* the top of the collector, and the path between collector and tank is as direct as possible.

The bottom collector manifold is piped to the bottom of the storage tank, ensuring that the connecting pipe has at least a slight rise throughout its length. Likewise, the top of the collector bank is connected to the storage tank at a position point one-third of the way down from its highest point. Larger than normal pipe sizes are used (1 to 1.5-inch diameter) depending on the system's volume, the vertical distance between tank and collector, and the number of elbows and other constrictions in the piping load.

In general, larger volumes, greater height differences, and more piping bends require larger diameter piping in order to reduce the pipe's flow resistance. Cold inlet water is piped into the tank bottom, and the tank's hottest water is drawn off at its highest level, and piped through a small conventional water heater that boosts the water temperature if necessary.

Sunlight striking the absorber plate inside the collector heats the water in the collector's tube grid. The heated water tends to rise by natural convection, just as heated air rises in a windowbox air collector. The heated water rises into the storage tank, drawing cold water from the bottom of the tank down to the bottom of the collector. This "thermosiphon" loop continues as long as there is enough energy coming into the collector to heat the water in the tubes above the inlet temperature. As soon as heating ceases, the circulation stops. Back-siphoning is prevented by the elevation of the storage tank above the collector. Water in the collector quickly cools due to the collector's rapid heat loss. This "plug" of cold, dense water will not move until heated the next day. The warm water in the storage tank will not flow downward unless displaced by warmer water. Thus the system remains at rest until the sun's energy is again available to power its circulation.

It is apparent that a thermosiphon system is most appropriate for older houses having large attics and multiple roof levels on which to locate the system's collectors. Another option, used by the Day and Night Company in their early systems (all of which were thermosiphon), was to disguise the system's storage tank as a chimney, located above the collector bank on the house's roof. However, its moderate cost (competitive with pumped systems at $20 to $25 per square foot of collector area) and essentially maintenance-free operation make it a very attractive option if there is any way you can economically meet its structural requirements.

Pumped-Circulation System

The flat-plate collector on your roof, connected to a storage tank in your garage by a small diameter pumped-circulation loop is the inevitable replacement for today's conventional water heaters. Already you can look in the yellow pages under "Solar Energy Equipment," and, in many regions, find designers and contractors ready to install a package unit in your house that will last twenty years, provide 50 to 75 percent of your family's hot water (if you follow the conservation tips outlined above), and cost $2000 or less.

A pumped solar water system is a smaller version of the solar mechani-

Figure 12-38. **Pumped Solar Water Heater**

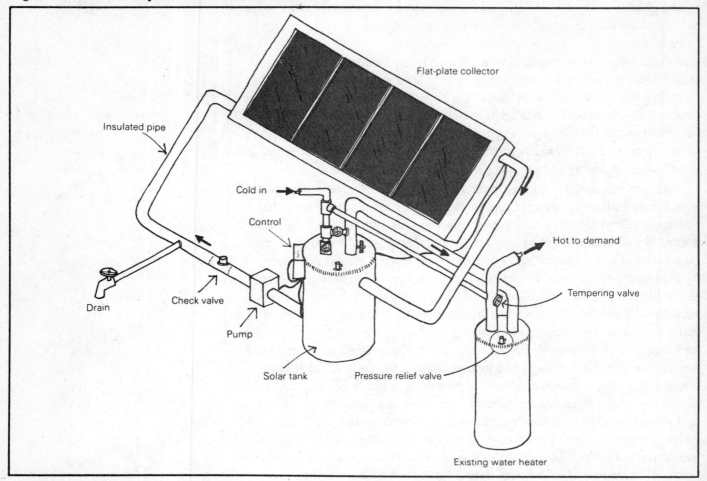

Flat-plate collector

Insulated pipe

Cold in

Control

Hot to demand

Drain

Check valve

Pump

Tempering valve

Solar tank

Pressure relief valve

Existing water heater

cal system described for space heating. An array of two or three collectors is piped in parallel to ¾ to 1-inch-diameter manifolds at the top and bottom of the array. A well-insulated storage tank (sized in the 60 to 120 gallon range rather than in the 200 to 1000 gallon sizes used for heating systems) is located in the garage or utility room, preferably either adjacent to the house's existing hot water heater or in its place, if the system's storage tank is equipped with integral auxiliary heating elements. A small pump is switched by an inexpensive, solid-state control unit that operates the system whenever energy can be added to it by the sun. Cold- and hot-water connections to the storage tank are identical to those for conventional systems. Indeed, most storage tanks are redesigned versions of the major manufacturers' standard lines.

The system's operation is identical to that for a solar heating system save for freeze protection. The simplest method of freeze protection is to circulate warm water through the collector array whenever a sensor signals a near-freezing temperature in the water at the bottom of the collector. This is adequate for a region having few nights with below-freezing temperatures, but would result in a 10 to 20 percent reduction in a system's yearly output if used in a cold-winter climate region.

Collectors can also be drained at night, either manually or by automatic operation of three solenoid valves—two close to block the circulation loop and one opens to drain the collectors. This option is not failsafe, as it is prone to both human forgetfulness and stuck or frozen solenoids. Its automatic version is also quite expensive.

Another expensive option, but one that is offered on many standard package systems, is the use of an antifreeze solution as the system's heat-transfer fluid. A solution of water and ethylene glycol (automotive antifreeze) is circulated through the collector rather than water. It transfers heat to the potable water in the storage tank by passing either through a finned heat exchanger inside the tank or through a tacket surrounding the tank and welded to its surface. The construction of the heat exchanger differs from that used on space heating systems because of the proximity of potable water to highly toxic antifreeze. A double-wall heat exchanger is required on potable water systems, so that the possibility of cross-contamination of one fluid stream by the other is minimized. A failsafe measure is to use a nontoxic fluid, such as polypropylene glycol (often used as a food additive). However, its high viscosity and poor thermal capacity make it harder to pump and less efficient in carrying heat than the common toxic fluid, which itself has a low enough performance to affect the system's design.

Antifreeze protection can also be used by the thermosiphon system, but a performance penalty is paid for the fluid's lower heat capacity and high viscosity. Antifreeze's main drawback, however, is the necessity for its periodic replacement. If left in the collector loop for more than a year you run the risk of its chemical buffers being exhausted, thus allowing the chemical to begin corroding the collector or heat exchanger.

A pumped system is suitable for any house which, for reasons of climate or structure, cannot make use of a thermosiphon system and which needs a combination of automatic control and high performance. Almost every house that presently has a conventional hot water heater can be adapted to one of the three options. An excellent time to change over is

Figure 12-39. **Solar Storage Tank Heat Exchangers**

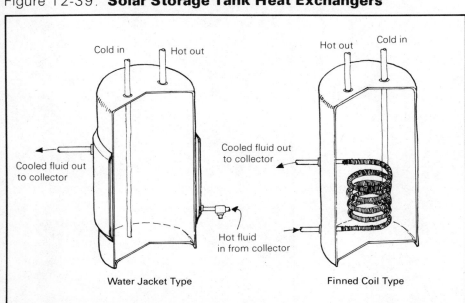

Cold in   Hot out   Hot out   Cold in

Cooled fluid out
to collector

Cooled fluid out
to collector

Hot fluid
in from collector

Water Jacket Type   Finned Coil Type

when replacing your rapidly aging existing unit. You can dedicate part of the cost of a replacement to a new, small auxiliary heater, and the rest to help defray the cost of a solar unit. You can also combine a solar heating and hot water system, thus realizing substantial savings on the cost of collectors, controls, and pump.

Note

Many more design options have been omitted than were presented in this chapter: solar cooling and roof-pond heating/cooling to name two. Rather, the focus has been on presenting generic options that are particularly suited for your existing home and that are good investments in terms of today's economy. For a wider range of options, especially those particularly suited to new construction, and for specific system design guidance, you should consult several of the solar design references listed in the bibliography.

Part Four:
The Interfaces

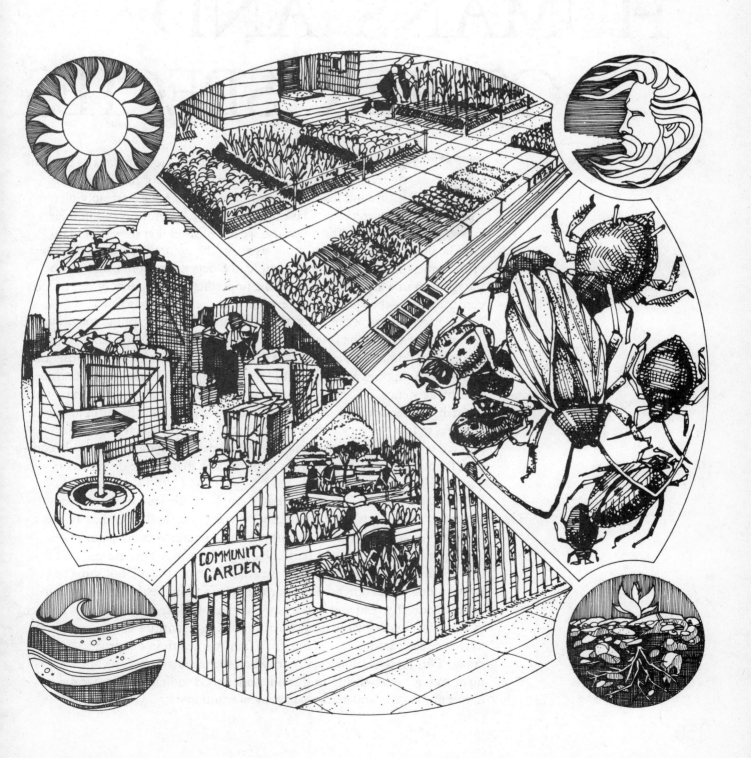

13. MANAGING WILDLIFE, OR HUMANS AND OTHER SPECIES

Urban environments encourage us to view humans as the center of the universe and all other forms of life as satellites around that hub. The household dog, the African violet, even the city landscapes exist where they do and in their present form because we are pleased that they should do so. The urban condition conditions us to see the natural world as composed of the tame and welcome—for example, the dependent domestic rose and the goldfish in a garden pool—and the unpredictable invaders of our orderly constructions—the voracious caterpillar and the pernicious weed.

There are two serious negative consequences of accepting this urbanized point of view. One is that it obscures the true interdependence of life forms. Our human survival is not a matter of subjugating and tolerating the nondomestic species around us; it is actually *dependent* upon their continued healthy existence. The recycling of nutrients that feed plants and ultimately nourish us, the cleansing of the gases and other pollutants harmful to our welfare, in fact the very stability of climate and soils, which we take for granted when erecting our urban islands, all depend upon innumerable complex food webs involving millions of organisms that can be described as "wildlife."

The second consequence is that a simplistic division of the world around us into "pests" and "nonpests" obscures our understanding of the ways in which our own activities have helped to create circumstances encouraging the problems that particular organisms may pose for us.

Both insights are essential if we are to manage the relationships between humans and other species for our comfort and aesthetic satisfaction. To methodically feed and house a population of cockroaches in one's kitchen as if they were pets while periodically applying quantities of toxic materials to reduce their numbers, risking one's family's health in the process, is crazy. This kind of situation occurs when the true nature of the other organism and our relationship to it is not understood sufficiently to reveal alternative and more permanent management solutions.

We need to take a step toward sanity—toward harmonious coexistence with all life on this planet and an appreciation of its natural rhythms and balances. To begin, we must review our attitudes towards other living creatures. The first place to apply our new insights is in our own personal environment, the integral urban house and garden and our community.

Toward a Personal Philosophy of Pest Management

Creating a New Perspective: The word *pest* usually signifies that, from the human point of view, a particular plant or animal is in the wrong place at the wrong time, or that it is present in too great a number. The current traditional response to pests is "Kill it! Get rid of it!" which in this chemical age means using a pesticide.

We need to reconsider two aspects of our traditional methods of pest control. First we must take another look at those living organisms we have designated as undesirable to see if they really are the problem we think they are. Second, if we *do* conclude that the greatest human and environmental good requires deliberate efforts to control a certain pest, we must reevaluate our methods in the light of current information on the effects that any particular pesticide or pest-killing method has on other organisms, including humans, and on the total environment.

What's a Pest?   Our decision to call a particular plant or animal a pest may be based on too narrow a view of natural communities. We may be receiving indirect benefits from the presence of that organism that we are not able to perceive. A classic example of our ignorance is the regular poisoning of ants around house foundations rather than using caulking, sticky barriers, and other exclusion methods to prevent the ants from entering the home. Ants may be an annoyance indoors, and some species may enhance certain aphid populations in the garden by protecting them from their natural enemies. But many ants aerate the soil with their tunnels; kill fly larvae and other undesirable insects they encounter in the mulch, soil or garden debris; and, as venerable termite enemies, often protect house foundations by preventing these more destructive insects from building new colonies. When the young fertilized queen termite lands adjacent to some likely wood in which to build her colony, she loses her wings and must seek a protected crevice in which to lay her eggs. Until the first workers hatch and begin to care for her, constructing the chambers that will protect her from her enemies, she is extremely vulnerable. During this period of vulnerability, patroling ant scouts can be valuable in preventing trouble before it starts. Once the termite colony has been established, humans must break it open to enable the ants to enter and kill and carry off the termites for food. We have seen one common ant species do this, the Argentine ant *Iridomyrmex humilis,* and we suspect that this behavior can be arranged using some other ant species as well.

Examples of attempts at eradicating an animal without appreciating its true value are too numerous to list here, and it seems that attitudes of rural people may be just as unenlightened as those of urbanites in this respect. Consider the treatment of the coyote, which still has a bounty on its head in some areas, and is pursued with toxic baits capable of killing many other organisms, and deadly traps as well. Contrary to the prejudices of some ranchers, the presence of these predators is known to have an upgrading effect on a herd of animals, by occasionally culling out a weak, sick, or old individual. And more important from the ranchers' standpoint, numerous studies of the stomach contents of coyotes have shown that their regular diet is largely composed of rodents. Wherever coyotes are killed off the rodent population, which competes directly with domestic stock for the same vegetation, increases significantly. This situation often leads to large-scale programs to poison rodents, which, in turn, can result in more undesirable environmental repercussions as other animals that feed upon rodents are affected.

The same narrow view, based on ignorance of the total picture, has characterized many traditional efforts to eradicate hawks, mountain lions, and other predators. Through our family or school education, we are taught to consider some forms of life friendly and others a menace. Our textbooks speak of "good" and "bad" insects. When these attitudes are held in common by all those around us, we may never stop to question their basis in fact.

A less obvious, but similar situation exists in our prejudices towards certain plants. Numerous common urban garden "weeds" are edible and should be tried as potherbs rather than hastily discarded as a nuisance. In several studies in orchards, clean-cultivation (the regular plowing under of weeds) has been shown to destroy predators and parasites of serious orchard pests such as the Oriental fruit moth and the colding moth. In these cases, the "weeds" are actually desirable plants, since they serve as alternate hosts for important insect species that can help to keep potentially damaging insects under control. These plants should be encouraged as permanent cover crops rather than eliminated, as is frequently the custom.

Entomophobia: An unreasonable fear of insects is called *entomophobia*. Extreme cases may take the form of a neurosis in which the presence of the insects is totally imaginary. It is surprising how many otherwise normal people share this revulsion for "creepy-crawly" things. To the frightened individual, any observed insect is considered a pest (see Box 13-1).

We remember visiting a woman who had called the health authorities because her lawn was undergoing the twice-yearly emergence of the March fly (*Bibio* species, a member of the fly family Bibionidae). She described them as looking like "little black worms," an indication that she had not observed them closely enough to see that they were winged insects. The woman seemed very upset and spoke emotionally about this horrible occurrence. She had been spraying her lawn heavily with chlordane, a chlorinated hydrocarbon. Yet she was the first to admit that the lawn itself was beautiful and seemed totally undamaged by the fly, and, further, that the insecticide she had been using was not affecting the repeated appearance of the insects. Though she realized that her spraying was not solving anything and was assured that the flies did not represent a known human health problem, her disgust at the sight of the flies made her quite willing to douse the entire area repeatedly with contaminants that threaten many other forms of life.

A lawn is an example of a monoculture. Wherever large quantities of a

Box 13-1 **Insect Fear (Entomophobia)**

Most people harbor some fear of insects, while in some individuals the fear has been cultivated into hysterical syndromes. This phenomenon needs to be understood in relation to some biological facts. In the following tables, a simplistic grouping of plants and animals by species indicates that a total of about 1.4 million species exist. (Known viral and rickettsial species number at most in the thousands.) If we divide the number of insect species (listed as 46. Arthropoda) into the total of all species known, we find that 63 percent of all living species are insects. If most people are afraid of insects, this means that most people are afraid of the largest proportion of living things. Given this orientation it is little wonder that the most common response to "pest" insects is to reach for the pesticide.

Table A. **The Plant Kingdom**

Divisions	Common Name	Number of Species
1 Cyanophycophyta	Blue-green algae	
2 Chlorophycophyta	Green algae	
3 Euglenophycophyta	Euglenoids	
4 Charophyta	Charophytes	All algae: 19,000
5 Phaeophycophyta	Brown algae	
6 Rhodophycopyta	Red algae	
7 Chrysophycophyta	Diatoms	
8 Pyrrhophycophyta	Dinoflagellates	
9 Schizomycota	Bacteria	
10 Myxomycota	Slime molds	
11 Acrasiomycota	Cellular slime molds	
12 Chytridiomycota	Uniflagellate fungi	
13 Oomycota	Water molds	All fungi: 50,000
14 Zygomycota	Bread molds	
15 Ascomycota	Sac fungi	
16 Basidiomycota	Club fungi	
17 Deuteromycota	Imperfect fungi	
18 Hepatophyta	Liverworts, hornworts	6,000
19 Bryophyta	Mosses	14,000
20 Psilophyta	Psilophytes	8
21 Microphyllophyta	Club mosses	1,000
22 Arthrophyta	Horsetails, sphenopsids	10-25
23 Pterophyta	Ferns	9,500
24 Cycadophyta	Cycads	100
25 Ginkgophyta	Maidenhair tree	1
26 Coniferophyta	Conifers	550
27 Gnetophyta	———	71
28 Anthophyta	Flowering plants	250,000
	Approximate total	350,000

Source: Bold, *The Plant Kingdom*.

Table B. **The Animal Kingdom**

Phylum	Common Name	Number of Species
29 Protozoa	Protozoans	30,000
30 Mesozoa	Mesozoans	43
31 Porifera	Sponges	5,000
32 Coelenterata	Coelenterates	10,000
33 Ctenophera	Comb jellies	
34 Platyhelminthes	Flatworms	10,000
35 Nemertinea	Ribbon worms	550
36 Entoprocta	———	60
37 Aschelminthes	Round worms	12,000
38 Acanthocephala	Spiny-headed worms	500
39 Bryozoa	Moss animals	4,000
40 Phoronidea	Phoronids	
41 Brachiopoda	Lamp shells	260
42 Mollusca	Mollusks	45,000
43 Annelida	Segmented worms	8,700
44 Sipunculoidea	Peanut worms	250
45 Echiuroidea	Echiurids	60
46 Arthropoda	Joint-footed (including the insects)	891,000
47 Chaetognatha	Arrow worms	50
48 Echinodermata	Echinoderms	5,500
49 Pogonophora	Beard worms	43
50 Hemichordata	Tongue worms	70
51 Chordata	Chordates	40,000
	Approximate total	1,062,000

Source: Information compiled from Storer and Usinger, *General Zoology*.

363

single plant are grown in continuous blocks, insect problems can be greatly multiplied. The most stable environment is a complex one, in which many kinds of plants and the animals that feed upon and among them can survive. In such a situation a wealth of predators and parasites that feed on the pests are encouraged to stay around too. Monocultures, or large single-species stands, are relatively unstable because they attract few herbivorous species. These become more serious pest problems than if plant mixes were maintained with multitudes of herbivores and natural-enemy complexes.

When the concept of a stable, complex environment is understood, then alternative, nonchemical methods of pest control suggest themselves. For example one might break up a continuous lawn with other plants in beds or borders. A different approach would be to examine and modify the composition or care of the lawn itself (see page 386 on "Lawn Insects").

However, even these reasonable alternative pest-control methods do not deal with the problem identified above—the irrational fear of "bugs." Spiders and snakes are two other groups of animals whose simple presence can arouse a hysterical reaction in humans. Unfortunately, fear alone is the basis for many unwise attempts to control such "pests."

Worse still, our irrational fears, ignorance, and traditional prejudices are exploited by those who sell pesticides. Some of these people want us to regard certain animals and plants as serious pests whose eradication is worth our money and energy. As with the "problem" of bad breath, dramatized and sold to the public by the mouthwash manufacturing companies, our pest problems may be based solely on our belief in a persuasive television commercial or other advertising display. But if the label on the insecticide bottle says, "Kills Earwigs!" does that automatically mean that earwigs should be killed?

The Natural Control of Pests: Basic to an understanding of natural control is the perception that most populations of insects, disease organisms, and plants that are potential pests are already under control. Climate, weather, food supply, suitable habitat, and competition among species—all act as limiting factors upon the size of pest populations at one time or another. Biological factors, however, are especially important because they can respond to changes in the numbers of the pests. All insects, for example, have diseases as well as predators and parasites (usually other insects) which control their population numbers within certain limits. If this were not so, the plant-eating insects would have consumed their host plants long ago. In fact, nearly all plants have aphids, spider mites, and other insects feeding upon them. If we are not aware of this, it is usually because the insects are present in such low numbers, kept low by many natural controls, including those mentioned. Therefore, a good pest-management program recognizes the natural controls present and facilitates them or at least integrates all pest-management strategies so that these natural controls are disrupted as little as possible.

Natural enemies of pest organisms can generally be grouped into three categories based on size, mode of life, and feeding methods. The categories are microbes, parasites, and predators. Microbes are those organisms that are smaller than their prey and reproduce inside them. This category in-

Figure 13-1. **Three Important Insect Predators**

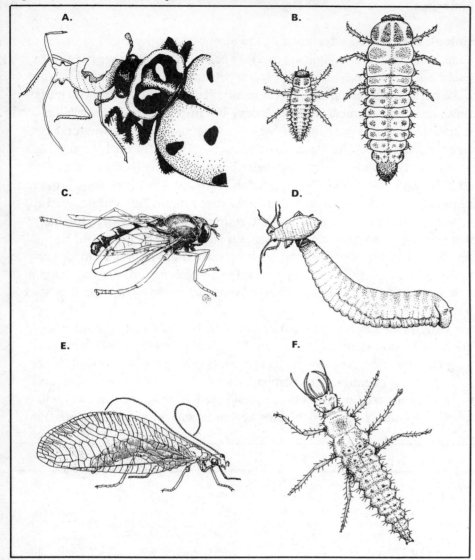

A. The adult lady beetle, Hippodamia convergens, *eating an aphid. All lady beetles occur in the beetle family Coccinellidae. There are about four hundred species of lady bugs in North America and each one feeds on a certain species or spectrum of herbivores.*

B. Larvae of lady beetles. Although these insects are very common, few people know how to recognize the young or larvae.

C. Flower fly, family Syrphidae. The adult syrphid, or hoverfly, can easily be mistaken for a bee. A little study, however, will reveal subtle differences in flight patterns and structure. Large syrphids can be more than half an inch long.

D. A flower fly larvae feeding on an aphid. These larvae are frequently difficult to find, particularly among an aphid colony.

E. The California green lacewing, Chrysopa carnea. *The adult green lacewing is a beautiful insect, about three-quarters of an inch long with golden-colored eyes. It is found on leaves near aphid colonies. These insects are included in the ''nerve-winged'' insect order Neuroptera along with ant lions and dobsenflies. Some species feed on living prey in the adult stages while others only feed on honeydew.*

F. A lacewing larvae. The jaws or mandibles are hollow and are used to suck up the body fluids of its prey.

cludes viruses, bacteria, fungi, protozoa, and nematodes.

Predators and parasites are both insect-eating insects. Predators are usually larger than the insects they eat, eat many insects during their lifetime, and are usually capable of eating many kinds of insects. They tend to be opportunists and consume whatever is in greatest supply, moving on to new areas or shifting to other species when their food supply, a given pest population, is reduced in numbers. Examples of predators are ladybird beetles, lacewings, and syrphid flies (see Figure 13-1). Parasites tend to be smaller than the insects they feed on, live inside of or on the surface of their prey (feeding only on one insect during their lifetime), and frequently live in or on only one particular species or closely related species of host. Parasites are very valuable in insect management, first because they are so species-specific, thus only affecting the pest-insect populations and none of the other organisms present, and also because they are effective even when the pest insect is present in low numbers. Because insect parasites are so tiny most people are not aware of them, and there are no common names for them.

Most are members of the order Hymenoptera and are often referred to as miniwasps.

Biological Control: Technically, the term biological control can refer to the natural control of organisms by other organisms such as we have just described, or to deliberate manipulations by humans of the natural enemies of the pests. Such biological control manipulations fall into four categories: conservation, augmentation, inoculation, and importation. Conservation can be achieved by manipulating the habitat so that the survival of natural enemy populations is increased. Providing nest boxes for birds (many birds eat insects when they are feeding their young, regardless of their normal adult diet) is a good example. Vegetation on roadsides and in waste areas can frequently provide habitat and shelter for many natural enemies; therefore, protecting such vegetation rather than routinely killing it with herbicides may be a good conservation approach. Of course, this tactic should be weighed against the possible role such vegetation has in producing or harboring pest populations. Where pesticides have been used, any reduction in their application will help to conserve beneficial insects that remain or start to repopulate the area.

Augmentation refers to tactics that increase the already existing populations of natural enemies of the pest. Using nursery plants and food sprays are good examples. Nursery plants are plants grown for the purpose of producing natural enemies. If old cabbage-family plants that have bolted and are heavily attacked by the cabbage aphid are left in the garden, they will operate as a nursery for lady beetles, syrphids, and the tiny miniwasps that

---

Box 13-2. **Bacillus thuringiensis**

Bacillus thuringiensis (B.t.) is a naturally occurring and commonly distributed bacterial species that causes disease in certain caterpillars. Over the past twenty years B.t. has been developed into a potent microbial insecticide. It was first discovered as a silkworm pathogen in 1901, but it was not seriously developed commercially until the 1950s. The isolation and development of a more potent strain in the late 1960s stimulated manufacturers to develop it as a pest-control tool. Today the commercial product is a blend of strains.

About 150 insects, mostly moths and butterflies, show susceptibility to B.t. The bacteria is registered for use against more than 30 insect pests of agricultural, horticultural, and forest plants. Current production in the United States is in the range of hundreds of tons. The bacteria is widely available in nursery and hardware stores all across the country under such common trade names as Biotrol[R], Dipel[R], and Thuricide[R]. The advantages of b.t. are its selectivity and its harmlessness to vertebrates. Many pesticides trigger more pest problems by increasing the mortality rate of natural enemies of the target insect, but B.t. does not kill the natural enemies of the pests.

To be used properly, the material must be applied to plants at the stage when the insect eats the most foliage so that the pest receives the highest dosage. Those caterpillars that eat a lethal dose frequently do not die immediately but first become paralyzed and may not die until many days later, depending upon temperature conditions. However, they stop eating immediately and cause no further damage.

Since the insects susceptible to this disease must eat it to be affected, nothing will be achieved by spraying B.t. around when the moths (which do not eat leaves) are seen to fly. Since the material is sold as a living spore, it must be kept cool and dry, and it definitely deteriorates with age. Many failures in the use of B.t. have resulted because the users didn't really understand these facts.

Two of us (the Olkowskis) have used this material very successfully on a range of caterpillars and a variety of plants in urban integrated pest-management programs in California. However, the reader is cautioned that even though the material is safe for nontarget animals, including humans, it should not be overused. Every time you temporarily wipe out a local pest insect you destroy the food needed by its natural enemies. When the latter die out there are none around to catch the next pest that flies in, and since the natural enemies of a pest are slower to propagate than the pest itself, you always risk creating new problems when you try to eradicate a pest. Use all insecticides, even safe biological ones, only as a last resort and only as spot treatments where damage is intolerable. Then if problems persist use them on successively larger scales.

attack these aphids. Using the commercially available microbial insecticide (*Bacillus thuringiensis*) (see Box 13-2) is also an augmentation tactic against the cabbage looper. This bacteria is a naturally occurring organism that is "artificially" increased for the purpose of killing off pest insects. Placing garden prunings covered with parasitized insects in a protected location for the winter will allow a release of the beneficial insects the following spring. Food sprays as a means of augmentation are discussed on page 380.

Inoculation is a tactic useful where natural enemies can be introduced earlier in the season than they would ordinarily occur so that they can reproduce on their prey and prevent a pest build-up. Inoculation tactics are used much as pesticides are—repeatedly. Importation, discussed below, does not have to be repeated regularly. An example of this would be using a fish species in a backyard pond to reduce mosquito development. Releasing commercially raised natural enemies is probably best handled in an inoculative method. To use such a method successfully, timing, dosage, and thorough biological knowledge of pest and natural enemies is needed, as well as good microclimatic information. Inoculation is discussed further under the appropriate headings in the remainder of this chapter.

Importations: When an insect is repeatedly present every season in numbers great enough to cause serious economic or aesthetic damage, often it has invaded from another area, leaving its natural enemies behind. In classical biological control introduction programs, the native area of the pest species is sought out and attempts are made to locate adopted or even species-specific natural enemies. Such species are incapable of feeding on any other insect or only feed on a small group of closely related similar species. Thus they do not cause disruptions in the environment but if effective can prevent the disruptions caused by pesticide use. Such organisms are often internal parasites of the pest insect. Still others are ectoparasites, living on the outside of their prey. These parasites are imported through a careful quarantine procedure insuring that no other organism is accidentally introduced. If the parasite of the invaded pest is successfully established in the new area, some measure of permanent control may be achieved. Once a natural enemy has been located, imported, and colonized, it must be allowed to freely attack the pest. During this phase, the situation must be monitored and the process evaluated. In agriculture, forestry, and landscaping in urban areas, successful biological control importations have been conducted against insects and weeds, and will probably be extended to many other groups of organisms in the future (see "Tree Pests," page 391). A classic example is the control of the cottony-cushion scale insect on California citrus trees by the vedalia lady beetle brought from Australia in 1888 (see margin). Another is the control of St. John's wort, or Klamath weed, by *Chrysolina* beetles imported from France. Table 13-1 summarizes one hundred years of experience in introducing natural enemies.

However, biological control agents may not always be found, or those found or bought and introduced may be incapable of holding down a pest population to acceptable levels some or all of the time. Therefore, the best approach to solving pest problems is ultimately a mixture of strategies, including biological control tactics of some sort, combined with a decision-making process. Such an approach is called integrated pest management.

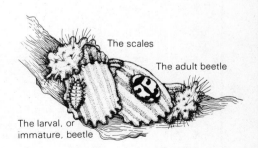

The scales

The adult beetle

The larval, or immature, beetle

The vedalia beetle and an immature larval form. The beetle and larva here are feeding on the cottony-cushion scale. The predator confines its attack to the eggs of the scale.

367

Integrated Pest Management (IPM): An integrated pest-management system is a decision-making process that utilizes all suitable techniques and information to suppress or prevent the build-up of pest population numbers. The aim is either to reduce pest populations and maintain them at levels below those causing aesthetic or economic injury, or to manipulate the pest populations so that they are prevented from causing such injury.

The essential features of an integrated pest-management system are listed in Box 13-3. An example of how a series of methods are combined in a program against a garden pest is given in Box 13-4.

To Spray or Not as a Last Resort: We can learn some valuable lessons from the classic example of DDT, first hailed as a "miracle" solution to insect pest problems and then gradually revealed to be the cause of at least as many problems as it cures. Consider for example the movement of pesticides on a global scale, as illustrated in Figure 13-2. The undesirable effects of pesticide use are found both on the target insects and on the nontarget species in their environment, that is, humans and wildlife. Figure 13-3 shows, for example, how the reduction in eggshell thickness for the pere-

Box 13-3. Essentials of an Integrated Pest-Management System

1. Monitoring (regular observation of) the pest, or potential pest populations (a) to learn the life cycle of the pest in any particular area, (b) to identify and assess the presence of natural enemies of the pest, (c) to determine if populations are rising or falling, and (d) to establish the level of the pest population causing aesthetic or economic injury in order to determine at what point treatment must be initiated (in other words, finding the action level).

2. Timing of treatments so as to be most effective against the pest and least disruptive of the natural controls.

3. Spot treatment, that is, confining treatments to only those areas where the pest problem has reached the action level, with the aim of not disturbing natural controls in other areas.

4. Using the most selective materials or processes available, in order to cause as little injury to natural controls as possible.

5. Techniques to enhance natural controls.

6. The search for and development of alternative pest-management tactics.

7. An integrated package that pulls all these components together so they operate smoothly.

The techniques that can be combined into an integrated pest-management program are these:

1. Educational. In cases where the mere presence of a few insects is causing concern and no significant damage to plants is involved, information about the situation is frequently adequate to help overcome fear of the insects and increase tolerance for their presence.

2. Cultural. Planting pest-resistant species and using maintenance practices such as watering and fertilizing to enhance natural controls and otherwise reduce pest problems.

3. Physical. Using physical methods to reduce pest populations; for example, pruning to remove a tent caterpillar colony. A particularly ingenious physical method of physically controlling a pest is illustrated.

4. Biological. Deliberately introducing and/or manipulating parasites, predators, and pathogens in maintaining another organism's density at a lower average than would occur in their absence or without manipulation.

5. Chemical. Using biocides (that is, insecticides, fungicides, herbicides, or rodenticides) that temporarily suppress pest populations to lower densities than would otherwise occur. The ideal chemical tools are nontoxic to humans and selective in that they will only kill the target species.

Physical pest control. An ingenious method of control for weevils injuring

plum and apricot trees, devised by Colonel T. Forest of Germantown, Pennsylvania in the early 1800s. "Having a fine plum tree near his pump (he) tied a rope from the tree to his pump handle, so that the tree was greatly agitated every time there was occasion to pump water. The consequence was that the fruit on his tree was preserved in the greatest perfection."

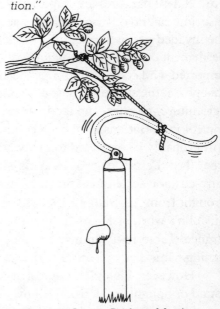

Source: Quote, Dethier, Man's Plaque. Illustration, Flint, van den Bosch. A Source Book on Integrated Pest Management.

grine falcon coincided with the widespread use of DDT. This correlation was verified by laboratory studies. In addition, after DDT was banned, eggshell thickness increased. However because of its persistence, many years will pass before DDT is eliminated from our bodies and the world eco-

---

Table 13-1. **Condensed History of Biological Control Projects**

The following table is organized to present records of particular natural enemy importation projects, first by the initial area where the natural enemies were tried and found successful to some degree, and then by the subsequent areas where the natural enemies were spread further. The parasite *Aphelinus mali*, which attacks the wooly apple aphid *Eriosoma lanigerum*, for example, was first discovered in eastern North America, and was introduced into Europe where it successfully reduced aphid populations. By 1960, it had been spread to twenty-five countries.

The data are also presented according to whether the introduction occurred on an island, such as Fiji or the West Indies, or on a continent, such as North America or Australia. This is important because some critics have said that the importation strategy is most effective on islands. These data question that statement. The evidence suggests that the strategy has been effective wherever it is supported.

A. Insect Control [in Number of Importations]

Degree of Success	After Initial Releases			After Subsequent Releases		
	Islands	Continents	Total	Islands	Continents	Total
Complete	12	19	31	36	67	102
Substantial	32	41	73	58	86	144
Partial	25	28	53	36	45	81
Total	69	88	157	129	198	327

B. Weed Control

Degree of Success	After Initial Releases			After Subsequent Releases		
	Islands	Continents	Total	Islands	Continents	Total
Complete	5	5	10	7	6	13
Substantial	7	7	14	9	17	26
Partial	0	5	5	4	14	18
Total	12	17	29	20	37	57

Source: Laing and Hamai. "Biological Control of Insect Pests and Weeds by Imported Parasites, Predators, and Pathogens."

Figure 13-2. **Long Distance Transport of Pesticides**

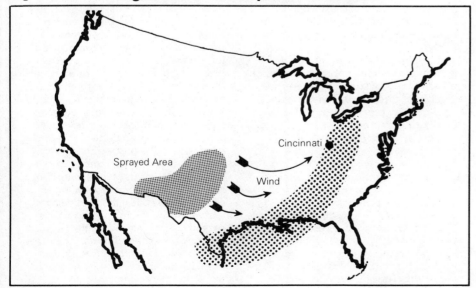

Insecticides (*DDT, DDE, chlordane, dieldrin,* and *heptachlor epoxide*) sprayed in western Texas for agricultural pest control were picked up by a large dust storm in Texas and deposited in Cincinnati, Ohio, with a light rain the following day at a level of 1.3 parts per million. At the time the dust fall occurred in Cincinnati the dust cloud resulting from the storm stretched for 1500 miles in a 200-mile wide band extending easterly from the southern tip of Texas north to Lake Erie.

Source: Flint and van den Bosch, *A Source Book on Integrated Pest Management.*

Box 13-4. **Integrated Pest-Management of the Garden Snail**

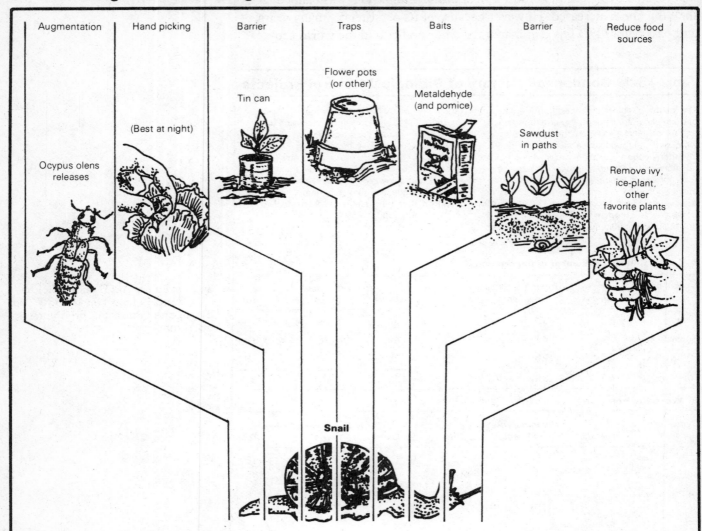

One of the major pests in gardens along the Pacific Coast of California is the common garden snail, *Helix aspersa*. This animal was deliberately introduced from France into the San Francisco Bay Area in the 1850s as a potential source of food. As with most invaded pests, it left its natural enemies behind and, released from restraint, populations were free to spread and grow to damaging numbers wherever sufficient moisture and food were available.

Keeping down the numbers of snails can become a full-time occupation if you want to raise any young, tender seedlings or other succulent plants during the rainy season. Constant use of a poison bait only results in the creation of a local population of snails resistant to the material, since the susceptible ones die and only those that can detoxify the pesticide live to breed the next gen-

eration. In any event, the snails are good travelers and will soon migrate into any environment suited to them no matter how thoroughly they have been cleaned out of the area previously.

What is needed is an integrated pest-management approach in which a variety of tools and strategies are combined through the use of a decision-making process that includes a monitoring system.

Start by surveying your overall garden environment. Are you encouraging snails to breed in some areas while fighting them in others? You may need to begin your snail-management program by doing some habitat manipulation. Some plants such as ivy and certain succulents, especially when used in massed plantings as ground covers, provide particularly favorable breeding areas. The soil surface remains

shaded and moist, and the plants themselves may provide unusually good food. If you observe large numbers of snails, particularly young ones, in a suspected area, you are probably encouraging their breeding there. Such plantings can be replaced, or reduced, the latter either in terms of total area, or by thinning, to decrease the amount of favorable habitat. Thinning may have the desirable affect of increasing aeration, simply by drying out the stems and ground surface around the plant.

Snails like to breed under wooden boards that are in contact with the soil. Their large transparent eggs can be easily seen there at certain times of the year. Wood should be picked up and stored off the ground. Or, in wet weather, if the boards are used for walking on in the garden, dry sawdust placed underneath the wood will very effectively reduce snail breeding in those areas.

Fine dry sawdust, in general, makes very effective barriers. This is the next strategy that should be considered. Hydrated lime and fine wood ashes are two other common materials used as barriers. Ferrous ammonium sulphate, which degrades into useful plant nutrients, is sold for the same purpose. All such barriers are caustic or irritating to the snail's mucous membrane. Each of these materials may inhibit plant growth if large amounts are placed close to growing plants, however; thus, it is best to use these materials as borders to the beds, if at all. Sawdust makes particularly good pathway material, since when placed two or more inches deep, it will help to prevent compaction where you walk. While it slowly decomposes it will act as an effective herbicide, starving weed seedlings for nitrogen. Yet once decomposed it can be incorporated into the soil, improving the soil structure just as other decomposed organic materials do.

Another kind of barrier may be created by sinking a tin can, open at both ends, into the soil around each young vegetable seedling. Snails can climb up and over the cans perfectly well, of course, but they frequently do not do so. Preliminary experiments seem to show they are less likely to discover the succulent seedlings protected inside.

Physical controls should always be considered when the pest is large and the area is small to medium in size. In this case, handpicking is the best method to use. The most effective job can be done at night, with a flashlight. After crushing them, the snails may be fed to the chickens or used in the compost pile. A bed of young vegetable seedlings can be bordered by a walkway of fine dry sawdust and the area within checked in the evening once a week. After watering the garden, or following heavy rains, the sawdust can be renewed and the area handpicked clean of snails in the evening once again.

Cultural controls may also have an effect on the size of the pest population. In this case watering techniques may need to be modified, since the drier you can keep the soil and plant surfaces the lower the overall humidity of your garden and the less favorable to the snail. Of course you can't do anything about the frequency or duration of the winter rains, but during the rest of the year you can water your garden as infrequently as possible. When you do water, do so long enough to wet the deeper layers of the soil. Then the plant roots will travel downward into the soil and be less susceptible to drying or other damage at the surface.

Compost mulches at the soil surface between the plants will help to retard evaporation from the soil surface and reduce the need for frequent sprinkling. Grouping plants in the garden according to their greater or lesser need for water may help to avoid any unnecessary irrigations.

Traps are another strategy that should be tried. Overturned clay flower pots are quite effective for this if the soil surface of the beds is uneven enough to permit snails to climb inside through spaces under the rim. The pots should be set close to the plants that the snails have been known to feed on, placed on the shadiest side. During the day the snails will leave the plant and fasten themselves to the cool inner sides of the clay flower pot. Periodic inspection of these pots will allow you to find and destroy the snails inside. They can be crushed inside the pot with a stick or the handle of a trowel or stepped on, and fed to the chickens or put in the compost.

We have observed dead and decomposing snails attracting other snails to the area. It may be yeast that is acting as the bait. It is the yeast odor that draws the snails into stale beer. Unfortunately, beer is not only an expensive bait, it is only effective when used as a pit trap, that is, when the container is sunk into the ground so that animals actually fall into it. The disadvantage of a pit trap is that you may trap beneficial organisms such as earthworms and ground beetles as well.

More reliable as bait but having all the disadvantages of a true pesticide is metaldehyde, a common component of many commercially sold snail baits. It is regarded as somewhat less objectionable than arsenic, the old-time bait still sold for this purpose, which you should avoid at all costs since it is directly poisonous to people, remains unchanged in the soil for a long time, and can be absorbed through the skin (while you are weeding, for instance). Nevertheless, metaldehyde should be used with caution, kept away from food plants, and used as infrequently as possible. Otherwise, as mentioned before, you will simply breed a local population of snails that is resistant to it.

It is best to use such a poison bait just to protect newly transplanted seedlings or particularly susceptible, valuable plants. Once the seedlings have grown to the size where they can sustain some damage, you should stop using the baits and rely on handpicking and trapping. That way the poison will be effective the next time you need to use it.

Also, use the pellets rather than the powdered form of the bait, as you can control the placement more accurately and are less likely to breathe the stuff while applying it. If there is a chance that a pet or child might be attracted to the pellets, try placing them inside a semiflattened tin can that is partially buried among the plants so it is inconspicuous. Metaldehyde has been known to make dogs sick if they eat it.

So, there you have an integrated pest-management program for the garden snail. The accompanying figure illustrates the program. In summary the components of the program are these:

1. *Monitoring* or regular checking to see when and where the damage is occurring and whether it is serious enough to warrant treatment.

2. *Habitat modification* wherever possible in the form of reducing or eliminating favorite breeding places of the pest.

3. Use of *barriers* to reduce the migration of additional pest individuals into the area or on to the plants.

4. *Physical controls*, in this case in the form of handpicking in the evening to eliminate a portion of the pest population.

5. *Cultural controls*, that is, reducing frequency of applying water to the garden.

6. *Traps* placed in strategic places to reduce pest numbers.

7. As a last resort, the use of a poison, choosing the *least toxic* one available, metaldehyde, in the best *formulation*, a pellet bait, and *timed* to be most effective and least likely to cause the development of resistant populations. Use only when young seedlings or extremely susceptible valuable plants are likely to suffer intolerable damage.

Ideally, biological control importation should also be a part of this program. In this case, importation would require research into the snail's na-

Box 13-4. **Continued**

tive European habitats to determine which, if any, natural enemies might be imported. This technique, described in more detail in the text, is obviously not one that the home gardener can be involved with directly, but individuals can encourage their state and federal government as well as private foundations to support this kind of research.

Does this treatment of the snail sound like more work than just using a pesticide? It *is* more work, and similar kinds of integrated pest-management programs in commercial agri-

culture would provide jobs for thousands of people who could train themselves to work for the farmer on a per acre basis as pest-management specialists. Farmers who use such trained pest managers to develop integrated pest-management programs for their crops do as well or better than farmers relying exclusively on chemical controls, and the use of poisons is greatly reduced. The appeal of the chemical pesticides is that they seem to be such a simple solution, but of course they are not a solution at all. They must be

used over and over again, eventually causing more problems than they cure. The only sane answer to managing our relationship with other forms of life that seem to be competing with us for food and fiber, reducing the aesthetic value of our landscape, or causing public health problems, is to develop effective integrated pest-management programs that can reduce the pest populations safely, such as this one that you can use in your own garden against the common garden snail.

Figure 13-3. **Effects of DDT on the Peregrine Falcon and Sparrowhawk**

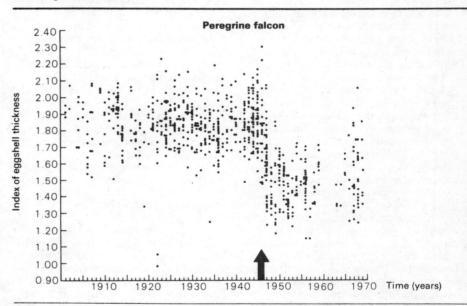

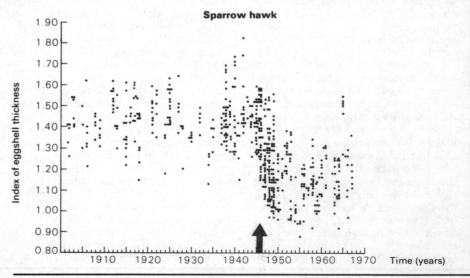

Changes in thickness of egg shells of falcon and hawk in Great Britain. Arrows indicate first use of DDT. (From Ehrlich and Ehrlich, 1970)

Source: Flint and van den Bosch, *A Source Book on Integrated Pest Management.*

system. The important thing about this situation is that the poison was used on a global scale before it was discovered to be dangerous to many life forms including our own.

It is now clear that the widespread use of insecticides, regardless of industry's insistence to the contrary, can cause the following types of disruptions.

Pest Resurgence (see Figure 13-4A):   Resurgence occurs when the predators and parasites that would naturally control the pests are temporarily removed or drastically reduced in numbers. The home gardener commonly experiences this phenomenon without realizing what is happening. In treating aphids on shrubs, for example, the first spraying may kill off the predators such as lacewings and syrphid flies and the tiny parasites that kill the aphids from within. Although the aphids appear to have been wiped out, in fact

Figure 13-4. **Effects of Chemical Treatment on Target Pest and Predator**

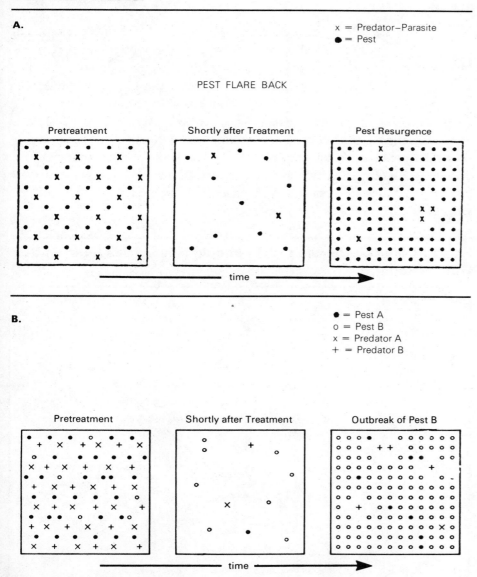

A.

x = Predator–Parasite
● = Pest

PEST FLARE BACK

Pretreatment   Shortly after Treatment   Pest Resurgence

time

A. Target pest resurgence. *Diagrammatic sketch of the influence of chemical treatment on natural enemy pest abundance and dispersion, and resulting pest resurgence. The squares represent a field, orchard or garden immediately before, immediately after and some time after treatment with an insecticide for control of a pest species (represented by solid dots). The immediate effect of the treatment is a strong reduction of the pest, but an even greater destruction of its natural enemies (represented by x's.) The resulting unfavorable ratio and dispersion of pest individuals to natural enemies permits a rapid resurgence of the former to damaging abundance.*

B.

● = Pest A
o = Pest B
x = Predator A
+ = Predator B

Pretreatment   Shortly after Treatment   Outbreak of Pest B

time

B. Secondary pest outbreak. *Diagrammatic sketch of the influence of a chemical treatment on natural-enemy, pest abundance and dispersion with resulting secondary pest outbreak. The squares represent a field or orchard immediately before, immediately after and some time after treatment with an insecticide for control of pest A (represented by solid dots). The chemical treatment effectively reduces pest A as well as its natural enemy (x), but has little or no effect on pest B (o). Subsequently, because of its release from predation by predator B (+), pest B flares to damaging abundance.*

Source: Flint and van den Bosch, *A Source Book on Integrated Pest Management.*

373

some always escape contact with the poison, and other unsprayed aphids fly in from neighboring areas. What probably *have* been thoroughly decimated are the natural enemies of the aphids; there are always fewer of them and they are slower to increase their numbers. The remaining aphids can now multiply with fewer restraints upon their population. Therefore, after a period of time passes the aphids are back, only worse than before. Another spraying causes the population to bounce back still more quickly as more natural enemies are eliminated. (Aphids don't need to mate during the growing season. The individual insects you see upon the plants are most likely to be all females with female embryos within them all ready to be born within a short period of time. Aphid parasites, or miniwasps (see page 383), must find a member of the opposite sex, mate, search out an aphid of the right kind, and lay eggs within it to survive. Obviously, this is a far slower process.) In general, a time lag will always occur between the appearance of first noticeable populations of the plant-eaters and the development of sufficient numbers of their parasites or predators necessary to reduce the pest population satisfactorily.

New Insect Pests: Pesticide use can also be responsible for the development of new insect pests (often called secondary pests) previously unimportant insects that multiply rapidly in the absence of their former competitors or the natural controls killed off by the chemicals (see Figure 13-4B). Although you may only be aware of one or two insects present in large numbers upon a particular plant, in actuality, many other potential pest species are likely to be feeding there also. They are not obvious because their natural enemies keep their populations down. Pesticide use against the primary pest may accidentally kill off those other natural enemies, thus releasing new species of plant pests. Mites are a common secondary pest that become problematic when pesticides are used (see page 387).

Figure 13-5. **The Increase of Pesticide Resistance over Three Generations**

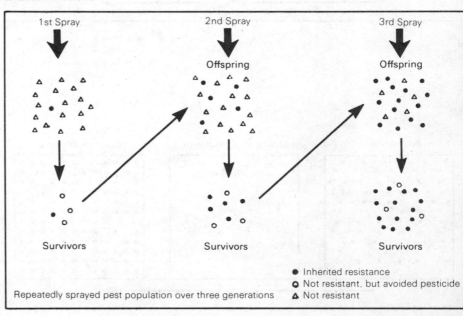

Resistance: A third problem resulting from pesticide use is the development of resistant insect strains that cannot be controlled by heavier doses of the same poison (see Figure 13-5).

It is attempts to cope with these phenomena that result in the "pesticide treadmill," that is, the use of pesticides leading to more pesticide use, leading to more pesticide use, leading to more, and so on.

The importance of the resistance problem alone can be understood when you realize that in California out of twenty-five insect pests, each of which in 1970 was reported to cause over a million dollars worth of damage, 72 percent of these insects were already resistant to insecticides (van den Bosch, personal communication. Clearly, chemical control is no permanent solution.

Furthermore, the implications for the field of public health are important. As with antibiotics used to control human infections, too casual or too frequent use of the powerful pesticide chemicals can render them powerless as tools when they are really needed and their temporary use might be justified. With key mosquitoes already resistant to methyl parathion, and rats becoming resistant to warfarin, we could face a major emergency if serious outbreaks of malaria, encephalitis, or plague should occur.

One of the most significant and severe threats to public health is the phenomenon of biomagnification. Biomagnification is the process by which poisons can be passed along food chains and accumulate in toxic levels after several such passages. Figure 13-6 presents data on the biomagnification of DDT. Figure 13-7 illustrates the concept of biomagnification using the chemical DDD as an example.

Describing in detail the current research on the effects of the new chemical pesticides upon humans and wildlife is outside the scope of this book. The reader seeking to gain an appreciation of the ways in which mod-

---

Figure 13-6. **DDT Concentration in a Lake Michigan Food Chain**

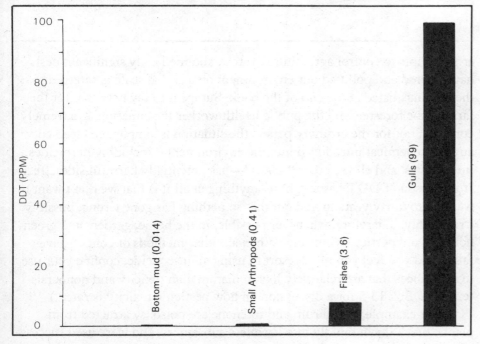

DDT load in gulls is about 240 times that of small arthropods. In 1969, Coho salmon from Lake Michigan were found to contain DDT at 4 to 6 times the tolerance standard for human consumption.

Source: Berry, Osgood, and St. John. *Chemical Villains.*

Figure 13-7. **DDD*Concentrations in the Clear Lake Food Chain**

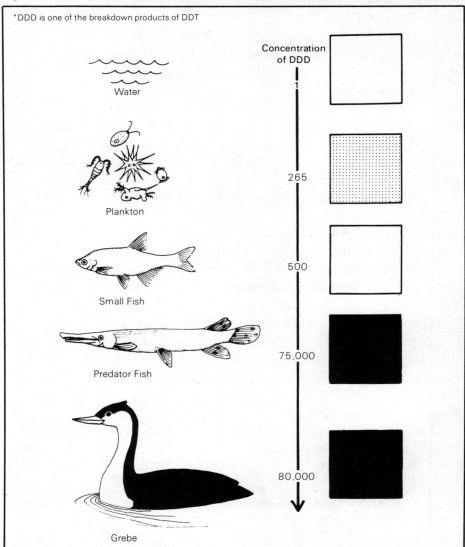

*DDD is one of the breakdown products of DDT

Water

Plankton

Small Fish

Predator Fish

Grebe

Concentration
of DDD

1

265

500

75,000

80,000

DDD was concentrated in plankton at a level 265 times its concentration in water. In small fish the concentration was 500 times, in predator fish 75,000 times and grebes 80,000 times the DDD level in the lake's water.

Source: Flint and van den Bosch. *A Source Book on Integrated Pest Management.*

ern attempts to control agricultural, forest, and medically significant pests have altered and polluted our environment on a global scale is referred to the readings listed at the end of the book. Suffice it to say here that for the farmer, the forester, and the public health worker the situation is extremely complex, but for the ordinary person the situation is simple and clear-cut: any new chemical introduced into the environment—including herbicides, insecticides, and all the other "-cides"—has potentially harmful side-effects. If the lesson of DDT has taught us anything at all it is that we don't want to wait ten to thirty years to find out that something has gone wrong, possibly irreversibly. Therefore, whenever possible, in the home, garden, and greenhouse, avoid pesticides entirely! When all other methods of control have failed and you feel you must resort to using an insecticide, confine your use to substances that are relatively low in mammalian toxicity and nonpersistent. (See Box 13-5 for a discussion on how pesticide toxicity is rated.)

For example, pyrethrum and rotenone are poisons extracted from plants, break down rapidly into harmless substances, and were used successfully before "miracle" synthesized pesticides made their appearance. Pyrethrum, sorptive dusts such as silica gel which have a drying effect on insects, and diatomaceous earth, which works mechanically as an abrasive, are generally considered "low hazard" insecticides. In fact, although pyrethrum has long been regarded as very safe, some recent data suggest that it may be more hazardous to mammals than had been realized previously. Take great care to avoid eating or breathing any of these substances. Aerosol sprays should certainly be avoided.

Rotenone is known to be more toxic to humans than pyrethrum, and is very toxic to fish. Therefore, it should not be used around ponds or streams, or used as a flea powder on dogs that play in the water.

Always check the label on insecticides to make sure that the chemical you want is not mixed with other pesticides. Fungicides and insecticides and particularly insecticide-herbicide combinations, should be avoided. When you have a specific insect problem, the addition of a fungicide or a herbicide as a prophylactic may have a disruptive effect on the environment. Treat for specific problems and only when they actually occur.

Piperonyl butoxide, a synergist used to increase the effectiveness of insecticides, is a common additive in insect sprays that has always been regarded as safe, until recently; it is now coming under suspicion as possibly hazardous.

The sections that follow provide more specific suggestions on how to handle particular pest problems.

Box 13-5. **LD$_{50}$**

LD$_{50}$ is a notation referring to the lethal dose of any given substance that kills fifty percent of the organisms tested. It is a measure of toxicity, and is usually expressed in milligrams of poison per kilogram of body weight (mg/kg). An LD$_{50}$ of 1.0, as with parathion, is more toxic than an LD$_{50}$ of 3000, as with pyrethrum. A poison with an LD$_{50}$ of 1.0 mg/kg eaten by a 150-pound (70 kg) man, means it will take about 68 milligrams of that poison to kill one-half of the subjects exposed to it:

1 mg/kg · 150 lb 0.45 kg/lb

= 67.5 mg

One needs to proceed carefully, however, when extrapolating the LD$_{50}$ found for one type of animal to that for another. The animals tested to determine pesticide toxicity ratings are usually rats, but dogs, chickens, rabbits, monkeys, pheasants, ducks, sparrows, and others are also used. The route of administration for the poison can also vary, from oral, dermal (on the skin), interocular (in the eye), interdermal (in the skin), and internasal (into the nose). Thus, using this index of toxicity, the common organophosphate insecticide malathion has an oral LD$_{50}$ (using rats) of 2800 mg/kg.

The reliance upon the measurement of LD$_{50}$ exclusively as an indication of how hazardous a material is has recently come under serious question, since carcinogenic, mutagenic, and teratogenic (birth-deforming) effects are not indicated by LD$_{50}$ ratings. However, given the choice between two compounds, select the one with the largest LD$_{50}$, if you must use any poison. If you need to determine the LD$_{50}$ of an acaricide (mite-killer), attractant, chemosterilant, defoliant, fungicide, herbicide, insecticide, molluscicide, nematicide, plant growth regulator, repellant, or rodenticide, look it up in the *Pesticide Index*, fifth edition, edited by W. J. Wiswesser, and published by the Entomological Society of America, 4603 Calvert Road, Box AJ, College Park, Maryland 20740.

Kicking the Garden Pesticide Habit: If you and your environment are already "hooked" on synthetic chemical insecticides, you may have to endure a transitional period during which pest damage becomes very noticeable while you learn new methods of management and a natural balance is slowly restored. It may take more than a single season for populations of controlling predators and parasites to reestablish themselves.

Whether you have been using chemical sprays or not, the cycle of a

What to Do When Damage Is Severe

1. Determine who the real culprits are. Sometimes it is easy to be fooled. In an example from our own garden, an earwig crawled out of a hole in a tomato, and closer examination revealed that a cutworm was curled up in the dark interior. However, a night-time visit to the tomato plant with a flashlight showed that snails and slugs were eating holes in the fruit. Our conclusion: the snails and slugs probably should be controlled, some of the abundant foliage could be spared to the cutworms, the earwigs were merely busy in the mulch and could be ignored. In fact, when slugs and snails were controlled (by hand-picking at night), there was little further fruit damage.

2. Use handpicking, trapping, barriers, or other mechanical methods whenever possible (see Figure 13-8). Remember, a few of the less desirable insects must be kept around if you want the animals that control them to be present and available to deal with future damaging outbreaks.

3. Incorporate plenty of organic materials (compost, leaf mold, manure, and so on) into your soil to develop humus. This will help provide a wealth of microorganisms as well as nutrients needed by the growing plants. If you put mulch on the soil, the microhabitat needed by many insect predators will develop.

4. Learn to recognize the natural predators and encourage their presence. A healthy environment is a complex one—the greater the variety of animal and plant species the better.

5. Stick to growing resistant varieties and plants that are suited to your area. If you are short of time or interest in solving pest problems in the ways suggested above, then grow native plants that require little maintenance and vegetable varieties known to be relatively pest-free in surrounding gardens. Recognize that your area may be too cold, too hot, too wet, too dry, too sunny, too shady, too acid, too alkali, and so on, for a particular plant where you are trying to grow it. A variety unsuited to its location may have a lower resistance to insects and disease. And, finally, eliminate the plants that repeatedly become infested from your garden rather than struggling to maintain them with chemical crutches that may poison you or the environment.

natural enemy will normally lag behind the pest it feeds upon. This can be a painful wait if you are the garden enthusiast who has selected and nurtured each plant and then you think you see them threatened by insects. *The best thing to do may be nothing.* If you are patient, natural controls may have a chance to catch up.

In the pesticide-free garden there will be some visible insect damage. Learn to appreciate signs of insect activity as a reminder that you share this planet with other living creatures. If you want perfect flowers, buy plastic ones. (Perfection has its costs even then. However, the problems caused by certain plastics in the environment deserve another essay.) Living plants can easily sustain a fair amount of leaf-pruning when mature. Seedlings can be started indoors and then set out, surrounded by protective barriers (see Cutworms and Root Maggots).

Natural Enemies in the Garden: The numbers of insects and other organisms important in pest control are so numerous and the animals themselves frequently so inconspicuous, either because of size, natural camouflage, or habit, that it would take an immense volume to describe them all. Many creatures play a role in saving us from being overrun with insects and other organisms injurious to people and their activities: snakes, spiders, wasps, salamanders, hawks, owls, ravens, seagulls, weasel (these last four are all enemies of rats in the wild), toads, flower flies, centipedes, ground beetles, lacewings, ladybird beetles, dragonflies, praying mantids, bats, raccoons, badgers, and 'possums, to name only a few. Surprisingly enough, every urban area has its share of even the larger of these pest-controlling animals.

However, many of the species are so obscure from the point of view of the ordinary person that it takes a highly trained specialist to recognize them and describe their function. For example, there is a soil fungus that traps and kills plant-root-destroying nematodes (roundworms). What average busy people have the time to brief themselves on this commonplace and yet miraculous phenomenon? It is simpler for us to recommend the addition of plenty of compost to the garden than to go into the details of exactly what animals, fungi, and other soil organisms valuable in pest control are likely to be in the compost. Refer back to Figure 13-1 for illustrations of some important common but rarely recognized helpful insects. A good book for readers who wish to learn about this subject in greater depth is *Beneficial Insects* by Lester A. Swan. The photographs are very clear and helpful for identification. This and other recommended readings are listed in the bibliography.

Importing and Attracting Beneficial Insects: Some gardeners swear that they have been greatly aided in pest control by commercially purchased ladybird beetles and praying mantids. However, when released in home gardens these insects usually migrate to other places. The few that remain may not become established or have a noticeable impact on pests, because their numbers are too small or they were released at the wrong season. On the other hand, the larvae of lacewings remain where they are released, so that if you have plenty of insect food for them to live on (aphids, for instance) they

Figure 13-8. **Useful Traps for Sampling and Detecting Pest Insects**

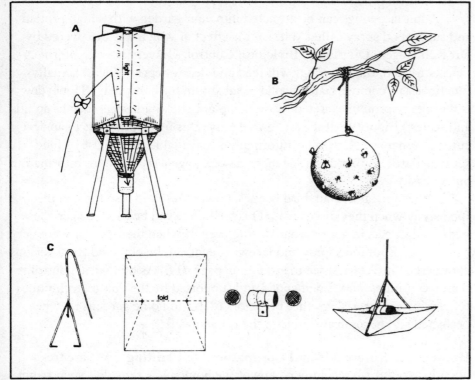

(A) A light trap, (B) "a sticky red sphere", (C) a pheromone trap. As shown, the latter can be made with wire and cardboard, and baited with a virgin female placed in a small screened cage in the center. Attracted insects are trapped by sticky adhesive.

Figure 13-9. **Agricultural Use of Food Spray**

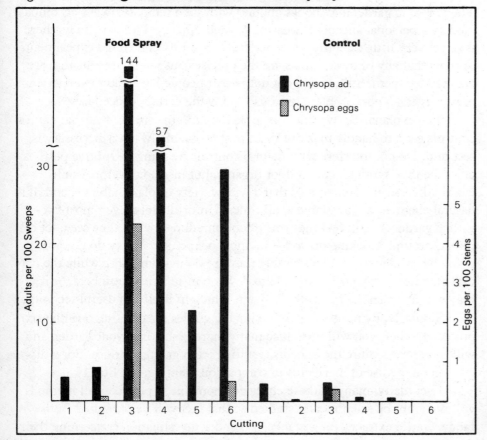

Use of artificial food supplements to increase predator populations in infested fields. This graph shows the mean number of lacewing (Chrysopa carnea) adults and eggs in an alfalfa plot sprayed with food supplements and an unsprayed field. Samples were taken in 1967. Food supplement consisted of yeast hydrolosate + sugar + water and was applied once a week.

Source: Hagen, Sawall, and Tassan. "The Use of Food Sprays to Increase Effectiveness of Entomophagous Insects."

may provide considerable control during the season. More work, however, is needed to "perfect" such techniques before they can be used as widespread insect-control practices.

Adult lacewings can be attracted into your garden with a high protein and sugar food spray called Wheast, the effect of which was discovered by Dr. Ken Hagen, Division of Biological Control, University of California. Once attracted, the lacewings will feed and deposit eggs. Wheast actually functions as a commercially available substitute for honeydew. (Honeydew is the sugary protein excreted by certain plant-sucking insects such as aphids and scales.) Figure 13-9 shows how effective this food spray was in an agricultural situation. No similar information is available for the use of food spray in garden situations. (See margin note, page 411, for more information on Wheast.)

Other predators (ladybird beetles, flower flies) will also feed on the food spray when they discover it. This technique can be used to keep these beneficial insects in your garden during periods when their prey are not very numerous. (Both food spray and lacewing eggs can be obtained from various commercial insectaries; see margin note, page 414.) As biological control research continues, and is demanded and supported by the public, techniques for rearing and releasing other predators useful in home gardens may be perfected and become available to the urban dweller.

Homemade Botanicals and Companionate Planting: We are frequently asked if we recommend any of the homemade remedies such as hot pepper sprays for aphids or planting marigolds to keep bean beetles away. The "organic gardening" books abound with such recipes, always accompanied by a personal anecdote swearing to their efficacy. Unfortunately, there is as yet very little scientific evidence from carefully controlled experiments to show that any of these rituals are the precise cause of the results that are claimed for them. Still, we do not doubt that people have had the experience of witnessing a pest problem diminish following certain procedures.

The explanation, we think, is to be found in the simple fact that natural controls exist to handle many of these pest problems. What is necessary is restraint. Do not interfere with natural controls by using disruptive pesticides, be they synthetic, natural, or organic, but instead develop a sufficiently diverse environment so that a wide variety of plant habitats, and thus natural enemies, are available at all times. Unfortunately, even most "organic" gardeners still feel they must "do something" when they see a lot of insects around. Cooking up and spraying a pepper spray may do no more than give gardeners that feeling that they are doing something while the natural enemies of the pest have time to develop in sufficient numbers, or it may merely wash the bugs off the plants which in itself is a useful technique.

Similarly, by religiously following the guides for planting one plant to protect another, you will introduce many more plants into your garden and will therefore acquire the benefits resulting from greater variety. For a discussion on the use of marigolds in companion planting, see Box 13-6.

Eventually, many of these cherished homemade pest-control methods will no doubt be scientifically studied so that fact will be separated from fancy. Garlic extracts, for instance, are under investigation concerning their

Box 13-6. **Marigolds and the Question of Companion Planting**

The entrance to the Integral Urban House in Berkeley is bordered by a self-seeding bed of marigolds. Many visitors ask, "Is it true that planting marigolds in the vegetable garden will keep insects away?"

This is one of the many common myths about "companion planting." Like all myths, it is an elaboration upon a kernel of verifiable truth, the elaboration serving a particular goal. The goal in this case is achieving reduction of damage on food plants without having to resort to using toxic insecticides. Unfortunately, this desire may be naively broadened until the goal becomes a simplistic desire to get rid of all insects. Of course, that would be undesirable even if possible, since most of the insect species and other closely related arthropods in the garden are either directly or indirectly beneficial to humans.

Will marigolds keep *pest* insects away? This idea apparently arose from the fact that both small marigolds (*Tagetes patula*) and large marigolds (*T. erecta*) have a root exudate that discourages certain plant-infesting nematodes (long, thin, white worms) such as the meadow, or root lesion nematodes (*Pratylenchus penetrans*). Now, nematodes are not insects, and the kinds that infest plants are not all that common. Usually they become a problem when a highly susceptible plant, strawberries would be an example, is grown season after season in the same soil so that the populations of nematodes build up.

A study done by the Connecticut Agricultural Experiment Station showed that when soils are so infested, planting the field solidly with marigolds for an entire season, and then plowing the marigolds under, will give good nematode control for two to three years—better than any other method used for the purpose, in fact. However, they also found that planting the flowers for shorter periods, or merely interplanting them among the other crops, did not have the same effect. It had to be a solid planting, much as you would plant wheat.

Rotating your crops is another way of reducing nematode infestations, since plants vary greatly in their susceptibility to infection. Another possible tactic (practical for the gardener but not for the farmer) is to introduce large amounts of compost or other decomposing organic matter into the soil. There are a number of fungi that trap and kill nematodes, and the organic material may provide a favorable environment for these fungi.

The nematodes referred to here are not the large visible ones you might see when turning over soil that has a lot of organic matter in it; those are the beneficial nematodes. Rather, they are microscopic in size and are found in nodules along the plant roots. A symptom of nematode infestation is the overall stunting of a plant that just fails to grow properly.

Returning to marigolds once again, the myth is that they repel insects, but actually the bright yellow orange varieties seem attractive to a certain moth, at least around Berkeley. This is not to say, however, that planting marigolds would increase damage in the garden. There is no data on that one way or another.

potential utility in mosquito control. But even if such a botanical becomes more useful there is no guarantee that it too could not be mishandled. Some of these botanicals, or plant-derived insecticides, may be no more selective than the synthetic chemicals they are used to replace. Although they may not pose the same environmental and human hazards, they still can cause insect problems because they may kill a broad spectrum of insects, thus eliminating the predators and parasites along with the pests.

It is important to emphasize that since even "low hazard" botanicals may seriously, if only temporarily, disturb the natural relationships among the insect populations their use should be confined to spot applications on the smallest possible area, and only when all else has failed and you cannot possibly sustain the level of damage or do without the infested plant.

Now that a theoretical framework has been presented, we shall turn to specific pest problems that have come to our attention. This list is not comprehensive, since a discussion of the many organisms considered "pests" is outside the scope of this book. Instead of an exhaustive treatment, a number of common animals are discussed as examples, with appropriate management techniques explained. We hope you can generalize from these to other specific problems you may have that are not mentioned here. The categories of pest problem discussed in this chapter are:

• *In the garden:* ants; aphids; cutworms; cabbage looper, imported cabbage worms, and tomato hornworm; earwigs; gophers; lawn insects and diseases; leafhoppers; mites; sowbugs (pillbugs); root maggots; scales, whiteflies, and other sucking insects; snails and slugs; ticks; tree pests; wasps; and weeds.

• *In the house:* ants; bedbugs; cockroaches and other pantry pests; fleas; flies; and mosquitoes; moths and carpet beetles; rats and mice; and spiders.

• *In the greenhouse:* mites, aphids, whiteflies, and mealybugs.

In the Garden

Ants: Very useful scavengers that not only clean up dead animals and debris in the garden (and in the house too, if they are permitted), but also aerate the soil and prey on other insects. In her very interesting book *Gardening Without Poisons,* Beatrice Trum Hunter points out that certain ant species are used to control caterpillars in Chinese citrus orchards, and that red ants are used in forest management in Europe because of their predatory habits. She goes on to say, "Ants feed extensively on many insects that pass all or part of their lives in the soil. They destroy a high percentage of the larvae of fruit flies and house flies. Because they will attack many insects that come within foraging range of their nests, they have a great influence on insect populations over and above what they eat."

There are two ways that ants can become a nuisance in the garden. In some cases they transport aphids in from another source, and these supply them with nutritious honeydew, and they may protect both aphids and scales by discouraging the natural enemies that would otherwise keep these pests in check.

If you determine that due to one or the other of these activities some ants are definitely having an injurious effect on a particular plant, you can keep them off a tree or shrub by the use of Stickem (the trade name of a sticky, adhesive substance), tree bands, or similar products. When the weather is not too damp, a pyrethrum-silica gel dust can be used to ring a plant stem and in some cases may be effective for as long as several weeks—probably long enough to let the natural enemies of the aphids and scales take control of the situation.

An ant stimulating an aphid to excrete honeydew by palpating with its antennae. All ants occur in the order Hymenoptera, family Formicidae and are related to bees and wasps.

A. An aphid "mummy." A parasitic miniwasp has emerged through the hole it chewed in the dead aphid's cuticle. This hole is very ragged, signifying that a hyperparasite emerged. An even-sided hole indicates that a primary miniparasite emerged.

B. An aphid parasite laying an egg inside an aphid. The parasitic insect that develops in the aphid kills it by consuming its internal tissues.

Figure 13-10. **An Aphid "Mummy" and Aphid Parasite**

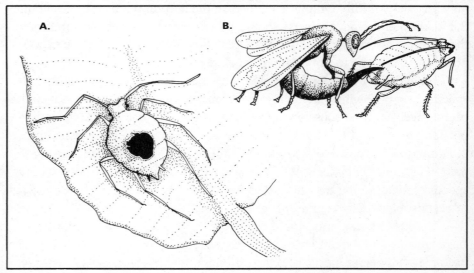

A.

B.

An occasional problem with ants in one corner of your garden should not be regarded as a signal to try to wipe out all the ants wherever you may find them in your yard. At the same time that some are tending aphids, others may be busily engaged in projects that are decidedly beneficial and they should be left alone to do their job.

If you have trouble with stinging ants that are causing extreme human discomfort, you may feel driven to use some sort of poisonous bait at each nest. If you are thinking of using arsenic, a common ingredient in commercial ant baits, keep in mind that this very dangerous poison doesn't break down, but rather accumulates bit by bit and can be absorbed through your skin—when you are weeding, for instance! Sometimes flooding the nests can help discourage ants, since it can disrupt their colonies. We have heard of a case where fire ants were driven from a backyard by repeated hosing of their nests.

Aphids: These soft-bodied, sucking insects are a very important source of food for many helpful garden insects. A few should be allowed to stay around just to encourage the presence of beneficial insects that feed on them. If they are particularly heavy on certain sections of a plant (often the growing ends of the branches), these may be pruned off. Wear a pair of garden gloves and run your hand over a flower bud and squash the aphids. A stream of water may wash them off. It is important that you do not use any chemical spray that would kill off the ladybird beetles, lacewings, flower fly larvae, and other aphid-eating insects. In any case, chemical control of aphids is temporary and you would soon experience a resurgence of the pests.

For your own understanding of the aphid-control process, learn to recognize a "mummy." This is an aphid which has been stung by an aphid-killing wasp (see Figure 13-10); it appears swollen, is sometimes a metallic color, and is stuck tight to the plant. Within this stung aphid, more parasitic wasps are developing. The sight of these mummies here and there among the normal population is a sign that help has arrived, and should encourage you to hold off on the poisons, particularly when the proportion of mummies to aphids is high.

Frequently, aphids will be particularly heavy on vegetable plants that are old and going to seed. If these plants are allowed to remain standing and to die naturally, several generations of many species of various aphid-eating predators can be raised on them. These will then fly off and help control the aphid populations on other plants. Since garden books generally advise cleaning up and disposing of any weakened and pest-ridden plants, this idea of harboring "predatory-nursery plants" may be a new one to you. Of course, with many plant diseases, destroying infected specimens may be a very good practice, but with aphids it is another story. In any case, merely destroying every aphid colony may not be best.

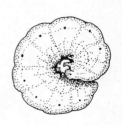

Cutworms: These night-feeding caterpillars are the young of a number of small brown and orange-brown marked moths. When disturbed, the larvae have a characteristic way of curling up and playing dead. Cutworms are chewing insects. You can deter them from cutting seedlings off at ground level by encircling the stem with a three-inch wide strip of paper shoved one

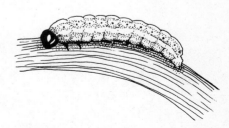

A cutworm in the curled position and crawling on a stem. Cutworm is a general term for a group of caterpillars.

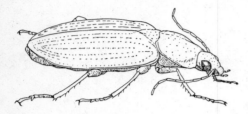

A ground beetle, family Carabidae. All ground beetles are predators. Many people mistake them for roaches and kill these beneficial species. Although there are small species a few millimeters long, many carabids are relatively large, some up to an inch long.

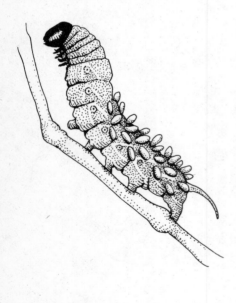

inch into the ground, about one-half inch away from the stem. Toilet paper rolls can be used for this.

Some cutworms climb up on the plants to feed. If you see damage on the margins of the leaves and suspect cutworms, try spotting them at night with a flashlight and picking them off by hand. This is a simple but very effective way of controlling them in the small garden.

In the daytime, cutworms frequently can be found burrowed in the soft dirt or mulch within a foot or so radius of the plant they were feeding on the night before. Scraping the surface mulch away gently with trowel or fingers will often reveal most of them. However, we have found cutworms a foot deep in the soil.

Baits are an old-time remedy for cutworms. A common recipe is a mixture of hardwood sawdust, wheat bran, and molasses moistened with water. To this may be added one of the botanical (or plant-derived) insecticides. A bait containing *Bacillus thuringiensis* is now available. However, going to such lengths should not be necessary if you are protecting the very young plants with collars, giving a weekly night check, and collecting cutworms by hand. Although the damage done by these insects is unsightly, a little leaf pruning by cutworms on a well-established plant will do no harm.

Among the natural enemies of cutworms are the large shiny black ground beetles. These stay pretty well hidden during the day, but can frequently be seen scurrying away when you lift up overturned flower pots, or similar traps, set among the plants to trap slugs and snails (see Box 13-4). Do not kill these valuable natural enemies and teach everyone you know to protect them.

Cabbage Loopers, Imported Cabbage Worms, and Tomato Hornworms: These and certain other caterpillars are susceptible to the disease caused by *Bacillus thuringiensis,* sold as a wettable powder under such trade names as Dipel, Thuricide, and Biotrol. The insect larvae must eat it to be affected, so the plants they are feeding on must be thoroughly covered. If hand-picking is not sufficient for managing a caterpillar invasion, you may wish to try this pathogen.

Since the disease affects only the young of moths and butterflies, it is a remarkably selective control and safe for other insects and animals in the garden, including you. Contact your local agricultural extension office or university entomology department to learn which pests it is effective against in your area and how you can obtain the *Bacillus* spores.

Earwigs: Don't be frightened by the useful earwig. There is a lot of folklore about earwigs, particularly in Europe, which may explain irrational dislike some people have for them. Possibly it is their looks—be assured they will not bite you with their "pinchers." Encouraged by the advertising of commercial products to poison them, which suggests that earwigs should be destroyed, people spend a great deal of energy trapping and killing them.

Earwigs prey on other insects as well as feeding upon plant material. They are frequently blamed for damage caused by others, so you should make an effort to catch them in the act of destroying something before concluding they are at fault. Even the damage they do commit must be weighed against their predatory benefit. As with cutworms (the culprits that are frequently doing the damage for which earwigs are blamed), the best way to observe the activities of earwigs is at night with a flashlight. You can trap them by putting out rolled-up newspapers for them to hide in on the ground in the areas where you see them active or suspect them. The following day, collect the papers and either burn them or shake them into a bowl of hot soapy water to drown. If you don't feel a need to kill them, they can be released at some distance.

We have observed that earwig damage to young seedlings is often a greater problem where the ground is bare around the plants as compared with heavily mulched gardens, even though the latter may support large earwig populations. One possible reason for this is that earwigs, being omnivores, have alternate sources of food in the mulch. In some areas, a parasite (the diptera *Bigonicheta setipennis* in the family Tachinidae) is present, and it may prefer the cooler moist environment that the mulches create. Whatever the reason, mulches alone may give adequate control in some cases.

Earwigs are interesting animals to observe. They appear to be midway between solitary and social insects. (Bees are examples of the latter.) A mother earwig will hover over her eggs to defend them if necessary, and will re-collect them into a pile if they are scattered. When they first hatch, the young will stay together for a while before dispersing and leading quite solitary lives.

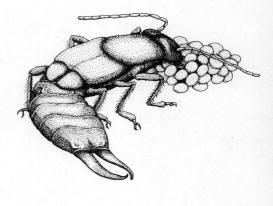

Gophers: Gophers such as ground squirrels and moles and other rodents can cause some real, sudden garden tragedies, and it is not surprising that they have become important pests, considering how relentlessly the predators that control them are hunted down and eliminated. Protect badgers, owls, hawks, snakes, and coyotes; they are all important in rodent control. Even the domestic cat can help.

For the suburbanite troubled with gophers in the flower or vegetable garden or a small home orchard, exclusion may be the solution. The following excerpt is from a very detailed booklet on the control of pocket gophers, ground squirrels, tree squirrels, mice, kangaroo rats, muskrats, rabbits, and moles, published by the California Agricultural Experiment Station Extension Service (see bibliography).

The gopher, Thomomys genus. Rodents in this genus are only found in western United States.

A fence of small-mesh wire sheet metal, or concrete extending about 24 inches below ground and about ten to twelve inches above will usually give protection. In lighter soils, greater depth may be desirable. If the fence is extended 36 inches above ground, it will also exclude rabbits.

Young trees can be protected against gophers by a cylinder of wire netting (one-inch or smaller) 12 inches in diameter and 18 inches tall that is stuck in the hold around the tree when planted; the top of the wire should be a little under the surface of the ground to avoid difficulty later in cultivating around the tree.

It is popularly believed that certain plants, particularly French marigolds and the Gopher plant, *Euphorbia lathyrus,* will repel gophers and moles. However, we do not know of any controlled experiments testing the effectiveness of these plants. "Euphorbias" have a bitter milky juice which might indeed discourage rodents. You may wish to find out for yourself if planting a border of such plants around a bed you want to protect will actually exclude gophers from the area within.

If exclusion is too difficult, then trapping is the only other safe way to control field rodents. According to the same booklet quoted above, trapping is probably as effective as any other method of control, in spite of the sophisticated poisons that have been developed for the same purpose.

The first step in trapping gophers is locating the gopher's main tunnel. Precise directions on how to do this, set the traps, and mark them are all detailed and well-illustrated in the publication mentioned above. What follows is a summary of that material.

The wire clutch snap trap is sold in most hardware stores, and is probably the best trap available for the cost. Two or more traps are needed. The traps must be set with special care. Wear gloves to prevent human smells from "contaminating" the devices. (Traps could be washed in soapy water or wiped with a rag soaked in shaving-lotion or cologne to remove any smells they may have accumulated before each use.) Dig into transverse or foraging tunnels. Start at a fresh mound or probe with a wire to find the tunnels, initially. Attach strong twine or rope to the trap and to a driven stake to prevent the rodent from pulling it deep into the tunnel. Traps should be placed in the tunnel facing in opposite directions. Use a board to cover the traps and be sure to exclude light. If the gophers see light, they will push soil toward the light and trip the trap without being caught. If no gopher is caught within three days, pull out and reset the trap in a new location. A stream of water from a garden hose is sometimes successful in flushing the gopher out of his tunnel. They then are easily killed with a shovel or stick. Do not pick them up, however, because they can bite.

Lawn Insects and Diseases: In general, we tend to discourage the planting of lawn around urban dwellings unless it serves a specific purpose other than status display. Fir bark, sand, or similar materials may be superior for children to play on, a wood or cement deck easier and less damp for sunbathing or entertaining, and a vegetable garden a more productive use of the space for the urban household. Also, for every geographic area, native plants that consume less energy and resources usually can be used to create an attractive and low-maintenance ornamental ground cover. (See page 426 for a discussion of lawns.) However, if you are devoted to keeping a lawn for one reason or other, at least consider ways to reduce pesticide use in its maintenance.

In recent years the manufacturers of lawn fertilizers haved used as a major selling point the addition to their wares of various pesticides, fungicides, and sometimes selective herbicides. These mixtures should be avoided. It is as important beneath the grass as it is everywhere else in the garden that a wealth of life inhabit the soil, and the use of any poisons is likely to cause more trouble than they are supposed to prevent or cure.

Before you panic and tear up a perfectly good lawn or spread pesticides around your property at the sight of insects on your lawn, remember the woman whose lawn was "black with worms" mentioned earlier, and be sure that the insects you see are actually causing some irreparable damage.

Brown spots, for instance, may be the result of dog urine rather than a fungus or insect pests.

When lawns suffer ailments of one sort or another, the amount and method of watering should be considered first. Lawns should be soaked deeply; the sprinkler should be on for at least an hour in one spot. Also, they should be watered infrequently. With respect to frequency, you will have to be guided by the type of soil that you have—sandy soils may require weekly watering while clay "adobes" may go comfortably for three weeks without attention. The aim of watering well but infrequently is to send the roots of the grass deep into the ground where hot sun or traffic cannot hurt them, while the surface remains relatively dry and inhospitable to many lawn pests. This hardiness cannot be developed if you stand around hand-sprinkling every other night or so. Also, experiment with mowing heights to see if your variety of lawn grasses is more resistant to insects and disease problems under different regimes. Remember that adequate fertilizing is important.

If attention to all these factors does not cure a highly visible and annoying problem, you may not have the best variety of grass for your area. Your local agricultural extension advisor may have a recommendation for you on the most hardy, pest-resistant grasses or other ground covers for your neighborhood.

Leafhoppers have piercing mouthparts like aphids, are active jumpers, and can usually fly considerable distances. Some species are frequently involved in transmitting viral plant diseases.

Leafhoppers: The leafhoppers compose a highly visible but somewhat overrated insect group. Most plants can be literally covered with leafhoppers and suffer no appreciable damage. These insects are typical of those the gardener may decide represent a problem just because they can be so noticeable. Yet they are just part of the natural fauna of the garden, and as with others we have discussed, experience a population build-up that may bring them to your attention and then a decline due to various environmental factors the details of which you may not be aware.

Some leafhoppers can carry virus diseases of certain plants. However, in the home garden with a variety of plants and consequently many insect predators, using insecticides against leafhoppers should not be necessary and may cause more problems than you started with.

If leafhoppers seem to be ganging up on new flower buds or other growing tips (on camellias, for instance), douse them with a water spray. The young (usually paler) leafhoppers do not fly, and if washed to the ground can be crushed there or picked up by predators.

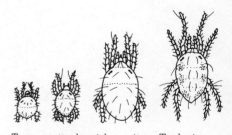

Two-spotted spider mites. Technically mites are not insects and are more closely related to ticks. Young mites have six legs but older stages like the adults have eight legs.

Mites: Mites are very tiny relatives of the spiders, so small, in fact, that they may be easily taken for specks of dust until they are observed to move. Common on the undersides of some vegetable leaves, such as beans, as well as on some ornamentals, they will often not make their appearance until a plant begins to lose its vigor.

Plant-feeding mites may become a problem in any circumstance where disruptions or exclusion diminishes the numbers of their many natural enemies. Common pesticides such as Sevin used against other pests may trigger mite outbreaks. Mites became a problem in commercial strawberry cultivation when increased mechanization encouraged growers to switch to plowing up all the plants at the end of each season and starting anew in the spring. Previously, they had grown each year's crop from the suckers produced by the last season's plants, much as many home gardeners do. With the older system, a large number of mite predators would build up in the fields and migrate to the young plantlets on the ends of the new year's suckers. These would survive there to control the pest mites when the older plants were selectively removed. Mite outbreaks have also been experienced along dirt roads and in forest areas that have been sprayed for mosquitoes.

Of course, the most artificial or disrupted environment of all is one indoors, and mites may become a serious problem in greenhouses and on house plants. Washing with soap and water is effective if the situation has not become too severe. Misting with a fine spray of light vegetable oil (for example safflower or sesame oil) is also successful in some instances. Test the oil on a few leaves first, as some plants may react adversely. But, as was pointed out in the section on home-made sprays (page 380), even such innocuous substances can have undesirable effects, since they are not selective and kill a broad spectrum of insects—including those such as a ladybird beetle which feeds on mites—that are the natural controls.

Buying and/or cultivating mite predators may be the solution for some mite problems. This technique is discussed in the section on greenhouse pests.

Sowbugs (Pillbugs): These little animals with eight legs are crustaceans, relatives of the crabs and lobsters. They feed on decaying organic material and turn it back into soil nutrients. You will find them in abundance, particularly if you mulch your plants. Some may curl up into a ball when disturbed. The chief importance of these creatures is their role in breaking down complex plant material so that its constituents are once again available to other plants as food.

Since they eat rotting material, sowbugs can become a problem whenever garden vegetables remain damp and their outer cells begin to decay. Thus, sowbugs may begin to eat into the undersides of pumpkins or other winter squashes where they sit upon the damp ground, or damage succulent bean seedlings and the like that are slow in unfolding and enlarging themselves during cool, moist weather, or that have been kept covered with a flower pot for too long after transplanting. In such cases the solution is to create drier conditions, often through superior aeration. Many squashes can be grown on fences or trellises, and the drying effect of the wind may be enough to reduce pest damage. Old leaves that are starting to fade may be removed by hand to improve air circulation. Maturing squashes sitting on the ground may be elevated slightly by placing one or two pebbles beaneath them. Bean seedlings can be started indoors and planted in their container so that the seedling itself is slightly above ground level.

There are specific chemical formulations for the control of these organisms. As in many other cases (chemicals to kill earthworms, for example) the fact that a product is available and promoted should not give gardeners the idea that one should regard this very beneficial animal as a pest.

Root Maggots: Imagine this scenario: Your vegetable members of the

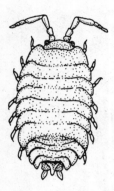

Sowbugs (or Pillbugs) are crustaceans, and thus are more closely related to crabs and crayfish than insects. When they curl up they look like a pill or miniature armadillo. They prefer to feed on decaying plant matter but are known to nibble more succulent plant parts and plant roots.

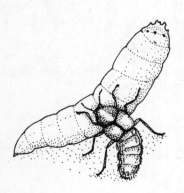

Here the root maggot larvae is shown being attacked by a rove bettle in the genus *Aleochara*. The cabbage-root fly, *Hylemia brassicae*, originated from Europe.

cabbage family are growing nicely; then suddenly, although there are no visible pests, they wilt and die. When you pull them up you find small, fat, white wormlike animals, maggots, tunneling into the root. You may experience a similar disaster with early onions.

The maggots are the larvae of flies that lay their eggs at the base of the plant stem on the ground. The eggs hatch and the larvae burrow into the root section of the plant. The maggots are preyed upon by beetles, and when persistent chemical poisons are used, these beetles may be wiped out. In their textbook, *Life in the Soil*, Jackson and Raw describe a classic example of the problems caused by the use of pesticides to control pests:

In field experiments it was observed that cabbages growing on plots previously treated with DDT, Aldrin, or BHC were damaged more by cabbage root maggot than those growing on plots that had never been treated with insecticides. It was also observed that carabid [ground,] and staphylinid [rove] beetles were less numerous on treated plots for several months after the insecticide was applied. . . . By decreasing the number of predatory beetles without controlling the pest, insecticide treatments resulted in more cabbage root fly damage.

The best method of beating the maggot problem is to raise seedlings in a coldframe or screened-in area until their root development is sufficient to enable them to stay ahead of any root-maggot damage. The same may be achieved by starting seedlings under cones constructed of screening (approximately ten inches high and in diameter) to keep the flies away until the plants have become well-established and too large for their individual screen protectors. These cones must be shoved into the earth at least an inch all around to prevent the flies from slipping under the screen to lay their eggs.

The time of the year may also influence the amount of trouble you may experience with root maggots. With the cabbage family (and the related radishes) a crop planted early enough may be unharmed but a second summer crop may suffer. With onions just the reverse may be the case. This may differ considerably from area to area, so you should experiment with planting dates when dealing with maggot problems.

Scales, Whiteflies, and Other Sucking Insects: Like aphids, scales, whiteflies, and other sucking insects are an important food for many garden inhabitants. If you avoid using pesticides you should have plenty of insect predators around to bring most epidemics under control within a few weeks of their appearance. Admittedly, waiting out a pest epidemic is difficult, and especially with these insects because they are so painfully noticeable and there is a general feeling, in this culture at least, that the very presence of insects is bad. This value judgment may be enhanced if one knows that these are insects that suck the juices from the plants. Another, and perhaps more environmentally sound perspective, suggests that these insects are an inevitable accompaniment of certain plants at certain times of the year.

Sometimes a light pruning of the affected areas is helpful. During the dormant period, a commercial oil spray is effective against scale. To kill mealybugs, paint them with a brush dipped in rubbing alcohol. (This is also a simple, effective way of dealing with these insects on house plants; also,

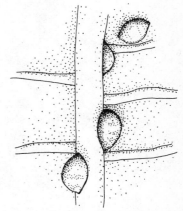

Scales are like aphids with shells formed as a protective layer over them. Adult scales, pictured here, are immobile, but the young can crawl about before settling down.

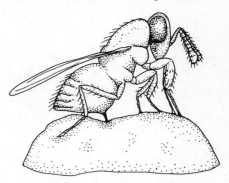

A fly laying "root-maggot" eggs

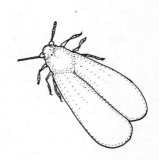

An adult whitefly. This is a harmless, gnat-sized creature sometimes found in large numbers. The whitefly looks like a tiny snowflake.

389

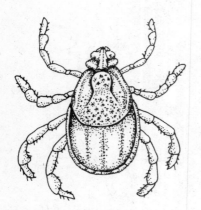

A male brown dog tick. A male of the brown dog tick can frequently inhabit homes. These organisms are not insects but are more closely related to mites and spiders. They are about a quarter of an inch long at most.

they can just be picked off with tweezers.)

If ants are swarming over the same area and seem to be keeping some of the predators and parasites away, use a deterrent such as Stickem or a pyrethrum and sorptive dust on the ants to keep them temporarily under control. The ladybird beetles, parasitic wasps, and lacewings are among the important controls for both scale insects and mealybugs. Whiteflies are discussed in greater detail in the section on greenhouse pests, pages 417–18.

Snails and Slugs: The brown garden snail, *Helix aspersa,* was introduced from Europe into several locations in California, for culinary purposes, sometime between 1850 and 1860. Subsequently, the snail has been discovered in many areas of North America. This omnivorous mollusk long has been considered a pest of home gardens in many areas, judging by the quantities of pesticides used against it and by the comments of gardeners. In one situation we know of the brown garden snail actually became a street hazard. Excessive snail populations have caused passing vehicles to skid, necessitating the expensive removal of streetside plantings where snails live. Recent studies indicate that a snail population subjected to regular baiting programs are less susceptible to pesticide treatments than populations rarely or sporadically treated.

Recently, a team from the biological control laboratory at the University of California at Riverside discovered that a predatory beetle, *Ocypus olens,* appears to be an effective limiting factor in some field locations. Currently, procedures are being designed to mass-produce these beetles. A predatory snail discovered in Southern California (but not necessarily native to that area) is also being studied for snail control.

An integrated pest-management program against snails is described in Box 13-4.

Ticks: Not strictly garden pests, although you may have trouble with them in a large suburban lot or home orchard, ticks are a common feature of the natural scene and you may encounter them frequently if you love the outdoor life. In some parts of the country they are numerous, and particularly because of the possibility that some ticks may be spreading human disease, chemical methods of control are sometimes applied against them.

The best solution is for people not to picnic on the ground or sleep out in areas where ticks are known to occur. If this is not possible, use repellents—diethyltoluamide and ethyl hexanediol are two common ones believed to be safe by the FDA.

When you are traveling in suspect areas there are a number of other precautions besides using repellents you may wish to observe. When hiking, stay on the trails, out of dense shrubbery and high grasses. Check out a proposed campsite for ticks by dragging a white flannel or other cloth over the grasses and other plants and then examine to see if ticks are present. Wear clothes made of denim, or other tightly woven fabrics, and tuck in loose ends—pants into the socks or boottops and the shirt under the belt.

When you return home or to your camp after a walk where ticks might occur, check yourself and your pets very carefully. Ticks frequently take a while before they settle down and embed themselves, and they are easily caught and destroyed during this period. If they have already attached themselves, remove them as soon as possible, treating them as you would a large sliver. Use an antiseptic and a pair of tweezers or some paper formed into tweezers to protect yourself from any disease should the body of the tick become crushed in the process. Alcohol or petroleum jelly applied directly sometimes induces the tick to detach itself slowly. Take your time removing the tick, since it is important that none of its head remain in the wound. This is best achieved by exerting a slow and steady pull. *Do not twist.* Twisting will separate the head and leave it in to infect the wound.

A relatively rare phenomena is a temporary paralysis in humans and animals caused by certain tick species. The tick must be removed promptly to avoid serious consequences. If you cannot extract it entirely, or if you are in an area where tick-borne diseases are common, seek out the advice of a doctor.

Ticks are often associated with certain types of plants. If such plants occur on or adjacent to your property, some vegetation management (not herbicides or pesticides!) may be called for. In such cases, it is a good idea to get the advice of your local and state health departments as well as the agricultural extension service office. Frequently, however, the solutions these offices advise will be nothing but the older, simplistic chemical spray methods, the very ones you wish to avoid. But by making clear that you are seeking other approaches, you may be able to get some information or at least stimulate some thought on alternate solutions. Fish and game departments often have information on wildlife-vegetation complexes that may be helpful in choosing plants to substitute for those in areas that are now tick-infested.

Contrary to some prominent advertising by pesticide manufacturers, with rare exceptions ticks and other parasites severely handicap only those animals that are weak or old. This is plainly seen in deer populations, for example. With animals (even humans) as with plants, one must evaluate the tick situation in terms of the total environment. Some plants and animals are weak because of age, genetic constitution, population pressures that cause the group to overexploit its environment, or other factors that make them unsuited for the particular area in which attempts have been made to cultivate them. A combination of physiological and social stresses may make any organism more susceptible to parasites such as ticks, and more seriously affected by those parasites it does pick up.

Tree Pests: Each tree supports a complex association of diverse life forms, and interfering with these natural communities by using insecticides can have undesirable effects felt at ground level as well as on the tree sprayed. Some chemical particles inevitably drift over adjoining vegetation so that flower and vegetable gardens in the area may experience considerable poison "fallout." One such experience could have the effect of destroying the careful nurturing of organic controls in your unsprayed garden.

Birds can be a great aid in controlling tree pests, and it is a good idea to make efforts to attract them as regular all-year visitors. Your local Audubon Society may be able to advise you on which birds would be most valuable and how to encourage them to stay around.

Washing with water or water and soap is useful for cleaning out aphid infestations; and ringing trees with sticky materials is useful for excluding ants. Pruning may also be a valuable tool for reducing pest habitat when sucker growth supports large aphid populations or tent caterpillars make silken nets that may be aesthetically disturbing.

With some caterpillar pests, you may wish to introduce the biotic agent *Bacillus thuringiensis* (see Box 13-2). If you use the services of a commercial pest control operator, you will need to specify this product.

Two of the authors (the Olkowskis) have developed integrated pest-management programs for tree pest insects in five communities in Central California (Palo Alto, Davis, San Jose, Modesto, and Berkeley) which have been instrumental in reducing pesticide use by 90 percent on city-owned streetside trees. These programs incorporate classical biological control or the introduction of pests' natural enemies as part of their strategies.

The first of the successful biological control importations within these city programs was against the linden tree aphid. This project is instructive in many ways since it typifies many of the urban insect pest problems that trigger pesticide use in these areas. What was involved was not actual damage to the trees, since the linden can comfortably support huge aphid populations, but rather the nuisance created by the sticky honeydew that the aphids excrete and which drops onto the tops of cars and onto sidewalks and driveways. The spots are further disfigured by a black mold that grows on the honeydew. A city with linden trees may receive an outcry from irate citizens demanding action in dealing with the "mess."

Since these lovely shade trees were originally imported from Europe, and their aphid pests were accidentally brought in also, we sought out parasitic wasps from France and Italy to control these aphids. Of course, it was necessary to get the city to stop spraying insecticides so as not to kill the introduced wasps or the native predators.

With each such introduction, even if it is successful, it still may take several years before the insect population drops down below the "aesthetic injury level," the point where there are so few aphids that they no longer create a nuisance. However, with the introduction of the linden aphid parasite, this aphid ceased to be a problem in the release areas by the next season (1972), and the populations have remained under control since that time with no further attention of any kind being needed. The City of Berkeley estimated a savings of $22,500 a year based on the cost of spraying these trees at 1971 prices.

Since that time, the same urban street tree research unit, under the authors' direction, has successfully controlled another aphid, and is very optimistic about the results of recent introductions of the natural enemies of the Elm Leaf Beetle (*Pyrrhalta luteola*), which is a major problem all across the country.

Clearly, classical biological control has a role to play in managing shade-tree pests, but as with all other suitable strategies, it must be integrated into an overall management program to achieve the best results.

Wasps: Most people are well aware of the importance of honey bees in the pollination of fruit, but few realize how very important wasps are in insect

A wasp. Contrary to popular opinion, wasps are all beneficial since they are predatory on other insects. Some species are scavengers as well and as a consequence are attracted to human garbage.

control. In spite of the possibility of being stung, every effort should be made to coexist peacefully with them. *Polistes* (commonly called "paper wasps") are slender elongated wasps that are major predators of many kind of harmful leaf-eating caterpillars. Yellow-jackets and hornets are all beneficial. Parasitic wasps—miniwasps—are important in control of all garden pests. See the section on aphids above. On picnics, take a chunk of meat (chicken, tuna, or liver are good) and set it off to the side. This will serve to attract wasps away from the picnic table. Wasps also like highly sugared liquids such as soft drinks.

If you are still worried about your reactions to wasp or hornet stings after taking these measures, consider having yourself immunized rather than dousing your entire area with insecticides. (Remember the story of the king who was so delighted with the feel of leather under his bare feet that he ordered the entire country paved with leather from border to border—whereupon a wise man suggested he tie a piece of leather under each of his feet to achieve the same effect!)

Immunization has proved very successful in helping allergic people. The Allergy Foundation of America has reported that "progression to more serious reactions was halted for over 97 percent of treated persons, and in most instances, responses were noticeably lessened or reduced to that of a normal person." You can contact this organization at 801 Second Avenue, New York, New York 10017, for literature and general information on desensitizing treatments for insect stings.

If you feel it is absolutely necessary to destroy a ground wasp nest, six or more ounces of kerosene or gasoline can be poured into the nest opening. Do not light it. A cloth should be dropped over it to hold the fumes in. Locate the nest in the daytime and mark its position, but destroy it late on a dark night after all the wasps have returned to the nest and the insects are quiet. Destroying a nest is really a two-person job. As soon as one person pours in the fluid, the other person should throw dirt over the opening with a shovel, and then both should leave the area speedily in case another entrance to the colony exists. Do not point a flashlight beam or stream of water from a hose at a nest, for the insects will swarm out and sting you severely. Obviously, destroying a wasp nest is rather dangerous and you may prefer to call in a professional. If you do, indicate that you wish unleaded gasoline to be used rather than a chemical insecticide, since the latter may persist in the area and cause other problems.

It should be emphasized, however, that quite aside from any direct danger to someone who may disturb a nest, killing wasps is a very serious step to take, as you may be destroying some of your major allies in insect control.

Weeds: As the word is generally used, "weeds" are extremely hardy, sometimes invasive plants that are growing where they are not wanted. Many of our serious weeds in the United States are plants that were introduced here either on purpose or accidentally. Removed from the natural biological controls of their homeland (such as the insects specialized to eat them at every stage in their growth), they have a competitive advantage here.

There are already some extremely successful cases of importing insect

If you are one of those people who are highly allergic to stings from wasps you can avoid them by taking some simple measures:
   1. Don't wear perfumed material, such as hair spray, suntan oils, or aftershave lotion.
   2. Wear white or very light clothing rather than bright colors.
   3. Walk around, rather than through, wild and other flower masses.
   4. Avoid areas where food and cooking odors are attracting wasps, such as outdoor barbecues and open refuse containers.

natural enemies of economically important weeds. The most famous is the control of klamath weed (*Hypericum perforatum*), a poisonous range plant in the West, by two imported species of beetle in the genus Chrysolina from the weed's native habitat in Australia. The more recent successes with controlling alligator weed (*Alternanthera phylloxeroides*), a pest plant of southern waterways, and an agricultural weed, puncture vine (*Tribulus terrestris*) by using the same classical biological-control methods have made people somewhat more aware of these techniques. Nevertheless, this work is as little-appreciated and as under-funded as similar biological-control work on insect pests, largely because of the American infatuation with the chemical cure, plus the huge profits made from selling pesticides.

Of course, these biological-control techniques are not available to the home gardener, who can only obtain such permanent control of noxious weeds through encouraging government and private applied research in this direction. But by knowing a bit about the nature of the weeds one is combating something *can* be done in the backyard. For example, some weeds propagate vegetatively, and the cultivator must be extremely careful not to break them up and replant the pieces in the process of turning the soil. Many other weeds require a dormant period, buried in the earth away from the light, warmth, and oxygen of the soil surface before they will germinate. (One of the ways in which our common vegetables were improved over their wild ancestors was to create varieties that will germinate immediately without

---

Box 13-7. **A Summary of Weed Management Practices**

Mulching

Covering the soil with some material to prevent seed germination due to exposure to light. Covering the soil with impervious layers of newspaper, plastic, or other nonpenetrable materials can reduce weed/seed germination and survival of seedlings. Use of a high-carbon substance, such as sawdust, can create an unfavorable carbon to nitrogen ratio that will reduce the viability of many plants, and is best for walkways.

Minimal Soil Disturbance

Since every time the soil is turned, weed seeds lying dormant beneath the surface are brought up and exposed to germinating conditions, less tilling may help to control certain weeds.

Competitive Exclusion

One of the best ways to exclude weeds from a particular area is to grow a plant or a series of plants there that thrives in that area and that can out-compete any weeds. A variant of this method is to prevent the situations from developing that foster weeds—for instance, disturbed soils or excessive stress or damage to already existing plant cover.

Handpicking

This is probably the most common practice, yet it is remarkable at times that this technique is not used more frequently. The major difficulty is the tenacity of some of the weeds and thus the need for certain types of tools, such as handweeders, and so on. Hoes are more effective in cultivating young seedlings. They should be kept sharpened and handled so that the blade slides forward toward the user, almost horizontally and a fraction of an inch under the soil surface, cutting off the seedlings at ground level.

Digging

Use of a digging fork to loosen the soil around the roots of certain weeds or turning the weeds under before they begin to seed is useful sometimes if the plant is killed in the process, or afterwards by lack of oxygen or moisture from being buried.

Mowing

By cutting some weeds off with a mower or cutting device before they flower, some species can be reduced in intensity of growth pattern or prevented from dispersing seeds. Controlled grazing by animals can achieve the same effect in pastureland.

Burning and Flooding

Both fire and water have been used successfully to control various weeds under agricultural conditions. While these techniques may be less applicable to urban areas, there are some situations where they might be usefully applied.

Biological Control

Use of plant-eating organisms to kill or suppress weeds is well established as a most powerful technology. However, this method is usually beyond the reach of most home-scale plant cultivators. For a review and introduction to this field see Huffaker and Messenger, *Theory and Practice of Biological Control*. For a review of weed control on a larger scale see the book *Weed Control* published by the National Academy of Sciences.

needing a dormant period.) Most can last many years, resting there, and will spring to life only when exposed. Thus, by turning the soil as little as possible, letting the soil animals incorporate the organic material into the earth and create good soil structure, and placing mulches on top of the surface to smother any weed seeds there, you can reduce the amount of weed-seed germination.

Once weeds have germinated, physical controls are most useful. Pull out unwanted plants by hand, chop them down with a hoe, or smother them out. Anything that will cut out the light—paper, a thick layer of compost, a cloth, old linoleum—will successfully smother large patches of weeds and those around and between desirable plants. If smothering is not effective, for example, with Bermuda grass and similar plants, dig the plants out, removing new patches by hand as soon as they are noticed. An information sheet on weed control prepared by Dr. Lloyd Andres, chairman of the USDA Biological Control of Weeds Laboratory, suggests that with a few other persistent perennial plants that resist smothering, such as wild morning glory, "properly timed controls . . . can quickly weaken the plant. In the first week of its growth, morning glory utilizes more food reserves than it manufactures. Vigilance, and the periodic removal of this new growth will eventually exhaust the root reserves." We tried this tactic and found it moderately successful against morning glory (also called field bind weed).

The information sheet continues, "Weed control chemicals have very limited application in the average home garden. Besides being dangerous to handle, they can destroy valuable garden plants along with the weeds. Of greater concern may be the fact that their effect upon soil organisms which your garden needs is unknown. . . ." Still, if all the mechanical methods of eradication have failed and you feel you must resort to an herbicide, choose one that is relatively low in mammalian toxicity and is nonpersistent. Oils are often effective. If commercial herbicides are employed, you must take great care to use them safely. What follows are two ways of using such chemicals with minimal contamination of the soil or other plants.

With trailing herbs, the growing tips can be placed in a small container containing the herbicide. When dealing with brush-type plants such as blackberry and poison oak, prune the branches almost down to the ground level (using gloves), then paint remaining stem tips with the herbicide. Be prepared to give repeated treatments to any new shoots as they appear. Be sure to store the herbicide, gloves and paintbrush away from seeds, fertilizers, and other general gardening materials.

If you are preparing a large new seed bed outdoors, wet the area thoroughly, allow the weeds to sprout, hoe the weed seedlings while they are still small, and then plant the seeds you desire, disturbing the soil as little as possible. Mulch between the seedlings as soon as they have their second pair of leaves, adding more material as they grow so the surrounding ground is heavily shaded, discouraging new weed growth.

Box 13-7 summarizes the various nonherbicide methods of managing weeds.

In the House

Intruder or Guest?: When we talk of pest problems inside the house, we are dealing with a different situation from the environmentally complex and healthy garden. In our opinion, anyone has the right to exclude other creatures from one's own living quarters if one finds them undesirable. The question is, To what lengths are you willing to go to keep your home devoid of other forms of life? For, in fact, we live in the midst of the rest of nature, and humans have had house companions since our days in the cave.

Unbidden House Guests, written and published by Hugo Hartnack, a scientist and professional pest exterminator, is a quaint book with an old-fashioned flavor that might lead you to believe it was originally written long before the actual publishing date of 1943. In the early sections of the book, along with some speculations on other animals from which people may have inherited their own pests, Hartnack includes a thought-provoking discussion of our attitudes towards pests which led us to the title of this section. He points out,

Live animals are invited to live in the house: dog, cat . . . bird . . . fish. Things of animal origin are welcomed by the thousands. . . Live and fresh plants are brought into the house, potted plants, cut flowers, fresh vegetables, baking yeasts. . . . In most cases, the plant or animal which shows up in the house without being invited, or stays there against our will, is looked upon with dismay. This feeling ranges from unawareness of any attitude toward the intruder, to hopelessness and terror . . . the bee is helpful, and mankind owes it much. Uninvited within the house, it intrudes. The white mouse kept by a boy in its cage is a pet. When it flees and roams the house, it is no longer welcome. . . . A mealworm bred or kept as fish food is welcome, between sacks of grain, an intruder. . . . No animal in itself is a pest. The way each of us feels about a visitor determines whether the animal is a pet or a pest; or in the old Latin words, hospes *or* hostis, *a guest or a foe.*

It is particularly ironic to realize how, in pursuit of the suburban dream house, we have literally gone out of our way to establish ourselves in countrylike settings that teem with the very insects and other animals to which we have such an aversion. While some of our insect pests seem quite dependent on man-created environments for their comfort and survival, in other cases we have moved into their homes and now are kicking them out!

What Price Are You Willing to Pay: Will you risk the health of your family and pets because insects are frightening or distasteful to you? Pesticide companies and their distributors thrive on your fears and lack of information about the toxicity of their products. Protect your home environment, and don't let persuasive advertising for such products tempt you to bring these poisons into your house.

The first principle of good pest control in the home is exclusion: use screens for flies, structural repair for rodent problems, and so on. If this isn't completely effective, use mechanical means: fly-swatters, traps, and so on. As a last resort, you might use a chemical, but in that case it is imperative to apply the smallest amount of the least hazardous material directly where and *only* when the problem is present. *Avoid cure-alls,* such as hanging pesticide strips; these "miracle" devices dispense a *continuous* cloud of pesticide vapor. Obviously, any continuously emitting device, or other method that sends the material at random into the air, such as aerosol dispensers, violate the above basic principles of good control.

A serious threat is posed by commercial pest-control operators who are eager to sign you up for a regular dosing of your entire premises. "The only good bug is a dead bug," is an example of their brand of overkill. If such companies were to sell regular check-ups, providing homeowners with education about how to correct situations as well as providing alternative control strategies themselves, using chemicals only as a last resort, they would find their business growing rapidly in an era of increased government restriction on pesticides and public concern over health effects from these toxic materials. Our feeling is that the private pest-control operator should stop relying on selling a product and start capitalizing on selling a service.

Where to Start: Let's talk about *preventive measures,* the most important of which is good housekeeping. Food and garbage (mainly sweets and grease) should be kept covered, out of reach of insects and rodents. Dark, damp storage areas filled with odds and ends encourage many pests that do not thrive in dry, well-ventilated places. Look for hitchhiking insects in the packages, bags, and bundles you bring home. Screen your doors and windows and plug up as many cracks and crevices in your walls and foundations as you can. In summary, exclude potential house pests and modify your home environment so they are no longer attracted to live and breed there.

Ants: If ants never start visiting your kitchen, you've won the battle before it begins. Do not leave food or dirty dishes around to attract them. In some places, one unwashed jelly spoon can bring an invasion overnight. Wipe up all food smears on counters, furniture, and the outsides of food containers.

A sudden ant invasion may be brought on by the first rains in the fall or by heavy garden irrigation close to the house. At the first sign of ants indoors, remove whatever food seems to be attracting them. Follow each line back to the point where they are entering the house and seal their entrance cracks with putty or petroleum jelly.

The botanical insecticide pyrethrum and the desiccant silica gel dusts are very effective against ants. In one commercial product (Silox), the narrow-mouth squeeze container allows you to blow a fine dust very neatly into narrow crevices. Avoid breathing this dust and confine its use to inaccessible areas, such as cracks between floor molding and wall and other places where it could not accidentally come in contact with food.

Be wary of ant baits such as stakes or little jars that contain arsenic; this is an accumulative poison, and children may be tempted to play with the containers. While arsenic is supposedly now on the EPA restricted list, until recently it was widely available, and undoubtedly stocks still in hand will be sold off over a long period of time. Mirex, another common ant bait, degrades to kepone, a potent nerve poison.

Bedbugs: According to a USDA leaflet on the subject, it has never been

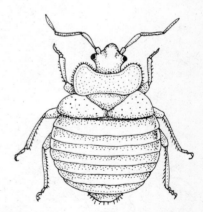

Bed bugs have piercing mouth parts, and usually hide near the bed in wall cracks or similar areas. They move to the host at night to take a blood meal. No human disease transmission has been proven despite many attempts. They are also called mahogany flats because of their reddish color and depressed body form.

397

proven that bedbugs cause any human disease. Their bites can cause an unpleasant itch, and if they are present in sufficient numbers, their characteristic smell may be noticeable.

Bedbugs do not necessarily live in the bed, unless it is an old wooden one likely to have many convenient cracks and hiding places, but they can be found throughout the room they are infesting, living in crevices of the floor, walls or furniture, behind baseboards, window and door casings, pictures, and picture moldings, and in loosened wallpaper, cracks in plaster, and partitions. Their presence can frequently be deduced by their excreta, which looks like dirt specks, along ledges and beneath cracks.

If what you desire is simply protection for a night or two in a hotel or rented room, placing a line of vaseline around the feet of the bedstead will prevent bedbugs from climbing up into the bed at night to feed. For permanent control it is necessary to thoroughly patch up all the cracks and crevices—a good coat of latex paint will do this—and to dust with pyrethrum in and around all of the areas where the bugs are established. A liquid spray can also be made of eight ounces of 0.2 percent pyrethrum mixed with one quart of water.

The pamphlet on bedbugs cited above is well illustrated and gives valuable details about the insects themselves. Unfortunately, like so many other interesting leaflets on pest control published by national and state agencies, the recommendations for chemical usage are way behind the times. For ex-

Figure 13-11. Cockroaches, the Common Indoor Pest

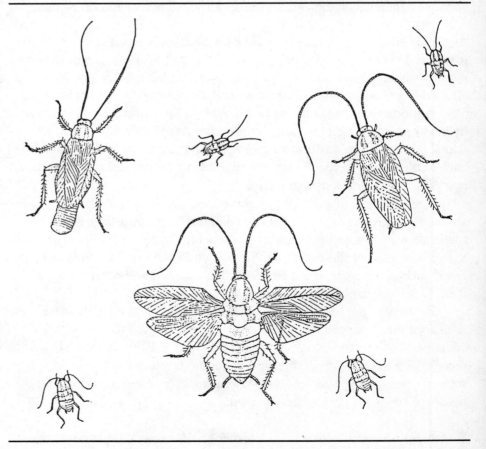

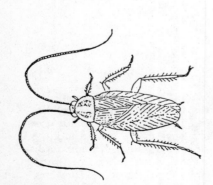

Most domicilary species of cockroach originated in Africa.

ample, the pamphlet suggests first the use of DDT and lindane, although a later paragraph does mention that pyrethrum is also effective against bedbugs. This leaves it up to the public to educate themselves on the difference between the highly toxic synthetic chemicals and a botanical with a very low mammalian toxicity. Ironically enough, another USDA pamphlet, *Controlling Household Pests*, admits that bedbugs may have become resistant to the more persistent chemicals, DDT and lindane, and that these substances are thus used against them less and less.

Cockroaches: The insect order Blattaria, (Figure 13-11) which is a very ancient group—probably as old as 340 million years. (In comparison, humans are probably not over a million years old.) About 3500 cockroach species are already named and about 4000 may still be discovered. Most of these species function as part of the decomposer community responsible for chewing up detritis to make it useful again. Only a small number have adapted to the human habitat, while others live in caves, mines, animal burrows, and ant and termite nests.

Four species of cockroaches are commonly found infesting human habitations and other structures: the German (*Blattela germanica*), the American (*Periplaneta americana*), the Oriental (*Blatta orientalis*), and the brown-banded (*Supella longipalpa*). As adults, these species are winged, but seldom fly, range in size from 0.5 to 1.5 inches (1.25–3.75 cm) in length, and vary in color from reddish or yellowish-brown to black, each with its distinguishing markings. Most prefer dark, moist places near food and water, and run rapidly when exposed to light. Table 13-2 summarizes the basic biological characteristics of these species.

Cockroaches are considered obnoxious, or nuisances, and have been suspected of carrying many types of human pathogens, but the outcome of

Source: Compiled from Cornwell, *The Cockroach, Volume I: A Laboratory Insect and Household Pest.*

Table 13-2. **Basic Biological Characteristics of Cockroaches**

Characteristics	German Roach *Blatella germanica*	Brown-Banded Roach *Supella longipalpa*	Oriental Roach *Blatta orientalis*	American Roach *Periplaneta americana*
Number of eggs/egg case	37	16 (12 hatched)	Up to 18	14
Number of egg cases/female	4–8 (7 average)	5–18 (11 average)	5 to 10	6 to 28 (12 average)
Total eggs per female	259	176	270 maximum	163 average
Incubation period of egg cases	17 days	74 days at 77°F 37 days at 86°F	44 days	59 days at 77°F 35 days at 86°F
Adult life-span	128 days, males 153 days, females	115 days, males @86°F 90 days, females	60 to 270 days	102 to 588 days (450 days average)
Period from hatching to adult	40 days at 86°F	164 days at 77°F 92 days at 84°C	533 days at 77°F 316 days at 86°F	210 days at 86°F
Preferred temperature range	86°F	80°F	68°F–84°F	Upper limit 92°F
Preferred indoor habitat	Warm, moist area; in larders, restaurants, ships, occasionally outdoors under rubbish, in dumps, goldmines and caves	High locations in heated rooms; desk and bureau drawers, behind pictures, on bookshelves, behind wallpaper, bedding, cupboards, bedrooms	Basements and cellars, service ducts, crawl spaces ovens, hot-water pipes, behind baths and sinks	Warm, moist areas, common outdoors in warm areas, out-buildings, woodpiles; occur in bakeries, latrines, sewers, restaurants

numerous studies still leaves the issue unresolved. Nevertheless, the roaches' lifestyle where they regularly contact and feed on a variety of waste materials render them potential health hazards. Numerous government pamphlets still recommend highly toxic chemicals for control of these pests. Millions of apartment, home, and office building managers and owners in big cities across the country continue to contract for repeated spraying of their premises. Yet the evidence before their very noses is plain enough—all these pesticides fail to make more than a very temporary dent in the roach populations, which must shortly be treated all over again. In the meanwhile people are exposed to toxic materials very close at hand.

As with the management of any other insect, an approach that relies exclusively on insecticides is bound to fail. An integrated pest-management approach must be taken that includes habitat modification as its number one strategy. Clean all infested rooms thoroughly, store food in glass or metal containers (roaches can eat through paper boxes), stop sources of water leakage, dry up spilled liquids thoroughly, and fill or repair cracks and holes in woodwork, around pipes, edges of sinks, and so on.

If you are serious about reducing cockroaches in your apartment, buy a can of putty and one of latex paint and go over your entire kitchen patiently and thoroughly as a first essential step. Every crack or crevice you close up will reduce the overall carrying capacity of that environment as far as cockroaches are concerned. It is actually possible to reduce their numbers to a tolerable level in your own apartment in this way, even though none of your neighbors do the same. Building them out and cleanliness cannot be overstressed.

Detailed studies by Dr. Walter Ebeling at the University of California (see the bibliography at the end of the book) show that roaches learn to avoid insecticides and bait-insecticide mixtures. This avoidance reaction is apparently due to the roaches' ability to sense the poisons. Although the roaches are killed by various insecticides, the local infestation is not eliminated unless the treatment is extremely thorough. It is questionable, however, whether you want to subject your family and immediate environment to the pesticides commonly used for roach control at the levels necessary to wipe out an infestation. Furthermore, if you have not modified the environment by eliminating the little dark cracks and crevices so dear to these creatures, sooner or later a new population will move in from neighboring apartments.

Boric acid is a relatively low-hazard substance that you might consider using if sanitation alone has failed to solve the problem. Boric acid kills cockroaches when they walk into it and then clean it off their bodies. Apparently, they do not learn to avoid it because it has no smell when used by itself. Although it is almost nonvolatile and not absorbed by the skin, if enough is eaten, it can kill people or pets. Therefore, confine powder to cracks and the dark, narrow, inaccessible areas that roaches use as hiding places. Do not put down heavy trails of powder, or more than half a teaspoon in any one place. Boric acid can also be dissolved in water and used to mop the floor. Use two cups of boric acid to two gallons of warm water and one-half cup of detergent. For very heavily infested areas, both the mopping and dust methods may be necessary together. Don't expect immediate re-

The flour bettle, *Tribolium confusum.* Besides being a pantry pest it is widely used as a laboratory animal.

sults. Boric acid will be slow to act and you may need to repeat the treatment, but in the long run it is very effective, as it kills the young after they emerge from the egg cases.

Remember, boric acid can be poisonous if eaten in sufficient amounts. Avoid treating areas frequented by children and pets. Keep boric acid dry, in airtight containers. Label all containers clearly and store them on a high shelf or in a locked cabinet with all other potentially dangerous cleaning products that must be kept from toddlers. If the boric acid becomes lumpy, force it through a screen before using.

With severe roach infestations, you may decide to seek professional help. Get estimates from several pest-control operators and question them carefully about what they propose to do. Avoid those operators who rely solely on chemicals for roach control without stressing sanitation and removal of hiding places, and who are not familiar with the use of boric acid for this purpose. You may wish to refer them to the paper by Dr. Ebeling, which describes at some length the use of boric acid for cockroach control.

Other Pantry Pests: Other common pantry pests, such as the beetles and little moths that feed on grain products and dried fruits, may enter your household with the product they feed upon. Of course, if they are present

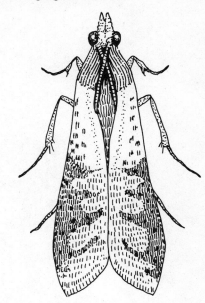

The Indian meal moth will crawl down the insides of screw-top jars to get at the contents.

Box 13-8. **Using Heat and Cold to Kill Stored Product Pests**

Both low and high temperatures can control food pests. Insect activity ceases at temperatures of 40° to 50°F. Prolonged exposure to a temperature of 40°F [4.4°C] will kill most food insects and even the most resistant are killed within three weeks if placed in a deep freeze. An exposure of two to three days will kill the more susceptible species which make up the greatest number that attack stored products. Food materials stored at this temperature will remain free of infestation.

To kill all stages of insect life in stored products, expose to temperatures of 120° to 130°C [248°F to 266°F] for two hours. However, the insect itself must be subjected to the heat for the required time. Be sure to reach and maintain the proper temperature at the center of the material being treated. To insure rapid heat penetration, spread the material in as thin a layer as possible and stir it from time to time. (Heat may be injurious to protein quality, so this method should be reserved for luxury items that are used for reasons other than the nutrition they offer—pine nuts would be an example.)

You can sterilize (disinfect) small quantities in an oven, but be careful not to scorch the product. In many cases you can obtain the desired temperature by merely turning up the pilot light in a gas oven. A longer exposure may be necessary for sufficient heat penetration.

If you use the oven, keep the temperature as low as possible; the usual resulting temperature of 180°F [82°C] will cause a rapid kill. You may open the oven door slightly to keep the temperature from rising too high. Use a thermometer to check the temperature increase.

To kill insects infesting dried fruits, drop the fruit in boiling water for about one minute. Spread the fruit to dry before storing.

The following suggestions, from the same booklet, offer a useful method of storing walnuts or other nuts in quantity in households where nut-infesting moths are a problem.

Preservation with dry ice: Carbon dioxide can be used to treat and preserve walnut and other nutmeats. You can obain it as dry ice (solid carbon dioxide). See classified section in telephone book.

Put a single layer of kernels in the bottom of the jars. . . . [Put some chips of dry ice on] the layer of kernels a short distance from the side of the jar where it can be seen after the jar is full. (Jars may crack if the dry ice is against the glass.) Use about one-half cubic inch of dry ice for pint jars, one cubic inch for one-quart jars, and two cubic inches for two-quart jars.

Fill with kernels, shake down—fill as full as possible. A quart jar will hold 12 to 14 ounces.

Put on the lids and screw them down until they begin to tighten. Then turn them back until slightly loose. Lids must be loose to allow the air and excess gas to escape and to prevent explosion of the jars.

Allow jars to stand undisturbed until all dry ice is gone.

Screw lids down tightly.

Store in as cool a place as possible.

CAUTION: Do not handle dry ice with bare hands—it will freeze the skin quickly. (Wear gloves)

Do not seal the jars until all dry ice has disappeared.

Source: This material is reprinted from University of California Agricultural Extension Service, *Common Pantry Pests and Their Controls.*

only in the egg stage, you will not be aware of them until they hatch at a later date and the larvae become visible.

Check incoming packages of dry cereals, flour, rice, and so on for adult pests. Whole-grain cereal products are more attractive to insects than refined ones. Just as in cockroach control, store all dry staples in tightly covered metal, glass, or plastic containers. If an infestation is discovered, check all dry goods, including dog food, bird seed, and spices. Dispose of contaminated products. Vacuum all shelves and cupboards with the crevice attachment. As with fleas, it is extremely important that vacuum sweepings be emptied as soon as possible outside the house, so that the insects do not escape, and so that reinfestation does not take place. Wash shelves and containers thoroughly before restocking. Insects may be killed by both heat and cold. Some practical suggestions on how to employ temperature as well as low-oxygen environments to manage pantry pests is given in Box 13-8.

Fleas: Fleas are common house inhabitants, particularly if you choose to have pets. Although cats and dogs each have their own flea species, the cat flea, *Ctenocephalides felis,* moves over to the dog very readily. Thus, much of the dog's scratching will frequently be due to the cat flea. This flea also feeds on humans. There is no simple, safe way to eliminate fleas from pets, and even if you could, scratching by animals is a normal behavior. Eradication as a strategy is an obsolete approach to these problems. Instead, temporary

Figure 13-12. **The Life Cycle of a Cat Flea**

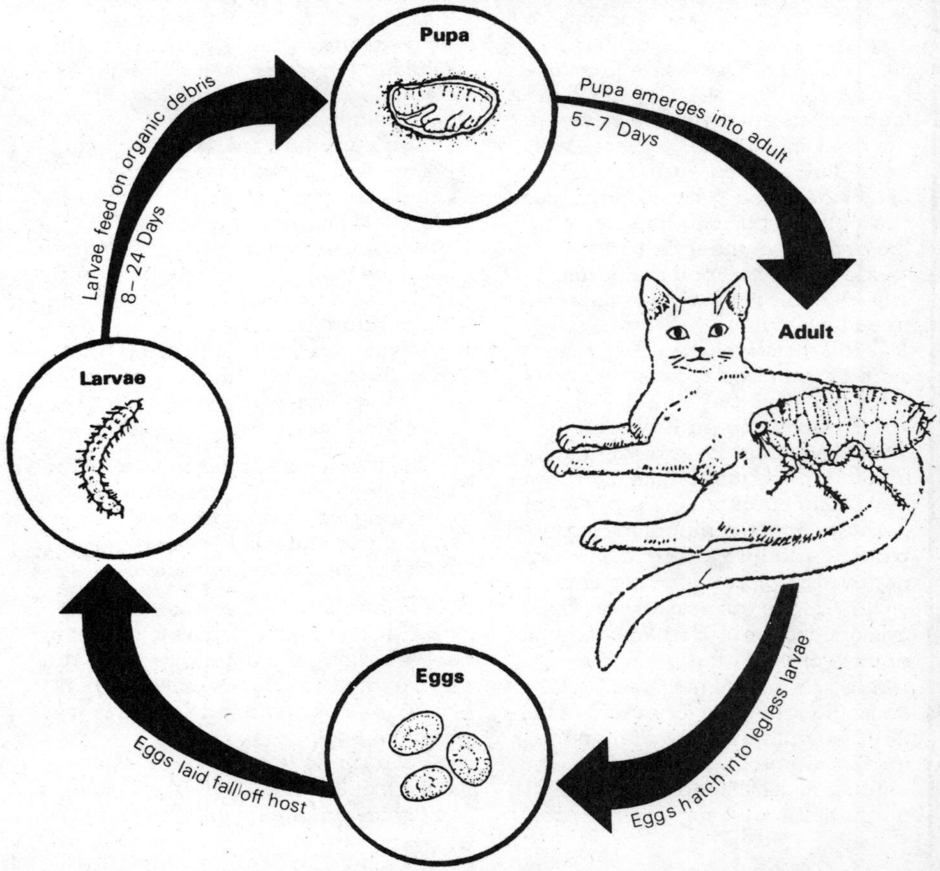

Pupa

Larvae feed on organic debris
8–24 Days

Pupa emerges into adult
5–7 Days

Adult

Larvae

Eggs

Eggs laid fall/off host

Eggs hatch into legless larvae

suppression when serious problems develop is the recommended method.

Fleas generally fall into two general classes—those that prefer to live on the animal and those that live in their nest, and each flea species differs in this regard. The adult cat flea rides its host, sucks its blood, and lays eggs that fall off the cat into the surrounding environment. The adult flea also sucks more blood from the host animal than she needs. This is excreted by the flea and dries, making the little black specks common throughout the fur of the cat or dog, and particularly visible in the white undercoat. These blood specks fall off the animal eventually, landing in the same areas where the flea eggs have been deposited. The eggs hatch and the young flea larvae, which look like tiny white worms, feed on this dried blood as a source of protein.

In order to prevent and/or reduce flea infestations and eradicate the dried blood and other food sources for the developing young, the eggs and

---

Figure 13-13. **How Organophosphorus Insecticides Affect the Nervous System**

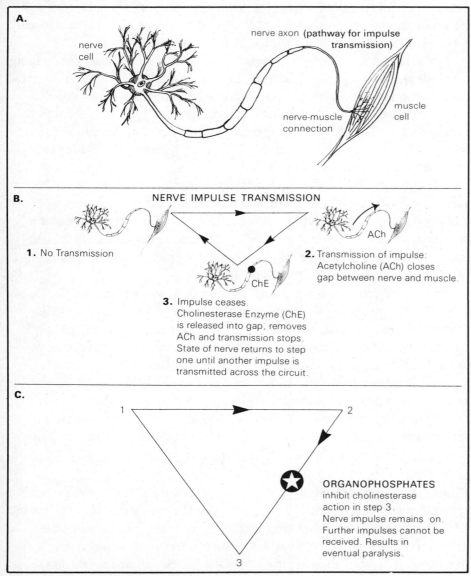

A.

nerve cell

nerve axon (pathway for impulse transmission)

nerve-muscle connection

muscle cell

B. NERVE IMPULSE TRANSMISSION

1. No Transmission

2. Transmission of impulse: Acetylcholine (ACh) closes gap between nerve and muscle.

ACh

ChE

3. Impulse ceases. Cholinesterase Enzyme (ChE) is released into gap, removes ACh and transmission stops. State of nerve returns to step one until another impulse is transmitted across the circuit.

C.

1

2

3

ORGANOPHOSPHATES inhibit cholinesterase action in step 3. Nerve impulse remains on. Further impulses cannot be received. Results in eventual paralysis.

Organophosphorus poisoning in insects or man is due to cholinesterase inhibition. Figure A shows nerve-muscle connection. Figure B shows normal, nerve impulse, transmission and figure C shows the action of a cholinesterase-inhibiting organophosphorus insecticide on nerve impulse transmission.

Source: Flint and van den Bosch. *A Source Book on Integrated Pest Management.*

An eighteenth-century flea trap to be worn around the neck. Fleas entered the outer perforations (bottom left) and were caught on a sticky tube inside (top left). No record of the effectiveness of this trap remains. However, we do know that fleas were a constant harassment to people of all classes during this period in Europe.

Source: After Lehane, *The Complete Flea.*

other life stages (see Figure 13-12) need to be removed and destroyed. Cleaning, daily if necessary, and vacuuming and washing thoroughly to remove debris from cracks, rugs, and pet bedding is essential. Soap and water work well. Upholstery and rugs that cannot be laundered can be shampooed in place, or vacuumed or steamed. After vacuuming, it is important to empty the vacuum cleaner and any other sweepings outside the house. Place the debris in a tightly closed bag, and burn it in the fireplace or put it in the middle of a hot compost or in the garbage can. Otherwise, you may simply be spreading the infestation from one place to another, within and outside the house. Vacuumed fleas clearly should not be placed where they can hop back onto the pets, which would then redistribute them. The animals themselves can be washed, at home or by a grooming parlor if the job is too much to handle at home. Obviously, if an all-out campaign against fleas is planned, the animals should be washed at the same time a thorough house-cleaning takes place.

A flea trap of questionable effectiveness is shown in the margin, and indicates the extent of some of the flea population during previous periods in history. A shallow pan of water placed where adult fleas are numerous will trap fleas, but obviously without additional efforts to clean the area affected such methods will not be enough to effectively reduce populations.

The use of flea collars is definitely not recommended. Like the hanging pesticide strips, these collars are impregnated with DDVP (dichlorvos) and emit a continuous poisonous vapor that affects both pets and people. The active ingredient in these products is a cholinesterase inhibitor, the significance of which is explained in Figure 13-13. However, if you are already using such a device, remove it from your pet and discard it and adopt a maintenance program as outlined above.

If your pet should suffer an intolerable flea outbreak that cannot be solved by cleaning both the house and the animal, and you feel you must use a flea collar (how did the animal survive for millions of years without this poisonous device?), then put it on for a minimum period (a day or so). As soon as possible, remove the collar, put it in a tightly capped jar, and store it in a cold area until you feel you must use it again.

We are frequently asked about herbal repellants against fleas (for example, eucalyptus nuts). There is so far no data that we know of showing any of them to be effective. What confuses the picture for the lay person is that flea populations rise and fall with the seasons, and no matter what you do or don't do when infestations are bad, the numbers will drop away later anyway. Furthermore, susceptibility to fleas varies from person to person, and with each person from time to time.

If fleas are really annoying you, and cleaning up the animals and the area won't solve the problem, there is only one safe solution: stop keeping pets in the house or don't keep them at all.

Flies: The housefly and the greenbottle fly (Figure 13-14) are the most common flies in urban areas. These species and a number of related ones are attracted to garbage, manure, and other decomposing material. The flies gain entry to homes through opened doors and windows, and through cracks in screens. They can also ride in on someone as they come into the house.

Figure 13-14. **The Housefly and Greenbottle Fly**

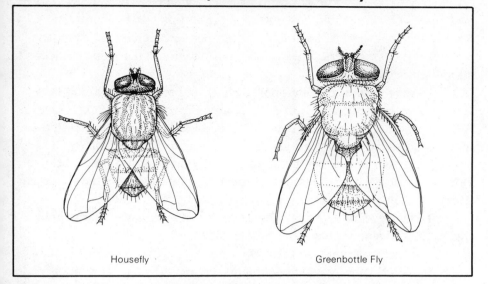

Housefly   Greenbottle Fly

The housefly, Musca domestica, readily invades homes, probably by tracking aromas from the kitchen.

The greenbottle fly, Phaenica sericata, develops in kitchen garbage after it is placed in the garbage can. Commonly seen feeding on dog manure, this species readily enters homes.

Old-fashioned beaded curtains are fairly effective in brushing flies off of a person or animal as they come through a passageway.

Although many people use aerosol "bug bombs" to kill flies, a fly swatter will usually do just as well and is much safer. The propellants in aerosol cans, like the Freon compounds, are suspected of being destructive to the ozone layer of the earth's atmosphere and have been removed from commerce for this reason. The ozone layer helps screen out ultraviolet rays from the sun, and damage to it could greatly alter life patterns on this planet.

Tight window screens and springs on screen doors are important in keeping flies out of the house also. Outdoor traps can help to reduce the local population and/or draw them away from specific outdoor eating areas, house entrances, and so on.

However, an excessive number of flies around the house indicates that the areas where they are developing must be found and the decomposing material treated so it will not continue to produce them. Composting kitchen wastes as well as other organic refuse is one way to prevent such potential fly sources from actually becoming a nuisance (see pages 118–139). A careful inspection of the outdoor areas, particularly where improper composting is taking place or where chickens or rabbits are being raised, will frequently show some of the key fly-breeding sources. Each source then will need to be analyzed to prevent fly development.

Ultimately, however, the major fly source in urban areas is the garbage can. In hot weather here in California a single can will produce a thousand flies per week (documented by the State Public Health Department). Unless municipal organic-waste practices are changed, large fly populations will continue to be major problems in urban areas.

Mosquitoes: Although proximity to lakes, rivers, streams, and marshes will inevitably bring a certain number of mosquitoes into the home, the buzzing, assiduous pest that ruins your night's sleep is probably there due to poor water management on your own property. If there isn't a water-filled ditch, can, tire, gutter, ornamental pond, tree hole, or the like on your prem-

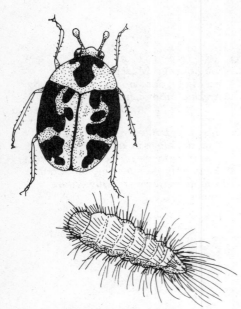

Adult carpet beetle and larvae, family Dermestidae. Archeologists frequently keep a culture of Dermestidae to clean bones that are studied for clues about early societies and prehistoric environments. These beetles also attack dead insects, so the entomological collector needs to prevent such damage.

Pet foods are frequently life-supporting factors for rats and mice. Here the house mouse, *Mus musculus*, is pictured by the kitty bowl to illustrate that the presence of a cat does not necessarily mean no mice. Cats need to be trained by their mice-killing mothers if they are to be effective mousers.

ises filled with the developing young (wigglers), then such a breeding place is probably to be found nearby on your neighbor's property. Efforts to solve mosquito problems should be directed at preventing water accumulations by removing containers that could hold water, regularly removing leaves and other debris from gutters, and stocking ponds with fish that will eat the mosquitoes as they develop.

The next level of prevention is to check and repair your window screens. Even small, one-eighth-inch holes will permit mosquito passage. Also repair other holes in the outside "skin" of the house. If you learn to spot mosquitoes flying toward you, it is possible to capture them by hand or by clapping your hands together. Because mosquitoes rest on wall surfaces indoors, particularly after taking a blood meal, you can sometimes kill them there, since they are usually more sluggish when full of blood.

The last level of defense involves the use of repellents. Diethyl toluamide, the active ingredient in the brand called Off, is an effective, safe compound that is very useful at night, to protect exposed portions of the body. Aerosol bombs, especially outdoors, are not effective, and indoors add toxic materials to your living space, besides increasing propellent levels in the environment.

Moths and Carpet Beetles: Moth larvae do not feed very avidly on clean wool. It is the spot of gravy on the coat or dress that they attack first. Therefore, if you wash or dry clean woolens before storage, your moth problems should be minimal. If you must use a moth deterrent, naphthalene is safer than paradichlorobenzene (PDB). Do not use any product containing a persistent pesticide that can be absorbed through the skin. Be wary of commercial cleaners' "moth-proofing" services.

Cedar chests are only sufficiently protective when they are new and are still giving off a strong smell, and even then the vapor is only effective against young larvae. As it ages, the advantage of a chest is related to how tightly it can be sealed. All closets or containers for woolen storage should be as airtight as practical. If naphthalene is used, it should be placed as high up in the container as possible, since the vapors tend to move downward.

The USDA bulletin on controlling household pests has this to say about moths and carpet beetles:

To control these pests, you must practice good housekeeping. . . . Give close attention to rugs and carpets, drapes and upholstered furniture, closets, especially those in which woolens and furs are kept, radiators and the surfaces behind them, corners, cracks, baseboards, moldings and other hard-to-reach surfaces. The vacuum cleaner is your best tool for most of this cleaning. After using it, dispose of the bag contents promptly; they may include eggs, larvae or adult insects.

In addition to cleaning rugs and carpets frequently, it is advisable to rotate them occasionally. Rotation is important because insects usually feed under heavy pieces of furniture where cleaning is difficult, rather than in the open, where regular cleaning, light, and movement of people keep down infestations.

An old but effective method of ridding woolen articles of insects and their eggs and larvae is to brush and sun the articles. Brush thoroughly, especially in seams, folds and pockets. If they cannot find protection from the light, any larvae missed in brushing will fall to the ground from clothing left hanging in the sun.

Rats and Mice: Sanitation and exclusion are the answers to rodent pests. Successful rat control can be achieved only by diligently following the practices of proper garbage disposal and food storage, eliminating places that rats like to live in, and constructing rat-proof enclosures for people and animals.

Rats will make their homes in piles of lumber or stones, in garbage dumps, in marshy areas, and along stream banks as well as in indoor heaps

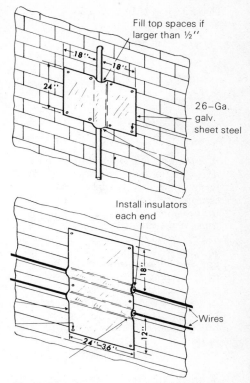

Fill top spaces if larger than ½"

18" 18"

24"

26–Ga. galv. sheet steel

Install insulators each end

18"

12"

24"–36"

Wires

These flat guards for small pipes and wires stop rodent access by creating a barrier rats cannot cross.

The sewer is one of the basic means rats use to distribute themselves in urban areas. Rats can move up the inside of sewer pipes to enter homes from the toilet.

Source: Scott and Borom, *Rodent-Borne Disease Control through Rodent Stoppage.*

Figure 13-15. **Sewer Access by Rats**

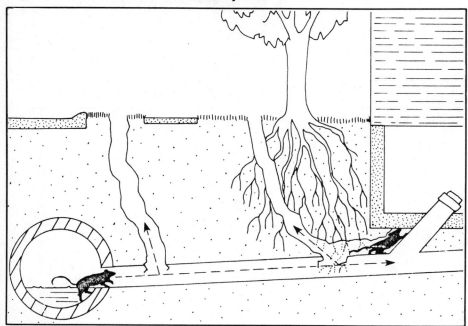

Figure 13-16. **Sealing Around Pipes**

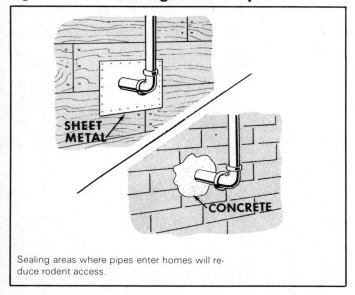

SHEET METAL

CONCRETE

Sealing areas where pipes enter homes will reduce rodent access.

Figure 13-17. **Constructing Concrete Sills**

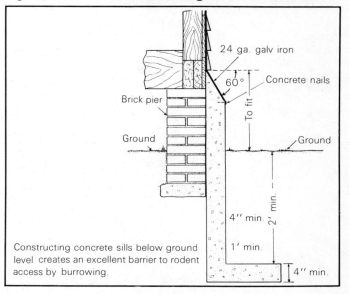

24 ga. galv iron

60°

Concrete nails

Brick pier

To fit

Ground

Ground

4" min.

2' min.

1' min.

4" min.

Constructing concrete sills below ground level creates an excellent barrier to rodent access by burrowing.

Figure 13-18. **Rat Excluders in Double Walls**

A common type of building construction with open space between floor joists (a), giving rats free access to double walls; wooden 2-by-4 stops (b) are sometimes employed, but as these have an important function in fire control, noncombustible material should be used; in old buildings galvanized sheet metal (c) may be cut to fit and nailed into place between studs, joists, floor, and sill; in buildings under construction noncombustible stops of cement and cinders (d) or broken bricks (e) are inadvisable, but preferably a good grade of rich cement (f) is recommended.

Source: Scott and Borom, *Rodent-Borne Disease Control through Rodent Stoppage.*

Figure 13-19. **History of Norway Rats in Baltimore**

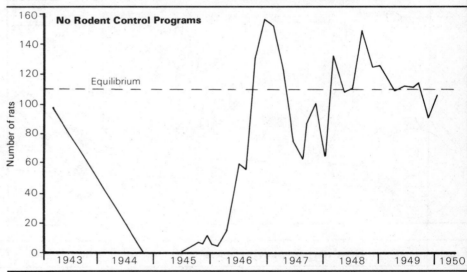

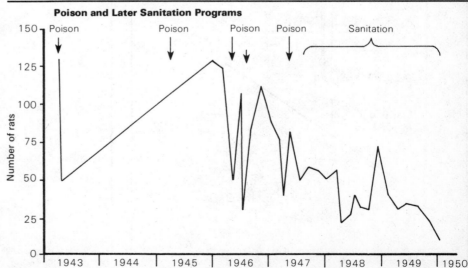

The top graph shows the normal changes in populations of city rodents not subject to control. The bottom graph illustrates the rebound effect of poison campaigns and the more substantial lowering of rodent populations as a result of habitat modification or "sanitation."

Source: Brown, *Biological Factors in Domestic Rodent Control.*

of rubbish in basements or attics. House mice make their indoor nests of miscellaneous shredded fiber material, contaminating and destroying household goods as they do so.

If you suspect that you already have one or the other of these rodents around, trapping is the temporary method to use for getting rid of them until you have sealed off their entrance to the house. Poisoning is undesirable because of the stench the dead rodent may leave if he dies in some inaccessible part of the property, not to mention the possible danger to children and pets. Baits for the traps can be any type of human food; what the rodents have shown preference for in your own pantry may be a clue. Rolled oats and other cereals, corn meal, bread crumbs, fried bacon, peanut butter, nut meats, apples, and raisins are all possible baits. The food can be tied to the trigger or scattered around and over it. Be aware, however, that trapping ultimately will have little permanent effect upon rodents. In fact, studies have shown that, just as with cockroaches, a given area will be able to support a certain number of rodents according to the amount of favored habitat and food it provides (see Figure 13-18). When rodents are trapped, those remaining in the area increase their reproductive rates to replace those lost, having more frequent and larger litters until their previous population size is attained once more.

As with other house pests, the only permanent answer is to build them out of your home. For detailed information on how to do this, see *Rodent-Borne Disease Control through Rodent Stoppage*.

Spiders: Fear of spiders is as widespread as it is unfounded. If you see a spider running towards you, don't panic—he is not about to attack. In all probability he can't even see you. Most spiders have very poor eyesight. While some kinds that run and catch prey—jumping spiders, for instance—can see for almost a foot, most are so nearsighted they cannot see objects beyond three inches away. They have to wait for their prey to come to them, blundering into and entangling itself in the silken web the spiders spin for this purpose.

Spiders are carnivorous, feeding mainly on insects. Because of their importance in insect control, they should never be harmed if possible. (Luckily, they are difficult to kill with home pesticide products. We heard of a person who once called the Berkeley Health Department to report hysterically, "I emptied the entire 'bug bomb' on him and he's still moving!")

Tidy housewives who deplore the sight of dusty spider webs should realize that when the web becomes noticeable because it is catching dust, it is probably no longer in use. When removing clean spider webs, do so carefully, so that the little occupant is not harmed and will live to control your insect pests another day. If you cannot bear to have a spider in the house, catch it in a jar (they cannot crawl up easily on glass) and liberate it outside.

Even the two poisonous spiders found in the United States, the black widow and the brown recluse spider, are very shy, and will retreat rather than harm you if they can manage to get away. Black widows may occasionally be found inside the house, although they are more common outside in piles of litter or around the house foundations and in outhouses. The female, the only one that might bite humans, is nocturnal, timid, and sedentary,

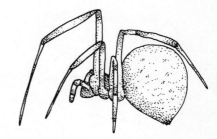

A common house spider eats many other insect invaders of the home. These beneficial organisms should not be killed.

rarely leaving her silken web voluntarily. Willis J. Gertsch, in his classic book on spiders written for the lay person, *American Spiders,* says of the black widow, "They ordinarily make no effort to bite even when subjected to all kinds of provocation. Although charged with viciousness, they are never aggressive and make no effort to attack, preferring instead to retreat and lie perfectly still. . . . The danger lies in the fact . . . [that] they may be accidentally squeezed against the body in some way."

The brown recluse spider is found inside; it may hide under piles of miscellaneous material such as clothes that have lain undisturbed for long periods on the floor of closets or other cool dark areas. Shaking out such garments before putting them on will keep you from inadvertently threatening any spiders that may be hiding there. These spiders avoid light and try to escape when discovered. They also are reluctant to bite, and when observed to do so do not necessarily release venom.

Fear of spiders can be overcome. By reading about them and observing their actions, one can learn to respect and value them and even enjoy the knowledge that they are patrolling the dark recesses of the house destroying many potential house pests. A good inexpensive little booklet on spiders that includes some interesting suggestions for teaching children about them is *Spiders,* by Verne N. Rockcastle.

In the Greenhouse

The major pest problems in the commercial greenhouses of the world are remarkably similar, because the environments and crops are similar. The home-scale grower can also expect many of the same problems. These are the two-spotted spider mite, *Tetranychus urticae;* the greenhouse whitefly, *Trialeurodes vaporariorum;* aphids, (*Myzus persicae,* the green peach aphid, and *Aphis gossypii,* the cotton aphid, among others); and a group of lesser problems.

In this section, we discuss these major pest problems and their management in some detail so that you can use these examples as models for dealing with other problems you may encounter. For a discussion of specific

Table 13-3. **Factors That Encourage Pests or Their Natural Enemies**

The Pest Herbivore	The Natural Enemies
High-density monoculture increases probability of greater pest damage.	Closely spaced plants can allow for fast and effective dissemination by natural enemies.
The greenhouse provides a protected environment where pests can easily adapt.	Controlled conditions can help in selecting natural enemies most suited to the greenhouse environment and crops.
Parasites and predators are prevented from entering the greenhouse.	Once parasites and predators occur inside, they cannot disperse to areas outside the greenhouse.
Pests are prevented from attacking other plants because they cannot migrate outside.	Natural enemies cannot migrate to attack other pests on other crops outdoors.
Pests can live in protected locations within greenhouses, for example, on and in benches.	Some natural enemies can also hide in greenhouse structures.
Pests can be transferred from the plant propagation house or other sources to the greenhouse.	Natural enemies can be distributed easily, for example, with plant propagating material that is moved through such houses.

but less common problems consult the book by Hussey *et al.* called *Glasshouse Pests.*

In working out pest-management programs for indoor situations, the different factors that can affect pest and natural enemies should be kept in mind. These are listed out in Table 13-3.

Nontoxic Control Methods: Physical methods of exclusion and destruction of plant pests always should be tried first before chemical tools. Screens on greenhouse windows and doors have both advantages and disadvantages in this respect. They will prevent the natural predators and parasites of the area from finding their way into the structure and seeking out the pest, but they will also prevent the entrance of many plant pests and keep inside where you want them any predators and parasites of the pests especially released for control purposes. On the whole, we recommend screening all greenhouse openings when possible, since this can help make releases of natural enemies successful.

Ants can easily be excluded from tables and benches with Stickem (see the ant excluder, page 311), and less easily from ground areas by caulking all baseboard cracks. The best strategy here is to give thought to ant exclusion in the original construction of the greenhouse by carefully sealing the seams where concrete footings and foundation sills meet the walls of the house as well as other areas with cracks opening to the outside.

Insects are cold-blooded, so crushing them by hand is particularly easy when the air is cold, since they cannot move quickly and readily escape. Whiteflies can easily be wiped off the leaves at such times. One person we know of suppresses the whitefly population by sucking them off the leaves with a vacuum cleaner in the early morning when they are cold. Physical removal is a good approach; sacrificing a section of an entire plant is well worthwhile if pruning it out will end the infestation. Where plants are in containers, they may need to be moved outdoors for a time during mild weather to see if their natural enemies will find the pests. Also, they may be inverted and washed in soapy water.

Some animals, such as slugs and sowbugs, will be found feeding at night. This is the best time to pick them off. Carry a flashlight if your greenhouse does not have lights. Sowbugs are primarily interested in decaying vegetation, but on occasion they will eat the surface of many different types of tender vegetation if it is moist. Keeping the ground surface from getting soggy and permitting good air circulation around the base of the plants by thinning and removing drying leaves along the ground level can reduce damage from these animals.

Drip-irrigation would seem to be a good way of reducing favorable habitat below soil level for both slugs and sowbugs since a moist soil surface is their preference. Copper-based anti-fouling paints (available in boat stores) are repellent to slugs and snails, and can be used on wooden structures to prevent attack by these mollusks. Baits (nonarsenical) are probably the only safe way to use poisons in a food-raising greenhouse. They are effective against slugs and snails as well as other animals and should be placed in flat containers set at soil level, rather than on the soil itself, in order to avoid contaminating the soil.

Wheast, a Predator Aid

Using Wheast: Wheast can be obtained by writing CRS Food Service and Supply Company 6043 Hudson Road, St. Paul, Minnesota 55119 (ask for CRS Formula #57), or Rincon Vitova Insectories, Inc. Box 45, Oak View, California 93022

Wheast is flour-like in consistency. It should be stored in a cool, dry place, in tight, insect- and rodent-proof containers. To prepare Wheast for use, mix it into a paste, using equal parts of water, sugar, and Wheast (one gallon water: one pound wheast: one pound sugar). This mixture can be smeared on various surfaces (wax paper is often used). The paper strips can be taped or attached to plants or rearing containers. The Wheast mixture can also be made more watery and painted or sprayed on plants and other surfaces directly. Since ants also may be attracted to the wheast, use Stickem or other ant excluders where the feeding syrup is concentrated.

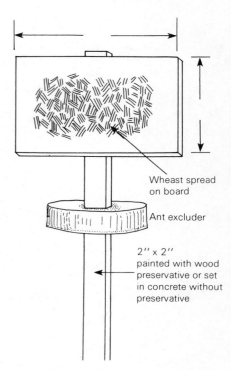

Wheast spread on board

Ant excluder

2″ x 2″ painted with wood preservative or set in concrete without preservative

Wheast Feeding Station

A beneficial insect feeding station, baited with Wheast. An ant guard is attached to prevent ants from eating the bait. This is an experimental method now being studied as a way to augment certain natural-enemy populations.

Spiders in the greenhouse should be encouraged in general, since they are general predators important in insect control. Frogs, particularly tree frogs, and salamanders can play a similar role. Tiny flies, or fungus gnats, inevitably show up sooner or later where decomposing vegetation is present as with many soil mixes. We have seen them in abundance in our greenhouse, but have not been able to verify that they are doing any damage. Ignore them.

One biological method is to release into the greenhouse large numbers of a general predator, either green lacewings or ladybird beetles, and to maintain them in the house by artificial feeding. They become permanent residents, so to speak, always there to keep down the herbivores that might reach pest numbers if left uncontrolled. We have received verbal reports of the success of this method using both of these predators. To maintain them in the greenhouse, all openings must be screened, and feeding stations of Wheast set out. This high-protein substance is available commercially, as a by-product of the cheese industry, and is used to feed bee colonies during the winter (see page 308 and margin). We use it, mixed with honey or sugar, painted on a flat, inclined board and mounted on a stick surrounded by an ant excluder.

Another approach is to buy predators and/or parasites anew each time a serious infestation is discovered, or at regular intervals when they can be expected. In this case, natural enemies specific to each pest should be obtained. Green lacewings and the specific predators of the common greenhouse mite, the two-spotted spider mite can be raised in home cultures. Raising pest predators is fascinating and offers income possibilities as well, but, as with the raising and care of any animal, it requires attention and some understanding of what you are doing. Before undertaking the culturing of these predators, it might be wise to learn methods of using those already available commercially.

In different plant and greenhouse situations, different predator rearing and release techniques may be required. Our experiences with some of these insects may help you develop your own procedures.

The Two-Spotted Spider Mite: The two-spotted spider mite (also called the red spider mite or glasshouse spider mite) is in the family Tetranychidae. This family of mites contains a good many plant feeders, among which the two-spot probably has the greatest range of host plants—over 150 host-plant species. The different stages in the life cycle of this species are sketched on page 387. Mites can be thought of as small ticks. This species, as you can see in the drawing, has a series of different stages—starting after the egg, first it has six legs, later eight. This latter is the characteristic number distinguishing spiders, ticks, and mites from insects, which only have six.

Mites are visible as tiny mobile specks running on leaf surfaces or across their silken webs. In heavy infestations, you can easily see them moving on webs by shining a light upon the leaf. A good hand lens is a key piece of equipment for anyone starting out to learn to manage pest problems. (The lens should have a magnification of at least 10X. If you are buying one, it is worthwhile to spend the extra money for a metal holder, since the plastic ones do not last long.)

The mature female two-spot can lay about a hundred round, shiny, cream-colored eggs. These can give rise to other females in eight days at optimal temperatures, 85° to 95°F (29° to 32°C). Although the mite's reproduction rate is relatively low, it does have a short development time, which means rapid population growth is possible in warm conditions. This is the main reason why mites can be such a severe problem. The adults can survive near their growth threshold (the temperature at which growth first starts) of 54°F (12°C) for more than two months. At temperatures much below that they need to undergo diapause (a state of arrested development akin to hibernation) or they will die. This species also has a diapausing egg from which new adults can develop in the spring.

Mites cause plant damage by feeding on individual plant cells, which are virtually stabbed to death. The mites do not have jaws nor even tubes for mouthparts like mosquitoes or aphids; instead they have solid, rodlike ice picks with which they stab surface cells and then suck up the released fluids. The stabbed cells die and show up as pale light-green "chlorotic" areas, first as pinprick-sized spots, and later, as the spots coalesce, entire chlorotic pale leaves will become common. Learning to recognize the damage in the early stages is important, since, if predators are to be released, it is desirable to do this before the populations are so great that webs are conspicuous and leaves

Box 13-9. **Raising Predatory Mites**

Because they are not cheap and must be ordered by mail, and because we have a constant mite problem in our greenhouse, we finally began raising our own predatory mites. In a screened cage, away from our main greenhouse, we raise bush beans in six-inch pots and infect them with the pest mite.

The cage can be a frame of wood set on a wooden base with organdy gauze stretched over the frame to permit light to reach the plants within. The organdy will prevent the mites from being blown around in the air of the house and infecting other plants. Tightly seal the edges of the organdy, and trim the door to the cage with foam or other weatherstripping. If the bean-plant pots are set in a dry pan which in turn is set in a larger pan of water, the pest mites will be unable to crawl out (two sizes of aluminum broiler pans can be used for this).

In another area, away from the cage, start the bean seedlings and allow them to grow several inches tall. Four or five seedlings can be started in a single pot. When a pot has a good growth of leaves on which to support the pest mite,

move it into the cage and lay on it a leaf or two clipped from a plant already infested.

New plants must be started and added to the cage every month or so because, without the controlling predators, the pest mites quickly kill off the beans before the plants get very large.

We raise the predator mites themselves right in our greenhouse. We use stainless steel pans filled with water. In the center, on a dry elevated platform (a saucer on another dish) we keep our predatory mites. (The moat of water keeps them there.) We started this culture by placing on it some bean leaves infested with pest mites and shaking on predatory mites we bought initially. At least once a week, we add more infested bean leaves to the little platform in the center of the pan, and at least once a week we take out leaves from the platform and distribute them around on the leaves of the plants we are trying to protect. In other words, we don't wait for an infestation to start, we practice preventive mite control routinely! This system has worked satisfactorily for several years, and the only continuing cost is the bean

seeds. A summary of the system follows.

1. Obtain and plant seeds (bush beans are usually used, but you can experiment).

2. Encourage healthy bean-plant development.

3. Move pot with healthy bean seedlings to screened cage.

4. Infect beans with two-spotted spider mites (*Tetranychus urticae*).

5. When bean plants are heavily infested, clip off a few leaves and carry to mite predator culture in greenhouse.

6. Regularly replace bean seedlings within screened cage that are killed by mites.

7. Regularly remove leaves from predator culture and distribute around greenhouse.

Important note:
Always move from pest culture in screened cage *to* predator culture. Never the reverse. If predatory mites are accidentally carried to the pest mite culture (on hands or clothing, for example) you can lose the supply of prey and subsequently the whole system.

are being lost.

During cold weather, the mites will leave the plants and hibernate in the cracks and crevices of the greenhouse benches or the interior structures of the house. They will also lay overwintering eggs. When the cold weather ceases, the pest mites will begin to feed. In greenhouses where mite damage was serious late in the previous fall, it is particularly important to be alert to this first feeding damage produced by the mites, and order predators to be shipped immediately.

Predators of the Two-Spotted Spider Mite: Some of the most voracious mite killers are other mites. Probably the best-known member of the predatory mite family Phytoseiidae, *Phytoseiulus* ("Phyto sēē ĕeyulus") *persimilis* is used extensively in greenhouse pest management, particularly in Europe. Other mites in this family include species of the genera *Amblyseius, Metaseiulus,* and *Typhlodromus* which frequently can be found feeding on two-spotted spider mites in predatory mite cultures shipped from commercial sources. The life-cycle of phytoseiids is shorter than that of tetranychids under similar conditions (less than six days). They produce fewer eggs (a maximum of two eggs per female per day, up to about sixty total eggs).

If you order predatory mites by mail, they may come in thin plastic tubes. Cut one end of the tube and tap or shake the predators out over the plants where the early signs of infestation have been noticed.

The main problem with using predatory mites is that they don't survive well. After they clean up all adult pest mites they may die off, thus becoming unavailable to control the new infestation that hatch from eggs laid by the first generation of pests. This is especially important with the first generation in the spring where hibernating eggs may provide continuing additions of new pests for many weeks.

Developing a Mite-Management System: Because the predator mites die before a new pest mite infestation develops from the original generation's eggs, an overall strategy must be developed. The simplest method is to order a new batch of predators each time you need them, though this is expensive. A second approach is to raise the pest mite on some isolated plants grown specifically for the purpose and add pests to your greenhouse periodically to feed the predators and keep them from dying out after they've cleaned up the pest adults in the greenhouse. This is somewhat tricky since, without a great deal of close scrutiny, it may be difficult to determine where the predators are in the greenhouse.

A third approach is to raise both pest and predator. This is slightly more trouble, but, surprisingly enough, not really difficult. You'll need a spot away from the greenhouse (a shelf or table in a sunny window in the house can do) where you can set up a wooden (or even cardboard) box screened with organdy mesh. (Ordinary window screen is too coarse.) In this box you raise the plants that you infest with the pest mite. In a small pan in the greenhouse fitted with a foam rubber section surrounded by a water moat you raise the predatory mite. The system is described in Box 13-9.

In large commercial greenhouse operations in Europe, growers have found that they can best gain control of the plant-feeding mites by releasing predator *and* pest mites directly into the house, in sequence. The pest is put out first, to make sure there will be enough food for the predator, and then the latter is released regularly when pest populations have started to build up. For more information on the commercial systems, see the bibliography.

Aphid Pest Problems: The greenhouse aphid species will vary with the plants that are grown, and thus the natural enemies will also vary. However, one aphid species is particularly common in indoor settings on many plants throughout the world: the green peach aphid, *Myzus persicae.* This species, like many other aphids (family Aphididae) over-winters in the egg stage in cold climates. In the spring the egg hatches and a female emerges which, when mature, can give birth to other females without having mated. As you can imagine from these facts, aphids have very high population growth rates. Within a week or two, especially with the warmer indoor temperatures, high aphid "blooms" may be found where previously no aphids were noticed. These female generations can continue until fall conditions trigger changes through which males and females are produced. These mate and the females lay the over-wintering eggs. In greenhouse situations, egg-laying generations may not occur because the environmental conditions may not provide the appropriate cues that trigger the aphids to change. This is particularly true if there are artificial lights simulating spring conditions (long day lengths—up to seventeen hours). Without artificial lights, the usual life-cycle will probably occur but will be advanced according to how warm the greenhouse is kept.

Aphids' Natural Enemies: Aphids' natural enemies are numerous and encompass many families of insects and other noninsect species. The most common insect families are the well-known lady beetles (Coccinellidae), lacewings (Chrysopidae, the green lacewings, and Hemerobiidae, the brown lacewings), and the hover fly family, Syrphidae. In addition to these predatory insects, two families of miniwasps also parasitize aphids, the Aphididae and the Aphelinidae. The aphidiids are all aphid parasites (about three hundred known species), but only about fifty aphelinid species attack aphids. Representatives of both families occur indoors. In order to learn to use these insects against the aphids that damage your plants you will need to find and learn how to identify the natural enemies. Some of these are illustrated in this chapter. You can learn about others from local entomologists and discover some yourself by making careful observations in aphid colonies. Each of the stages of the natural enemy is important, since gauging how many are present requires an assessment of total numbers wherever possible. In making your own observations, look for species that feed on the aphids and then try to make a judgment about what their impact could be.

Watching a hungry lady beetle adult wade into a group of feeding aphids is like watching a lawn mower cut swathes in extra-tall grass. One can easily see that such organisms are of major importance. However, lady beetles are, in general, opportunists and crop aphids from many different sources; they fly away to better feeding grounds when the number of aphids decreases below a certain point. Lady beetles can sense such levels, judging by their behavior. The first, or lowest, level is the survival level. Here the adult beetles just eat an occasional prey and with it manage to avoid starvation. Next is a feeding and more-vigorous-search-for-food level. Above that

Figure 13-20. **Life Cycle of the Green Lacewing at 75°F**

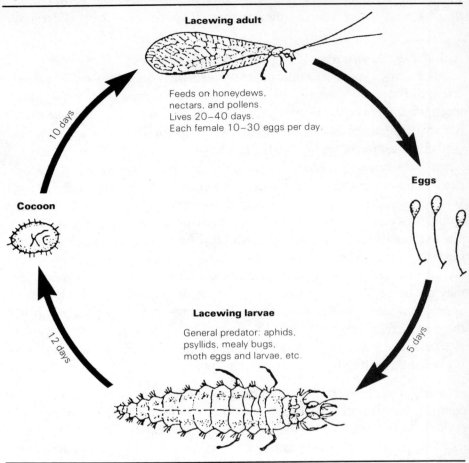

Lacewing adult

Feeds on honeydews, nectars, and pollens. Lives 20–40 days. Each female 10–30 eggs per day.

10 days

Cocoon

Eggs

12 days

5 days

Lacewing larvae

General predator: aphids, psyllids, mealy bugs, moth eggs and larvae, etc.

Source: Tassan and Hagan "The Influence of Food Wheast and Related *Saccharomyces Fragilis* Yeast Products on the Fecundity of *Chrysopa Carnea*."

is the active feeding and egg-laying level, while above that is the feeding-frenzy level, where many more aphids are killed than are eaten. By close examination you can determine what the condition of your natural-enemy population is—whether it is reproducing satisfactorily, just nibbling, or barely surviving. Such an assessment can help you understand just what is occurring when you see a lady beetle within a colony.

Although lady beetles are important predators, the parasites are frequently the key regulating factors, since they can search out and destroy prey at low densities. This is important in preventing aphid outbreaks. Parasites are usually passed over by the neophyte grower because they do not, on the surface, appear to have a significant impact on the aphid population. Dissections of aphids to assess parasitism rates is one way to assess their impact directly. But this involves a microscope and some skill.

Lacewings, on the other hand, offer the potential for home use—in particular *Chrysopa carnea*, the Golden-Eyed Green Lacewing, which is available from commercial sources. These insects have relatively wide host ranges, are easily reared in mass, and can be shipped through the mail without too much trouble. *C. carnea* is widely used in Europe in greenhouse aphid control, and will probably become more widely used here in North America as biological controls become more popular.

The green lacewing lays its eggs on stalks, presumably to protect them from cannibalistic larvae that have hatched previously. The adult does not prey on aphids, but feeds on honeydew. As with other predators, lacewing populations normally lag behind the populations of their prey, and thus to be useful must be introduced in anticipation of increases in pest numbers. The life cycle, with detailed information on the biology of this species, is shown in Figure 13-20.

The Greenhouse Whitefly: The *Trialeurodes vaporariorum,* is related to aphids and scales, and is a well-known and persistent pest in houses on indoor plants the world over. A short summary of the biology of this insect and its best-known natural enemy, *Encarsia formosa* is given in Box 13-10. The home greenhouse manager may be able to control whiteflies with a release of *Encarsia formosa,* the whitefly parasite obtained from a commercial source, with additional releases if the parasite dies out. Greenhouse temperatures, however, play an important role for both small- and large-scale structures. Below 75°F (24°C), the whitefly is favored. At 64°F (18°C), the reproduction rate of the whitefly is ten times that of *Encarsia formosa,* although both develop at the same rate. At 78.8°F (26°C), the reproductive rate is equal, but the parasite rate of development is twice that of the host. Below 55.4°F (13°C), *Encarsia* cannot establish.

In one experiment on tomato plants, with the release of one parasitized whitefly scale per square foot, the whitefly population was controlled in nine weeks. In another experiment, releasing prey, as discussed in the section on

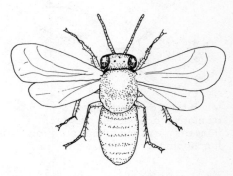

Encarsia formosa, the parasite of the greenhouse whitefly. This species is commercially available.

Box 13-10. **The Greenhouse Whitefly**

The whitefly, *Tricaleurodes vaporariorum,* gets its name from the white, powdery wax covering of body and wings and its gnatlike size and behavior. The adults can collect in large numbers, usually on the upper foliage, and fly about in little swarms when disturbed. Females live for 30 to 40 days and are attracted to young foliage to feed. They have piercing mouthparts and feed by penetrating phloem tubes (the pathways through which sugars are transported inside plant tissue). Plant nutrition greatly affects their reproductive rates—the better-fed host plants promote higher whitefly reproductive rates.

The whiteflies' small (0.2 to 0.25 millimeter; .008 to .009 inch) yellowish eggs become black in two days. At 86°F (30°C), eggs will hatch in four days, while they will incubate for thirty days at 46°F (8°C). Females lay about 25 eggs per day, up to a total of 150 to 500 eggs. The eggs are attached to the leaf by a short stalk—normally on the undersides of the leaves, but also on the upper surface of a main stem. The eggs are usually found grouped into small circles, 20

to 40 eggs per circle. This arrangement occurs because the female lays her eggs while still feeding with her mouthparts embedded in the plant. Thus, she lays an egg and rotates slightly, lays another egg, and so on.

The newly hatched larvae is flat, light green, and has bright red eyes. It moves around for 2 to 3 days before settling permanently next to a leaf vein. After molting and losing its legs and antennae, the developing whitefly looks like a flat scale, adhering closely to the leaf. Other molts follow until the adult emerges. The whole life cycle takes about three weeks at 70°F (21°C), or four weeks at 60°F (15°C).

Like aphids, whiteflies have characteristic families of natural enemies. The most well-studied whitefly natural enemy is the aphelinid *Encarsia formosa.* This species was discovered in Britain in 1927, but probably originated in the United States. For many years, it was used without adequate data, and only recently is the species being studied carefully. The parasite female senses its potential larval host, or as they are called, "scales," with its

antennae or ovipositor (egg-laying apparatus), and lays its eggs, one per host, in the scale. The egg hatches inside the whitefly scale, and the parasitic larvae kills it by eating its internal tissues. The scales turn black about nine to ten days after being parasitized. Whitefly eggs, active first stage larvae, and pupae are never attacked; only the developing sedentary whitefly scales are parasitized. Like many parasites, *E. formosa* prefers a particular stage of its host. The older scales are preferred, but when severe competition for these occurs, younger scales are probed with ovipositors, though no eggs are laid. Nevertheless, the young scales are killed by this repeated probing.

The other way this parasitic species has an impact on its prey is through host-feeding. Like other members of the family Aphelinidae, this parasite opens a wound in its host and drinks the body fluids. This can provide nourishment when scales are sparse, particularly since such feeding on its host can occur on scale pupae as well as larval forms.

mite management above, at a rate of eight whiteflies between each pair of cucumber plants, a uniform distribution was obtained. Thereafter, *Encarsia* was released at the rate of eight per plant. Within twelve weeks, control was accomplished except where honeydew production was heavy and interfered with the parasites. The honeydew, however, may be easily removed with a water spray.

On tomatoes, 10 adult whiteflies per apical leaf appears to be the highest tolerable level. On cucumbers, 40 whiteflies per upper leaf produced no honeydew. Even at 135 flies per upper leaf, no mold developed on the honeydew. (The black sooty mold grows whenever sufficient honeydew is present and microclimactic conditions permit.) Thus about 50 to 60 whiteflies per leaf can probably be tolerated on cucumbers without economic loss. These figures are included here to indicate the number of pests that have been observed to be tolerable under commercial situations because you will need to judge levels for your own plants.

Some parasites that attack greenhouse whiteflies can live under cooler temperatures. In our garden, one species (*Eretomoceris* sp.) got into our greenhouse accidentally and controlled our whiteflies there. If someone learns to raise and market them, this species could be a valuable addition to the greenhouse biological control option.

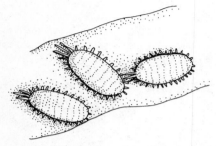

Mealybugs are sometimes common on many indoor plants. The projections are waxy secretions, probably functioning as protective devices.

Mealybugs: Mealybugs probably got their name from their powdery appearance. Many of the species secrete waxy substances that cover their bodies. Mealybugs are related to scales and aphids. They are soft-bodied sucking insects and have well-developed legs throughout their lives but no pupal stages. Some mealybugs lay eggs and others give birth to living young, as mammals do. Eggs are often laid in crevices about the plant. The newly hatched or borne young look like small replicas of the large adults. With some species the shape of these insects is difficult to perceive because of the waxy powder covering their bodies, but the true shape can be revealed by wetting them with a drop of alcohol. Some mealybugs are common pests on indoor and greenhouse plants, while other species are known on commercial crops.

Although both green and brown lacewings will also attack mealybugs, the lady beetle *Crytolaemus montrouzieri* is specific to mealybugs and has been particularly useful in their control. This black and red beetle, first introduced from Australia in 1892, has been raised in mass-production systems by growers and private groups in California since 1916, when the discovery was made that the beetle could be successfully reared on mealybugs developing on potato sprouts.

To raise these ladybugs yourself for a mealybug-control program keep the potatoes warm and dark. You may need to buy "organic" potatoes to make sure they have not been sprayed to prevent sprouting (usually the growth regulator maleic hydrazide is used). As some potatoes become soft and rotten, other newly sprouted ones can be added to the culture. When the potatoes are sprouted, place mealybugs and then beetles on them in turn. Periodically take off as many adult or larvae lady beetles as are needed to suppress pest populations in the greenhouse.

Dick Tasson of the Division of Biological Control, University of California, Berkeley, suggests that although you can place mealybugs and lady beetles together in an appropriate container, as we have done, the culture will last longer if the mealybugs on the potato sprouts are raised separately. Keep the predator lady beetles in a smaller container, with a piece of tissue paper or toilet paper for the beetles to hide under. In this way the predator beetles will not get stuck in the oozing potatoes, and the culture will be better controlled. At regular intervals you should harvest the mealybugs by picking up the potatoes in one hand and sweeping the insects off with a small brush with the other. The harvest rate should be kept at about 90 percent so that some are left to replenish the culture.

Harvested mealybugs can be refrigerated for days and stay fresh enough to use as food for the predators. A mealybug culture is also very useful if you are raising lacewings, because the young mealybugs are smaller than the young lacewings and thus make a good food source for starting lacewing cultures.

What If Your Problem Isn't Mentioned Here?

Pest problems vary greatly from area to area. Only a few specific examples could be covered in this book. Hopefully, you will be able to generalize from the examples given here to other situations you encounter.

The most successful alternative methods to chemical control are usually those where careful on-the-spot consideration is made of *all* the factors operating to create that particular problem. Often, you may have to experiment with a number of different possible solutions to find the best one for your own situation. You will need ingenuity and plenty of common sense. Start by asking yourself, "Do I really need to kill that animal (or plant)?" Respect for the importance of every single living creature in principle will help you to tolerate the presence of those life forms that appear to be only a nuisance and whose precise importance in the natural scheme of things you may not know.

14. THE FRONT YARD

In most residential areas a space exists between the street and the front of the house—the front yard—where sunlight falls and plants are, or can, be raised. This is a sensitive area, an interface between the private and public lives of the residents, and often subject to conflicting demands of territory, status displays, and community access. These demands give the front yard its special character and problems. The challenge is to develop subsystems of the integrated household that usefully incorporate this space into the life-support of the house, and still communicate the desired message from the residents to the passing crowd of the need for privacy and security.

Various living and nonliving components are commonly used in this space to perform many functions—for example, signs to guide passing pedestrians; fences and hedges to screen the household from sight and to block traffic noise and the toxic chemicals from automobile exhaust; gates to keep the public out and to restrain certain household members such as animals and young children; and trees to provide shade, decrease wind velocity, and enhance the aesthetic appeal of the property (see Table 14-1). Compared with nonliving structures used in this area, vegetation has the advantage of providing microclimate modifications by increasing humidity and gas exchange, thus affecting human comfort in a positive way. But plants, being alive, may also pose special maintenance problems. They may introduce irritants such as pollen and wildlife or their products. For example, the honeydew excreted by certain shade tree aphids and related insects occasionally may be copious enough to create problems when picked up on shoes and tracked into the house.

The Curbside Space

If we begin at the street and work back toward the house, the first space available is often a long narrow stretch of earth. It is bounded by curb and sidewalk along its length, and by driveways or walks at either end. Some communities strictly regulate the use of this area and restrict what can go in it; others leave its use entirely to the discretion of the residents. Some suburban areas, giving themselves over totally to the automobile, have eliminated a path for foot traffic entirely, so that this curbside space blends indistinguishably into the privately owned land surrounding the front of the house.

This strip, often rigidly defined by cement on all sides, may be the habitat of a shade tree, frequently but not always selected, planted, and maintained by the city parks or public works department. The choice and care of such a tree may be a source of major interaction between the residents and the city, since, by its very size and placement, a large tree is capable of dominating the entire front area, determining the amount of shade the yard and house receives, and thus profoundly affecting both the indoor and outside microclimate. In addition, because of competition from the tree's roots and deposits of leaf and branch litter, the kinds and amounts of other vegetation that may be grown in this area are also affected. Curbside shade trees may greatly affect the aesthetic and thus the market value of a property, a fact well-demonstrated by the dramatic visual change wrought by Dutch elm disease in areas where it has caused rows of stately streetside elms in towns across the United States and Europe to die suddenly.

The most important function of the curbside space may be providing access to the street or to parked cars. Thus, compaction from foot traffic may be its distinguishing characteristic. The primary requirements in this case would come from a desire to reduce mud, dust, or other impediments that could damage shoes and clothing or hinder easy passage. This desire for

Table 14-1. **The Front Yard—A Functional Analysis**

Element	Street	Medium Strip	Sidewalk	Front Yard	House Entrance
Function	Broadway	Access to street / vehicles	Pedestrian passage	Public interface, status display	Aesthetic enhancement, climate modification
Common Constituent	Cement / asphalt	Turf, concrete, soil	Concrete	Lawn / ornamentals	Shrubs, flowers
Alternative use	Vehicular traffic and bike path separate from each other	Dense vegetation for sound and air pollution barrier	Woodchip, tan-bark path for biological recovery	Edible ornamental plants / alfalfa	Dwarf citrus, espalier fruit trees, and vine crops

easy street access has led to the use of tough, low-growing ground covers such as grasses or, where low maintenance is desired, replacement of vegetation with inert materials such as cement, stones, bricks, and the like. Some homeowners may attempt to reduce maintenance by applying toxic materials, such as commercial herbicides, to reduce weeds. Many a lovely shade tree has been accidentally killed through use of such products on the ground surrounding it. The same lethal effect may be achieved by using this area as a waste recipient by dumping gasoline, cleaning agents, and so forth on the soil. The proximity of this space to the curbside gutter, a traditional place for disposal of wastes, may make this tempting.

Passageways

Perhaps as a reaction to the mud and dust of primitive frontier-town conditions, or as a product of the U.S. urban and suburban passion for sanitizing nature and rendering it less disorderly or hostile to the pursuits of humans, the general choices for passageway materials have been impermeable cement or asphalt. However, the illusion of permanence that these substances give may be broken by enlarging tree roots and shifting earth foundations, thus necessitating costly repairs to the sidewalk. These materials provide smooth surfaces for rollerskating, bicycling, skateboarding, strollers, shopping carts, and so on, but they are in fact unhealthy for extensive walking or running. In addition, impermeable surfaces create a problem when plant debris falls on them because lack of contact with the ground prevents normal decomposition. Disturbing the monotony of these cherished passageways with leaves and twigs results in the obsessive sweeping so dear to the neighborhood sentinel. Precious resources may be consumed in these efforts through the use of water washes from the garden hose or, worse yet, blowers with motors powered by fossil fuels.

Table 14-2. **Urban Run-off**

Width of Sidewalk	Annual Rainfall in Inches							
	6″	12″	18″	24″	36″	48″	60″	72″
2 feet	750	1500	2250	3000	4500	6000	7500	9000
3 feet	1125	2250	2375	4500	6750	9000	11,500	13,500
4 feet	1500	3000	4500	6000	9000	12,000	15,000	18,000
5 feet	1875	3750	5625	7500	11,250	15,000	18,750	22,500
6 feet	2250	4500	6750	9000	13,500	18,000	22,500	27,000

Annual Run-off from 100 feet of sidewalk (in gallons per 100 linear feet of sidewalk)

One of the most serious consequences of impermeable surfaces is that they inhibit the absorption of water. While they eliminate the problem of muddy feet, cement and asphalt simultaneously create the problems associated with run-off. Water that would otherwise sink into the ground where it falls, replenishing the soil water and cleansing itself of any air-borne or other pollutants by passing through layers of biological and physical filters, is channeled away. Problems of erosion, pollutant concentrations, and mosquitoes and other pest problems develop as the water is captured in ditches, gutters, catch basins, or storm sewers and is finally deposited into the nearest river, lake, or oceanside tidelands. As Table 14-2 shows, this run-off may be considerable, especially where sidewalks and driveways are broad.

What alternatives exist for these public and semipublic passageways? Permeable asphalts and cement are being developed in which the fine particles have been removed from the compound, permitting water passage. However, products strong enough for use as roadways have not yet been perfected. Gravel is a common substitute for driveways, particularly in more rural areas. It requires occasional renewal, since on steep surfaces it may wash away. Bricks are often used as walkway material. If they are set in sand between wooden curbs or edges, they will allow the passage of water. As with stone tile or wood stepping stones, control of undesirable grasses that may grow up in cracks or crevices between the bricks needs to be given some thought. The same problem might be created by the use of beds of small stones instead of vegetation in the curbside space. An increasingly common way to deal with unwanted plant growth has been to lay down a heavy sheet of polyethylene plastic beneath the stones or other permeable surfaces, but this defeats the goal of permitting water penetration, and is a questionable use of fossil fuels. A better solution is encouraging low, hardy plants, such as mosses, that may begin to grow voluntarily in those areas, or deliberately seeding in plants that can compete well with grasses, such as sweet alyssum.

At the Integral Urban House in Berkeley one of our favored choices for heavily used walkways has been wood chips. This waste product is readily available in many cities, since it is created by running through a machine called a "chipper" the debris from the pruning of city trees. During certain times of the year, this pruned-off material may constitute a significant percentage of the plant debris produced by municipalities. The usual repository of these materials is the city dump. Recycling them for use as walkways and mulch seems preferable.

The chips make an attractive, pleasingly complex-looking surface. The same effect may be achieved by using bark products sold commercially as mulch. All such materials must be bordered by wood, metal, or stone edging to prevent it from migrating out into surrounding spaces.

The use of such organic material as a walking surface has many advantages. Rain and other water can percolate down through it, along with oxygen, permitting the soil organisms beneath the surface to survive. The continued existence of these organisms makes it easy to grow plants in those areas once again, should you desire to change the position of the walkway. Decomposition will proceed slowly on the underside of the chip layer, eventually adding nutrients to the soil and furnishing a home for earthworms and other highly desirable animals. Initially, however, the high carbon content of these materials will help suppress weeds in the pathway itself.

The effect of walking on such a surface is similar to walking on the soil itself. Feet are kept dry and clean when the ground is wet, but somewhat more care is required than when walking on the smoother surfaces of cement or asphalt. However, with more awareness of where you put your feet, surface irregularities are less likely to cause you to trip and stumble than when you encounter an unexpected break or bump in a surface you expected to be

Figure 14-1. **Some Mineral Cycles in the Front Yard**

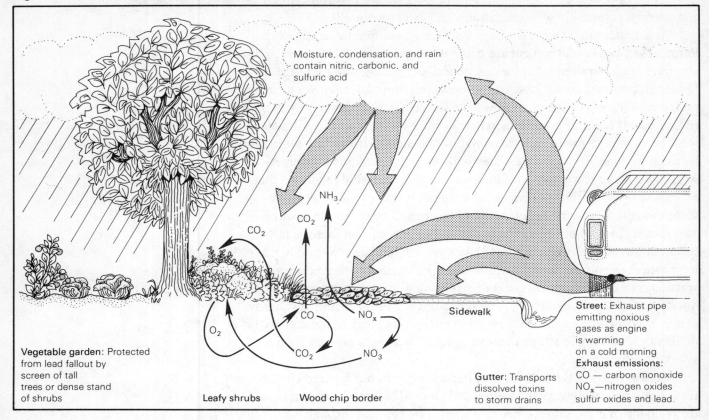

Moisture, condensation, and rain contain nitric, carbonic, and sulfuric acid

NH_3

CO_2

CO_2

O_2

CO NO_x

CO_2 NO_3

Sidewalk

Vegetable garden: Protected from lead fallout by screen of tall trees or dense stand of shrubs

Leafy shrubs

Wood chip border

Gutter: Transports dissolved toxins to storm drains

Street: Exhaust pipe emitting noxious gases as engine is warming on a cold morning
Exhaust emissions:
CO — carbon monoxide
NO_x—nitrogen oxides
sulfur oxides and lead.

The illustration shows the cycling of minerals in a biologically active surface compared with their runoff from an impermeable one. Automobile exhaust from a car warming its engine on a cold morning settles on an adjacent sidewalk or wood chip pathway, or is released into the atmosphere. Moisture in the air reacts with the pollutants to produce harmful acids such as sulfuric and nitric acid. Photochemical effects energized by the ultraviolet spectrum of sunlight produces still other pollutants. Periodic rains move the dissolved toxicants from the air onto the land. Runoff from the sidewalk and other impervious surfaces carry the pollutants into the city's gutters, and then into the storm drains, and ultimately into a body of water of some kind. Where wood chips or some other biologically active surfaces exist, rainfall is absorbed by the medium and the microorganisms thriving on the organic substrate detoxify many of the dissolved pollutants and can render some harmless or useful for plant growth. Although these relationships appear logical, research is needed to determine how much real benefit such walkways can provide. The decreased amount of permeable and bi- perfectly smooth.

Most important, permeable organic surfaces provide an active microbial filter, adding to the physical filtering effects of the soil particles and sifting out and in some cases breaking down contaminants picked up by rain falling through polluted city air. The microbial community of a soil surface rich in organic material may also enhance air quality by converting carbon monoxide, a component of car exhausts that is poisonous to many organisms, to carbon dioxide, which is a compound beneficial to plant life. (This point was made by Dr. Oen C. Huisman, Department of Plant Pathology, University of California, Berkeley, in a personal communication with the authors.) This idea is illustrated in Figure 14-1.

Screens and Barriers

A great variety of screens and barriers are in use in cities. Nonliving barriers may range from a simple row of stones painted white to guide the nighttime traveler, to formidable fences or walls of wood, stone, brick, or concrete. Their vegetation counterparts may range from a border of blooming annuals that provides primarily a psychological barrier by marking the property limits or edging a pathway, to impenetrable hedges of rose bushes, cacti, or other thorny bushes.

Most critical to the comfort of the residents are barriers to invasion of privacy in the form of the sight or sound of the passing traffic. While the former may be easy to achieve, the latter is far more difficult, but it is also more crucial in terms of the health of the occupants within.

Noise: What is noise? A subjective assessment might include the notion of unwanted sound. From a psychological point of view, one person's music may be another person's noise. But noise is also a physical phenomenon, a disturbance, in the form of a flow of energy through matter.

Table 14-3 shows the intensity (loudness) of a number of common indoor and outdoor noises to which urban people may be deliberately or unintentionally exposed. With industrialization, a wide variety of labor-saving and automatic machines and appliances have become a source of noise within the home. Heating, cooling, and plumbing systems, television, music, dogs barking, people talking, and clocks ticking are all examples of indoor noise sources one becomes accustomed to ignoring and enduring in ordinary living or working settings.

As an environmental pollutant, noise is one of the most insidious, precisely because human beings tend to adjust to continuous high noise levels by screening them out of their consciousness. Noise does its damage to the body slowly. Thus, one grows accustomed to increasing deafness, remaining unaware that loss of hearing is occurring until it becomes quite severe. According to the Environmental Protection Agency, as many as 80 million Americans are harmed by noise, many of them while at work. Our personal observations indicate that most people are unaware that their health as well

ologically active surfaces in cities place human health and environmental quality in jeopardy. Urban environments are becoming simplified to the point where they are without any capabilities of biological renewal. The least we can do to help restore the biological vitality of these areas is to recognize the importance of soil and organic matter as nutrient cyclers and pollution detoxifiers, and to protect the existence of natural surfaces.

Table 14-3. **Sound Levels and Human Response**

Source: U.S. Environmental Protection Agency, "Noise Pollution."

Example	Noise Level (Decibels)	Response	Hearing Effect	Conversational Relationship
Deck of an aircraft carrier, jet operation	140	Painful limit of amplified speech		
Foghorn at 3 feet	130			
Jet takeoff (200')	120			
Discotheque				
Riveting machine	110			
Jet takeoff (2,000')				
Garbage truck	100			Shouting in ear
N.Y. subway station				
Heavy truck (50')	90	Hearing damage after 8 hours		Shouting at 2'
Pneumatic drill (50')			Hearing impairment begins and gets worse	
Alarm clock	80	Annoying		Very loud conversation at 2'
Freeway traffic (50')	70	Telephone use difficult		Loud conversation at 2'
Air conditioning unit (20')	60			Loud conversation, 4'
Light auto traffic (100')	50	Quiet		Normal conversation, 2'
Bedroom	40			
Soft whisper (15')	30	Very quiet		
Broadcasting studio	20			
	10			
	0	Threshold of hearing		

What comes with a carriage and goes with a carriage, is of no use to the carriage, and yet the carriage cannot move without it?—an old riddle, (see next page).

Box 14-1. **Noise Control Strategies**

1. **Source reduction.** Muffle or redesign engines for jet aircraft, cars, and trucks; redesign or use smaller motors for appliances and home and office machinery; and use hand tools whenever possible rather than heavy power equipment.

2. **Use modification.** Reroute traffic around residential areas; redirect air routes; deny landing rights to loud aircraft; and time noisy activities so as to affect fewer people.

3. **Sound interruptions.** Use barriers (with a mass of at least 15 kilograms per square meter) to absorb or redirect noise; use soft, heavy materials in designing buildings and rooms to absorb noise and echoes; and eliminate flat surfaces and squared corners wherever possible.

4. **Protect the receiver.** Use ear plugs and earphones to muffle sounds or increase the distance between the receiver and the noise source.

5. **Education.** Make people aware of noise and its effects; file nuisance complaints about noisy neighbors, dogs, lawn mowers, and so on; and help create municipal antinoise laws.

as their daily productivity is being damaged by the noises they are regularly exposed to. They don't take noise seriously.

All inhabitants of modern industrial nations—as compared to tribal members living in remote jungle clearings—are likely to experience premature loss of hearing. On the average, men lose their hearing, at least of the higher frequencies, earlier than women. However, much of that loss is unnecessary and could be avoided by requiring that machines be constructed so that noise production is reduced, and that adequate soundproofing be integrated into building design.

More than loss of hearing is involved in exposure to noise, however. There is plenty of evidence that irritability, inability to concentrate, and general physiological stress may be produced by lengthy exposure to high-intensity sounds. While interior furnishing such as rugs, curtains, and any complex surfaces that prevent echoes can reduce noise originating within the room, traffic noise and other sounds from outside the house can be reduced only by distance or by mass placed between the noise source and the hearer.

Unfortunately, front yards are frequently too small to permit the erection of high walls of soil or concrete. City laws may prohibit high barriers in any case. To achieve any appreciable reduction in noise level using vegetation, several rows of high shrubs and trees between the source and the house are necessary. Such plantings may have various effects upon the dwelling's microclimate, acting as a windbreak and thus reducing heat loss from the house if the barriers are located to the windward, or providing shade if they are on the sunny sides. Planting areas that might be used for growing food and other processes utilizing solar energy will be affected by these barriers, so careful planning is needed. A summary of approaches to noise reduction is given in Box 14-1.

Raising Food in the Front Yard

Lawns: With interest in food-raising increasing, many people have begun to use their front yards for this purpose. In general, it has always been our feeling that the front lawn is a great waste of space. When all the fossil-fuel inputs are accounted for, an ornamental lawn turns out to be a considerable investment in terms of ground preparation (some areas require the importation of topsoil by truck after the house is completed because of the soil damage sustained during the construction), as well as seeding, fertilizing,

Answer: Noise

pest management, watering, mowing, and trimming.

The maintenance of some 16 million acres of lawns in America represents an enormous investment of energy and natural resources. Consider the amount of water, chemical fertilizer, pesticides, gasoline, and human labor devoted to the maintenance of such an expanse of vegetation. In fact, a study entitled "The Energetics of a Suburban Lawn," by John Howard Falk, concluded that the energy inputs into a lawn of a Walnut Creek, California, home amounted to 573 kilocalories per square meter of turf per year. That rate of energy use exceeds the rate for the commercial production of corn on an equivalent amount of soil. The tragedy is that the product of all that energy expenditure, the grass clippings, frequently ends up in plastic sacks by the curb waiting to go to the dump. Wiser gardeners either let grass clippings fall where they are cut, to act as a mulch, or rake them up, together with leaves, to use in the compost. See Box 14-2 on using grass clippings.

Grass serves many functions, some of them aesthetic or psychological. A grassy expanse in front of the house is a status symbol that is firmly entrenched in the minds of those who are descended from northern European cultures. Historically, lawns are associated with the manor house and those wealthy enough to be able to own and preserve some fields for looks alone. A lawn is a boast that the owner is not forced to pasture animals upon the green. Doubtless, in areas where natural rainfall is sufficient and mowing is feasible green grass is unsurpassed as a groundcover for reducing erosion.

Box 14-2. **Using Grass Clippings**

Grass clippings piled by themselves are slow to decompose, since the small, even-sized pieces tend to compact and exclude air, causing the interior of the pile process to go anaerobic. The odors thus generated may attract flies, which will breed in the pile. One of the species attracted to such conditions could be the biting stable fly, *Stomoxys calcitrans*, which in the adult stage can suck the blood of humans the same as a very large mosquito.

If grass clippings are to be used in a slow compost, some coarser materials, such as leaves, should be mixed in to allow more oxygen to circulate. An English system for handling such grass and leaf accumulations is to pile them up in a ring several feet out from and around the dripline of a shade or fruit tree. This composting method is suitable for cool, rainy climates; the decomposition will proceed slowly, primarily through the action of fungi. Material used to create the first pile in the circle during the spring will be ready for use the following year. Plant nutrients leached out of the pile by rains wash down to the roots of the tree. (For a more detailed discussion of composting, see Chapter 6.)

Grass clippings also make a good poultry food. At least a third of the calories in a chicken's diet can profitably be made up of grass without adversely affecting egg-laying efficiency. As with any green vegetable matter used as chicken feed, the vitamin A in grass clippings will turn the egg yolks a deep yellow-orange.

Where artificial watering means that lawn maintenance requires pumps, and consequently use of fossil fuels, or where terrain makes clipping difficult, other low-growing groundcovers (such as birdsfoot trefoil) should be investigated. These may offer the same spacious vista while being well-adapted to the soils, climate, diseases, insects, and other pests native to the area, as well as requiring very little maintenance.

Of course, few other ground-covers can offer the pleasure of grass for walking, playing, and sitting upon, or the resistance to the wear and tear of these activities. But ironically enough, the lawn in front of the house is rarely used for this purpose. The area is often perceived as being too visible

Figure 14-2. **Yearly Energy Budget of a Lawn Compared to an Alfalfa Patch**

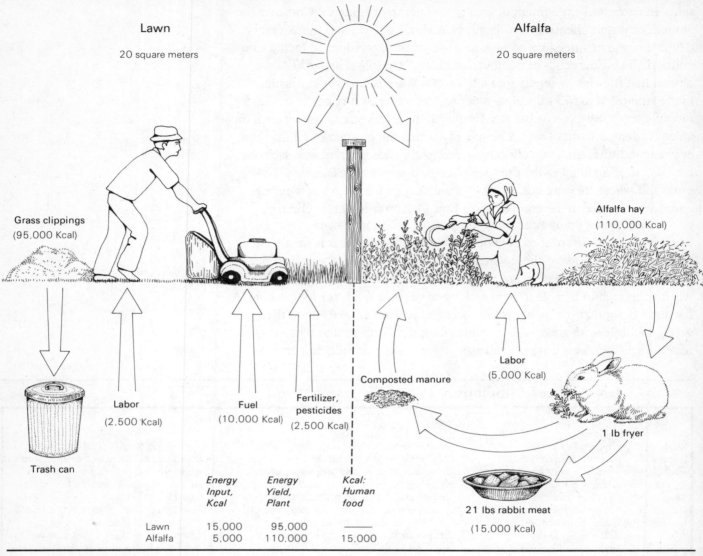

Lawn
20 square meters

Alfalfa
20 square meters

Grass clippings
(95,000 Kcal)

Alfalfa hay
(110,000 Kcal)

Labor
(5,000 Kcal)

Composted manure

Trash can

Labor
(2,500 Kcal)

Fuel
(10,000 Kcal)

Fertilizer,
pesticides
(2,500 Kcal)

1 lb fryer

21 lbs rabbit meat
(15,000 Kcal)

	Energy Input, Kcal	Energy Yield, Plant	Kcal: Human food
Lawn	15,000	95,000	—
Alfalfa	5,000	110,000	15,000

Note: All notation represents annual totals.

to be a setting for household recreation activities. For this reason, as well as for those of space economy in a hungry world, where the front yard receives enough sun we have often recommended that it be used for raising food to sustain people or other animals.

Suitable Food Plants for the Front Yard: At the Integral Urban House, we have found alfalfa to be a very satisfactory substitute for a lawn. Our experience has been that even on this small a scale and using only hand labor in the cultivation and harvesting of the plant, the alfalfa beds are more productive per unit area than a lawn, while requiring only one-third as much energy for maintenance. The alfalfa plant is a legume, and requires no nitrogen fertilizer, in contrast to most lawns. All other essential nutrients can be supplied to the alfalfa in sufficient amounts by applying a compost topdressing about twice during the season of most active growth.

We determined that for every unit of energy invested (exclusively human work) in the production of alfalfa, twenty-two units of energy were returned in crop production. In the case of the lawn, as documented in the study by Howard Falk mentioned above, each unit of energy invested (part human work, part fuel, and part chemical fertilizer) returned six units of energy as lawn clippings. If the grass clippings are discarded as wastes, the net production efficiency of the lawn would be more accurately described as zero (see Figure 14-2).

The alfalfa produced enough digestible nutrients per square meter to support the production of one pound of usable rabbit meat. The twenty-one square meters of median strip in front of our Integral Urban House produces twenty-one pounds of meat per year. In addition, the rabbit manure is composted and provides enough top-dressing to maintain the alfalfa crop, a benefit not considered as a part of this study.

Edible and Other Usable Ornamentals: Of course, not everyone will be interested in sporting a green of alfalfa for their front yard, but we have found several plants that provide both an ornamental display of foliage and flowers and a source of human or animal food. Along the front entrance of Integral Urban House, strawberries make an attractive ground cover. They are evenly spaced over the bed, and stepping stones allow us to hop from place to place when harvesting the fruit. A high border of chrysanthemums provides color, and the clippings are relished by the chickens. We use rhubarb chard for brilliant color accents in the garden, and perennial foundation plantings of artichoke and true rhubarb to provide food as well as pleasing textures and colors. Similar edible ornamentals suitable to different climates could well be used in other areas of the country.

For high hedge material, we have been growing mulberry trees, which we have dwarfed by planting them very close together and pruning severely. As mentioned earlier, we use foliage from this hedge to feed silkworms. In some areas of the country where the winters are mild, hedges of nonrunning bamboo are a possibility. The prunings from bamboo provide stakes to support plants in the garden. The flexible quality of these stakes, especially while still green, makes them useful for a variety of jobs around the house, as well as for decorative crafts. We have used flexible split-bamboo strips to support netting over the beds, to keep birds away, as well as to create tube-like greenhouses, as mentioned earlier (Chapter 7, Food Plants Outdoors). If a shade tree is part of your design for the front of your house, by all means consider using one that will provide fruit or nuts if such can be found that will grow in your area. The idea is to make use of each planting in as many ways as possible besides pure decoration. Now, after whipping up your enthusiasm for planting vegetables in place of front lawn, we would like you to stop and consider whether it's really a good idea to do so.

Lead and the Front Yard Vegetable Garden: There may be a very good reason not to grow vegetables in your front yard: lead pollution. Lead is now a common constituent of the air we breathe (see Table 14-4). In many urban areas, general air quality is a problem in and around the entire house. This is particularly true in neighborhoods that are both industrial and residential, in areas close to heavily traveled roads, in all residential communi-

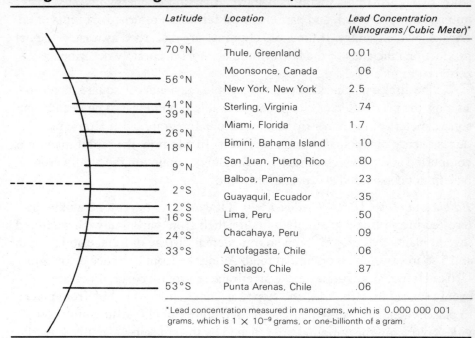

Table 14-4. **Lead Concentrations in Surface Air from Sites along the 80th Longitudinal Meridian, 1967**[*]

Latitude	Location	Lead Concentration (Nanograms/Cubic Meter)[*]
70°N	Thule, Greenland	0.01
56°N	Moonsonce, Canada	.06
	New York, New York	2.5
41°N 39°N	Sterling, Virginia	.74
26°N	Miami, Florida	1.7
18°N	Bimini, Bahama Island	.10
9°N	San Juan, Puerto Rico	.80
2°S	Balboa, Panama	.23
	Guayaquil, Ecuador	.35
12°S 16°S	Lima, Peru	.50
24°S	Chacahaya, Peru	.09
33°S	Antofagasta, Chile	.06
	Santiago, Chile	.87
53°S	Punta Arenas, Chile	.06

[*]Lead concentration measured in nanograms, which is 0.000 000 001 grams, which is 1×10^{-9} grams, or one-billionth of a gram.

This table illustrates the worldwide distribution of average levels of lead in surface air along the eightieth longitude meridian. The different cities which lie on the meridian are indicated. Notice that the whole world has considerable levels of lead, while highly industrialized and metropolitan cities such as New York, Miami, and Santiago have particularly high levels.

Source: Lovering, *Lead in the Environment.*

Figure 14-3. **Lead Emissions in the US, 1968**[*]

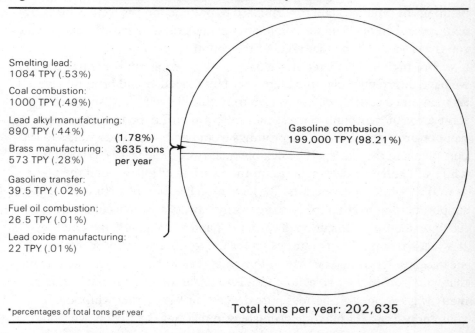

Smelting lead: 1084 TPY (.53%)

Coal combustion: 1000 TPY (.49%)

Lead alkyl manufacturing: 890 TPY (.44%)

Brass manufacturing: 573 TPY (.28%)

Gasoline transfer: 39.5 TPY (.02%)

Fuel oil combustion: 26.5 TPY (.01%)

Lead oxide manufacturing: 22 TPY (.01%)

(1.78%) 3635 tons per year

Gasoline combusion 199,000 TPY (98.21%)

[*]percentages of total tons per year

Total tons per year: 202,635

Source: Lovering, *Lead in the Environment.*

ties where geography and weather combine to create frequent temperature inversions that trap a layer of polluted air over the entire area, and in residential areas in the path of prevailing winds that carry contaminants from industrial developments. Logically, we could have considered this subject at any point in this book where food-raising outdoors was discussed. However, because the source of much of this pollution is the gasoline engine of the automobile, and the common urban pattern is for houses to front upon the street, we decided to discuss this problem along with considerations on the

Figure 14-4. **Lead Concentration of Chard from Vegetable Gardens in Berkeley, California, 1976**

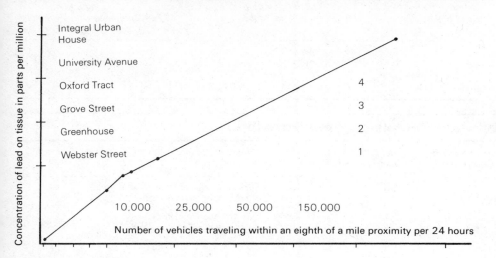

Location in Berkeley, California	Amounts of lead on plant tissue in parts per million (chard)	Concentration of traffic within eighth-mile proximity/24 hours
Webster St. near Claremont Ave.	.22	2,000
Greenhouse. Ellsworth St. near Dwight Way.	.48	7,000
Grove St.	.63	15,000
Oxford Tract. Virginia St. near Oxford.	.71	16,000
University Ave. University Ave. near Sacramento	1.14	32,000
Integral Urban House. 5th St. near Cedar (5 blocks from freeway).	3.57	139,000

Table 14-5. **Average Lead Content of Gasoline, 70–71**

	Grams per Gallon	
	1970	1971
Regular gasoline	2.43	2.22
Premium gasoline	2.81	2.67
Low-lead and no-lead gasoline	———	0.75

In filtered cigarettes, 24.1 ppm of lead has been reported. Smokers inhale 1.0 to 3.3 μg of lead per cigarette or 20 to 66 μg per pack. This lead in tobacco is believed to have originated with lead arsenate sprays used years before against insect pests.

Source: Waldbitt, *Health Effects of Environmental Pollutants.*

Source: Student Research Report, Department of Conservation of Natural Resources, University of California, Berkeley.

use of the front yard for food production.

Unquestionably, the combustion of leaded gas in automobile engines is the most important source of lead pollution in urban areas (see Figure 14-3). The average car, burning leaded gasoline, emits 5 pounds of lead into the air for every 30,000 miles traveled, or an average of 50 milligrams of lead per minute of traveling time. Approximately 180,000 tons of lead are poured into the air each day in the United States from autos, trucks, and buses. Throughout a city such as Cincinnati, this may mean 4101 pounds (1860 kilograms) of lead per day from gasoline—that is, 1.6 micrograms of lead for each cubic meter of air inhaled. Table 14-5 indicates the amount of lead per gallon of gas consumed. Knowing the gallons of gas used per mile, you can calculate the amount of lead contributed for each trip.

Lead is poisonous to humans and a problem in many living systems. In a student research project, samples of unwashed chard leaves from different areas in the city of Berkeley were tested for lead and correlated with traffic on neighboring streets (see Figure 14-4). Since the Integral Urban House is

Table 14-6. **Lead Content of Ashed Vegetables Collected near Roads**

Distance from Road (Feet)	Lead Content in (Parts per Million)	Percent Reduction, Compared with Vegetables Grown at Road's Edge
1–25	80	——
25–50	66	18
50–500	45	44
more than 500	20	75

Source: Lovering, *Lead in the Environment.*

Table 14-7. **Effects of Lead and Other Metals on Plant Growth**

Plant	Solution pH	Metal Contents at Harvest (Ppm, Dry Weight)*	Height at Harvest Inches	Cm	Effects of Metal on Growth
Sweetpea	7.6	8200	60	152	Thin vines, no chlorosis, brittle roots,
	5.8	11	41	104	healthy, slightly chlorotic
Tomato	7.6	1500	31	79	Healthy, buds still developing,
	5.8	130	14	36	healthy, white tips on leaves
Bluegrass	7.6	2400	14–24	36–60	80% alive, still growing dk-blue-green smooth leaves
	5.8	2400	10–15	25–38	95% alive; still growing dk-blue-green rough leaves
Violet	7.6	430	7.5	19	Dark green, glossy; healthier than
	5.8	12	6	15	control plant; seed pods developed dark-green leaves

Note: The plants were grown in artificial medium—vermiculite, which contained 25 parts per million lead. Control plants were germinated and grown in a nutrient solution at pH 7.6; their lead contents in the dry weight at harvest were as follows: sweetpea, 18 ppm; tomato, 18 ppm; bluegrass, 33 ppm; violet, 13 ppm.

*Note that remarkably high levels of lead uptake result from growing in materials lacking in soil humus. 25 ppm of lead is not very high for urban soils.
Source: Lovering, *Lead in the Environment.*

only six blocks from the freeway, not surprisingly the garden suffered the highest level of lead contamination.

However, other factors besides the proximity of the freeway may account for high levels of lead found on the vegetables at the Berkeley Integral Urban House. The house is located in a mixed industrial-residential neighborhood and is bordered by a paint factory, galvanizing plant, tannery, two trucking companies, a ceramic factory, welding shops, an ink factory, and two sand-and-gravel works. All these plants are polluting the area heavily with by-products of vehicle traffic and industrial processes. In contrast, the vegetables with the least lead in this analysis were grown in the backyard of an upper-middle-class, exclusively residential area from which through traffic has been diverted.

Table 14-6 shows how the amount of lead on vegetables decreases with the distance from roads. Table 14-7 shows how the amount that plants take up from an artificial growing medium varies with the acidity (pH) of the medium and the variety of plant. The appearance of the symptoms of lead contamination also varies with different kinds of plants. Another factor, not mentioned on this table, is the influence of organic matter in the soil. High concentrations of organic matter bind heavy metals, preventing them from entering food chains—another good reason for using a substantial amount of compost in the garden. Although this study shows that plants can take up lead through their roots, additional work is needed to relate this effort to different soil types and conditions.

Do the data cited here mean that one shouldn't grow food in urban areas? The fact is, if growing vegetables in this area is too dangerous, living

Figure 14-5. **A Model of Major Lead Pathways in the Environment**

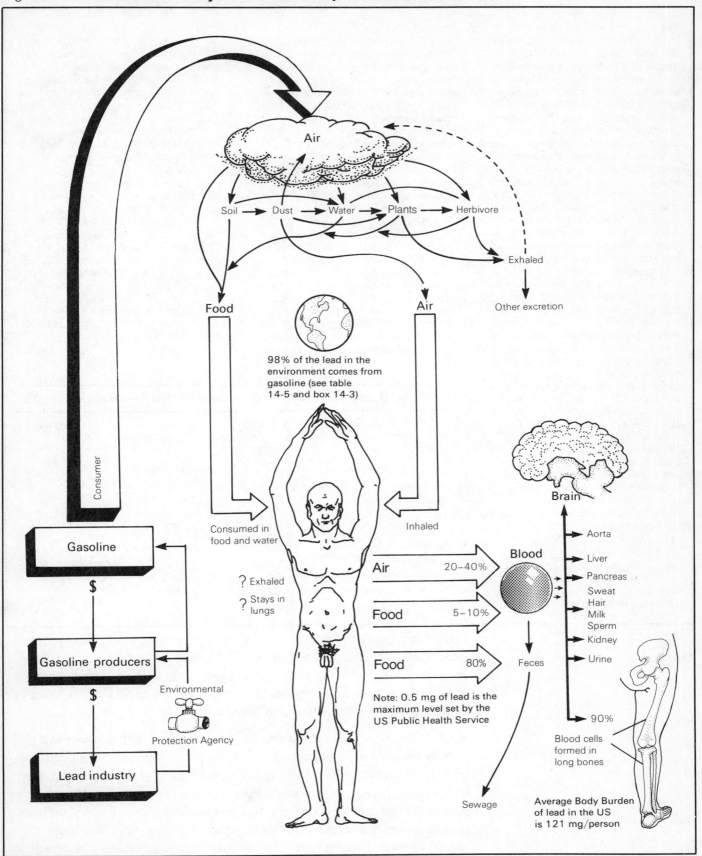

Box 14-3. **Lead in the Human Body**

The average total daily uptake of lead for humans is estimated to be 300 micrograms per day, 20 micrograms of which comes from water and beverages. Using a 10 percent absorption rate, about 30 micrograms per day finds its way into your bloodstream from this route. Background levels of lead in the food supply if humans had not contaminated the environment have been estimated at .01 microgram per gram of food. Presently, the level is .2 microgram per gram, or twenty times higher than this estimate. Of course, the actual amount of lead intake is a function of the source of the food and water and personal physical differences, so they can actually be much higher than this average amount.

Figure 14-5 in the text illustrates the major sources and routes of lead uptake of importance to urban food producers. This figure indicates that if equal amounts of lead occur in air and in or on food and water, the most important route into the body and subsequently the bloodstream is through the lungs. This has been shown to be the case in the study summarized in Table A. About 20 to 40 percent of inhaled lead is absorbed through the lungs, while 5 to 10 percent is absorbed through the gastrointestinal tract. The lung route is even more important if one realizes that there appears to be little way for most of the remaining lead not absorbed into the bloodstream to leave the lungs, while ingested lead is largely passed out in the feces.

Observed clinical symptoms of low-grade lead poisoning (anemia, intestinal cramps, neurological damage, hypertension) start to be observed at blood levels of 60 to 80

micrograms per 100 milliliters of blood, and health can be damaged at levels of 40 micrograms in children. Ten percent of the blood level samples in the 1- to 16-year-old groups tested in Los Angeles exceeded 40 micrograms per 100 milliliters, and some were up to 60 mcg/100 ml.

Absorption of lead through the gastrointestinal tract appears to be regulated to some extent by the same processes controlling calcium and phosphorus absorption. Some antagonism to lead uptake occurs in the alimentary canal when calcium is present. Thus it is important that urban diets be high in calcium, which is found in a number of foods and can also be taken as a supplement.

Once lead enters the bloodstream, it tends to accumulate in the bones. There it may affect the formation of blood cells. Over 90 percent of the human body burden (in the United States the average burden is 121 micrograms) occurs in the bones.

The tissues and organs that accumulate lead, in descending order, are the liver, kidney, pancreas, lungs, bone, spleen, testes, heart, and brain. Many mysteries still remain concerning the entry of lead into the body, routes of dispersal in the body, and excretion levels. Lead poisoning, which often goes undetected, may result in mental retardation in children, early aging, kidney damage, and hypertension.

A laboratory that uses atomic absorption spectroscopy to detect lead does tissue analysis for the general public. (See Harrison and Win, "Determination of Trace Elements in Human Hair by Atomic Absorption Spectroscopy.") If you would like an analysis of your hair (which is the tissue most easily sampled and tested) and want to learn more about the testing procedure, write to Dr. G.G. Gordon, P.O. Box 187, Hayward, California 94543.

Table A. **Body Burden Lead Levels in the 1–16 Age Group**

Measurement	Sex	Los Angeles	Lancaster	L.A./Lancaster ratio
Blood lead	M	24	11	2.2
(μg Pb/100 ml)	F	17	10	1.7
Lead in hair	M	107	17	6.3
(short scalp hair)	F	70	12	5.8
Urine lead	M	18	10	1.8
(μg Pb/liter)	F	16	14	1.1
Fecal lead	M	1.7	1.4	1.2
(μg Pb/gram)	F	1.1	1.6	0.7

Note: Lancaster, California is a rural desert town in contrast to Los Angeles, which is a large metropolis. The average air lead levels in Los Angeles is 6.3 micrograms per cubic meter (μg/m³) while, in Lancaster, it is 0.6 μg/m³). Soil lead levels are 30 times higher in L.A.

Source: Council on Environmental Quality, 7th Annual Report.

here might just be too dangerous also. Most of the lead your body accumulates is taken in through your lungs, as Figure 14-5 shows. The vegetables are in the air for only a few months, but you are growing and living in it season after season. If it is too dangerous to raise vegetables in your front yard, it might be too dangerous to breathe there too.

What to Do About Lead Pollution: What should you do if you live in a heavily polluted environment? The following are some general guidelines:

1. If your street is heavily traveled, don't raise vegetables out in front of the house if you can find another place to raise them. Obviously, the same advice goes for side or back yards that lie along busy streets. Do plant high hedges to trap heavy lead particles in the air. Whenever possible these should be placed between the street and the garden or wherever they will

slow down winds blowing from lead-emitting sources.

2. Incorporate plenty of organic matter in the soil to bind lead and other heavy metals there so that they will not be taken up by plants.

3. Wash vegetables grown in gardens near busy streets very carefully. The studies of University of California students determined that 20 to 80 percent of the lead was removed by washing. A touch of vinegar in the wash water is helpful for rinsing off the lead. Any vegetable that has been protected by an outer covering (peas in a pod, corn on the cob, the inner leaves of cabbage, and so on) is less likely to have picked up lead fallout from the air. Exposed vegetables from areas known to be contaminated should be peeled or thoroughly washed before eating.

Box 14-3 describes the effects of lead on the human body. If you are concerned about yourself and your children becoming poisoned by the lead in the air where you live, either stop breathing or start working actively to get the lead out of gasoline. Of course, such efforts will take you out of your integral urban house and into the larger community.

15. THE INTEGRAL URBAN NEIGHBORHOOD

The logical extension of the integral urban house idea is the integral urban neighborhood, which itself leads to the development of communitywide or municipal-scale programs of resource management and local self-reliance. True, it is important to test and perfect the idea on the scale of a single household. But once the technologies have been proven, they ought to be advanced on the neighborhood level and ultimately on the citywide level. The idea of establishing integral urban neighborhoods is not particularly unique. Both private and nonprofit organizations as well as state and federal agencies are exploring the potential for implementing appropriate technologies on the community level. For example, in the Bronx, in New York City, a neighborhood community development association is rehabilitating condemned tenements and installing solar and wind energy facilities. And in Oakland, California, neighborhood community centers are teaming up with governmental agencies in establishing a citywide ecosystem-management program that proposes to integrate programs in waste recycling, community food raising, and housing rehabilitation, the overall goal being improvement of the urban environment and creation of jobs in new businesses for the unemployed.

Just as the home can be interpreted as an ecosystem, so may a neighborhood. Basic life-supporting processes in which resources are consumed and wastes are produced prevail on both scales. As with the individual integral home, the objective of the integral neighborhood is to provide for a high quality of human existence with minimal destruction to the environment. The advantages of a community-scale resource-management project are many. First, several homes and lots taken collectively will yield a high degree of complementarity and diversity unlikely on the individual home basis. One home's yard may be well suited for extensive garden activity, while another, because of shading of trees and adjacent buildings, may be best suited for composting and animal raising. Second, the element of economy of scale becomes apparent when the retrofit of an entire neighborhood of homes is undertaken. Construction materials may be purchased in sufficient quantities to dramatically reduce unit costs. Construction time for the simultaneous fabrication of three or four solar water heating systems in all probability will not be three or four times as long as for just one. Third, the maintenance of life-support systems may be shared by several families, thus freeing the individuals involved for the imposing responsibility of daily care. This is particularly important in reference to the raising of livestock, the watering of a garden, or the maintenance of a sanitary composting system.

An integral urban neighborhood, as we envision it, would have several components of a comprehensive program of sound resource management: housing weatherization and solarization, community food raising, environmental landscaping, waste recycling, and ecological pest management. The following list presents an idea of the scope of possibilities:

1. Housing weatherization and solarization: weatherstripping of windows and doors of the homes, insulation of ceiling and walls, increase of solar gain through skylights and south glass, attached greenhouses to south sides of buildings, installation of solar water and space heating systems, and use of wind power where appropriate.

2. Community food raising: jointly maintained vegetable garden, animal raising facilities, and fruit orchards.

3. Environmental landscaping: planting of deciduous vegetation along the south-facing sides of homes; utilization of water-conserving mulches on all planted areas; cultivation of low water use and low-maintenance vegetation; minimal use of concrete, asphalt, and other impermeable surfaces for walking paths.

4. Waste recycling: community-scale composting projects for garden and household wastes, neighborhood recycling centers.

5. Ecological pest management: alternate approaches to pesticide use for the control of indoor/greenhouse and garden pests. The professional phrase for this type of pest control is integrated pest management and is discussed in Chapter 13.

The integral urban neighborhood concept has more than a technological character; it has a social character as well. A community garden links people not only to the soil, but to each other. A municipal composting program not only conserves valuable materials and makes good use of natural resources, but can create new jobs. A citywide program of home weatherization goes beyond the conservation of fuel and materials; it ultimately results in the saving of money.

The authors have had personal experience with three aspects of integral urban neighborhoods: community gardening, municipal composting, and recycling projects. In this final chapter we will report on our experiences in hopes that it will inspire you to go beyond the confines of your individual home and begin thinking about the next step.

Community Gardening

There are good reasons for establishing community gardens, in areas where the homes are provided with small backyards and, more importantly, where a predominance of apartment houses and other multiple-unit dwellings means many people have no access to outdoor growing space. Working collectively to raise food can make efficient use of tools, seed and water. It can also encourage positive neighborhood interactions in the development of currently unproductive urban open space. The urban community garden can provide a setting in which chronically underemployed groups in the urban society, youth and the elderly, are able to engage in work that enhances both personal and community self-reliance.

Much urban space that might be suitable for community gardening has been overlooked. Besides the obvious vacant lots and parks, there are vast stretches of ornamental lawns supported at great expense on the grounds of hospitals, public schools and colleges, and other municipal, county, and state institutions as well as privately owned, temporarily unused space. It may take two to three years to reclaim the soil in some of these latter spots, and permission to use the site might be granted for one season only, so starting a garden there would not be worthwhile. A three- to five-year agreement regarding use or sufficiently undisturbed soil to start with would make the situation more suitable for a large-scale effort.

The best place to begin looking for available land is your town's housing authority. It is likely that the city government owns small parcels of land that would be suitable for a community gardening effort. The city council or local board of supervisors should be petitioned for the use of public land. Rarely do available sites combine all of the ideal characteristics, but to aid in making a choice, the desirable qualities are listed in the margin.

Qualities to look for in urban sites:

1. Good exposure to sun
2. Access to water
3. Minimal exposure to heavy traffic (to reduce lead, noise, and other pollution)
4. Adequate fencing against potential damage from dogs and vandals, or the potential for being inclosed and/or protected
5. Minimal compaction of the soil
6. Minimal amount of trash (building debris, glass, and so on) mixed with the soil
7. Little or no competition with roots of trees or tall hedges
8. Accessible to a vehicle for hauling supplies such as compost material or lumber
9. Protection from wind, if necessary
10. Owner is supportive of program

Establishing the Garden: The first step after the site has been selected and permission has been obtained for its use is the development of some protection. Strong fencing is obviously the best, and certainly a must where stray dogs might dig up the seed beds or attack livestock. However, in some situations either the social climate of the neighborhood or the willingness of nearby residents to supervise the area could make fencing less essential. We stress this aspect because we have seen community garden attempts destroyed by low morale when produce is stolen or the garden damaged due to a lack of protection.

The second step is the establishment of a water line. The final details of the irrigation system within the plot itself may have to be worked out after the overall plan for the garden is developed. However, it is essential to make sure that sufficient water at adequate pressure is available to the site itself. Generally, a line pressure of at least 35 psi (pounds of pressure per square inch) is necessary for effective operation of overhead sprinklers, and 2 psi is sufficient for drip irrigation. If the plot is a large one, spigots may have to be established throughout the garden, since long hoses, which tend to damage plants as they are dragged to and fro, are best avoided. Ideally, no area should be more than twenty-five feet from a spigot.

People often wonder about the feasibility of digging a well so that the garden can have its own water supply, perhaps pumped from the ground with a windmill. Considerations in this regard are groundwater depth, water quality (proximity to sewage leaching fields could be important here), and the cost of pumps and well-digging operations. Water needs vary according to air temperatures, wind, soil type, and plants grown (as well as the techniques for growing them, as described in Chapter 8), but if rain does not contribute substantially to garden watering you may need to plan on pumping in approximately 200 gallons of irrigation water per week for every 300 square feet of garden space. If the community garden is composed of 50 300-square-foot plots (each 15 × 20 feet) then an average of 220,000 gallons of water would be required for a 5-month growing season from April through September. Analyze the situation. If the water table is shallow and easily tapped, and the cost of city water is high enough to justify the expense of a well and pump, then a well may be appropriate. Wells become increasingly attractive during periods of acute water shortages when consumption is rationed.

Unquestionably, community gardeners may be tempted to overwater, since individual water use is generally not monitored. The only solution is to encourage conservation techniques by demonstration as well as verbal reminders through whatever type of meeting or media is used to communicate among the participants. In a university-sponsored vegetable garden for married students on the University of California at Berkeley campus a number of years ago, the entire plot was laid out in furrows following the standard agricultural model for this part of California. The garden was then irrigated by university maintenance people on a regular weekly schedule. There are many good reasons for irrigating in this way. Vegetable plants differ in their water requirements, and rarely is one watering schedule suitable for every type of plant. Under the U.C. system, many plants received more water than they needed. Furthermore, the plowing of furrows imposed an arbitrary pattern upon the individual planting schemes, wasted good growing space, and destroyed efforts to mulch, plant intensively, and use other good water-conservation and gardening strategies. It also inadvertently taught people an inefficient gardening style. Regardless, however, we were sad to see this project ended.

Individual Versus Cooperative Efforts: A fundamental decision has to be made in the initial planning of the garden: will the land be divided into parcels and distributed to individuals and/or families or will the entire lot be maintained cooperatively? There are advantages and disadvantages to both schemes, and ultimately the choice will be made according to the people involved in each garden, their perception of their individual vs. community needs, the degree of mutual trust they enjoy, and their overall primary objectives in becoming involved in the project.

Gardens encouraged by public institutions will doubtless favor individual plots, since this approach is generally the more familiar (and less threatening) one. As a legacy of the civil rights and anti-Vietnam War movements and as a relative of the gradually evolving anti-nuclear movement, a group that comes together to deal with the problems of increasing neighborhood self-reliance stands a good chance of sharing other common goals that can form the basis for political action by its members. It doesn't take long for members to compare notes and perceive the need to tackle many supposedly individual or neighborhood problems at the higher levels of government and big business where the power ultimately lies. Therefore, it is our

Figure 15-1. **Cleminatina Towers Community Garden in San Francisco**

The garden is maintained by the residents of an adjacent apartment house complex. The garden had been in existence for five years.

assumption that the cooperative approach will rarely be initiated or encouraged by a sponsoring organization outside the neighborhood. Any impetus in the direction of cooperative gardening styles would have to come from within the community itself.

The advantages of the individual-parcel approach are that it permits participants a great deal of choice as to gardening styles and varieties of vegetables grown without their having to appeal to a committee or a manager for a decision. It solves the problem of food distribution, since people take only what they can grow personally, and sometimes a competitive spirit may arise, encouraging optimum productivity from each plot. In any case, people tend to be reasonably responsible toward the upkeep of an area they feel is their own, if only for a season.

The disadvantages of the individual style are primarily those of duplication of effort and materials. Resources may be used less wisely. Food, and even land, may be wasted. Everyone buys his own tools but uses them only a fraction of the time. It is more difficult for the group to acquire and disseminate information about new and superior gardening techniques, or of insect management that reduces pesticide use, for example. Most important, the participants feel less of a sense of community and the garden is harder to use as a stepping stone towards addressing other neighborhood issues of energy and resource use and undertaking specific activities for local improvement.

The disadvantages to cooperative gardens are inherent in a society that stresses the individual in an "every man for himself" sense. Resolving such conflicts as distrust of others—particularly over issues of equitable division of labor and produce—disputes over techniques to be used and similar issues can be time-consuming without working models for cooperative action. The successful gardens we are personally familiar with in which everyone works together are usually run along rather authoritarian lines. Participants often become like students in a class or the followers of a garden guru who holds power through a mixture of personal charisma and the infusion of mystical dogma into horticultural expertise. Still, we would like to believe that the hierarchal absolutism common to both universities and religious cults is not essential to the success of a neighborhood garden that is farmed cooperatively. Certainly, the benefits in efficiency of land and resource use and the sense of community self-reliance and realignment of local power would seem to be worth the effort.

Components of the System: Regardless of whether other nonvegetable components such as rabbits, chickens, bees, and the like are introduced into the community garden, some sort of waste-management system will need to be devised to provide compost. In some cases, for example, the San Francisco Community Gardens, compost of plant debris or from manure of municipally maintained horse stables may be brought to the gardens from a central point where it has been produced. Often it is desirable to have compost made on the site. The bin system described earlier can be used very satisfactorily on sites up to a certain size. Five compost bins serviced a collectively run University student garden we developed in which thirty-five students were involved on a rotating basis. The planting area was approximately 150 feet by 200 feet (but a considerable area was given over to footpaths and meeting areas because of the heavy traffic within the garden). But if the garden becomes too large, processing all the waste materials through a bin system may be difficult. Still, this may be a matter of who is managing the system. Several years ago, one of us (Javits), using only three bins for an entire twelve-month period, composted the entire daily food wastes of 150 people living in three housing cooperatives, and we understand that the system is still being maintained at the time of this writing. In this event, a windrow system may be used as described in the next section on municipal or large-scale composting.

Other useful additions to a community garden are lockable tool sheds,

1. Program justifications including (a) a solution, in part, to the city's waste-management problems; (b) an environmentally sound management strategy; (c) economic feasibility, in terms of reduced need for land-filling or incineration, and savings on water and herbicides (as a result of using the finished compost as mulch)

2. A site plan and description of operating procedure

3. A proposed budget, including costs and anticipated income derived from dumping charges and sale of finished compost

4. An environmental impact assessment procedure

5. A method for evaluating the project after a year of operation

Windrows are aerated and repositioned by an equipment operator at the City of Berkeley Municipal Composting Site.

protected bulletin boards for communications, shaded benches on which the elderly (and everyone else) may relax, sandboxes or other recreational provisions to occupy very young children, and a solar-heated greenhouse for starting young seedlings early in the season, as described in Chapter 9.

The Department of the Interior, Bureau of Outdoor Recreation, has shown an interest in community gardens, and has been active in accumulating information about those already in existence. Doubtless, many states will become involved in setting up community garden coordinators. The responsibilities of the person holding this post in California (within the state's Office of Appropriate Technology) is to "assist communities throughout the state in obtaining land, funding, equipment and technical assistance necessary to establishing community-tended vegetable gardens."

Municipal Composting: There are many reasons why a community might decide to establish a municipal or large-scale composting system. Not everyone has sufficient space, time, or interest in maintaining a home composting operation. Furthermore, some types of plant debris, particularly tree trimmings and heavy brush, are too difficult to compost using a bin system, because of either size or coarseness. The large machinery needed to deal with such materials is only cost- and energy-effective on a municipal scale. Also, a city-operated composting program can recycle a large mix of materials generated by the municipal agencies such as the parks and recreation de-

Figure 15-2. Windrows of Decomposing Plant Debris

partments, as well as by large landowners, landscape contractors, and tree pruners. Municipal sewage sludge, assuming that it is not too high in heavy metals, can be mixed with the plant debris. The finished compost can be made available to city gardeners and to individual citizens.

We like to refer to these municipal composting systems as leaf banks to impress upon people that the materials are precious, a resource to be conserved. The materials are deposited in the bank as plant debris and then withdrawn as compost. We know of a local example of a leaf bank (in the city of Piedmont, California) where in fact only leaves are used. They are deposited there by the municipal tree crews and then after a year's slow composting in the piles where they were dumped, the leaf-mold is availabale free to citizens. However, a greater range of plant debris saved in the leaf bank is more desirable, and this requires some sorting and processing.

Preparing to Establish a Leaf Bank: The first step in bringing a composting program to your city is to establish a citizens' advisory committee that can assess the present state of affairs and prepare a proposal to be submitted to the city council or other appropriate decision-making body. This committee should evaluate the existing methods of handling plant debris to determine if an alternative is indeed necessary. If it decides that a leaf bank composting system is desirable, the next step is to determine the characteristics of the plant wastes generated by citizens, municipal agencies, and private landscapers and gardeners.

Next, the cost of establishing and maintaining the system must be estimated. It is important that the projected costs be compared with those of the existing disposal methods for these materials. In many cases, plant debris is taken to a land-fill whose life expectancy can be predicted. The costs attendant on establishing a new disposal site when the current one is filled up may indeed justify the cost of establishing a compost site.

However, promoting municipal composting programs exclusively on the basis of the income they might generate in the selling of the end-product has proven to be a poor tactic. Rather, the positive impact these programs have on helping to alleviate solid waste disposal problems should be stressed. While it is true that revenue can be generated from the sale of the finished compost, the most important thing about a leaf bank system is that it is an alternative to existing methods of managing these wastes. People are already paying to get rid of these wastes without expecting a useful product to be ultimately returned to them. So a composting program designed to break even or be subsidized, in view of the potential benefits, is a highly desirable method of waste reclamation. Certainly, the system should not be expected to generate income in addition to the good it does the community. Since abundant documentation exists on the problems and costs associated with "sanitary" land-fills as well as the benefits to be derived from compost (including savings in water, fertilizer, and cultivation labor costs when compost is used around trees and shrubs in parks and other municipally owned grounds), making a good case for the desirability of a composting project in your community should not be difficult. Still, in cases where the cost of the new system is much greater than the present one—all current costs considered, including purchase of soil amendment and mulch by the city—then you may need to explore potential markets for the finished product (see Box 15-1).

After assessing the need and analyzing the costs, the next step is preparing a proposal. It should include the items listed in the margin.

Site Layout: A site layout should include accommodations for a project office, a place to receive and inspect incoming plant debris, an area sufficiently large to store two week's worth of material received, a place for storage of shredding and other equipment, an asphalted or cement pad for placement of the compost windrows, and an area for curing the compost and distributing it to citizens.

Operating Procedure: The Berkeley Composting System: An operating procedure must be developed for the various management tasks necessary to complete the composting process. The tasks involved are receiving and storing the material, and shredding, composting, and distributing it. The system has to be monitored for objectionable odors, fly-breeding, and the harboring of rats. In cases where the composting system will be maintained by city personnel, a substantial program of education and training in how to manage such a system may be required. We use the program in Berkeley, in which one of us (Javits) has been involved as a technical consultant, as an example of how the process might be organized.

Berkeley's composting program processes plant debris, leaves and weeds, tree trimmings, and brush generated by city agencies, landscape contractors, professional gardeners, and private citizens. No attempt is made to compost household wastes such as kitchen garbage. Although the program is selective and therefore not comprehensive, this factor does simplify operational and maintenance procedures and minimizes potential fly production and generation of odors. An average of 100 to 150 cubic yards of material is delivered daily to the 80,000-square-foot facility located adjacent to the city's land-fill operation. A 50-cent tariff is charged for each cubic yard delivered. This revenue is used to help offset the program's operational costs.

Box 15-1. **The Boundary Problem**

A central concept used in changing social institutions is the necessity to draw the boundary around enough of a system to insure that the problem can feasibly be solved within it. Two of us (the Olkowskis) learned this technique initially in the process of developing municipal pest-management programs designed to reduce pesticide use. As long as the vegetation-management people focused only on the bug and the plant the problem often seemed unsolvable without synthetic chemical tools. The point was to enlarge the boundary to include these factors: natural enemies of the pest insects; fertilizing, watering, and other techniques; other species of plants and their management; the union's concern for

safer working conditions; citizens' efforts to reduce medical expenses resulting from ailments caused by toxic materials in the environment. When these factors were identified as part of the pest-management system, many new management strategies as well as sociopolitical goals made possible solutions that were not previously obvious.

An exact parallel exists with regard to the establishment of leaf bank compost systems. If only the cost of machinery and labor to process the materials are considered, the cost may be prohibitive. But if the boundary is drawn large enough to include the cost of present waste-management and city-owned vegetation-maintenance programs, the need for

jobs in the community, and the value of the end-product to the citizens, then all the dynamics of the situation are changed, costs and benefits may be assessed differently, and the problems inherent in establishing the program are more likely to be seen as solvable. As in all such situations, educating the politicians, general public, and municipal staff, if they are to be involved, is absolutely essential. It is a tenet of our personal belief system that most people will modify their views and behavior and accept and be willing to financially support new systems when they understand that the change is truly in their own interest.

Customers receive a voucher that entitles them to one cubic foot of finished compost in return for each cubic yard of fresh material delivered.

The incoming material is heterogeneous, varying in particle size, moisture level, and carbon-to-nitrogen ratio. The site attendant carefully inspects each incoming load, determines its best use, and directs the customer to a particular place on the pad for dumping. Large branches and tree trunks are removed from the piles of received material, sawed into logs, and sold to the public for firewood. Clean sawdust from local lumber yards and cabinet shops is stockpiled and made available to people who want uncomposted material for their own compost or absorbent litter in their animal pens. Clean wood chips delivered to the site from tree-pruning contractors and the municipal public works department are also stockpiled for use by the public or by some other city agency as mulch. Weeds, grass clippings, brush and leaves, and tree trimmings having a diameter of two inches or less are ground to uniform particle size.

The most critical part of the entire composting process is the shredding of the mixed plant debris. Shredding increases the surface area of the coarse material and therefore hastens the decomposition process, reduces volume, improves water and heat retention of the compost windrows, makes handling of the material by heavy equipment easier, and produces a more attractive product. Although the most vital element in the process, shredding is also the least refined. It was difficult to find grinding equipment designed to effectively shred mixed plant debris to the size and at the speed required and at the cost the city could afford. Machines in the right price range with an adequate grinding rate of thirty to fifty cubic yards per hour have been developed to shred homogeneous material such as hay or paper, but these were found to be unsuitable for mixed plant debris. Berkeley, with the aid of State of California funds, finally purchased a Farmhand Tub Grinder. This is a heavy-duty piece of machinery boasting a massive hammer mill. However, in its original form the grinder could not handle material with mixed particle size, moisture content, and texture. City engineers and technicians have modified the machine's grinding mechanism so that it can satisfactorily process up to forty yards of debris per hour, which is the rate required for operation of the project.

A front-loader tractor equipped with a two-yard bucket and grapple hook is used to load plant debris into the hopper of the tub grinder. The material is ground to a 1.5-inch particulate size and then assembled in a windrow (extended pile) with a basal width of 16 feet, height of 8 feet, and length between 40 and 80 feet. Since compaction and shredding reduces the volume of the material by 300 to 500 percent, a 175-cubic yard windrow accommodates five days worth of receipts (500 to 750 cubic yards). The windrows are oriented parallel to each other and at a distance from one another of forty feet from center to center. See Figure 15-3.

Composting: Immediately following assembly and placement of a windrow on the asphalt pad, the surface of the material is moistened with a 6-inch layer of water. A windrow with a surface area of 960 square feet requires 3600 gallons of water (the amount is reduced during the rainy season). An

The volume of a windrow can be computed by the formula:

.625 × height × basal width × length

Therefore, a windrow having a height of 8 feet, basal width of 16 feet, length of 75 feet has an estimated volume of 4,800 cubic feet, or 175 cubic yards.

Figure 15-3. **Layout for Berkeley Municipal Composting Program**

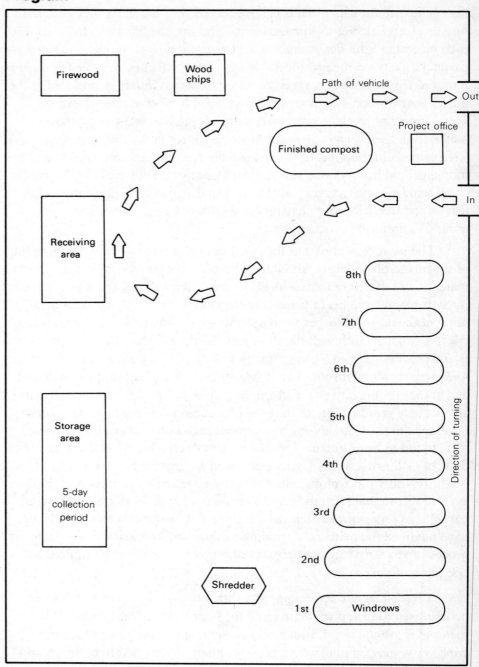

Each successive windrow is smaller due to loss of mass during decomposition.

additional 1800 gallons of water is applied to the windrow each of the first five times it is advanced on the pad. The moisture content of the compost is regularly tested, and sprinkling rates are adjusted to maintain a moisture level of 50 to 60 percent. Each cubic yard of shredded plant debris requires about 75 gallons of water throughout the composting process, and this must be supplied by the program unless, of course, it rains. Rainbird sprinklers were installed to water the compost.

The windrows are turned and advanced on the pad whenever a fresh windrow is prepared, usually every five days. The pad accommodates eight

Figure 15-4. **Operational Cycle of Berkeley Composting Program**

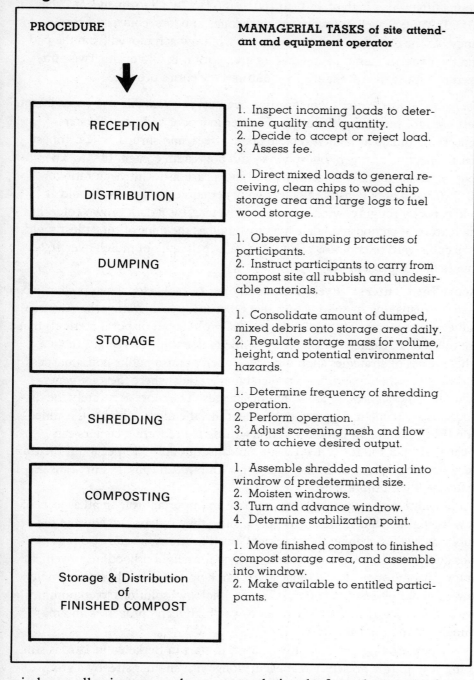

PROCEDURE	MANAGERIAL TASKS of site attendant and equipment operator
RECEPTION	1. Inspect incoming loads to determine quality and quantity. 2. Decide to accept or reject load. 3. Assess fee.
DISTRIBUTION	1. Direct mixed loads to general receiving, clean chips to wood chip storage area and large logs to fuel wood storage.
DUMPING	1. Observe dumping practices of participants. 2. Instruct participants to carry from compost site all rubbish and undesirable materials.
STORAGE	1. Consolidate amount of dumped, mixed debris onto storage area daily. 2. Regulate storage mass for volume, height, and potential environmental hazards.
SHREDDING	1. Determine frequency of shredding operation. 2. Perform operation. 3. Adjust screening mesh and flow rate to achieve desired output.
COMPOSTING	1. Assemble shredded material into windrow of predetermined size. 2. Moisten windrows. 3. Turn and advance windrow. 4. Determine stabilization point.
Storage & Distribution of FINISHED COMPOST	1. Move finished compost to finished compost storage area, and assemble into windrow. 2. Make available to entitled participants.

windrows, allowing seven advancements during the forty-day composting period. The front loader advances the windrow by pushing the material from one position to another. The equipment operator carefully mixes the windrow as it is advanced so that materials that were on the cooler outside of the windrow in its former position are incorporated into the hot center of the reconstituted windrow. The heat of decomposition insures that weed seeds, plant diseases, and fly eggs or larvae are destroyed. When the windrow reaches the last position on the pad it has completed the most intensive part of the composting cycle.

The site operators can determine whether the windrow has stabilized (finished decomposing) by checking its temperature (it will have dropped from a fifteen-day high of 150° to 160°F [66° to 78°C] to an end-of-cycle 90°F [32°C]) as well as by observing changes in odors, color, and consistency. At the completion of the cycle the windrow is removed from the pad and the material stored in an adjacent area until it is sold or otherwise utilized by city agencies. Figure 15-4 outlines the entire process.

Compost Characteristics: The finished compost is a valuable soil amendment, best used for increasing the organic matter in a poor soil or as a water-conserving mulch around vegetable plants, trees, and shrubs. The compost has a collective nitrogen, phosphorus, and potassium content of 2 to 3 percent, a good balance of trace elements, and a carbon-to-nitrogen ratio of 30:1. It has a bulk density of 600 pounds per cubic yard and will hold at field capacity roughly twice its weight in water. It is a dark brown color, has the texture of composted horse manure, and has the odor of forest leaf mold. One cubic yard of compost will provide a 2-inch layer of mulch over 162-square feet of garden.

Recycling Centers: Every community needs to develop a comprehensive plan for managing its solid wastes that takes into consideration the resource value of these materials. A plan to gradually phase out disposal methods that are relics of an earlier "throw-away" ethic is essential. To replace them a whole series of strategies should be developed to raise public consciousness and facilitate the separation of recyclable materials where they are generated: in homes, stores, schools, and businesses. The more accurately the distinctions are made in separating the materials, the more valuable the collection. For example, in Berkeley at this writing the recycling centers can receive $30 per ton for collections of tin cans, but only $15 per ton if the tin ones are mixed together in the same bin with bimetal cans. ("Tin" cans are really steel with tin linings.)

Community recycle centers can play an important role in all aspects of developing such a comprehensive plan, since they function to educate the public as well as channel the material flow. These centers can also provide jobs and youth training and act as a catalyst for neighborhood improvement in low-income areas. Recycling centers can help people understand simple low-capital, low-energy, "appropriate-technology" solutions to community problems as contrasted with the expensive "high tech" processes and machinery often urged at City Hall.

The recycling center that we helped to start in Berkeley in 1970 is still going strong. It is presently managed, along with another site, by a group calling itself the Community Conservation Center (see Figure 15-5). The two sites recycle an average of 2000 tons of reusable waste per year. Their bright blue and white posters suggest the outline of the San Francisco Bay, and are intended to remind citizens that materials that are recycled do not end up in the dumps which fill the Bay.

Personnel are paid to do the work of the center: supervising the use by the public, maintaining the site, storing the materials collected, keeping records, and so on. The organization has slowly managed to inch salaries upwards as the prices they receive for materials gradually rise. However, along

The legend on the posters gives the locations and hours as well as a list of the materials accepted for recycling:

Glass: separated by color; no metal neckrings or caps

Cans: aluminum, crushed; tin (actually steel cans with tin linings), flattened; bimetal, smashed

Paper: newspaper, tied in six-inch bundles; cardboard, unwaxed and flattened

Bottles: California wine bottles —fifths (all shapes), half-gallons, gallons (these are sterilized by a local group called "Encore!" and reused by local wineries)

Figure 15-5. **A Community Recycling Center in the City of Berkeley**

Maintained by the community Conservation Center.

with the rise in value of some of the secondary materials has come increased pilfering from the sites, and staff have had to guard their stored materials more vigilantly. (Prices paid for old newspapers nearly doubled in a few months during the fall of 1978, for example.) The City of Berkeley contributes some truck drivers from the Department of Public Works as well as truck rentals and maintenance for a total of just slightly less than the center's total budget.

Two of the center's on-going problems are occasional vandalism and the general untidiness of the sites. However, the personnel feel that the extreme accessibility of the centers encourages greater citizen participation than would occur if the center were in a more protected and less obvious site in the industrial area.

It is particularly worth noticing that in addition to taking glass of various colors (this is sorted into separate bins of brown, white, and green at the center itself), wine bottles are cleaned and reused as they are. The basic rationale is that high-quality products should be used as long as possible. We mentioned this idea earlier in connection with the concept of recycling paper, but glass bottles offer a particularly good and obvious opportunity for reuse. At present most glass containers are thrown away after being used once. A tremendous amount of materials, energy, and labor has been in-

Box 15-2. **The Oregon Bottle Bill**

The Oregon Bottle Bill was the first legislative effort in the United States to attempt to encourage the reuse of glass, plastic, and metal containers. The law requires that the refund value be embossed on each container, that certain containers be banned (those with detachable metal pop-tops), and that redemption centers be established to receive reusable containers.

The bottle bill works in Oregon! The evidence that it is valid and effective is overwhelming. Rumors and misinformation circulated by opponents continue, however. The facts, in contrast to the objections raised against the bill, follow:

1. Beverages in returnable containers cost less. Post-bottle-bill price increases were due to increases in sugar prices.

2. Sales have not fallen, but have increased.

3. Overall employment has increased (by 365 jobs), but some specific jobs have been eliminated.

4. A net savings of 1.4 trillion Btu per year has been documented. This is enough energy to heat the homes of 50,000 Oregonians for a year. Projected savings on a national level would save 70,000 to 80,000 barrels of oil *each day!*

5. Highway litter has been reduced. The number of containers entering the solid-waste stream has been reduced by 88 percent. Garbage reduction has been estimated at 7 to 10 percent.

6. The bill caused no increases in state or local government.

7. The bill was enthusiastically received by the public. Ninety percent of the population approve of the law, and 95 percent participated in its implementation. Oregon retailers and distributors have cooperated and supported the law, helping to make the transition smoother. The bill has enhanced community awareness and commitment to environmental concerns, facilitated recycling and resource recovery operations, and attracted public involvement in community air quality standards and the protection of open space.

To quote from the law itself, "The Bottle Bill gives some Americans a chance to demonstrate their real priorities: a good life and clean environment based not on consumerism but on conservation. The public does not demand a throw-away economy; it has merely responded to aggressive advertising and marketing techniques which promote waste of natural resources."

For further information about the bottle bill, write to the Oregon Department of Environmental Quality, Recycling Information Office, 1234 S.W. Morrison, Portland, Oregon, 97205, or call (503) 229-5119.

vested in their fabrication, distribution, and disposal.

Currently, "bottle bills"—which set prices for returnable containers and outlaw disposable ones—are being contemplated by various state legislatures as a way to reduce litter and to save energy. Industries that depend upon disposable containers are fighting these bottle bills at every turn. We believe that these laws will eventually become common and disposable bottles will become a thing of the past. The Oregon Bottle Bill is a model. It is a very successful piece of legislature now having a highly positive effect on energy savings, litter reduction, and jobs within that state (see Box 15-2).

A next step in the process of change would be to develop less destructible containers that would survive many uses without breaking. Such a product could be plastic (if the problem of plasticisers migrating into the contents could be avoided), metal, or glass of sufficient strength to be recleaned and reused without breaking. At present, the initial bottle bill in Oregon shows a recycling pattern of over twenty reuse cycles for a glass beverage container. Containers that theoretically never wear out would surely use up less energy in the society as a whole than replacing glass containers after twenty or more cycles. At this stage however, reusing glass containers is a step in the right direction.

The ultimate objective is to have a social policy requiring that material goods be designed to last as long as possible and made of substances that permit recycling when they can no longer be used in their original form. At least two highly cherished assumptions of our present society are challenged by this goal: the right to make objects that become obsolete or break down quickly so the consumer has to buy another, and the right to have an endless variety in the shapes of manufactured items (such as bottles) rather than a few standard sizes used over and over for everything.

Figure 15-6. **Summary of the Major Material Recycling Paths**

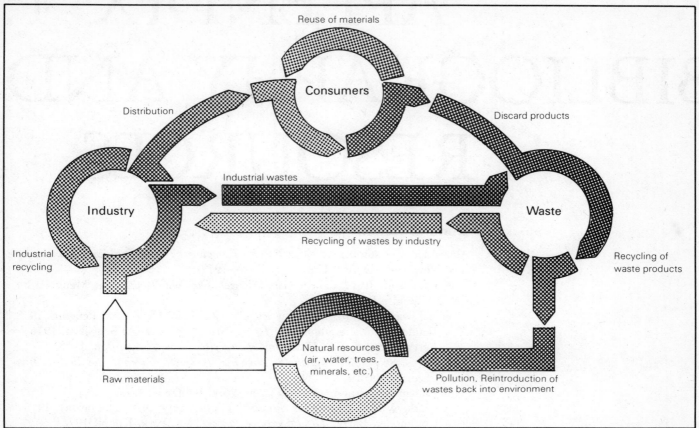

Figure 15-6 provides a model on which to construct the major recycling pathways for our society at some future time. The overall plan indicates that there are priority recycling paths, the use of which should be maximized before other paths are used. One of the most obvious examples would be the industrial recycle pathway (arrow 3). If this pathway were maximized, wastes would be recycled as close to the point of generation as possible. Waste paper from a paper mill recycled within the plant that generates the waste is such an example. This is already done to a fair degree within industry, but often only after vigorous prodding by some antipollution law. The homeowner's role here would be that of an intelligent consumer who purchases from industries that recycle and make durable items, or as a member of a particular industry who tries to encourage and develop recycling programs where none existed before.

The overall objective of organizing our social use of resources around maximum recycling is to reduce wastes and the costs now borne by society, which has to manage those wastes. Ultimately, by developing material-use systems that more closely emulate self-regenerating natural systems the society could begin to develop a steady-state economy—or a solar economy, if you will. The experiment surely seems worthwhile. If we wait longer, we may not have a choice.

Many other neighborhood or municipal projects will spring up in the future. We hope this book will stimulate people to think about the transformation of our destructive way of life.

APPENDIX 1: BIBLIOGRAPHY AND RESOURCES

General Readings

Alexander, Christopher, et al. *A Pattern Language: Towns, Buildings, Construction.* New York: Oxford University Press, 1977.

Anderson, Bruce, and Riordan, Michael. *The Solar Home Book.* Menlo Park, Calif.: Cheshire Books, 1976.

Baldwin, J., and Brand, Stewart, eds. *Soft Tech.* New York: Penguin, 1978.

Bender, Tom. *Environmental Design Primer.* New York: Schocken, 1976.

Berry, Wendell. *The Unsettling of America.* New York: Avon, 1978.

Burns, Scott. *The Household Economy: Its Shape, Origins, and Future.* Boston: Beacon Press, 1977.

Callenbach, Ernest. *Ecotopia.* New York: Bantam, 1977.

Clark, Wilson. *Energy for Survival.* Garden City, N.Y.: Doubleday, 1975.

Commoner, Barry. *The Poverty of Power.* New York: Knopf, 1976.

Darrow, Ken, and Pam, Rick. *Appropriate Technology Sourcebook.* Rev. ed. Stanford, California: Volunteers in Asia, 1978.

Hackleman, Michael, and House, David. *Wind and Wind Spinners.* Culver City, Calif.: Peace Press, 1975.

Harman, Willis. *An Incomplete Guide to the Future.* San Francisco: San Francisco Book Co., 1976.

Henderson, Hazel. *Creating Alternative Futures: The End of Economics.* New York: Berkley Publishing Corp., 1978.

Howard, Sir Albert. *The Soil and Health: A Study of Organic Agriculture.* New York: Schocken, 1972.

Hyams, Edward. *Soil and Civilization.* New York: Harper and Row, 1976.

Illich, Ivan. *Energy and Equity.* New York: Harper and Row, 1974.

Illich, Ivan. *Tools for Conviviality.* New York: Harper and Row, 1974.

Jeavons, John. *How to Grow More Vegetables Than You Ever Thought Possible on Less Land Then You Can Imagine.* Palo Alto, Calif.: Ecology Action, 1974.

Lappé, Frances Moore. *Diet for a Small Planet.* New York: Ballantine, 1975.

Lappé, Frances Moore, and Collins, Joseph. *Food First: Beyond the Myth of Scarcity.* Boston: Houghton Mifflin, 1977.

Leckie, Jim; Masters, Gil; Whitehouse, Harry; and Young, Lily. *Other Homes and Garbage.* San Francisco: Sierra Club Books, 1975.

Leopold, Aldo. *A Sand County Almanac.* New York: Ballantine, 1977.

Lovins, Amory. *Soft Energy Paths: Toward a Durable Peace.* San Francisco: Friends of the Earth, 1977.

McHarg, Ian L. *Design with Nature.* La Jolla, Calif.: Natural History, 1971.

Merrill, Richard, ed. *Energy Primer: Solar, Water, Wind, and Biofuels.*

Menlo Park, Calif.: Portola Institute, 1975.

Odum, Eugene P. *Fundamentals of Ecology.* Philadelphia: W.B. Saunders Co., 1971.

Odum, Howard T. *Environment, Power and Society.* New York: John Wiley & Sons, 1971.

Rainbook: Resources for Appropriate Technology. By the editors of *Rain* magazine. New York: Schocken, 1977.

Roszak, Theodore. *Person-Planet: The Creative Disintegration of Industrial Society.* Garden City, N.Y.: Doubleday, 1978.

Schumacher, E.F. *Small Is Beautiful: Economics As If People Mattered.* New York: Harper and Row, 1976.

Vegetable Gardening. By the editors of Sunset Books and *Sunset* magazine. Menlo Park, Calif.: Lane Publishing Co., 1975.

References

Chapter One

Ehrlich, Paul R., and Ehrlich, Anne H. *Population, Resources, Environment: Issues in Human Ecology.* San Francisco: W.H. Freeman and Co., 1962.

Epstein, S.S. "Potential Carcinogenic Hazards Due to Contaminated Drinking Water." In *Biological Control of Water Pollution,* edited by Joachim Tourbier and Robert W. Pierson, Jr. Philadelphia: University of Pennsylvania Press, 1976.

Harris, R.H. "Carcinogenic Organic Chemicals in Drinking Water." In *Biological Control of Water Pollution,* edited by Joachim Tourbier and Robert W. Pierson, Jr. Philadelphia: University of Pennsylvania Press, 1976.

Chapter Two

Dasmann, Raymond F., et al. *Wildlife Biology.* New York: John Wiley & Sons, 1964.

Elton, Charles. *Animal Ecology.* New York: Halsted Press, 1966.

Thomas, William L., Jr., ed. *Man's Role in Changing the Face of the Earth.* 2 vols. Chicago: University of Chicago Press, 1971.

Von Bertalanffy, Ludwig. *General System Theory: Essays on Its Foundation and Development.* Rev. ed. New York: Braziller, 1969.

Chapter Three

Ashbrook, Frank G. *Butchering, Processing and Preservation of Meat.* New York: Van Nostrand Reinhold, 1975.

Cervinka, V.W.; Chancellor, J.; Coffelt, R.J.; Curley, R.G.; and Dobie, J.B. *Energy Requirements for Agriculture in California.* California Department of Food and Agriculture, Sacramento, with University of California, Davis, 1976.

Logsdon, Gene. *Small Scale Grain Raising.* Emmaus, Pa.: Rodale Press, 1977.

Wiest, J.D., and Levy, F.K. *A Management Guide to PERT/CPM.* Englewood Cliffs, N.J.: Prentice Hall, 1969.

Chapter Four

ABT Associates. *In the Bank . . . or up the Chimney? A Dollars and Cents Guide to Energy-Saving Home Improvements.* U.S. Department of Housing and Urban Development. Washington, D.C.: 1975.

A Community Planning Guide to Weatherization. Community Services Administration. Washington, D.C.: 1975.

Antonioli, P.S., and Farrar, L.C. *Heating with Wood.* National Center for Appropriate Technology, Butte, Mont.: 1977.

ASHRAE Handbook of Fundamentals. 2nd printing. New York: American Society of Heating, Refrigerating and Air Conditioning Engineers, 1974.

Crawley, Gerald M. *Energy.* Riverside, N.J.: MacMillan, 1975.

Dahlin, D. *The Working Woodburner: Home Heating and Cooking with Fireplaces and Wood Stoves.* Point Richmond, Calif.: Interactive Resources, Inc., 1976.

Energy Savings Through Automatic Thermostat Controls. Energy Resources Development Administration, No. EDM-1023. Washington, D.C.: 1977.

Factors Affecting Automotive Fuel Economy. Environmental Protection Agency, Office of Air and Waste Management, No. AW-455. Washington, D.C.: 1976.

Gay, Larry. *The Complete Book of Heating with Wood.* Charlotte, Vt.: Garden Way Publishing Co., 1974.

Home Energy Saver's Workbook. Department of Energy. Washington, D.C.: 1977.

McCullagh, James C., ed. *Pedal Power: In Work, Leisure, and Transportation.* Emmaus, Pa.: Rodale Press, 1977.

1978 Gas Mileage Guide. Department of Energy. Washington, D.C.: 1977.

Ott, John. *Health and Light.* Old Greenwich, Conn.: Devin-Adair Co., 1976.

Residential Energy Consumption, Single Family Housing. Report No. HUD-HAI-2. Columbia, Md.: Hittman Associates, Inc., 1973.

Shelton, John W., and Shapiro, A.B. *The Woodburner's Encyclopedia.* Waitsfield, Vt.: Vermont Crossroads Press, 1942.

Spies, H.R., et al. *350 Ways to Save Energy (and Money) in Your Home and Car.* New York: Crown Publications.

Tips for Energy-Savers in and around the Home, on the Road, in the Market Place. Federal Energy Administration, Document No. 0-566-806. Washington, D.C.: 1975.

Vivian, John. *Wood Heat.* Emmaus, Pa.: Rodale Press, 1976.

Chapter Five

Javits, Tom; Fricke, Tom; Leon, Sheldon; and Matthews, Scott. *Grey-Water Use in the Home Garden.* Berkeley: Farallones Institute, 1976.

Milne, Murray. *Residential Water Consumption.* Water Resources Department, Report No. 34. Davis: University of California, 1976.

The Nation's Water Resources. Water Resources Council. Washington, D.C.: 1968.

Water Conservation in California. State of California Resources Agency, Department of Water Resources, Bulletin No. 198. Sacramento: 1976.

Chapter Six

Golueke, C.G.; Oswald, W.J.; Dugan, G.L.; Rexford, C.E.; and Scher, S. *Final Report on Photosynthetic Reclamation of Agricultural Solid and Liquid Wastes.* Sanitary Engineering Research Laboratory. Berkeley: University of California, 1972.

Gotaas, H. *Composting.* World Health Organization, Monograph No. 31. Geneva: 1953.

Lowe, R.A. *Energy Conservation Theory in Improved Solid Waste Management.* U.S. Environmental Protection Agency. Cincinnati: 1974.

Poincelot, R.P. *The Biochemistry and Methodology of Composting.* Agricultural Experiment Station, Bulletin No. 754. New Haven, Conn.: 1975.

Stoner, Carol H., ed. *Goodbye to the Flush Toilet.* Emmaus, Pa.: Rodale Press, 1977.

Van der Ryn, Sim *The Toilet Papers,* Santa Barbara, Calif.: Capra Press, 1978.

Waldbott, George L. *Health Effects of Environmental Pollutants.* St. Louis: C.V. Mosby Co., 1973.

Chapter Seven

Angelico, R., and Sonogy, J.C. "Prevention of Atherosclerosis by Diet: Present State and Conclusions, Outlines of Dietary Prevention of Atherosclerosis." In *Diet and Atherosclerosis,* edited by Cesare Sirtori, Giorgio Ricci, and S. Gorini. New York: Plenum Press, 1975.

Berry, James W.; Osgood, D.W.; and St. John, P.A. *Chemical Villains: A Biology of Pollution.* St. Louis: C.V. Mosby Co., 1974.

British Crop Protection Council. *Pesticide Manual.* England: Boots Co., 1977.

Farm Chemical Handbook. Willoughby, Ohio: Meister Publishing Co., 1977.

Guthrie, Helen A. *Introductory Nutrition.* 2nd ed. St. Louis: C.V. Mosby Co., 1971.

Knott, James Edward. *Handbook for Vegetable Growers.* New York: John Wiley & Sons, 1957.

Leonard, Jon N.; Hofer, J.L.; and Pritikin, N. *Live Longer Now: The First One Hundred Years of Your Life.* New York: Grosset and Dunlap, 1974.

Manske, D.D., and Johnson, R.D. "Pesticide and Other Chemical Residues in Total Diet Samples." *Pesticide Monitoring Journal* 10(1972): 134–48.

Merck Index. Rahway, N.J.: Merck & Co., 1976.

Mount, James L. *The Food and Health of Western Man.* New York: Halsted Press, 1975.

Report of the Secretary's Commission on Pesticides and Their Relationship to Environmental Health. U.S. Department of Health, Education, and Welfare. Washington, D.C.: 1969.

Sanitary Engineering Research Laboratory, Report No. 69-1. Berkeley: University of California.

Suburban and Farm Vegetable Gardens. 2nd. rev. ed. U.S. Department of Agriculture, Home and Garden Bulletin No. 9. Washington, D.C.: 1970.

Sutton, H.E., and Harris, M.I. *Mutagenic Effects of Environmental Contaminants.* New York: Academic Press, 1972.

Taylor, Ronald L. *Butterflies in My Stomach: Insects in Human Nutrition.* Santa Barbara, Calif.: Woodbridge Press, 1975.

Watt, B.K., and Merrill, A.L. *Composition of Foods.* U.S. Department of Agriculture, Agricultural Handbook No. 8. Washington, D.C.: 1963.

Chapter Eight

Bogart, Jean; Briggs, George M.; and Calloway, Doris Howes. *Nutrition and Physical Fitness.* 9th ed. Philadelphia: W.B. Saunders Co., 1973.

Carlson, Anton J., and Johnson, V. *The Machinery of the Body.* Chicago: University of Chicago Press, 1941.

Conservation Tillage. Ankeny, Iowa: The Soil Conservation Society, 1973.

Donahue, Roy L.; Shickluna, J.C.; and Robertson, L.S. *Soils: An Introduction to Soils and Plant Growth.* 3rd ed. Englewood Cliffs, N.J.: Prentice Hall, 1971.

Doubleday Research Association. *Newsletter.* Essex, England.

Evans, H.J., and Barber, I.F. "Biological Nitrogen Fixation for Food and Fiber Production." *Science* 197(1977): 332–39.

Hellige Soil Handbook. New York: Hellige, Inc., 1931.

Janick, Jules; Schery, R.W.; Woods, F.W.; and Rutton, V.W. *Plant Science.* San Francisco: W.H. Freeman and Co., 1969.

Keyes, John H. *Harnessing the Sun to Heat Your House.* Dobbs Ferry, N.Y.: Morgan & Morgan, 1974.

Knott, J.E. *Handbook for Vegetable Growers.* New York: John Wiley & Sons, 1957.

Palm, Charles E. *Weed Control.* National Academy of Sciences, Publication No. 1597. Washington, D.C.: 1968.

Pimentel, David, et al. "Food Production and the Energy Crisis." *Science* 182(1973): 443–49.

Russell, E.W. *Soil Conditions and Plant Growth.* 9th ed. New York: John Wiley & Sons, 1961.

Schaller, Friedrich. *Soil Animals.* Ann Arbor: University of Michigan Press, 1968.

Soil Biology: Reviews of Research. UNESCO. New York: 1969.

Stallings, J.H. *Soil Conservation.* Englewood Cliffs, N.J.: Prentice Hall, 1957.

Stout, Ruth. *How to Have a Green Thumb Without an Aching Back.* Rev. ed. New York: Cornerstone Library, 1970.

Van Riper, J.E. *Man's Physical World.* San Francisco: McGraw Hill, 1971.

Williamson, Samuel J. *Fundamentals of Air Pollution.* Reading, Mass.: Addison-Wesley Publishing Co., 1973.

Chapter Nine

Atkinson, Robert E. *Dwarf Fruit Trees, Indoors and Outdoors.* New York: Van Nostrand Reinhold, 1972.

Fisher, Rick, and Yanda, Bill. *The Food and Heat Producing Solar Greenhouse.* Santa Fe, N.M.: John Muir Publications, 1977.

Jensen, Merle H. "Energy Alternatives and Conservation for Greenhouses." *Horticultural Science* 12: 14–24.

Jorden, William. *Windowsill Ecology.* Emmaus, Pa.: Rodale Press, 1978.

Journal of the New Alchemists. Nos. 1–5. Woods Hole, Mass.: New Alchemy Institute, 1974–1978.

Smith, Miranda. *Self Reliance* 11. Washington, D.C.: Institute for Local Self-Reliance, 1976.

Chapter Ten

Carson, Ron, and Carson, Ceanne. *Countryside Magazine,* November 1977.

From Chick to Layer—A Complete Guide Book for Poultry Raisers. Mt. Morris, Ill.: Poultry Tribune.

Gotaas, H. *Composting.* World Health Organization, Monograph no. 31. Geneva: 1953.

Minnish, Jerry. *The Earthworm Book.* Emmaus, Pa.: Rodale Press, 1977.

Nutrient Requirements of Poultry. National Academy of Sciences, Agricultural Board. Washington, D.C.: 1971.

Olkowski, Helga, and Olkowski, William. *City People's Book of Raising Food.* Emmaus, Pa.: Rodale Press, 1975.

Templeton, George S. *Domestic Rabbit Production.* Danville, Ill.: Interstate, 1968.

Chapter Eleven

Beekeeping in the United States. U.S. Department of Agriculture, Agricultural Handbook No. 335. Washington, D.C.: 1971.

Mraz, Charles. "Bee Venom Therapy." American Bee Journal 117(1977): 260.

Root, A.I. *ABC and XYZ of Bee Culture.* Medina, Ohio: A.I. Root Co., 1966.

Wells, F.B. "Hive Product Uses—Venom—Part IV." *American Bee Journal* 117(1977): 10–13.

Chapter Twelve

Anderson, Bruce. *Solar Energy: Fundamentals in Building Design.* New York: McGraw Hill, 1977.

Barber, E.M., Jr., and Watson, Donald. *Design Criteria for Solar-Heated Buildings.* Guilford, Conn.: Sunworks, Inc., 1975.

"The Climate Controlled House." *House Beautiful.* Series of monthly articles, October 1949 to January 1951.

Crowther, Richard L., et al. *Sun/Earth: How to Apply Free Energy Sources to Our Homes and Buildings.* Denver: Crowther Solar Group, 1976.

Daniels, Farrington. *Direct Use of the Sun's Energy.* New York: Ballantine, 1974.

Duffie, John A., and Beckman, William A. *Solar Energy Thermal Processes.* New York: John Wiley & Sons, 1974.

Eccli, Eugene, ed. *Low-Cost, Energy-Efficient Shelter: For the Owner and Builder.* Emmaus, Pa.: Rodale Press, 1976.

In the Bank . . . Or up the Chimney? A Dollars and Cents Guide to Energy-Saving Home Improvements. U.S. Government Printing Office, No. 023-000-00297-3. Washington, D.C.

Kreider, Jan F., and Kreith, Frank. *Solar Heating and Cooling: Engineering, Practical Design, and Economics.* Washington, D.C.: Hemisphere Publishing Co., 1976.

Olgyay, Victor. *Design with Climate: Bioclimatic Approaches to Architectural Regionalism.* Princeton, N.J.: Princeton University Press, 1963.

Shurcliff, William A. *Solar Heated Buildings of North America: 120 Outstanding Examples.* Church Hill, N.H.: Brick House Publishing Co., 1978.

Sunset Books. *Do-It-Yourself Insulation and Weatherstripping for Year-Round Energy Saving.* Menlo Park, Calif.: Sunset Books, 1978.

Watson, Donald. *Designing and Building a Solar House: Your Place in the Sun.* Charlotte, Vt.: Garden Way Publishing Co., 1977.

Wright, David. *Natural Solar Architecture: A Passive Primer.* New York: Van Nostrand Reinhold, 1978.

Chapter Thirteen

Andres, Lloyd. Information sheet on weed control. U.S. Department of Agriculture, Biological Control of Weeds Laboratory. Mimeographed. Alvarez, Calif.: 1974.

Berry, James W.; Osgood, D.W.; and St. John, P.W. *Chemical Villains; A Biology of Pollution.* St. Louis: C.V. Mosby Co., 1974.

Bold, Harold C. *The Plant Kingdom.* Englewood Cliffs, N.J.: Prentice Hall, 1970.

Brown, R.Z. *Biological Factors in Domestic Rodent Control.* U.S. Department of Health, Education, and Welfare, Public Health Service Publication No. 773. Atlanta, Ga.: 1960.

Common Pantry Pests and Their Controls. U.S. Department of Agriculture, Cooperative Extension. Berkeley: 1974.

Controlling Household Pests. U.S. Department of Agriculture, Home and Garden Bulletin No. 96. Washington, D.C.

Cornwell, P.B. *The Cockroach: A Laboratory Insect and Household Pest.* London: Hutchinson and Co., 1968.

Dethier, V.G. *Man's Plague.* Princeton, N.J.: Darwin Press, 1976.

Ebeling, Walter. *Journal of Economic Entomology.* 60(1967): 1375-90.

Flint, M.L., and Van den Bosch, R. *A Source Book on Integrated Pest Management.* Department of Health, Education, and Welfare, Office of Education, Grant No. G007500907. Washington, D.C.

Gertsch, Willis J. *American Spiders.* New York: Van Nostrand Co., Inc., 1949.

Hagen, K.S.; Sawall, E.F.; and Lassan, R.L. "The Use of Food Sprays to Increase Effectiveness of Entomophagous Insects." Tall Timbers Conference Proceedings. *Ecological Animal Control by Habit Modifications* 2(1970): 59-81.

Hartnack, Hugo. *Unbidden House Guests.* Tacoma, Wash.: Hartnack Publishing Co., 1943.

Huffaker, C.B., and Messenger, P.S. *Theory and Practice of Biological Control.* New York: Academic Press, 1977.

Hunter, Beatrice T. *Gardening Without Poisons.* 2nd ed. Boston: Houghton Mifflin, 1972.

Hussey, N.W.; Read, W.H.; and Hesling, J. *Glasshouse Pests.* New York: American Elsevier Publishing Co., 1969.

Jackson, R.M., and Raw, Frank. *Life in the Soil.* New York: Crane-Russak Co., 1966.

Keh, Benjamin. "Loxosceles Spiders in California." *California Vector News.* California State Health Department, May, 1970.

Laing, J.F., and Hamai, J. "Biological Control of Insect Pests and Weeds by Imported Parasites, Predators, and Pathogens." In *Theory and Practice of Biological Control,* edited by C.B. Huffaker and P.S. Messenger. New York: Academic Press, 1977.

Rockcastle, Verne N. "Spiders." *Cornell Science Leaflet.* New York State College of Agriculture, Ithaca, N.Y. 60, No. 1.

Scott and Broom. *Rodent-Borne Disease Control Through Rodent Stoppage.* U.S. Department of Health, Education, and Welfare, Public Health Service, National Communicable Disease Center. Atlanta, Ga.: 1965.

Storer, I.I., and Usinger, R.L. *General Zoology.* San Francisco: McGraw Hill, 1965.

Swan, Lester A. *Beneficial Insects.* New York: Harper and Row, 1964.

Tassan, R.L., and Hagen, K. "The Influence of Food Wheast and Related *Saccharomyces Fragilis* Yeast Products on the Fecundity of *Chrysopa Carnea.*" *Can. Ent.* 102(1970): 806–11.

Wiswesser, W.J., ed. *Pesticide Index.* 5th ed. College Park, Md.: Entomological Society of America, 1976.

Chapter Fourteen

Falk, John Howard. "The Energetics of a Suburban Lawn." *Ecology* 57(1976): 141–50.

Lovering, L.G., ed. *Lead in the Environment.* U.S. Department of the Interior, Geological Survey, Professional Paper No. 957. Washington, D.C.: 1976.

Noise Pollution. U.S. Environmental Protection Agency. Washington, D.C.

Shayler, Pat. "Lead Sampling in Berkeley." Research report. Department of Conservation of Natural Resources. Berkeley: University of California, 1975.

Waldbott, George L. *Health Effects of Environmental Pollutants.* St. Louis: C.V. Mosby Co., 1973.

Resources

Rachel Carson Trust
8940 Jones Mill Road
Chevy Chase, Md. 20015

(A nonprofit organization for the purpose of researching human health and the hazards of pesticide pollution worldwide)

Domestic Technology Institute
P.O. Box 2043
Evergreen, Colo. 80439

(Construction drawings for freestanding solar greenhouses)

Farallones Institute:
Integral Urban House
1516 5th St.
Berkeley, Calif. 94710

Rural Center
15290 Coleman Valley Rd.
Occidental, Calif. 95465

San Francisco Center
Fort Mason Building 312
Laguna & Marina Blvds.
San Francisco, Calif. 94123

(Classes, workshops, publications, technical plans)

Garden Way Publishing Co.
Charlotte, Vt. 05445

(Plans for assembly of hives and honey extractors)

Institute for Local Self-Reliance
1717 18th St. N.W.
Washington, D.C. 20009

National Center for Appropriate
Technology
P.O. Box 3838
Butte, Mont. 59701

New Alchemy Institute
P.O. Box 47
Woods Hole, Mass. 02543

Office of Appropriate Technology
State of California
1530 10th St.
Sacramento, Calif. 95814

Peoples' Development Corporation
(East Eleventh Street Project)
500 East 167th St.
Bronx, N.Y. 10456

APPENDIX 2: CONSTRUCTION AND WORKING PLANS

Working Plans: Window Greenhouse

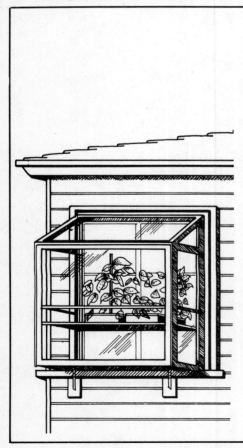

For city dwellers who enjoy gardening, a window greenhouse can provide an ideal habitat for propagating and growing food and ornamental plants. Attached to a south-facing window, the greenhouse can extend the growing season of food plants by maximizing use of the sun's energy during the shortest winter days. Attached to an east window, the greenhouse will provide a suitable climate for growing and maintaining most common houseplants as well as for starting seeds and cuttings.

These window greenhouse construction drawings were designed for double-hung windows or for the casement type which open toward the *interior* of the house. It is difficult to give specific construction dimensions for the greenhouse since existing house windows vary in size and configuration. Thus the builder should measure his/her house windows and use these drawings as suggested detailing guidelines.

Materials Needed

*1"x3" Douglas fir or pine for frame.
*1"x1" Douglas fir or pine for frame.
*1"x1" Douglas fir or pine for shelf.
*1/2 A.C. exterior glue plywood for base.
*3/16" acrylic sheets for glazing.
*3/4" pine corner trim
 36—3/4" #10 galvanized metal screws with galvanized washers and rubber gaskets.
2—11" galvanized butt hinges
10'—1/8" foam weatherstripping
 1 pint white exterior enamel paint
 1 tube clear butyl sealant
*Quantities depend on size of window

Construction Procedure

1. Measure window and dimension out greenhouse design.
2. Acquire materials.
3. Build wood frame of greenhouse.
4. Paint wood frame white.
5. Cut and install glazing.
6. Trim.
7. Construct potting shelf.
8. Install and caulk onto house.

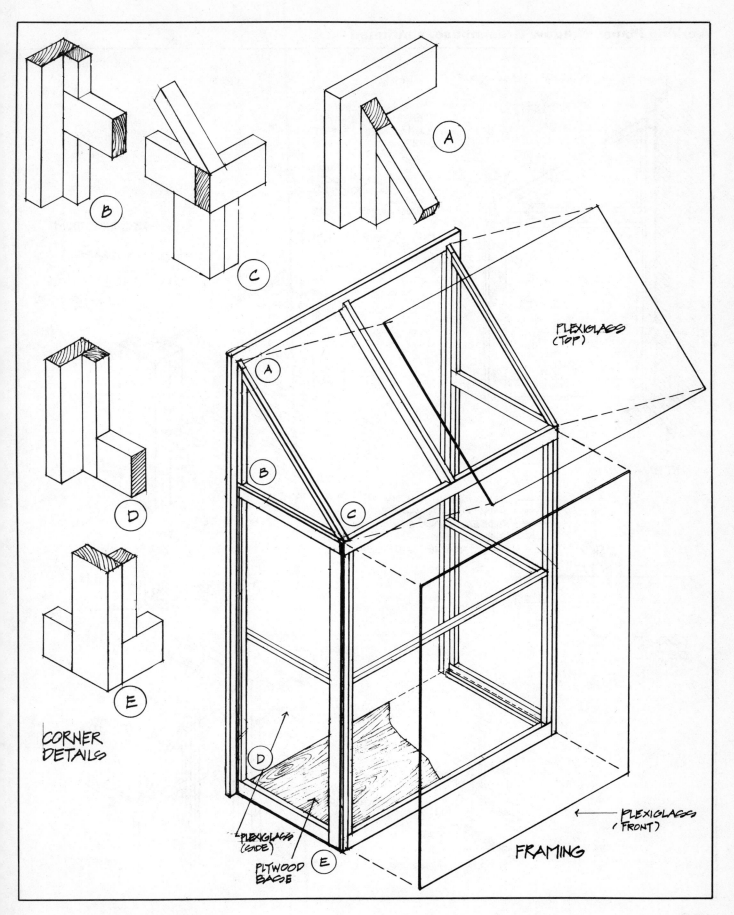

A

B

C

D

E

CORNER
DETAILS

PLEXIGLASS
(TOP)

PLEXIGLASS
(SIDE)

PLYWOOD
BASE

PLEXIGLASS
(FRONT)

FRAMING

461

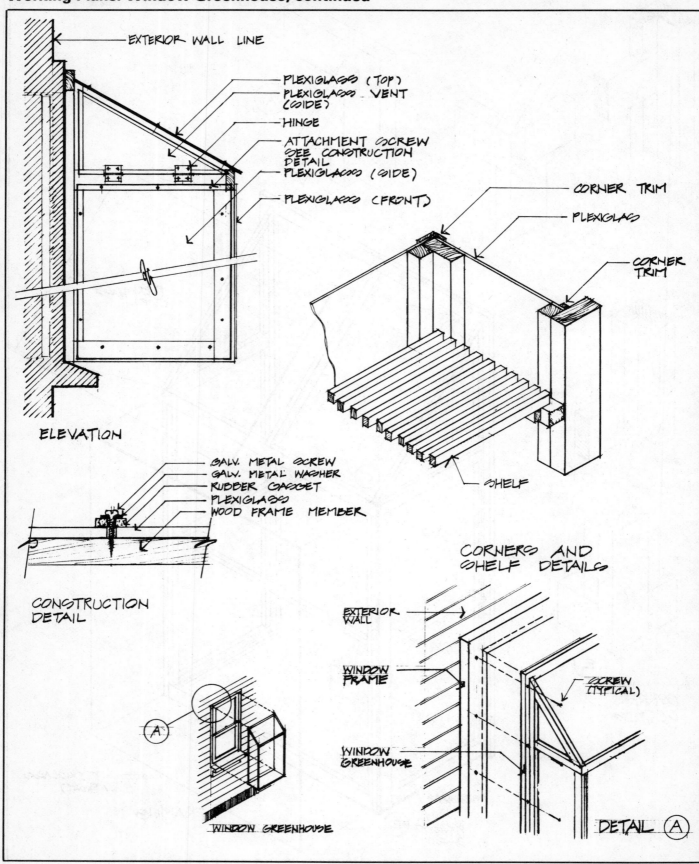

EXTERIOR WALL LINE

PLEXIGLASS (TOP)

PLEXIGLASS VENT (SIDE)

HINGE

ATTACHMENT SCREW SEE CONSTRUCTION DETAIL

PLEXIGLASS (SIDE)

PLEXIGLASS (FRONT)

ELEVATION

CORNER TRIM

PLEXIGLAS

CORNER TRIM

SHELF

GALV. METAL SCREW
GALV. METAL WASHER
RUBBER GASKET
PLEXIGLASS
WOOD FRAME MEMBER

CONSTRUCTION DETAIL

CORNERS AND SHELF DETAILS

EXTERIOR WALL

WINDOW FRAME

WINDOW GREENHOUSE

SCREW (TYPICAL)

A

WINDOW GREENHOUSE

DETAIL A

462

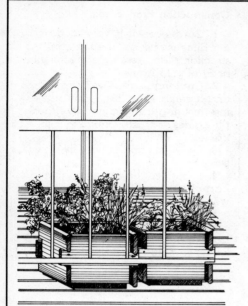

When garden space is in short supply, try gardening in containers. By using this technique you can grow plants on decks, patios, cement driveways, windowsills, rooftops and other unused spaces. And the selection of plants adaptable to container-growing is practically limitless. With proper management most vegetables, herbs, fruits and ornamental plants can be grown in containers, including such perennials as berry vines and dwarf fruit trees.

Choosing a Container

Containers should be durable, resistant to decay, large enough to contain mature plants and designed to provide good drainage. Containers meeting these requirements are available at nurseries and garden supply stores. Less expensive containers can be found among recycled materials such as soy tubs, wine barrels, used tires, machine packing boxes, five-gallon bakery and paint buckets and even milk cartons. These containers are available free or inexpensively in most communities and make roomy, attractive garden containers. To provide drainage, drill ½" holes around one-quarter of the bottom surface of the container. Set the container on wooden blocks or a pebble-filled saucer to insure adequate air and water exchange in the plant's root zone.

Soil Mixes

A loose, well-drained soil mix is essential to successful container gardening. We use a homemade mix composed of 1/3 sifted garden soil and 2/3 sifted compost. The garden soil is rich in mineral nutrients, and the compost provides drainage, nutrients, and a balanced microbial population which enhances nutrient availability and buffers against soil-borne disease organisms. For gardeners wishing to purchase commercial mixes we recommend using Vita Bark brand potting mix and adding perlite equal to 25 percent of the soil mix volume to increase drainage.

Fertilizing

A dilute solution of manure or compost tea added every four or five weeks maintains an excellent level of plant growth in our compost-rich container garden. Containers filled with commercial potting mixes will not have equally high levels of major and minor plant nutrients and will probably require weekly additions of dilute compost tea to maintain adequate plant growth. If using chemical fertilizers, avoid heavy applications for container-grown plants are particularly sensitive to fertilizer burn due to the confinement of their roots.

Watering

Container-grown plants are unable to tap deep soil water reserves and must be checked every few days (and daily in hot weather) to ascertain their water needs. We have found drip irrigation techniques ideal for large container plantings as the slow application rates allow water to be absorbed by the soil rather than lost through the container's drainage holes. If watering by hand, place hose nozzle close to soil, keep water pressure low, and give the plants a long, slow drink. Avoid wetting the foliage, and water in early morning to minimize water losses to evaporation.

Assembling the Farallones Planter Box

1. Determine the desired size of boxes, whether they be large or small.

2. Acquire 1" x 12" redwood boards. Measure and cut to size.

3. Screw boards together according to the plan provided.

4. Drill drainage holes. Locate and plant.

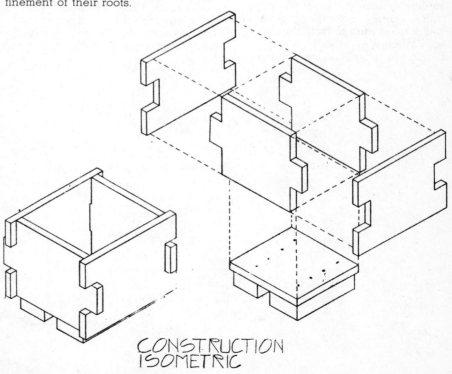

CONSTRUCTION ISOMETRIC

Working Plans: Garden Cold Frame

A good way to extend the growing season is by using a cold frame. Properly constructed, cold frames utilize a transparent glazing material such as glass or plastic to permit the passage of sunlight into the frame where it is stored in the soil floor. At night, the stored solar heat is radiated out of the soil and warms the surrounding plants.

Working with this heat storage principle, gardeners can start seeds in cold frames weeks before the beginning of the growing season. Similarly, the end of the growing season can be extended by sowing fall salad crops in cold frames and harvesting them throughout the winter.

To ensure successful operation of a cold frame, maintain proper temperatures and air circulation levels by opening the cover of the frame in the morning and closing it at night. Most plants prefer temperatures in the 65°F to 80°F range. On bright, sunny days, temperatures inside cold frames can rise as high as 10°F to 100°F despite cold outside temperatures. Thus, a daily check of the cold frame is a good idea. During warmer weather it is often necessary to cover the glazing material with whitewash, lath strips or saran cloth to reduce daytime temperatures and intensity of sunlight striking plants in the cold-frame. During severely cold weather it is a good idea to insulate the cold frame at night with a heavy blanket or other insulating material.

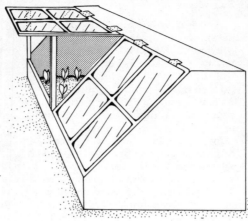

Be sure, also, to avoid excessive watering of plants in cold frames. When closed, cold frames can become very humid, creating conditions favorable to damping off disease and other plant pathogens. In general, plants in cold frames should be watered only as often as necessary to keep them from wilting. There is no easy formula for determining watering frequency since age and type of plant, soil mix, time of year, number of plants in the frame and degree of daily ventilation all play a role in determining daily moisture needs. By checking the plants daily (optimally mid-mornings and afternoon) you'll soon learn the rhythm of water use by the plants and be able to supply additional moisture at the proper times.

Construction Procedures:

1. Cut pieces of ½″ plywood as per dimensions specified in construction plan. Assemble pieces into body of cold frame.

2. Cut lengths of 1″ x 3″ board and assemble into frame for glazing. Install glazing material, either plexiglass or plastic. Hinge to cold frame.

3. Cut vents and fit with fly screen.

4. Locate cold frame in sunny part of garden. Paint to protect wood.

5. Optional procedure is to use salvaged window pane or glass door and build wooden frame to accommodate its size.

Material List

1 SHEET ½' CDX PLYWOOD
GLAZING MATERIAL & FRAME
48 SQ. IN. SCREEN
2 • 2'' BUTT HINGE

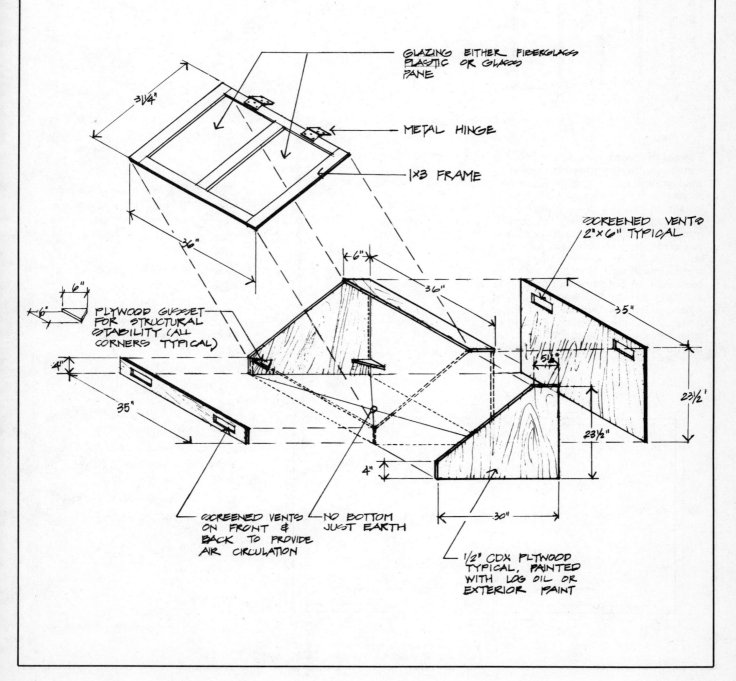

GLAZING EITHER FIBERGLASS
PLASTIC OR GLASS
PANE

METAL HINGE

1×3 FRAME

31/4"

36"

6"

6"

6"

PLYWOOD GUSSET
FOR STRUCTURAL
STABILITY (ALL
CORNERS TYPICAL)

4"

35"

SCREENED VENTS
ON FRONT &
BACK TO PROVIDE
AIR CIRCULATION

NO BOTTOM
JUST EARTH

36"

SCREENED VENTS
2"×6" TYPICAL

35"

5½"

23½"

23½"

4"

30"

1/2" CDX PLYWOOD
TYPICAL, PAINTED
WITH LOG OIL OR
EXTERIOR PAINT

Working Plans: Solar Greeenhouse

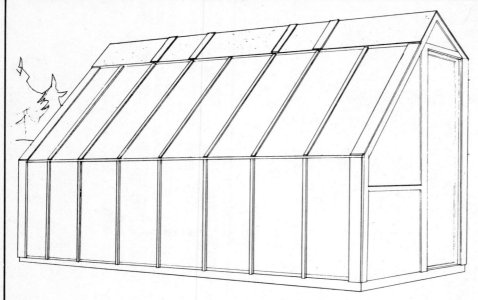

Construction Materials for a 8' x 16' Greenhouse

Quantity	Description of Materials
480'	2'' x 4'' D.F. Construction Grade—12' Lengths
128'	2'' x 4'' D.F. Construction G.—16' Lengths
24'	2'' x 6'' D.F. Construction G.—16' & 8' Length
12' Sheets	½'' 4' x 8' A-C Ext. Plywood
2 Sheets	½'' 4' x 8' C-DX Plywood (roof)
48'	4'' x 4'' RDW Foundation G.—16' Lengths
32'	1'' x 6'' RDW—8' Lengths
216'	¼'' x 4'' RDW Bender Board
450''	RDW Lath
272'	1'' x 4'' RDW Construction Grade—8'
138'	R-11 Fiberglass Batts 22'' Wide Foil Faced
120	6 Mil Polyethylene Standard
450	6 Mil Clear Polyethylene—Greenhouse Type
32'	1'' x 1½'' Edge Flashing
100	15 lb. Roofing Felt
100	90 lb. Roll Roofing—Green
140	1' R.G.D Styrofoam Insulation
10	55 Gal Drums—Black
200	Filon 50' x 4' Roll
8 lbs	16D Common Nails
2 lbs	8D Common Nails
5 lbs	6D Galvanized Box Nails
3 lbs	4D Galvanized Box Nails
4 lbs	¾'' Roofing Nails
4 Sets	Butt Hinges 3'' Long
8 Sets	Butt Hinges 2'' Long
3 Tubes	Butyl Sealant
3 Gal	White Latex Paint—Exterior
2 Gal	Redwood Stain Log Oil
1½ Yards	Coarse Gravel

RDW: Redwood
D.F.: Douglas Fir

The solar greenhouse differs from conventionally designed and operated greenhouses in that it does not rely on outside sources of energy for winter heating and summer cooling. Glazing is selectively applied to surfaces with southern exposure to permit entry of light and heat. Insulated walls on all northern exposures reduce nighttime heat loss. Manually operated vents promote natural convection to help keep the interior cool. Steel drums filled with water act as thermal mass and help to moderate daytime-nighttime temperature fluctuations. Opaque south roof sections are calculated to permit winter sun but exclude summer sun. A gravel floor is dampened to promote evaporative cooling. A modular design promotes efficient and uncomplicated construction. For more information, see Chapter 12.

*Note: Greenhouse should be sited on an unobstructed location with the long glazed axis facing approximately 15° east of south.

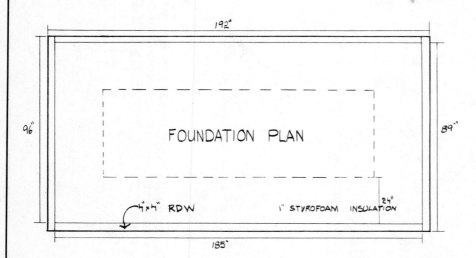

Greenhouse size may be enlarged by increments of four feet depending upon need. I.e. 8' x 20' or 8' x 24'

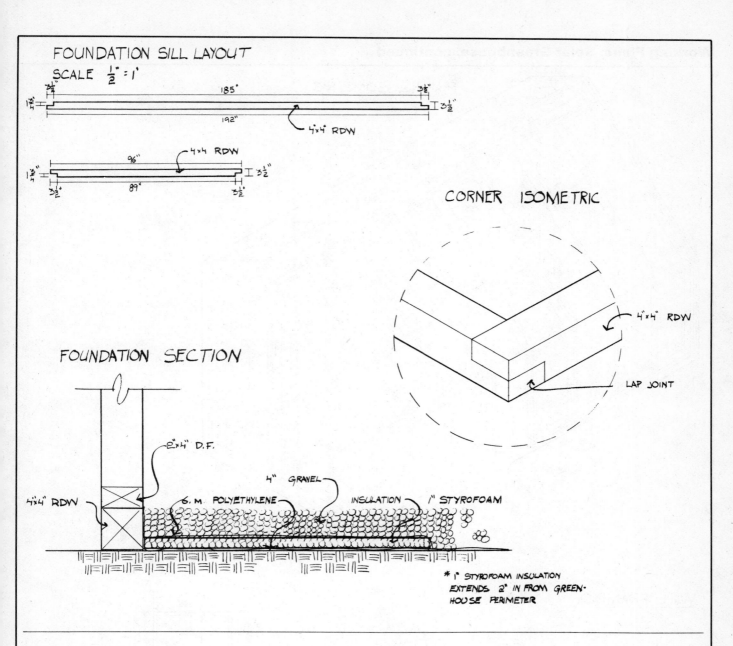

FOUNDATION SILL LAYOUT

SCALE ½" = 1'

185'

192"

4"x4" RDW

3½"

96"

4"x4" RDW

89"

3½"

CORNER ISOMETRIC

4"x4" RDW

LAP JOINT

FOUNDATION SECTION

2"x4" D.F.

4"x4" RDW

4" GRAVEL

6. M. POLYETHYLENE

INSULATION

1" STYROFOAM

* 1" STYROFOAM INSULATION EXTENDS 2" IN FROM GREEN-HOUSE PERIMETER

Sheathing Schedule

	Exterior	Middle	Interior
A	Filon	Air Space	6 Mill Polyethylene
B	½' A-C Plywood	R-11 Fiberglass	6 Mill Polyethylene
C	½' C-DX Ply with Roofing	R-11 Fiberglass	6 Mill Polyethylene
D	6 Mill Polyethylene	1'' Styro-foam	4'' Gravel

467

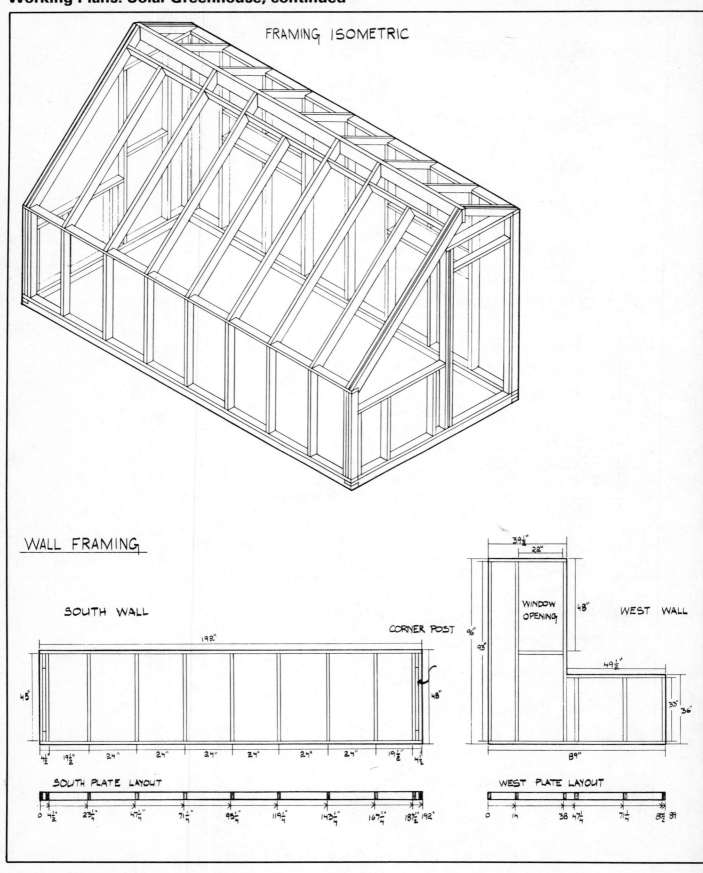

FRAMING ISOMETRIC

WALL FRAMING

SOUTH WALL

CORNER POST

192"

45"

48"

4½" 19½" 24" 24" 24" 24" 24" 24" 19½" 4½"

SOUTH PLATE LAYOUT

0 4½" 23½" 47½" 71½" 95½" 119½" 143½" 167½" 18½" 192'

WEST WALL

39½"
22"

WINDOW
OPENING

48"

96"
93"

49½"

33"
36"

89"

WEST PLATE LAYOUT

0 14 38 47½" 71½" 8½" 89

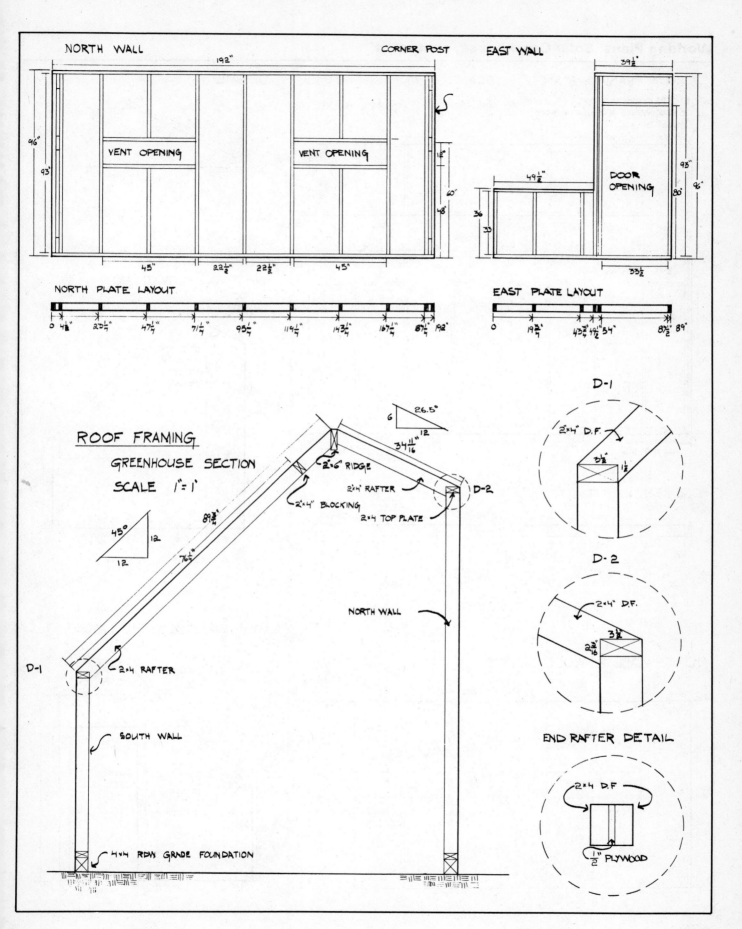

NORTH WALL

CORNER POST

EAST WALL

192"

96"

93"

VENT OPENING

VENT OPENING

12"

60"

48"

45"

22½"

22½"

45"

NORTH PLATE LAYOUT

0 4½" 20⅜" 47½" 71½" 95½" 119½" 143½" 167½" 87½" 192"

39½"

DOOR OPENING

49½"

93"

80"

96"

36"

33"

33½"

EAST PLATE LAYOUT

0 19¾" 43¾" 49½" 54" 87½" 89"

ROOF FRAMING

GREENHOUSE SECTION

SCALE 1"= 1'

26.5°

6

12

34 11/16"

2"×6" RIDGE

2"×4" RAFTER

2"×4" BLOCKING

2"×4 TOP PLATE

D-2

89¾"

45°

12

12

76½"

2×4 RAFTER

D-1

NORTH WALL

SOUTH WALL

4×4 RDW GRADE FOUNDATION

D-1

2"×4" D.F.

3½"

1½"

D-2

2"×4" D.F.

2 3/16"

3½"

END RAFTER DETAIL

2×4 D.F

½" PLYWOOD

469

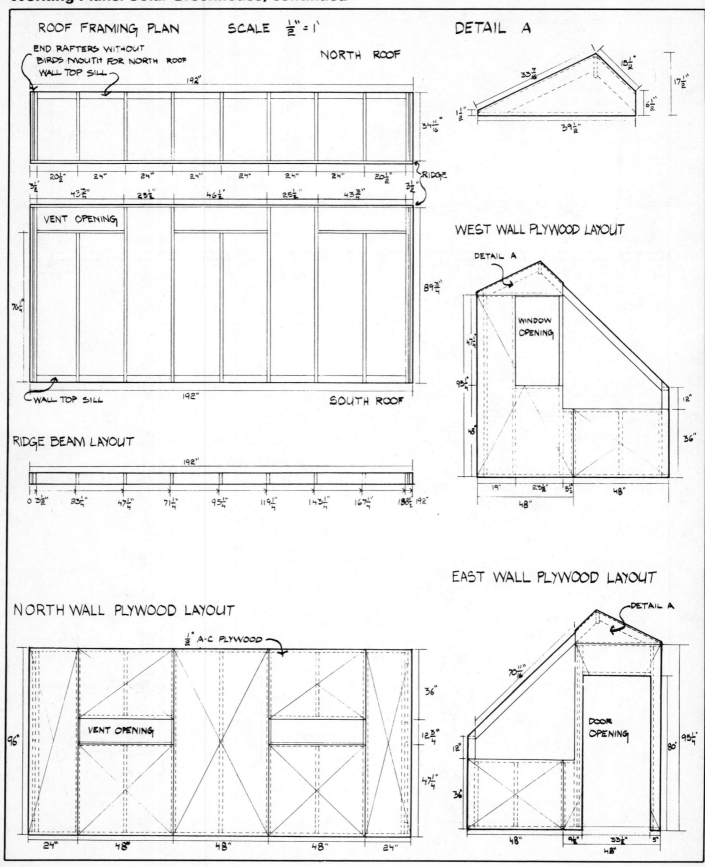

ROOF FRAMING PLAN   SCALE $\frac{1}{2}"=1'$ DETAIL A

END RAFTERS WITHOUT BIRDS MOUTH FOR NORTH ROOF WALL TOP SILL

NORTH ROOF

192"

34 $\frac{1}{16}$"

20 $\frac{1}{2}$" 24" 24" 24" 24" 24" 24" 20 $\frac{1}{2}$"

RIDGE

3 $\frac{1}{2}$" 43 $\frac{3}{4}$" 25 $\frac{1}{2}$" 46 $\frac{1}{2}$" 25 $\frac{1}{2}$" 43 $\frac{3}{4}$" 3 $\frac{1}{2}$"

VENT OPENING

76 $\frac{1}{4}$"

89 $\frac{3}{4}$"

WALL TOP SILL   192"   SOUTH ROOF

RIDGE BEAM LAYOUT

192"

0 3 $\frac{1}{2}$" 23 $\frac{1}{2}$" 47 $\frac{1}{2}$" 71 $\frac{1}{2}$" 95 $\frac{1}{2}$" 119 $\frac{1}{2}$" 143 $\frac{1}{2}$" 167 $\frac{1}{2}$" 188 $\frac{1}{2}$" 192"

NORTH WALL PLYWOOD LAYOUT

$\frac{1}{2}$" A-C PLYWOOD

VENT OPENING

96"

36"

12 $\frac{3}{4}$"

47 $\frac{1}{4}$"

24" 48" 48" 48" 24"

DETAIL A

33 $\frac{7}{16}$" 15 $\frac{1}{2}$"

17 $\frac{1}{2}$"

1 $\frac{1}{2}$" 6 $\frac{1}{2}$"

39 $\frac{1}{2}$"

WEST WALL PLYWOOD LAYOUT

DETAIL A

WINDOW OPENING

47 $\frac{1}{4}$"

93 $\frac{3}{4}$"

12"

48"

36"

19" 23 $\frac{1}{2}$" 5 $\frac{1}{2}$" 48"

48"

EAST WALL PLYWOOD LAYOUT

DETAIL A

70 $\frac{11}{16}$"

DOOR OPENING

12"

36"

80"

93 $\frac{3}{4}$"

48" 9 $\frac{1}{4}$" 23 $\frac{1}{2}$" 5"

48"

BENCH FRAMING

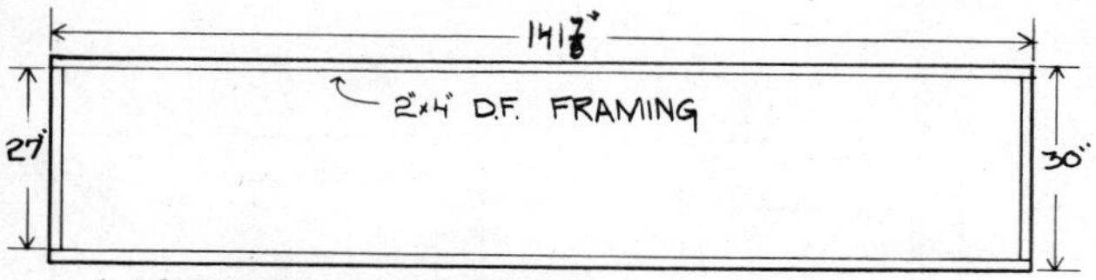

141⅞"

2"x4" D.F. FRAMING

27"

30"

NORTH BENCH
SCALE ½" = 1'

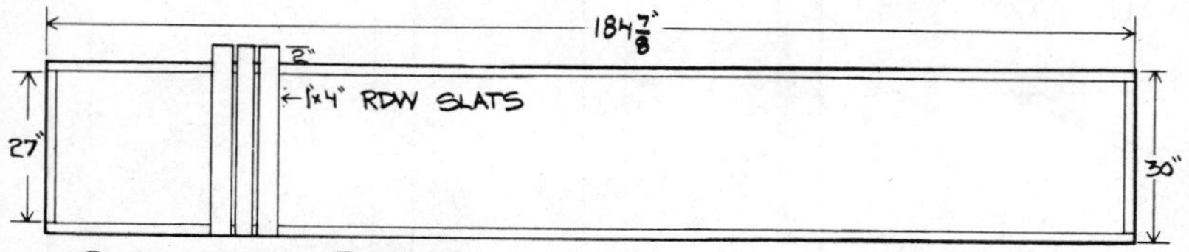

184⅞"

2"

1"x4" RDW SLATS

27"

30"

SOUTH BENCH
SCALE ½" = 1'

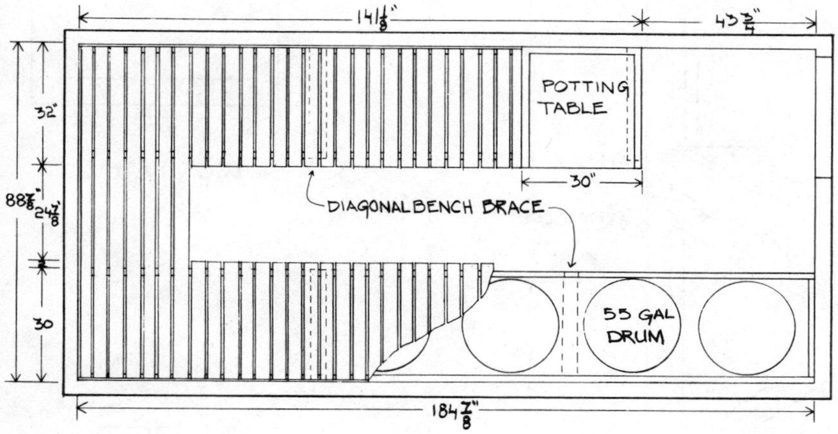

141⅛"

43¾"

POTTING TABLE

32"

30"

88⅞"
24⅞"

DIAGONAL BENCH BRACE

55 GAL DRUM

30

184⅞"

BENCH SECTION

INSULATION

½" PLYWOOD A-C

1"x4" RDW

1"x4" RDW SLATS
2" OVERHANG
2"x4" FRAME

2"x4" DIAGONAL BRACE

55 GAL. DRUM

36"

31¾"

3½" GRAVEL

4"x4" RDW FOUNDATION

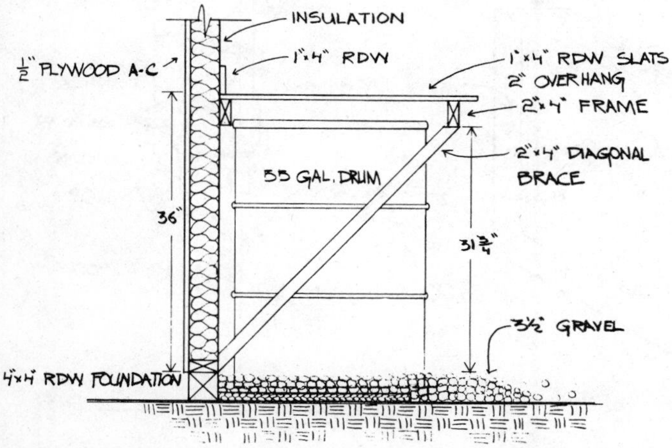

ISOMETRIC

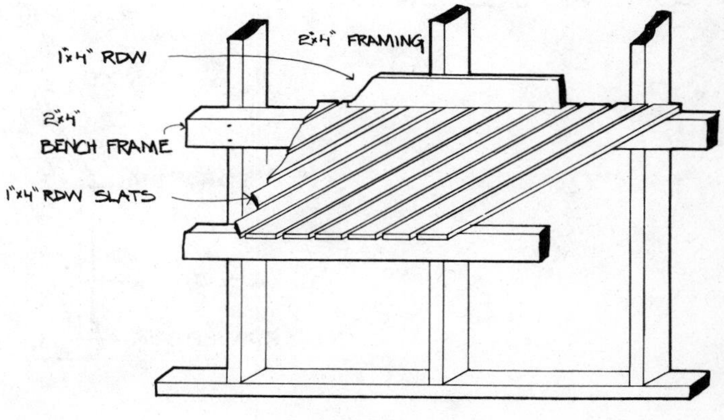

1"x4" RDW

2"x4" FRAMING

2"x4" BENCH FRAME

1"x4" RDW SLATS

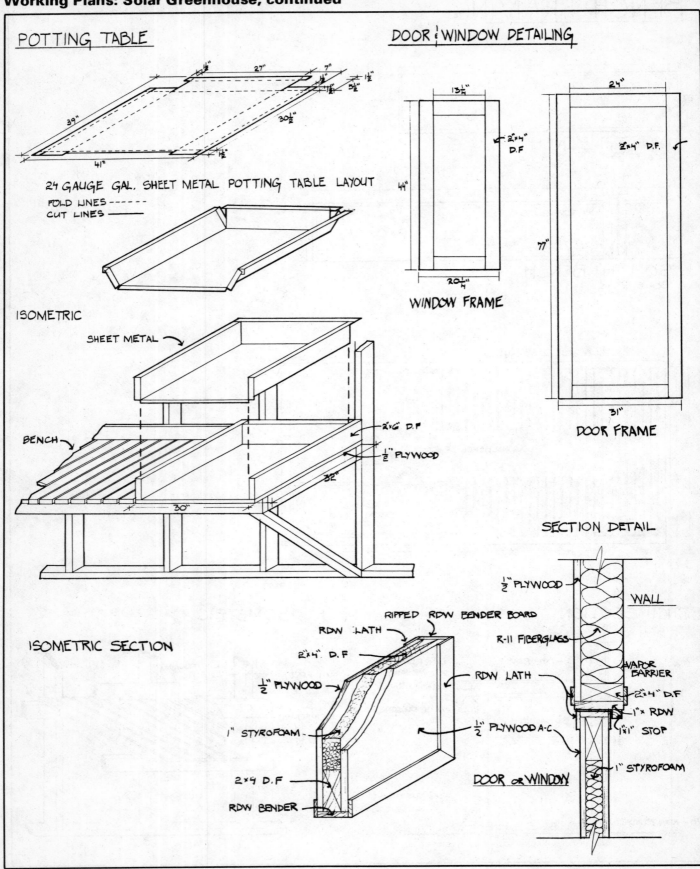

POTTING TABLE

DOOR & WINDOW DETAILING

24 GAUGE GAL. SHEET METAL POTTING TABLE LAYOUT
FOLD LINES ------
CUT LINES ———

ISOMETRIC

SHEET METAL

BENCH

2"x6" D.F
½" PLYWOOD

WINDOW FRAME

2"x4" D.F

DOOR FRAME

2"x4" D.F

ISOMETRIC SECTION

RIPPED RDW BENDER BOARD
RDW LATH
2"x4" D.F
½" PLYWOOD
1" STYROFOAM
2x4 D.F
RDW BENDER

RDW LATH
½" PLYWOOD A-C

SECTION DETAIL

½" PLYWOOD
WALL
R-11 FIBERGLASS
VAPOR BARRIER
2"x4" D.F
1"x RDW
1"x1" STOP
1" STYROFOAM

DOOR or WINDOW

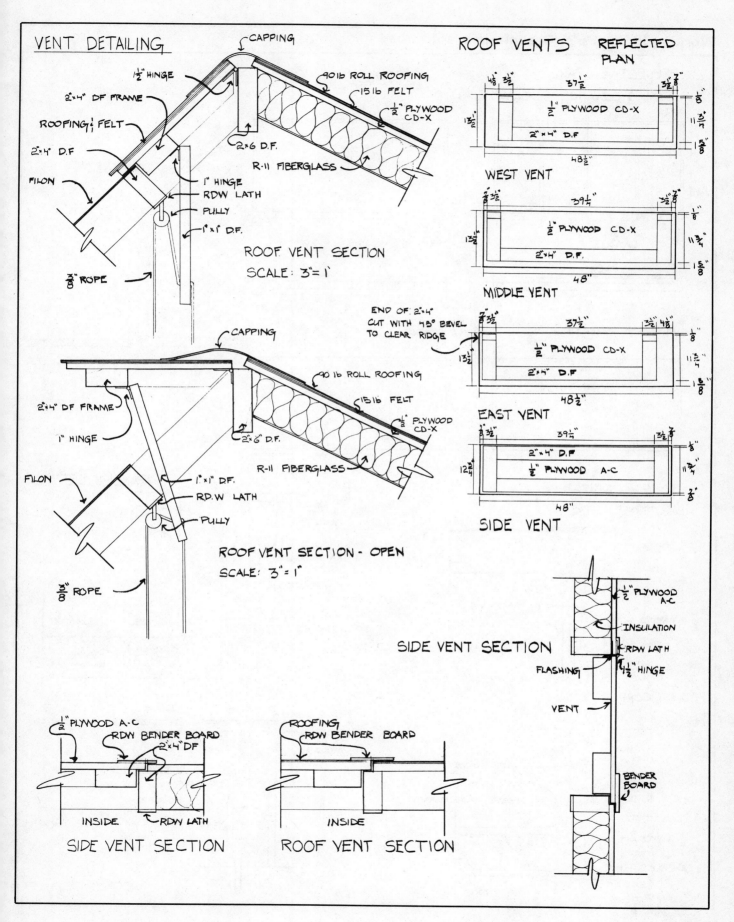

VENT DETAILING

CAPPING

½" HINGE
2"×4" DF FRAME
ROOFING FELT
2"×4" D.F
FILON
⅜" ROPE

90 lb ROLL ROOFING
15 lb FELT
½" PLYWOOD CD-X
2×6 D.F.
R-11 FIBERGLASS

1" HINGE
RDW LATH
PULLY
1"×1" D.F.

ROOF VENT SECTION
SCALE: 3" = 1'

ROOF VENTS REFLECTED PLAN

4⅛ 3½   37½   3½ ⅞
13½ ½" PLYWOOD CD-X ⅛
     2"×4" D.F.   11¾
48½   1⅝

WEST VENT

⅞ 3½   39¼   3½ ⅞
13½ ½" PLYWOOD CD-X ⅛
     2"×4" D.F.   11¾
     48   1⅝

MIDDLE VENT

⅞ 3½   37½   3½ 4⅛
END OF 2"×4"
CUT WITH 45° BEVEL
TO CLEAR RIDGE
13½ ½" PLYWOOD CD-X ⅛
     2"×4" D.F   11¾
     48½   1⅝

EAST VENT

⅞ 3½   39¼   3½ ⅞
12¾ 2"×4" D.F   ⅛
     ½" PLYWOOD A-C   11¾
     48   ⅞

SIDE VENT

CAPPING

2"×4" DF FRAME
1" HINGE
FILON
⅜" ROPE

90 lb ROLL ROOFING
15 lb FELT
½" PLYWOOD CD-X
2"×6" D.F.
R-11 FIBERGLASS
1"×1" D.F.
RD.W LATH
PULLY

ROOF VENT SECTION - OPEN
SCALE: 3" = 1'

SIDE VENT SECTION

½" PLYWOOD A-C
INSULATION
RDW LATH
FLASHING
1½" HINGE
VENT
BENDER BOARD

½" PLYWOOD A-C
RDW BENDER BOARD
2"×4" DF
INSIDE
RDW LATH

SIDE VENT SECTION

ROOFING
RDW BENDER BOARD
INSIDE

ROOF VENT SECTION

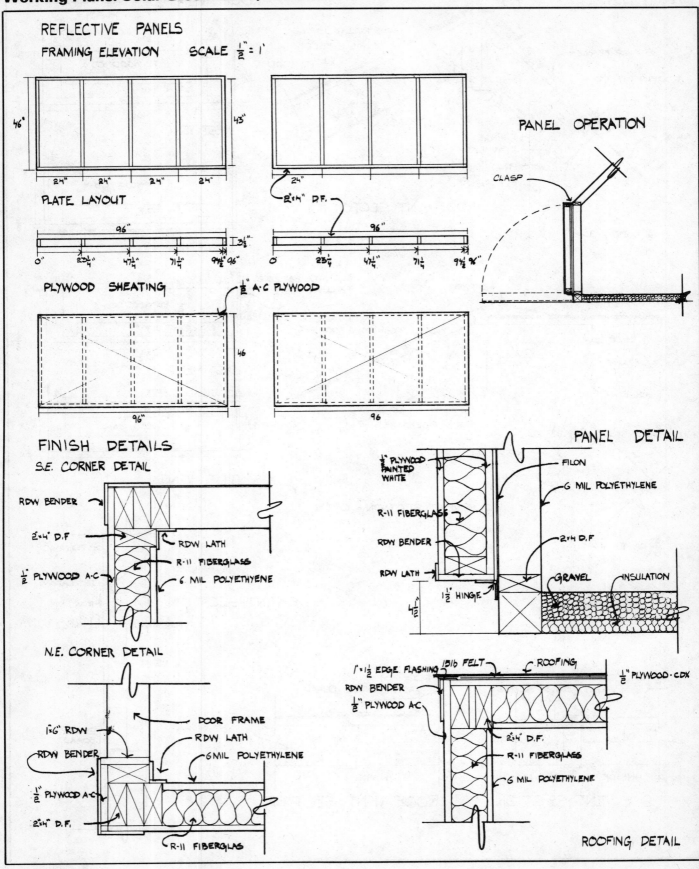

REFLECTIVE PANELS

FRAMING ELEVATION   SCALE ½" = 1'

PLATE LAYOUT

PLYWOOD SHEATING   ½" A·C PLYWOOD

PANEL OPERATION

CLASP

FINISH DETAILS

S.E. CORNER DETAIL

RDW BENDER
2×4" D.F
½ PLYWOOD A·C
RDW LATH
R·11 FIBERGLASS
6 MIL POLYETHYENE

PANEL DETAIL

½" PLYWOOD PAINTED WHITE
R·11 FIBERGLASS
RDW BENDER
RDW LATH
1½" HINGE
4½"
FILON
6 MIL POLYETHYLENE
2×4 D.F
GRAVEL
INSULATION

N.E. CORNER DETAIL

1×6" RDW
RDW BENDER
1½" PLYWOOD A·C
2×4" D.F.
R·11 FIBERGLAS
DOOR FRAME
RDW LATH
6 MIL POLYETHYLENE

1"×1½ EDGE FLASHING
RDW BENDER
½" PLYWOOD A·C
15lb FELT
ROOFING
½" PLYWOOD·CDX
2×4" D.F.
R·11 FIBERGLASS
6 MIL POLYETHYLENE

ROOFING DETAIL

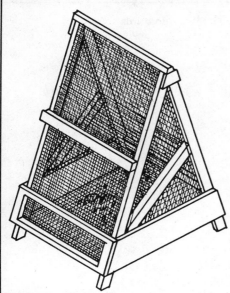

Baiting the Trap

Place any type of food or liquid that will attract the flies (buttermilk, molasses and syrups, sweet-smelling fermenting foods, meat, fish and kitchen scraps, animal manures, etc.) in a saucer or plate under the A-frame trap. Position the dish in the middle. If it is too close to the edge, the flies will find it easy to feed at the outer edges and will escape the trap altogether. The objective is to attract the flies into the lower area of the trap where the contrast between light and dark will be greatest. You can elevate the dish on some bricks and/or boards in order to get the bait three to four inches up into the trapping area.

The secret of successful baiting is to keep the bait wet! Since flies have sponging mouthparts, and have to take in liquid nutriment, the bait becomes much less effective as it dries out. To keep your traps going, you may have to moisten the bait every day or so, depending on the type you use, or—replenish them often with fresh materials. Remember, the trap will work only as well as the bait you use.

You may have to do some experimenting to see which baits work best for your fly species, location and conditions. Not all flies are alike in their food preferences. Blow flies, or calliphorids, (medium- to large-bodied shiny-metallic colored flies), feed primarily on carrion (dead tissue of animals, or meat scraps, etc., as in garbage cans), whereas the typical house flies (the

medium to small greyish-brown bodied flies with striped backs) are attracted to a wide variety of food wastes and animal manures.

To avoid "putting all your bait in one basket," you might want to use a combination of baits. For instance, combine something sweet and smelly (fermenting) with meat scraps, or dead snails, or fish heads, etc., *and* with some animal manure. Dog droppings are usually all too available; chicken manure mixed with broken eggs works particularly well for the blow flies.

Mixtures of cornmeal and molasses will ferment and attract house flies, *Musca domestica*, the common green bottle flies, *Phoenicia seriata*, and others. The advantage of this mixture over others is that the flies cannot breed in it as they can in the other baits; the disadvantages of this bait is its cost. It also takes a while before it ferments and becomes attractive. Yeast can be added to speed the process.

Placement of the Trap

Locate the trap so the bait will not compete with some other nearby food source and perhaps not trap many flies. If you must place your trap near competing food sources (an animal yard, for instance), then beef up your bait accordingly.

If possible, place the trap in the sunshine—most flies are more active in sunlit areas. Or, if you notice cool-weather flies seeking shaded areas during hot weather, move your traps around accordingly. In general, try to notice how the fly activity varies during different times of day. This will help you place traps as well as sticky tapes (a good way to trap the swarms of adult male flies which hover around).

Place the traps away from areas where you do not want a lot of fly activity—away from doorways and entrances, for example. Once the traps are working well, there will be quite a few flies buzzing around them.

If you are concerned about children and pets, build a shelf to elevate the trap or place it on top of a drum or barrel to get it up off the ground.

Cleaning the Trap and Harvesting the Flies

Emptying the trap of dead flies is very easy using the lift-up panel. The dead flies can be used as food for chicken and other fowl. They are high in protein (as are the garbage and food wastes they feed upon).

The birds are naturally adapted to eating flies. However, to avoid any possibility of infecting your chickens with disease organisms which may survive inside the adult flies, it is advisable to "cook" the flies before feeding them to your birds. (Most disease organisms don't survive from the fly's maggot stage to the adult stage, but a few do.) The flies can be cured by placing them in a glass jar with a lid or plastic bag and letting them "cook" in the hot sun for a few days. (Glass is better, however, as it does not release fumes when heated, while plastic does.) You can put them in aluminum foil and roast them at high temperatures in the oven or in a fire for thirty minutes. Or, you may just want to compost the flies in your compost pile, or bury them in the soil, if you have no other way of recycling them.

Important

This trap will not work miracles! It will not, in all likelihood, solve your fly problems, which are part of a much larger picture of inadequate or inappropriate waste management at a community level. However, this trap *does* enable you to take large quantities of flies out of egg-laying circulation without the use of pesticides, sprays or pest-strips.

Effective, permanent fly control is possible without heavy reliance on pesticides. "Integrated fly management" combines special waste management practices with release of beneficial insects which prey only on flies. Establishment of these parasites and predators results in "biological control" of fly populations to keep them well-below intolerable levels. Integrated fly management is not an instant solution, but it is the only environmentally-sound strategy.

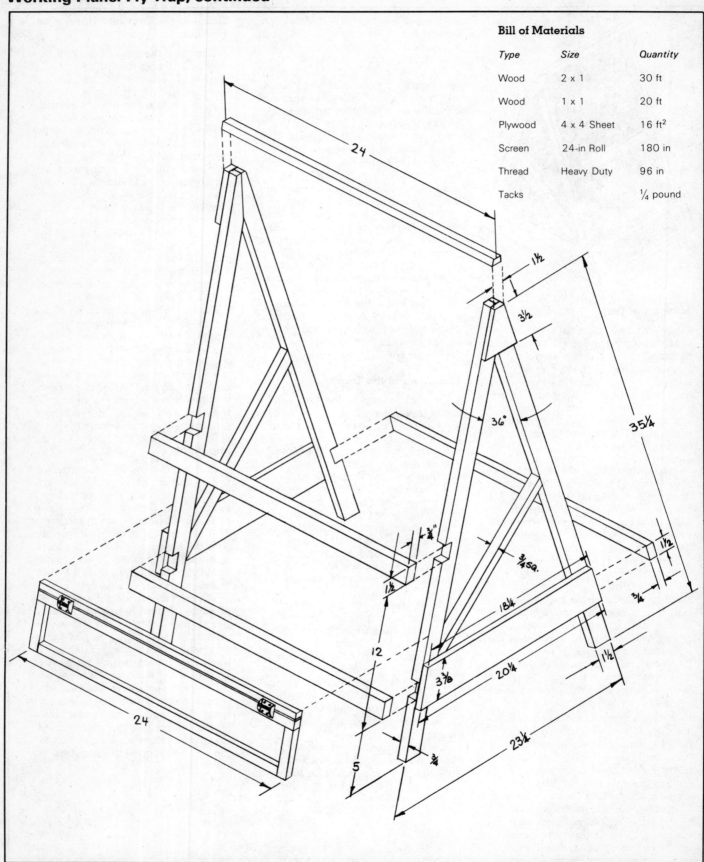

Bill of Materials

Type	Size	Quantity
Wood	2 x 1	30 ft
Wood	1 x 1	20 ft
Plywood	4 x 4 Sheet	16 ft²
Screen	24-in Roll	180 in
Thread	Heavy Duty	96 in
Tacks		¼ pound

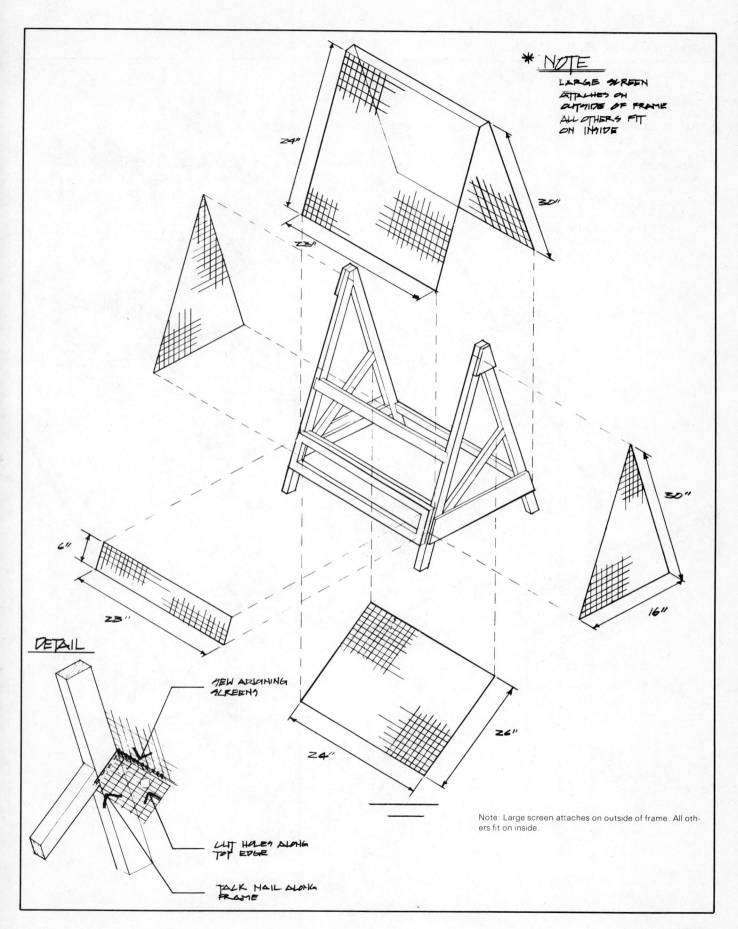

NOTE

LARGE SCREEN
ATTACHES ON
OUTSIDE OF FRAME
ALL OTHERS FIT
ON INSIDE

24"

30"

23"

30"

6"

23"

16"

DETAIL

SEW ADJOINING
SCREENS

CUT HOLES ALONG
TOP EDGE

TACK NAIL ALONG
FRAME

24"

26"

Note: Large screen attaches on outside of frame. All others fit on inside.

477

Working Plans: Solar Oven

Cooking food in a solar oven is a practical method of taking advantage of free energy from the sun. Simple and inexpensive to construct, a solar oven is essentially an insulated box with a surface of glass or other transparent material which faces the sun at an angle favorable to maximum capture of solar energy. At northern California's latitude of 37°, a 45° slope on the oven's front surface produces satisfactory heat gain. White reflector panels help to focus sunlight on the oven's transparent face composed of two panes of glass. An interior of blackpainted sheet metal absorbs collected solar energy and intensifies the heat within.

The solar oven chamber sits on a lazy-susan swivel plate allowing the oven to be rotated to take advantage of maximum sun angles. On a clear day, temperatures in the solar oven can reach 350°

The solar oven is capable of baking most foods usually cooked in conventional gas and electric ovens.

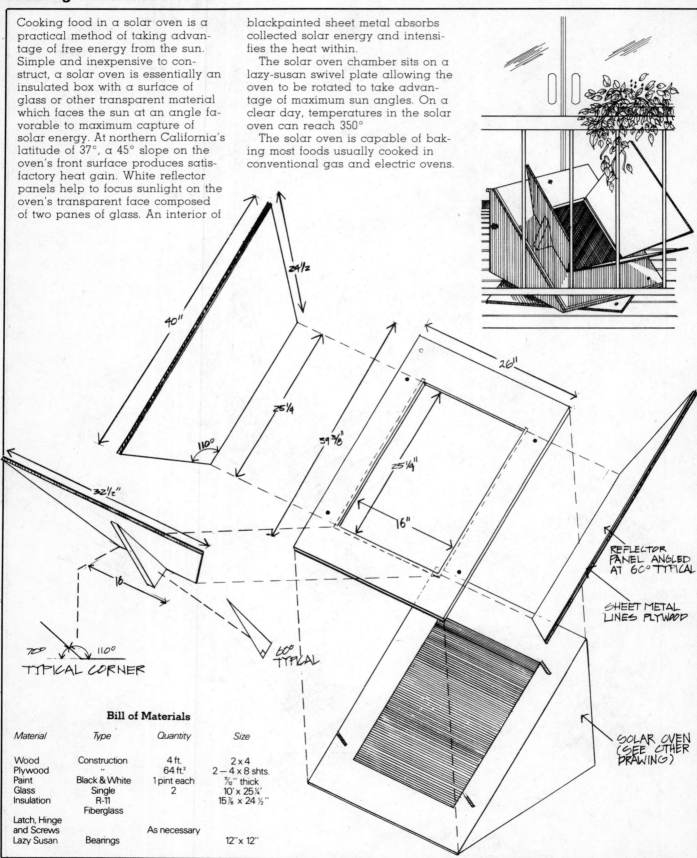

TYPICAL CORNER

70° 110°

16

24½

40"

110°

25¼

32½"

39⅜"

26"

25¼"

16"

60° TYPICAL

REFLECTOR PANEL ANGLED AT 60° TYPICAL

SHEET METAL LINES PLYWOOD

SOLAR OVEN (SEE OTHER DRAWING)

Bill of Materials

Material	Type	Quantity	Size
Wood	Construction	4 ft.	2 x 4
Plywood	"	64 ft.²	2 — 4 x 8 shts.
Paint	Black & White	1 pint each	⅞" thick
Glass	Single	2	10' x 25¼'
Insulation	R-11 Fiberglass		15⅞ x 24½"
Latch, Hinge and Screws		As necessary	
Lazy Susan	Bearings		12" x 12"

Breads and cookies do very well, although they usually require 50 percent longer baking times. Grilled cheese sandwiches and homemade pizza are other favorite foods which do well in solar ovens. However, if meat is to be cooked by this method, it should be tightly wrapped in aluminum foil to prevent heat losses around the meat.

Assembly of the Solar Oven

1. Cut out and assemble plywood pieces for the cooking chamber and door of the oven as per the dimensions in the construction drawings.

2. Place R-11 fiberglass insulation between interior and exterior surfaces of oven chamber and door.

3. Attach pieces of 24 gauge sheet metal to inside of chamber. Paint sheet metal surfaces with high temperature resistant flat black paint.

4. Cut out pieces of plywood for the three reflector panels and attach to reflector apron as per construction drawings opposite. Use wing screws to secure reflection panel unit to oven chamber.

5. Paint all exterior surfaces of oven and reflector panels with semi-gloss white enamel.

6. Set two panes of single strength glass on two sets of glazing strip placed ½″ apart as detailed on page 480. Caulk outside panens. with glazing compound. compound.

7. Place complete assembly on lazy-susan swivel unit as shown in plans.

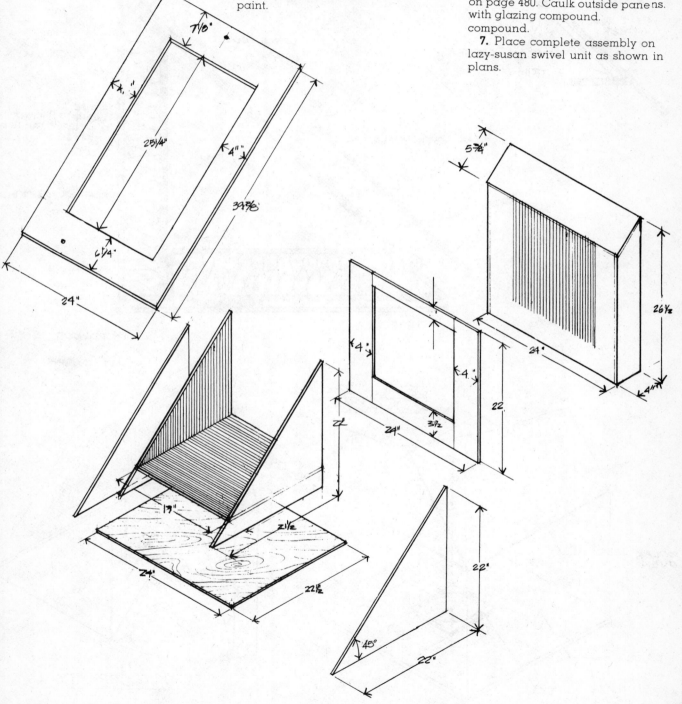

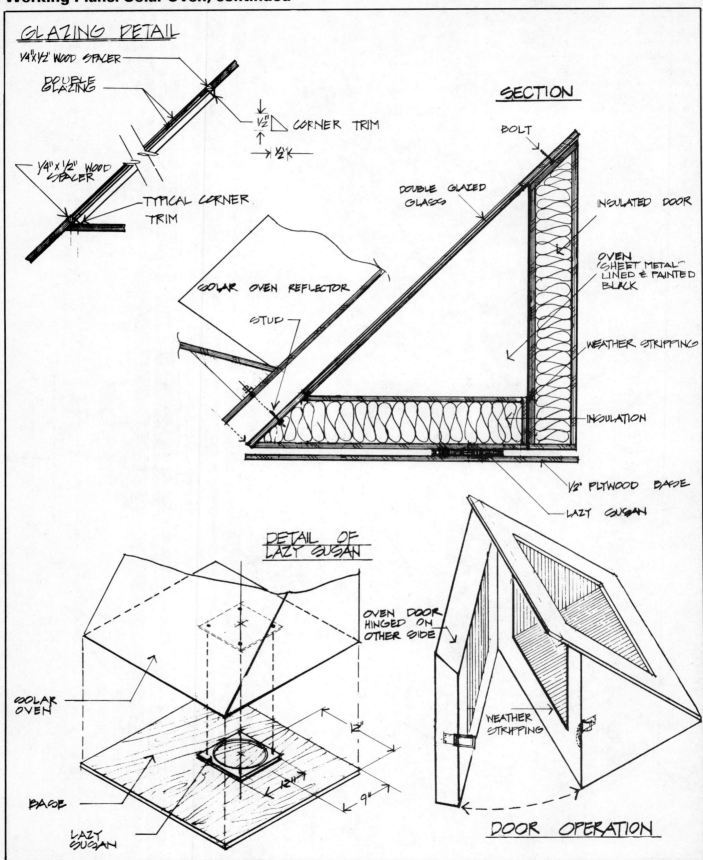

GLAZING DETAIL

1/4" X 1/2" WOOD SPACER

DOUBLE GLAZING

CORNER TRIM

1/4" X 1/2" WOOD SPACER

TYPICAL CORNER TRIM

1/2"

1/2"

SECTION

BOLT

DOUBLE GLAZED GLASS

INSULATED DOOR

OVEN (SHEET METAL) LINED & PAINTED BLACK

SOLAR OVEN REFLECTOR

STUD

WEATHER STRIPPING

INSULATION

1/2" PLYWOOD BASE

LAZY SUSAN

DETAIL OF LAZY SUSAN

SOLAR OVEN

BASE

LAZY SUSAN

12"

12"

9"

OVEN DOOR HINGED ON OTHER SIDE

WEATHER STRIPPING

DOOR OPERATION

480

Working Plans: Cool Closet

A cool closet offers an energy-efficient method for short term storage of fresh fruits, vegetables, breads and other baked goods. The closet is particularly useful for the homescale producer of fresh vegetables whose harvest is too great for storage in a refrigerator.

The closet is constructed on a section of the northernmost exterior wall of the house. The cool air enters the storage chamber through a low vent, rises up past the foods stored on lath board shelves, and leaves the closet through a top vent as described in the construction plan. The draft of cool air inside the chamber serves the double function of cooling the foods as well as removing any foul odors resulting from the ripening of the stored fruits and vegetables. The insulated walls of the closet help maintain it at a cool temperature level.

Construction Procedures

1. Determine appropriate place for attaching cool closet to exterior wall of kitchen or pantry.

2. Determine suitable size for your closet and calculate the dimensions of the attached construction plan. Typical cool closets are two feet deep and 16 inches wide. Height varies depending on storage needs and size of available wall space.

3. Mark top and bottom vent locations on exterior wall. Cut openings and install louvered vents as shown in construction plan.

4. Construct framework of closet using 2 x 4 studs and cross members. Apply ½" sheet rock to interior. Insulate all surfaces with R-11 fiberglass. Apply siding or sheet rock to exterior.

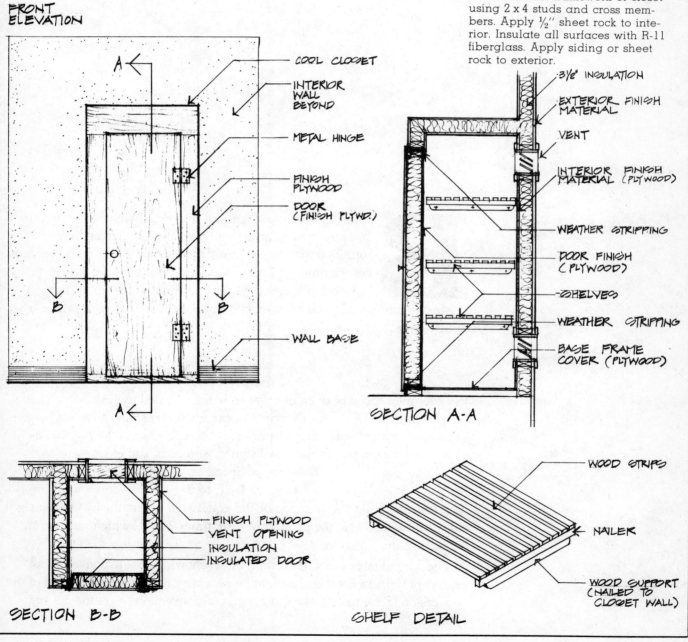

FRONT ELEVATION

- COOL CLOSET
- INTERIOR WALL BEYOND
- METAL HINGE
- FINISH PLYWOOD
- DOOR (FINISH PLYWD.)
- WALL BASE

SECTION A-A

- 3½" INSULATION
- EXTERIOR FINISH MATERIAL
- VENT
- INTERIOR FINISH MATERIAL (PLYWOOD)
- WEATHER STRIPPING
- DOOR FINISH (PLYWOOD)
- SHELVES
- WEATHER STRIPPING
- BASE FRAME COVER (PLYWOOD)

SECTION B-B

- FINISH PLYWOOD
- VENT OPENING
- INSULATION
- INSULATED DOOR

SHELF DETAIL

- WOOD STRIPS
- NAILER
- WOOD SUPPORT (NAILED TO CLOSET WALL)

APPENDIX 3: UNITS OF MEASUREMENT

Because different conventions historically have been used to measure various quantities, the following tables have been compiled to sort out the different units. This first table identifies the units typically used for describing a particular quantity. For example, speed might be measured in "miles/hour."

Most quantities can also be described in terms of the following three basic dimensions:

$$\text{length} \quad L$$
$$\text{mass} \quad M$$
$$\text{time} \quad T$$

For example, speed is given in terms of length divided by time, which can be written as "L/T." This description, called "dimensional analysis," is useful in determining whether an equation is correct. The product of the dimensions on each side of the equal sign must match. For example:

$$\text{Distance} = \text{Speed} \times \text{Time}$$
$$L \quad = L/T \times T$$

The dimension on the left side of the equal sign is length, L. On the right side of the equal sign, the product of L/T times T is L, which matches the left side of the equation.

The second table is a Conversion Table, showing how to convert from one set of units to another. It might be necessary to take the reciprocal of the conversion factor or to make more than one conversion to get the desired results.

482

Measured Quantities and Their Common Units

Length(L)	Area(L^2)	Volume(L^3)	Pressure($M/L/T^2$)	Energy(ML^2/T^2)	Power(ML^2/T^3)
mile(mi.)	sq. mile(mi^2)	gallon(gal.)	atmosphere(atm.)	British thermal	Btu./min.
yard(yd.)	sq. yard(yd^2)	quart(qt.)	pounds/sq. inch(psi)	unit(Btu.)	Btu./hour
foot(ft.)	sq. foot(ft^2)	pint(pt.)	inches of mercury	calories(cal.)	watt
inch(in.)	sq. inch(in^2)	ounce(oz.)	cm. of mercury	foot-pound	joule/sec.
fathom(fath.)	acre	cu. foot(ft^3)	feet of water	joule	cal./min.
kilometer(km.)	sq. kilometer(km^2)	cu. yard(yd^3)		kilowatt-hour	horsepower(hp.)
meter(m.)	sq. meter(m^2)	cu. inch(in^3)		(kw.-hr.)	
centimeter(cm.)	sq. centimeter(cm^2)	liter(1)		horsepower-hour	
micron(μ)		cu. centimeter(cm^3)		(hp.-hr.)	
angstrom(Å)		acre-foot			
		cord(cd)	**Time(T)**	**Energy Density(M/T^2)**	**Power Density(M/T^3)**
		cord-foot	year(yr)	calories/sq. cm.	cal./sq. cm./min.
		barrel(bbl.)	month	Btu./sq. foot	Btu./sq. foot/hr
			day	langley	langley/min.
Mass(M)	**Speed(L/T)**	**Flow Rate(L^3/T)**	hour(hr.)	watthr./sq. foot	watt/sq. cm.
			minute(min.)		
pound(lb.)	feet/minute	cu. feet/min.	second(sec.)		
	(ft./min.)				
ton(short)	feet/sec.	cu. meter/min.			
ton(long)	mile/hour	liters/sec.			
ton(metric)	mile/min.	gallons/min.			
gram(g.)	kilometer/hr.	gallons/sec.			
kilogram(kg.)	kilometer/min.				
	kilometer/sec.				

Table of Conversion Factors

Multiply	By	To Obtain:	Multiply	By	To Obtain:
Acres	43560	Sq. feet	"	3.15×10^{-8}	Watts/sq. cm.
"	0.004047	Sq. kilometers	Calories(cal.)	0.003968	Btu.
"	4047	Sq. meters	"	3.08596	Foot-pounds
"	0.0015625	Sq. miles	"	1.55857×10^{-6}	Horsepower-hours
"	4840	Sq. yards	"	4.184	Joules (or watt-sec.)
Acre-feet	43560	Cu. feet	"	1.1622×10^{-6}	Kilowatt-hours
"	1233.5	Cu. meters	Calories, food unit		
"	1613.3	Cu. yards	(Cal.)	1000	Calories
Angstroms(Å)	1×10^{-8}	Centimeters	Calories/min.	0.003968	Btu./min.
"	3.937×10^{-9}	Inches	"	0.06973	Watts
"	0.0001	Microns	Calories/sq. cm.	3.68669	Btu./sq. ft.
Atmospheres(atm.)	76	Cm. of Hg(0°C)	"	1.0797	Watt-hr/sq. foot
"	1033.3	Cm. of H_2O(4°C)	Cal./sq. cm./min.	796320.	Btu./sq. foot/hr.
"	33.8995	Ft. of H_2O(39.2°F)	"	251.04	Watts/sq. cm.
"	29.92	In. of Hg(32°F)	Candle power		
"	14.696	Pounds/sq. inch(psi)	(spherical)	12.566	Lumens
Barrels(petroleum,			Centimeters(cm.)	0.032808	Feet
U.S.)(bbl.)	5.6146	Cu. feet	"	0.3937	Inches
"	35	Gallons(Imperial)	"	0.01	Meters
"	42	Gallons(U.S.)	"	10.000	Microns
"	158.98	Liters	Cm. of Hg(0°C)	0.0131579	Atmospheres
British Thermal			"	0.44605	Ft. of H_2O(4°C)
Unit(Btu)	251.99	Calories, gm	"	0.19337	Pounds/sq. inch
"	777.649	Foot-pounds	Cm. of H_2O(4°C)	0.0009678	Atmospheres
"	0.00039275	Horsepower-hours	"	0.01422	Pounds/sq. inch
"	1054.35	Joules	Cm./sec.	0.032808	Feet/sec.
"	0.000292875	Kilowatt-hours	"	0.022369	Miles/hr.
"	1054.35	Watt-seconds	Cords	8	Cord-feet
Btu/hr.	4.2	Calories/min.	"	128(or 4 × 4 × 8)	Cu. feet
"	777.65	Foot-pounds/hr.	Cu. centimeters	3.5314667	Cu. feet
"	0.0003927	Horsepower	"	0.06102	Cu. inches
"	0.000292875	Kilowatts	"	1×10^{-6}	Cu. meters
"	0.292875	Watts(or joule/sec.)	"	0.001	Liters
Btu/lb.	7.25×10^{-4}	Cal/gram	"	0.0338	Ounces(U.S. fluid)
Btu/sq. ft.	0.271246	Calories/sq. cm.	Cu. feet(ft^3)	0.02831685	Cu. meters
		(or langleys)	"	7.4805	Gallons(U.S., liq.)
"	0.292875	Watt-hour/sq. foot	"	28.31685	Liters
Btu/sq. ft./hour	3.15×10^{-7}	Kilowatts/sq. meter	"	29.922	Quarts(U.S., liq.)
"	4.51×10^{-3}	Cal./sq. cm./min(or	Cu. ft. of H_2O		
		langleys/min)	(60°F)	62.366	Pounds of H_2O

Table of Conversion Factors, continued

Multiply	By	To Obtain:
Cu. feet/min.	471.947	Cu. cm./sec.
Cu. inches(in.^{3})	16.387	Cu. cm.
''	0.0005787	Cu. feet
''	0.004329	Gallons(U.S., liq.)
''	0.5541	Ounces(U.S., fluid)
Cu. meters	1×10^6	Cu. centimeters
''	35.314667	Cu. feet
''	264.172	Gallons(U.S., liq.)
''	1000	Liters
Cu. yard	27	Cu. feet
''	0.76455	Cu. meters
''	201.97	Gallons(U.S., liq)
Cubits	18	Inches
Fathoms	6	Feet
''	1.8288	Meters
Feet(ft.)	30.48	Centimeters
''	12	Inches
''	0.00018939	Miles(statute)
Feet of H$_2$O(4°C)	0.029499	Atmospheres
''	2.2419	Cm. of Hg(0°C)
''	0.433515	Pounds/sq. inch
Feet/min.	0.508	Centimeters/second
''	0.018288	Kilometers/hr.
''	0.0113636	Miles/hr.
Foot-candles	1	Lumens/sq. foot
Foot-pounds	0.001285	Btu
''	0.324048	Calories
''	5.0505×10^{-7}	Horsepower-hours
''	3.76616×10^{-7}	Kilowatt-hours
Furlong	220	Yards
Gallons(U.S., dry)	1.163647	Gallons(U.S., liq.)
Gallons(U.S., liq.)	3785.4	Cu. centimeters
''	0.13368	Cu. feet
''	231	Cu. inches
''	0.0037854	Cu. meters
''	3.7854	Liters
''	8	Pints(U.S., liq.)
''	4	Quarts(U.S., liq.)
Gallons/min.	2.228×10^{-3}	Cu. feet/sec.
''	0.06308	Liters/sec.
Grams	0.035274	Ounces(avdp.)
''	0.002205	Pounds(avdp.)
Grams-cm.	9.3011×10^{-8}	Btu.
Grams/meter^2	3.98	Short ton/acre
''	8.92	lbs./acre
Horsepower	42.4356	Btu./min.
''	550	Foot-pounds/sec.
''	745.7	Watts
Horsepower-hrs.	2546.14	Btu.
''	641616	Calories
''	1.98×10^6	Foot-pounds
''	0.7457	Kilowatt-hours
Inches	2.54	Centimeters
''	0.83333	Feet
In. of Hg(32°F)	0.03342	Atmospheres
''	1.133	Feet of H$_2$O
''	0.4912	Pounds/sq. inch
In. of Water(4°C)	0.002458	Atmospheres
''	0.07355	In. of Mercury(32°F)
''	0.03613	Pounds/sq. inch
Joules	0.0009485	Btu.
''	0.73756	Foot-pounds
''	0.0002778	Watt-hours
''	1	Watt-sec.
Kilo calories/gram	1378.54	Btu/lb
Kilograms	2.2046	Pounds(avdp.)
Kilograms/hectare	.893	lbs/acre
Kilograms/hectare	.0004465	Short ton/acre
Kilometers	1000	Meters
''	0.62137	Miles(statute)
Kilometer/hr.	54.68	Feet/min.
Kilowatts	3414.43	Btu./hr.
''	737.56	Foot-pounds/sec.
''	1.34102	Horsepower
Kilowatt-hours	3414.43	Btu.
''	1.34102	Horsepower-hours
Knots	51.44	Centimeter/sec.
''	1	Mile(nautical)/hr.
''	1.15078	Miles(Statute)/hr.
Langleys	1	Calories/sq. cm.
Liters	1000	Cu. centimeters
''	0.0353	Cu. feet
''	0.2642	Gallons(U.S., liq.)
''	1.0567	Quarts(U.S., liq.)
Lbs./acre	.0005	Short ton/acre
Liters/min.	0.0353	Cu. feet/min.
''	0.02642	Gallons(U.S., liq.)/min.
Lumens	0.079577	Candle power(spherical)
Lumens(at 5550Å)	0.0014706	Watts
Meters	3.2808	Feet
''	39.37	Inches
''	1.0936	Yards
Meters/sec.	2.24	Miles/hr.
Micron	10000	Angstroms
''	0.0001	Centimeters
Miles(statute)	5280	Feet

INDEX

Walkways, 36, 422–24; garden, 130, 156, 164, 172, 180, 192

Walls: bottle, 41; drum, 334, 335; garden, 161; insulation of, 72–73; rat excluders in, 408; for solar-energy collection, 60, 67, 330–36, 466, 468–70; Trombe, 332–36; tube, 335

Washing. *See* Cleaning

Washing machines: water management with, 92, 99, 101, 193

Wasps: parasitic, 366, 374, 382, 383, 390, 392, 393, 415; predatory, 392–93

Wastes, 5, 6, 49–52, 110–43; in aquaculture, 292, 298; on farms, 148; from plants, 30, 60, 111, 128, 134, 246, 249, 252, 443–48. *See also* Composts; Garbage; Manures; Recycling; Sewage

Water, 5, 6, 30, 32, 33, 63; aquaculture, 292, 293, 294–96, 298–99; for bees, 308; for chickens, 282, 290–91; chlorine in, 226–27, 229; for community gardens, 438–39; in composts, 136; conservation of, 88–109, 112, 115, 180, 197–98, 352; cost of, 51; for indoor plants, 226–27, 228–30; for lawns, 387, 427; mosquito-attracting, 405–6; nitrate in, 218; passageways obstructing, 422–23; in photosynthesis, 28; plant retention of, 91, 158, 159, 161, 177, 179–80; for rabbits, 266, 267; recycling of, 52, 63, 97–109, 112; residential consumption of, 23, 88–95; in solar heating systems, 235–46, 241, 346–47, 348, 349, 350; U.S. consumption of, 88; vegetable consumption of, 197; waste transport by, 93, 96–97, 112, 115, 119. *See also* Greywater; Humidity; Irrigation; Moisture control; Rainfall

Water dam toilet device, 97

Water glass: egg preserving, 281

Water heaters, 80, 92–93; breadbox, 352–54; insulation of, 81, 84, 352; solar, 36, 37, 60, 62, 343, 351–58

Water meters, 51

Water softeners, 193–94, 227

Weathering: of rocks, 188–89

Weatherizing, 5, 6, 66–76, 82–83, 312–16, 437

Weatherstripping, 67–68, 322, 323, 437

Webbing: in integral system, 20

Weed Control (National Academy of Sciences), 394

Weeds, 393–95; beneficial uses of, 362; biological control of, 367, 393–94; for chicken feed, 249; in composts, 120, 127, 128, 129, 135; mulch control of, 164, 192, 394, 395

Wellesley-Miller, 24

Wells: for community gardens, 438–39

Wheast, 380, 411

Wheat: raising of, 56–57

White Cornish Cross chickens, 280

Whiteflies: in gardens, 389–90; in greenhouses, 410, 411, 417–18; indoors, 233

White Leghorn chickens, 280

Wilting point: in soil, 196

Windbreaks, 82, 91, 161, 179–80, 197

Windowbox solar collector, 326, 327–29

Windows, 26; double-glazed, 322–23, 350; greenhouses in, 86, 237, 341, 342, 460–62; skylight, 224, 225, 228; for solar collection, 60, 62, 67, 322–30; storm, 67, 76; weatherizing with, 66, 67–68, 76, 82, 86, 322–27, 350

Windowsill Ecology (Jorden), 234

Wind power: 39, 298–99

Windrows, composting, 125–26, 441, 442, 445–48

Wire: for rabbit cages, 262–66

Wiswesser, W.J., 377

Wood: for compost bins, 131, 132–33; in rabbit cages, 258, 262

Wood-burning: heating by, 81

Wood chips: for walkways, 36, 172, 423

Wool: moth-attracting, 406; rabbit, 246

Worms: in gardens, 381, 383–84; manure, 258–59, 301

Wright, David, 330

Wright, Frank Lloyd, 330, 340–41

Yanda, Bill, 238–40

Yusho disease, 140

Zinc: in food plants, 203; in soil, 201, 221